Shamanic Wisdom
in the Pyramid Texts

Shamanic Wisdom
in the Pyramid Texts

The Mystical Tradition of Ancient Egypt

Jeremy Naydler

Inner Traditions
Rochester, Vermont

Inner Traditions
One Park Street
Rochester, Vermont 05767
www.InnerTraditions.com

Library of Congress Cataloging-in-Publication Data
Naydler, Jeremy.
   Shamanic wisdom in the pyramid texts : the mystical tradition of ancient Egypt /
Jeremy Naydler.
      p. cm.
   Summary: "A radical reinterpretation of the Pyramid Texts as shamanic mystical
wisdom rather than funerary rituals" —Provided by publisher.
   Includes bibliographical references and index.
   ISBN 0-89281-755-0 (pbk.)
   1. Mysticism—Egypt. 2. Shamanism—Egypt. 3. Egypt—Religious life and
customs. 4. Pyramid texts. I. Title.
   BL2443.N39 2005
   299'.3182—dc22

                                                        2004023223

Printed and bound in the United States at Lake Book Manufacturing, Inc.

10 9 8 7 6 5 4 3 2 1

Text design by Virginia Scott Bowman and layout by Priscilla Baker
This book was typeset in Janson, with Augustea and Trajan used as display typefaces

CONTENTS

PREFACE AND
ACKNOWLEDGMENTS

This book began seven years ago with the overly ambitious aim of reinterpreting not only the Pyramid Texts, but also the Coffin Texts and the Book of the Dead, seeing them as documenting mystical experiences rather than simply funerary beliefs. As research progressed, and the original project was transformed into a Ph.D. thesis in religious studies, its scope narrowed to a reinterpretation of the Pyramid Texts alone and, like previous interpreters, I found myself gravitating to the texts in the pyramid of Unas. At the same time, I also had to think a great deal more about mysticism and the methodologies appropriate to studying it. The Ph.D. thesis, entitled "Mysticism in Ancient Egypt: the Pyramid Texts Re-examined," forms the basis of the present book. While I have reduced the number of references, cut out or rewritten various sections, and generally tried to streamline the prose, the lineaments of the doctoral thesis are never far beneath the surface. This is not therefore a "popular" book on ancient Egyptian mysticism, nor was it ever intended to be. Egyptian mysticism is both too serious and too neglected a subject to be taken lightly, and the stakes are too high to warrant anything less than a thorough reexamination of the source material, and a comprehensive critique of the way this has been interpreted within Egyptology during the twentieth century.

I wish to express my profound gratitude both to the supervisor of my thesis, Dr. Leon Schlamm, and to Dr. Alison Roberts, who kindly agreed to take on the role of Egyptological consultant. I could not have wished for two more committed guides, who have been as demanding and challenging as they have been inspirational and supportive. Through their conscientiousness and meticulous attention to detail, I have been saved from countless errors and pointed toward new avenues of reflection and research. Where errors and shortcomings remain, the responsibility for them is mine alone.

My thanks also go to Louanne Richards for her loving support and encouragement, and for listening and responding to every chapter as it emerged, and then all too often reemerged several weeks or months later. Thanks also to Dr. Felix Padel for his enthusiastic response to the whole text, and his recognition of its implications; to Sam Betts, for his sustained interest and for his comments, especially on chapter 5; to Deborah Clarke for her feedback on chapter 1; and to Maura Maguire for hearing various chapters and for the warmth and consistency of her encouragement, especially during the long bleak weeks of "the siege of Stalingrad." Thanks also to Allegra Wint for her crucial help during the last year.

My first real engagement with the texts of the pyramid of Unas was between 1991 and 1993, during which time a small group of us met regularly to read and discuss them. To the members of this group—Hélène Goodfellow, James Hunt, Jean Semlyen, Dr. Felix Padel, and Anthea Bazin—I owe a debt of gratitude, for those meetings planted the seeds of this book. I am also grateful for the comradeship of K. A. and Anthea Bazin over years of struggling with the Unas hieroglyphs, as well as for the rich discussions this entailed. My indebtedness extends to so many students over the years, at Reading and Southampton Universities—too many to name but without whom I doubt if this work would have been embarked upon. I mention only the late Peter McGhie, who had the rare ability, when reading the Pyramid Texts, to convey the awesome, archetypal power of their content to all who were present.

I am grateful also to the late Dr. Kathleen Raine, who supported my initial application to work toward the Ph.D., and thereafter provided many opportunities for me to share this work through the Temenos Academy, and was consistently supportive over many years. I am grateful, too, to Stephen Overy, administrator of the Temenos Academy, for arranging the series of London seminars on the Pyramid Texts between 2001 and 2003, at which it was possible to experience just how "alive" the Pyramid Texts can be today, as well as to share and receive feedback from the various participants on work that was by then already well advanced.

I am grateful to both Dr. Alison Roberts and Claudia Böse for their help with translations of several long passages of German text, and to Iain Geddes for kindly volunteering to produce figure 8.8. I want also to express my gratitude to my mother, Elizabeth Naydler, for financial assistance during the first year of the thesis.

While this book steers a course that is in many ways counter to that of mainstream Egyptology, I am nevertheless indebted to the generations of Egyptologists who have dedicated themselves to discovering, transcribing, editing, translating, and commenting upon the Pyramid Texts—in particular, Gaston Maspero, Kurt Sethe, Samuel Mercer, Alexandre Piankoff, and R. O. Faulkner, without whose labors the present study would not have been possible. I would like also to acknowledge the contribution of the non-Egyptologist William Fix, whose analysis of the Unas texts in his book *Star Maps* decisively influenced the direction taken in this study. Finally, special thanks to Cannon Labrie, Doris Troy, Erica Blomquist, and Jeanie Levitan at Inner Traditions for the care and dedication with which they have prepared this manuscript for publication.

As the Pyramid Texts have already been translated into English three times, I have liberally used these already published translations, which are credited in the notes. On occasion I have felt the need to produce a fresh rendering of a passage, and these translations for which I myself am responsible are left uncredited.

DECEMBER 2004

ABBREVIATIONS

ADAIK   *Abhandlungen des Deutschen Archäologischen Instituts Abteilung Kairo*

ÄgAb   *Ägyptologische Abhandlungen* (Cairo)

AN   *Archéo-Nil* (Paris)

ASAE   *Annales du Service des Antiquités de l'Égypte* (Cairo)

BAAA   *Le Bulletin Annuel de "L'Atelier d'Alexandre"* (Alexandria)

BÄBA   *Beitrage zur Ägyptischen Bauforschung und Altertumskunde* (Cairo and Wiesbaden)

BD   The Book of the Dead. For translations, see bibliography.

BO   *Bibliotheca Orientalis* (Leiden)

CH   Corpus Hermeticum. For translations, see bibliography.

CT   The Coffin Texts. For translations, see bibliography.

CW   *Collected Works of C. G. Jung* (Bollingen Series XX), 20 vols., trans. R. F. C. Hull, ed. H. Read, M. Fordham, G. Adler, and W. McGuire (Princeton: Princeton University Press, 1953–1979)

DE   *Discussions in Egyptology* (Oxford)

JARCE   *Journal of the American Research Center in Egypt* (New York)

JEA   *Journal of Egyptian Archaeology* (London)

JNES   *Journal of Near Eastern Studies* (Chicago: University of Chicago Press)

JWCI   *Journal of the Warburg and Courtauld Institute* (London)

KMT   *KMT: A Modern Journal of Ancient Egypt* (San Francisco)

LÄ   *Lexikon der Ägyptologie*, 7 vols., ed. W. Helck and E. Otto (Wiesbaden: O. Harrassowitz, 1975–89)

MÄS   *Münchner Ägyptologische Studien*

MDAIK   *Mitteilungen des Deutschen Archäologischen Instituts, Abteilung Kairo* (Mainz: Verlag Philipp von Zabern)

NHC   Nag Hammadi Codices. For translation, see J. M. Robinson, ed., *The Nag Hammadi Library in English.*

OMRO   *Oudheidkundige Mededelingen uit het Rijksmuseum van Oudheden* (Leiden: Rijksmuseum van Oudheden)

Or   *Orientalia* (Rome: Pontificium Institutum Biblicum, 1920–)

PT   The Pyramid Texts. For translations, see bibliography.

RAIN   *Royal Anthropological Institute News* (London)

RHR   *Revue de l'histoire des religions* (Paris)

SPAW   *Sitzungsberichte der Preussischen Akademie der Wissenschaften, Philosophisch-historische Klasse* (Heidelberg)

UGAÄ   *Untersuchungen zur Geschichte und Altertumskunde Ägyptens* (Leipzig and Berlin)

Utt.   Utterance of Pyramid Texts, as cited in R. O. Faulkner, *The Ancient Egyptian Pyramid Texts* (Oxford: Oxford University Press, 1969)

§   Section of Pyramid Texts, as cited in K. Sethe, *Die altägyptischen Pyramidentexte*, 4 vols. (Leipzig, 1908–1922), often referred to in Egyptological studies as "Pyr." Sethe's divisions are also followed in the translations of Mercer, Piankoff, and Faulkner.

ZÄS   *Zeitschrift fur Ägyptische Sprache und Altertumskunde* (Leipzig, Berlin)

PART 1

MYSTICISM IN ANCIENT EGYPT

1 INTRODUCTION: THE ENCOUNTER WITH THE SACRED

Religious Egypt

Many people today find themselves by one route or another drawn to ancient Egypt. It is a civilization that seems to have the ability to "come alive" for us in a way that other ancient civilizations do not. Egypt seems to welcome us in, to invite us to live imaginatively into the life of its people; we feel the magic of its landscape, we are awed by its monumental architecture, and we marvel at its rich cultural and artistic legacy. One reason it holds a fascination for us is that its culture is so accessible and yet belongs to an era of history that is so very remote from our own. Egypt is forever elsewhere, its life has been lived, and yet at the same time it can become tantalizingly present to our imagination. When it comes to ancient Egyptian religion, however, we can have an additional feeling. Something can stir in us that is not quite the same as the fascination we feel when drawn to other aspects of Egyptian culture. We can feel that we are not simply engaging with something that belongs to the past, or even belongs specifically to ancient Egypt. We can feel that we touch a dimension of human experience that directly, perhaps disturbingly, impinges upon us today.

The religious life of the ancient Egyptians was never really separate from the rest of their lives: The whole culture was infused with religious awareness, with an awareness that the spirit world interpenetrated all spheres of existence. Ancient Egypt was a sacred culture, and this, more than anything else, is the key to its perennial allure. When we "go back" to ancient Egypt, we are also "going down" to a deeper, more archaic level of human experience that is closer to the gods, closer to a half-forgotten awareness of transpersonal beings and primal encounters with archetypal realities.

As today we haltingly move toward a reawakened awareness of the inner worlds, it is as if the Greco-Roman foundations of Western culture no longer seem deep enough to secure what is beginning to unfold spiritually in our own times. A different kind of anchorage is necessary for the next phase in our development. Egypt provides this anchorage: not the "daily life" Egypt that so readily captures the imagination of children, but the more potent "religious" Egypt that calls to us from deep within our own souls.

This book is an answer to that call. It is an exploration of the religious Egypt that lies at the foundations of the Western esoteric tradition. Its focus is on the earliest body of religious literature that has survived not only from ancient Egypt, but from anywhere else in the world: the Pyramid Texts. Up until now these texts have been regarded as funerary texts, for use in the funerary liturgy of the dead king or to aid him in his afterlife journey. This book argues that they are mystical texts that contain a shamanic wisdom based on the experiences of the living king, thrust into extreme psychological and existential predicaments and perilous encounters with alternate realities. Such experiences constitute the basis of ancient Egyptian mysticism.

It is both a curious and a lamentable fact that the subject of mysticism in ancient Egypt has come to be a controversial one. From the beginning of the twentieth century, there has been a broad consensus within Egyptology against the existence of any form of mysticism in ancient Egypt, and this remains the situation today. While there have been occasional challenges to the antimysticism consensus over the years, they have not yet succeeded in dislodging it, and Egyptologists tend to view mysticism as a dangerous subject best avoided. And so, instead of mysticism, attention is focused on the funerary beliefs of the Egyptians. Indeed, the counterpoise to the denial of mysticism in ancient Egypt is the undue weight given to the funerary interpretation of ancient Egyptian religious texts and rituals. This emphasis on the funerary interpretation has served only to depotentize Egyptian religion and to distort our understanding of ancient Egyptian religious sensibility. It does this by treating as mere belief or external ritual what were, for at least some Egyptians, intense inner experiences ritually undergone while still alive.

If we are to understand the character and significance of these experiences, we need to approach them not simply from an Egyptological standpoint—as products of the culture of ancient Egypt. We need to approach them from the standpoint of the phenomenology of religion, as specifically religious phenomena that reveal extraordinary possibilities of human consciousness. While the cultural milieu in which these experiences took place is obviously relevant to any understanding of them, knowledge of the cultural milieu alone is not sufficient if we are really to understand these experiences. The aim of this book is therefore to go to a level deeper than historical and cultural conditions, in order to focus on the existential situation of the human being. In the case of the Pyramid Texts, this human being is the king—his state of consciousness and his relationship to the spiritual sphere. In this respect the approach of the present study differs fundamentally from that of Egyptology: for in the following pages, we shall be aiming to engage with and understand the Pyramid Texts from an existential and experiential standpoint, in the belief that only then does the shamanic wisdom that they contain become evident, and only then does it become possible truly to understand the nature of the mystical tradition of ancient Egypt.

Mysticism and Ancient Egypt

During the twentieth century, the word *mysticism* has, broadly speaking, been defined in two different ways by scholars. On the one hand, there have been those who have understood it in terms of states of consciousness called "unitive" or "unitary," in which union with the ultimate source of reality is experienced.[1] In such states of consciousness, the mystic goes not only beyond ordinary sensations, thoughts, and passions, but also beyond spiritual visions, illuminations, nonordinary states of consciousness, and possible accompanying paranormal phenomena.[2] The distinction between the unitive state of consciousness and visionary or paranormal states is one that is regularly made in modern studies of mysticism. Visionary or paranormal states have frequently been held by both practitioners and scholars alike to be of marginal significance, and are often regarded as distractions from the true goal and real meaning of mysticism—namely, mystical union or identity with the godhead. From this point of view, visions and voices, raptures and ecstatic trances, are not mystical phenomena, and a distinction must be maintained between the "visionary" and the true mystic. The former is still caught in duality, whereas the latter has transcended all distinctions between subject and object and enjoys the nondual consciousness of "oneness," or absorption in the Absolute.[3]

This understanding of mysticism as a state of total absorption in the godhead, empty of any imaginative or visionary content, has dominated scholarly studies of mysticism during the twentieth century.[4] Were we to accept it, we would have to regard most of the religious literature of ancient Egypt as falling completely outside the sphere of mysticism. There is, however, a much broader and more inclusive way of understanding the meaning of the term *mysticism* that is both more helpful and more appropriate in approaching the subject of mysticism in ancient Egypt. It encompasses a wide range of unusual or nonordinary experiential states, which include visions, out-of-body experiences, otherworld journeys, encounters with spirits, initiatory death and rebirth, as well as the more unfathomable states of divine union, or *unio mystica*. According to William James, for instance, mystical experiences are not just peak experiences of union but should be seen as belonging to a spectrum ranging from revelatory insights and déjà vu at one end to more overtly religious ecstasies and unitive experiences at the other. He argued that images, whether symbolic or literal, play an enormous part in mysticism, which was for him essentially "a vivid sense of the reality of the unseen."[5]

William James is just one of a number of twentieth-century scholars who have sought to embrace visionary and various kinds of paranormal and supernormal experience within a broad definition of mysticism. Among them, we may include Mircea Eliade, Henry Corbin, Gerda Walther, and more recently J. B. Hollenback and Andrew Rawlinson.[6] Such experiences as encountering angels or spirits, being lifted up beyond the sphere of the earth and ascending through the heavens, or the intense inner experience of being spiritually reborn are evidently felt to be important mystical events in their own right by those who have experienced them. They reveal domains of spiritual reality that have often had a shattering impact on their conception of the world and a radically transforming effect on their lives. While these experiences may not be described in terms of union or identity with the Absolute, they nevertheless entail a breakthrough in plane, in which a level of reality that most people are not normally aware of forcefully impinges upon their consciousness. For scholars to dismiss or set aside these spiritual domains in order to focus exclusively on a transcendent state of union, or *unio mystica*, could be seen as a kind of spiritual reductionism that would sacrifice a qualitatively rich and ontologically significant dimension of experience for the sake of a rather purist attachment to the essentially ineffable culminative experience. The tendency of many scholars to focus more or less exclusively on the latter has had the effect not only of bypassing whole realms of spiritual experience but also of misunderstanding what is bypassed, for it has too often entailed the reinterpretation of what are really visionary cosmologies as mere intellectual constructs. This tendency is characteristic of a mentality that devalues the image and the imaginal realm in favor of that which is aniconic and abstract.[7]

How mysticism is defined reflects the mentality that defines it. It also reflects what that mentality values. It has been proposed, for example, that mysticism simply did not exist before the Upanishads, thereby dismissing at a stroke all religious literature prior to the Upanishads as "premystical" because it (arguably) lacks reference to the "soundless, formless, and intangible" experience expressed in the Upanishads.[8] Since the Upanishads were composed at a period when Egyptian civilization was already in decline (well over 1,500 years after the Pyramid Texts), the Pyramid Texts along with most other ancient Egyptian religious literature would—on this view—have to be classed as "premystical." All this tells us is that the narrow definition of mysticism cannot cope with archaic spirituality, such as is found not only in the Pyramid Texts but within both very ancient and also surviving tribal cultures in which shamanism is practiced. It is too "concrete" in the sense of being highly colored by visions, locutions, dramatic journeys into the spirit world, and so on. But archaic spirituality could and should be regarded as "mystical" to the extent that it involves supernormal states of consciousness in which experiences take place in, or in relation to, a transcendent dimension. Such experiences may not all be "unitive," they may not be "soundless, formless, and intangible," but that is not to say they are not numinous, for they might involve awesome encounters with spirit beings. They might also involve the devastating experience of being dismembered, or devoured by spirits, and then being "reborn" with a new spiritual identity. To quibble over whether experiences like this deserve to be called "mystical" is to betray a peculiar and quite unnecessary prejudice that would exclude a vast and important range of human spiritual experience from the domain of mysticism.[9]

While ancient Egyptian civilization was not tribal, its religion does share important elements with the archaic spirituality of tribal religions.[10] One of these common elements is that ancient Egyptian spirituality expressed itself in very concrete visual imagery and clearly functioned in relation to numerous spirits and deities. Rather than deny that mysticism existed in ancient Egypt, on the grounds that there appear to be no ancient Egyptian references to the kind of nondualistic experience of mystic union that we find in the Upanishads, Shankara, or Meister Eckhart, it is surely more fruitful to accept that while the experience of union or identity with the Absolute is an extremely important mystical experience, it is not the only kind of experience that may legitimately be called mystical. We then free ourselves to examine what kind of mystical tradition may have existed in ancient Egypt and what types of mystical experience may have been fostered there.[11] If we set up Meister Eckhart or Shankara as providing the norm of what mysticism is, then we deprive ourselves of the means to understand the mystical significance of the visionary experiences of Black Elk, or the coronation text of the Egyptian pharaoh Thutmosis III, which describes the living king rising to heaven in the form of a falcon.[12] Are we simply to look askance at these examples of archaic spirituality and declare them "premystical" or merely inferior visionary episodes because, as Rudolf Otto pointed out, "Eckhart never saw 'visions' or experienced 'occult facts,' nor does Shankara appeal to such experiences"?[13]

When we inquire about the existence of a mystical tradition in ancient Egypt, then, we need to bear such questions in mind. Egyptologists who have denied that mysticism of any kind existed in ancient Egypt have invariably adhered to a typically limited conception of what mysticism is. Erik Hornung, for example, in asserting that "no trace of mysticism can be found in ancient Egypt," explains: "The Egyptians never succumbed to the temptation to find in the transcendence of the existent release from all imperfection, dissolution of the self, or immersion in and union with the universe."[14] While "release from all imperfection," "dissolution of the self," and "immersion in and union with the universe" may be considered legitimate mystical aims in some mystical traditions, they are certainly not the aims of all mystical traditions.[15] If we cannot find these aims in ancient Egypt, perhaps we can find something else that may with equal legitimacy be described as mystical. We would, for example, look in vain for anything equivalent to the modern concept of "self" in ancient Egypt, that might be subject to a mystical dissolution. What we do find are a number of different psychospiritual components or aspects of the human being, one of which—the *akh*—represents a state of inner spiritual illumination.[16] If ancient Egyptian religious texts stress the importance of attaining the condition of becoming *akh*, then it seems unwise to deny that this has anything to do with mysticism on the grounds that the texts are not referring to the "dissolution of the self." Something similar could be said in relation to the idea of "release from imperfection," for it is an aim that would have made little sense to the Egyptians. The Egyptian state was constantly fine-tuned (through royal ritual) to harmonize with the cosmic order of Maat. While "release" from imperfection was not part of the Egyptian worldview, the perfecting of the imperfect world through attuning it to Maat certainly was.[17] Why should we regard the former as a mystical aim and not the latter? Again, it is unlikely that the ancient Egyptian would have made much of the idea of "union with the universe," for the universe was not conceived independently of the gods, of which it was regarded as an epiphany. Union with gods we do meet, but union with the universe is a notion quite alien to the Egyptian mentality.[18] If, then, the religious literature describes union with gods rather than "union with the universe," are we really entitled to deny that mysticism existed in ancient Egypt?

In order to inquire into whether or not a mystical tradition existed in ancient Egypt, it is necessary to set aside some of the preconceptions that have dominated the study of mysticism in the twentieth century so that we allow ourselves to become aware of the form that mystical experience may have taken in ancient Egypt. We need to recognize that there are many types of mysticism, and ancient Egypt presents us with a specific mystical sensibility that to call by any other name would mean to miss its true significance. The type of mysticism that existed in ancient Egypt is perhaps best described as "visionary mysticism." It entailed direct experience of the spirit world through states of consciousness in which the soul left the body in an ecstatic flight, to encounter ancestors, gods, and spirits, and to experience an inner rebirth. Insofar as we are dealing first with direct experience, rather than a set of beliefs or conjectures, and second with a living relationship to a spiritual dimension of existence perceived as utterly real, it seems justifiable to describe these experiences as mystical, and the literature in which they are expressed as mystical texts.[19]

The main argument of the following chapters is that the earliest corpus of ancient Egyptian religious literature—the Pyramid Texts—gives voice to a mystical tradition that has strong affinities with shamanism, which, as Mircea Eliade has pointed out, is the mysticism of archaic spirituality.[20] Although the present study entails a reinterpretation of core religious texts that hitherto have been regarded as exclusively funerary, the aim is not to deny the funerary status of the Pyramid Texts, for there is little doubt that they were used in a funerary context. The aim is rather to show that they were also mystical texts and could—and did—serve mystical as much as funerary ends. The reason why it was possible for these texts to be both mystical and funerary is that the realm of death was, for the Egyptians as for so many other ancient peoples, a realm of invisible forces, powers, and beings. It was a spirit realm that existed in a more interior way than the outwardly manifest world that we perceive with our senses, but it was nevertheless regarded as completely real. One of the central contentions of this book is that beyond the funerary rites and the cult of the dead, there also existed the possibility of certain individuals entering into a more conscious relationship with this spirit realm, bridging the gap between worlds in an altered state of consciousness. It was this conscious crossing of the threshold between the world of the living and the world of the dead that constituted the essence of ancient Egyptian mysticism, and it was this spiritual experience, rather than Egyptian "funerary beliefs," that determined the content of the Pyramid Texts.

A Question of Boundaries

One of the primary aims of approaching the Pyramid Texts from the standpoint of the phenomenology of religion is to position ourselves as far as possible within the religious consciousness from which these texts originated. The aim is to try to "stand inside" the religious consciousness of the ancient Egyptians of the Old Kingdom. Insofar as the Pyramid Texts are religious phenomena, we shall be attempting to understand them on their own terms, on their own religious plane of reference. And it is assumed at the outset that the religious plane of reference has reality, meaning, and value.[21] One of the things that distinguishes the phenomenological approach from others is that it aims to follow the religious material through to its origins in actual human experiences. What it seeks to avoid is the explanation of religious material in the nonreligious terms of historical or cultural determining influences—a fashionable if paradoxical endeavor of both modernism and postmodernism.[22] Our focus, then, will be less on social, political, economic, and other cultural influences on religious forms of experience and expression—important though these undoubtedly are—than on the essentially spiritual content of the religious experience. Through this approach, levels of existential meaning in the Pyramid Texts, which up until now have been unrecognized, are given the chance to reveal themselves.

Now, it could be argued that it is possible to understand the religious experience of the ancient Egyptians only by studying the whole society within which such experience took place—its language, its literature, its history and art, its political and economic organization, and so on. At the conclusion of this argument is the view that only Egyptologists are qualified to pronounce on the nature of Egyptian religion, for only they have the necessary expertise in all these fields.[23] There need be no difficulty in accepting that all the above-mentioned factors would have had an effect on how the Egyptians interpreted and explained their religious experiences to themselves. Religious experience is mediated through—and to a greater or lesser extent conditioned by—these cultural forms that are reassuringly analyzable. But simply to explain religious experience in terms of these conditioning factors would be to miss something essential. That "something essential" is not reducible to ordinary social, political, historical, or cultural circumstance, but belongs rather to the nature of human consciousness and its capacity to become receptive to numinous, and thoroughly nonordinary, levels of reality.[24]

It is for this reason that the study of ancient Egyptian religion should not be regarded as the exclusive preserve of Egyptology. Few people could doubt that the academic discipline of Egyptology is the only reliable mediator and transmitter of knowledge concerning ancient Egyptian culture today, and the present study is greatly—and gratefully—indebted to the scholarly diligence of Egyptologists. Egyptology is the necessary foundation on which any inquiry into the nature of ancient Egyptian religious life must depend. Egyptology does, however, cover a great many different subject areas—language, history, literature, art, and so on, as well as religion—and this breadth of scope is not just a strength but also a weakness.[25] It is a strength insofar as Egyptologists are obliged to maintain an overall perspective, but it is a weakness insofar as that as soon as one enters deeply into any single subject area, an invisible boundary line is crossed, at which point one is no longer simply working within the field of Egyptology but has moved into an area that falls within another specialist discipline, be it art history, social anthropology, political history, or—as in the present case—the history of religion. It is not, however, merely a question of the boundaries of academic disciplines and their respective methodological tools that concerns us here. In the case of ancient Egyptian religion, a point comes when one is no longer simply studying ancient Egyptian religion, but *encountering the religious dimension* as such. One is, in other words, encountering a realm of experience that—while it may be expressed in Egyptian terms—is by no means uniquely Egyptian.[26]

The interpretation of religion requires not simply breadth of knowledge of the culture in which that religion flourished, nor even thorough acquaintance with its religious forms, but also a feeling for, and a personal interest in, the nature of religious experience. Religion—even a so-called dead religion (as ancient Egyptian religion may seem)—is not so much another academic subject to be covered as a universe of human experience to be encountered, engaged with, and affected by. While it may be studied academically, the deeper understanding arises only when the academic is prepared to allow him- or herself to be existentially challenged by the material that is being studied.

The question is: To what extent is the Egyptologist—whether as an "allrounder" or a specialist—prepared to become vulnerable to such a challenge? Underlying this question, and it is only a question, not an accusation, is the issue of motivation. If a scholar is particularly attracted to the religion of Egypt, is this because the religion of Egypt answers a longing in his or her own soul, or is it merely because it is an interesting "field" to be covered? This question needs to be asked, because the task of studying and trying to understand the religious world that the Egyptians inhabited may well lead to depths of engagement that take the researcher beyond the sphere of Egyptology into the sphere of religion, and an exploration of that dimension of reality with which human religious experience is concerned.

It is in such circumstances that the issue of boundaries arises. When does an Egyptologist become a historian of religion? When do the methods used in the discipline of Egyptology need to be supplemented or even replaced by methods that belong to the phenomenology of religion? And if the Egyptologist does not adopt these methods, is there a danger that the significance of certain phenomena—especially those associated with religious experience—may not be fully appreciated by him or her? The phenomenological study of ancient Egyptian religion differs from Egyptology in this respect: The phenomenologist does not set out simply to describe, nor even simply to interpret, but rather to enter into dialogue with the ancient texts and thereby risk being changed.[27] This existential risk—which arises when one opens oneself to the religious universe of the Egyptians—is intrinsic to the phenomenological endeavor of following the texts through to their experiential origins.

The experiential root of Egyptian religion is not safely located in the distance of a civilization long since past, but belongs to the very structure of the human being as a religious being. In becoming receptive to it, we provide the soil in which it can begin to grow within ourselves, and become part of our inner orientation toward the world of spirit. In other words, we also grow with it. As the historian of religion W. Brede Kristensen once stated, "When religion is the subject of our work, we grow religiously."[28] Perhaps it would be more accurate to say: "When religion is the subject of our work, we *need* to grow religiously"—for if we do not, then the subject of our work will elude us. The study of religion is not like the study of chemistry or biology. It requires that something within us awaken that should it remain unconscious would prevent us from gaining the necessary understanding of the subject. In conventional academic disciplines, the call to spiritual awakening may be ignored, or at least set to one side of the researcher's work, to be pursued in his or her leisure time. For the person who wants to understand religion, the normal, common-sense, "everyday consciousness" is not adequate. It is only a religious consciousness that can unlock the inner meaning of the religious forms of the past.

Subjective Engagement

There is, then, something potentially problematic in a purely Egyptological approach to the study of Egyptian religion: namely, that unless the Egyptologist adopts a frame of mind that takes the whole sphere of human religion and religious experience seriously, then the attempt to penetrate ancient Egyptian religion with real understanding is unlikely to succeed. But in taking religion and religious experience seriously, one has crossed over into a subject that is no longer strictly speaking Egyptology. One is studying something more universally human, from which we cannot exclude ourselves. To paraphrase W. Brede Kristensen again, when religion is the subject of our work, we cannot exclude ourselves from it.

The path taken by the researcher studying ancient Egyptian religion will at some stage arrive at this borderland between Egyptology and the study of religion, and here the researcher will have to decide whether or not to make the crossing. If the decision is made to cross, then the first thing that one encounters is the great dilemma that faces all who embark on the study of religion. The dilemma could be expressed as follows: The degree to which one is able to understand the meaning of the texts is dependent upon the degree to which one "subjectively" engages with them. To the extent to which one wishes to preserve the detached stance of "objectivity," the meaning of the texts will remain more or less unpenetrated.[29]

This dilemma has been referred to by Jan Assmann, who, writing in 1995, noted that few Egyptologists are prepared to stray from merely editing primary sources to producing a "fully developed exegesis" of their meaning. Assmann pointed out that such ventures into hermeneutics (the art of interpretation) are fraught with the dangers of arbitrariness and subjectivity that most Egyptologists wish to steer clear of.[30] In particular, Egyptology has always been sensitive to the fact that its subject matter has a tendency to attract esoteric interpretations with which the scientifically minded scholar feels profoundly ill at ease.[31] Yet Egyptology cannot avoid hermeneutics. Any translation of an ancient Egyptian text will at the same time be, like it or not, an interpretation. And any attempt to understand the religious ground from which that text was produced will necessarily involve an activity—a "subjective" activity—of interpretation. The issue here has to do with the extent to which one is prepared to step into the religious universe of the Egyptians, and relinquish—even challenge—the position of being a "neutral" observer located in the nonreligious universe of modernity.

But let us stay with Assmann. As one of the foremost scholars of New Kingdom religion, his notion of how the Egyptologist gains an understanding of ancient Egyptian religious material is highly instructive, for he clearly delineates the borders that Egyptologists shrink from crossing and which, once crossed, proclaim that one has moved into territory that is no longer strictly Egyptological. The other side of the border is the terrain of the phenomenology of religion. Assmann explains what he, as an Egyptologist, means by "understanding" religious material in the following way:

> By "understanding" I do not mean empathy or "tuning into," which may deceive one into thinking that one has reached the destination without having realised that a journey is either possible or necessary. Rather I mean analysing and sorting the material that has been transmitted to us, so that by reducing its complexity we may uncover meaningful and, as such, intelligible contexts.[32]

For Assmann, keenly aware of the dangers of subjectivity in interpretation, the key to objective understanding is classification and structural analysis of texts. By contrasting "analysing and sorting the material" with empathizing and "tuning in to," he makes clear one of the major differences between the methodology of the Egyptologist and the one that will be taken in this study. It is not that the phenomenological approach avoids analysis and classification of material. This is important in itself and provides the necessary "control" for all subsequent phenomenological work.[33] The phenomenologist does, however, seek through the material also to empathize and tune in to the religious consciousness that produced it. Where the Egyptologist is content to subject this material to analysis and classification, to "reduc[e] its complexity" and to uncover "intelligible contexts," the phenomenologist will attempt to relive the original experience, no matter how complex it is and how far it may be from what is familiar to us today.[34]

From a phenomenological standpoint, the method of reducing complexity and uncovering intelligible contexts seems guaranteed to steer the researcher away from the specifically religious significance of the phenomena being studied, for it is surely only by acknowledging complexity and by moving our focus away from what is merely contextual to what is essential that we put ourselves in a position to recognize the mystical dimension of ancient Egyptian religion. This is precisely what the phe-nomenological method enables us to do, whereas were we to pursue the methodology advocated by Assmann, the power, the intrinsic numinosity and existential meaning of this dimension would be missed. Through fol-lowing the phenomenological method, a new kind of understanding can be gained that is both more receptive to and more engaged with the mystical content of the Pyramid Texts than would be possible if we adhered to methodological approaches such as that put forward by Assmann.[35]

The aim of this study, then, is to move beyond describing and classifying the content of the Pyramid Texts in order to encounter the human situation, the existential and experiential ground, from out of which this content has arisen and to which it ultimately refers. When, for example, we read in utterance 223 of the Unas Pyramid Texts, of the king being told to wake up, stir himself, and rise up, it is not enough simply to note that this is an allu-sion to a particular episode in the Osiris myth, and that the king is at this point identified with Osiris. Certainly to stop at this point may be a great temptation. One could, of course, elaborate further on the social, political, and funerary contexts of this episode of the myth, or devote oneself to extended commentary on the grammatical structure of the text, and in so doing one would no doubt make a valid contribution to scholarly knowl-edge. In all likelihood, one would in the process have also safely neutralized the text's existential significance and saved oneself from too unsettling an exposure to its real import. But for the phenomenologist, there is a further question to be asked, and that is: What does it mean existentially and expe-rientially for the king as Osiris to wake up, stir himself, and rise up? To ask this question in a thoroughgoing manner is to deepen our involvement with the religious dimension of what is being described. We attempt to penetrate further into its meaning by allowing its meaning to penetrate into us. The king, in being identified with Osiris, has crossed the threshold of death, and yet in utterance 223 he is told to raise himself, stand up, and eat. Here do we not knock on the door of a realm of experience that is both unfamiliar and terrifying? Truly to expose ourselves to the inner meaning of utterance 223 is to risk releasing the full power of a *mysterium tremendum*.

While it may be quite appropriate for the Egyptologist to hold back from attempting such an encounter and to focus on analyzing and sorting the religious data as an end in itself, for the phenomenologist this encounter is crucial in order to gain the kind of understanding that he or she is seeking. This is not to criticize Egyptology, but simply to distinguish two different kinds of approach to the same subject matter. Within the dis-cipline of Egyptology, it may be sufficient to define *understanding* as "analysing and sorting the material" in order to reduce complexity and "uncover meaningful and . . . intelligible contexts." But the methodology of analysis and classification by itself will result in a mode of understanding that inevitably remains external to the living content of the religious text. For the phenomenologist, one has not fully understood the specifically religious significance of a text until one has, in the words of Mircea Eliade, "laid bare the existential situation" underlying a symbol, rite, or myth.[36] For the phenomenologist, no amount of analytical and classificatory work will result in true understanding unless there is a mobilization of all one's emotional and intuitive faculties in order to empathize and tune in to the nature of the experience that is being described.

Shamanism in Relation to Ancient Egyptian Religion

The spiritual universe of the ancient Egyptians does in fact have a great deal in common with that revealed in the literature of shamanism. In the shamanic literature, we read account after account given by people for whom the spirit world is a reality, just as it was for the ancient Egyptians. In shamanism, as in ancient Egyptian religion, we are only marginally concerned with belief systems, for central to shamanism are actual human experiences. It is simply not possible to approach an understanding of these experiences unless one accepts that they relate to a dimension of existence of a different order from the sense-perceptible world that normally captures our awareness. Thus, as we shall see in the course of this study, a certain alliance exists between shamanism and ancient Egyptian religion that sets them both apart from the later, faith-based religions.

The role of the shaman as mediator between the "nonordinary" reality of the spirit world and the ordinary reality of the sense-perceptible world is in many respects paralleled in ancient Egypt by the Egyptian king, whose role is similarly to act as mediator between worlds.[37] Such important shamanic themes as the initiatory death and dismemberment followed by rebirth and renewal, the transformation of the shaman into a power animal, the ecstatic ascent to the sky, and the crossing of the threshold of death in order to commune with ancestors and gods are all to be found in the Pyramid Texts, as we shall see. If within shamanism these motifs correspond to actual experiences undergone by the shaman, then one fails to do justice to the same motifs in the Pyramid Texts if one locks oneself into an interpretative stance that can see them only as the expression of Egyptian "funerary beliefs."

This is not to say that religious life in Old Kingdom Egypt should be summarily reclassified as a type of shamanism. There are several elements in classical shamanism that are absent from ancient Egyptian religion, both during the period of the Pyramid Texts and later. Most obviously, we do not find the single figure of the shaman in Egypt, entering into trance states in order to retrieve souls, heal the sick, or journey into the spirit world, in the way in which this is described in classical shamanism. Moreover, classical shamanism is, strictly speaking, a phenomenon of tribal hunter-gatherer societies, usually organized in small, scattered units.[38] The social organization of ancient Egypt was very different from this. We do, though, find a variety of figures in ancient Egypt, be they priests, magicians, healers, or the king himself, who, taken together, fulfilled practically all the roles of the traditional shaman, using more or less the same means.[39] Furthermore, it could be argued that we misunderstand shamanism if we see it merely as a sociological phenomenon. As Mircea Eliade has pointed out, shamanism should be classed as a type of mysticism.[40] It is in this sense that it seems justifiable to speak of shamanic content in the Pyramid Texts, for, as we shall see, the type of mystical experience that the Pyramid Texts describe is frequently paralleled by similar accounts in the literature of shamanism. Indeed, it seems that a right understanding of the Pyramid Texts is not possible without recognizing how profoundly shamanic are the experiences they describe.

So while Egyptian society, including its highly structured religious organization, may not correspond to traditional tribal cultures in which classical shamanism is practiced, the mystical experiences that we meet in the Pyramid Texts have a distinctive quality that to call by any name other than "shamanic" would be to do them an injustice. To the extent that we try to penetrate the quality of the spiritual life that is presented to us in the Pyramid Texts, and in particular the kind of consciousness within which it arose, it seems impossible to avoid reference to shamanism. By showing that certain features of the ancient Egyptian Pyramid Texts have a distinctively shamanic quality, and indeed express a distinctively shamanic wisdom, the religious landscape of Old Kingdom Egypt receives illumination from the perspective of a specific kind of mystical tradition. From this perspective we are able to see better the lived relationship of the pharaoh in particular to the "nonordinary" reality of the spirit realm.

The inner meaning of the Pyramid Texts can also be illumined from the perspective of other mystical traditions of the Mediterranean world, such as the ancient Greek and Hellenistic mystery cults, the mystical philosophy of Platonism and Neoplatonism, and the Hermetic tradition. While these mystical traditions are not usually classified as shamanic, they do have many shared characteristics with shamanism.[41] For example, crossing over the threshold of death, the ascent of the soul to the sky, the encounter with ancestors and gods, and the critical experience of spiritual rebirth are all attested in these mystical traditions just as they are in shamanism. If we find corresponding motifs in the Pyramid Texts, then we have all the more reason to consider that they may be referring not to "funerary beliefs" but to actual mystical experiences. For if the spirit world is a reality, then human beings may become conscious of it, and journey into it, through a diversity of means and from within a wide range of different religious frameworks.

Of all the different religious frameworks, shamanism could be regarded as the most primal, and could be seen as a substratum of what came to expression in more urbanized and hierarchically organized, formal religious structures such as developed in ancient Egypt.[42] But Egyptology has been and remains remarkably resistant to the idea that there was any shamanic element in ancient Egyptian religion. Few Egyptological studies of ancient Egyptian religion refer to shamanism, and if they do, it is usually in dismissive terms.[43] It is hoped, then, that the present study may contribute to a softening of this resistant attitude, and may lead to an acceptance that not only was ancient Egyptian religion mystical, but that the type of mysticism that existed in Egypt had strong affinities with shamanism.

The Call to Awakening

Reference has been made to the attempt to "lay bare the existential situation" as crucial to understanding the specifically religious significance of a text. Intrinsic to any existential situation is both the act of experiencing and the object experienced. The interpretation of religious texts requires that we recognize that not only do they arise out of actual religious experiences, but that they also refer to spiritual realities that need to be understood precisely as such.[44] The fact that cosmic and spiritual realms such as the Dwat (Underworld), and the Akhet (the place of spiritual illumination), and so on may not be realities to the modern world should not lead us to categorize them as belonging merely to "cosmologies," "cosmographies," or "ideologies," or anything else. Although this may be how they seem to the modern scholar, for the Egyptians they were indubitable realities.[45] It is a guiding assumption of this study that in order to understand the Pyramid Texts, we need to overcome what Henri Corbin has called the "agnostic reflex" that seems to have become a kind of guarantor of academic respectability, and which has a paralyzing effect on the mind, closing it off from the dimension of experience to which the Egyptians were so open.[46] If we are concerned with mystical experience, we should be concerned also with that to which this experience refers. The use of the term *mysticism* in this book therefore incorporates both awareness of and relationship to the spiritual dimension of existence that is perceived to have reality and power. For the ancient Egyptian religious consciousness there were experiential realms that most moderns are unaware of. The focus of this study, then, returns to experiences and the transpersonal realities to which these experiences refer.[47]

Insofar as this book will be concerned both with the religious consciousness of ancient Egypt and with the nature of the inner worlds toward which that consciousness was directed, its focus is not simply on the past. It is on structures of human consciousness and the objects that are revealed to these structures of consciousness. The religion of ancient Egypt puts us in touch with dimensions of reality that, though they have been excluded from the worldview of scientific materialism, are no less real for falling outside the dominant conceptual and experiential framework of our times. Those who allow themselves to engage with it fully know that ancient Egyptian religion has the capacity to connect us with something buried and half forgotten within ourselves. For Mircea Eliade, this was one of the most important reasons for studying the history of religions. He referred to the latter as a "meta-psycho-analysis" that can lead to an "awakening" to the existence of great spiritual riches and a "renewal of consciousness."[48]

The culture and religion of ancient Egypt exercises such an enormous fascination for people today largely because of the depth and integrity of its spiritual life, which so contrasts with that of modern secular culture. It is therefore incumbent on us to try to unveil those layers of experience and wisdom that have to a large extent been excluded from the purview of the Egyptological establishment and which, as we shall see, constitute the mystical core of ancient Egyptian religion. This can put us in touch with a whole dimension of human experience that few of us today come near to experiencing, but with which many of us feel we need to reconnect. There is a universe of experience that exists only a little way below the threshold of modern awareness of which the Egyptians were intensely aware. If we take this experiential universe seriously, our dialogue with the religion of the ancient Egyptians may serve to pierce the veils of complacency with which the modern secular mentality surrounds itself.

The root concern of this study, therefore, is not just to understand a mode of consciousness that is remote from us in time, but also to reflect on ourselves, the peculiarly godless predicament that we find ourselves in, and the spiritual restlessness that accompanies it. The study of ancient Egyptian religion serves as a mirror to our own consciousness. Through entering into dialogue with the ancient Egyptians, our presuppositions concerning the possible range of human experience may well be shaken by the presentiment that it could be so much greater. While what follows is intended to shed light on the religious experience of the ancient Egyptians, this in itself can wake us up to levels of our own humanity, and to objective spiritual realities with which the contemporary world has long since lost contact.

2 EGYPTOLOGY: THE DEATH AND REBIRTH OF MYSTICISM IN ANCIENT EGYPT

Mysticism and the Realm of Death

For the Egyptians, death was not simply something that happens to people when they come to the end of their life. It was conceived as a realm, which they called the Dwat,[1] that exists alongside the physical realm that we inhabit during our lifetime. The Dwat is an invisible region that borders on, and interpenetrates, the world of the living. In this region are to be found gods and demons as well as the spirits of the dead. Furthermore, it is only through having entered this region that the experience of inner spiritual illumination (becoming *akh*) can come about.[2] Whereas today we tend to have a temporal conception of death as something that intervenes and cuts off our life at a certain moment in time, the Egyptian conception of death was not simply temporal; it was also spatial. The space occupied by the dead was, however, conceived of as a deeply interior space. In contrast to the modern secular awareness of the world, the Egyptians were aware that the world they lived in was not simply physical, not simply visible, but both physical and nonphysical, both visible and invisible. And even more unlike the modern view, they regarded the invisible or interior world as in many respects more important and more real than the visible, exterior world.

It was more important because it was regarded not only as the terminus of old, worn-out life but also as the source of new life. It was the source of all that comes into manifestation on the material plane, somewhat similar

20

to the Platonic world of archetypal forms. For the Egyptians, then, life on the material plane was considered to be more than just interrelated with the Dwat—it was utterly dependent upon it. To understand both the origins and the fate of the things that come into being in the physical world, the Egyptians believed that it was necessary to know the nature of the invisible world of the Dwat.

There is a New Kingdom esoteric text that appears in the tomb of Ramesses VI, and elsewhere, that makes it very clear that this interior realm of the Dwat, into which people go when they die, was the object of intense interest for the Egyptian priesthood. The title of this text is the Book of What Is in the Underworld (Dwat), and in its introductory sentences we read that the text is concerned with "the knowledge of the power of those in the Dwat" including "knowledge of their sacred rituals to Ra, knowledge of the mysterious powers, knowledge of what is in the hours as well as their gods. . . ."[3]

Now, it might be argued that the whole of this text along with the contents of all the rest of the massive body of literature dealing with the Egyptian "otherworld" is not knowledge at all, but mere priestly speculation about something essentially unknowable. But it could equally well be maintained that this knowledge was the outcome of the type of mystical experience that involved crossing the threshold of death while still alive, an experience that is so characteristic of shamanism. There is evidence, which will be presented in the next chapter, that rituals existed in ancient Egypt that served the purpose of projecting the soul across the threshold of death even when still alive. These rituals, although portrayed primarily as royal rituals in which the king was the main participant, are unlikely to have been exclusively royal for the simple reason that they were devised and directed by, and then recorded under the supervision of, the priesthood. Unless there were also initiates into this mystical knowledge within the priesthood, it is hard to see how such kingship rituals could have been spiritually effective. It is also hard to see how the literature, with its detailed descriptions of the geography of, and the experiences of the human soul in, the world of the dead, could have come about unless there were priests who had direct awareness of this realm.

In this respect, the following comments of Mircea Eliade in relation to the role of the shaman in tribal communities are also pertinent to our understanding of the role of the priesthood in ancient Egypt and the origin of esoteric texts such as the Book of What Is in the Underworld:

> It is thanks to his capacity to travel into supernatural worlds and SEE superhuman beings (gods, demons) and spirits of the dead that the

shaman is able to contribute in such a decisive manner to the KNOWLEDGE OF DEATH. It is likely that many features of the "funereal geography," as well as certain themes of the mythology of death, are the result of the ecstatic experiences of the shamans.[4]

Whether we regard such ecstatic experiences as capable of producing genuine knowledge depends to a large extent on our own philosophical position, but it is certainly the case that within shamanic cultures this was, and is, regarded as a valid route to the acquisition of authentic knowledge. In ancient Egypt, this also seems to have been the case. Kingship rituals were by no means just pageantry, but entailed the king undergoing powerful inner experiences. In chapter 1, reference was made to the coronation text of Thutmosis III. In this text the king claims to have risen up to heaven in the form of a falcon and actually *seen* there the secret image of Ra and *beheld* the transformations of the sun god "on his secret ways of heaven."[5] We may, of course, dismiss this as merely an empty piece of royal bombast, but it could also be seen as a description of a genuine mystical experience.

The titles of various ancient Egyptian high officials from all periods indicate that many of these officials may also have had direct knowledge of spiritual realities. One such title was master of secrets, or in its longer form master of secrets of heaven, earth, and the Dwat, which we find, for example, in the titulary of the New Kingdom vizier Rekhmire, of whom it was claimed: "There is nothing on earth, in heaven or in any part of the Dwat of which he does not have knowledge." It certainly seems more likely that the type of knowledge referred to here had an experiential basis than that it was merely a memorizing of the content of sacred texts.[6] In other words, it was mystical knowledge—knowledge that was the result of direct experience of spiritual realities. According to the Egyptian priest Chaeremon, who, living in the first century A.D., is an important late source for our understanding of the tenor of the inner life of the priesthood, the priests of Egypt were in "constant contact with divine knowledge and inspiration."[7] His account of the type of knowledge pursued in the temples will be considered later in this chapter, but it is worth noting here that Chaeremon describes it as both "divine" and "inspired."

It was because of the perceived mystical basis of ancient Egyptian religion that across the ancient Greek and Hellenistic world, ancient Egypt had a reputation for being the fountainhead of esoteric knowledge and wisdom.[8] Many Greek and Roman accounts of ancient Egyptian religion are not only respectful and sensitive toward its deeper spiritual import, but they also affirm that mystical experience was the wellspring of this esoteric wisdom. Indeed, not a single commentator seems to have thought the funerary cult held a paramount place in ancient Egyptian religious life. Instead of the funerary cult, we find writers such as Herodotus, Plutarch, and Iamblichus referring a great deal to mysteries, initiation, and mystical experience.[9] The Egyptian priests are portrayed as spiritual practitioners who had direct knowledge of realities beyond the physical. According to our Greek and Roman sources, this knowledge was less the result of philosophical reasoning or speculation and more the result of direct experience.[10] Thus, Greek religion and philosophy were often portrayed as but a pale reflection of the earlier Egyptian wisdom.[11]

The Greek and Roman commentators had the advantage of direct or indirect contact with contemporary Egyptian priests, a possibility denied to us. Furthermore, they were living during a period when there was still a flourishing mystery tradition that some of our most important sources were acutely sensitive to, or into which they were themselves initiated.[12] There is therefore not just a historical proximity to ancient Egypt but also an experiential proximity in these ancient sources, the lack of which puts us at a distinct disadvantage when it comes to understanding the religious experience of the ancient Egyptians. In most other respects, our knowledge of ancient Egyptian culture is far more accurate and comprehensive than that of the ancient Greeks and Romans, who, with a few notable exceptions (like Pythagoras), were not able to read hieroglyphs. But in the sphere of religious experience, the ancient commentators were spiritually far closer than we are to the Egyptians, and for this reason their testimony carries considerable weight.[13]

Egyptology: Mysticism Denied

The revival of interest in ancient Egypt during the Renaissance was largely because it was seen as the source of a wisdom of both greater antiquity and greater profundity than that of the Greeks. The Renaissance knowledge of Egypt depended on ancient commentators such as Plutarch, Diodorus, and Iamblichus, supplemented with newly discovered and freshly translated texts, most importantly the *Corpus Hermeticum*.[14] This dependency on classical sources continued into the eighteenth century, with the consequence that until the end of the eighteenth century, the standard view of Egypt among academics differed little from the view held in antiquity—that Egypt was the source of both Greek culture and Greek religion and that it harbored a wisdom more profound than that of the Greeks.[15] Thus, when Charles-François Dupuis, one of the most politically influential scholars of the French Revolution and Napoleonic period, promulgated the idea that Greek religion and philosophy were simply embellishments of a wisdom whose source was Egyptian, this was not seen as particularly radical.[16] Indeed, this was the belief of many members of the battalion of scholars who went to Egypt with Napoleon's expedition, and quite possibly of Napoleon himself. The dream of unlocking a lost ancient knowledge that could then be integrated within contemporary European culture was almost certainly part of the agenda of the French conquest.[17] The direct result of the conquest of Egypt was that Egyptian hieroglyphs were eventually deciphered, and the modern discipline of Egyptology was born.

In the beginning, Egyptology was still aligned to the ancient perception of Egypt as harboring a tradition of deep wisdom that was the inspirational fount of Greek religion, mythology, and philosophy—particularly Platonism and Hermetism. Early Egyptologists like Champollion, de Rougé, and Brugsch had a genuine reverence for Egypt as the source of a sublime metaphysics and theology.[18] But this reverential attitude toward Egyptian religion was gradually displaced by a far more critical approach as Egyptology established itself as a professional academic discipline. The attitudes of late-nineteenth- and early-twentieth-century Egyptologists like Maspero and Erman differ markedly from those of the earlier "romantics." Their interest in Egypt was not fired by religious motivations, and the ancient religious texts that they now published for the first time seemed to have no affinity at all with the intellectually precise treatises of the Greek philosophers. Maspero, who was the first to publish the Pyramid Texts, confessed that despite trying, he was unable to discover any profound wisdom in ancient Egyptian religious texts. After years of grappling with them, he had to admit in 1893 (the year before his publication of the Pyramid Texts) "that they [Egyptian religious texts] did not show any of the profound wisdom that others had seen in them. I cannot be accused of wanting to depreciate the Egyptians and I am convinced that they were one of the great people of humanity, one of the most original and the most creative, but they always remained semi-barbarians. . . ."[19]

Adolf Erman was of a similar opinion. He pointed to the "conflicting ideas," "jumble," and "confusion" that he found in the Pyramid Texts, which he felt were simply exacerbated in the Book of the Dead. Referring to the latter, he declared the confusion to have become so great "that it now scarcely repays the labor of attempting to disentangle it."[20] For Erman, the Greeks' reverential attitude toward the Egyptians could only be explained as being due to their having been deliberately hoodwinked by the charlatan Egyptian priests, who knew that if they simply kept quiet, the Greeks would read into their religion all sorts of wonderful mysteries that were actually not there:

> The more taciturn and reserved was the behaviour of the priests, the more did the Greeks believe that they possessed wonderful secrets; and when in time they learned these mysteries and understood what was contained in the sacred writings concerning Osiris and Isis, Typhon and Horus, their faith in the wisdom of the Egyptians was so deeply rooted that they were unable to look with unprejudiced eyes at those myths so devoid of spirituality. They interpreted them according to their own philosophical ideas, instead of perceiving their emptiness.[21]

From the 1880s onward, more and more of the sacred literature of ancient Egypt was translated and made available to the modern world. But for the translators, who were working within an increasingly positivistic milieu, these texts seemed to reveal only a desultory mix of primitive magical spells and a confusion of hymns, offering formulae, prayers, fragments of myth, and disparate instructions for carrying out arcane rituals. To many of the first generations of scholars, the sacred literature of ancient Egypt seemed so muddled, haphazard, and obscure that any residual hopes of rediscovering some "forgotten wisdom" or "secret knowledge" came to seem like childish fantasies, which were now exploded.

Thus it was concluded that the ancient Egyptian mind was "prephilosophical," incapable of coherent or systematic thought and given to expressing itself in rather crude imagery. Far from being a treasure house of sublime wisdom or a repository of lost secret knowledge, ancient Egyptian religious literature seemed to be riddled with primitive superstitions and muddled, if somewhat grandiose, beliefs.

The sentiment expressed by the Egyptologist T. Eric Peet, writing in the 1930s, is fairly typical of the conclusions reached by scholars after half a century of labor:

> In the eyes of the Greeks, the Egyptians possessed a reputation for wisdom. As time goes on and we learn more about the Egyptian mind and its products it becomes increasingly difficult to understand this. . . . Theology, for instance, consisted of a mass of myth and legend in which the deeds of the gods, neither better nor worse than those of any other pantheon, were preserved. . . . The fact is that the Egyptians never disentangled philosophy from the crudest theology.[22]

This view of the ancient Egyptian mind to a large extent remained the dominant one among Egyptologists for much of the twentieth century. It was complemented by a second view, that the Egyptians were practical people with a basically materialistic outlook on life. This is why their theology was so undeveloped. For T. Eric Peet, "The Egyptian mind was practical and concrete, and concerned itself little or not at all with speculations regarding the ultimate nature of things."[23] It is an opinion that we find repeated over and over again. The Egyptians, far from being the guardians of a secret wisdom, were actually an ignorant lot who had not yet discovered philosophy or science and concerned themselves with only the practical affairs of daily existence. As another Egyptologist, B. L. Goff, writing in the late 1970s, was to put it,

> In ancient Egypt, as also elsewhere in the ancient world, there was no knowledge of consistent laws governing the operation of everything around us. Men knew that the world was complex. Much in their experience seemed inconsistent. They and their associates were often inconsistent. . . . Thus polytheism seemed a realistic conclusion from their observation of the complexity of the world; and inconsistency seemed of its essence. . . . Thus what appears to us contradictory did not seem invalid to the ancient Egyptians. Furthermore they were practical, not philosophical people.[24]

Goff's argument seems to be that, owing to a certain weakness in the ancient mind, due (we must suppose) to the fact that it did not have the advantage of a modern training in scientific thinking, the Egyptians solved the problem of a complex and apparently inconsistent world by creating an equally complex and inconsistent polytheistic mythology. Thanks to modern science, we have now advanced beyond this stage of bafflement by the world, and have attained precisely what eluded the Egyptians—a knowledge of the "consistent laws governing the operation of everything around us."

This assessment of the level of knowledge, or rather blind ignorance, of the ancient Egyptians was shared by many non-Egyptologists as well. Otto Neugebauer, in his monumental *The Exact Sciences in Antiquity*, first published in 1951, put it like this: "Ancient science was the product of very few men; and those few happened not to be Egyptian."[25] The same opinion is echoed by the philosopher Bertrand Russell in his book *The Wisdom of the West*: "Both Egypt and Babylon furnished some knowledge which the Greeks later took over. But neither developed Science or Philosophy.

Whether this is due to lack of native genius or to social conditions is not a fundamental question here. What is significant is that the function of religion was not conducive to the exercise of the intellectual adventure."[26]

In the second part of the twentieth century, however, the view of the ancient Egyptian mind as "prephilosophical" and incapable of accessing worthwhile knowledge became less and less sustainable. As scholars like Alexandre Piankoff, Erik Hornung, and Jan Assmann began to penetrate the subtle, complex, and highly intricate levels of meaning in New Kingdom religious literature, it became clear to them and others that, in the words of Hornung, "Egyptian thought steers clear of monocausal simplification, convincing instead through refinement and association, through mastery of both word and image."[27]

Russell was wrong. The Egyptians *were* concerned with philosophical questions: questions about being and nonbeing, about the meaning of death, about the nature of the cosmos and human nature, and about many other philosophical, cosmological, and theological issues.[28] In the view of James P. Allen, writing in the late 1980s, we should lament less the intellectual deficiency of the ancient Egyptians than of modern Western thought, which has created a dichotomy between objective scientific knowledge and philosophy on the one hand and subjective religious experience on the other. This dichotomy simply did not exist in ancient Egypt, where religion and philosophy formed a unity.[29] Jan Assmann went so far as to assert that in ancient Egypt there was, after all, "an esoteric body of knowledge."[30] For scholars like Piankoff, Hornung, Assmann, and Allen, what was required was a detailed analysis and sorting of the religious material so as to uncover what is meaningful and intelligible beneath what initially appears to be confused and confusing.

Although within contemporary Egyptology the tide has been turning in attitudes toward ancient Egyptian religion, there is still a long way to go, for while scholars of Egyptian religion may now be more inclined to see intelligibility and meaning, they do not see mysticism. They do not see knowledge that has an intrinsic validity because it has arisen from direct spiritual experience. Thus, despite Assmann referring to a body of "esoteric knowledge," he views this knowledge as esoteric by virtue of its restricted access rather than because of its intrinsically mystical content.[31] And Hornung has consistently denied the existence of mysticism in ancient Egypt.[32] Both Piankoff and Allen, who have worked extensively with the symbolism and cosmology of the Pyramid Texts, follow the same line; they do not question the general assumption that they are funerary texts reflecting complex beliefs concerning the afterlife.[33] Here, then, it seems we come to the boundary, referred to in chapter 1, over which Egyptology is reluctant to step. The boundary lies between intellectual analysis on the one side and empathetic "reliving" of the spiritual experiences that are expressed in the religious texts on the other.

Egyptology in the latter part of the twentieth century has on the whole been highly resistant to investigating the experiential dimensions of Egyptian religion. Furthermore, it is not unusual still to encounter Egyptological studies that report only incoherence, inconsistency, and confusion in ancient Egyptian religious texts.[34] On the whole, it would be fair to say that such perceptions are less dominant than they were, but the attitudes that characterized Egyptology during the late nineteenth and first part of the twentieth century are deeply ingrained and form a kind of substructure to the whole edifice of the discipline. Underlying much Egyptological thinking during the nineteenth and twentieth centuries, it is possible to detect presuppositions—to a large extent shared by the general culture—that still exercise a considerable influence on the way in which ancient Egyptian religious material is interpreted. Three can be isolated as having had a determining influence on attitudes within mainstream academic Egyptology since its inception in the nineteenth century. We have met them all in the previous pages. They are, first, that since the Egyptians lacked modern scientific method, they must also have lacked true knowledge of the world. Second, because Egyptian civilization was historically earlier than that of the Greeks and Romans, it was more primitive and less advanced, just as modern civilization is more advanced than that of the Greeks and Romans. Underlying this assumption is the idea of progress, which tends to color negatively modern perceptions of the past. The third assumption is that the character or temperament of the Egyptians was practical rather than mystical. This assumption, along with the other two, has had particularly serious consequences for the study of Egyptian religion and the way in which Egyptian religious texts have been understood.

The three presuppositions have led to many of the deeper, more mystical aspects of ancient Egyptian religion being passed over or neutralized by being subsumed under the general rubric of "funerary beliefs." Those Egyptologists who have addressed the mystical aspects of ancient Egyptian religion have run the risk of being marginalized from the mainstream. What is at issue is more than just the level of knowledge or ignorance (and, by implication, degree of "primitiveness") of the *ancient Egyptians*. It is also a question of the satisfactoriness of *our own* scientific knowledge, and of the culture that is based upon it, and whether perhaps the Egyptians really did know important things about which we today are abominably ignorant.

The Knowledge of the Egyptians

For several centuries a fundamental assumption of modern Western culture has been that the way to attain reliable knowledge is through science rather than through religious or mystical experience, and that science was a product of Greek, not Egyptian civilization. The first part of this assumption can be traced back at least as far as Francis Bacon's *The Advancement of Learning* (1605), which set forth the vision of a "universal science" within which all knowledge would be incorporated through a slow, cumulative process, fueled by continuing and systematic research.[35] In this paradigm, scientific knowledge is purged of personal opinion, feeling, or value judgment in order to attain an impersonal and objective description of reality. It does this by pursuing a methodology that stresses empirical observation, the ability of third parties to repeat observations and experiments, and the formulation of explanatory theories that will be open to modification or refutation by subsequent observations. Its objectivity is thus guaranteed, whereas the insights, visions, or revelations of religious or mystical experience are viewed as irredeemably subjective, impossible to verify or repeat by third parties, and thus unreliable sources of knowledge.

The second part of the assumption, that it was the Greeks who invented the one and only reliable method of attaining knowledge called science, began to take root considerably later—during the eighteenth century, when William Warburton and others first argued that the Egyptians were unable to think scientifically or philosophically.[36] Up until that time, it was still widely believed that the Egyptians possessed a knowledge and wisdom that was superior to that of the Greeks—superior because it was based on contemplation and/or mystical experience of the divine order.[37] But slowly the view took hold that it was the Greeks who laid the foundations of the scientific pursuit of knowledge and that the cultures of Mesopotamia and Egypt that existed before that of Greece were "prescientific" and "prephilosophical." As such, they could hardly be credited with having had much in the way of "real knowledge."

When the Egyptologist B. L. Goff stated that in ancient Egypt "there was no knowledge of consistent laws governing the operation of everything around us," he was voicing an opinion widely held by twentieth-century Egyptologists and ancient historians that there was no real knowledge in Egypt.[38] This opinion is very deep rooted, and emerges in otherwise open-minded studies of ancient Egyptian culture, such as Barry Kemp's *Ancient Egypt: Anatomy of a Civilization* (1989). There we read, with reference to ancient Mesopotamia and Egypt, the almost casual remark that these ancient cultures "have arisen and run successfully for long periods without much true knowledge of the world at all."[39]

The assumption, of course, is that only modern scientific knowledge is "true knowledge." During the nineteenth and twentieth centuries, it was argued that in these ancient cultures, where the guardians of learning were priests, knowledge remained at a primitive level because of the stranglehold of superstition, magic, and uncritically held beliefs that supposedly characterized pre-Greek societies. The reason why there was no "true knowledge" was that it was totally inhibited by their religious outlook and theocratic power structures.[40] The implication here is that a religious culture such as that of ancient Egypt is necessarily an ignorant one.

This assumption has had such a strong hold that even when the historian of science Otto Neugebauer and the Egyptologist J.-Ph. Lauer were forced by the evidence on the ground to admit that the Egyptians were using such mathematical relations as pi and phi in the construction of buildings, instead of concluding that the Egyptians had a theoretical knowledge of these mathematical relations, they put it down merely to "practical knacks" and "utilitarian empiricism." In other words, the Egyptians were using these numerical relationships without actually being aware of the fact they were doing so.[41] This reluctance to admit that the Egyptians were as capable of logical and mathematical thinking as the Greeks sits uneasily with the extraordinary precision with which ancient Egyptian monuments, such as the pyramids, were built. It is also in stark contrast to the testimony of the Greeks themselves. According to no less an authority than Aristotle, Egypt was "the cradle of mathematics," and the priests of Egypt invented geometry, arithmetic, and astronomy.[42] Ancient sources testify that prominent Greek thinkers (like Thales, Pythagoras, Plato, and Eudoxus) learned their philosophy and science from the Egyptians. Eudoxus—like Pythagoras before him—was a renowned mathematician and astronomer who spent sixteen months studying in Egypt before returning to Athens to teach at Plato's Academy.[43]

In the early days of Egyptology, there was a greater willingness to accept that the Egyptians did have an understanding of mathematical principles such as pi as well as advanced astronomical knowledge, and this can be seen in the writings of Jomard, Piazzi Smyth, Norman Lockyer, and Flinders Petrie.[44] But during the twentieth century, advocacy of such views became increasingly heretical, and a growing rift emerged between "mainstream" Egyptology, which was dismissive of claims that the Egyptians had the capacity either to think in terms of abstract mathematical relations or to make very accurate astronomical observations, and "outsiders," who usually did not have a formal qualification in Egyptology and so could easily be dismissed as cranks or "pyramidiots." Foremost among the latter was R. A. Schwaller de Lubicz, who, despite his detailed study of the theoretical principles and practical application of ancient Egyptian mathematics in *The Temple of Man (Le temple de l'homme)* and his studies of ancient Egyptian esotericism and symbolism in this and other works, remains virtually ignored by the Egyptological establishment.[45] In *The Temple of Man*, Schwaller de Lubicz argues like many before him that the learning of the Greeks was largely derivative of, and lagged behind, the much more comprehensive metaphysical understanding of the Egyptians. His explanation for the difference between the Egyptian and the Greek methods of acquiring knowledge is that the Greeks isolated and abstracted the analytical faculty from its metaphysical and symbolic locus in the Egyptian religious consciousness. It was not so much that the Greeks were more intellectually rigorous, but rather that they were less spiritually aware than the Egyptians. Thus the science that they inaugurated was a science from which the sacred dimension had been expurgated.[46] According to Schwaller de Lubicz, the Egyptians had the same intellectual abilities as the Greeks, but they put these at the service of an overriding metaphysical and symbolic sensibility, ever directed toward "the eternal vital moment" that constantly escapes analytical inquiry.[47]

It is significant that the explanation given by Schwaller de Lubicz corresponds very closely with an account of the Egyptian priest Chaeremon, who lived in the first century A.D. Though an Egyptian, Chaeremon was steeped in Hellenic culture and went out of his way to explain Egyptian temple life in terms comprehensible to non-Egyptians. Some allowance, therefore, has to be made for his speaking the language of Platonic and Stoic philosophy, which by the first century A.D. had become the lingua franca of discourse about spiritual matters. According to the account he has left to us, the Egyptian priests "dedicated their entire lives to the thought and contemplation of God. . . . The fruit of their contemplation of God was knowledge; and through contemplation and knowledge they attained to a way of life at once esoteric and old-fashioned."[48] Through this "constant contact with divine knowledge and inspiration," the priests of Egypt pursued "a life of wisdom." Chaeremon then explains that it was within this sacred context that they practiced astronomy, studied arithmetic and geometry, and devoted their lives to "scholarly investigation."[49]

Chaeremon's Egyptian priests are portrayed as philosopher-priests, pursuing a life of wisdom through the contemplation of God. This should be understood as his way of making accessible to his Greco-Roman audience the fact that the path to "divine knowledge" pursued by the priests involved the cultivation of elevated states of consciousness different from normal discursive reasoning based on sense experience. The ancient Egyptians valued and prioritized mystical knowledge acquired through exalted states of consciousness, and this—as we shall see—is to a large extent what is documented in the sacred texts that have come down to us. The reason why such knowledge was valued so highly is that the world was understood by the ancient Egyptians to be interpenetrated by divine forces. The gods were the moving causes behind and within the phenomenal world. Thus knowledge of the gods, in a universe recognized to be a manifestation of divine powers, was the only knowledge truly worth having: All other knowledge was secondary to it.

The ancient Egyptians clearly had a quite different conception of knowledge from that of modern science, which seeks to reduce phenomena to their material causes and sees explanations as successful to the extent that these material causes are laid bare. Ancient Egyptian "science" was above all directed toward the immaterial causes that lie behind the events of the world, and the goal of knowledge was the experience of these spiritual causes or powers. Such knowledge was therefore a pursuit of priests, practiced in a sacred context, and in this respect differed fundamentally from modern secular science. In ancient Egypt it was inconceivable that knowledge could be pursued in isolation from religion, for all real knowledge was religious. To ask the question of whether or not the Egyptians pursued scientific knowledge in anything akin to the modern sense, or had the ability to "think scientifically," is actually to miss the far more fundamental question of *what the reality was in which they lived*. It was precisely their awareness of interior, spiritual dimensions of existence that demanded methodologies of knowledge that bear little comparison with those of modern materialistic science. In Egypt, the rational faculty was subservient to a contemplative, inspirational, and, as shall later become apparent, *ecstatic* contact with the divine.

The Idea of Progress

The assumption that modern materialistic science provides the only sure path to acquiring knowledge, and that true knowledge began with the Greeks not the Egyptians, to a large extent rests on a second deeply rooted assumption: that human history constitutes a steady progress not only of knowledge, but also of social organization and psychological and spiritual maturity. Just as our knowledge today is considered to be more accurate and comprehensive than that of the past, so too our social and political forms are deemed more just and humane, and people today assume that they are more psychologically developed and more enlightened than peoples of the past. Thus the idea of progress not only works to our advantage, but it also disadvantages the past, for the earlier the culture, the more primitive it must have been.

This contrasts with the way ancient cultures tended to view the past, which was that history involves a gradual decline from an original golden age in which human beings lived in harmony with the gods. Whereas we tend to think of history as inevitably entailing progress and advancement, in ancient times history was viewed as entailing an ever greater falling away from a much higher spiritual condition.[50] The modern idea of progress can be traced at least as far back as Francis Bacon, who saw progress and science as indissolubly linked. Bacon was one of the first to chide his contemporaries for referring to the Greeks and Romans as the "ancients" when they were really the youth of world history.[51] This reversal of perspective took some time to filter through, but by the mid-nineteenth century, through the writings of Condorcet and then later August Comte, the idea of progress had become an unquestioned presupposition in the worldview of educated Europeans.

Comte gave a particularly full and compelling account of human history in terms of the idea of progress. In his massive, six-volume *Cours de philosophie positive* (1830–42), three stages of history are set out, as seen from the vantage point of the modern scientific and materialistic worldview. In the first and most primitive stage, the peoples of antiquity, in struggling to understand the world around them, explained natural phenomena by reference to imaginary deities; in the second stage—beginning around the time of the Renaissance—reference to imaginary deities was superseded by an abstract philosophical interpretation of the world; and in the third stage, which corresponds to the modern period, philosophizing gives way to scientific observation and experiment. Thus, humanity passes through a theological stage during which the mind invents, a metaphysical stage in which the mind abstracts, and finally a scientific stage when it submits itself to positive facts.[52] Each stage is subdivided into different periods, the theological, for example, having three periods—of fetishism, polytheism, and monotheism. Ancient Egypt belongs to an early phase of the polytheistic period, and Greece and Rome belong to a later phase. The long theological stage is succeeded by the much briefer metaphysical stage in the fifteenth century, the work of which was largely to clear away the debris of the past and prepare for the new age of scientific positivism beginning in the nineteenth century.[53]

What Comte set forth was a general perspective that corresponded to a certain feeling that had its origins in the sixteenth century and which, by the nineteenth and twentieth centuries, had rooted itself in the European psyche: that the present was more enlightened, more knowledgeable, and more civilized than the past. While his ideas were adapted, refined, and modified by successive thinkers, he had nevertheless articulated the archetypal idea of progress for the modern age. Two years after Comte's death, Darwin's *Origin of Species* (1859) was published. The theory of evolution served only to reinforce the view of the past as necessarily inferior to the present.[54] With the idea of progress extended into the sphere of biology, scientific thinking for the first time became historical. Science and history could thus join forces insofar as they both conceived of their subject matter in terms of evolutionary progress, of organisms on the one hand and humanity on the other. It was this conception that lay behind the efforts of late-nineteenth-century anthropolgists like Edward Tylor and Sir James Frazer to categorize developmental stages in human culture, from the more primitive or "lower" to the more civilized and "higher" in the evolutionary scale. Judging the past in terms of the modern scientific mentality, Tylor, for instance, argued that the animistic belief in spiritual beings is characteristic of all "low races."[55] Such belief arose from inadequate observation and faulty reasoning. This was due to gross superstition and the inability to distinguish between waking and dreaming, one of the main factors that led, in his view, to "the whole monstrous farrago" of primitive religion.[56] Frazer, like Tylor, viewed the peoples of antiquity as thinking logically but erroneously. He concluded that it was due to a certain innate stupidity that they subscribed as long as they did to the magical view of the world. In time the more intelligent and thoughtful turned away from magic to embrace religion, though in ancient Egypt magic and religion remained inseparably intertwined.[57] Like Comte, Frazer envisaged three phases in the march of human progress. Just as magic would be superseded by religion, so religion would be superseded by science, for the advance of scientific knowledge would inevitably lead to the decline of religious faith.[58]

While Frazer's view of a secular endpoint of human progress was not necessarily shared by historians of religion, it was part of the atmosphere in which the history of religion was studied. During the late nineteenth century, at the time when Egyptology was establishing itself as an academic discipline, the concept of an evolution of religion from elementary or primitive early stages (totemism, fetishism, shamanism) to the later stages of a more refined and elevated religious consciousness was promulgated in various theories.[59] But instead of religion giving way to science, "lower" religious forms could be understood to give way to "higher," with "ethical monotheism" being regarded as the most advanced religious sensibility. Thus, for Sir John Lubbock, writing in 1870, atheism—far from being the endpoint of the evolutionary journey—was rather the most primitive stage, out of which developed fetishism, totemism, shamanism, and anthropomorphism (idolatry), with ethical monotheism being the most developed and final stage.[60] The view that ethical monotheism is the most advanced form of religious consciousness naturally had a tremendous appeal to historians of religion, many of whom were Christian. But it often entailed a dismissive attitude to such "primitive" features of historically earlier religions as shamanism and magic.[61]

Since Egyptology was established as an academic discipline in the nineteenth century, it is hardly surprising that we find evolutionary ideas reflected in the interpretation of ancient Egypt, and especially ancient Egyptian religion. Most nineteenth- and early-twentieth-century Egyptologists were initially classicists, and in approaching Egypt as it were from the territory of Greece, they had to allow that the Egyptians belonged to an earlier historical phase and for this reason could not be as "advanced" as the Greeks. Thus not only were the Egyptians "prescientific," but Egyptian religion was necessarily more primitive, contaminated with magic, superstition, and animal worship. As we have seen in the cases of Maspero and Erman, the difficulties faced by scientifically minded scholars in translating the religious literature led to a perception of the ancient Egyptians as unable to think systematically or philosophically. This is why they expressed themselves in muddled and unclear language. The following (relatively charitable) assessment by James Henry Breasted in his classic study of Egyptian religion, *The Development of Religion and Thought in Ancient Egypt* (1912), is typical of nineteenth- and early-twentieth-century attitudes:

> The Egyptian did not possess the terminology for the expression of a system of abstract thought; neither did he develop the capacity to create the necessary terminology as did the Greek. He thought in concrete pictures, he moved along tangible material channels, and the material world about him furnished nearly all of the terms he used. . . . As we contemplate the earliest developments in human thinking still traceable in contemporary documents, we must expect the vagueness, the crudities, and the limitations inevitable at so early a stage of human development.[62]

For Breasted, the development of religion and thought in ancient Egypt was essentially an evolutionary development, though only partially realized, that showed the struggle to advance from polytheism to monotheism, from superstitious worship to moral idealism, from collective to individual consciousness, and even (albeit in the sphere of the afterlife) from autocracy to democracy. It is significant that for Breasted, as for so many contemporary Egyptophiles, the pharaoh Akhenaten is seen as a peculiarly "modern" ancient Egyptian, an idealist and Romantic whose sensitivity he compared to that of Wordsworth and Ruskin.[63] Akhenaten, it will be recalled, launched an assault on the traditional religion of Egypt that was almost as devastating as that of Christianity some 1,500 years later. For Breasted, however, Akhenaten represented a climax of Egyptian civilization, and after the glorious inflorescence of his reign, Egypt entered its final phase of decline, a fading flower unable to sustain its brief flirtation with modernity.[64]

Sir Alan Gardiner, writing some fifteen years after Breasted, in 1927, filled out the picture of a people still in the childhood of human development. Just as children are averse to philosophizing, so it was with the Egyptians:

> Despite the reputation for philosophic wisdom attributed to the Egyptians by the Greeks, no people has ever shown itself more averse from speculations or more wholeheartedly devoted to material interests; and if they paid an exaggerated attention to funerary observances, it was because the continuance of earthly pursuits and pleasures was felt to be at stake, assuredly not out of any curiosity as to the why and whither of human life.[65]

The Egyptians were, for Gardiner, "a pleasure-loving people, gay, artistic, and sharp-witted, but lacking in depth of feeling and idealism."[66] Depth of feeling and idealism are typical late-adolescent qualities that presumably were lying dormant until they were developed by the Greeks.

Although these attitudes would be regarded by most Egyptologists today as outmoded, they nevertheless can often be detected not far beneath the surface of contemporary accounts of ancient Egyptian religion. We shall consider in the next section the influence of Gardiner's view that the Egyptians were not speculative but practical, and that they were concerned with material interests rather than affairs of the spirit. Underlying it is the Frazerian theory of the religious consciousness of antiquity as being, during the magical phase, directed by practical concerns. This theory still informs the thinking of contemporary commentators on Egyptian religion. For example, in Barbara Watterson's popular reference work, *The Gods of Ancient Egypt* (1984), the Frazerian view of the developmental phases of religious life reappears, with the Egyptians beginning as animists, moving on to adopt magic, until "eventually, theories were developed that turned magic into religion." The Egyptians, however, "never entirely lost their primitive instincts and remained a very superstitious people in whose lives and religious practices and beliefs magic always played an important part."[67] While certainly magic played an important part in Egyptian religious life, should we accept that this was due to the Egyptians being a "superstitious people" in the grip of "primitive instincts"?

Twentieth-century psychological approaches to historical development, such as those initiated by Freud and Jung, have also tended to conform to the evolutionary paradigm and the idea of progress in its earliest Baconian form, in which history is viewed as a maturation from the childhood of the ancients to the adulthood of the moderns. Freud's theory of individual psychological development incorporated the Baconian-Frazerian idea that it recapitulates human history—from the "childhood" (magical phase) of humanity, through an "adolescence" (religious phase), to its "adulthood" (scientific phase). For Freud the modern child, still thinking animistically, presents a picture of the peoples of the past; only those modern adults who have fully adapted themselves to the scientific worldview could be regarded as mature human beings. Furthermore, the magical rites and spells of the earlier phase are characterized as corresponding psychologically to the obsessional notions and protective formulas of modern neurotics.[68] This adds an interesting psychological twist to the idea of progress: namely, that the steady advance of humanity has been from psychopathology to true sanity (i.e., acceptance of the scientific worldview). Thus, in the late 1970s, Julian Jaynes would contend that in antiquity human consciousness was essentially schizophrenic and that Egyptian civilization was controlled and directed by hallucinated "bicameral voices."[69] A similarly unflattering view of the position of the ancient Egyptians in the unfolding of the historical process is given by the transpersonal psychologist Ken Wilber, who dismisses the whole society as mad![70]

More influential than Freud has been Jung's portrayal of the religious life of antiquity as involving the projection of inner psychic contents onto the figures of the gods. For Jung, the development of consciousness is necessarily a process of "world despiritualization" as these projections are returned to the psyche.[71] Jung's evolutionary view of history, as developed in Neumann's *The Origins and History of Consciousness*, sees the history of humanity as involving the liberation of individual consciousness from its original state of fusion with the collective unconscious. The polytheistic religion of ancient Egypt corresponds to a stage in which the original state of fusion begins to dissipate, as the ego begins to find itself.[72] For Neumann, as for Freud, the whole historical process is reflected in the development of each individual, and thus history is presented in terms of a movement from humanity's childhood to its maturity in the present day.[73]

While most Egyptologists today would avoid adjectives such as *superstitious* and *primitive* to characterize the spiritual life of the ancient Egyptians, the idea of progress nevertheless remains a deeply ingrained presupposition of modern culture. As long as the worldview of modern materialistic science retains its dominance in the Western mental outlook, and succeeds in extending itself throughout the rest of the world, it is extremely difficult to envisage condescending attitudes toward the past being fully dislodged. Despite the more sympathetic and less judgmental appreciation of the religious world of antiquity that has been shown in the second half of the twentieth century, mainstream archaeology and ancient history are still conducted from within the dominant materialistic and evolutionary paradigm. Although it is certainly possible to produce nonjudgmental accounts of ancient religious life, and many Egyptologists do succeed in doing this, the problem is deeper than one of merely writing an objective account of a religious world long since past. The real problem is that the religious outlook of the ancient Egyptians is directly opposed to the modern secular outlook, and a full-hearted engagement with ancient Egyptian spirituality leads us into a worldview that challenges at every turn the correctness of modern assumptions, not least of which is the idea of progress.

It scarcely needs pointing out that the Egyptians themselves would not have regarded their culture and religion as belonging to an early and immature stage of human development. As we have already seen, their view of history was the opposite of the modern view. When they looked back into the past, they had the idea that conditions on earth more and more approximated conditions in heaven the further back in time one went. Thus the king lists show that the reigns of the first kings of Egypt, who were gods rather than humans, lasted for enormous spans of time, cosmic rather than earthly in their duration. In the Book of Sothis, for example, Ra reigned over Egypt for a full 30,000 years before he was succeeded by a series of twelve gods who altogether reigned for just under 4,000 years. As history moved toward the time when human beings would take over the rulership of Egypt, the reign of the kings gradually diminished in length. The twelve gods were succeeded by eight demigods and then finally the human god-kings who together ruled for roughly 2,500 years.[74] Other Egyptian chronological records concur with the basic principle of the diminution in the lengths of reigns as the kingship is slowly transferred from heavenly hands into the hands of gods incarnate in mortal flesh—the pharaohs.[75] Far from seeing their origins in some lowly primate progenitor, the time of origins was for the Egyptians a golden age in which human beings were much closer to the world of the gods and lived in harmony with Maat, the goddess who personified the spiritual order of the cosmos.[76]

Modern secular culture has little conception of history as decline because history, post-Egypt, has been a triumphant progress of secularization. And Christian theologians, despite a more or less critical stance toward secularization, have tended to hail the development of ethical monotheism as the most advanced form of religious consciousness. The ancient view of "history as decline" does not resonate well with modern progressive attitudes. And yet a sympathetic treatment of ancient Egyptian religion requires that we set aside these modern assumptions and make the attempt to see the world from the standpoint of the Egyptians themselves. Not only that, it requires that we make a further effort—to raise up an Egyptian mirror to our own times and try to see ourselves as the Egyptians might see us.

We have already observed how according to Hornung, Egyptian thought "steers clear of monocausal simplification, convincing instead through refinement and association, through mastery of both word and image."[77] There is a Hermetic text (dating from around the second century A.D.) that goes considerably further in describing the quality of Egyptian thought. It gives the Egyptian view of their own mental and linguistic capacities in comparison to those of the Greeks. In this text, which purports to summarize many Egyptian secret teachings, it is stated that "it will be entirely unclear when the Greeks eventually desire to translate our language into their own and thus produce in writing the greatest distortion and unclarity. But this discourse, expressed in our paternal language, keeps clear the meaning of its words. The very quality of the speech and the sound of Egyptian words have in themselves the energy of the objects they speak of."[78]

The text then goes on to contrast the "empty speech" of the Greeks with the spiritually empowered language of ancient Egypt. The Greek language is too feeble, too arrogant, and too superficial to be able to convey the mysteries expressed in the original Egyptian.[79] In this passage we are given a glimpse of how the Egyptians viewed their own tradition and contrasted it with the "abstract terminology" of their successors.

In his *Timaeus,* Plato gives an account of a series of conversations between the Greek statesman Solon and certain Egyptian priests, which occurred when Solon visited Egypt in the sixth century B.C. On one occasion an aged Egyptian priest abruptly turned to Solon and said to him: "O Solon , Solon, you Greeks are never anything but children, and there is not an old man among you." When Solon asked him what he meant, the priest said: "I mean you are all young in mind. . . ."[80] Far from revering them as more developed and mature than his fellow Egyptians, we sense the exasperation of the old Egyptian priest who dismisses the Greeks as mere "children." It is worth pondering whether our contemporary instant-gratification culture of supermarkets, mobile phones, and global air travel would have seemed to him more mature or, on the contrary, even more infantile than the culture of the Greeks.

Were the Egyptians Practical Rather Than Mystical?

In line with the Frazerian view of the most primitive spirituality being "prereligious," the Egyptians have been constantly characterized as practical people whose preferred relationship to the divine world was through result-oriented magic rather than through religious piety or faith, let alone mystical experience. The typical view is not that there was no religion in ancient Egypt, but rather that Egyptian religion was so interfused with magic that it never rose to the levels of mystical spirituality attained by the Greeks or of the enlightened theologies of the later monotheistic religions. Egyptian "practicality" is supposed not only to have determined their predilection for magic, but also to have deflected them from mysticism. At the same time, it was responsible for their extraordinary achievements in the arts, crafts, social organization, and so on.

Within Egyptology there is a long tradition of paying special attention to "daily life in ancient Egypt." From Wilkinson's *The Ancient Egyptians: Their Life and Customs* (1854), Erman's *Life in Ancient Egypt* (1894), Pierre Montet's *Everyday Life in Egypt in the Days of Ramesses the Great* (1946), and Manchip White's *Everyday Life in Ancient Egypt* (1963) to Eugen Strouhal's *Life in Ancient Egypt* (1992), a picture is presented of farmers, artisans, scribes, and priests in a physical and social context more or less removed from a spiritual one. They serve to promote a picture of ancient Egypt that particularly suits the modern secular mentality, bent on denying or ignoring the reality of the world of gods and spirits that was so present to the ancient Egyptians. This tendency to portray the purely practical aspects of Egyptian civilization while more or less ignoring the spiritual life has far more to do with what modern sensibilities feel comfortable with than accurately reflecting the tenor of Egyptian culture. When, for example, the Egyptologist J. A. Wilson remarked on the "cheerful urbanity" of the ancient Egyptians and commented that for them the "active, extroverted life they lived was the great reality, and they light-heartedly refused to accept any extinction of that life,"[81] we need to question whether this characterization reflects the true nature of the Egyptians. Ancient Egyptian religious texts testify that the "great reality" for the Egyptians was less a happily active and extroverted life than the cosmic order of the universe presided over by Maat and a living awareness of the spiritual presence of the gods. To pass over the testimony of the religious writings and to characterize the ancient Egyptian attitude toward death as one of lighthearted refusal is to remold the ancient Egyptians into a form palatable to modern saccharine tastes.

The view of the Egyptians as practical, cheery, and extroverted, not bothering their heads about ultimate questions, is often put forward in the context of the interpretation of tomb paintings. As practical people, engrossed with the activities of daily life, one of their most central spiritual preoccupations is supposed to have been the materialistic wish that these practical pursuits continue to be enjoyed after death. By portraying their daily-life activities on the walls of tombs, it is claimed that the Egyptians hoped magically to ensure that these activities would continue into the afterlife. Because of their lack of spiritual sophistication, they not only naively pictured the afterlife as a continuation of the pleasures of life on earth, but also actually believed that by representing scenes of daily life in their tombs, these scenes would become realities in the otherworld. So, according to William Murnane's *The Penguin Guide to Ancient Egypt* (1983), "these scenes reflect the ancients' belief that they could 'take it with them,' projecting an ideal of the good life into the world beyond death." Beyond this, however, was a further practical concern:

> [T]heir main *raison d'être* was practical. . . . Creating a picture of these offerings, of the servants who presented them and ultimately, of the means of production that brought them into being were all logical extensions of the same concern, that is to guarantee these materials for the tomb owner's use forever. A wide variety of rather humdrum activities thus came to be illustrated in most private tombs.[82]

In other words, since the tomb owner required endless supplies of the good things of life, images of them had to be provided in abundance; but to make completely sure that these things would never run out, the whole process of their production had to be portrayed as well.

Such an interpretation clearly not only implies that the Egyptians naively denied the reality of death, but it also excludes any thought that the experience of daily-life activities was injected with spiritual content, and that their portrayal in tombs was more likely to have had a symbolic rather than a merely practical meaning. While the infusion of apparently profane activities with sacred content has long been recognized as a characteristic of the religious mentality of ancient peoples by historians of religion, Egyptologists have tended to see the spheres of the sacred and the profane as separated from each other. Despite the fact that, since the 1970s, this tendency has been challenged from within Egyptology by scholars such as Derchain, Westendorf, Ritner, and Wilkinson,[83] it remains deeply entrenched. The standard religious interpretation of the so-called daily-life activities in tomb paintings is still that they served in a magical way the naive wish fulfillment of a happy afterlife of hunting and fishing or magically provided all the material needs of the *ka* after death. This literalistic approach fails to take into account the symbolic resonance that all daily-life activities had for the Egyptians, and in fact tells us far more about the modern commentator, who prefers to see the Egyptians as basically materialistic and their art as devoid of spiritual meaning, than it does about the ancient Egyptians.[84]

It is from within the safety of the view that the Egyptians were essentially pragmatic and materialistic, and that their religious consciousness did not rise above the level of rather crude magical thinking, that it then becomes possible to justify ignoring the spiritual life of the Egyptians in order better to concentrate on their more tangible achievements in the arts. I. E. S. Edwards summed up the presumption admirably:

> However primitive and materialistic the Egyptian conception of the Afterlife may seem, it must be conceded that it was responsible for the production of some of the greatest artistic masterpieces in antiquity. Without the impetus provided by a practical motive, it is doubtful whether a fraction of the statues, reliefs or inscriptions which are now so universally admired would ever have been produced.[85]

The attitude that while we may legitimately admire the wonderful artistic achievements of the Egyptians, the beliefs that gave rise to them are not worth our serious consideration has its origins in the early struggles of Egyptologists with the religious material that seemed to them so confused and abstruse. Gardiner regarded art and craftsmanship as "the noblest of her [ancient Egypt's] achievements" whereas Egyptian religion was but a "wil-o'-the-wisp by reason of its mystery and in spite of its absurdity."[86] Cyril Aldred, in his three-volume study, *Art in Ancient Egypt* (1968–72), made the observation that the tomb paintings of the Old and Middle Kingdoms were founded on beliefs discoverable in "the lower layers that we can trace in the ancient rubbish-mound of Egyptian religion."[87] Erman was no less dismissive of Egyptian religion: It was "an unparalleled confusion" and the gods "meaningless puppets," but her people he nevertheless hailed as "intelligent, practical and very energetic."[88] Despite the fact that more sympathetic and penetrating studies of Egyptian religion were made during the second half of the twentieth century, this assumption of Egyptian practicality has to a large extent remained dominant, determining the favored topics of research and thereby reinforcing the stereotype.

It reappears again in Hornung's *Conceptions of God in Ancient Egypt* in a passage already referred to in chapter 1. Just where Hornung denies any Egyptian tendency toward mysticism, he promotes the view that the Egyptian mentality was essentially pragmatic:

> Several writers have stressed quite correctly that no trace of mysticism can be found in ancient Egypt. The Egyptians never succumbed to the temptation to find in the transcendence of the existent release from all imperfection, dissolution of the self, or immersion in and union with the universe. They remained active and, to us, startlingly matter-of-fact; any sort of ecstasy appears quite alien to their attitudes.[89]

The denial of mysticism in ancient Egypt is here clearly allied to the affirmation of Egyptian down-to-earth practicality, extroversion, and a "matter-of-fact" attitude to life.

Hornung is one of several influential Egyptologists who have argued that there was no mystery cult in ancient Egypt equivalent to the mysteries of the Greek and later Greco-Roman world, and we shall return in chapter 3 to discuss his view and the views of others on this important subject. Whether there were mysteries or mysticism in ancient Egypt is becoming one of the most pressing questions currently debated both within and outside the Egyptological establishment. The way it is answered does not affect only the way in which Egyptian religion and the Egyptian character are understood. It affects also the way in which Egyptology conceives of its own task. If the Egyptians are to continue to be portrayed as down-to-earth and cheery souls unperturbed by the greater questions of life, then mysticism of any kind will be foreign not only to them but also to Egyptology. If, on the other hand, it is accepted that there is a mystical core to Egyptian religious life, and that the Egyptians were indeed religious people, then mysticism itself would become part of the agenda of Egyptological research. Due consideration would have to be given to the far-reaching parallels between the transcendental experiences reported in the literature of shamanism and ancient Egyptian religious texts. Gnosticism, the religious philosophies of Platonism, Hermetism, and Neoplatonism, as well as esoteric traditions such as alchemy and freemasonry, would need to be reevaluated both in terms of the possible influence exerted by Egyptian religion on them and also for the light that they might reciprocally shed on our understanding of ancient Egyptian religion.[90]

It is partly because of the long association of interest in Egyptian mysticism with such esoteric and metaphysical perspectives that the question of the existence of mysticism in ancient Egypt has become so loaded. For the modern professional Egyptologist, taking Egyptian religion seriously is fraught with the danger that one comes to be perceived as taking magic and occultism seriously, and hence aligning oneself with the old Hermetic-Neoplatonic respect for ancient Egyptian spirituality that academic Egyptology definitively rejected at the end of the nineteenth century.[91] As John Baines has pointed out, Egyptology began at the time of the decipherment of the hieroglyphs to break away from the earlier Hermetic, Neoplatonic, and esoteric axis and increasingly needed to define itself as anti-metaphysical and anti-esoteric precisely insofar as it was scientific. Thus the denial of mysticism in Egypt became at the same time the affirmation of the scientific respectability of Egyptology, and remains so today.[92]

There is, then, more to the denial of mysticism in ancient Egypt than at first meets the eye. A major factor in this denial is the historical struggle of Egyptology to be accepted as a credible academic discipline, which required that it distance itself from the earlier European metaphysical and esoteric traditions. It is this factor *in the history of Egyptology* that is at the root of its rejection of mysticism in ancient Egypt and the corresponding portrayal of the Egyptians as happy-go-lucky, practical, and extroverted. Such a portrayal conveniently masks the spiritual reality in which the Egyptians lived, and saves the Egyptologist from the embarrassment of having to engage with a religious consciousness that, for the modern secular mentality, is profoundly challenging.

The Rebirth of Egyptian Mysticism

Despite the long established consensus within Egyptology against the existence of mysticism or mystery rites in ancient Egypt, there have been some Egyptologists who have taken a different view. Back in 1922, Alexandre Moret interpreted several Egyptian rituals, both royal and nonroyal, as rituals of death and rebirth on the lines of the later Greek and Hellenistic mystery cults. He argued that although they are often documented on tomb walls, in funerary papyri, and on mortuary stelae, what they describe are rituals performed during a person's life.[93] A generation later, S. Mayassis argued that Egyptian religion was essentially mystical, and at its core were initiatory rites that involved suffering the trial of death while still alive.[94] For both Moret and Mayassis, the key to understanding mysticism in ancient Egypt was the concept of the "voluntary death" undergone before one's actual physical death. This was the necessary preliminary to the experience of a mystical rebirth, or "going out into the day." Whereas for everyone the experience of dying is a kind of initiation, for those who undergo the "voluntary death" during life, the way to spiritual rebirth is opened and the celestial destiny of the soul is ensured. It is in this crucial respect that the initiate differs from the uninitiated.[95] Neither of these authors, however, made much impact on attitudes within the Egyptological establishment, which was sharply antagonistic toward such interpretations of Egyptian religion.[96]

A generation after Mayassis, in 1982, the Egyptologist Edward Wente opened up again the question of Egyptian mysticism in an article entitled "Mysticism in Pharaonic Egypt?" published in the *Journal for Near Eastern Studies*. In this seminal paper, Wente argued that certain New Kingdom texts, despite being located in royal tombs, were not just funerary texts, for they were not originally designed for the use of the dead king. Rather, they were "originally designed for use upon earth as well as in the otherworld and were only secondarily adapted as specifically royal funerary literature."[97] According to Wente, these texts served the mystical aim "to bring the future into the present" so that the "realities of death and movement into the netherworld with attendant rebirth could have been genuinely experienced in this life now." Wente saw that although these texts are located in tombs, this does not mean that we should automatically assume they are funerary texts.[98]

This important insight of Wente's, for which Moret was the precursor, has been taken up in a more limited way by other Egyptologists, including Jan Assmann. In his book *Egyptian Solar Religion*, Assmann argued that the

New Kingdom Underworld books that appear in the royal tombs—texts such as the *Amduat* or Book of What Is in the Underworld—were originally designed to serve the sun cult, and that "the 'mysteries' of the solar journey are their real and original meaning and purpose."[99] For Assmann, however, the term *mysteries* has less to do with mysticism than with "restricted knowledge," and his denial of the existence of mysteries (and thereby mysticism) in ancient Egypt is unequivocal.[100] Nevertheless, Assmann has established an essential principle: that the location of a text in a tomb does not automatically mean that it is a funerary text.

More recently, Alison Roberts has made the case for a mystical as opposed to a funerary interpretation of these New Kingdom texts, based on a detailed analysis of the Book of Night. This was first inscribed by Seti I in the Osireion at Abydos, and subsequently appeared on the ceilings of Ramessid royal tombs at Thebes and then Twenty-second Dynasty royal tombs at Tanis. By the time of the Twenty-fifth Dynasty, it began to be included in the decoration of private tombs at Thebes, so its funerary associations were obviously very strong. According to Roberts, however, the journey through the body of the sky goddess, Nut, that the text describes was concerned primarily with the "mysteries of return to primal origins and cosmic rebirth": "As such, it leaves not the slightest shadow of doubt that this heavenly journey through the body of Nut, though normally shown in a funerary context, was deeply important for living Egyptians, giving them the power to experience consciously the process of death and rebirth during their lifetime on earth."[101] For Roberts, the same point applies to the rest of the corpus of New Kingdom Underworld books, including specific chapters of the Book of the Dead: They were essentially mystical texts, often grounded in ritual practices, for use by the living.[102]

A similar perspective has also been taken by Walter Federn on certain of the Coffin Texts. Despite their location on the sides of Middle Kingdom coffins, he sees the whole genre of spells concerned with transforming into animal or divine forms of the sun god, along with a great many other spells, as originally nonfunerary and for use by the living. The "transformation texts" should be viewed as meditations for the purpose of acquiring spiritual powers, in a manner akin to the Indian concept of *samadhi* in various Yoga-Sutras.[103] Furthermore, Federn argues for the existence of initiation rites in ancient Egypt comparable to those of shamanism, involving the experiences of death, dismemberment, and rebirth.[104]

There is, then, an alternative stream of thought within Egyptology that is inclined to interpret the so-called funerary texts as nonfunerary mystical texts. It has always been in a minority, and yet the scholarship of these

Egyptologists is not in question; it is rather that their views have simply not been compatible with the underlying philosophical orientation of the discipline. In its efforts to steer clear of mysticism, Egyptology has used the funerary interpretation as a bulwark against the infiltration into Egyptological thinking of mystical and esoteric perspectives. But all the signs are pointing toward the total collapse of the funerary interpretation of ancient Egyptian religious texts. It is becoming less and less possible to view the New Kingdom Underworld texts as purely funerary, as Assmann has now established, and a mystical interpretation of these along with the Book of the Dead seems more and more difficult to keep at bay. The Coffin Texts, from which many of the spells in the Book of the Dead derive, are equally vulnerable to mystical interpretation, as Walter Federn has shown. Only the Pyramid Texts, which are the originating source of many of the Coffin Texts, remain to hold off the total demise of the funerary interpretation of ancient Egyptian religious literature. As the present study will attempt to demonstrate, a purely funerary interpretation of the Pyramid Texts is, however, no longer sustainable.

3 THE MYSTICAL VERSUS THE FUNERARY INTERPRETATION OF ANCIENT EGYPTIAN RELIGION

A Clash of Views

If the so-called funerary texts of ancient Egypt, of which the Pyramid Texts are the earliest example, were not simply for the use of the dead but also for the living, this implies the existence in ancient Egypt of a certain type of mysticism in which the living had experiences—probably in a highly charged ritual context—that would normally occur only after one had died. The fact that a ritual context formed the framework within which such mystical experiences were induced, and that these rituals were implicitly secret, entitles us to refer to them as "mystery rites" or "mysteries."[1] These experiences were of a direct encounter with spiritual realities normally veiled by the conditions of human physical existence. The direct experience of the spirit world, of the forces and energies that it contains and of the gods and ancestors who dwell in it, required that the normal conditions of daily life and daily consciousness be suspended. Ancient Egyptian mysticism involved a crossing of the threshold of death while still alive in order to stand within the spirit world and to know oneself as a spirit. The experience of spiritual rebirth required that one consciously undergo the experience of dying.

While scholars generally accept that this "voluntary death" was one of the central aims of the Greek and Hellenistic mystery cults, Egyptology has resisted the idea that any such initiatory rites or experiences existed in Egypt. The keynote against any such rites in ancient Egypt was struck by Siegfried Morenz, who, in his influential book, *Egyptian Religion*, compared the role of Isis and Osiris in the Hellenistic mysteries with their role in ancient Egypt in the following way. Whereas the later Hellenistic mysteries "sought to elevate the mystic to the divine plane by associating him with Isis and Osiris," in ancient Egypt "the deceased becomes Osiris and enters into God by the performance of the funerary rites." Between ancient Egypt and the Hellenistic world a radical transformation took place, and "[t]his transformation consists in the following: in Egypt it was the DEAD, whereas in the Hellenistic world it was the LIVING who were so consecrated and thereby saved from their state of worldly terror."[2] The argument of Morenz is that where we find mysticism in the Hellenistic world, we find funerary rites in Egypt.

More recently, both Erik Hornung and Jan Assmann have reiterated Morenz's view. Hornung, recognizing the implicitly mystical content of Egyptian "funerary" literature, has argued that transcendental experiences—such as entering the realm of the gods—must have been understood by the Egyptians as being attainable only after a person's death. This has for many years been the standard interpretation within Egyptology, to be found in the work of Piankoff, Mercer, Frankfort, Faulkner, James P. Allen, and many others. It is held that ancient Egyptian attitudes differed profoundly from those prevalent during the Greek and Hellenistic period. As Hornung put it: "While in the later period a few select individuals become initiates by undergoing a symbolic death, in the Pharaonic period each person enters the realm of the gods and learns the secrets of the afterlife through his or her actual death. . . . Knowledge about the afterlife is no secret teaching. Although it contains many mysteries, it is not part of a mystery cult. . . ."[3] For Hornung, then, mystical experiences were believed (especially during the New Kingdom) to be available to all—there was no secret mystery cult—but unlike the Greeks, the ancient Egyptians had to wait until they died before they could actually have any of these mystical experiences. Thus we meet in the religious texts such important inner events as spiritualization and divinization of the soul, as well as vision of and union with gods, but these transcendent experiences are all postmortem. As such, they should be understood as belonging to an elaborate system of belief rather than lying on the experiential path of the mystic. By displacing mystical experiences from this life into the afterlife, it becomes possible to uphold the view that no matter how mystical dead Egyptians may have been, living Egyptians were practical, extroverted, and, in Hornung's memorable phrase, "startlingly matter-of-fact."[4]

Concomitant to this approach is an assessment of the "funerary" literature of the Egyptians as essentially mere conjecture. It could not have been based on any actual experiences, for it did not arise out of—it was not the expression of—something lived. It must have been arrived at through priestly speculation. This is explicitly stated by Jan Assmann, for whom the esoteric knowledge of the New Kingdom Underworld books is essentially speculative "cosmography." It is, for him, a pseudoscience based on nothing more than "pure speculation," and its formulation reflects less any spiritual reality than "the typical bureaucratic and systematic style of Egyptian daily life, transposed to the next world."[5] For Assmann, as for Hornung, any form of trance or ecstasy, mystical contemplation or attempt to unite with the numinous was foreign to the ancient Egyptians.[6]

Hornung and Assmann articulate the consensus within Egyptology today. For both of them the experiential world of the ancient Egyptians—given that they were so evidently a highly religious people—seems to have been unusually limited. It was augmented by a speculative and highly imaginative "science" of the afterlife that could have had no basis in actual experience. Egyptian religion then appears a matter of faith, the product of imaginative construction rather than of mystical practice.

The trouble with this view of Egyptian religion is that the essentially religious—the lived encounter with the numinous or the sacred—is effectively denied. The Egyptians are regarded as oddly impervious to mystical experience, and seemingly unaware of the potent effects of initiatory rites that everywhere else in the ancient world were absolutely integral to religious life. As we have seen, some Egyptologists—a dissenting minority to be sure—have suggested that there is another way of interpreting ancient Egyptian religion, in which it is viewed as based on experience rather than faith, and experience of a very specific kind. This other way makes just as much sense—often considerably more sense—of the religious material than does the more usual funerary interpretation. More to the point, this other way enables a religious content to be revealed that is otherwise sequestered and, in a sense, held captive by the funerary interpretation. The aim of this chapter is to set forth the kind of perspective that seems to be required in order that this deeper religious content may be released to view.

Mysticism and the Experience of Death

In chapter 2, we saw that according to some of the most important Greek and Roman commentators, Egyptian religion was a highly mystical religion, and that through certain of its rites people were led to profound spiritual experiences. Whereas modern scholars tend to see the core of ancient Egyptian religion as focused on the needs of the dead, the Greek and Roman commentators saw it as focused on the needs and experiences of the living. These experiences were the source and foundation of the knowledge and wisdom of the Egyptians that was generally revered throughout the ancient world. It was, however, understood by these ancient commentators that the central mystical experience, which could be regarded as the backbone of Egyptian religion, was of a type that closely parallels the experience of death.[7] What this means is that if a given religious text appears to be concerned with postmortem experiences, we need to look at it very carefully, because it could be describing mystical experiences of the living that parallel those that a person will undergo after death. In this respect the fundamental tenor of ancient Egyptian mysticism is accurately transmitted in the Hermetic tradition, in which mystical experiences are described that could otherwise easily be mistaken for postmortem experiences.[8] Over the last forty years a great deal of work has been done to show that the Hermetic writings do in fact transmit genuine ancient Egyptian doctrines, one of which was that "the human being can become established on high without even leaving the earth."[9]

The association of mystical experience with the experiences that one will have at death is by no means an unusual association, only to be found in a few Hermetic texts. It is also central to shamanic initiation rites, which often involve not only the experience of dismemberment or reduction to the state of a skeleton but also a descent to the Underworld or an ascent to Heaven, and the further experience of spiritual rebirth.[10] This initiatory pattern in which the main mystical experience was to travel into the realm of the dead was common throughout the ancient world. It was the central experience of initiation into the mysteries.[11]

A well-known philosophical example of the teaching concerning the mystical-experience/death-experience parallel can be found in the dialogues of Plato, particularly important because of their influence on later mystics and mystically inclined philosophers. Plato was reputed to have spent thirteen years studying in ancient Egypt under the tutelage of priests, so an Egyptian source of this teaching cannot be discounted.[12] It is most clearly expounded in his dialogue *Phaedrus*, which has been called "the

51

basic text of mysticism in the true sense,"[13] for it describes in most evocative and elated language the ascent of the human being to the divine world. This ascent is accomplished by the soul "growing wings." In this beautiful image of the soul becoming winged, and hence capable of moving upward, away from the earth and the world of matter, Plato affirms that the human being has a celestial, as well as a terrestrial, home. The way to return to our celestial home is by cultivating the spiritual qualities of "beauty, wisdom, goodness, and every other excellence." Through nourishing ourselves on these sublime qualities, we not only "grow wings" but also realize our own immortality, lifting ourselves beyond the sphere of the earth to the stars. There the winged soul meets Zeus and a "host of gods and spirits" at the summit of the arch of the heavens. Going beyond even this arch, it contemplates an indescribable reality: "the reality with which true knowledge is concerned, a reality without colour or shape, intangible but utterly real, apprehensible only by intellect *(nous)* which is the pilot of the soul."[14]

Plato's description of this mystical ascent of the soul is also—and he is quite explicit about this—a description of the postmortem experience of souls once released from physical embodiment. Thus, in the same passage, he goes on to describe the periods of time between incarnations and the forces of destiny that will then lead a soul from a spiritual state of enraptured vision into a particular type of physical incarnation.[15] Plato nevertheless stresses that for the philosopher, who is the true lover of wisdom, the task in life is diligently to cultivate virtue, so as to grow the wings that will bear the soul upward toward the supreme vision of reality granted normally only after death.[16] In this dialogue, then, Plato weaves together his description of the mystical ascent of the soul to the stars culminating in its vision of the indescribable reality beyond with a description of postmortem experiences. The mystical vision is precisely of that dimension of existence that is experienced when the soul finally separates itself from the body at death. Normally, this dimension is concealed from us, but it harbors a reality that the philosopher aims to become conscious of *while still living*, through practicing a moral and intellectual discipline that breaks through the veil created by sense-based consciousness.

It is for this reason that in another dialogue, *Phaedo*, Plato goes so far as to define the profession of true philosophers as radically inclusive of the experience of dying: "True philosophers make dying their profession, and to them of all people death is least alarming . . . [for they are] glad to set out for the place where there is a prospect of attaining the object of their lifelong desire, which is Wisdom. . . . If one is a real philosopher, one will be of the firm belief that one will never find Wisdom in all its purity in any other place [than the next world]."[17] For Plato, the goal of philosophy ("wisdom") cannot be attained in the normal embodied state of consciousness, but is accessible only to the soul that has become free of the body. Since this is the state of the soul once it has died, the experience of death becomes the aim of Plato's mystical philosophy. Thus, in the same dialogue, he writes, "Ordinary people seem not to realise that those who really apply themselves in the right way to philosophy are directly and of their own accord preparing themselves for dying and death."[18]

Turning back to the *Phaedrus*, we find Plato comparing the beatific vision to initiation in the mysteries. He even uses the terms *mystai* and *epoptai*—terms taken from the Eleusinian mysteries that refer to two levels of initiate—in the following passage, in which the ultimate vision is described: "then resplendent beauty was to be seen . . . a joyous view and show, and [we] were initiated by initiations that must be called the most blessed of all . . . celebrating these . . . encountering, as *mystai* and *epoptai*, happy apparitions in pure splendour, being pure ourselves."[19] The reference to the Eleusinian *mystai* and *epoptai* is significant because Plato is clearly implying that the type of experience that he is describing is comparable to what was experienced in the Eleusinian mysteries. The Platonic philosopher "preparing for dying and death" is like the initiate undergoing the rites of the Eleusinian mysteries. It is worth briefly considering what occurred in the Eleusinian mysteries, for this may shed more light on the relationship between the type of mystical experience that Plato is referring to in *Phaedrus* and *Phaedo* and the experiences referred to in ancient Egyptian religious texts.

The Eleusinian Mysteries and Other Mystery Religions

The Eleusinian mysteries were celebrated from at least the eighth century B.C. at Eleusis, near Athens, and continued into the Hellenistic period. While there is some reason to believe that they were established at a much earlier date—in the second half of the fifteenth century B.C.—and that their origin was Egyptian, neither an earlier dating nor an Egyptian origin is accepted by the majority of scholars today, for lack of firm evidence. Nevertheless, the possibility of an earlier Egyptian origin of the Eleusinian mysteries should not be dismissed out of hand, and there are some who have no difficulty with this view.[20] But whether or not they had an Egyptian origin is a side issue to the present argument. Eleusis was just one of many mystery centers that flourished throughout the Greek and Greco-Roman world. Like the other mystery religions that were constellated around the cult of a certain god or goddess, the Eleusinian mysteries were based upon the myth and cult of Demeter and her daughter Persephone. The key event of this myth is Persephone's abduction by Hades, the god of the Underworld, and her eventual release from the clutches of Hades and restoration to her mother and the Upperworld. The birth of a divine child seems also to have been a crucial event. In other words, the central themes of the myth are of Persephone's death and resurrection, and the birth of a new "principle" in the form of a divine child.[21]

The rites celebrated at Eleusis fell into three parts.[22] The "lesser mysteries" were celebrated in spring and their purpose was mainly instructional and purificatory. The "greater mysteries" occurred the following autumn and lasted nine days, during which time candidates experienced a reenactment of the myth of Persephone's descent into, and release from, the Underworld, and the birth of the divine child, announced by the hierophant. From the accounts that have come down to us, it is clear that the mysteries were intensively participated in, and the candidates (mystai) felt inwardly identified with Persephone. Finally, a full year later, came the highest level of initiation, the epopteia or "vision," which led to the second grade of initiate that Plato mentions, the epoptai.

While the broad course of events that took place at Eleusis is fairly well known, much less is known of the details of what actually occurred in the mysteries, because the initiates were sworn to secrecy. We do know, however, from Aristotle, that what happened to the initiates was not that they gained some kind of intellectual understanding, but rather that they had a transformative experience that had a strong emotive charge. Aristotle writes that initiates were "not expected to learn something but to experience emotions and a change in the state of mind (diatethenai)."[23] From other ancient writers we have cryptic statements indicating that participation in the mysteries conferred on the initiates a blessing that set them apart from the uninitiated, particularly in a changed attitude toward death. For example, Pindar, Sophocles, Isocrates, and the anonymous Homeric Hymn to Demeter all confirm that people initiated into the mysteries felt that they had a quite different relationship to death from the uninitiated. They no longer feared death, but looked forward to it as the beginning of a new life.[24] We have already seen that Plato implies that the initiate experienced in initiation something similar to what would otherwise be experienced after death: a sublime mystic vision. To this we may add a corroboratory statement of Plutarch: "The soul at the point of death has the same experience as those who are being initiated in great mysteries."[25]

Plutarch was referring to either the Eleusinian mysteries or the Hellenistic mysteries of Isis, probably both.

While some scholars have been very cautious in making any pronouncement as to what actually occurred in the initiations at Eleusis, others have been more willing to follow through the implications of the various testimonies that have come down to us. According to Carl Kerényi, the climax of the Eleusinian mystery rites was a "beatific vision" comparable to the medieval Christian mystical *visio beatifica*.[26] It was, that is to say, a "mystical seeing" that conferred upon the initiate a certain beatitude. Walter Burkert has suggested that of the "things shown" *(dromena)* to the initiates at Eleusis during the nocturnal ceremonies, the most important was a certain insight into the nature of death.[27] This view is in contrast to the overly literalistic interpretations of commentators both ancient and modern who have held that the things shown were simply ritually charged objects like an ear of wheat or a representation of a phallus. It seems far more likely that the hierophant enabled the initiate to glimpse a transcendent reality that, as Cicero put it, showed one "how to live in joy, and how to die with better hopes."[28]

We therefore have considerable documentary support for the view that is implied in Plato's *Phaedrus* that one of the main purposes of initiation in the Eleusinian mysteries was to bring one almost to the point of death, so that one stood at the threshold of the spiritual world and was enabled to see into it, and to catch a glimpse of a transcendent reality beyond anything normally experienced in ordinary life. Paralleling the Eleusinian mysteries, the Hellenistic mysteries of Isis seem to have had a very similar aim. Apuleius, writing in the second century A.D., is explicit on this point. In *The Golden Ass* he describes in some detail the inner experiences that accompanied initiation:

> Then the High Priest ordered all uninitiated persons to depart, invested me in a new linen garment and led me by the hand into the inner recesses of the sanctuary itself. . . . I approached the very gates of death and set one foot on Persephone's threshold, yet was permitted to return, rapt through all the elements. At midnight I saw the sun shining as if it were noon; I entered the presence of the gods of the Underworld and of the Upperworld, stood near and worshipped them.[29]

In the writings of Plato, in the Greek Eleusinian mysteries, and in the Greco-Roman Isis mysteries, we therefore find a shared understanding that there is a kind of mystical experience that closely parallels the experience of death. So closely does it parallel the experience of death that in the accounts of Plato, Plutarch, and Apuleius a person would seem to be brought experientially to the very brink of death. For Plato, death was understood to involve the separation or withdrawal of the soul from the experiential world mediated by the senses. As a consequence of this withdrawal, a new range of experiences becomes possible, no longer conditioned by the physical environment or by bodily incarnation. For both Plato and the mystery religions that we have been considering, it is clear that it was regarded as possible for people, *while still alive*, to enter a state of consciousness in which the soul becomes separated from the body for a short period. During this period of separation, people could have profound experiences that they would not otherwise have until they died, the most important of which was an intense realization that there is an element in their nature that is immortal.

This understanding of the relationship between a certain type of visionary mystical experience and what is experienced at death is well attested to in the shamanic tradition too.[30] And we have already seen that it was central to the Hermetic tradition. There is compelling evidence that various Greco-Roman and Hellenistic mystery cults all shared the same perspective.[31] It is highly probable that more than a thousand years earlier in ancient Mesopotamia a similar initiatory encounter with death was central to the Akitu, or New Year festival. During this festival, the death and resurrection of the god Marduk were reenacted. He descended into the Underworld and was mourned for three days before he rose again triumphantly. The role of Marduk was taken by the king, who was ritually disrobed and "confined in the mountain"—the ziggurat—for the prescribed length of time, and then liberated to the jubilation of the gathered crowds.[32]

Here, then, we seem to have a mystery rite that in essential respects, both mythological and experiential, parallels the Greek and Hellenistic mystery rites. Where it differs from the Greek and Hellenistic models is that apparently only one person, the king, went through the experience of death and resurrection on behalf of the whole community. Given the overall context of the Akitu, which means literally "power making the world live again," it is likely that what the king underwent, and later on in the festival enacted in the Sacred Marriage Rite, was felt to affect the whole country and its populace.[33] In this respect, the affects of the Akitu bear comparison with certain passages in the Pyramid Texts that indicate that through the king's transformation and rebirth, the land of Egypt was renewed, the grass was made green, and the fields became fertile.[34] These considerations should cause us to approach the ancient Egyptian Pyramid Texts with an awareness that, although they appear concerned with the fate of the soul after death, they may belong to a similar mystical tradition to the Mesopotamian Akitu, and that the experiences the pharaoh underwent were regarded as benefiting the whole country. According to this mystical tradition, in crossing the threshold that separates the world of the living from the realm of the dead, a connection was made with the vitalizing energies that are mediated by the dead into the world of the living.

The fact that the mystical "near-death" experience appears to have been central not only in the mystery rites of Greek and Hellenistic times but also in ancient Mesopotamia clearly weakens the argument of Morenz, Hornung, Assmann, and others discussed at the beginning of this chapter that implies that such rites were a post-pharaonic development, for the Mesopotamian Akitu goes back to the third millennium B.C., was already well established at the time of the Egyptian Middle Kingdom, and probably dates back to before that period.[35] If we find these rites in Mesopotamia, then the likelihood that something similar also existed in ancient Egypt is considerably increased. There is, however, a good deal of evidence to suggest that this same understanding and ritual practice flourished in many other ancient cultures contemporaneous with pharaonic Egypt, such as the Minoan, Ugaritic, Hittite, and so on.[36] Against such a background, it would seem odd if in Egypt similar mystery rites and initiations did not take place, especially given the enormous significance that the religious life had for the Egyptians and the reputation of Egypt throughout the ancient world for being a fount of esoteric wisdom. We therefore need to look further into whether the reasoning of Egyptologists who refuse to accept that a comparable mystical tradition existed in ancient Egypt is as compelling as at first sight it may seem.

The Funerary Interpretation of the Osiris Myth

In ancient Egyptian mythology, the god who presided over death and rebirth was Osiris, and it is he who would have been a central point of reference for the kind of initiatory rites that we have been considering had they taken place in Egypt. As is well known, Osiris is regarded by modern scholars as a god central to the funerary religion of Egypt. We need, therefore, to look at the figure of Osiris in order to ascertain whether this "funerary" god might not also have played an initiatory role in an Egyptian mystical tradition. We shall begin by examining certain key passages in the Pyramid Texts and then look at some important kingship rituals in which Osiris had a prominent part.

Osiris and Horus

According to the widely accepted current view, the myth of Osiris's death and resurrection, and the birth of his son Horus, was not an initiatory myth but a myth that underpinned the funerary cult. It was originally a myth that applied solely to the king and his successor to the throne. While reigning, every king of Egypt was regarded as a living Horus, but when the king died he became assimilated to Osiris, and his successor then assumed the title of Horus. This view—or doctrine, as it has become—is concisely stated by H. W. Fairman in his essay "Kingship Rituals of Egypt": "Horus was the son, the avenger, and the successor of Osiris, and so every living king was Horus, and every dead king was Osiris, for Osiris was the good king, who had been murdered by his evil brother Seth, but whose throne had eventually been assigned to his son Horus as a result of a lawsuit before the gods themselves."[37]

For Fairman, the Osiris myth involves three main protagonists: Osiris, his brother, Seth, who murders him, and his son, Horus, who avenges him. We should add to this, of course, Osiris's wife, Isis, whose role is crucial to Osiris's resurrection and the birth of Horus. For Fairman, these mythological figures should be viewed as archetypes that certain key individuals come to embody: In particular, the living king is Horus, the dead king is Osiris. In time, this myth became adopted beyond the narrow sphere of the kingship by increasingly broad social strata within Egyptian society. By the New Kingdom, scribes and petty officials, physicians, priests, and temple chantresses, men and women, all hoped to become assimilated to the god Osiris when they died.

This purely funerary interpretation of the Osiris myth and Osirian rites has been expressed and reiterated so many times by so many eminent Egyptologists that it could be described as a cornerstone of the modern Egyptological understanding of ancient Egyptian religion. To challenge it is to seriously risk aligning oneself with cranks, pyramidiots, past-lifers, and other heretics with whom no respectable academic would want to be associated.[38] At the same time, however, it is comparatively rare to find a reasoned and documented defense of this position. The tendency is for the scholar of Egyptian religion simply to state the position that the dead king is Osiris and the living king is Horus as if it were an indubitable fact. In this respect it has a status similar to the theory of evolution in biology, informing not only the way in which a wide range of data are consciously interpreted but also the way in which they have come to be automatically perceived.

It is difficult to say exactly when this interpretative stance became a mode of perception. We meet it already in the writings of Erman at the end of the nineteenth century, and when J. H. Breasted published his classic study of Egyptian religion, *The Development of Religion and Thought in Ancient Egypt*, in 1912, he felt little need to argue for the funerary interpretation of the Osiris myth.[39] While Breasted refers to a great many utterances from the Pyramid Texts, his interpretation of them is always within the framework of the funerary interpretation of the Osiris myth. Within the Pyramid Texts, however, there are a great many references to the supposedly dead king as Horus. While Breasted acknowledges this awkward fact, he explains it by simply arguing that this was more the exception than the rule and focuses on what he calls "the favorite belief" of the Osiris faith, that the dead king became Osiris and "rose from the dead" as Osiris did. The amount of references to the "dead" king as Horus in the Pyramid Texts, however, militates against simply dismissing them as exceptions to the general rule.[40] It is, moreover, often instructive to examine exactly under what circumstances the "dead" king is in the Horus role. To take one example, which appears in the pyramid of Unas, the king states:

I am Horus, my father's heir.
I have gone and returned. . . .[41]

Elsewhere, it is as Horus that the king "rests in life in the West (i.e., the Underworld)" and then, like the sun, "shines anew in the East."[42] In both these passages, a nonfunerary interpretation in which the king mystically "dies" by entering into and then returning from the realm of the dead is just as plausible as a funerary interpretation. But however we interpret them, their existence is incontrovertible evidence that the "dead" king is not always an Osiris. Given the abundance of references to the "dead" king as Horus, it is indeed surprising to find it stated so categorically by those who uphold the funerary interpretation that the dead king is always Osiris.[43] Perhaps, though, it is not so surprising, for if the dead king is sometimes—indeed frequently—a Horus, the implication is that he may not in fact be literally "dead." And if he is not literally dead, then the texts may not be simply funerary texts.

The Resurrection Texts

In support of the "favorite belief" theory—that the dead king "became Osiris and rose from the dead as Osiris did"—Breasted refers the reader to utterance 373 of the Pyramid Texts, which begins:

> Oho! Oho! Raise yourself, O King;
> Receive your head, collect your bones,
> Gather your limbs together,
> Throw off the earth from your flesh. . . .[44]

Certainly the passage would appear to be describing the king rising from the dead, but can we be certain that this rising from the dead is a post-mortem event? What is actually being described is the "re-membering" of his dismembered body—head, bones, and limbs. Suppose the king has only temporarily "died" in the mystical sense of traveling through the dismemberment experience that identifies him with Osiris. The experience of dismemberment and re-memberment is, after all, well documented as a feature of shamanic initiations worldwide.[45] Should we not at least consider the possibility that a similar experience was undergone in ancient Egypt? An initiatory interpretation of this passage is not actually such a wild alternative reading, for at the end of the very same utterance it is stated quite categorically:

> Rise up, O King, for you have not died![46]

For Breasted, however, there is little doubt that this and other passages asserting that the king is in fact alive are simply expressing the "favorite belief of the Osirian faith," that through identifying with Osiris after one has died one wins through to an eternal postmortem "life." Breasted goes on to quote a famous utterance that appears in the pyramid of Unas in order to demonstrate that the union of the dead king with Osiris assures the king, despite his death, of eternal life. The utterance reads:

> He lives, this Unas lives!
> He is not dead, this Unas is not dead!
> He is not gone down, this Unas is not gone down.[47]

As Breasted says, "These asseverations are repeated over and over, and addressed to every god of the Ennead, that each may be called upon to witness their truth. . . ."[48]

When we are presented with statement after statement affirming that the king (as Osiris) has not died, has in fact overcome death, and indeed "lives," surely it is incumbent upon the reader of the Pyramid Texts to ask whether the texts may, *perhaps*, be wanting to convey the fact that the king is indeed not dead. Does it not, after all, require a certain straining of the meaning of these statements to interpret them as descriptions of a king who is dead? To put it another way, if the ancient Egyptians wanted to convey that the king had not in fact died, but had been through an experience that brought him close to death, and that he had come through this experience, and was indeed alive, then how else could they have stated it? Yet for Breasted and for all subsequent Egyptologists adhering to the funerary interpretation, there is no question that these statements, insisting as they do that the king is alive, nevertheless refer to the dead king. Indeed, it is regarded as so obvious that they are referring to the dead king that they can be quoted in support of the funerary interpretation of the Osiris myth.

In the Pyramid Texts, there are a great many utterances, in addition to utterance 373 quoted above, in which the king as Osiris is told to wake up, stand up, shake the dust off his feet, and take possession of his body. These "resurrection utterances" are usually understood simply as an expression of "the human protest against death"—a denial of its reality.[49] Within Egyptology, this has become the standard view. We meet it, for instance, in J. Gwyn Griffiths's detailed and authoritative study of the Osiris myth and cult, *The Origins of the Osiris Cult* (1980). For Griffiths, those utterances in which the king is told to rouse himself and take possession of his body are to be understood as "the earliest expression in literature of a belief in life after death."[50] But it is surely a somewhat odd conception of life after death that sees the pharaoh stand up and shake off the dust, and—most significantly—take possession of his body (the Egyptian word for *body* used in the utterance to which Griffiths refers is *djet*, which normally means "the living body").[51] It sounds so much like the king actually reviving that to interpret it otherwise we would have to impute to the text a naive denial of the reality of death. That is to say, the Egyptians, despite all appearances to the contrary, insisted that the dead king actually stood up again in his physical body. This is indeed the way Griffiths chooses to explain it:

> The Osirian system is clearly connected with the body of the dead king and desiderates continued life for his body. Death indeed is not usually admitted. As Osiris, the tired god, was able to revive from his sleep, so the king will awake and stand and take possession of the body which temporarily had left his control. Death is really only a sleep, then, a phase of tiredness; and the firm denial of it in other references shows that it is denied both as a state and an occurrence.[52]

Rather than projecting onto the Egyptians a naive denial of physical death, we would surely do better to consider the possibility that there is a mystical and initiatory aspect to these texts. Indeed, it is precisely by not considering this mystical and initiatory aspect to Egyptian religion that we are led to the questionable interpretation of the Egyptians' naively denying the physical reality of death. Could it be, then, that the denial is after all on *our* side rather than on the side of the Egyptians? Much is at stake here. What is at stake is not just our interpretation of ancient Egyptian religious attitudes; it is also our own modern, predominately secular presuppositions about the possible range of human religious experience.

Horus Who Is in Osiris

Another example from the Pyramid Texts will, perhaps, make the point clearer. Like the previous example of the status of the "resurrection" texts, it also has to do with the way in which the relationship of the king to Osiris and Horus is conceived. According to the standard Egyptological view, the living pharaoh is never merged with Osiris.[53] In the Pyramid Texts, there are, however, suggestive utterances in which an offering is made to "Horus who is in Osiris."[54] In terms of the orthodox funerary interpretation, it is difficult to make sense of this phrase, since Horus is supposed to be the king who succeeds his dead predecessor, so how can he be "in" him? From a mystical perspective it would, needless to say, have far-reaching significance, for it implies that although the king is in the condition of Osiris, the Horus principle is nevertheless within him as well. Horus, in other words, is the inner possibility of Osiris.[55] Rather than go down this route, Griffiths, in seeking to defend the funerary interpretation, proposes the theory that there were originally two myths, one concerning Horus and the other Osiris. Passages that refer to "Horus who is in Osiris" simply provide evidence of the fusion of these two myths that became muddled in these utterances.[56]

While the case may certainly be made for the separate origins of a Horus myth, featuring the conflict of Horus and Seth and the main elements of the Osiris myth, it is surely disingenuous to argue that the merging of these two myths in the Osiris religion was the result of some kind of muddle, an illegitimate intrusion or "transference" due to historical and political factors. If there really were originally two separate myths (and this has by no means been proved), then it is highly unlikely that their fusion was due to an error. To suggest that their fusion was the result of purely political pressures also seems far less likely than that the motivation for their fusion was religious, for the simple reason that the outcome was to deepen the religious significance of the two myths. *If* there was a fusion of two originally separate myths, then this was surely done deliberately, and it was done because it was viewed as giving to both an additional level of meaning. To ignore this additional level of meaning while favoring an explanation of the texts as the product of political and historical forces, combined with priestly ineptitude (in unintentionally muddling up two quite different myths), scarcely does justice to their religious content.[57] But to take this religious content seriously, we would have to think in nonfunerary terms.

The Throne of Osiris

One final example that illustrates the problems inherent in the funerary interpretation of the Osiris myth is used by both Breasted and Griffiths. In the Pyramid Texts there are passages in which the king is said to receive "the throne of Osiris." Breasted quotes from the pyramid of Pepi II:

> **O King, how good is this,**
> **how great is this**
> **which your father Osiris has done for you!**
> **He has given his throne to you,**
> **and you give orders to those whose seats are hidden,**
> **you lead their august ones,**
> **and all the spirits follow you.[58]**

According to Breasted, the meaning of this passage is that it is "the dead king who receives the throne of Osiris and becomes, like him, king of the dead."[59] Certainly, there can be no doubt that the text affirms that Osiris gives his throne to the king, but the text does not itself say that the king is dead. This is assumed by Breasted to be the case because it is Osiris who gives his throne to the king, as a consequence of which the king gives orders to "those whose seats are hidden," which Breasted interprets as meaning "the dead." Let us assume that he is right that "those whose seats are hidden" are the dead. This does not mean that the context of Osiris's gift of the throne is necessarily funerary, for if the living king had ventured into the realm of the dead in a mystical experience of the type we have already examined, then it could of course be the living king who receives the throne of Osiris. Breasted admits that there may be a certain ambiguity in the whole concept of the king receiving the throne of Osiris, because in some passages the king seems to be receiving it as the heir of Osiris— that is, as Horus![60] But it does not occur to him that this ambiguity arises out of a far more fundamental ambiguity in the identities of Horus and

Osiris, which is that one and the same king can actually be referred to both as an Osiris and as a Horus. Osiris and Horus do not therefore have to be the dead king and his successor—they could be just the one king experiencing himself as aligned now to Osiris and now to Horus.[61]

Underlying the whole question of the king acquiring the throne, whether as Osiris or as Horus, is the significant fact that several utterances in the Pyramid Texts are clearly linked to, derived from, or are versions of coronation texts.[62] If coronation texts are part of the corpus of the Pyramid Texts, this should lead us to question the funerary nature of the texts associated with them, especially when it is now seriously proposed that key elements in the coronation rites undergone by the king were tantamount to initiation rituals.[63] And yet Egyptologists have with very few exceptions followed Breasted in interpreting the "throne of Osiris" motif in an exclusively funerary context. Griffiths, for example, discusses a similar text to the one referred to by Breasted, from the pyramid of Unas:

> **O King, you have not departed dead,**
> **you have departed alive;**
> **sit upon the throne of Osiris,**
> **your sceptre in your hand,**
> **that you may give orders to the living. . . .**[64]

The text clearly states that the king has "departed," but that he has not departed dead. He sits on the throne of Osiris with an *'aba* (lotus bud) scepter in his hand, so that he may give orders to the living. The words "alive" and "living" are unequivocal in the pyramid of Unas, where this text first appears. They are both written with the ankh sign, which in the case of "the living" is written three times to denote plurality.

Here, then, is a passage that could well be seen as having an initiatory import: The king's accession to the throne of Osiris could mean that he has mystically passed through the Osirian death (his departing) and subsequent rebirth (the lotus-bud scepter symbolizing, among other things, his rebirth). Griffiths, however, holds doggedly to a funerary interpretation of this passage. The ankh sign denoting "life" should, he suggests, be taken as a euphemism for the dead. Thus the pharaoh who has "departed alive" is the dead pharaoh and the term *living* (plural *ankhs*) is best interpreted as "giving an affirmation about the glorified dead."[65] But while the Egyptians did use the ankh to refer to the dead, they also used it to refer to the literally living.[66] In accepting possible equivocation in the use of the ankh, we have also to accept that it must sometimes have meant the literally living, or else it would no longer have retained the meaning "living," and would have always simply meant the dead. In order for a word to be used equivocally, it must sometimes mean what it says. So we cannot be sure whether "the living" in this particular passage are in fact the dead—it depends on our interpretative stance. Likewise, when it comes to the king being alive or dead, it is not clear-cut, for we notice that the ankh (in the singular) is contrasted with the word for "dead," *met*, and it is explicitly stated that the king has not departed dead *(met)* but alive *(ankh)*. In this case, it is surely perverse to claim that the king who has "not departed dead" really is dead on the grounds that he is referred to as having "departed alive"! Once again perhaps we should ask ourselves: What if the Egyptians wanted to convey that the pharaoh really was alive, and not dead. How else could they have done it, other than by writing the word *alive* and explicitly contrasting it with the word *dead?*

For Breasted, Griffiths, and a great many other Egyptologists, the Egyptians never came to terms with the brute fact of death. This is why the words *living* and *alive* were used when they really meant their opposite. Rather than accepting that the king really was dead, the Egyptians embraced the "fiction" that the dead king was in fact alive. This is a view that is constantly reiterated in standard reference works.[67] But suppose it isn't a fiction. For those who support the funerary interpretation it *has* to be a fiction, because if it were not a fiction, then the Pyramid Texts would cease to be simply funerary texts, but would have to be regarded also as mystical texts concerning the journey of the living pharaoh into the spirit world. The origins of the Osiris myth and cult would not be funerary but shamanic.

The Mystical Embrace of Osiris and Horus

At this point, a brief summary of the argument so far may be helpful. First of all, there are many statements in the Pyramid Texts that apparently refer to the "dead" king as Horus. Either this means that the king could continue to be identified with Horus after his death or that the funerary interpretation of the texts in which he is identified as Horus is incorrect, and these texts are actually referring not to the dead but to the living king. Second, there are many statements in the Pyramid Texts in which the king, although identified with Osiris, is nevertheless said to be alive and not dead. However we interpret these passages in which either the "dead" king is Horus or the king as Osiris is said to be alive, it would seem that a degree of flexibility is needed in the way we approach them. While every dead king may have been regarded as Osiris, we cannot ignore the evidence that suggests there were circumstances in which he was thought of as Horus, with the possible implication that he may not in fact have been literally dead. Likewise, while every living king may have been officially regarded as Horus, there could have been occasions when he was identified with Osiris, in which case he may have been temporarily merged with Osiris even though he was alive. We need, therefore, to loosen up the generally accepted view that the living king is Horus and the dead king Osiris, and to become open to the possibility that the identifications of the king with Horus and Osiris were not rigidly bound to the king's being physically alive or dead. One very important implication then follows. This is that the status of the Pyramid Texts, and thereafter the Coffin Texts and the Book of the Dead, as well as the royal New Kingdom Underworld books, may not have been exclusively funerary. They might also have had a mystical significance.

In the last section we have seen that a mystical interpretation of certain passages of the Pyramid Texts in which the "dead" king is in the Horus role appears to be just as plausible as a purely funerary interpretation. But it is difficult to see how it would be possible to substantiate the mystical interpretation. How such passages are interpreted depends to a large extent on the presuppositions of the interpreter regarding the nature and purpose of the Pyramid Texts as a whole. The situation is different, though, in the case of the living king becoming united with Osiris, for here we can look at evidence from sources that clearly involve the living king, but at the same time show him to be identified with Osiris.

The most instructive sources that we can turn to are kingship rituals in which there is absolutely no question that the king, as chief participant, is alive and not dead. There are several rituals that are relevant to the question of whether the living king ever underwent an Osiris identification, but two in particular are of sufficient antiquity to have been performed during the period when the Pyramid Texts were composed. The first is described in a papyrus, discovered in a Middle Kingdom tomb but which probably originated in the First Dynasty. It is generally referred to as the Ramesseum Dramatic Papyrus, and it details an elaborate royal ritual in forty-six scenes, with thirty-one vignettes, culminating in the coronation of Horus and the raising of Osiris. The second is a kingship ritual, known as the Sed festival, for which we have records going back to the very earliest dynasties. This ritual, often described as effecting a renewal of the kingship, was enacted throughout Egyptian history. We shall look first at the Ramesseum Dramatic Papyrus ritual and return in the next section to consider the Sed festival.

The Ramesseum Dramatic Papyrus describes and comments on a ritual performed for the Twelfth Dynasty king, Sesostris I, but since it probably derives from a First Dynasty ritual it, or something like it, may have taken place during the Old Kingdom, at the time the Pyramid Texts were committed to writing.[68] The ritual was originally interpreted by Sethe as being performed by the king shortly after his accession (and before his coronation), when he visited the important cities of Egypt. Thus, according to Sethe, it took place between the death of one king and the coronation of the next king. This view is also held by Henri Frankfort, who calls it a "mystery play of the succession."[69] It has also been argued, however, that it was closely linked to the Sed festival, and may in fact have been performed on the eve of the Sed festival. If this is the case, then it was not linked simply to the royal succession, but also to the renewal of the kingship within the reign of an already living king.[70]

The ritual began with preliminary rites during which food offerings and sacrifices were prepared, and royal insignia, such as scepters, staff, and a mace, were brought out from a shrine and carried in a procession. After this, there are scenes symbolizing the dismemberment of Osiris, in which grain (symbolizing Osiris) is trampled by oxen, then loaded onto asses and taken away. The use of asses symbolizes Seth's subordination to Osiris, and this theme is taken further with the raising of the *djed* column, witnessed by the king, and signifying the demise of Seth. Offerings are now made to Horus, and a fight—possibly a wrestling match—between the "children of Horus" and the "followers of Seth" is enacted, with the victory going to Horus. There follows an offering procession in which produce from the three spheres of nature, animal, plant, and mineral, are brought to the king and presented to him, each as an "eye of Horus." These include milk and meat; bread, wine, and wood; precious stones; and metals. The next event is the coronation of the king in a ceremony that involves his taking hold of two scepters, symbolizing the elemental energy of Seth, a golden *shen* ring or headband, and two feathers that are tied to his head. Priests sing a chant to the sacred Horus eye, which is now—through the crowning of the king—symbolically restored. Shortly after this, the king eats a *hetep* meal (i.e., a meal of sacred offerings), as if to empower him for the next phase in the ceremonies. In fact, all of the components of this first half of the ritual may be viewed as serving the single purpose of empowering the king for the more challenging and arduous events that are to come.

What occurs next is the most significant part of the ritual. It begins with a lector priest bringing a special garment called a *qeni* (worn over the chest and back and knotted at the shoulder), which is then placed on the king.

The text identifies the *qeni* (illustrated in figure 3.1) with Osiris. It is filled with the spiritual potency of Osiris. So, as this garment is placed over the king, it signifies the ritual union or "embrace" of the Horus-king and Osiris. The king says:

I have embraced this my father
who has become tired,
so that he may become quite healthy again.[71]

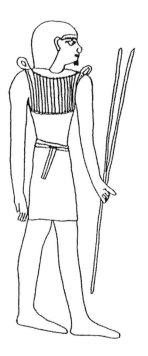

Figure 3.1. The qeni *is shown here worn by a* sem *priest during a ceremony of Opening of the Mouth. In the ritual described in the Ramesseum Dramatic Papyrus, the* qeni *is identified with Osiris and placed on the living king.*

The embrace is protective of Osiris, restoring to him health and strength, but it is also a mutual act that has an invigorating and renewing effect on the Horus-king, as we shall see.

It is worth dwelling on the meaning of this embrace, for it really is the kernel of the whole ceremony. According to Frankfort, we should understand that it is "no mere sign of affection, but a true fusion, a communion between two living spirits, *unio mystica*."[72] Frankfort implies that the two archetypes, or archetypal energies, of Osiris and Horus are at this moment virtually indistinguishable, for what occurs is essentially an inner event in the consciousness of the king, an awareness that his royal power arises from this mystical fusion of the two archetypes within his own being: Osiris, the archetype of death and renewal, and Horus, the archetype of the reborn human spirit. Frankfort describes this phase in the ceremonies as "an excellent example of those *rites de passage* which . . . guide man's personality from an earlier to a new state of life."[73]

We know, however, of the mystical embrace of Osiris and Horus from other sources in addition to the Ramesseum Dramatic Papyrus. One is a New Kingdom "Ancestor Ritual" performed in the Eighteenth and Nineteenth Dynasties. Another is a text from the eighth century B.C. known as the Memphite Theology, which was inscribed on a basalt stone and is generally regarded as originating at least as far back as the New Kingdom, and possibly dating to the Old Kingdom.[74] Because of its possible greater antiquity, it is the latter that we shall touch on here. Much of the Memphite Theology is concerned with the creation of the world by the god of Memphis, Ptah, but at both the beginning and the end of this text part of the Osiris myth is briefly related, in which Osiris is saved from drowning by Isis and Nephthys. We also read of how Osiris entered "the Secret Gates" of the Underworld and walked "on the path of Ra" before arriving at "the palace" and "coming to earth at the Royal Fortress" (Memphis). After this, "his son Horus arose as king of Upper Egypt, arose as king of Lower Egypt, in the embrace of his father Osiris and of the gods in front of him and behind him."[75] There is little reason to doubt that what is described here closely parallels the Ramesseum Dramatic Papyrus ritual.[76] What is particularly interesting is the allusion to a sequence of three mystical Osirian phases after the god has been saved from drowning: (1) entering the Secret Gates of the Underworld; (2) walking on the paths of Ra; and (3) finally "coming to earth" at the Royal Fortress. These Osirian phases are then followed by Horus arising as king, presumably through a coronation ceremony, and at the same time "in the embrace of his father Osiris."

Now, these sources describing the mystical embrace of Horus and Osiris in a coronation ceremony are closely paralleled in the Pyramid Texts. There is, for example, a passage in the Pyramid Texts that presents the embrace of Osiris and Horus as having an utterly transformative effect on the Horus-king. Through the embrace, he becomes a shining spirit *(akh)*:

> **O Osiris, this is Horus in your embrace,**
> **and he protects you.**
> **He has become *akh* through you,**
> **in your identity of the *akhet***
> **from which the sun emerges.**[77]

The Egyptian word *akhet* is usually translated as "horizon," because this is where the sun first shines each morning, but it is also, in a religious sense, the "place" of spiritual transfiguration. Not only the sun god Ra but also the human soul undergoes this transfiguration after the sojourn in the dark netherworld, referred to in the Memphite Theology.[78]

While we cannot be sure that the embrace of Osiris and Horus that is described in the Pyramid Texts involved the ritual of the *qeni* garment, it would certainly seem to be related to a kingship ritual very similar to that described in the Ramesseum Dramatic Papyrus. In this ritual, what occurred outwardly in ritual act was intended to correspond to some inner experience of mystical union of the gods Horus and Osiris within the consciousness of the king. Both the Memphite Theology and the Pyramid Texts amplify what this inner experience probably entailed. The quotation from the Pyramid Texts is particularly explicit, for it states that Horus, who is held protectively in the embrace of Osiris, is made shining (akh)—like Ra—through this embrace. Whether Osiris is identified with the dead king, who spiritually embraces his successor, or is thought of as a condition of soul that the living king experiences in order to undergo an inner rebirth and to "become akh" is immaterial to the crucial fact that insofar as we accept that the embrace was actually experienced by the Horus-king, what he experienced was a fusion with Osiris.

In the ritual described by the Ramesseum Dramatic Papyrus, the embrace is immediately followed by the bringing in of the products of Osiris's symbolic death—bread and beer, made from the trampled grain. Different kinds of cloth are also brought in, one of which (colored purple) is identified with the restored and awakened Osiris and worn by the king. Then the king orders certain priests, called the Embracers of the Akh[79] (who wear jackal and baboon masks), to create a great ladder that reaches up to the sky, and it is on this ladder that the Osiris-king now ascends. As the king climbs, the priests swing clubs to drive back Seth—an action that at the same time appears to produce the rungs of the ladder. This ladder, then, is partly symbolic but it probably did exist physically in some form, so that the king's ascent, as an awakened Osiris, was dramatically enacted. Climbing up to the sky on a ladder or stairway is typical of shamanic rituals, for which many examples can be found worldwide.[80] It is interesting, therefore, that references to the ascent of the king to the sky by means of a ladder are also to be found in the Pyramid Texts, once again linking them both with the kingship ritual of the Ramesseum Dramatic Papyrus and a typically shamanic motif.[81] With this ascent of the Osiris-king, the ritual now draws to a close, ending with a huge feast in which, of course, the living king is the main participant.

As there can be little doubt about the fusion of Osiris and Horus in the qeni garment episode, we may conclude that in this part of the ritual, at least, we have an example of the living Horus-king being united with Osiris. And this momentous event clearly has ramifications that affect, and probably determine, all the other episodes in the ritual, both before and after. Whether we understand Osiris to be the living king's dead predecessor or the god or spiritual power that exists independently of the dead king and with which the dead king became fused is probably not a question that should be posed in either/or terms. The "embrace" was felt to involve an identification of the living king with the god Osiris, facilitated by and through the royal ancestor or ancestors. The effect of the "embrace" was that as the consciousness of the living king extended itself into the sphere of the dead, it became "the same" as the consciousness of the king's dead predecessors—that is, open to the world of spirit.

The Sed Festival

The Sed festival is known from very early dynastic sources, and was celebrated throughout ancient Egyptian history. It is a festival for which there is a wealth of information from ancient sites, wall reliefs, tomb paintings, and hieroglyphic records.[82] The festival may have originally been celebrated in the thirtieth year of the king's reign, and seems to have served the function of renewing or reinvigorating the kingship. But there are so many exceptions to the thirty-year rule that it is difficult to say exactly what the circumstances were that meant that the holding of the Sed festival would be deemed appropriate.[83] The name given to the festival probably derives from the short kilt with a bull's tail that the king put on for its culminating rites.[84] The festival lasted five days and took place immediately after the annual Osiris rites, at the time of the retreat of the Inundation. The series of rites that made up the festival centered on the person of the king, and the most important of them seem not to have changed from the earliest dynasties through to the late period.[85]

The preparations for the festival began a long time before its actual celebration, for it was necessary either to found a new temple or to construct a "festival hall" within the precincts of an already existing sanctuary specially for the festival. The main buildings required were a festival hall, a court containing shrines for the gods of Egypt, and a "palace" or robing chamber for the king's use. In addition to these buildings, a special chamber was included among the Sed festival buildings in which the most secret rites were undergone. We know from the reliefs of Niuserre that his chamber contained a bed, but there is evidence to suggest that in certain cases a sarcophagus may have been used.[86]

For the five days immediately preceding the festival, a fire ceremony called "lighting the flame" served to purify the festival precincts. The festival proper began with a great procession of the king and priests that also included statues of gods representing the different regions, or nomes, of Egypt. The first two days of the festival then alternated between the king visiting the gods in their shrines and retiring to his palace to undergo ritual purification and change of dress and insignia. The purpose of these formal visits of the king to the gods in their shrines was for him to renew his spiritual connection to the nomes of Egypt. According to the requirements of the ritual, the king would appear as king of the south or the north, burning incense before the shrines of the gods, making offerings to them and receiving from them the blessings of a long life and a long reign.

During or soon after these opening rites, there was also a coronation ceremony in which the king was crowned four times facing the four cardinal directions.[87] It seems likely that, as with the coronation ceremony described in the Ramesseum Dramatic Papyrus, this coronation served the purpose of empowering the king for the main ritual that was shortly to follow. Also serving to empower the king was the ritual meal that he ate soon after the coronation. Finally, he donned a special Sed festival robe and walked in procession around the whole Sed complex, symbolically taking possession of it. The king then entered a pavilion or shrine with the standards of the jackal god Wepwawet, the Opener of Ways, who at this point in the ceremonies begins to play a prominent role. There now also appears a *sem* priest (who conducts funerary rites) along with two other priests, one of whom is called "the opener of the mouth" and the other "the one who carries the *qeni*."[88] As we have already seen in relation to the Ramesseum Dramatic Papyrus rites, the *qeni* is the garment through which Horus is united with Osiris in a mystical embrace.

The next phase in the ceremonies, called by Eric Uphill "the secret rites in the tomb," involves the king first going through a purification rite and then entering a building, or chamber, possibly his tomb. It constitutes the central event of the festival.[89] In figure 3.2, King Osorkon is purified by *sem* priests wearing leopard skins. Since *sem* priests normally conduct funerary rites, a funerary context may well be indicated. But so also may rites of a more shamanic nature, since one of the specialties of the *sem* priest seems to have been to make contact with the realm of the dead.[90] The king is pictured wearing a long robe and the white crown, which probably should here be interpreted as the white crown of Osiris. He also wears an Osirian beard, which is usually absent in other portrayals of him during the festival. Figure 3.3 shows a standard representation of Osiris, for comparison.[91]

In the next scene in the reliefs of King Osorkon's Sed festival, the king, having entered the "tomb," comes face-to-face with twelve important deities (fig. 3.4). These are, from top to bottom and right to left Ra, Atum,

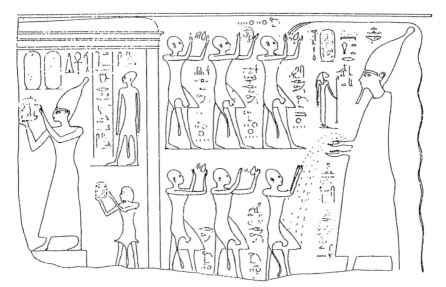

Figure 3.2. The "secret rites" of the Sed festival. King Osorkon II is purified by sem priests before entering a shrine or tomb. He wears the white crown and a long funerary robe from which his hands protrude, and is also shown with an "Osirian" beard, absent from most of the portrayals of him in other scenes.

Figure 3.3. Osiris with Isis. Osiris wears the white crown (he is not normally, if ever, depicted wearing the red crown) and is shown here with a beard. Notice the way in which his hands are shown, protruding from his tight mummy garment. He holds the crook, flail, and was scepter.

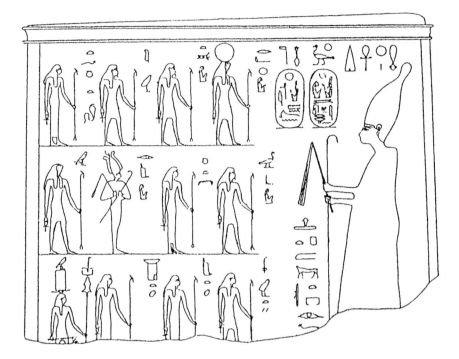

Figure 3.4. The "secret rites" of the Sed festival. King Osorkon II enters a shrine or tomb during the Sed festival and meets twelve major deities. The fact that the meeting takes place here rather than before the shrines of the deities suggests the visionary nature of this encounter.

Shu, and Tefnut; Geb, Nut, Osiris, and Horus; and Seth, Isis, Nephthys, and the king's *ka*. In front of the king are written the words "Resting inside the tomb," apparently followed by the beginning of a broken sentence: "May he make (*iry*) . . ." The word translated as "tomb" here is *is*, a common word for tomb in Old Kingdom inscriptions, though the translation "shrine" has also been suggested.[92] If, as may be the case, the tomb here is not Osorkon's actual grave but some kind of shrine or chapel, the funereal character of the reliefs surrounding the two scenes (figs. 3.2 and 3.4) is notable. We have already observed the presence of *sem* priests in the previous two phases of the ceremonies. Higher up on the wall above the image of the king "resting inside the tomb" in figure 3.4 a procession of *sem* priests and men carrying mummiform *shabti* figurines adds to the funerary atmosphere of the event.[93] And yet the king, who is portrayed standing up, is clearly not in a state of unconsciousness, but actively "making" or "doing" something.[94]

That the king, alone in the "tomb," should at the same time find himself in the presence of the twelve major deities of the Egyptian pantheon is suggestive of a mystical experience rather than simply another ceremonial event. This is corroborated by the fact that whereas in the earlier phases of the festival the king visited the gods of the different nomes of Egypt in their shrines, now it would seem that he is communing with the major gods of the pantheon directly, for these gods, appearing in front of the king, have no shrines. They are portrayed as living presences ranged before the king's awakened inner vision. Perhaps it is merely a coincidence that in the Pyramid Texts there is one utterance in particular that refers to just such an array of deities as Osorkon here encounters. It is utterance 219, in which each of the deities is addressed in turn, beginning with Atum and Shu and Tefnut, and moving on to Geb, Nut, Isis, Seth, and Nephthys and so on. The list of gods does not coincide exactly, but it is close enough to bear comparison. We have had cause to refer to this utterance earlier in this chapter, when discussing the "resurrection texts." It will be remembered that in it each of the gods is addressed, and it is stated again and again that the king is not dead but "lives."

We need to turn to the Sed festival reliefs of the Fifth Dynasty king Niuserre if we are to understand better what exactly occurred during these "secret rites in the tomb." In figure 3.5, the damaged relief shows King Niuserre in a chamber that contains a bed ornamented with lion heads. It

Figure 3.5. The "secret rites" of the Sed festival. King Niuserre stands beside a double bed ornamented with the heads of lions. It also has lion legs and paws. The shaded areas are where the relief has been damaged. The significance of the lion bed is that it is of the type that Osiris lies on when undergoing his death and rebirth.

also has lion legs and paws. He is not, however, shown lying on it. Unfortunately, the lower half of his body is lost, but comparison with adjacent fragments indicates that Niuserre is standing beside the bed, thus emphasizing his conscious relationship to it. The importance of this bed is that it is of the type that is closely associated with Osiris. It is, for example, frequently used as a funerary bier on which the deceased lies, as in figure 3.6.

The lion bed was also used in the depiction of the mystical stages of Osiris's death, disintegration, reconstitution, revitalization, and resurrection that are found on the walls of temples such as the temple of Seti I at Abydos, Hathor's temple at Denderah and Isis's temple at Philae. Figure 3.7 shows one of a sequence of ten reliefs from Denderah, depicting ten phases of the Osiris myth. This image portrays the union of Osiris with Isis (in the form of a kite hovering above him) on the lion bed, leading to the conception of Horus. It is events such as this, therefore, that are symbolically associated with the lion bed, not simply funerary rites. The "posthumous" conception of Horus is an important mystical occurrence in the Osiris myth that has profound implications, for it signifies the generation of a new spiritual principle. Whether it formed part of the "secret rites" is, however, impossible to answer with certainty. In the Niuserre reliefs, the bed is actually depicted four times, suggesting at least four "Osirian" stages, possibly more, as only fragments of relief survive.

The next scene (fig. 3.8) in the Niuserre reliefs shows King Niuserre in a

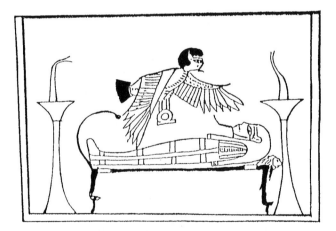

Figure 3.6. A mummy lies on a lion-headed bier that also has lion legs, paws, and tail. The mummiform figure is the New Kingdom scribe Ani, who wears the Osiris beard and was identified with Osiris throughout his papyrus, from which the image is taken. Above Ani hovers the winged form of his ba, *or soul-bird.*

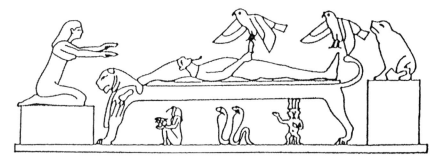

Figure 3.7. The conception of Horus, one of a sequence of ten reliefs in the western roof chapel at the temple of Hathor, Denderah. Osiris (or the Osiris-king), wearing the white crown and Osirian beard, lies on a lion bed similar to the one depicted in the Sed festival "secret rites." Here he unites with Isis, who appears in the form of a kite hovering over him. From their union the god Horus will be born.

Figure 3.8. King Niuserre is reborn as a god from the lion bed. The text above the bed (top left) reads, "The birth of a god; giving the head . . ." The restoration of the head was the most critical symbolic act in the re-membering of the dismembered Osiris. The shaded areas are where the relief has been damaged.

similar position to the one he has in figure 3.5, standing beside the same bed. But now, above the bed is written "The birth of a god, giving the head . . ." These enigmatic words refer to the experiences of the king in the tomb. The tradition of Osiris losing and then regaining his head is an extremely ancient one, and was important within the funerary cult. Headless, Osiris languishes in the Underworld; the restoration of his head corresponds to his rebirth and solarization. There can be little doubt that these words confirm that the king is here identified with Osiris, and undergoes the archetypal process by which the god becomes spiritually empowered, assuming a new identity as Horus.[95] The king thereby acquires a new awareness of the spiritual world, able to perceive a reality that is beyond the range of normal consciousness.

The ritual of "giving the head" is, significantly, referred to in the Pyramid Texts. Indeed, many of the references to the king as Horus in the Pyramid Texts may well be best understood in precisely this context.[96] Underneath the bed two men are shown with their arms held low in front of them in a gesture of homage to the newborn god-man who stands before them. Above the men are written the words "*sesefetch* oil 2 jars." *Sesefetch* oil was one of the seven holy oils and is mentioned in the Pyramid Texts in association with the healing and revivification of Osiris (see fig. 7.8).[97] There is in fact so much visual and circumstantial evidence in these reliefs depicting the "secret rites" that the king undergoes an Osiris identification that to deny it would require that one literally close one's eyes to the meaning that is displayed at every turn.

According to Eric Uphill, this phase in the rites was the supreme moment of the Sed festival. He suggests that to understand what occurs next in the rites, we should consider a scene in the cenotaph of Seti I at Abydos that features one of the stages in the Osiris myth (fig. 3.9).[98] It shows Seti dressed in a shroudlike garment, such as was used by the king during his entombment in the Sed festival, stretched out on a lion bed. We have to imagine that at this point in the rites the king has been lying on his back on the bed and then turns around so that he is lying on his stomach. In the Abydos relief, the Osiris-king is shown having rolled over and now lying on his stomach like a sphinx while "his son" the god Horus presents him with the symbols of life, stability, and dominion attached to the end of a long staff. Over the bed there is just one hieroglyph, of two pieces of wood joined and lashed together, meaning "Awake!" Below the bed are spread the royal regalia, clothing, and weapons that the king would take up after his rebirth. What is depicted is the spiritual awakening of the king after his symbolic death during the

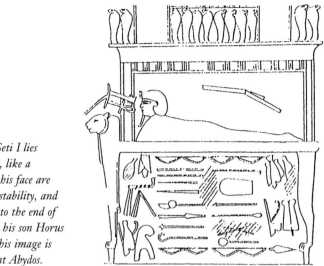

Figure 3.9. King Seti I lies prone on a lion bed, like a sphinx. In front of his face are the symbols of life, stability, and dominion attached to the end of a long staff held by his son Horus (off the picture). This image is from his cenotaph at Abydos.

Sed festival. It is, needless to say, the living king who is depicted as an Osiris awakening.

This scene, being part of the standard sequence portraying the phases of the Osiris myth, is not unique to the cenotaph of Seti. It is one of a type that recurs elsewhere. Thus a similar image can be found in the sequence of ten reliefs at Denderah, to which reference has already been made. The Denderah version of this same event is reproduced in figure 3.10.

After "the secret rites," the king discards the Osirian garment and puts on his usual royal dress. There is evidence from at least one record of the Sed festival that what follows is the raising of the *djed* column, symbolizing the god Osiris, which through the period during which the king was in the tomb had been lying on the ground. Now, at dawn on the morning of the fourth day of the festival, the *djed* is raised.[99] The king then embarks on the famous running ceremonies, known as the "dedication of the field," to which we shall return in chapter 4. In one hand, he holds a document called "the secret of the two partners" (the two partners being Horus and Seth, whom he has integrated within himself), and then runs or lopes across a demarcated area symbolizing the land of Egypt. During this rite, the king wears a kilt with the bull's tail. Finally, on the fifth and last day of the festival, there is a great procession culminating in a second coronation, confirming the king's status as the Horus-king, lord of the Two Lands, uniter of heaven and earth. Arrows are shot to the four cardinal directions, and a

Figure 3.10. The king turns over on his stomach to face Horus, who rouses him from his initiatory sleep. Notice the seven royal crowns underneath the bed, with the cobra and sundisk to the right. The image closely parallels an image in the cenotaph of Seti I, described above. This relief is from a sequence of ten at Denderah, and probably illustrates an important phase in the most secret rites of the Sed festival.

large public feast with music, dancing, and general celebration brings the festival to its conclusion.

The Sed festival reliefs of Osorkon II and Niuserre, as well as the Osiris reliefs in the Cenotaph of Seti I and the chapels at Hathor's temple at Denderah, all support the view that during the Sed festival the king became identified with Osiris. We have seen, as well, that certain passages in the Pyramid Texts relate to episodes in the Sed festival. On the basis of this accumulation of evidence, Eric Uphill has argued that it is probable that a large proportion of the Pyramid Texts that are concerned with lists of offerings of food, oils, and drink, of royal clothing, regalia, and symbolic objects, as well as the ritual presentation of the "Eye of Horus" and the Opening of the Mouth ceremony all belong as much to the Sed festival as to the funerary rites of the king.[100] If this is the case, and if it is also the case that key events described in the Pyramid Texts such as the restoration of the dismembered body of the king and his spiritual rebirth were also key events of the Sed festival, then it seems we must seriously consider the possibility not only that was the living king identified with Osiris during the Sed festival, but also that the Pyramid Texts may be as closely linked to the Sed festival as they are to the funerary rites of the king. Once again, then, if we read the Pyramid Texts as mystical initiatory texts, we could find that they make considerably more sense than if we read them simply as funerary texts. Since the Coffin Texts and the Book of the Dead are in the same genre as— and indeed are to a large extent derived from—the Pyramid Texts, the same inference may apply to them as well. A radical re-reading of the "funerary" literature of ancient Egypt would therefore seem to be required.

4 THE PYRAMIDS AS THE LOCUS OF SECRET RITES

The Living in Relation to the Dead

In chapter 3 we have seen that key passages in the Pyramid Texts along with certain kingship rituals, most notably the "secret rites" of the Sed festival, provide powerful evidence that there existed in ancient Egypt the same type of mystical tradition that existed in other contemporaneous and later ancient cultures: namely, a tradition in which experiences were induced in a living person (in the case of the Sed festival, the king) that normally would only occur at death. Initiation within this mystical tradition was regarded as giving to the initiate an immediate experience of spiritual realities that for most people would be experienced only after their death. Since the focus of the present inquiry is the Pyramid Texts, it is incumbent that, as well as texts and rituals, we look at the tradition of pyramid building in Old Kingdom Egypt and ask the vital question: Were the pyramids and their surrounding buildings and ceremonial courts built simply to serve the royal funerary cult, or could they also have served mystical ends? Could they, for example, have been used for the performance of rites such as those of the Sed festival, involving the living king?

In this chapter, we shall review some of the evidence that supports the possibility that the pyramids and pyramid complexes of the Old Kingdom were indeed intimately connected with the Sed festival. This evidence does not necessarily preclude their subsequent use in the funerary cult of the king. But equally, evidence of their use in the funerary cult does not preclude the possibility of their prior use by the living king for the conducting of mystical rites. Initiation within this mystical tradition was in obvious respects at the same time a preparation for death, which would as a result be approached more consciously. For the king to be buried in the same place where he first underwent initiation would not be in the least contradictory. Before examining the evidence for the association of the pyramids with the Sed festival, however, it is necessary to look a little further both into the spiritual context in which the "secret rites" took place and, in the next section, into the broader content and meaning of the Sed festival as a whole.

It is often felt today that the ancient Egyptians were obsessed with death, and in a way this is correct. But as we have already seen, the Egyptians understood death very differently from us. For the modern person, brought up in the secular and humanist culture of the West, it seems obvious that death is something that follows life. We live our lives for, hopefully, seventy or eighty years and then we die. What occurs then is unknown to us, though we may have strongly held beliefs about survival or lack of survival after we have died. But the conception of death that most of us unquestioningly subscribe to is a temporal conception. Death awaits us at the end of our lives. Even those of us who believe in reincarnation tend to think of this in temporal terms, as repeated incarnations spread across a time line. It seems so obvious that it does not occur to many of us to question this modern way of thinking about death as a punctuating factor of our living in time.

For the Egyptians, however, it was not so simple, for as we have seen, their conception of death was not simply temporal; it was also spatial. Death was a realm—not a physical realm but a subtle realm that they referred to as the Dwat.[1] Furthermore, the realm of the dead was for them an ever present factor of life, interpenetrating the world of the living. In the realm of the dead, invisible forces, powers, and energies—gods and demons as well as the spirits of the dead—are active, and their activity impinges directly on the world of the living. The Egyptians were intensely aware that the world they lived in was more than just the world perceptible to the senses. It included a vast and complex supersensible component as well.

It would be a mistake, then, to regard the Dwat as simply the realm of the dead. It is the habitation of spirits, of beings that are capable of existing nonphysically. These include the essential spiritual energy or life energy of those beings and creatures that we see around us in the physical world. In the Dwat, everything is reduced to its spiritual kernel. Just as the forms of living plants, when they die, disappear from the visible world as they are received into the Dwat, so when the young plants unfold their forms again in the new year, they unfold them from out of the Dwat. This "hidden realm" (literally *amentet*, another term for the realm of the dead) is the originating source of all that comes into being in the visible world.

The Egyptians conceived of the Dwat as a deeply interior realm and pictured it in various ways, one of the most evocative being as a region existing within the body of the cosmic goddess Nut. Nut is both the nurturing mother who gives birth to all things that come into manifestation and the devouring mother who swallows all things back into herself at the end of their lives.[2] In the Dwat, then, the essential forms of things exist inwardly in a more interior space—a space that is prior to the external space into which they will unfold when they enter the world of physical manifestation. As for plants, so also for animals. Even the river Nile has its source in the Dwat.[3]

Therefore the Dwat, as much as it is the realm of death, is the source of all that comes to exist in the material world. The lord of this realm of death, which is also the realm of rebirth and rejuvenation, is Osiris. Thus the realm of Osiris, where the dead dwell, was by no means only a place where exhausted and tired-out life languished in a state of passive inertia. It was where things also existed in a state of energized inwardness, poised to burst forth again into manifestation.[4] The Egyptian understanding of the realm of the dead, then, was that it was the source of the fertility of the land, the growth of crops, and the increase of herds. And the dead were not just passive in this realm, but were felt to have a special role as the guardians of the forces of life, and hence the well-being of the whole land of Egypt. This is the meaning behind the ancient Egyptian cult of the dead: It was not simply about remembrance; it was about ensuring that a connection between the manifest world and its vital spiritual kernel was maintained, for the dead were the conduits of this inner spiritual vitality to the outwardly manifest world.[5]

In the ancient Egyptian social order, there was one person who had a particularly important role in relation to the dead, and that was the king. His primary function was to keep the visible and invisible worlds linked together. The king had to live as much in relation to the spirit world as he did in relation to the visible world. He was, as god-man, the mediator between the worlds.[6] For the king to properly fulfill his function, it was essential that the veil or barrier between the worlds did not exist for him, for his responsibilities included precisely those aspects of the well-being of the country that were dependent on the beneficent flow of vitalizing energies from the spirit realm into the realm of the living. The king was ultimately responsible for the well-being of crops and animals, the annual flooding of the Nile, and the fertility of the land.[7] It would therefore be a mistake to think of the kingship as a political institution in the modern sense, for the most important role the king fulfilled was in fact magical or shamanic. It was the fulfillment of this role that provided the underlying reason for kingship rites such as the Sed festival.

The Meaning of the Sed Festival

The Sed festival served several interrelated purposes. While it is often referred to as being concerned with the renewal of the kingship, and the impression is given that it was designed to prove that the ageing king, after thirty years of his reign, still had sufficient energy to rule the country, this does not give us the whole picture. As we have already seen, the festival was not necessarily celebrated in the thirtieth year but could be celebrated much more frequently. Despite the undoubted symbolic importance of the thirty-year period, we know of kings who celebrated the festival several times in their reign at much smaller intervals than the thirty-year interval.[8] So the festival was not simply about the rejuvenation of the ageing king. A major part of the festival consisted in the king visiting the shrines of the assembled gods of Egypt. These gods, made present in their statues, were brought ceremonially to the festival site from all over Egypt. They represented the spiritual energies of the landscape, which were embodied in the human and semihuman forms of their divine statues. The king was thus engaged in a ritual communion with the spirits of the land of Egypt.[9] The underlying purpose of this was to reach across to the more subtle spirit world that upholds and vitalizes the physical world, in order to ensure a beneficent connection with it and an unhampered flow of energies from it into the physical.

The central rite of the Sed festival needs to be understood in this context of the king's harmonizing the relationship between the invisible and visible worlds for the benefit of the whole country. As we have already seen in chapter 3, the central rite involved the king crossing the threshold between worlds in order to stand in direct relationship to the normally hidden spiritual powers. In the mystical tradition described in chapter 3, for which we have rich documentation from the Greek and Hellenistic period, we know that it was deemed necessary for the human being to come to the very brink of death in order for these spiritual powers to be revealed in an ecstatic visionary experience. It would seem that it was just such an experience that was induced in the king during the most secret rites of the Sed festival. The Sed festival had at its core a mystical ritual that served the purpose of bringing the king into a conscious relationship with the spirit world. As such, it could be regarded as an Egyptian precursor of the later Greek and Hellenistic practices. But it differed from these in certain fundamental respects.

Having successfully undergone the "secret rites," the king went on to perform the famous Sed "dance," so often portrayed in reliefs. Known as the "dedication of the field," it is usually assumed that the purpose of the dance was to prove the ageing king's vitality. But this is to overlook a more profound level of its meaning. Through this dance, the performance of which involved the king crossing a large courtyard that symbolically represented the country of Egypt, he magically linked the heavenly with the earthly world. Often in reliefs depicting the king performing the Sed dance, three sets of hoops or cairns are depicted, between which the king runs. These are territorial markers representing the boundaries of his kingdom. In addition to these, one also often finds paired glyphs representing the two halves of the sky.[10] In figure 4.1, the boundary markers can be seen just in front of and behind the king's feet, while the half-sky glyphs can be seen above and to the right of the king. Under each of them is the *shen* sign, signifying eternity. The king is here depicted wearing the traditional costume for this part of the festival: a short kilt with a bull's tail, symbolizing his integration of the virility of this animal. By means of the dedication of the field dance, the king brought the flow of vitalizing energies into the country through his participation in two worlds. Because of the presence of the sky hieroglyphs, it is quite possible that the "field" that was being dedicated through the dance was not just the land of Egypt but was also a spiritual or heavenly field.[11] This is made explicit in a Ptolemaic text in the temple of Edfu that describes the Sed dance of the king as follows:

> **He runs crossing the ocean**
> **and the four sides of heaven,**
> **going as far as the rays of the sun disk,**
> **passing over the earth,**
> **giving the field to its mistress.**[12]

The word *field* is frequently used in both the Pyramid Texts and later religious literature to refer to nonphysical regions traversed by the dead.[13] As it was into these regions that the king mystically traveled during the "secret rites," the purpose of the Sed dance may have been to confirm his power over them, and to revitalize the whole land by bringing it into connection with hidden sources of life in the spirit world. In this respect, we can discern an obvious parallel between the perceived conse-

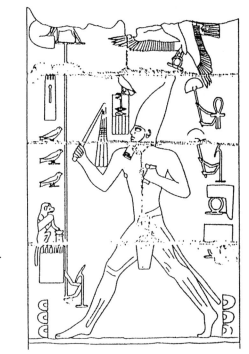

Figure 4.1. King Zoser performs the Sed festival rite of "dedicating the field," preceded by the standard of Wepwawet, the Opener of the Ways. He runs between sets of three hoops or cairns, shown either side of his feet. Behind him, two glyphs (the lower one is damaged) depict the sky. One of three reliefs in a passage underneath his pyramid at Saqqara.

quences of the Sed festival and the Mesopotamian Akitu, through which a renewal of the powers of fertility throughout the land was felt to be accomplished.[14]

Driving home the fact that the Sed festival was concerned with establishing the king's power over both the physical world and the spirit world, the coronation ceremonies undoubtedly had cosmic associations. The coronation dais on which the throne was placed is always portrayed as stepped, and symbolized both the primordial hill that emerged from the ocean of Nun at the beginning of creation and a stairway linking earth and heaven.[15] In contrast to European tradition, the coronation of the king of Egypt was not a once-only event at the beginning of his reign. The Sed festival was one of several that included coronation ceremonies, the purpose of which was the confirmation or reinvestment of the king with the awesome divine-human power of his office.[16] It is likely that the king underwent a coronation ceremony at least twice during the course of the festival: once before the "secret rites" and then a second time at the end of the ceremonies as a grand finale to the whole festival.[17]

One important aspect of the coronation was that it involved a confirmation of the king's solar status as "son of Ra." Insofar as the coronation dais symbolized the primordial hill that emerged from the ocean of Nun at the beginning of creation, the king in ascending it and being crowned upon it was reenacting on earth the primordial appearance of Atum-Ra. The king became the human embodiment of the sun god. One of the purposes of the Sed festival was to empower the king as a manifestation of the sun god on earth. His "solarization" was an implicit part of the ceremonies—in some cases made quite explicit.[18] It was probably for this reason that it was felt appropriate by Niuserre to have depictions of his Sed festival in his sun temple.

The crowning itself was a cosmic event that was regarded as accomplishing the union of the Above and the Below, thereby infusing the earth with the fructifying energies of the spirit realm. This union of heaven and earth during the coronation ceremonies was accompanied by these words, spoken by an attendant priest: "Horus appears resting on his southern throne / and there occurs a uniting of the sky to the earth." The same formula was repeated once for each of the four cardinal directions toward which the king duly turned.[19]

Coronations were always themselves double events in that they included the king being crowned with both the white crown and the red crown. The symbolism of the two crowns extends beyond their simply representing Upper and Lower Egypt, for the crowns, respectively, carried notions of spiritual and temporal power.[20] In addition to this, the white crown has specifically Osirian associations, as the god is normally depicted wearing it, rather than the red crown. Horus, by contrast, is usually shown wearing the double crown that integrates both white and red. During the coronation ceremony, the king wore either a short tunic or a long "Osirian" cloak, probably the same as the cloak that he wore during the "secret rites." This in itself could imply that he was crowned not simply as Horus, but also as Osiris, lord of the spirit realm. The coronation of the king wearing the long Osirian cloak can be seen in figure 4.2, which shows King Osorkon's coronation shortly before the "secret rites." Compare this with figure 4.4, which shows King Niuserre crowned in the short tunic, worn for the second coronation sometime after the "secret rites."[21]

After each of the coronations, or possibly as part of the coronation ceremonies, food offerings were brought to the king. In the Osorkon Sed festival inscriptions, we read that the king retired to a special Hall of Eating after one of his coronations.[22] A Hall of Eating is also mentioned in the reliefs and inscriptions of the Sed festival of Amenhotep III.[23] It is

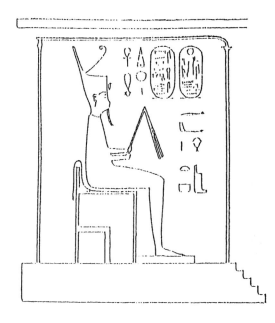

Figure 4.2. King Osorkon II is crowned with the red crown and wears the long Osirian cloak, shortly before embarking on the phase of the festival known as the "secret rites."

unlikely that the meal that took place there would have been a straightforward meal, for it occurred within a highly charged sacred context. The food that the king ate was the choice produce of the land, and his ingesting it would have had deep symbolic connotations, for it meant that he became empowered with the vital substance of the whole country. Since it was he who was ultimately responsible for the vitality of the substances he now ceremonially ate, in eating them he thereby completed the circle of fertility.

It is likely that at the conclusion of the festival a second banquet was an integral part of the general festivities, for there was a large public reception that, in the case of the Osorkon reliefs, seems to have been associated with some form of agricultural ceremony and the presence of women bearing jars of produce.[24] Similarly, there is evidence that at all three of the Sed festivals of Amenhotep III, large quantities of food were consumed. According to Eric Uphill, "Probably a great amount of public entertainment was provided by the king at the festival, with mass meals on a scale large enough to include the whole population of the capital."[25]

One important implication of this is that when we come across reliefs of offerings, offering bearers, or the king receiving offerings, the context may not, as is usually assumed, be funerary. There are, for example, many depictions of offerings in the Sed festival reliefs of Niuserre, evidently

Figure 4.3. Sed festival offerings placed before Niuserre, the top of whose crown can be seen to the right. The offerings include figs, jars of wine, and the produce of the fields. Sun temple, Abu Gurob, Fifth Dynasty.

presented to the living king.[26] Figure 4.3 shows one such relief fragment from within the substructure of the obelisk of Niuserre's sun temple, where all the reliefs are devoted to the Sed festival rites. The offerings are shown stacked up in front of the king, the top of whose crown can be seen to the right of the picture.

The Sed dance, the coronations, and the sacred meal point to levels of complexity within the Sed festival that show it to have been about more than simply the mystical initiation of the king. While the mystical experience induced in the "secret rites" was central to the festival, this episode had a specific purpose and consequences that went far beyond the king's personal life. The main purpose of the Sed festival was to link heaven and earth, the spirit world and the mundane world, through the king's fully inhabiting—and, indeed, mastering—both. The consequence was that the whole land of Egypt would flourish, animals and crops multiply, and the fertility of the earth be ensured.

The Sed Festival and the Step Pyramids

We need to look next at the evidence for the Sed festival being associated with the pyramids of Old Kingdom Egypt, for this obviously has a direct bearing on how we should interpret the Pyramid Texts. Owing to the dominance of the interpretation of the pyramids as tombs and their adjacent temples, shrines, and causeways as serving the mortuary cult of the king, this evidence has generally been overlooked. Recently, however, there has been greater openness among Egyptologists to the idea that royal temple complexes, previously considered to have been built for the cult of the dead king, were in fact built at the beginning of his reign specifically for his cult while still alive. The Egyptologist Stephen

Quirke, for instance, has suggested that the expression "mortuary temple" is no longer accurate and should be discarded in favor of "temple for the royal cult."[27] This suggestion is especially pertinent to the pyramid complexes of the Old Kingdom that, from the Fourth Dynasty on, included substantial "mortuary" temples. If it can be shown that the pyramid complexes were closely linked to the Sed festival, then a reappraisal of the purely funerary interpretation of the pyramids and their associated temples will also have to be made. None of the evidence we are about to examine is new; it has simply been neglected because the full significance of the connection of the pyramids with the Sed festival has not been sufficiently considered.

Zoser's Pyramid Complex at Saqqara

The very first pyramid to have been built, if we accept the orthodox chronology, was the pyramid of Zoser at Saqqara during the Third Dynasty. This pyramid was not a "true" pyramid, in that it did not have smooth sloping sides, but rather a series of "steps." It is likely that these steps symbolized the primordial hill that emerged at the beginning of time from the waters of Nun. In mounting this hill, the creator god, Atum-Ra, brought light and life into manifestation from out of the primeval chaos and darkness that characterize the pre-creation world. The primeval hill is represented hieroglyphically as a mound with a series of steps. It is known from textual evidence that in the vicinity of several temples there was a simulacrum of the primordial hill. Since they were not made of lasting materials, they have long since vanished, but it is probable that they had stepped sides.[28] For the Egyptians, the creation of the world did not just happen once at the beginning of time, but was constantly being repeated. Every year saw the land disappear under the floodwaters of the Nile and then miraculously reappear fertilized and renewed. Likewise, every night the sun god was absorbed back into the waters of the Nun to be reborn from them the following day.

How, then, does the stepped mound relate to the Sed festival? We have already seen that the Egyptian king was an image of Ra on earth. Ra was mythologically the "first king" of Egypt and every king was his successor, occupying the same throne. Each morning, when the king ascended the stairs of the House of the Morning he was enacting on earth what Ra was enacting in the heavens at sunrise.[29] During the Sed festival coronation rites, the king was similarly reenacting the solar rebirth, the coronation dais on which he was crowned being an image of the stepped primordial

Figure 4.4. The coronation of King Niuserre at his Sed festival. The depiction of the double throne surmounting a double staircase, symbolizing the primordial hill, is typical of Sed festival representations. The shaded areas are where the relief has been damaged.

hill. In figure 4.4, King Niuserre is shown on the coronation dais wearing the short tunic and crowned with the white crown during his Sed festival. So symbolically important to the kingship was the stepped mound that it was as much a symbol of the Sed festival as it was a symbol of the primordial hill. Thus it was sometimes used on its own by the Egyptians to represent the Sed festival (see fig. 4.5). From one point of view, then, the step pyramid was nothing other than the Sed festival coronation dais built on a truly massive scale.[30]

Zoser's whole pyramid complex at Saqqara was in fact constructed as a Sed festival site. It is replete with robing chambers, chapels for the visiting gods of the regions of Egypt, a court for the performance of the Sed festival dedication of the field ceremonies, a coronation dais, and so on (see fig. 4.6). There is absolutely no doubt as to the fact that the buildings and ceremonial spaces around the pyramid were designed with the king's Sed festival firmly in mind. Many of the structures are, however, simulations in stone of original features that would have been made in mud brick or wood. Not all, but some of the buildings have been described as symbolic "dum-

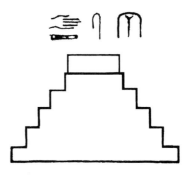

Figure 4.5. *The primordial mound and the Sed festival coronation dais both have the same form, that of a stepped pyramid. Here it is shown with the hieroglyphs of the Sed festival above it.*

mies" that were probably not used for the actual Sed festival celebrations of the king, but served a purely commemorative purpose. This has led many Egyptologists to conclude that the whole site was designed solely for the use of the king in the afterlife.[31] The so-called dummies, however, are not completely unusable. The "dummy" chapels, for example, have entrance corridors, statue niches, and receptacles for the torches that would have been lit at the beginning of the ceremonies. There are likewise several important structures on-site that were definitely not "dummies" but fully serviceable buildings.[32] It is, therefore, just as plausible that the site was used for the performance of Sed festival rites during the king's lifetime as that it was designed only for Zoser's postmortem use.

Underneath the Step Pyramid, there is a maze of corridors and passages constructed around a central granite vault, from which mummy remains were retrieved. These, however, proved to have been placed there many

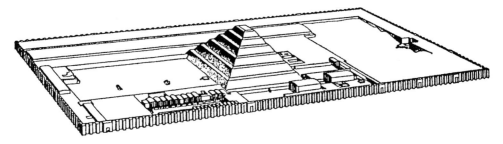

Figure 4.6. *The pyramid complex of Zoser at Saqqara incorporated many Sed festival elements. In the foreground, the row of dummy chapels can be seen lining the sides of a courtyard that also contained the coronation dais. The Houses of the North and South are to their right. A robing chamber known as Temple T is to the rear of the pyramid. The "southern tomb" is located at the center of the enclosure wall on the left, opposite the pyramid, across a large ceremonial courtyard.*

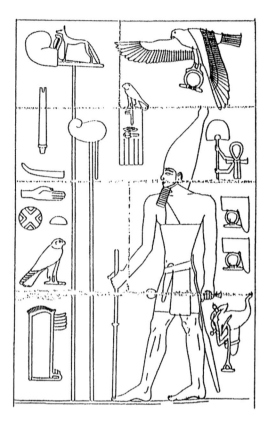

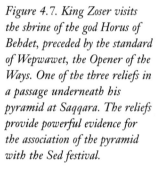

Figure 4.7. King Zoser visits the shrine of the god Horus of Behdet, preceded by the standard of Wepwawet, the Opener of the Ways. One of the three reliefs in a passage underneath his pyramid at Saqqara. The reliefs provide powerful evidence for the association of the pyramid with the Sed festival.

centuries after Zoser's reign.[33] There is, in fact, no evidence that the king was buried in the pyramid. Rather, the reliefs and inscriptions within the pyramid all relate to the Sed festival. In one of the subterranean corridors are three niches with reliefs, two of which show Zoser wearing the short Sed kilt with the bull's tail and performing the dedication of the field ceremony (shown in fig. 4.1) while the third shows him standing before a shrine (fig. 4.7). As these are the only reliefs inside the pyramid, there could be no stronger evidence to demonstrate that the interior of the pyramid was as much associated with the Sed festival as were the buildings and architectural spaces in its vicinity.

Similar reliefs are also to be found in the so-called southern tomb at the south edge of Zoser's pyramid complex. This has led some Egyptologists to suggest that the southern tomb may have been used for the "secret rites" during the Sed festival.[34] But the argument could equally well be made that the pyramid itself was used for this purpose. There is no compelling reason to select the southern tomb in favor of the pyramid, as it merely replicates the decoration—and to some extent the layout—of the passages and chambers within the pyramid itself.[35]

The Pyramid of Sekhemkhet

The next pyramid to be constructed after that of Zoser, though it was probably never completed, was that of Sekhemkhet. This was also a stepped pyramid, and was at the center of a large complex on a similar scale to that of Zoser, and built very close to it at Saqqara (see fig. 4.18). Sekhemkhet's pyramid is of special interest because when it was excavated in the early 1950s, it clearly had not been entered before. The doorway on the north side was still sealed, and huge limestone blocks barred the entrance to the inner chamber. Among the debris on the corridor floor were gold bracelets, gold beads, and a magic wand covered in gold leaf. Of even greater significance were fragments of an alabaster dish inscribed with the words "Sed festival . . . Ii-en-Chnum."[36] We know that Ii-en-Chnum was a courtier of Zoser who must have also held office under Sekhemkhet.[37] The presence here in the corridor of Sekhemkhet's pyramid of this courtier's alabaster dish commemorating his attendance at a Sed festival would seem to imply an association between the Sed festival and the pyramid.

The door to the inner chamber of Sekhemkhet's pyramid was, like the main entrance door, still sealed. When the inner chamber was breached, an alabaster sarcophagus in the center of the chamber was found, but it was also sealed. On top of it were plant remains, but around it there were no burial artifacts. When the sarcophagus was finally opened, it was found to be completely empty.[38] Here, then, is an example of a pyramid that was definitely not a tomb, and yet it contained a sarcophagus. Although the sarcophagus had evidently not been used for the burial of the dead king, this does not mean that it had not been used at all. In chapter 3, reference was made to the possibility that a sarcophagus was used in the Sed festival "secret rites."[39] While it cannot be proved, it is surely not unreasonable to suppose that the empty sarcophagus of Sekhemkhet, placed within a pyramid that was in the center of a complex designed on similar lines to Zoser's pyramid complex, could have been used in the "secret rites" of the Sed festival.

The Seven Provincial Step Pyramids

Step pyramids continued to be built into the early part of the Fourth Dynasty. There are seven step pyramids that are attributed to either Huni

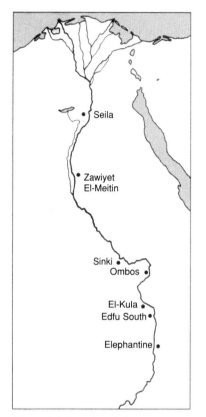

Figure 4.8. Location of the seven provincial pyramids, attributed to Huni and Sneferu. None of them is believed to have been built as a tomb, as they lack internal chambers.

(the last king of the Third Dynasty) or Sneferu (the first king of the Fourth Dynasty). Referred to as the "seven provincial pyramids," they are located in different provinces across Egypt, from Seila near the Faiyoum in the north to Elephantine in the south (fig. 4.8). All of these pyramids stand alone, without adjoining buildings, ceremonial courts, or temples. Most of them are small, though the pyramid at Seila (which is attributed to Sneferu) is about the same size as the Fifth Dynasty pyramid of Unas. The others are approximately half this size. The interesting thing about these seven provincial pyramids is that none of them has any entrances, internal corridors, or chambers. Their purpose could not therefore have been to have served as tombs. It has been suggested that these pyramids were representations of the primordial mound, but it is likely that they were also emblems of the king's power, set up near to his provincial palaces.[40] As we have already seen, what makes them into emblems of royal power is the fact that as well as representing the primordial mound, they also represent the coronation dais. Whether the seven provincial step pyramids were connected with the celebration of the Sed festival is impossible to say. But their existence reinforces the fact that the funerary cult of the king was by no means the only, nor even the primary, purpose of building a pyramid.

Fourth Dynasty Pyramids and the Sed Festival

During the Fourth Dynasty, the step pyramid underwent transformation into the "true" pyramid with smooth, sloping sides. But the purely funerary function of the pyramid is no less questionable during the Fourth

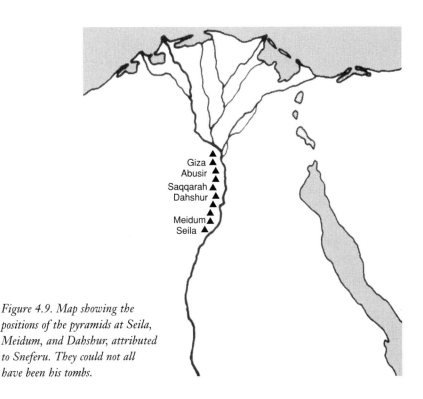

Figure 4.9. Map showing the positions of the pyramids at Seila, Meidum, and Dahshur, attributed to Sneferu. They could not all have been his tombs.

Dynasty than it is during the Third. The first king of the Fourth Dynasty, Sneferu, apparently built three pyramids in addition to the pyramid at Seila and probably several other of the provincial pyramids already discussed. To Sneferu is attributed the pyramid at Meidum as well as the Bent Pyramid and the Red Pyramid at Dahshur. Clearly not all of them could have been his tombs, and we would have to be peculiarly attached to the funerary interpretation to argue that they were nevertheless all intended to be tombs, but for reasons unknown to us the king kept changing his mind and sallied forth once again to construct yet another tomb for himself. Rather than go along with the "vacillating king theory," Mark Lehner has argued that the Meidum pyramid was built as a cenotaph, not as a tomb.[41] No remains of a sarcophagus were found, nor were any mummy remains, and the chapel beside the pyramid was extremely small: more like a commemorative chapel than a mortuary temple. If we accept Lehner's assessment of the Meidum pyramid, then what about the two pyramids at Dahshur?

The Bent Pyramid

The Bent Pyramid at Dahshur was the first pyramid to have a valley temple built some way from the pyramid and linked to it via a causeway. It also was the first to have a small satellite pyramid within the pyramid complex (fig. 4.10). This may have served a similar function to the "southern tomb" of Zoser's (and later Sekhemkhet's) complex, which was possibly to have housed a *ka* statue of the king.[42] While the presence of the satellite pyramid might at first encourage us to see the Bent Pyramid as the tomb of the king, there are certain factors that require us to proceed with caution. First of all, there was no trace of a sarcophagus in either of the pyramid's chambers, nor was there any sign of human remains. This alone, of course, does not amount to conclusive evidence that the pyramid was not used as a tomb, but then nor does it provide any evidence that it was. Second, the chapel adjacent to the pyramid was little more than a shrine, on a similar scale to the one at Meidum, and hence more appropriate for a cenotaph than a tomb.[43] Third, two stelae were found beside the satellite pyramid; one of them was inscribed, but only uninscribed fragments of the other were found. It is almost certain that two identical stelae were also placed in the chapel adjacent to the main pyramid and again at the entrance to the valley temple.[44] These stelae, each surmounted by a Horus falcon, proba-

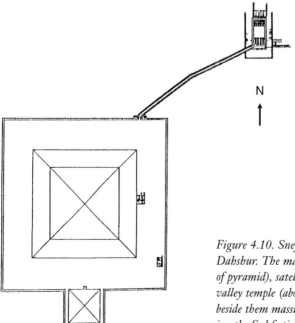

N
↑

Figure 4.10. Sneferu's Bent Pyramid at Dahshur. The main pyramid chapel (right of pyramid), satellite pyramid (below), and valley temple (above right) each had placed beside them massive stelae of Sneferu wearing the Sed festival tunic.

Figure 4.11. Stela of King Sneferu, from the Bent Pyramid complex, showing him seated on a throne wearing the short tunic of the Sed festival. The hieroglyphs read, from top to bottom, "Lord of Truth, King of Upper and Lower Egypt, the Two Ladies, Lord of Truth, Horus of Gold."

bly all bore the same simple inscription as the more or less intact one found beside the satellite pyramid. It has Sneferu's name and titles, alongside an image of the king seated on his throne. The six stelae, then, served to link the different parts of the pyramid complex. It is, however, the image of Sneferu seated on his throne that is of particular interest, for there can be no doubt that it shows the king wearing the short tunic of the Sed festival and seated on the Sed festival throne (fig. 4.11).

This is not the only piece of evidence linking the Bent Pyramid to the Sed festival. The valley temple of the pyramid is remarkable not only for

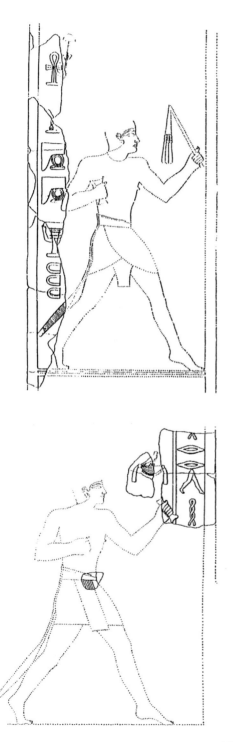

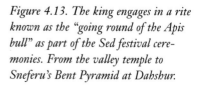

Figure 4.12. King Sneferu "dedicates the field," an important rite of the Sed festival. Reconstruction from the valley temple to the Bent Pyramid.

its being the first of its kind to be built, but also for the reliefs that were carved on its walls and especially on the ten pillars at the north end of the central hall. Despite their fragmentary nature, there is no doubt that they portray the king performing Sed festival rites.[45] In figure 4.12, for example, the position of the king's elbow and foot, along with the bull's tail of the Sed festival kilt, the three cairns, and the two half-sky glyphs all enable a reconstruction to be made of the king performing the dedication of the field rite.

Figure 4.13 shows the king holding the parchment or decree that legitimates his power over the land of Egypt. This part of the ceremony was known as the "going round of the Apis bull," and provides the earliest evidence that the Apis bull, symbol of the fertility of the land and the virility of the king, was present in the Sed festival ceremonies.[46] In figure

Figure 4.13. The king engages in a rite known as the "going round of the Apis bull" as part of the Sed festival ceremonies. From the valley temple to Sneferu's Bent Pyramid at Dahshur.

4.14, the king is shown embraced by Seshat. The embrace of the king by this or another goddess is commonly represented in sequences of reliefs depicting the Sed festival, and this would appear to be one of the first of such representations. These few examples of reliefs from the valley temple of the Bent Pyramid, combined with the stelae already referred to, can leave us with little doubt that the whole complex was profoundly oriented toward the celebration of the Sed festival.

The Red Pyramid

To the north of the Bent Pyramid at Dahshur is Sneferu's Red Pyramid, which is generally believed to have been his actual tomb. The temple adjacent to the pyramid was more substantial than any previous pyramid temple, and closer in scale to the "mortuary temples" of later Fourth Dynasty kings. While the valley temple has not yet been sys-

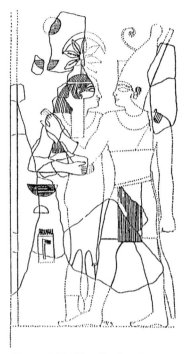

Figure 4.14. King Sneferu is embraced by the goddess Seshat as part of the Sed festival ceremonies. From the valley temple to the Bent Pyramid, Dahshur.

tematically excavated, excavations at the base of the pyramid and of the pyramid temple have revealed two interesting facts that link the site to the celebration of the Sed festival. First of all, there is compelling evidence, from fragments of casing stone inscribed with graffiti, that the pyramid was built during the thirtieth year of Sneferu's reign.[47] As the thirtieth year had the symbolic significance of being the year when the king was officially obliged to celebrate the Sed festival, we can hardly regard the construction of the pyramid in this year as simply a coincidence. Second, as if to confirm the suspicion of a Sed festival connection, the excavation of the pyramid temple in 1982 uncovered reliefs of Sneferu wearing the same kind of Sed festival tunic as he does on the stela found at the Bent Pyramid (fig. 4.11).[48] Could it be that the Bent Pyramid and the Red Pyramid were therefore both locations in which the king underwent Sed festival rites? There is no reason why the king could not have celebrated his Sed festival more than once, since his reign appears to have been thirty-four years long.[49] If, as is generally believed, the king was obliged to hold a Sed festival every three years after the thirty-year festival, then Sneferu would have had to have celebrated the Sed festival at least twice. But we also know that the thirty-year rule was not strictly adhered to, and some kings celebrated the festival before the thirtieth year of their reign.

The evidence points toward two conclusions concerning Sneferu's pyramids. First, whether or not the Red Pyramid or any of the other pyramids attributed to Sneferu were actually used as his tomb, there is good reason to believe that the two pyramids at Dahshur were both associated with the celebration of Sneferu's Sed festival. Second, if—as seems likely—Sneferu celebrated his Sed festival at least twice, then this may account for the fact that he built two pyramids at Dahshur. This seems a more likely explanation for the construction of the two pyramids at Dahshur than abrupt changes of mind about where his tomb should be located. This is not to suggest that none of Sneferu's pyramids was used as his tomb, but only that the primary reason for their construction lay in the need to create a new site for the celebration of the king's Sed festival.

The Giza Pyramids

Sneferu was the father of Khufu (or Cheops), the king to whom the Great Pyramid at Giza is attributed. So much has been written about this and the other pyramids on the Giza plateau that it is perhaps wise to restrict the discussion here to a very few salient points. Regarding the pyramid of Khufu, there is little evidence that it was used as a tomb. This lack of evidence does not mean that we should conclude that it was not used as a tomb, but it does mean that we should not automatically assume that it was. One lidless and empty granite sarcophagus hardly constitutes proof that the king was buried here. The design of the pyramid, with its three chambers, the mysterious "air shafts," and extraordinary Grand Gallery, does not support the tomb theory any more than it supports the many other more or less ingenious theories that have been proposed over the years, though some are clearly less convincing than others. The Great Pyramid could have been a tomb, but it equally may have been used for other purposes, perhaps as well as being used as a tomb. In order to ascertain its use, it is important not to neglect the whole pyramid complex of which it is a part. The presence of a full-scale "mortuary temple" adjacent to the pyramid, a causeway, and a valley temple has seemed to lend support to the funerary interpretation. But, as we have seen in the case of the Bent Pyramid and the Red Pyramid, their presence does not exclusively support the funerary theory. In the case of Khufu, we do in fact have some interesting and important evidence from both the causeway and the upper temple that directly connects the pyramid with the Sed festival.

Excavations of the causeway revealed two relief fragments that portray Khufu performing ceremonies of the Sed festival.[50] Part of the fragment from the northern wall of the causeway, which depicts the king seated and enthroned wearing the characteristic Sed festival garment, is reproduced in figure 4.15. This fragment is particularly interesting because it includes four lines of text. Some of the text is damaged, but it contains the following two phrases, the first of which refers to the king, the second to his pyramid:

The great wild bull
The Splendour of Khufu[51]

The epithet "the great wild bull" is frequently used of the king in the Pyramid Texts, in the context of both his superabundant virility on earth and his overwhelming power in the heavens.[52] The fact that this statement appears close to the relief of the king engaged in Sed festival rites and immediately above the name of Khufu's pyramid ("The Splendour of Khufu") has led Selim Hassan, who conducted excavations at Giza for a great many years, to comment with all due scholarly caution: "It appears as though this scene had some connection with the pyramid."[53] Yes, it certainly does appear that way, and it is hard to find any reason to dissent from Hassan's conclusion. But this is not the only evidence for a connection of the Sed

Figure 4.15. Khufu, wearing the short Sed festival tunic, sits enthroned. Part of a fragment from the northern wall of the causeway to his pyramid at Giza.

festival with Khufu's pyramid. The presence of a Sed festival robing chamber within Khufu's pyramid complex is attested to in inscriptional records, and its probable location is known.[54] Fragments of blocks from both the temple adjacent to Khufu's pyramid and the valley temple have been recovered, all of which are carved with Sed festival reliefs and inscriptions.[55] They provide important evidence in support of the view that there was a functional relationship between the pyramid and Sed festival rituals that could have taken place in the upper temple court.[56] The Great Pyramid may or may not have been used by Khufu as his tomb, but it seems almost certain that it was connected somehow with the celebration of the king's Sed festival.

As for the pyramids of Khafre and Menkaure, the paucity of inscriptional or relief evidence for these pyramids being used either as tombs or in connection with Sed festival rites means that it is difficult to make any pronouncement as to their use, save that it was probably similar to that of the Great Pyramid. It seems very likely that the pyramid temple of Khafre with its large open court was—like that of Khufu—used for Sed festival ceremonies.[57] A Sed festival robing chamber was also integral to Khafre's pyramid complex.[58] As with the Great Pyramid, both pyramids had adjacent temples and valley temples linked by a causeway. As with the Great Pyramid, both pyramids also contained empty sarcophagi, though in the sarcophagus of Khafre some bones of a bull were found, apparently thrown into it at a much later period. The sarcophagus of Menkaure was empty when found, and was later lost at sea.[59]

Zawiyet el-Aryan

It is this recurrent feature of empty sarcophagi with no trace of an original burial that so weakens the funerary interpretation. Even when sealed sarcophagi have been found, they have failed to reveal any sign of a mummy. This was not only the case with Sekhemkhet's pyramid at Saqqara, already discussed, but it was also the case with the large but unfinished Fourth Dynasty pyramid at Zawiyet el-Aryan, just south of Giza. Apparently belonging to a little-known king named Nebka or Bikka, when discovered the sarcophagus had its lid sealed in place with mortar and was covered with a thick layer of clay. All around it and above it limestone blocks were still in position, but when the sarcophagus was opened, it was found to be empty.[60] Now, it could be argued that both the sarcophagus in Sekhemkhet's pyramid and the one in the pyramid at Zawiyet el-Aryan were empty because the pyramids were unfinished and thus the pharaoh had to be buried elsewhere. But this hardly explains why the sarcophagi were put there in the first place, if they were not going to be used; nor why they were so carefully sealed and protected as if they were already regarded as in some sense sacred. While it cannot be proved, it is surely possible that they were used before the king died. Although such a possibility cannot be entertained by those who subscribe to the "tombs and tombs only" view of the pyramids, it is consonant with the evidence that the pyramids of both the Third and Fourth Dynasties were connected to the celebration of the Sed festival, and that central to the Sed festival rites was the king's undergoing initiatory "secret rites" while he was still alive.

Fifth and Sixth Dynasty Pyramids and the Sed Festival

Userkaf's Pyramid Complex at Saqqara

After the Fourth Dynasty, the center of pyramid building moved away from Giza. The first king of the Fifth Dynasty, Userkaf, built his pyramid adjacent to the pyramid complex of Zoser at Saqqara, while subsequent kings concentrated on Abusir as their preferred site for the building of pyramids (fig. 4.9). Relief fragments from Userkaf's pyramid temple at Saqqara show birds in a papyrus thicket and the king fowling, hunting, and throwing the harpoon. There are also scenes of offering bearers, and of the slaughter of oxen and other horned animals.[61] The latter may well belong to Sed festival ceremonies, since both the slaughter of animals and the presentation of offerings were an important part of Sed festival rites.[62] At the same time, bird catching and hunting were symbolically charged activities concerned with both fertility and regeneration. Furthermore, they had festival associations, for the phrase "a catch of wild birds" is hieroglyphically identical to the phrase "to be festive," each deploying the same hieroglyph of an open booth surmounting an alabaster bowl used for purification.[63] The principal excavator of Userkaf's pyramid complex, C. M. Firth, believed that the site was connected to the Sed festival, though he regarded the satellite pyramid as the locus of the "secret rites" rather than the main pyramid.[64] As is so often the case, no trace of a royal mummy was found in Userkaf's pyramid, though it did contain one empty basalt sarcophagus.

Sahure's Pyramid Complex at Abusir

While little can be stated with certainty regarding the Sed festival associations of the pyramid complex of Userkaf, the pyramid site of his successor, Sahure, at Abusir, provides specific evidence of a Sed festival connection. Like the pyramid temple of Userkaf, the temple of Sahure's pyramid was covered with reliefs of the king hunting, fishing, and fowling. There were also scenes of the king victorious over Asiatics and Libyans. One relief shows the king in the act of slaying a captured Libyan. This motif, while it may at first seem unconnected with the Sed festival, reappears in Pepi II's pyramid temple alongside his Sed festival reliefs (see fig. 4.21). Like the hunting, fishing, and fowling scenes, a literal "smiting of the Libyan" may not have been a part of the Sed festival ceremonies, but that does not mean it bore no relationship to the festival. It is a motif in ancient Egyptian depictions of the king that goes back to the very earliest dynasties, and in the act of slaying the enemy, the king is always portrayed wearing the short Sed festival kilt with the bull's tail. This is the case, for instance, in one of the earliest depictions of the motif—the Narmer palette (fig. 4.16)—in which the action of the king is clearly echoing that of the falcon god Horus

Figure 4.16. One of the earliest depictions of the Egyptian king, wearing the Sed festival kilt with the bull's tail and "smiting the enemy" (usually a Libyan or an Asiatic). This image is from the Narmer palette, but the motif was a recurrent one, and in Sahure's pyramid temple it reappears again.

above and to his right. The scene clearly illustrates the king's indomitable prowess.[65] One of the consequences of his performing the Sed festival rites was that this godlike power was reinstilled into him. We have inscriptional evidence to this effect from Osorkon's Sed festival gateway, where we read of the king: "thou appearest on the throne of Horus . . . thou hast smitten the Libyans."[66]

Nearby the relief of the king smiting the Libyan in Sahure's pyramid temple is a relief of the bearded king in an open booth, wearing the short Sed festival tunic and sitting on a throne. He wears the red crown and holds a flail in one hand (fig. 4.17). The relief of the king is similar to the one depicting Sneferu in figure 4.11, though Sneferu wears the double crown

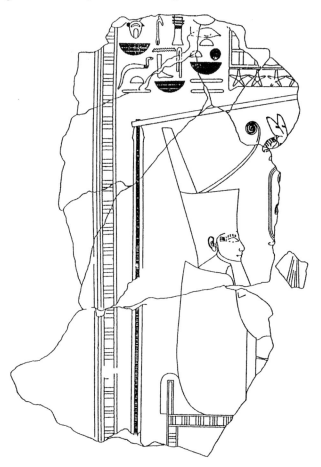

Figure 4.17. King Sahure sits in an open booth, enthroned and wearing the short Sed festival tunic. He holds a flail in one hand and wears the red crown. Relief from his pyramid temple at Abusir.

and is beardless. The presence of this relief, and other relief fragments from both the temple adjacent to Sahure's pyramid and the valley temple, strongly suggests that this pyramid complex, like that of Zoser, Sekhemkhet, Sneferu's two pyramids at Dahshur, Khufu's pyramid complex at Giza, and possibly several other Third and Fourth Dynasty sites, was associated with the celebration of the king's Sed festival.[67]

Niuserre

No reliefs have survived from the pyramid temple of the king who succeeded Sahure, Neferirkare, because it was left uncompleted at his death, as was his pyramid. The same goes for his successor, Reneferef (Neferefre). To the next king, Niuserre, however, we owe detailed reliefs of the Sed festival. But these were not placed in his pyramid temple but in the open sun temple nearby, at the center of which was an enormous obelisk. As the platform on which the obelisk was placed was a truncated pyramid with sloping sides, and the obelisk itself was like a pyramid raised up into the air, it is not hard to see that it could have served a similar function to that of the pyramids of other pharaohs. Some of the reliefs depicting Niuserre's Sed festival were in the chapel adjoining the obelisk, while others were on the walls of corridors that ran around the inside of the large central court. Perhaps the sun temple was felt to be an appropriate location for the reliefs because the festival entailed the "solarization" of the king, who through the festival rites became closely linked to the sun god Ra. If the comprehensive Sed festival reliefs in the sun temple suggest that some of the festival ceremonial was celebrated within its precincts, it is possible that the "secret rites" took place in Niuserre's pyramid nearby.[68] There is some evidence linking his pyramid complex to the festival. For example, an alabaster vessel commemorating his Sed festival was found in the pyramid temple, and the king is also depicted there being suckled by the goddess Sekhmet—a motif that recurs in many Sed festival reliefs of other kings, though the goddess is not always Sekhmet (see fig. 4.22).[69]

Djedkare-Isesi

After Niuserre, the center of pyramid building moved back to Saqqara with the pyramid of Djedkare-Isesi. This pyramid is notable because it is the first one to provide positive evidence of an original royal burial. Human remains found inside the pyramid may well be those of the king.[70] From now on to the end of the Sixth Dynasty, Saqqara is the main site for the building of pyramids (fig. 4.18). In several of the pyramids, canopic chests (which would have held the viscera of the king) have been found, reinforcing the probability that they were used as tombs. This, however, does not mean that they were not also used for Sed festival rites, only that they were not exclusively used for these rites. As we have already seen, it is perfectly feasible for the same pyramid to have been used both for the Sed festival "secret rites" and then subsequently as the tomb of the king.

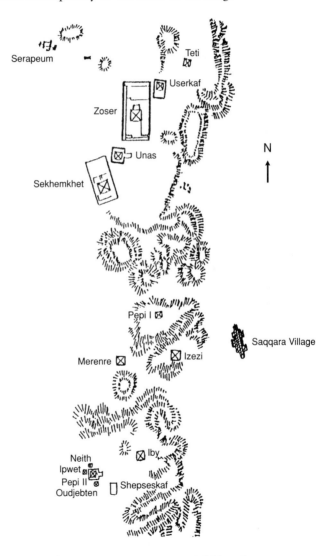

Figure 4.18. Map showing the Fifth and Sixth Dynasty pyramid fields at Saqqara.

Unas

Djedkare-Isesi was succeded by Unas, the last king of the Fifth Dynasty and the first to have his pyramid inscribed with texts. As the Pyramid Texts of Unas are the main subject of this study, the evidence for his pyramid complex being linked to the Sed festival will be examined in detail, in chapter 6. We shall therefore pass over Unas here and go directly to his successor, Teti.

Teti

Teti was the first king of the Sixth Dynasty and, like Unas, he and subsequent Sixth Dynasty kings covered the inner chambers of their pyramids with texts. The pyramids all followed that of Djedkare-Isesi in design, having a sarcophagus chamber, an antechamber, and a mysterious tripartite chamber that was uninscribed, adjoining the antechamber. Outside, there was the usual satellite pyramid, pyramid temple, and causeway leading to a valley temple. Excavations of the pyramid temple of Teti in the early twentieth century revealed very few surviving fragments of reliefs; nevertheless, one fragment shows Teti enthroned and wearing the Sed festival tunic.[71] Subsequent excavations in the 1970s produced further evidence linking the Sed festival with the pyramid temple in the form of an inscription on one of the pillars expressly mentioning the king's Sed festival.[72] Thus, despite the remains from the temple being so fragmentary, and the impossibility of establishing overall themes in the temple decoration, one certainty is that the Sed festival was both depicted in relief and referred to in inscription.

Pepi I

We know that Teti's successor, Pepi I, celebrated the Sed festival at least once, for we still have a large jar and ointment vase made on the occasion of his first Sed festival plus a host of other artifacts commemorating it.[73] Excavations at the pyramid temple revealed fragments of reliefs with themes similar to those found in the pyramid temple of Pepi II, which we shall shortly come to. The latter clearly depict scenes from the Sed festival, and it is likely that they follow precursors from the pyramid temples of both Teti and Pepi I, for which only fragmentary evidence survives. In the pyramid temple of Pepi I we have a fragment showing the slaughter of an ox, which we know from the Sed festival reliefs of Niuserre to have been part of the ceremonies.[74] There is also a fragment depicting the king holding a *seshed* cloth in his hand. This cloth symbolized the renewal of the spirit, and it is likely that it had Sed festival associations.[75] There is also a relief fragment showing the king being suckled by a goddess, a recurrent theme in Sed festival relief sequences, that expresses an obvious rebirth symbolism. This image comes from the north side of the temple court, which also had hunting scenes and the ubiquitous "smiting of the Libyan" by the king, another theme that, as we have seen, had Sed festival associations.[76]

Pepi II

Pepi I's successor, Merenre, had only a short reign, possibly of as few as four years, with the consequence that work on his pyramid temple was nowhere near completed at the time of his death.[77] Many of the surviving fragments of relief are simply outlined rather than modeled. It is likely that the king died before he was able to celebrate a Sed festival, as there is no evidence from any source for a Sed festival having taken place during his reign.[78] For this reason, we may pass on to the pyramid complex of his long-lived successor, Pepi II. Owing to his long reign (of possibly ninety-four years), Pepi II celebrated the Sed festival several times. A unique feature of this king's pyramid was an immense girdle more than six meters (twenty-one feet) wide, surrounding the pyramid and placed right up against its sides (fig. 4.19). As

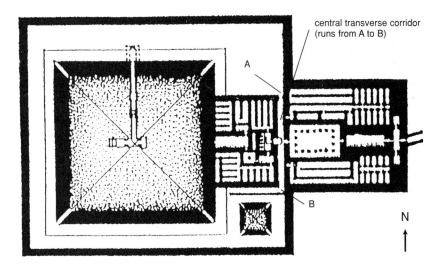

Figure 4.19. Plan of the pyramid and pyramid temple of Pepi II at Saqqara, showing the girdle wall around the pyramid and the central transverse corridor, where reliefs of the king's Sed festival were positioned. The corridor runs north–south and is located to the left of the enclosure wall that intersects the temple.

the girdle was built at a later date than the pyramid itself, it has been suggested that it was constructed to mark the celebration of one of the king's
Sed festivals.[79] While there is some evidence to support it, this hypothesis
cannot, of course, be proved. Of greater relevance is the fact that the pyramid temple contains some of the most explicit reliefs of a king engaged in
Sed festival rites of any of the Fifth and Sixth Dynasty pyramids.

The Sed festival reliefs of Pepi II were painstakingly reconstructed by
Jéquier in the 1930s from many fragments. These reliefs are to be found in
the corridor that runs between the outer and the inner temple, known as
the central transverse corridor (fig. 4.19). Here the king is depicted four
times performing the Sed festival dedication of the field ceremony. One of

*Figure 4.20. Relief showing the king performing the dedication of the field rite of the Sed
festival, and then being embraced by a goddess (probably Hathor). Reconstructed scene
from the central transverse corridor of Pepi II's pyramid temple.*

these depictions is reproduced in figure 4.20. To the left of the king running, he is shown in the embrace of a goddess, possibly Hathor. To the right, immediately adjacent to the dedication of the field scene, he is shown "smiting the Libyan" (see fig. 4.21). The fact that the embrace of the goddess and the "smiting of the Libyan" appear on either side of the dedication of the field rite indicates their close connection with the celebration of the Sed festival.

The motif of "the smiting of the Libyan" should be understood as a magical affirmation of the king's godlike stature rather than as a representation of an actual human sacrifice.[80] This is made clear from the fact that reliefs on the causeway as well as inside the pyramid temple closely emulate the reliefs in the pyramid complex of Sahure. In the central transverse corridor, the very same Libyan chieftains (bearing identical names) are

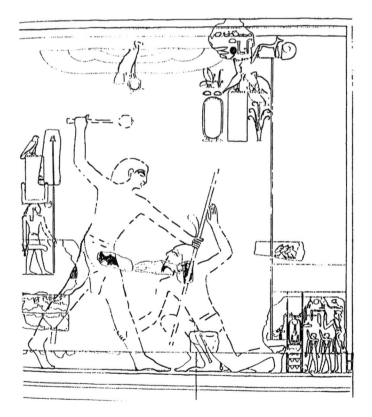

Figure 4.21. The king smites the Libyan, who was regarded as the archetypal enemy of Egypt. Note that the king wears the Sed festival short kilt with the bull's tail. Reconstructed scene from the central transverse corridor of Pepi II's pyramid temple, Saqqara.

taken prisoner, and the very same cattle are led away, as in the temple of Sahure.[81] The significance of this for the interpretation of Sed festival and related reliefs is that "the smiting of the Libyan" should be regarded as a pictorial statement about the prowess of the king, which, as a consequence of his having gone through the Sed festival ceremonies, is thoroughly proved. Here the king steps out of history to reenact timelessly the same feats of royal invincibility, for the Sed festival has the effect of aligning the king to the superhuman and supratemporal realm of the gods. The Libyans are the archetypal enemy, eternally defeated by each successive king, whose victory over them in the archetypal realm is reflected in their defeat in the mundane world of time and history. The alignment of the king to the world of the gods is at least part of the meaning of his being embraced by the goddess.

Also in the transverse corridor, the king is shown overseeing a ceremony that involved setting up a high pole (suggestive of the medieval Maypole) supported by four wooden stays up which young men are seen to be climbing. In later representations of this ceremony, the ithyphallic fertility god Min is always nearby. Since the effects of the Sed festival were meant to extend beyond the rejuvenation of the king to the reinvigoration of the whole land, it would have been perfectly appropriate to have included the raising of Min's pole in the Sed festival ceremonies.[82] In addition to this ceremony, there are depictions of the king being embraced by various gods

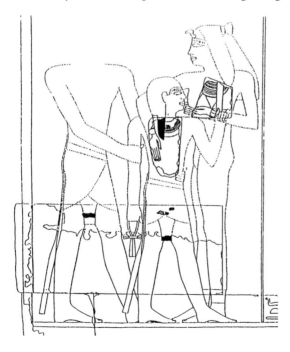

Figure 4.22. Pepi II, wearing the short Sed festival kilt with the bull's tail, is suckled by a goddess. Reconstruction of one of two reliefs in the central transverse corridor of his pyramid temple at Saqqara.

and goddesses. He is also shown twice being suckled by goddesses (see fig. 4.22). This is an important motif in the coronation rite that frequently recurs in Sed festival depictions, and is also prominent in the Pyramid Texts, as it graphically illustrates the king's spiritual rebirth.

While it is not certain that reliefs elsewhere in the temple of Pepi II refer to the Sed festival, it seems likely. In the antechamber, a square room with one central pillar, midway between the central transverse corridor and the pyramid, the king is shown having emerged from his tomb holding the *seshed* cloth in his right hand. He stands before the gods of the land, who each stand in front of their shrines, while bullocks (off this picture) are slaughtered nearby (fig. 4.23).[83] It has been suggested that since a *sem* priest is present (facing the gods to the right and just above the king), these reliefs

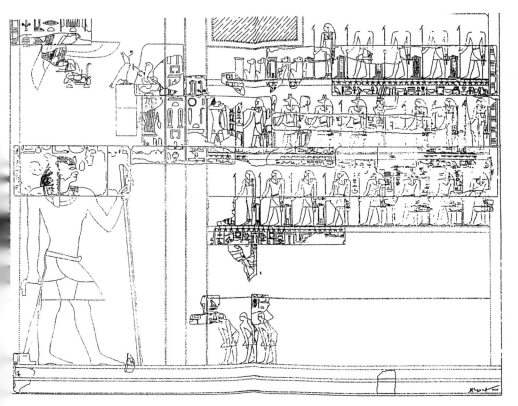

Figure 4.23. Part of a scene from the antechamber of Pepi II's pyramid temple, showing the king, holding the seshed *cloth (symbolic of his spiritual rebirth) in his right hand, standing in front of one hundred deities, priests, and officials. Reconstruction of relief in Pepi II's pyramid temple, Saqqara.*

portray the dead king in the hereafter, being received by the gods of Egypt and the souls of the dead. But we know that the *sem* priest also has an important role in the Sed festival "secret rites," and that central to the "secret rites" is a communion with the gods and the spirits of the dead that we find represented here in the antechamber.[84] There is, furthermore, a corroboratory piece of evidence pointing to a link between the antechamber and the Sed festival. In one of the surviving fragments from this chamber, the date of Pepi's Sed festival is specifically mentioned.[85]

In the sanctuary, the largest room in the inner temple, immediately adjacent to the pyramid, the reliefs are wholly dedicated to offerings of food brought to the king. As we have already noted, such scenes, although normally interpreted as funerary, are not necessarily so. They could equally belong to the Sed festival, for the presentation of such offerings to the king was an intrinsic part of the festival rites. Here, as with the interpretation of many of the other reliefs, there is scope for a variety of approaches to understanding their significance. However, given the extraordinary consistency with which the Sed festival was represented in Old Kingdom pyramid complexes, and given the prominence that the representations seem always to have had, it does appear likely that many motifs that hitherto have not been regarded as connected to the Sed festival were in fact intimately related to it. The "smiting of the Libyan," the embrace of the goddess, being suckled by the goddess, meeting the gods and spirits of the dead, raising the Min pole, and receiving food offerings all fall into the category of motifs that are not necessarily funerary but could be related to both inner and outer events of the Sed festival.

The Pyramid Texts and the Sed Festival

The pyramid complexes of Old Kingdom Egypt, from the Third through the Sixth Dynasty, consistently reveal an abundance of evidence that they were intimately connected with the celebration of the Sed festival. This does not mean that every depiction of a Sed festival ceremony on a given temple wall indicates that the ceremony depicted took place in that exact location. While this may have been the case with the upper temple courts of the Giza pyramid complexes, no one would argue that Zoser performed the dedication of the field underneath his pyramid in the narrow passageway where reliefs of him doing just this are found. Likewise, the central transverse corridor in Pepi II's pyramid temple could hardly have been the location for the Sed festival events that are depicted there. But the fact that Sed festival rites are recorded on stelae, wall reliefs, and temple columns in the pyramid complexes suggests that a vital connection must have existed between the pyramids and the Sed festival rites. As well as reliefs and inscriptional records, certain buildings have also been identified as specifically designed to serve Sed festival purposes. Again, this does not mean that all of the rites necessarily took place in the pyramid complex, for there were other sites that could have served as the venue for certain of the festival ceremonies.[86] But it does seem likely that some of the rites did take place within the pyramid complexes. It has been suggested, for example, that both the upper temple and the satellite pyramid served as a location for Sed festival rites, and there is strong evidence for the existence of Sed festival robing chambers within certain of the pyramid complexes.[87]

Of all the buildings in the pyramid complex, the pyramid itself is the most prominent both architecturally and in terms of its importance. While orthodox opinion tends almost unanimously to support the view that the pyramids were built for the sole purpose of being tombs to house the dead body of the king, there are three facts that militate against this interpretation. The first is that the construction of a pyramid was started right at the beginning of a king's reign, and it is almost certain that the temples connected to the pyramid functioned during the king's lifetime, serving the royal cult. Pepi II's pyramid complex provides a good example. It is inconceivable that the sanctuary that was demolished and then reused in the girdle later built around the pyramid was unused before it was demolished. It must have functioned for many years before it was demolished and its blocks used again in the construction of the massive girdle.[88] By that time the pyramid itself would have been already completed. That pyramids and their temples were constructed right at the beginning of a king's reign is clear from the case of Merenre, who reigned for probably only four or five years, and yet his pyramid along with a small entrance chapel and larger pyramid temple were already built.[89] Evidently, these buildings were not intended simply for the "mortuary cult" of the king. There must have been aspects of the royal cult that could have been enacted in them during the king's lifetime. As Stephen Quirke has noted:

> The evidence more strongly suggests that each king embarked on the construction of a temple for his own cult at the outset of his reign, that the temple would have been in operation during the reign, and that, far from coming into usage at the death of that king, the temple saw its income diverted and its cult begin to fall apart from the moment that he died and the new king sought to muster all possible resources for the benefit of his new cult temple.[90]

For this reason, it is highly misleading to refer to the pyramid temples as "mortuary" temples. Since the pyramid itself would likewise have normally been completed many years before the king's death, it is equally questionable to assume its sole purpose was to house the dead body of the king.[91] Second, if the pyramid temples and causeways were built to serve the pyramids, then it is probable that the reliefs that decorated them would relate not only to the temples but also to the underlying purpose of the pyramids. As a substantial proportion of the reliefs in the pyramid temples portray events linked to the Sed festival, it is hard to think of any good reason why we should not seriously consider the possibility that while the most public aspects of the Sed festival may have occurred at Memphis or Heliopolis, there were other aspects that may have been reserved for the pyramid and its related buildings. Rather than the temples attached to the pyramid serving the mortuary cult of the king, whose dead body was lodged inside the pyramid, it seems more probable that they provided the sacred environment that would support the ritual preparation for (and presumably also the aftermath of) the one episode in the Sed festival that could have involved the use of the pyramid: the "secret rites."

Now, it may be the case that many of the pyramids did serve as royal tombs, and the evidence for this is strong for the pyramids subsequent to, and including, the pyramid of Djedkare-Isesi. Even were we to accept that most pyramids were used as tombs, this would not weaken the central contention that they could have been used prior to the king's death as the locus of the "secret rites" of the Sed festival. Indeed, if anything, it would strengthen it, for there would be nothing contradictory for the building wherein the secret rites took place to be the tomb in which the king was later buried. That said, we should also leave open the possibility that a separate tomb could have been used. If it were admitted that the pyramid was the locus of the Sed festival "secret rites," this would explain why there was such an abundance of reliefs and inscriptions in the temples relating to the Sed festival. It would explain why sarcophagi seem to have been placed within their pyramids at a very early stage of the pyramid's construction. It would also explain the phenomenon of empty but sealed sarcophagi, and it would provide a viable alternative to the usual recourse to postulating robbery as the reason for the widespread absence of original burials in so many pyramids.

There is, finally, a third reason why we should not accept that the pyramids were built solely as tombs to house the dead body of the king. Evidence for a relationship between the pyramids and the Sed festival does not derive solely from reliefs and inscriptions in adjacent buildings. We have already seen that in the Third Dynasty pyramid of Zoser, reliefs within the pyramid itself portray the pharaoh engaged in Sed festival rites. Subsequent pyramids lack both reliefs and inscriptions, until the Fifth Dynasty pyramid of Unas and his Sixth Dynasty successors Teti, Pepi I, Merenre, and Pepi II. A significant proportion of the texts inscribed within the chambers of these Fifth and Sixth Dynasty pyramids do in fact reflect certain elements of the Sed festival. The dedication of the field dance, for example, is referred to both directly and obliquely in a number of the Pyramid Text utterances. In utterance 273–74, the king is described as a "Bull of Heaven" who eats the magic of the gods and "assembles his spirits." It is then said of the king that

> **he has travelled around the whole of the two skies,**
> **he has circumambulated the Two Banks.**[92]

Since in the dedication of the field dance two half-sky glyphs are frequently depicted along with the boundary marker cairns, this passage could be understood as expressing exactly what the king enacted during the ritual.[93] The reference earlier in the utterance to the king being the Bull of Heaven can also be seen to relate closely to the same dance, in which the king wears a kilt with a bull's tail, symbolic of his having integrated its powers. Sometimes in Sed festival reliefs the king is shown running with a bull, and it would appear that this ritual of running with the bull was integral to the Sed dance from an early date.[94] In the Pyramid Texts, the encounter of the king with the Bull of Heaven in a celestial meadow or field, and the integration of its vital energies, is an important motif.[95] It is not difficult to see how the dedication of the field dance could have been a ritual counterpart to this inner event.

In the Pyramid Texts there are also a number of utterances that are related to coronation rituals. In utterances 57–71, the king is presented with weapons, garments, and insignia, including a tailed loincloth and a cloak. These may of course be interpreted simply as funerary offerings, but it is interesting that the tailed loincloth is presented while the text refers to the "dance" of Horus.[96] The presentation of these garments along with weapons, scepters, maces, and staffs suggests a coronation ritual—quite possibly one of the coronation rituals of the Sed festival—rather than simply funerary offerings. Similarly, utterances 220 and 221 describe a ritual involving the crown of Lower Egypt, in which the crown is removed from its shrine and addressed as a goddess by the officiating priest and then by the king. The king says to the crown:

> **Ho crown, great of magic!**

Ho fiery serpent!
Grant that the dread of me be like the dread of you;
Grant that the fear of me be like the fear of you;
Grant that the acclaim of me be like the acclaim of you;
Grant that the love of me be like the love of you.
Set my *'aba* sceptre at the head of the living,
Set my *sekhem* sceptre at the head of the spirits,
And grant that my sword prevail over my foes![97]

These words certainly don't sound like the words of a dead man. They sound as if they belong to a coronation rite of just the type that was integral to the Sed festival ceremonies. In the Pyramid Texts, great prominence is given to the ritual offering of food and other substances to the king. In the pyramid of Unas, the whole of the north wall of the sarcophagus chamber is devoted to a long offering ritual. Most of what is offered is food. Since during the Sed festival there was a sacred ingesting of food by the king in a special "hall of eating," and since there are Sed festival reliefs depicting food offerings being brought and then set out before the king, it is quite conceivable that the offering ritual described in the Pyramid Texts was used during the Sed festival. It may also have been incorporated into the king's funerary rites, but it could well have been adapted for funerary purposes from a ceremony that originally took place during the king's Sed festival.[98] These are just three examples in which passages in the Pyramid Texts could relate to Sed festival rituals. More examples will be discussed in part 2. But on the basis of these three examples, all of which relate to major episodes in the Sed festival, it seems advisable not to close our minds to the possibility that there are other passages in the Pyramid Texts that relate to the very kernel of the Sed festival: the mystical experiences of the king during the "secret rites." We have already seen that the central experience in these "secret rites" was that the king was brought to the threshold of death in order to travel into the spirit world. We have also seen that from an experiential standpoint, the Sed festival "secret rites" bear comparison with shamanic initiation rites and belong to essentially the same mystical tradition that we find in the Eleusinian and later Hellenistic mysteries, the dialogues of Plato, and certain of the Hermetic dialogues. Within these sources, we can distinguish three main elements of this type of mystical experience that they all have in common:

1. *Cosmic ascent.* An experience of cosmic ascent, or ecstatic flight away from the earth and away from the physical realm. This is described in

terms of the soul rising up through the heavens to the stars. In Plato's *Phaedrus*, the climactic mystical vision occurs in the sphere of the fixed stars of the zodiacal belt, while the Hermetic texts give a detailed account of the ascent through the planetary spheres in order to attain the highest mystical experience.[99]

2. *Vision of the gods.* In this heavenly region among the stars, the mystic has a direct vision of the gods. In Plato, the procession of the Olympians is described. In Apuleius, who is a key source for the Hellenistic Mysteries of Isis, the gods of both the Underworld and the Upperworld are encountered. In the Hermetic texts again, celestial and spiritual beings become present to the initiate's heightened consciousness.[100]

3. *Spiritual rebirth.* The most important experience of all: The mystic knows that he or she is a spiritual being as well as a merely physical being. This direct experience of one's spiritual and immortal core is often expressed in the language of rebirth. The person feels that he or she has been born again spiritually.[101]

It is significant that all of these three elements are powerfully present in the Pyramid Texts. The motif of celestial ascent is prominent throughout the Pyramid Texts, the king ascending to the sky by means of a ladder, or on the smoke of incense, or by transforming himself into a bird or even a grasshopper.[102] The vision of the gods is likewise frequently attested to. We have already seen, in chapter 3, that during the "secret rites" a visionary encounter of the king with twelve gods seems to have taken place. The twelve gods who appeared before Osorkon correspond closely with the gods referred to in utterance 219 of the Pyramid Texts. But as well as this utterance there are numerous others describing the king meeting with gods, often with the gods paying homage to the human god-king in their midst.[103] Similarly, the important spiritual event of the king's rebirth in the spirit realm is often referred to in the Pyramid Texts, his "mother" usually being Nut, Sekhmet, or Isis in her celestial form as Sothis.[104] All of these themes we shall come back to in part 2, for they are all present in the pyramid of Unas. Their presence suggests that the Pyramid Texts, far from being funerary texts, were primarily concerned with mystical experiences of a type similar to those that the living king had during the "secret rites" of the Sed festival, for they can clearly be seen to belong to a genre of archetypal human experiences at the crossing point between this world and the spirit world.

This is not to say categorically that the Pyramid Texts should be regarded as "Sed festival texts," but rather that many of them do reflect the kind of ritual and mystical events that occurred during the Sed festival. Given the prominence of Sed festival depictions in Old Kingdom pyramid complexes, the Sed festival seems an appropriate point of reference for any reinterpretation of the Pyramid Texts as nonfunerary, but it is not necessarily the only point of reference. Other kingship ceremonies, such as those described in the Ramesseum Dramatic Papyrus, may also be reflected in the Pyramid Texts. The main point is that the Pyramid Texts should be read as referring primarily to rituals of the living king and the inner experiences undergone by him during these rituals. Since the Sed festival was one of the principal kingship ceremonies, and since there is clearly a relationship between the pyramids, the pyramid complexes, and the Sed festival, it stands to reason that some, possibly a great many, of the Pyramid Texts would refer to the more public Sed festival rituals and to its secret rites. The aim of this study, however, is not to attempt to pin down every Pyramid Text to a Sed festival episode, but only to show that the Pyramid Texts are best interpreted as relating to rituals and ritual experiences of the living rather than the dead king. In part 2, therefore, while noting likely Sed festival references in the Pyramid Texts, the main objective will be to show that the Pyramid Texts may more accurately and meaningfully be interpreted as mystical rather than funerary texts. But before embarking on a detailed examination of the Pyramid Texts, it is necessary to consider some of the methodological issues that this fundamental reinterpretation of a major corpus of ancient Egyptian religious literature raises.

5 A QUESTION OF METHOD

Phenomenology and the Ideal of Presuppositionless Inquiry

The previous chapters have not simply been about whether there is or is not compelling evidence for mysticism having existed in ancient Egypt. They have also been about how certain texts, images, and rituals are perceived and understood by us today, and so can either be seen or not seen as actually constituting this evidence. In the previous chapters, we have been concerned less with new discoveries that have been made, or new facts that have come to light, than with what is already known but not recognized or accepted as being evidence for a mystical tradition in ancient Egypt. Insofar as it is here presented as evidence, we are therefore challenging not accepted facts but rather accepted *interpretations* of facts. The inscriptions, the texts, the relief carvings, the architecture, the rituals, remain the same: All we are doing is once again questioning their meaning. In this respect what is really at issue here are the attitudes, concepts, and presuppositions that are brought to bear on the historical data and whether these attitudes, concepts, and presuppositions help to reveal or on the contrary serve only to obscure the religious experience of the ancient Egyptians.

To the extent that the concern here is, then, with the underlying question of perception and interpretation, we are also concerned with the question of methodology. Is there a methodological procedure by which we can set our cherished presuppositions aside in order to allow evidence that was previously "silent" to acquire a voice and speak? And in consciously pursuing such a method in the study of ancient Egyptian religion, could it be that the existence of a mystical tradition will be revealed precisely where previous approaches have been impelled to deny it? In other words, is one methodology more likely to enable us to perceive the existence of a mystical tradition in ancient Egypt than another? In general, Egyptologists have not overly concerned themselves with methodological questions, taking for granted that procedures appropriate in archaeology, such as "analysis and sorting the material," can equally well be followed in other spheres, such as the understanding of religion.[1] But we have already seen in chapter 1 that such an assumption is highly questionable. Historians of religion have, by contrast, devoted a great deal of thought to what kind of methodology is appropriate in the field of religious studies. It so happens that several of the most influential of these scholars have also been deeply interested in ancient Egyptian religion, as we shall shortly see. Their contribution is one that therefore deserves careful consideration.

In the study of the history of religions from the nineteenth through to the second part of the twentieth century, one of the most influential methodologies among scholars and historians of religion has been phenomenology. One way of defining phenomenology would be to say that it is a method of inquiry in which the inquirer attempts to place all presuppositions to one side, so that the phenomena he or she is investigating are able to reveal themselves uncolored by the inquirer's preconceptions, value judgments, or personal or cultural assumptions. Phenomenologists aim to take their lead from the phenomena, rather than from a favored hypothesis, theory, or assumption. The ideal of presuppositionless inquiry goes hand in hand with a certain devotion to the phenomena that one is attempting to understand, so that one considers them in their own terms or on their own plane of reference.[2] When these phenomena are religious, the phenomenological approach necessarily involves a defense of the autonomous status of religious phenomena against those who would explain them in the nonreligious terms of sociology or political theory, or by reference to historical or cultural conditions. In this respect, religious historians adopting the phenomenological approach proceed on the principle that there is a religious "plane of reference," and even though its precise existential status may be left open, this plane of reference is deemed to have reality, meaning, and value.[3] And this naturally provides the motivation for inquiring into it.

Insofar as it seeks to understand religious phenomena religiously, not sociologically, economically, politically, linguistically, biologically, and so on, the phenomenological approach to religion is inherently antireductionist. But within this basic orientation, it sees it as possible and indeed essential to practice a discipline of restraint with regard to the deployment of interpretative categories. The phenomenologist will aim to hold back from imposing judgments, concepts, and explanatory theories onto the phenomena in order to allow them to speak in their own voice. To approach religious phenomena *as religious* does not mean that the ideal of presuppositionless inquiry is thereby abandoned, but rather that it is practiced within an overall orientation that accepts that the spiritual dimension is real. This requirement is no different from that of the natural scientist who has to accept the reality of the physical dimension in order to investigate physical phenomena. However, unlike the common procedure within the natural sciences, the phenomenological approach to the realm of spiritual phenomena is not concerned to arrive at causal explanations. Rather, the goal of this approach is to attain deeper perceptions of the phenomena that it is directed toward. In the case of an ancient Egyptian text describing a religious experience, this deeper perception would require an imaginative reexperiencing of that experience, for the phenomenological approach is one of engagement and participation rather than detached analysis and theorizing.

One of the great pioneers of the phenomenological method was the German poet, playwright, and scientist Goethe, who developed the main principles of phenomenology in various essays on scientific method, and put them into practice in a number of scientific studies.[4] Goethe repeatedly warned against the dangers of the theorizing mind losing touch with the phenomena it is theorizing about. In his *Theory of Colour*, for example, he observed that "many would prefer to dismiss phenomena with a general theoretical precept or a quick explanation." What is required, he insisted, is that "we must deepen our involvement" with the phenomena.[5] While Goethe was the great pioneer of phenomenology, it was Edmund Husserl—a contemporary of such famous Victorian Egyptologists as Flinders Petrie, Breasted, Erman, and Maspero—who developed it into a fully fledged philosophy. For Husserl, the human mind's natural tendency to theorize and make value judgments is the first thing that the phenomenologist has to recognize. We naturally imbue the world with interpretative concepts as well as values such as beautiful or ugly, agreeable or disagreeable, pleasant or unpleasant, and so on, and it is this "natural standpoint" that the phenomenologist must suspend in order to approach phenomena freshly.[6] This involves what Husserl called the "phenomenological reversal of our gaze" away from the objects of consciousness imbued with our judgments and values to the act of consciousness by which they become (often without our realizing it) imbued with these judgments and values.[7] The phenomenological method thus initially requires us to engage in an act of critical self-reflection in order to objectify our own unconscious or semiconscious contribution to the appearance of the phenomena. Having become aware of this subjective contribution, we are then required to set it to one side, to "disconnect" it from any further investigation of the phenomena. This technique of setting to one side or "disconnecting" one's favored concepts, value judgments, and subjective reflexes from the act of consciousness by which one seeks to approach phenomena Husserl named the *epoché*.

Epoché is a Greek word that Husserl defines as "a certain refraining from judgment."[8] In practicing the *epoché*, we deliberately "disconnect" or "bracket" our projections onto the world so that whatever it is we are investigating can reveal itself as far as possible uncolored by our interpretative concepts. The *epoché* has two aspects to it. On the one hand it involves the phenomenologist objectifying the feelings, thoughts, and presuppositions with which he or she approaches the phenomena, whether as a cultural or personal reflex to them. Once objectified, they are set to one side, "disconnected," or "bracketed" as simply another, but quite different, potential object of study. On the other hand, the *epoché* involves the phenomenologist breaking through to a much more open, nontheorizing mode of awareness, freed of the encumbrances of emotional reaction, desire, prejudice, and value judgment. Husserl refers to this "pure" consciousness as the "residuum" of the phenomenological *epoché*. But though he calls it a residuum, it is not so much something left over as the basis of a new relationship to the world, in which consciousness, as the source of subjectivity, is experienced as being the source of true objectivity as well.[9]

These ideas of Husserl were influential on historians of religion searching for a methodology that would give their discipline a solid epistemological basis, quite distinct from positivist and materialistic approaches, which could not do justice to the subject matter of religion. Phenomenology provided a method that could protect their discipline from being taken over by the social sciences or reduced simply to cultural history. One of the first to embrace Husserl's phenomenological principles was the Dutch religious historian Gerardus van der Leeuw, who wrote several studies of ancient Egyptian religion during the early part of the twentieth century.[10] But it is his book *Religion in Essence and Manifestation* (1933) that is most remembered, and this work remains a model for the phenomenological investigation of religion. This is how van der Leeuw summarized the phenomenological approach: "The method is . . . an attempt to re-experience a certain entity as such, to transpose oneself into an object as an organic whole. . . . The criterion in all cases is the evidence *(Evidenz)* through which it is not so much we who discover the object, but the object that manifests itself to us."[11]

Both Husserl and van der Leeuw believed that it is possible for human consciousness to make itself receptive to the inner meaning of the objects toward which it directs its attention. For both of them, meaning is something that inheres within phenomena, rather than being something that the theorizing mind imposes on them in order to explain them. For van der Leeuw, the role of the phenomenologist is not to try to explain the phenomena in terms of a particular theory, but rather to deepen our involvement with the phenomena to the point at which it becomes possible to testify to the value and meaning intrinsic to them.[12] Like Goethe, van der Leeuw saw phenomenology more as a way of being than simply as a method. The phenomenological "restraint" *(epoché)* was for van der Leeuw far more than just a methodological device; it was "the distinctive characteristic of man's whole attitude to reality."[13] It is an inner discipline that one carries into all one's dealings with the world and with others. For him, the goal of phenomenology is "pure objectivity" in the sense of allowing the object to manifest itself in its essential nature, distorted neither by our preconceptions nor by our explanatory theories.

When it comes to the question of how we are to understand the meaning of ancient religious texts like the Pyramid Texts, the phenomenological approach would be to put to one side or bracket the general assumption that because these texts are inscribed on the inner chambers of certain Old Kingdom pyramids, they are necessarily funerary texts. They may or may not be funerary texts. The important thing is to approach them in such a way that the meaning inherent in the texts is able to show itself unencumbered by our preconceptions. For van der Leeuw, this would require that we submit ourselves to the rigors of the phenomenological *epoché* in which our favored theories and assumptions are recognized precisely as such, and set to one side. We are then in a position to engage freshly with the source material, allowing it to reveal its own intrinsic meaning to us.[14] Van der Leeuw considered this exercise to be as much a moral discipline of self-restraint as a spiritual discipline of self-transcendence. By means of it, the ordinary "knowing" in which the subject stands over against the object gives way to a different sort of knowing: "a 'knowing' which, driven by devoted love, is directed by the norm of the meaning that asserts itself."[15]

Among phenomenologists of religion, van der Leeuw was typical in seeing the aim of the phenomenological approach as being to testify to the inherent meaning in religious data, rather than to impose upon them causal explanations, make them conform to our preconceived hypotheses, or fit them into grand historical or sociological theories. His contemporary the Norwegian scholar W. Brede Kristensen was also keenly interested in ancient Egyptian religion and—like van der Leeuw—was living at a time when historians of religion (including Egyptologists) were trying to explain ancient religion from the standpoint of evolutionary theory. Kristensen saw it as his task to resist this trend. Just as we need to set aside our attachment to particular hypotheses, so we need also to set aside more general assumptions about past religions being more "primitive" than those of today, for general assumptions like this simply get in the way of understanding the religion from the standpoint of its adherents, which is the only route to perceiving its inner meaning.[16] To do this, it is necessary not only to set aside the more obvious theoretical baggage but also to set aside oneself—one's preconceptions, personal beliefs, and values. In *The Meaning of Religion*, Kristensen writes:

> The historian and the student of phenomenology must therefore be able to forget themselves, to be able to surrender themselves to others. Only after that will they discover that others surrender themselves to them. If they bring their own idea with them, others shut themselves off from them. No justice is then done to the values which are alien to us, because they are not allowed to speak in their own language. If the historian of religion tries to understand the religious data from a different viewpoint than that of the believers, he negates the religious reality. For there is no religious reality other than the faith of the believers.[17]

Another phenomenologist who also made important contributions to the understanding of ancient Egyptian religion was C. J. Bleeker. For Bleeker, the practice of the *epoché* was the central methodological tool for the study of the history of religion, because through it one can become receptive to the inner content of what one is studying. Far from making conjectures and framing hypotheses, the phenomenologist needs to adopt a listening approach: "In using the *epoché* one puts oneself into the position of the listener, who does not judge according to preconceived notions."[18] For Bleeker, the phenomenological approach enables the historian to "creep into the thought forms" and "under the skin" of those who are being studied.[19] This comes close to van der Leeuw's concept of a "second experience" of the event that is described in the documents and other sources that form the basis of historical research. It implies that human consciousness, if it can successfully set aside its own historical and cultural conditioning, would then be capable of placing itself inside the experience of another human being, whether living now or five thousand years ago.[20]

On Approaching the Phenomena with Empathy

One of the key ideas in the phenomenology of religion is that in order to understand religious phenomena, it is necessary to approach them with empathy. This has, predictably, elicited accusations of subjectivism from the critics of phenomenology, and we have seen in chapter 1 how Jan Assmann wished to exclude empathy from his definition of understanding ancient Egyptian religious material. The phenomenological response would be to point out that insofar as empathy enables one to "get inside" the religious experience or existential situation that one is endeavoring to understand, it is a quality that gives more, not less, objectivity.

For Husserl, the kernel of the phenomenological method is the attainment of a state of consciousness in which the division between subject and object is effectively transcended. In his main work on phenomenology, *Ideas*, published in 1913, Husserl introduced the idea of empathy as having the role of mediating intersubjective experience, but its role is relatively minor at this stage in his thinking. In *Ideas*, the *epoché* is the really crucial inner activity that enables us to reach into the "interiority" (or essence) of objects, through accessing a more "interior" level within them than that which the normal, unreflective consciousness with its "natural standpoint" is able to reach.[21] For Husserl, the quality of interiority that belongs to human consciousness, far from trapping us in our own subjectivity, presents a pathway into the innermost nature of the phenomena toward which consciousness directs attention. For this reason he called the consciousness that has submitted to the rigors of the *epoché* "transcendental." In *Ideas*, Husserl expresses an implicit confidence in the capacity of the human mind to free itself from subjectivity and grasp the essential being of another. The very nature of human consciousness is that it has the potentiality to place itself on the inside of the objects it focuses on, and when it succeeds in doing this, their inner meaning is revealed to it.[22]

Nevertheless, when the object of consciousness is another consciousness, Husserl saw that the *epoché* alone needed to be supplemented by the quality of empathy *(Einfühlung)*. The importance of empathy for Husserl is made clear in his late work *Cartesian Meditations*, where he writes: "To me and to those who share in my culture, an alien culture is accessible only by a kind of 'experience of someone else,' a kind of 'empathy,' by which we project ourselves into the alien cultural community and its culture."[23] In declaring the need for empathy in addition to the *epoché*, Husserl was expressing what contemporary phenomenologists of religion like van der Leeuw already knew: that a commitment of the whole person, not just the intellectual restraint of the *epoché*, is required in order to grasp the inner meaning of religious phenomena.[24] The intellectual rigor of the phenomenological *epoché* needs to be complemented by what might be described as a "discipline of the heart," in which one uses the natural human capacity to enter with feeling into the condition of another as an instrument for gaining a deeper, more intimate knowledge. As van der Leeuw expressed it: "All understanding rests upon self-surrendering love. Were this not the case, then not only all discussion of what appears in religion, but all discussion of appearance in general, would be quite impossible; since to him who does not love, nothing whatever is manifested. . . ."[25]

Clearly, the importance of empathy in the practice of the phenomenology of religion cannot be overestimated, for without it, it is not possible to understand experiential worlds foreign to one's own. The word *empathy* is Greek in origin (after *empatheia*) and it has the connotation of entering into (*em*) with passion or feeling (*pathos*). Empathy, then, is the power of projecting one's whole soul into, and thus inwardly identifying with, the object of contemplation. It is somewhat different from *sympathy*, which is literally "like feeling," or "feeling the same as" another (from the Greek *sympatheia*). The former is the precondition of the latter: One cannot share the same feelings as another unless one has first of all empathized with him or her. Just because phenomenology of religion is directed toward the experiential world of others, it cannot adopt a posture of emotional aloofness, for it would then condemn itself to remaining on the outside of its subject matter. Beyond the *epoché*, therefore, emotional involvement is necessary in order for an objective understanding (in the sense of becoming one with the object) to be possible. It is important to realize, however, that this emotional involvement is quite different from an emotional predisposition toward, or an emotional reaction to, the subject matter. It is rather a mobilization of one's emotional and affective faculties in the service of understanding. Thereby the subject matter is allowed to resonate again in the soul of the phenomenologist, and to become to a certain extent alive once more.[26]

It can be seen that phenomenology of religion proceeds quite differently from the natural sciences in this respect. From van der Leeuw onward, phenomenologists saw their task as not simply to describe and classify religious phenomena in a detached and impersonal way. The phenomena have to be "interpolated into our own lives" through "keen sympathy" with experience other than our own.[27] In the words of van der Leeuw, what is required is "not only the description of what is visible from outside, but above all the experience born of what can only become reality after it has been admitted into the life of the observer himself."[28] Because the observer, or subject, has to be fully involved in order for the object to fully manifest itself, it is necessary for him or her to pass beyond the stage of pure erudition to an empathetic and sympathetic reliving of the existential situation that gave rise to the religious material that is being studied. Among phenomenologists of religion, Mircea Eliade has been perhaps the most acutely aware of the inner challenge that this presents to the researcher: One cannot remain in the detached scholarly frame of mind if one is wanting to understand the extremities of human experience that—almost by definition—are present when the religious dimension is activated. According to Eliade, then, "The proper frame of mind for discovering the meaning of a typical human situation is not the 'objectivity' of the naturalist, but the intelligent sympathy of the exegetist, the interpreter. It is the *frame of mind* itself that needs to be changed. . . ."[29] This change in the frame of mind involves a movement from detached analysis to sympathetic engagement. For W. Brede Kristensen, such sympathetic engagement requires the mobilization of imagination, intuition, and the whole personality of the historian of religion. Only then can insight be achieved into the religions of the past *from the standpoint of their adherents.*[30]

Needless to say, the empathetic approach has only fueled criticism from those who would have the study of religion proceed on the model of the exact sciences. But while many phenomenologists of religion have reiterated the importance of empathy in order to understand the religions of the past, none of them has seen it as sufficient in itself.[31] Empathy needs to accompany exact and painstaking scholarship; it cannot replace it. It is clear that a distinction must be observed between the empathetic "entering into" a religious phenomenon in order to understand it in its own terms and critical reflection on the documents and other materials that provide access to the phenomenon.[32] In the case of van der Leeuw, who was the greatest advocate of empathetic involvement, it should be remembered that he was a committed and rigorous scholar. It was of paramount importance to him that phenomenologists have their feet on the ground: "If phenomenology is to complete its own task, it imperatively requires perpetual correction by the most conscientious philological and archaeological research. It must therefore always be prepared for confrontation with material facts. . . ."[33] Indeed, as soon as it withdraws itself from "control by philological and archaeological interpretation," it becomes pure art or empty fantasy.[34] These are statements that every phenomenologist would have to agree with, for only through the strict observance of such "control" is one's contact with the phenomena ensured. In order to live into the phenomena on their own plane of reference, control by philology and archaeology is as much a component of the phenomenological approach as are the *epoché* and the employment of empathy.

The Challenge to Phenomenology

One of the main criticisms lodged against the phenomenological approach to the study of religion is that it fails to recognize that all human experience is necessarily mediated by a series of social, historical, cultural, and personal filters and that it simply cannot escape these mediating filters. No matter how stringently the *epoché* is applied, no matter how empathetic the phenomenologist tries to be, and no matter how meticulous the scholarship, the phenomenological enterprise is fundamentally naive and misconceived, for precisely those conditioning factors that the phenomenological *epoché* seeks to bracket are in point of fact unbracketable. We are all situated in a certain cultural and historical milieu, and we are deluding ourselves if we think we can extract ourselves from it. If we "interpolate the phenomena into our own lives," as van der Leeuw advocated, then it is precisely into our lives that they are interpolated.[35] And there they will live in a very different way from the way in which they would live in someone else born into a different age or with a different cultural heritage. For this reason, the idea that we can arrive at a pure perception of the essence of a religious phenomenon, or grasp its inherent meaning, is fallacious. Our perception will always be colored in various ways by the various mediating factors to which we are inescapably subject.

According to this view, meaning is not inherent in the world, waiting for us to discover it; it is something that is bestowed upon the world by us, and to a far greater extent reflects our own nature than it does the nature of things. The meaning that we apprehend in phenomena is conditioned by precisely those historical, cultural, and personal factors that color our consciousness.[36] Our experience of the world is entangled with these factors and, try as we might, it is not possible to disentangle ourselves from them. Thus no phenomenon is "pure": It is sullied by the concepts, beliefs, and precon-

ceptions that human consciousness brings to it, and that constitute the very
nature of the phenomenon as it appears to consciousness. Every phenomenon is literally and irredeemably a *representation*, re-presented to consciousness by consciousness itself, laden with interpretative ideas and
concepts.[37]

From this standpoint, then, the study of the religious phenomena of the
past (or indeed any other historical phenomena) will always involve a large
component of projection on our part. A twentieth- or twenty-first-century
historian will discover meanings that will be quite different from those
apprehended by a nineteenth-century historian. As Gadamer has pointed
out: "When we read Mommson's *History of Rome*, we know who alone could
have written it, that is, we can identify the political situation in which the
historian organized the voices of the past in a meaningful way."[38] Our experience is not simply influenced, but it is informed and constituted by our
historical situation, the legacy of our education, cultural influences, our
previous speculations, and our own deeply held beliefs.[39]

But it is not just the objectivity of scholarly studies of the past that is
compromised on this view. Clearly the meaning that is given to a religious text, image, or ritual by the person who produced or enacted it is
equally compromised, for his or her experience is just as much colored by
social, political, and historical factors as is that of the contemporary
researcher. All religious phenomena should be seen as profoundly conditioned by the social and cultural contexts of a particular time and place.
If we want to reach viable explanations of religious phenomena—even if
we accept that there is an experiential dimension to them—then we
should examine these contexts that condition the phenomena, rather than
hazard a suspiciously subjective transposing of ourselves into the minds
of those who had an alleged religious experience. The study of the history of religion must therefore proceed within the sweep of the cultural
and historical sciences.[40]

This view, referred to as "contextualism" by its advocates, has been
termed "constructivism" by its opponents, because of its emphasis on the
degree to which religious experience is said to be constructed by the concepts and beliefs of those who have it.[41] For contextualists, mystical experience can never outrun the concepts and beliefs—many of them socially and
culturally determined—of the religious tradition within which the mystic
lives his life. According to this view, an ancient Egyptian king's mystical
union with Ra will in large part inevitably be determined by a complex
belief system, itself permeated with social and political factors, not least of
which is the belief that such an experience is quite out of the range of the

peasant. For this reason, mystical union with Ra cannot be equated with experiences of mystical union with the godhead in other religious traditions, with quite different social, political, and also religious conceptions from those of the Egyptians. The terms in which the ancient Egyptian understands what is happening are uniquely ancient and uniquely Egyptian. Comparison with other traditions such as shamanism and the later Hellenistic mystery traditions could only be misleading. The nature of an ancient Egyptian's experience will necessarily be quite different from the nature of other mystical experiences in other traditions.[42]

In order to understand ancient Egyptian religion, therefore, it will not be sufficient simply to know how the ancient Egyptians may have explained their religious beliefs and experiences to themselves. It is assumed, on this view, that they would not have been aware of the many sociological and cultural factors that determined the way in which their own beliefs and experiences were constructed. Wayne Proudfoot, for example, has argued that it is "perfectly justifiable, and is, in fact, normal procedure" to offer explanations of religious experience that do not conform to the concepts or beliefs of the person who has the experience and do not meet with his or her approval. For Proudfoot, "[I]t may be that the correct explanation requires no reference to religious realities," and Proudfoot would certainly regard it as preferable were this the case.[43]

In Proudfoot's view, if we are to understand the religious experience of the ancient Egyptians, then we need to move from the descriptions of this experience that we might find in ancient texts to an explanation in terms of modern sociology or political theory. If, for example, the coronation text of Thutmosis III describes the king transforming into a falcon and ascending to the heavens, a sociopolitical reading is more likely to make sense of the text than a literal reading. Even if there was an experiential component to it, that experience must itself have been largely constructed by the conceptual and symbolic apparatus of the pharaonic state, which required the king to transform precisely into a falcon and ascend to no other god than Ra. This kind of "explanatory reductionism" (as Proudfoot calls it), which effectively eliminates reference to the religious sphere, exactly parallels procedures in mainstream science in which explanatory theories do not necessarily bear any relationship to a person's lived experience. Just as an explanation of color phenomena is given in terms of angles of refraction or wavelengths of light, without needing to refer to what the human being actually experiences, so too a valid explanation of religious phenomena can be given in terms of social or political theory.

Within Egyptology, this reductionist approach to the understanding of religious material has often been taken. A well-known example is the case of the mythic conflict and reconciliation of Horus and Seth—a theme that occurs frequently in the Pyramid Texts. It is argued that the conflict can be explained as political and historical in origin. It simply reflects predynastic tribal conflicts that were eventually settled when the warring factions of the north and south of Egypt were united under Menes. Passages that refer to Horus and Seth being reconciled in the king can be explained as political, not religious, statements concerning the nature of the kingship that, after Menes, was conceived as a union of the "Two Lands" of the north and south of Egypt. In this way the specifically religious significance of the reconciliation of the two warring gods within the soul of the king is bypassed.[44]

Even were the reductionist prepared to admit that there was an experiential component to the myth of the reconciliation of Horus and Seth, this would still be regarded as mediated and molded by the belief system within which it takes place and the language used to express the belief system. For this reason, it has been argued that those wishing to understand religious experience would do better to study concepts and language rather than allegedly "pure" religious or mystical experiences. This has been proposed by Gavin Flood in his recent book, *Beyond Phenomenology*. The argument, taken by Flood to its nihilistic conclusion, leads to the view that in the study of religion, the locus of inquiry should not be "inner states" or states of "consciousness" at all, nor should it even be beliefs (which are too subjective), but rather it should be language and culture and "the realm of signs."[45] According to Flood, not only are religious practices completely embedded in nonreligious cultural practices, but consciousness itself is constituted in the "semiotic interaction of the social group," without which consciousness would not exist.[46] It stands to reason, therefore, that "for the explanation of religion, models from the social sciences have to be introduced and the data of religion have to be explained in terms of these models."[47] For Flood, therefore, the future of the study of religion lies in its closer proximity to the social sciences. We are finally relieved of any remaining doubts as to the terminus of the argument when he proposes that, because consciousness is constructed in human relationship, and human relationship is embodied, the study of religion would be better served if the word *spirit* were replaced by the word *body*.[48]

Standing Reductionism on Its Head

There is an irony in the fact that the supposedly more "objective" alternatives proposed by critics of phenomenology end up by effectively negating the object they are attempting to understand. In advocating that we explain religious phenomena in the nonreligious terms of the social sciences or linguistic anthropology, what is specifically religious is lost to view. Even more so if we follow Flood's advice and abandon talk of "inner states" and account for the phenomena of consciousness by reference to language and the "realm of signs," or simply cut out all talk of "spirit" and replace it with talk about "body." While all this may be advocated in the name of greater "objectivity," the object—the religious phenomenon—is in effect denied, if not completely eliminated.

The crucial issue here is whether it is possible to understand the religious sphere without deeply engaging with it and personally exposing oneself to it. Because the critics of phenomenology assume that religious experience is nonreligiously determined, their aim is to formulate nonreligious explanatory theories of religious phenomena rather than to allow the phenomena *as religious* to reveal themselves in their existential and experiential depth. By contrast, the phenomenological approach enables us to understand religious phenomena on their own plane of reference, rather than as epiphenomena of social, cultural, or historical conditions. It does this by avoiding explanations "in terms of" at all costs—even at the risk of slipping into subjectivism—in order to try to *see what is really there*. Yes, there will be sociological, linguistic, and cultural factors present, but the aim is to move through these to the deeper experiential component of the religious phenomenon, be it a text, image, or ritual. In the case of religious phenomena, theoretical explanations invariably take us away from the existential situation that they are expressing and direct us toward some other (sociological, linguistic, political, historical) phenomena, whereas the phenomenological approach will try to apprehend a phenomenon in relation to its own intrinsic meaning.[49]

There are, then, two quite different directions to go in. One is the direction of "explanatory reductionism," which leads away from the inherent meaning of religious phenomena as religious. The other is the phenomenological method, which leads to a deepened experience of the religious phenomena in their fullness or "intensive depth."[50] These two possible directions can be very clearly seen in the writings of Proudfoot, on the one hand, and Eliade on the other. Proudfoot's book, *Religious Experience*, is dedicated to finding the pathway that leads from a person's religious experience to a nonreligious explanation for it. The latter will ideally be cast in historical or cultural terms and will avoid all reference to such religious terms as "numinous," "holy," and "sacred."[51] What Proudfoot wants is to avoid evoking a sense of awe or mystery when discussing religious phenomena and to ensure that the explanation given for them is satisfying for the secular, scientific mind.[52] Eliade, by contrast, does not see understanding the meaning of a religious phenomenon as an additional act of interpretation. It is rather a penetration to a deeper level of the very same phenomenon, allowing this level to reveal itself. It is not that Eliade dismisses the sociological, economic, or political contexts as irrelevant, but that he sees that they keep us on the periphery of what is essentially religious, at a relatively superficial level of understanding. If we are to gain a deeper understanding of what is religious, then we need to find the underlying existential, or experiential, situation that is its ground of meaning.[53]

The way we do this is by practicing the inner discipline of the *epoché*. The phenomenologist holds that it is both necessary and possible to train ourselves to recognize, and to detach ourselves from, those personal and cultural factors that distort our perception of the phenomena we are trying to understand. Only then do we have the chance to perceive them in their own essence. But this requires, as Goethe put it, "an enhancement of our mental powers."[54] The phenomenological *epoché* provides the groundwork for just such an "enhancement of our mental powers" because it clears the way for a more intensive engagement with the phenomena.

How successful each phenomenological practitioner will be in practicing the *epoché* and how truly perceptive a phenomenologist's insights will be is not something that can be guaranteed. The method is not foolproof; it cannot be applied mechanically. But that is not to say that it is not scientific. Indeed, it is more truly scientific than the more mechanical approaches advocated by its critics, for if it were really the case—as they believe—that we are not able to free ourselves from our social and historical circumstances, then we would have to accept that all knowledge is relative to, if not merely a reflection of, these circumstances—in which case, it hardly merits being termed knowledge. But the very fact that it is possible to identify the conditioning factors that determine the way we experience the world implies that there is something within the human being that is able to transcend these conditioning factors. Otherwise we would not be able to become aware of them. If we are able to become aware of them, this presupposes that we are able to achieve an awareness that is not itself conditioned. The purpose of the phenomenological *epoché* is precisely to center consciousness in this unconditioned or "free" space that Husserl called "transcendental." It is from this transcendental awareness that it is possible to engage with the phenomena on their own terms, and this constitutes the basis of true objectivity.

In the phenomenological reengagement with the world, the dualistic spectatorial consciousness of the "natural standpoint" is suspended. This natural standpoint is the unquestioned premise of those who would see the study of religion conducted after the manner of mainstream science, as a sociological or historical discipline. In phenomenology, however, this consciousness undergoes a radical restructuring so that the opposition between subject and object is suspended.[55] It is suspended because the activity with which the transcendental consciousness is engaged occurs at a level deeper than (and philosophically "prior to") the dualism of subject versus object. The more the object's depth of meaning is laid hold of, the more the subject transcends the personal and cultural level. As van der Leeuw has stated: "The sphere of meaning is a third realm, subsisting above mere subjectivity and mere objectivity. The entrance gate to the reality of primal experience, itself wholly inaccessible, is *meaning: my* meaning and *its* meaning, which have become irrevocably one in the act of comprehension."[56]

In this respect, the phenomenological method rests on a nondualist epistemology, for the activity engaged in by the subject is seen as essentially a participation in the inherent meaning of the object. But this, of course, requires a discipline of consciousness, and it is this inner discipline of the *epoché* that sets phenomenology apart from those approaches to understanding the religions of the past that follow the methods of mainstream science. Phenomenology's relevance to the study of ancient Egyptian religion lies in the fact that it requires the researcher to change his or her own consciousness. The religious dimension cannot be understood by a consciousness that remains circumscribed by the "natural standpoint," that defines itself in opposition to the objects it investigates. And overcoming the natural standpoint is no easy task. Mircea Eliade has pointed out that the *epoché* has a similarity to certain spiritual disciplines practiced in religious traditions, where the aim is to liberate the mind from the conditioned world. He even goes so far as to compare the phenomenological method with initiation ceremonies in traditional cultures. In these ceremonies, the "profane" experience characteristic of the "natural man" is deliberately suppressed in a manner that parallels the phenomenological suspension of the natural standpoint. Just as through the initiation rites, the novice gains access to the sacred world—that is, to what is considered truly real and meaningful—so through the phenomenological *epoché*, the subject "succeeds in grasping the reality of the world."[57]

For the reductionist, the idea of a methodology that requires us to change our consciousness is wholly unpalatable. It has a "magical, occult ring to it" that sets it in opposition to mainstream scientific method.[58] It is a philosophical presupposition of contextualism that we are unable to escape the natural standpoint, which locks all our experience into the social and cultural conditions that are said to constitute it. As we have seen, for the reductionist even mystical experience is regarded as historically and culturally conditioned. And by that token, it is denied as a possibility to human beings.[59] By contrast, phenomenology recognizes that there is a spiritual kernel to religious experience that is not essentially conditioned, even though it may be expressed in the language and through the myths and symbols of a given culture. This spiritual kernel is identifiable as a certain type of human experience that we may meet in a wide range of cultures. Therefore, comparison with accounts of similar experiences in other spiritual traditions may well help to illumine our understanding of the experience as we find it described in one particular tradition. While cultural and historical factors will inevitably play their part in the way in which religious or mystical experiences are understood and interpreted by those who have them, we would be missing something essential were we to assert that they alone determine the content of a given religious experience. So, for example, in the coronation text of Thutmosis III—as in utterance 302 of the Pyramid Texts—it is not primarily political and cultural factors that determine that the king of Egypt transform himself into a falcon. The mystical ascent of the king to the heavens requires that he transform himself into a bird that soars upward, a fierce and regal creature that disdains the earth—a falcon and not a duck. The symbolic preeminence of the falcon is determined less by political than by spiritual requirements. It is a bird that belongs to the heavens, whose home is the sky. The political status of the falcon as the royal bird of power is determined by a perception of its soul qualities, which the king himself calls upon and identifies with in his mystical ascent to the sky. For this reason, in many shamanic traditions it is as an eagle (a close relative of the falcon) that the shaman ascends to the sky.[60]

In a religiously organized society like ancient Egypt, it is in fact impossible to understand social, political, and linguistic factors independently of the fundamentally religious orientation of the whole culture. Far from the religious life being conditioned by supposedly nonreligious contexts, there was nothing in the society that was not permeated by a thoroughgoing religious sensibility. The head of state was a god, the economic life of the country was to a very large extent managed by the temples, the language was literally "sacred writing," and magicians held important offices of state.[61] Furthermore, the most important events in the life of the king were religious rituals, the neglect of which would have been regarded as catastrophic for the well-being of the whole country.[62] Indeed, if our aim was to understand the political, economic, social, or linguistic contexts of ancient Egyptian civilization, then it would be necessary for us first to understand the *religious life*. The reductionist project of explaining the religious life in nonreligious terms needs to be stood on its head in the case of ancient Egypt, for every aspect of its culture was permeated by religion.

A Question of Motivation

If we accept, with the phenomenologist, that it is possible to study religious phenomena "on their own plane of reference" and if we accept that this plane of reference has reality, meaning, and value, then this clearly provides the motivation for studying religious phenomena, whether they be of the past or the present. Those, on the other hand, who seek to explain religious phenomena in the nonreligious terms favored by "explanatory reduction-ism" clearly have a different motivation, for they do not accept that the religious plane of reference has the requisite reality, meaning, and value that they are looking for. Thus, their motivation is quite different from that of the phenomenologist, for at the back of their approach to religious phenomena is their conviction that they are epiphenomena of something else, something that is not religious at all. What, then, could be the motivation for seeking to explain religious phenomena nonreligiously? It would have to be that we already subscribe to a nonreligious view of the world, and therefore want to explain all phenomena—including the phenomena of religion—in nonreligious terms.

In the case of the study of ancient Egyptian religion, it is likely that one or the other of these two motivations, each expressing a fundamental attitude to the world, will be operating. Both have been present in the study of the religion of ancient Egypt over the centuries. Broadly speaking, what motivated people to study ancient Egyptian religion from the Greek period through the Roman Empire and into the European Renaissance was the belief that ancient Egypt was a repository of spiritual wisdom. To study things Egyptian was potentially to access sublime mysteries and deep spiritual truths. It was therefore something worth doing to further the spiritual understanding of precisely those aspects of reality that the Egyptians knew about. There was, in other words, a belief that one could learn something of real value from the Egyptians.

By contrast, from the late nineteenth century on, when the study of ancient Egyptian religion became subsumed within the academic discipline of Egyptology, the spiritual enlightenment of the researcher or the researcher's contemporaries was no longer regarded as a valid reason for pursuing the research. As we have already seen in chapter 2, for Egyptology to establish itself as a bona fide academic subject, it had to abandon any prior affiliation with metaphysics and esotericism and subscribe to the worldview of scientific materialism. From the mid-nineteenth century, the Darwinian interpretation of the past as involving an evolution of higher forms of life and consciousness from lower forms became increasingly embedded in the disciplines of sociology, anthropology, and history. Inseparable from the idea of progress, which gained unquestioned supremacy from the nineteenth century onward, Darwinism ensured that no respectable academic would propose that past civilizations had superior knowledge or wisdom to our own. The trajectory of history was seen as a steady ascent from the primitive childhood of humanity, dominated by magic and superstition, to our present enlightened maturity, characterized by scientific rationalism, industrialization, and technological sophistication. To take the religion of ancient Egypt seriously would thus be to jeopardize both one's career and the standing of Egyptology within academia. Egyptology became handmaiden to a much bigger project—that of materialistic science—which was to explain both the outer and inner worlds in terms that excluded all reference to the spiritual as a real and operative dimension of existence. What this meant was that the data of Egyptian religion—the gods, the temples, the rituals, the religious texts, and so on—would be treated at a respectable distance and with the requisite detachment, laced every so often with the occasional condescending remark.

Now, in the last few decades attitudes within Egyptology have moved on, and this may be due in part to the gradual reawakening of the West to levels of reality other than the physical. In the course of the twentieth century, we have had the development of depth psychology and the opening up of Western esoteric and Eastern religious perspectives, along with an increasing disaffection with the worldview of scientific materialism. Whereas much of ancient Egyptian spirituality seemed uncongenial to the nineteenth- and then twentieth-century mind-set, now at the beginning of the twenty-first century to many people it seems far less so. There is the prospect today of people turning to ancient Egyptian religious texts and studying them because they believe that they will learn something from them that will have genuine spiritual relevance to their lives. Indeed, ancient Egyptian spirituality seems increasingly to have the ability to speak to us now almost in answer to our deepest, often only half-articulated questions concerning the struggle to reconnect with those subtle dimensions of existence with which the ancient Egyptians were so familiar.

It would seem, then, that at the beginning of the twenty-first century, a new motivation for studying ancient Egyptian religion is making itself felt. This new motivation is that Egyptian religion serves to put us in touch with precisely those dimensions of reality that are excluded from the worldview of scientific materialism—dimensions that are not outwardly observable, and yet are no less real for being invisible. In this respect, a new role for Egyptology could develop in the coming decades, if only it is able to shake off its deference to this worldview and once again embrace the attitude that ancient Egypt has much of value to teach us today. It is to this end that the phenomenological approach to ancient Egyptian religion can contribute, while at the same time broadening the contemporary understanding of the nature of mystical experience and the spiritual realities that are accessed by it. Ancient Egyptian religion has the capacity to connect us again with experiential worlds that the West has only recently begun to rediscover. As Mircea Eliade predicted back in the 1960s:

> Very soon the West will have not only to know and understand the cultural universes of the non-Westerners, but will have to value them as an integral part of the history of the human spirit and no longer consider them as infantile or aberrant episodes of an exemplary History of Man. Moreover, confrontation with the "other" helps Western man to know himself better. The effort spent on correctly understanding modes of thought foreign to the Western rationalist tradition, that is to say, in the first place on deciphering the meaning of myths and symbols, will be repaid by a considerable enrichening of the consciousness.[63]

Eliade has been criticized for approaching the study of the history of religions as a means of reinfusing the desacralized Western world with a new spiritual awareness, but it is inevitable that the religious outlook of the ancient Egyptians, as with any ancient or primal religious worldview, if taken seriously, will present a challenge to the prevailing secular and materialistic consciousness. Ivan Strenski has complained that Eliade's "creative hermeneutics" are nothing more than "a species of high-order propaganda, a sort of scholar's magic which seeks to change the way people see things."

In a revealing fit of pique, Strenski accuses Eliade of trying "deliberately to upset the everyday common sense views of existence."[64] It can indeed be upsetting to have one's commonsense views challenged, and it is not easy to change the way one sees things, but these discomforts hardly constitute grounds for regarding Eliade as wrong.

If we are not prepared to risk opening ourselves to the content of ancient Egyptian religion, then the methodology of explanatory reductionism is there waiting to be called on. It will take the researcher halfway to an actual engagement with the spiritual content of a religious document or ritual and then save the researcher from a direct encounter with it by concentrating on its historical or social context or its linguistic structure. By contrast, the phenomenological method—while not ignoring the historical, social, or linguistic contexts—will, through the deployment of the *epoché*, and through a combination of exact scholarship with an empathetic and imaginative "living into" the material, aim for an engagement with the existential content of the same religious phenomenon. It is for this reason that the phenomenological method is so challenging. It really is liable to "change the way we see things." And it is liable to do so especially when applied to the study of ancient Egyptian religion, which functioned within a worldview that has precious few affinities with that of modern or postmodern culture. In fact, the practice of the phenomenology of religion cannot leave the practitioner unchanged: It is an occupation that "has consequences," as Eliade himself was acutely aware:

> If these consequences are not always evident, it is because the majority of historians of religion defend themselves against the messages with which their documents are filled. This caution is understandable. One does not live with impunity in intimacy with "foreign" religious forms, which are sometimes extravagant and often terrible. But many historians of religions end up by no longer taking seriously the spiritual worlds they study; they fall back on their personal religious faith, or they take refuge in a materialism or behaviorism impervious to every spiritual shock. Besides, excessive specialization allows a great number of historians of religions to station themselves for the rest of their days in the sectors they have learned to frequent since their youth. And every "specialization" ends by making the religious forms banal; in the last instance it effaces their meanings.[65]

This "effacement of meanings" is precisely the agenda of those contextualists who proceed by the method of "explanatory reductionism" to a denial of the very subject they are purporting to study. Within Egyptology, despite the signs that things are beginning to change, there are still a great many Egyptologists who are not interested in the realities toward which Egyptian religion was directed, nor are they interested in the inner experiences that the Egyptians devoted themselves to attaining. Eliade's remarks are as applicable to both historians of religion and Egyptologists today as they were in 1969 when he wrote them.

The phenomenological approach to ancient Egyptian religious material provides the needed complement to standard Egyptological approaches, by recovering those layers of experience and wisdom that have to a large extent been neglected within the Egyptological establishment. To the extent that the phenomenological study of ancient Egyptian religion puts us in touch with what was regarded by the ancient Egyptians as essentially a sacred dimension of life, it presents us with a reality that is more than simply historical. The phenomenology and history of religions is one of the few "humanistic" disciplines that can have an utterly transforming effect on the researcher, for it can lead to an awakening to aspects of reality and possibilities of human experience that fall outside what has come to be regarded in the West as normal.[66] Although a culture of the past may be historically remote from us, it nevertheless still represents the experiences of human beings. These human beings may have been very different from ourselves, but we share with them our basic humanity. If, therefore, we are confronted by "existential situations" with which we are quite unfamiliar, because of our living in the modern secularized world, we thereby come to know something of our own human nature of which we are normally unaware and at the same time are presented with realms of spirit that few of us come near to experiencing.

This has extraordinary implications for us today, precisely because in the prevailing culture of the modern West (and increasingly the modern world), we suffer from chronic amnesia concerning spiritual realities with which the ancients were relating on a daily basis. Insofar as we are able to acknowledge cultures of the past, such as ancient Egypt, not only as part of our own history, but—as Eliade says—as part of what lies buried within the modern psyche, and insofar as we are able to incorporate and integrate them into our understanding of who we are today, we may open the way to reconnecting with that lost part of ourselves and that lost dimension of existence that was so present to the Egyptians and has become so absent from our modern awareness.

In this chapter, the phenomenological approach to the study of ancient Egyptian religion has been defended not only because it presents an honest attempt to understand religious phenomena on their own "plane of refer-ence," but also because it does not allow the researcher to remain distant or detached from the religious material. To appreciate the real significance of this material requires the full engagement of the researcher, and this is indeed potentially life changing. In practicing the phenomenological method, the researcher attempts to reach out to and unite with the "other" through under-standing and empathy, to the point of imaginatively reliving the experiences that he or she is trying to comprehend. In so doing, the phenomenologist can-not remain unaffected, cannot remain untouched by this encounter, for the encounter is not simply with a "historical other" but with an "existential other" that is closer to us than we would dare believe. It is this encounter with a buried part of ourselves, and with a hidden aspect of reality, that is the con-sequence of opening ourselves to the content of the material that forms the substance of the present study. It is to this material that we shall now turn.

PART 2

THE SHAMANIC ROOTS OF THE PYRAMID TEXTS

6 THE PYRAMID OF UNAS

The Pyramid Texts

The early sacred literature that survives from ancient Egypt includes tomb inscriptions, offering lists, and brief prayers, but there are no long consecutive religious texts until the Pyramid Texts appear in the pyramid of Unas at the end of the Fifth Dynasty, roughly 4,350 years ago. The Pyramid Texts are not only the earliest example of ancient Egyptian sacred literature—they are the earliest example of any piece of extended writing worldwide. They are of immense value to us today because they open a window onto the religious consciousness of human beings who lived under very different spiritual, psychological, and social conditions from ourselves. This religious consciousness plumbed depths of spiritual experience that we fail to appreciate if we regard the Pyramid Texts merely as representing the funerary beliefs of the ancient Egyptians. Only by setting aside this assumption does it become possible for the texts to reveal themselves as the prototype of a mystical tradition that is at the root not only of later ancient Egyptian religious life but also of subsequent Western mystical and esoteric traditions such as Platonism, Hermeticism, Gnosticism, and alchemy.

The Pyramid Texts were first discovered in 1881 by Gaston Maspero, engraved onto the walls of the inner chambers of several Old Kingdom pyramids at Saqqara. Maspero assumed from the beginning that the texts were funerary, and divided them into three types: ritual texts, prayers, and magic spells.[1] The pyramid in which the Pyramid Texts first appeared was that of Unas, the last of the Fifth Dynasty kings, whose thirty-year reign lasted from 2375 B.C. to 2345 B.C. If we accept the conventional chronology of the building of the Great Pyramid at Giza during the reign of Khufu, then the pyramid of Unas was built some 180 years later. The pyramid of Khufu, along with the other pyramids at Giza, do not have any texts inscribed within their chambers, although travelers to the Giza site in ancient and early medieval times claimed to have seen hieroglyphic inscriptions on the outer casing stones of the Great Pyramid.[2] As the casing stones have since been removed, little can be said about these possible earlier "pyramid texts."

What we do have are texts inscribed on the internal walls not only of the pyramid of Unas, but also of his immediate successor, Teti, the first of the Sixth Dynasty kings, and Teti's successors Pepi I, Merenre, and Pepi II. During the long reign of Pepi II, who was the last of the Sixth Dynasty kings, the privilege of having an inscribed pyramid was extended to his three wives, Neith, Ipwet, and Oudjebten, each of whom had a small inscribed pyramid close by that of Pepi. After the reign of Pepi II, only one more king inscribed a pyramid: This was the Eighth Dynasty king Iby, but the quality of the inscriptions in his pyramid is relatively crude compared to the finely crafted hieroglyphs of the earlier pyramids, especially those of the pyramid of Unas.

This means that the Pyramid Texts were employed in pyramids for approximately 180 years. After this, they continued to appear in various nonroyal tombs through to the Middle Kingdom. For example, in the cemetery surrounding the pyramid of the Middle Kingdom king Senwosret I at Lisht, there is a tomb of an official called Senwosret-Ankh that contains a fairly close copy of the texts of the pyramid of Unas. This means that either the pyramid of Unas remained unsealed for several hundred years or else—more likely—the texts existed as a separate corpus probably preserved on papyrus rolls.[3] In either case, the Unas texts were evidently regarded as an integral work in their own right, and seem to have acquired "canonical" status, unlike the selection of texts in the later Sixth Dynasty pyramids. Thus a copy of the offering liturgy from the Unas pyramid was made in the Late Period (in the Twenty-sixth Dynasty tomb of Pet-Amen-Apet) but no similar copies of texts from the other pyramids are known. Portions of the whole corpus of Pyramid Texts were, however, frequently used on the coffins of various Middle Kingdom nobles. Many of the Middle Kingdom Coffin Texts, and some passages in the New Kingdom Book of the Dead, are also clearly derived from the Pyramid Texts. The final appearance of Pyramid Texts is on the walls of the Philadelphus temple at Philae in the Ptolemaic period.[4]

Although the Pyramid Texts were first committed to writing in the Fifth Dynasty, it is virtually certain that they existed in oral form before this date. It has been argued that many are in fact predynastic.[5] Ascertaining their date of origin, however, is a difficult, if not impossible, task and is perhaps less important than recognizing that the texts existed as an independent corpus, many of them originally spoken in a ritual context rather than written. For this reason, a considerable number of the texts begin with the formula "Words spoken" (*djed medu*) and hence they are given the title "utterances." Although the name of the individual king frequently occurs in the utterances of his particular pyramid, in origin they probably did not apply to him personally, but were chosen from the preexistent corpus of words for recitation.[6] Altogether there are over 750 of these utterances, many of them paralleling or echoing others. The large number of utterances means that most contemporary readers are likely to feel a little bewildered when they first confront the sheer mass of the collected texts. Where does one begin?

The texts were first grouped together in utterances by Sethe, who produced the definitive edition of the Pyramid Texts in 1910.[7] Both Maspero and Sethe began the numbering of the texts in the sarcophagus chamber and ended in the entrance passageway. Despite subsequent scholars questioning whether this is in fact the right order of reading the texts, Sethe's method of numbering the utterances remains the standard one. Because Sethe's numbering system incorporates texts from all the different pyramids, references to Pyramid Texts using this system can seem a little like references of astronomers to asteroids, doing no more than giving each utterance a tag by which to identify it. It is not clear from the numbering alone which chamber each utterance is taken from nor even to which pyramid it belongs. The standard modern English translation of the Pyramid Texts by R. O. Faulkner follows Sethe's numbering, beginning with utterance 1 and ending with utterance 759, with no indication as to the location of each utterance within the pyramid nor any indication as to which pyramid or pyramids it occurs in. Many of these utterances in fact appear in more than one pyramid, and any single pyramid will have only a selection of the total on its walls. Quite possibly the same text will appear on different walls in different pyramids. It needs to be remembered, therefore, that the numbering of the utterances serves only to identify them, and it indicates neither the exact position of a text within a pyramid, nor necessarily the order in which the texts are to be read.

The whole question of the "right order" in which to read the Pyramid Texts has received considerable attention from scholars in the second half of the twentieth century. Because it has a direct bearing on how the texts themselves should be understood, a review of the scholarly discussion of this question will be given in the final section of this chapter. From a phenomenological standpoint, however, the best initial approach to the texts is without the encumbrance of the many rival theories concerning their interpretation, and to examine them simply as we find them on the walls of the corridors and chambers of the pyramid, through which and into which one walks. Approached in this way, the question of where to begin and where to end certainly seems at first not to be of paramount importance, for the Pyramid Texts are not like a book that one holds in the hand and reads from beginning to end; they are a book that we walk into, that encompasses us on all sides. In our first encounter with them, we find them architecturally located, and it may be that they do not in fact "begin" or "end" anywhere. The texts are wedded to walls and ask of us that we engage with them as architectural phenomena, with an awareness of where each utterance belongs in the inner structure and layout of the pyramid.

The pyramid itself is, of course, also spatially located. There are altogether nine pyramids with Pyramid Texts. They are all fairly close to each other at Saqqara, as can be seen from the map in figure 6.1. This whole area served as the necropolis of the Old Kingdom capital, Memphis, where the more public aspect of the Sed festival ceremonies would probably have taken place.[8] From the earliest times, Saqqara was sacred to the god Sokar, originally regarded as a manifestation of Osiris, but at the same time fused with Ptah, the god of Memphis. As a manifestation of Osiris, Sokar represented his power of rebirth, and was depicted as a falcon resting on, or breaking out of, a mound of earth, placed on a boat.[9] The whole area, then, was as much to do with rebirth as it was to do with death.

Of the nine pyramids at Saqqara, four are so badly damaged that whole sections of text are missing from certain walls. These four are the pyramids of Teti, Pepi I, Merenre, and Iby. The pyramids of the three queens of Pepi II are also not in the best state of preservation, and they suffer, along with that of Iby, from the added disadvantage of being single-chamber pyramids and therefore lacking an inscribed antechamber. Their texts are thus not as representative as the other pyramids, which all have antechamber texts. This leaves the greatest body of extant texts in the pyramid of Unas and the pyramid of Pepi II. Pepi II's pyramid is the largest and has by far the most utterances on its walls. But it has also sustained some damage, so the texts of this pyramid are incomplete. One might think that this is more than made up for by the greater amount of texts. The impression one gets, however, is that Pepi somewhat indiscriminately crammed as many texts as possible into his pyramid, often overriding earlier conventions as to the placement of utterances on walls oriented to one or another of the cardinal directions.

151

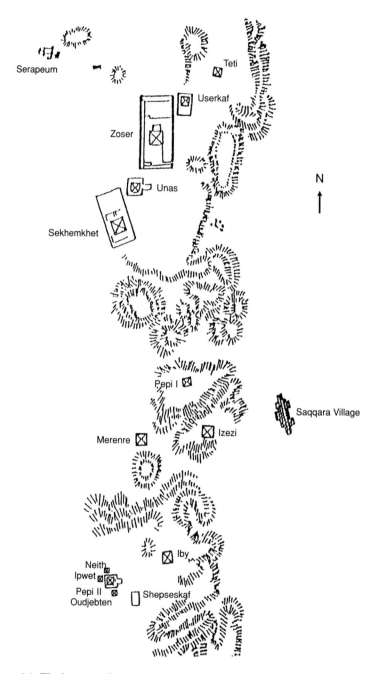

N

Figure 6.1. The locations of the main pyramids at Saqqara. The inscribed pyramids are (top to bottom): Teti, Unas, Pepi I, Merenre, Iby, and Pepi II, with queens Neith, Ipwet, and Oudjebten.

We are left, then, with the pyramid of Unas, which is not only the best preserved but also the one pyramid for which we have a complete set of utterances.[10] Unas's pyramid was also the earliest to have texts inscribed on its inner walls, and the placement of the texts seems to follow a clearer intention than in the later pyramids.[11] As we have already seen, there is evidence to suggest that the Egyptians themselves regarded the Unas texts, in contradistinction to the texts in the other pyramids, as having canonical status. In concentrating on this pyramid, we need not, however, ignore the others. Unas's pyramid probably served as the model or archetype of the later pyramids, which all emulated it in design and to a significant degree also in the thematic content of their texts. To enable the reader to pursue comparison between the Unas texts and those of the other pyramids, a list of utterances and their position in the chambers of their respective pyramids is given in appendix 2.

The Pyramid Temples and Causeway of Unas

The pyramid of Unas is generally assumed to have been his tomb, but this is by no means certain. When excavated by Maspero in 1881, the sarcophagus was found to be empty, and no traces of a burial were present.[12] There is, furthermore, a large mastaba tomb nearby that has quarry marks bearing the name of Unas on the backs of certain of the blocks. The internal arrangement of the mastaba is also similar to that of the pyramid of Unas.[13] The existence of quarry marks with the name of Unas is not in any way conclusive evidence that the tomb belonged to him, but it is something to be borne in mind when thinking about the possibility that his pyramid might have served a nonfunerary purpose. Equally suggestive is the fact that altogether five priests of the pyramid of Unas are known. All of them have the title Prophet of the Unas pyramid Nefer-asut ("beautiful of places") except one: the priest Akhet-hotep, who had two stelae in his tomb. On one he is called Prophet of the Unas pyramid Nefer-asut, but on the other he is called Prophet of the Unas pyramid Asut-asuti ("place of places"). Are we to conclude, then, that Unas had two pyramids?[14] Again, we are not in a position to judge since only one pyramid is known to us, but these scraps of information should at least make us proceed with caution when we approach the question of the exact purpose of the surviving Unas pyramid.

Like most Old Kingdom pyramids, the pyramid of Unas was approached from a temple in the valley below, adjacent to a canal (see fig. 6.2). The ancient Egyptian way of coming to the pyramid was first by boat, which would have moored alongside the valley temple. Very little survives

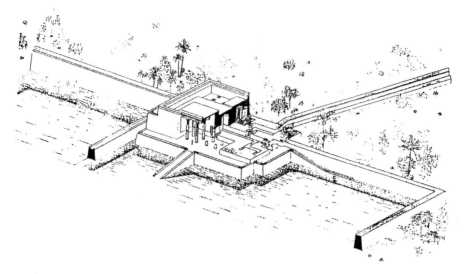

Figure 6.2. Reconstruction drawing of the valley temple of Unas. The temple was approached by boat. Here initial purificatory rites were probably performed before proceeding to the causeway (above right) that led uphill to the pyramid temple almost half a mile away.

today of the valley temple of Unas, but it was here that initial purification ceremonies probably took place and preparation was made for entering the pyramid. From the valley temple, one then proceeded uphill along a causeway. The causeway was really a long corridor with high walls and a roof that completely insulated from the world outside those who traveled its length. This insulation from the outer world was alleviated by just one feature: In the middle of the roof and running its whole length, there was a narrow slit through which light filtered. So, walking along this causeway for almost half a mile, it would have been impossible to see anything beyond the walls and ceiling by which one was enclosed. But on the inside of these causeway walls were beautiful reliefs illumined by the soft light allowed through the slit in the center of the roof. These reliefs showed deer being hunted by greyhounds, men and women bargaining at a fish market, metalworkers, archers, farmers hoeing, pitiful scenes of people starving, ships full of prisoners begging for mercy, other ships transporting granite columns for a temple, and then women bearing offerings in a long procession. It is as if the whole sweep of life was depicted on these walls—its pleasures and tribulations and the work of human beings in the world. Meanwhile, looking up, the causeway ceiling was decorated with golden stars against a blue background.

Excavations have shown that the causeway had two changes of angle. Just south of the second bend, there are two large boat pits, that—in all probability—once contained wooden boats.[15] These probably represented the day and night boats of the sun god, and could have been used in ritual "sailings" of the type that is known to have taken place during the Sed festival of Amenhotep III, who undertook a ritual journey in the night bark of the sun god Ra during his Sed festival (see fig. 7.16).[16] To the north of the causeway are many tombs, those nearest the pyramid belonging to the two queens of Unas, senior officials, and members of the royal family. These are located between the pyramid temple and the huge Sed festival complex of the Third Dynasty king Zoser farther to the north (fig. 6.3).

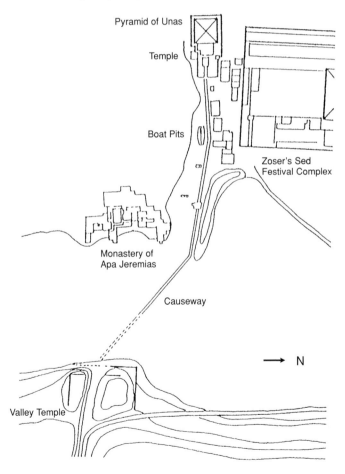

Figure 6.3. Map showing the valley temple, causeway, boat pits, pyramid temple, and pyramid of Unas at Saqqara.

The causeway leads directly to the entrance of the (now ruined) outer temple, which had to be visited and passed through in order to reach the pyramid (fig. 6.4). The pyramid itself was surrounded by a high temenos wall, and there was no way into it except through the temple. And as there was no way of entering the temple except from the causeway that was itself entered from the valley temple, it is clear that the actual approach to the pyramid, and the experiences that arose through approaching it in this particular way, was considered to be extremely important. From the beginning, as soon as one entered the valley temple, one was in an environment sealed off from the outside world. It was an environment in which the consciousness of the human being was compelled by the sequence of architectural spaces to become increasingly focused on the meaning of this westward journey uphill, toward the entrance to the pyramid.

Having arrived at the outer temple, one came first to a short corridor and then to an open court surrounded by pillars. On the other side of the court was the temenos wall of the pyramid, and the entrance through it marked the threshold between the outer and the inner temple. It was at this threshold that ran the long transverse corridor that, in the pyramid temple

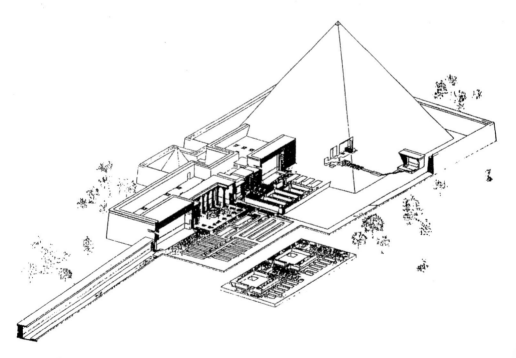

Figure 6.4. The pyramid temple and pyramid of Unas. Reconstruction drawing.

of Pepi II, was decorated with depictions of the king celebrating his Sed festival.[17] Farther west and closest to the pyramid, the main chambers and sanctuaries of the inner temple were located, all now in a state of complete ruin. This temple design (itself based on the temple of Unas's predecessor Djedkare-Isesi) became the model for the later pyramid temples. Thus comparison of the ground plan of the pyramid temple of Pepi II (seen in fig. 4.19) with that of Unas's pyramid temple (fig. 6.5) shows that Pepi's temple deviated only in minor respects from that of Unas. It seems likely that just as the design features of the pyramid temples were similar to each other, so also were the reliefs, in respect to both their subject matter and their location. It is probable, therefore, that the central transverse corridor of Unas's pyramid temple would have been adorned with reliefs illustrating the same Sed festival motifs as were later depicted in the central transverse corridor of Pepi II's pyramid temple. Likewise, the long rectangular sanctuary at the west end of the pyramid temple, abutting the east wall of the pyramid, was probably decorated with offering scenes.

In contrast to the many reliefs that survive intact from the causeway, the surviving reliefs from Unas's temple are few and fragmentary. They include, however, many of the same kinds of images that were found in a better state of preservation in the temple of Pepi II: images of gods and

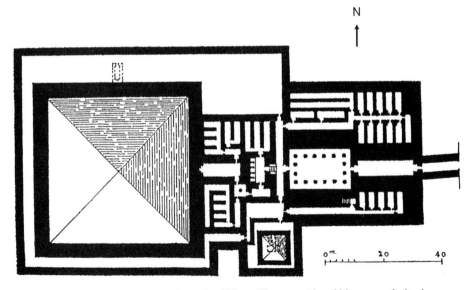

Figure 6.5. Plan of the pyramid temple of Unas. The pyramid could be approached only through this temple, and its integration into the temple complex was reinforced by the temenos wall that surrounded it and demarcated the inner temple sanctuaries from the outer temple.

Figure 6.6. Fragment of the king performing the dedication of the field dance of the Sed festival. Below the tableau of stars to the left, the roof of a chapel can be made out with the top of the king's head within it. In front of the chapel, the standard of the jackal god Wepwawet can be seen. Limestone fragment from the pyramid temple of Unas, Saqqara.

goddesses, processions of offering bearers, and various royal ceremonies, many of which are of the Sed festival.[18] This similarity of images reinforces the probability that the decoration of the temple of Unas was similar to that of Pepi's temple. In figure 6.6, two lightly dancing feet above a tableau of stars undoubtedly belong to the king, who is performing the dedication of the field dance. Underneath the stars, to the left, the king is apparently seated in a chapel, while in front of him the top of the standard of the jackal god Wepwawet, who played a prominent role in the Sed festival, can be seen.

In another limestone fragment, shown in figure 6.7, we meet again the familiar profile of the bearded king enthroned, wearing the short Sed fes-

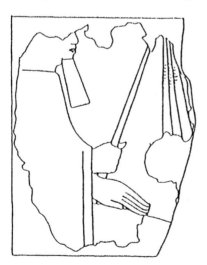

Figure 6.7. The king, wearing a false beard and the short Sed festival tunic, sits enthroned. Limestone fragment from the pyramid temple of Unas, Saqqara.

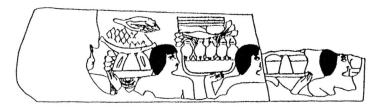

Figure 6.8. Limestone fragment showing offering bearers carrying trays of fruit. From the pyramid temple of Unas, Saqqara.

tival tunic and holding in his right hand the royal flail. This image closely resembles that of Khufu found at Giza (fig. 4.15) and of Sahure found at his pyramid temple at Abusir (fig. 4.17). Finally, in figure 6.8, another fragment depicts a procession of offering bearers carrying many kinds of fruits on trays as well as vases and containers. This relief is one of thirteen fragments depicting offerings and offering bearers.[19] We have already noted that in the temple of Pepi II, similar scenes were depicted in the sanctuary. They may or may not belong to the Sed festival, but as we have already seen in chapter 4, it is perfectly feasible that they do.[20]

The Pyramid of Unas

The entrance to the pyramid is at ground level on its northern side. To enter it, it is necessary to bend over awkwardly in order to clamber down the low entrance passage. A cross section of the entrance passage, vestibule, and horizontal corridor leading to the pyramid can be seen in figure 6.9. As with most pyramids, the angle of the sloping entrance passage appears to be quite deliberate. In Khufu's pyramid at Giza it is 28 degrees, in Khafre's pyramid it is 26 degrees, while Pepi II's has an angle of 25 degrees. In the

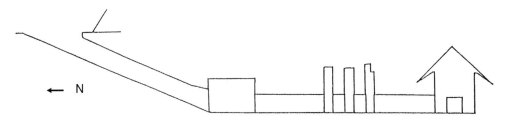

Figure 6.9. Cross-section showing the entrance passage, vestibule, and horizontal corridor leading to the pyramid of Unas.

pyramid of Unas, the angle of the entrance passage is 22 degrees. As these passages were each oriented to specific northern stars, they would be conceived better as exits than entrances. The Pyramid Texts clearly state that the king went on a celestial journey, the northern or "imperishable" stars being of special symbolic significance because of their visibility throughout the year.[21]

At the bottom of the sloping passage, there is a small vestibule that leads to a horizontal corridor. It is still not possible to stand upright, and the discomfort of having to bend and crouch makes one feel that both entrance passage and corridor were not designed entirely with the human form in mind. So far there are no decorations and no inscriptions on the walls. Halfway along the horizontal corridor, there are three granite portcullises that effectively sealed the pyramid. It is only after passing this barrier that we meet the first hieroglyphs, on the walls at the end of the horizontal corridor. It is the nature of the hieroglyphic script that it can be read either from left to right or from right to left, depending on which way the hieroglyphs are facing. The direction in which these hieroglyphs in the "entrance" passage are to be read is from the inside of the pyramid out, not from the outside in, a fact that adds to the impression that we are in an exit rather than an entrance.

At the end of the corridor, the first chamber of the pyramid to be entered is the antechamber (see figs. 6.10 and 6.11). The antechamber is right at the center of the pyramid. The exact center of the pyramid is the center point of the antechamber ceiling. Here it is possible to stand up, and

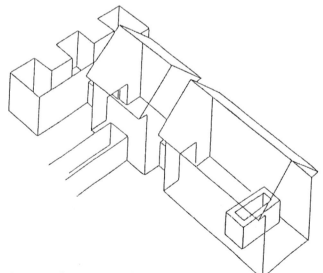

Figure 6.10. Drawing of the pyramid of Unas.

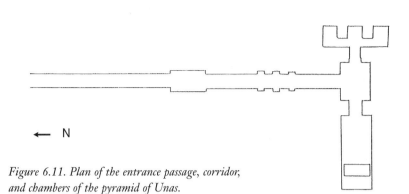

Figure 6.11. Plan of the entrance passage, corridor, and chambers of the pyramid of Unas.

← N

to have the experience of being encompassed on all sides by the blue-tinted hieroglyphs, which seem almost tangibly to emanate a magical power and to saturate the chamber with a mysterious potency. To the west of the antechamber is the sarcophagus chamber, similarly covered with hieroglyphs, while the large black granite sarcophagus occupies the far (west) end of the chamber (fig. 6.12). To the east of the antechamber, abutting the wall of the inner temple, is an undecorated and uninscribed triple chamber,

Figure 6.12. View into the sarcophagus chamber of the pyramid of Unas showing the black granite sarcophagus at its west end.

or *serdab*, the purpose of which is not known for certain. It has been suggested that the *ka* and *ba* statues of the king were installed in it.[22] In the pyramid of Unas, not only the triple chamber itself but also the entrance to it is undecorated and uninscribed. This is the case with all the later pyramids save one: the pyramid of Teti, who reigned immediately after Unas. In Teti's pyramid, on the walls of this opening to the *serdab* are texts that refer to the resuscitation of Osiris, the re-membering of his body, and his being clothed and anointed. As these texts read from the triple chamber outward toward the antechamber, they may furnish a clue as to what may have occurred within it.[23]

One of the interesting design features of the pyramid of Unas, which was copied in the later pyramids, is that the north and south walls of the chambers stop short of the ceiling and form a shelf a little way below it. By contrast, the east and west walls rise all the way to the ceiling. Since the ceiling was painted with stars, it symbolized the heavens, and this architectural difference between the north–south and the east–west relationship to the ceiling may have some bearing on the texts that the walls carry. The shelf can be seen in figure 6.12. This photograph also shows that in the sarcophagus chamber there are no texts in the immediate vicinity of the sarcophagus. Instead, we find the geometrical "palace-façade" designs that derive from the royal mastaba tombs of the First Dynasty. One of the recurrent motifs is that of two lotus flowers with their stems but no leaves, represented back to back (see fig. 6.13). This is a motif that occurs in many Old Kingdom tombs and on tomb artifacts, but especially on sarcophagi and around false doors. The significance of this is that the sarcophagus was a place of transition between the physical and spiritual worlds, while the false door was a place of communication between realms. The lotus, whose manner of growth involves passing out of the water element in order to flower in the air, touched by the rays of the sun, was preeminently a symbol of breakthrough from one world to another.

Just as some light is perhaps shed on the purpose of the undecorated and uninscribed triple chamber by referring to texts of a later pyramid that are placed in the opening between it and the antechamber, so it may also be possible to shed light on the significance of the symbolic designs on the walls around the sarcophagus in Unas's pyramid by referring to texts that are placed on the same walls in later pyramids. This time it is not to Unas's successor Teti that we must turn, for the west wall of Teti's sarcophagus chamber is, like that of Unas, uninscribed. But in other pyramids this same west wall is covered with texts. A significant proportion of these texts is concerned with precisely the themes that are found in the opening between the triple sanctuary and the antechamber in Teti's pyramid: namely, the resuscitation, re-membering, and reclothing of the king as an awakened Osiris.[24] In the pyramid of Pepi I, for example, the king is repeatedly urged to raise himself, to gather up his bones, and to take his head. He is then given a garment to wear.[25] As the same sequence of texts also occurs on the same west walls of the sarcophagus chambers of Merenre and Pepi II, they provide a strong indication that the sarcophagus adjacent to them was the location of an Osirian rite of re-memberment.

Comparison of the west ends of the north and south walls of later pyramids with the decorated but uninscribed west ends of the Unas north and south walls is less easy, as in the

Figure 6.13. An example of the so-called palace-façade design that appears on the alabaster walls surrounding the sarcophagus. This design features a "double lotus" motif.

later pyramids they are badly damaged or lost. But a similar tendency to place the most esoteric texts—those concerned with initiatory rites of death and rebirth—in exactly the areas that are left uninscribed in the pyramid of Unas can be discerned in the pyramid of Pepi II—which has the most complete surviving texts of the later pyramids. Thus, at the west end of Pepi II's sarcophagus chamber north wall, there are a series of texts in which the Osirian king is mourned by Isis and Nephthys, who also reassemble his members, give him his heart, and aid his ascent to the sky.[26] The west end of the south wall is more difficult to interpret because of the fragmentary nature of the texts that remain, but the texts do include a clothing ritual and an ascent to the sky.[27] All of these considerations may lead us to conclude that in the highly sensitive space surrounding the sarcophagus, certain ritual events took place that were—in the pyramid of Unas—regarded as too delicate to reveal in words. But in later times, after the reign of King Teti, the immediate vicinity of the sarcophagus—especially the west wall—was freed from this stricture, and what was only implied by the symbolic designs in the Unas pyramid was now openly expressed in words. It is for this reason that the pyramid of Unas contains so little textual reference to the Osirian re-memberment: It was considered too delicate a matter to put into words.[28]

The walls around the sarcophagus in Unas's pyramid on which the designs are carved are polished alabaster, whereas all the other walls of the pyramid are limestone.[29] The stone used in the pyramid, as in all ancient Egyptian sacred buildings, served a symbolic or magical as well as a purely functional purpose. Alabaster is a soft, almost translucent rock created through pressure being exerted on a more or less fluid mix of limestone and mud, which then solidifies through compression. The Egyptian word used to refer to it (*shes*) had the connotation of something precious. Alabaster was also referred to simply as *ankh*, which means "life," and it is interesting that *ankh was* ("the sap of life") is one of the designations of milk. That alabaster was referred to as *ankh* may not simply be because of its milky color, but may also—as Schwaller de Lubicz has suggested—be due to the manner of its formation, which he compared to cream rising to the top of milk, an image that also evokes the idea of gross matter (mud) undergoing a purification.[30] The main alabaster quarry from the Fourth Dynasty on was located about twenty-five miles southeast of Tel el-Amarna and was, interestingly, known as Hatnub, or "house of gold." This phrase was also used to designate the sarcophagus chamber in royal tombs.[31] We have good cause to believe, then, that the reasons for using alabaster rather than limestone around the sarcophagus were largely symbolic—one might even say alchemical—for this stone was regarded as capable of supporting the transformative processes that occurred in the sarcophagus chamber around the sarcophagus.

In Unas's pyramid, the sarcophagus that the alabaster walls surround is made of black granite. Granite is an igneous rock originating from very deep under the earth's surface. There it exists in a molten state, before being thrust up from the depths and cooling as it rises to the surface. As it cools, it condenses into a very hard stone. Schwaller de Lubicz has argued that the Egyptian word for granite (*match*, var. *mat*) is phonetically related to another word *mat*, to which he ascribes the meaning "to dream, discover, imagine, conceive." The implication is that for the Egyptians, granite may have had some symbolic connection with achieving visionary insight.[32] Whether or not this was the case, the color black was symbolically important as the color not only of death but also of fertility, new life, and spiritual resurrection.[33] This may well be the reason why black granite was chosen as the material for Unas's sarcophagus.

The third and by far the largest component of the pyramid is limestone. Limestone is a sedimentary organic rock of saltwater origin, composed of millions upon millions of shells of tiny organisms that lived in the seas that used to cover Egypt. These shells piled up as sediment on the seabed and, mixed with other deposits of sandstone and flint, formed the white cliffs that line the Nile valley. The Egyptians simply called it the "white" or "bright" (*hedj*) stone. As well as its denoting ritual purity, this stone was associated with the metal silver, which was also referred to as *hedj*.[34] Whether the builders of the pyramid used alabaster and limestone with the specific intention that these materials would symbolize, or in some way correspond to, the metals gold and silver is impossible to say with certainty. But the way that the granite, alabaster, and limestone are used in the pyramid does suggest that their deployment was far from arbitrary.

Location of Texts

The walls of the pyramid of Unas are inscribed with 228 utterances. Because three of these are repeated several times, there are altogether 234 utterances in total. Of these, there are two utterances that do not restrict themselves to one wall but straddle two walls, and there are two utterances that are regarded each as a combination of two (utts. 220–21 and utts. 273–74). For these reasons, scholars sometimes appear to disagree about the exact number of utterances in the pyramid. It is now generally accepted that many of the utterances belong to larger units or sequences of text, but the utterance nevertheless remains the organic basis of the Pyramid Texts.[35] The texts are to be found in the sarcophagus chamber, in the antechamber, in the passage between the two chambers, and at the end of the entrance corridor nearest to the antechamber. Unlike a modern printed book that can be read more or less anywhere on the planet, the Pyramid Texts are wedded both to the chambers and to the walls on which they are inscribed. A north-wall sarcophagus-chamber text could not be transposed to the east wall of the antechamber without losing a whole dimension of significance. The texts that a wall hosts derive an important dimension of meaning from the chamber that they are in and from the orientation of the wall on which they are inscribed. Furthermore, between north- and south-wall texts and between west- and east-wall texts, there exists a powerful dynamic, and the same thing goes for other walls: Texts on one wall will often relate in significant ways to texts on walls opposite, adjacent to, or even on the reverse side of them, as we shall see.

The Sarcophagus Chamber

In the sarcophagus chamber, although there are no texts in the immediate vicinity of the sarcophagus, there are some eighteen utterances above the designs of the west wall, on the west gable (fig. 6.14a). These eighteen texts are mainly protective spells against snakes and relate to similar spells at the other end of the pyramid on the antechamber east wall. A further 118 texts are to be found on the north wall of the sarcophagus chamber (fig. 6.14b). These constitute the earliest known offering liturgy, consisting of five parts: rites of purification, the opening of the mouth, a preliminary presentation of offerings, anointing with the seven holy oils, and a final "offering feast" consisting of bread, beer, meat, fruit, and so on. The offering liturgy takes up over half of the total amount of utterances in the pyramid, but most of these north-wall utterances are very short.

After the west-gable and north-wall texts, there are only nineteen more texts in the sarcophagus chamber. These constitute two sequences: The first is a sequence of twelve texts from the south to the east wall, the second is a sequence of seven texts on the east gable. On the south wall (fig. 6.14c) opposite the offering texts of the north wall, the sequence of twelve begins with seven texts that describe a series of mystical experiences in which the spirit of "Osiris Unas" travels to the southern stars, where he undergoes purification and rebirth. It is emphasized that Unas is "not dead." These texts are continued on the east wall (fig. 6.14d), where the mystical union of the king with the sun god Ra occurs in a cosmic setting. As well as this cosmic union with the sun god, the texts are concerned with the coronation of the king as Horus with the red crown and the return of his spirit to physical embodiment. The "solarization" of the king through his mystical union with Ra would seem to be the prerequisite for his coronation as a living Horus. Above the east wall, on the gable (fig. 6.14e), seven more texts describe the spiritual nourishment of the king, who lives on food provided by the gods and is suckled by a heavenly milk goddess, for he has been spiritually reborn.

The sarcophagus-chamber texts of the north and south walls both begin at the west end and read from west to east, while the texts of the west gable read from north to south and those of the east wall and gable read in the opposite direction: from south to north. These directions have a symbolic import: The movement from west to east is especially significant because this symbolically corresponds to a movement from death to life, paralleling the daily journey of the sun god, who "dies" each evening in the west and is "reborn" the following morning in the east. Whereas the north-wall liturgy is self-contained, the west–east momentum of the south wall texts is continued onto the east wall, where it becomes a movement from south to north. Utterance 219, at the east end of the south wall, actually spills over onto the east wall at its southern end and has to be continued in a northerly direction. The significance of the south–north axis is that the south is the direction of the southern constellations, which change through the cycles of the year, whereas north is the direction of the "imperishable" northern stars, apparently immune to time and change. The south is also a direction, like the west, particularly associated with the Dwat.[36] Whereas in the east the king experiences solar rebirth, in the north he experiences stellar rebirth. The north, however, also retains an association with the west insofar as it also provided a point of access to the Dwat.[37]

On the walls of the passageway between the sarcophagus chamber and the antechamber are eight texts. In the three texts on the south wall (fig. 6.14f), Unas crosses the threshold to the stars and joins Nut, the sky goddess. The five texts on the north wall (fig. 6.14g) describe Unas going forth with his *ka*, or vital spirit, under the protection of Thoth. Like the texts of the sarcophagus chamber, these texts read from west to east, continuing the syntactic momentum from the sarcophagus chamber toward the antechamber.

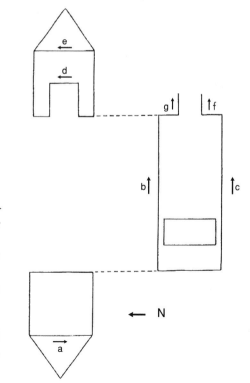

Figure 6.14. Diagram of the location of the texts on the walls of the sarcophagus chamber. The arrows indicate the direction in which the texts are to be read. (a) west gable: utts. 226–43; (b) north wall: utts. 23–57, 72–116, 117–71; (c) south wall: utts. 213–19; (d) east wall: utts. 219 (cont.)–224; (e) east gable: utts. 204–12; (f) passageway, south wall: utts. 244–46; (g) passageway, north wall: utts. 199, 32, 23, 25, 200.

The Antechamber

In the antechamber, there are altogether sixty-two texts. Beginning with the west gable, we find that the seven west gable texts (fig. 6.15a) are in fact thematically linked to the seven texts of the east gable of the sarcophagus chamber that they back onto. Not only do they share the same assumption that the king is newly born into the spiritual world, but each text can be seen to amplify the text to which it is juxtaposed on the other side of the wall. This is an example of what Schwaller de Lubicz termed "transposition," in which the complements of an idea given in one room are given on the other side of the wall in another room.[38] We shall return to discuss this practice in subsequent chapters. The same phenomenon can also be observed in the five utterances below the west gable, on the west wall (fig. 6.15b), which relate both thematically and spatially to the east-wall utterances of the sarcophagus chamber. Here the theme of the king overcoming death and moving from an Osiris consciousness to a Horus consciousness is linked to a second crowning, with the white crown. This is accompanied by another description of the king's mystical union with the sun god Ra.

These five west-wall texts constitute the first third of a fifteen-text sequence that is continued onto the south wall. Just as on the south wall of the sarcophagus chamber the most eastern text is continued onto the east wall, so in the antechamber the most southern text of the antechamber west wall is continued onto the south wall. This most southern text is utterance 260, just one vertical line of which is on the west wall, while all the rest is on the south wall. On the south wall of the antechamber (see fig. 6.15c), the dominant theme of the ten remaining texts is of the king's ascent to the sky and his crossing the Field of Rushes so that he may come before the gate of Nun, the ultimate source of existence. Opposite these south-wall texts, on the north wall (fig. 6.15d) are ten texts (with an eleventh very short text) that, although they read in the same direction as the south-wall texts (i.e., from west to east), are written with their hieroglyphs reversed. Normally, hieroglyphs "face" the direction in which they are to be read, but here they are all turned around—as if in an act of homage—so they face east, the direction of sunrise. These also treat of the king's ascent to the sky, his stellar rebirth, and his taking the form of a wild bull—symbolizing his fecundity and power—and journeying to the Akhet, the mystical place of inner illumination.

At the east end of the antechamber is the famous Cannibal Hymn on the east gable (fig. 6.15e), which has Unas absorbing the power of all the gods into himself as he ascends to the sky. The Cannibal Hymn comprises two utterances and is completed by a third in which the king opens the doors of the Akhet. The east gable also includes a spell against snakes, which means that altogether there are four utterances here. Beneath this, on the east wall, there is the entrance to the mysterious triple chamber (or *serdab*), which has no inscriptions or decoration. Around the entrance on the east wall of the antechamber (fig. 6.15f) are twenty-five utterances, most of which are protective spells against snakes, that echo those of the west gable of the sarcophagus chamber. This, as we shall see, is a further case of "transposition," in which texts of one wall complement those of another.

Finally, there are the texts on either side of the entrance corridor adjacent to the antechamber. These texts read from south to north—in other words, as if one were going out of the pyramid. On the west wall (fig. 6.15g),

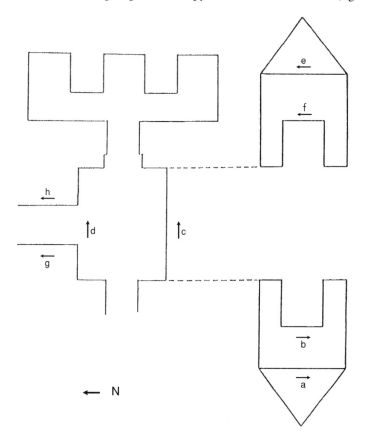

Figure 6.15. Diagram of the location of the texts on the walls of the antechamber. The arrows indicate the direction in which the texts are to be read. (a) west gable: utts. 247–53; (b) west wall: utts. 254–60; (c) south wall: utts. 260–72; (d) north wall: utts. 302–12; (e) east gable: utts. 273–76; (f) east wall: utts. 277–301; (g) entrance corridor, west wall: utts. 313–17; (h) entrance corridor, east wall: utts. 318–21.

in five texts Unas is identified with first Horus and then the crocodile god Sobek. He opens the doors to the sky, and he also gains power over water and the forces of fertility throughout the land. On the east wall (fig. 6.15h), in four texts Unas celebrates having achieved creative power over heaven and earth, he unites the two lands of Egypt, and he causes the plants to grow. The final utterance portrays Unas as the faithful companion of Ra.

A list of the utterances in the pyramid of Unas, their position, and a brief indication as to their content is given in appendix 1. One thing that even the short survey above shows is that while some texts clearly belong to a ritual (for example, the offering liturgy of the sarcophagus-chamber north wall) and some are magical spells (for example, the snake spells of the sarcophagus-chamber west gable and the antechamber east wall), in many texts we are being presented with descriptions of inner experiences. These experiences may of course have occurred within a ritual context, but the texts are clearly pointing to the existence of an experiential dimension that the king was assumed to engage with.

Second, we cannot fail to observe that these experiences are to a large extent cosmically located. There is a constantly reiterated theme of the king's ascent to the sky and of his becoming united there with powerful energies: the creative energy of the cosmic bull, the sky goddess who suckles him, and the radiant energy of the sun god Ra. A further observation can also be made: There is a recurrent theme of the king not only not being dead, but also being crowned as Horus-king of Egypt. Furthermore, while the setting for most of the utterances may be cosmic, there is also a strong earthy theme of the king's potency and his living and reigning over the Two Lands. The texts on the entrance corridor indicate that the king as a living Horus has gained power over the forces of fertility in the land of Egypt. Finally, it should be borne in mind that a considerable number of the texts in the pyramid of Unas retain the first-person form and were evidently meant to be spoken by the king himself, often in alternation with utterances spoken by the officiating priest.

All of these observations are compatible with a nonfunerary interpretation of the texts. Indeed, some of the texts would seem to positively require such a nonfunerary interpretation if we are to make sense of them. Nevertheless, most interpretative theories concerning the meaning and purpose of the Pyramid Texts have assumed that they are funerary texts. In the next section, we shall review some of the main theories that have been put forward regarding the interpretation of the Pyramid Texts.

The Interpretation of the Pyramid Texts

At the beginning of this chapter, we noted that the question of the "right order" in which to read the Pyramid Texts has received considerable attention from Egyptologists, as has the larger question of how the meaning of the texts should be interpreted. It is now time to review this literature, and we shall see how intertwined these two questions have been from the beginning of the many and varied attempts to interpret the Pyramid Texts. The first person to propose an order in which to read the texts was, as we have already seen, the German Egyptologist Kurt Sethe. Sethe was of the opinion that the texts begin in the sarcophagus chamber and end in the entrance passage. The reason why he held this opinion was that he viewed them as "transfiguration spells" (*Verklärungssprüche*) primarily for the king's use after death, to enable him to undergo the transition into life in the hereafter, the "coming forth by day." Rising from his sarcophagus, the resurrected king would make his way out of the pyramid-tomb, reading the texts inscribed on its walls on his way, and they would assist him in his transfiguration or spiritualization.[39] Because of the intrinsic magical power of the hieroglyphs, their presence within the pyramid freed the king from dependence on the funerary cult, making available to him what was essential for his inner transformation.[40] It seems that Sethe did not believe that the texts reflected the burial ritual as such, but regarded them as a loose collection of spells whose order was not determined by liturgical considerations.[41] In this respect Sethe differs from an influential group of later Egyptologists who sought to prove that the Pyramid Texts form the liturgical part of the burial ritual. We shall first consider the arguments of these Egyptologists, the most prominent of whom are Schott, Spiegel, and Altenmüller, before returning to consider the view favored by Sethe and others that the Pyramid Texts were for the use of the king after his death and express the beliefs of the Egyptians concerning his postmortem destiny. Finally, the rather different approach to be taken in this study will be outlined.

The Pyramid Texts Belong to the Burial Ritual

SIEGFRIED SCHOTT

The first person to put a detailed case for the texts being part of a ritual, and for this ritual determining not only their content but also their sequence, was Siegfried Schott. In his *Mythe und Mythenbildung im Alten Ägypten* (1945), Schott analyzed the Pyramid Texts into three different literary forms: the "dramatic texts" recited by the participants in a ritual drama, "hymns" that allude to the ritual drama but do not themselves represent actual dialogue, and "transfiguration spells" in which the scene of the ritual is the spirit world, about which the king himself speaks through the reciting priest. He speaks through the reciting priest because, for Schott, the king is of course dead and the ritual is his funerary rite.

Schott then set himself the task in *Bemerkungen zur Ägyptischen Pyramidenkult* (1950) of reconstructing as much of the Old Kingdom royal funerary ritual as he could, basing his reconstruction on passages in the Pyramid Texts that appear to be ritual instructions, allusions to ritualists and ritual implements, and semimythical localities within the texts. This task he undertook in collaboration with Herbert Ricke, who had specialized in the reconstruction of Fifth Dynasty pyramid temples. Just as Schott assumed the Pyramid Texts to be liturgical texts of the burial ritual, so Ricke understood the pyramid complex to be a "mortuary complex" dedicated to the funerary cult. On the assumption that the pyramid temples and causeways had been designed to serve different stages of the funerary ritual of the king, Schott put forward the idea that various parts of the pyramid complex were architecturally analogous to the various chambers within the pyramid. The valley temple corresponded to the vestibule, the causeway to the entrance corridor, the outer pyramid temple to the antechamber, and the inner pyramid temple to the sarcophagus chamber. By implication, the texts inscribed on the walls of the pyramid chambers would reflect the different stages of the funerary ceremonies conducted in the temples and causeway outside the pyramid and would reciprocally elucidate the function of the different parts of the funerary complex. Thus the ritual purpose of any given utterance could be deduced from its position in the pyramid, and equally the ritual function of any given part of the pyramid complex could be elucidated from the spells in the corresponding pyramid chamber.[42] Because Schott saw a direct relationship between texts and rituals, the order in which the texts should be read had to be the same as the most likely direction of the funerary procession through the pyramid complex, terminating in the inner pyramid temple, which corresponded to the sarcophagus chamber of the pyramid. Thus, far from reading the sarcophagus chamber texts first, as Sethe had supposed, Schott concluded that we ought really to read them last of all.[43]

Ingenious as it is, the trouble with Ricke and Schott's approach is that, in terms of methodological procedure, it starts out with a theory and then attempts to fit the various phenomena into it, rather than keeping faith with the phenomena and allowing the phenomena themselves to reveal their intrinsic meaning. First of all, it is by no means evident that the architectural features of the pyramid complex are reflected in the internal design of the pyramid. And the attempt to support this view by trying to show that Pyramid Texts in certain locations within the pyramid relate to rituals that were supposedly performed in locations outside the pyramid means that the texts are effectively press-ganged into serving a dubious hypothesis rather than being left free to speak with their own voice. Because the texts are required to reflect an assumed liturgical sequence, they are not allowed to hold other meanings or point to quite other experiential situations. It has been shown, furthermore, that there are so many examples of texts quite obviously not corresponding to the rites that they are supposed to correspond to that the whole enterprise is demonstrably unsupportable— not least because the location of utterances varies from pyramid to pyramid, whereas the overall architecture of the pyramid complex remains virtually unchanging.[44]

The view that the temples and causeway of the pyramid complex were designed to serve the different stages of the funerary ritual, from purification and embalming (valley temple) to funerary procession (causeway) and offering ritual (inner pyramid temple), is at best hypothetical and receives considerably less support today than it did fifty years ago. It has been challenged most notably by Dieter Arnold, who has argued that the burial rituals took place outside the pyramid complex, and that there was no funerary procession from the valley temple to the pyramid temple.[45] Arnold based his view on the methodological principle that the function of the pyramid complex should be determined not by referring to the texts concealed within the pyramid chambers but by examining the wall reliefs, statues, inscriptions, and architectural features of the complex itself, all of which refer remarkably little to funerary rites.[46] As we have seen, what they do consistently refer to are episodes of the Sed festival rather than funerary rituals. Even then it has to be accepted that there is no indication in the Pyramid Texts themselves as to exactly where their recitation was supposed to take place.

JOACHIM SPIEGEL

Despite these objections to Ricke and Schott, their attempt to pin the ordering of the texts to an actual order of ritual has been influential on subsequent interpretations of the Pyramid Texts. Accepting the difficulties of linking the texts to the stages of a supposed funerary ritual that took place in the architectural spaces of the pyramid complex, Joachim Spiegel has sought to show that the texts on the walls of the pyramid of Unas reflect burial rituals that took place solely in the internal chambers of the pyramid itself.[47] According to Spiegel, the placement of the texts reflects the sequence of the entry of the funerary procession into the pyramid, the celebration of burial rites, and a silent "resurrection ritual" performed on the king. Thus the texts are supposed to begin on the west wall of the entrance corridor, continue into and go around the sarcophagus chamber, and re-enter the antechamber on the south wall, ending on the east wall of the entrance corridor (fig. 6.16). This is of course a quite different order from that proposed by both Schott and Sethe.

For Spiegel, the chambers of the pyramid have a symbolic significance: The sarcophagus chamber represents the Dwat, and the antechamber the Akhet.[48] During the burial ceremonies in the sarcophagus chamber, the king's *ba* left his body to go through the Dwat (the sarcophagus chamber). There it was first united with Osiris and then changed itself from Osiris into Horus (reflected in the coronation ceremony on the sarcophagus-chamber east wall). It then traveled across the night sky, reaching the Akhet in the antechamber, and was finally received by Ra and Atum in the *serdab* (which symbolized Heliopolis), where the *ba* and *ka* statues were placed.[49] Spiegel believed that the burial and resurrection ritual occurred at night, beginning at sunset and continuing until sunrise, and took place on the last night of the waning moon. Thus in the final part of the ritual, the soul leaves the tomb altogether, and as it emerges it is greeted not only by the

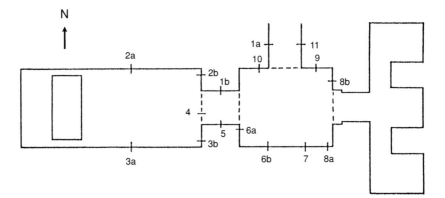

Figure 6.16. The order of utterances for rectitation in the pyramid of Unas, according to Joachim Spiegel: (1a) 317–13; (1b) 200, 25, 23, 32, 199; (2a) 23, 25, 32, 34–57, 72–79, 81–96, 108–71; (2b) 223–24; (3a) 213–19; (3b) 219; (4) 220–22; (5) 244–46; (6a) 256–58, 260; (6b) 260–63; (7) 267–71; (8a) 272; (8b) 300–301; (9) 302–6; (10) 307–12; (11) 318–21. The utterances of the silent ritual (not shown here) are: utts. 254–56 (antechamber west wall); 247–53 (antechamber west gable); 273–76 (antechamber east gable); and 277–99 (antechamber east wall).

dawn but also by the new crescent moon, which will act as its ferry across the heavens.[50]

Along with this spoken ritual, which is concerned primarily with the soul's union with the sun god, Spiegel believed there was a silent ritual that was celebrated simultaneously with the second part of the spoken ritual, beginning as the priests passed from the sarcophagus chamber into the antechamber.[51] This involved only the silent enactment of the rites, beginning with the smashing of the red vases in the passage between the two chambers. To this proposed silent ritual belong the antechamber west-wall and gable texts as well as the Cannibal Hymn (utts. 273–74) on the east gable of the antechamber, in which Spiegel understood the king to be claiming overlordship of the world in opposition to the sun god. The silent and spoken rituals represent Upper Egyptian and Lower Egyptian rituals, respectively, both of which would have been necessary for the complete royal funerary ritual.[52]

As with the theories of Schott and Ricke, it is difficult not to have the impression that Spiegel's reconstruction imposes an explanation on the texts, the meaning of which as a result becomes distorted. This becomes apparent when we encounter the same texts in quite different locations on the walls of other pyramids, where they obviously could not perform the ritual function that they are purported to perform in the pyramid of Unas.[53] Since it is central to Spiegel's approach that the texts on the walls of the pyramid of Unas reflect ceremonies that actually took place in the chambers themselves, are we to assume that the order of ceremonies changed in the other pyramids with each royal burial? Given the conservatism of the Egyptians in the matter of royal ceremonial, this seems unlikely, and we can only conclude that the arrangement of texts in the other pyramids fails to corroborate Spiegel's interpretation.[54] Furthermore, it may be questioned whether it is realistic to suppose that elaborate ceremonials such as coronation rites would have been performed in the limited confines of the sarcophagus chamber with a mere six officiants presiding.[55] As with the coronation rites, it is equally hard to imagine the offering ritual being performed in the sarcophagus chamber, with all those onions and cakes and joints of meat, jugs of beer, and vases overbrimming with wine. We only have to think of the difficulties of access to imagine how awkward it would have been to bring in all the items used in the offering ritual. And if, as seems likely, the ritual slaughter of a bull was an integral part of the funerary ceremonies, are we really to suppose that this enormous beast was somehow persuaded to enter the pyramid down the confined entrance corridor and then calmly allow itself to be slaughtered in the sarcophagus chamber without causing pandemonium? The more one thinks about it, the more implausible does Spiegel's idea seem that the inner chambers of the pyramid were the location of the long, complicated, and difficult rites.[56]

From a purely methodological standpoint, Spiegel's approach is vulnerable to the criticism that instead of beginning with the phenomena and allowing their intrinsic meaning to reveal itself, they are interpreted in accordance with a preconceived theory that already restricts their meaning within the straitjacket of a very particular conception of the royal funerary rituals to which they are supposed to correspond. The coronation texts on the east wall of the sarcophagus chamber are a case in point, for there is no indication in the texts themselves that they did in fact form any part of a funerary ritual. Yet for Spiegel, it is necessary to interpret them as part of the funerary rites because his theory demands that all the texts relate one way or another to them. No doubt his interpretation of these texts is, like that of Ricke and Schott, ingenious, but it fails to carry conviction because we have the sense that the texts are being forced to speak in a voice that is not their own. This forcing of the texts stems from the assumption that a satisfactory explanation must bring the whole collection under one overriding interpretative theory. But there are many texts that need more than simply tying into a supposed sequence of funerary rites if we are to make sense of them. The requirement that each text be fitted into this sequence puts an unbearable strain on the texts that cry out to be released from this kind of treatment.[57]

This is not to say that the texts in the Unas pyramid do not form a coherent unity, but if we are to find the key to their unity, we need to ensure that the texts, rather than our favorite theory, are both our starting point and constant reference point. We need also to accept the possibility that the texts may not form a coherent unity, and that we may understand them better if we desist from trying to turn them into one. The danger of attempting to relate the texts to the stages of the funerary ritual is that we assume they follow a kind of narrative sequence, whereas their positions in the pyramid may in fact be determined by other—for example, architectural and symbolic—principles.[58] In certain specific cases, such as the offering liturgy and the coronation texts, there can be little doubt that we are dealing with ritual texts, but as we shall see, these do not have to be understood as belonging to the funerary ritual. Furthermore, we should not assume that simply by exposing the possible ritual context of a given text, we have thereby uncovered its meaning. Even if we could posit in the case of each utterance the ritual, or phase of ritual, to which it corresponds, there still remains the dimension of inner experience that is the correlate of any ritual action. And this holds whether the king be regarded as dead or alive. As much as the utterances on the walls of the pyramids are seen as belonging in a ritual context, they need also to be understood as directed toward realms of spiritual experience.

HARTWIG ALTENMÜLLER

In comparison to Spiegel, the approach of Hartwig Altenmüller's *Die Texte zum Begräbnisritual in den Pyramiden des Alten Reiches* (1972) is only a little more promising. Although his starting point is a careful epigraphical analysis of the texts in the pyramid of Unas, and although he abandons Spiegel's assumption that these texts must reflect a ritual conducted inside the pyramid, Altenmüller is nevertheless convinced that the Unas texts as a whole reflect the stages of the royal funerary ritual, and that their meaning is explained only insofar as they can each be given their place within this ritual. Realizing that the utterances have not been inscribed consecutively but rather in several sections, Altenmüller—on the basis of a comparison with the later copy of the Unas texts in the Middle Kingdom tomb of Senwosret-Ankh—attempts to reconstruct a number of broad textual sequences. Three main sequences in the pyramid of Unas are isolated by him. The first comprises three parts: (1) the ritual for the funerary procession and actions on the mummy such as censing and opening the mouth (the sarcophagus chamber south and east wall as well as the antechamber north-wall utterances);[59] (2) the offering ritual (on the sarcophagus chamber north wall);[60] (3) the burial ritual on the west wall of the antechamber.[61] The second sequence is the ritual for the royal statue that is taken from the pyramid temple and placed within the pyramid (on the antechamber south wall and east gable);[62] the final sequence comprises spells to protect both the king in the afterlife and the whole sacred precinct of the pyramid (the snake spells at either end of the pyramid and the utterances on the walls of the entrance corridor).[63]

These sequences of texts in the pyramid of Unas are determined in part by the requirements of an order of ritual and in part by comparison with the later copy of the texts in the Middle Kingdom tomb of Senwosret-Ankh. The internal layout of the texts in the pyramid itself is in the end a secondary consideration. As much as we may feel relief that the obligations placed on the texts by Spiegel to conform to rituals supposedly performed within the pyramid chambers are removed by Altenmüller, we may also feel a certain unease that the texts are now being made to conform to other external criteria. While comparison of the Unas texts with the version in the tomb of Senwosret-Ankh may be helpful, we need to approach such a procedure with a good deal of caution, for the two versions do not corre-spond exactly; there is in fact considerable discrepancy between them. Reference to the versions in the other inscribed pyramids is surely just as important as reference to this much later and inexact copy of the Unas texts.[64] Altenmüller's proposed order in which the Unas texts are to be read is shown in figure 6.17. Here it can be seen that because Altenmüller based his order on the sequencing of the texts in the tomb of Senwosret-Ankh in tandem with his hypothesized order of royal funerary ritual, their coher-ence within the pyramid of Unas suffers. For example, Altenmüller's pro-posed funerary procession sequence straddles the south and east walls of the sarcophagus chamber and the south wall of the passage between the chambers and then leaps across to the north wall of the antechamber (the movement from *3* to *4* in fig. 6.17). From there we are supposed to return once more to the sarcophagus chamber and begin reading the texts on the north wall (see *5* in fig. 6.17). The placement of texts in the pyramid thereby appears to be completely haphazard and in terms of the architec-ture of the pyramid chambers seems to make little sense.

In order to support his interpretation of the Unas texts as burial ritual texts, Altenmüller argues that portrayals of the funerary ceremonies that appear on the walls of nonroyal Middle and New Kingdom tombs would have replicated the Old Kingdom royal funerary ritual and therefore pro-vide a guide to the interpretation of the Pyramid Texts. This must, how-

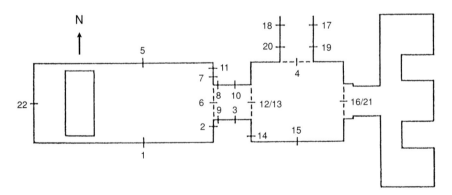

Figure 6.17. The order in which the utterances in the pyramid of Unas are to be read according to Altenmüller: (1) 213–19; (2) 219–22; (3) 245–46; (4) 302–12; (5) 23, 25, 34–42, 32, 43–57, 72–79, 81, 25, 82–96, 108–71; (6) 204–5, 207, 209–12; (7) 223; (8) 199; (9) 244; (10) 32, 23, 200; (11) 224; (12) 247–53; (13) 254–58; (14) 260; (15) 260–63, 267–76; (16) 273–76; (17) 321; (18) 317; (19) 318–20; (20) 313–16; (21) 277–301; (22) 226–43.

ever, remain largely conjectural since we simply do not have sufficient information on Old Kingdom royal funerary ceremonies to be able to reconstruct with any certainty the exact order of ritual.[65] Even were this conjecture correct, however, and we were to accept that these pictures illustrating the stages of the nonroyal funeral ritual of later times do in fact reflect the earlier royal funerary ritual, this still does not provide any guide to interpreting the Pyramid Texts unless we have already decided that they are burial texts. It is only because Altenmüller has already assumed that the Pyramid Texts are the texts of the royal funerary ritual that he looks for an exact correlation between these much later illustrations and the Old Kingdom texts. And so he attempts to explain every utterance in terms of some aspect of the illustrated funerary ritual, relying almost entirely on hazardous interpretations of mythological references and wordplay in the Pyramid Texts to determine which texts correspond to which pictures. Thus links are made between the utterance on the one hand and rituals, ritualists, implements, and mythologial localities on the other on the basis of little more than a series of unsupported presuppositions and a considerable amount of freewheeling speculation.

The weakness of Altenmüller's hermeneutical method is illustrated in his approach to the texts of the north wall of the antechamber, which are supposed to relate to the funerary procession. In utterance 304, we read of the king ascending to the sky on a ladder and being met there by the daughter of Anubis, an ostrich, the bull of Ra with four horns, and the personified Field of Offerings. According to Altenmüller, the daughter of Anubis should be interpreted as the embalming bed on which the mummy is placed; the ostrich is the sledge on which the *tekenu* (an enigmatic and much debated figure that appears in Middle and New Kingdom illustrations of the funerary ceremonies) is pulled; the bull of Ra with four horns represents the four canopic jars; and the Field of Offerings is the chest in which the Pyramid Text papyri are kept. Last but not least, the ladder on which Unas climbs up to the sky is not a ladder at all, but a funerary sledge with two ropes attached to its ends.[66] Through this methodological procedure, Altenmüller is able to resolve everything in the text into something else, in order that it be brought into conformity with the assumption that the north-wall texts belong to the funerary procession sequence as this is portrayed in the later Middle and New Kingdom private tombs. The fact is that direct connections between Pyramid Texts and the illustrations in later nonroyal tombs are extremely few and far between, as Altenmüller himself admits.[67] And even where we do find them, this does not allow us to assume that the text belongs to the ritual any more than a quotation

179

from the Bible or a favorite poem used in a funeral service today entitles us to view them as specifically designed for a funeral service. The appearance of the first lines of utterance 213, "O King, you have not departed dead, you have departed alive," in the tomb of Antefokar, vizier to the Twelfth Dynasty king Senwosret 1, is one of the extremely few examples that Altenmüller gives of a direct connection between text and illustration, for it appears just above a picture of the sarcophagus sledge in the funerary procession.[68] But does this single instance really permit us to conclude that utterance 213 pertained to this phase in the ceremonies or even that it was an exclusively funerary text? A similar excerpt from the beginning of utterance 252 appears in two quite different contexts in later tombs, thereby undermining the attempt to pin it to a particular episode in the funerary ceremonies.[69] In the case of utterance 213, we have only a single instance of its use in a later nonroyal Middle Kingdom tomb, but even if we met utterance 213 over and over again in exactly the same position, above the sarcophagus sledge in the funerary procession, in twenty nonroyal Middle Kingdom tombs, this would prove nothing concerning either its original existential significance in the Pyramid Texts or the ritual context in which this phrase was used in the royal rituals of the Old Kingdom. Neither these words nor the rituals to which they probably belonged have to be interpreted as exclusively funerary, and to assume that they should be on the basis of their adaptation to funerary rituals conducted several hundred years later is to risk missing altogether their original meaning.[70]

Schott, Spiegel, and Altenmüller all see the key to understanding the Pyramid Texts as lying outside the texts themselves. The key to understanding them lies in our ability to correlate the texts with the stages of the royal burial ritual. For Schott, the stages of the ritual are given in the architectural spaces of the pyramid complex. For Spiegel, because the burial ritual is envisaged as occurring within the inner chambers of the pyramid itself, the texts need to be read and interpreted in relation to its supposed phases in each of the chambers. For Altenmüller, the means by which we arrive at a correlation of text and burial ritual is discovered far from both pyramid and pyramid complex, in portrayals of the stages of a funerary ritual on the walls of distant Middle and New Kingdom nonroyal tombs. In none of these approaches are the texts in and of themselves seen as harboring their own inherent meaning. It is felt, rather, that in order to explain them, we must bring them into relationship with the funerary ritual: Only then will the texts make sense. The assumption common to all three approaches would appear to be that an explanation has been satisfactorily arrived at if we are able to explain one set of phenomena (the Pyramid Texts) in terms of another set of phenomena that are assumed to be related to the first set of phenomena (the funerary rites). It is supposed that by collating the first set of phenomena with the second, their meaning is then laid bare.

In chapter 5, a fundamentally different methodology was proposed. Essential to the phenomenological approach to understanding the Pyramid Texts is that it does not start by turning elsewhere for their elucidation, but assumes at the outset that the secret of their meaning lies in the texts themselves. The phenomenological approach attempts to keep faith with the phenomena, staying with them in order to comprehend them in their own depth. In the case of these ancient religious texts, their depth—the ground out of which they have arisen—is apprehended in the existential situations that the texts themselves describe. This is not to say that their possible ritual context is irrelevant. Far from it. But it is to say that merely to correlate the texts with different phases of the funerary, or any other, ritual does not in itself mean that we have understood them, for we have fallen short of apprehending their experiential and existential significance, which the texts themselves would reveal if only we opened ourselves to it.

The Pyramid Texts Reflect Beliefs about the Afterlife

WINFRIED BARTA AND OTHERS

Winfried Barta has shown that not only is it unlikely that the Pyramid Texts as a whole were "recitation texts" to be recited at different stages of the royal funerary ritual, but it is also extremely doubtful that they even belong to a funeral process at all.[71] In his book *Die Bedeutung der Pyramidentexte* (1981), Barta subjects the work of Schott, Spiegel, and Altenmüller to a withering critique, and argues that the purpose of the texts extended far beyond the short duration of the funeral ritual, and were meant to serve the king in the afterlife. The attempts of Schott, Spiegel, and Altenmüller to correlate the Pyramid Texts with funeral rites result in a misreading of their meaning, and we would do better to look elsewhere for the possible indications as to the liturgical content of the funeral ritual.[72] Barta thus frees the Pyramid Texts from the restrictions that they must necessarily suffer when forced to conform to the requirements of the funerary ritual, and they are once more able to breathe again. Their overall purpose is, according to him, to assist the king in the process of his divinization, providing essential knowledge and also magic power to the king in the afterlife.[73] For Barta, however, there is no question that the

181

realm of the dead might be accessible to the king while he is still living. The Pyramid Texts, though they may not be funerary texts, are nevertheless designed for the king's postmortem use: They are not yet mystical texts.

In holding this view, Barta returns to the more open attitude of Sethe, who also saw the Pyramid Texts as essentially "transfiguration texts" not specifically tied to the funeral ritual, but serving to aid the king in his spiritualization in the afterlife. It has to be said that, not only for Sethe but also for subsequent translators of the Pyramid Texts, the idea that they are all part of the funerary liturgy has seemed too narrow an interpretation. For Faulkner, the Pyramid Texts should be regarded not only as funerary literature but also, more broadly, as religious literature.[74] He believed that they are part of the "star-religion" of ancient Egypt, for they describe the king's postmortem journey to the stars, and his transformation into a star, indicative of his spiritualization.[75] For Mercer, who like Faulkner made a complete translation of all the Pyramid Texts, only the offering liturgy (on the north wall of the sarcophagus chamber of the pyramid of Unas) belongs to the funerary ritual. The other texts include magical and mythical formulas, hymns, prayers, and petitions, the purpose of which was "to guarantee the deceased king's resurrection and new birth, his transfiguration and divinity, his successful journey to heaven, and his immortality there with the other gods."[76] In this respect, although the king may be dead, for Mercer he is at least undergoing various spiritual experiences, and thus an existential meaning to the texts is acknowledged.

ALEXANDRE PIANKOFF

Similarly for Piankoff, who also translated the texts of the pyramid of Unas, these texts describe a journey of spiritual transformation that the king undergoes. For Piankoff, this journey entails the initial rebirth of the king from the primeval waters, his ascent to heaven, his traveling in the sun boat, his absorbing the substance of the gods, and his final exaltation as he is enfolded in the embrace of Atum.[77] The texts thus describe a postmortem mystical journey that culminates in a (postmortem) mystic union with the godhead, Atum. The sequence of this mystical journey determines the order in which the texts should be read, which, according to Piankoff, is the reverse order to that envisaged by Sethe and corresponds (but for quite different reasons) to the order proposed by Schott.[78] Piankoff argues that we should begin reading the texts in the corridor leading into the pyramid, for it is there that the king rises up from the primeval waters in the form of the crocodile god Sobek. In the antechamber, he ascends to heaven, where he meets various deities, and in the sarcophagus chamber he is divinized and

Ra-Atum takes him into his arms.[79] Thus the texts in the pyramid of Unas, if read in this way, provide a coherent narrative that is in accord with later New Kingdom royal texts that similarly deal with the different stages of the rebirth and spiritualization of the dead king.[80]

However, in seeking to interpret the texts as a continuous narrative, Piankoff—despite his lack of interest in pursuing the possible ritual accompaniments of the texts—could be said to have succumbed to a similar temptation to that of Schott, Spiegel, and Altenmüller. In both cases, an explanation of the texts is felt to have been arrived at once they are seen as belonging together as a whole and, as it were, "telling a story." But we need to be aware that the actual placement of the texts in the pyramid can also be understood from the perspective of the architectural symbolism implicit in the orientation of the chambers and the walls on which the texts are inscribed. And it is this that may determine their position in the pyramid as much as their following a narrative sequence. Indeed, it may be more appropriate to assume that the texts do not form a unity at all, but rather constitute a diversity of discrete units, albeit united by certain themes, but nevertheless more like an anthology of poems or prayers than either a narrative description of a mystical journey or as forming a liturgical sequence for the funerary rites.[81]

JÜRGEN OSING AND JAMES P. ALLEN

The approach to the Pyramid Texts that sees them more as an anthology of discrete units has been taken by Jürgen Osing and James P. Allen. Like Altenmüller, both Osing and Allen draw extensively on the Middle Kingdom copy of the Unas texts in the tomb of Senwosret-Ankh at Lisht in order to arrive at their own reading of the texts in the pyramid of Unas itself. But in contrast to Altenmüller, Osing and Allen argue that the order in which the texts are to be read is determined not by reference to hypothesized stages of a funeral ritual, but by the thematic relationship of the texts to the architectural symbolism of the two chambers of the pyramid.[82] The link between the texts and the internal architecture of the pyramid, which had been disrupted by Altenmüller, is thereby restored.

For Allen, the layout of the texts in the pyramid of Unas reflects the king's journey from death to new life, and to this extent they could be said to fall into a narrative sequence as they do for Piankoff. Just as the sun dies in the west, unites with Osiris in the Dwat, and is born again in the east, so—according to Allen—the texts should be read from the western sarcophagus chamber to the eastern antechamber, ending in the entrance corridor, where the king rises from the Akhet into the sky at dawn. This, of

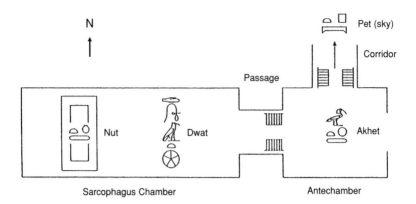

Figure 6.18. The layout of the texts in the pyramid of Unas, according to Allen, reflects the cosmology of the solar passage from west to east, night to day, and death to rebirth. Thus the western sarcophagus chamber corresponds to the Dwat, where the king's ba emerges from the sarcophagus (symbolizing the goddess Nut) and then travels to the antechamber, which corresponds to the Akhet, or place of solar rebirth. In the entrance corridor, the king rises from the Akhet into the sky at dawn.

course, is the reverse order to that proposed by Piankoff! But for Allen, who takes up Spiegel's interpretation of the sarcophagus chamber as representing the Dwat and the antechamber as representing the Akhet, or place of solar rebirth, the positioning of the units and sequences of text is determined by the symbolic meaning of the chambers, and it is for this reason that the utterances are seen by him to move in the opposite direction (fig. 6.18).[83] For both Piankoff and Allen, there can be little doubt that the texts on the walls of the two chambers and the entrance corridor reflect the process of the king's spiritual rebirth and inner transformation. But it is indicative of the inherent difficulty of interpreting these texts that two scholars, both of whom have freed themselves from the assumption that the texts have to reflect the stages of the burial ritual, should nevertheless still come up with such divergent views concerning the order in which they should be read. This in itself is enough to make us question whether the texts do in fact neatly divide themselves up thematically between the two chambers. As we shall see, despite the importance of the work of Osing and Allen in uncovering plausible sequences of texts, whether it is possible to arrive at an interpretation that convincingly shows the texts to form a coherent unity that "tells a story" with a beginning and an end remains an open question.[84]

Suspending the Funerary Presupposition

Leaving open the question of whether the texts tell a story, in the following chapters the utterances in the pyramid of Unas will be studied as far as possible from a phenomenological standpoint. Where this approach differs from all of those that we have just reviewed is that, first, it suspends the presupposition that these texts are necessarily funerary texts connected to a funerary ritual or to funerary beliefs concerning the postmortem experiences of the king in the afterlife. This radical suspension of a presupposition that has profoundly influenced all previous Egyptological analyses of the Pyramid Texts may, hopefully, serve to liberate a level of meaning in the Pyramid Texts that has hitherto gone unnoticed or else been simply ignored.[85] Second, the approach pursued in the present study will differ from previous approaches insofar as it is neither intended as a commentary on the Pyramid Texts, nor does it attempt a systematic interpretation of the texts in order to prove a particular theory, preconceived or otherwise. The aim is rather to allow, as far as possible, the texts to speak for themselves, so that the way we come to view their content is informed by what the texts themselves reveal regarding the existential situations they describe. It is these existential situations that provide the key to the deeper meaning of the Pyramid Texts. This is not to deny that much light may be thrown on the texts through uncovering the possible ritual contexts in which many of them undoubtedly belonged, but we should not forget that the rituals themselves were designed to accompany and to promote certain experiences.[86] It is in these inner experiences that the meaning of the texts resides, and it is therefore this experiential basis of the Pyramid Texts that we shall attempt to uncover in the following pages.

7 THE SARCOPHAGUS CHAMBER TEXTS

The North-Wall Offering Liturgy

The texts on the north wall of the sarcophagus chamber of the pyramid of Unas are a liturgy of offerings, usually thought of solely in funerary terms. Certainly the north-wall liturgy reflects the stages of an elaborate ceremony, but whether this ceremony was employed only in the funerary rites for the dead king or whether it also served the symbolic purpose of preparing the living king for a profound initiatory experience is less a matter of established fact than of interpretation. Lists of offerings do in general belong in a funerary context, and were common in tombs of the Fourth Dynasty.[1] On the north wall of the sarcophagus chamber, however, we have more than simply a list of food offerings: We have the earliest known form of a complete liturgy that was used again on the north walls of the Sixth Dynasty pyramids and in later tombs.[2] We have already seen that although a text may be placed in a tomb, this fact alone does not necessarily mean that its purpose was exclusively funerary. We have also seen that the presentation of offerings to the king was an important ritual component both in coronation ceremonies, such as we find described in the Ramesseum Dramatic Papyrus, and in ceremonies concerned with the renewal of the kingship, such as the Sed festival. In both cases the king underwent certain rituals that brought him into proximity with the realm of the dead while he was himself alive. In the case of the north-wall texts of the pyramid of Unas, we do not know all the circumstances in which such a liturgy was employed. Even though the Unas offering texts were duplicated in later tombs, we should bear in mind that if the experiences of initiation were regarded as approximating the experiences of physical death, then texts employed in rites of initiation would be similar in many respects to funerary texts. That this was indeed the case has been one of the main arguments pursued in part 1.

The north-wall liturgy comprises 118 utterances distributed over three registers (see fig. 7.1) and is divided into five parts.

THE TOP REGISTER

part 1: purification (utts. 23, 25, 32, 34, 35 and 36)

part 2: opening of the mouth (utts. 37–42)

part 3: transitional purification text (utt. 32) and preliminary presentation of offerings (utts. 43–57)

THE MIDDLE REGISTER

part 4: anointing with the seven holy oils (utts. 72–78) and adorning with eye paint and linen (utts. 79 and 81)

part 5: transitional purification texts (utts. 25 and 32) and beginning of the offering feast (utts. 82–96 and 108–16)

THE BOTTOM REGISTER

balance of part 5: conclusion of the offering feast (utts. 117–71)

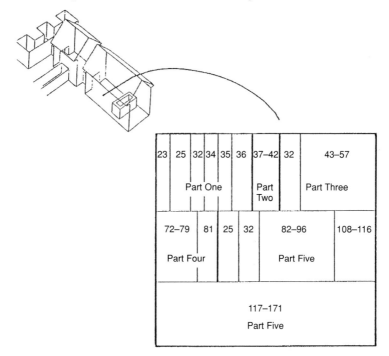

Figure 7.1. The Offering Liturgy on the north wall of the sarcophagus chamber of the pyramid of Unas is in five distinct parts distributed over three registers. The numbers refer to the utterances.

Each part of the Offering Liturgy was accompanied by certain ritual acts whose purpose it was to help the soul journey into the spirit world, while at the same time promoting a beneficial relationship between the soul as it is spiritualized and the realm of the living. What is preserved on the walls are the words spoken to accompany the performance of the rites, beginning at the west end of the wall and working eastward.

Part 1: Purification (Utts. 23, 25, 32, 34–36)

The ceremonies begin with a series of six purification rituals, four using water (utts. 23, 32, 34, and 35) and two employing fire through the burning of incense (utts. 25 and 36). The most important of these are utterances 25 (incense) and 32 (libation), both of which occur later on as markers of crucial stages of transition as the ceremonies proceed. Utterance 25 is a censing rit-

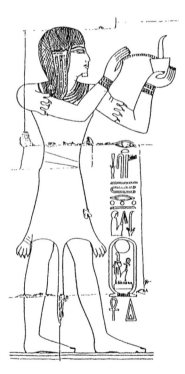

ual. It took place immediately after a preliminary cleansing ritual (utt. 23) involving water being sprinkled, probably over the king's head.[3] The censing described in utterance 25 that followed this purification by water was meant magically to bring about a union of the king with the royal *ka*, which was the bearer of the king's divinity. Thus through the censing rite, the king became inwardly divinized.[4] Thereby he could go forth with his *ka*, just as do the gods, with freedom to move in any direction he wanted. In the text, his *ka* travels accompanied by the gods of the four cardinal directions: Horus (north), Seth (south), Thoth (west), and Dunanwy (east). We shall return to the incense rite when we come to the texts on the north wall of the passage between the sarcophagus chamber and the antechamber. Here it is sufficient to note that censing was a ceremony performed not only on dead kings, but also on living ones at their coronation.[5] There is therefore no compelling reason to assume an exclusively funerary context for this rite (fig. 7.2).

Figure 7.2. A sem priest performs the incense rite. In utterance 25, this is to enable Unas "to go forth with his ka." New Kingdom relief, from the temple of Seti I, Abydos.

Utterance 32 follows immediately. It is a libation text in which natron-infused water is poured over the king's feet so that his heart becomes "cool." For the Egyptians this "cool water" had a heavenly origin. Its source was the Nun, mythologically the birthplace of Ra. In this utterance, it is also described as having issued from Osiris, so it has both the cosmic creative properties of the Nun and the renewing properties of Osiris, god of regeneration. As such, the libation has a baptismal significance, effecting the rebirth of "Osiris Unas" as a newborn Horus.[6] The water is said literally to be poured "under the sandals" of the king, a ritual that formed a significant part of the Sed festival ceremonies. As with the censing of the king, the pouring of the libation is not necessarily a funerary ritual. In figure 7.3, the jar of water that is poured under the sandals of King Niuserre is held by a *smer* priest, behind whom stands a *kheri heb* priest, both of whom usually preside over funerary rites. Here, however, the king is alive and the event is his Sed festival.

After the pouring of water under the sandals of the king, there are three further purificatory rites, two using water infused with natron (utts. 34–35)

Figure 7.3. A libation is poured "under the sandals" of King Niuserre as part of the Sed festival ceremonies. The liturgy on the north wall of the sarcophagus chamber of the pyramid of Unas describes a similar purificatory rite.

and the last one using incense (utt. 36). This final rite once again concentrates on the king's *ka*, freeing it to travel like a god in any direction it pleases.

Part 2: Opening of the Mouth (Utts. 37–42)

After this initial set of rituals, there are six texts for the rite of Opening of the Mouth (utts. 37–42), which together make up the second part of the liturgy.[7] The mouth is split open using an instrument called a *peseshkef*, illustrated in figure 7.4. The word *peseshkef* is composed of two parts: *pesesh* implies division and refers to either the shape or the function of the instrument (possibly both), while *kef* refers to the material out of which it was made—flint. Hence its name means "the divided (or dividing) instrument *(pesesh)* of flint *(kef)*".[8] Its exact purpose has been the subject of intense debate, but it was most probably used in midwifery to cut the umbilical cord. Its employment here would thus be to ritually confirm the king's rebirth and ensure his transition into a new life. According to the text, it is wielded both by Horus and Seth (utts. 37–38), and Seth's involvement may well be in his role of "demonic initiator," who severs one from one's past identity.[9] In the illustration, it is held by a *sem* priest wearing the ritual leopard-skin garment.

Figure 7.4. Opening of the Mouth with the peseshkef *instrument. From the tomb of Pet-Amen-Apet, Twenty-sixth Dynasty.*

Although it is usually thought of as being conducted on a dead person, to enable him or her to partake in funerary offerings, the Opening of the Mouth rite was essentially involved with opening a channel between the spirit world and the physical world. This is why it was used magically to animate statues of the gods or equally the *ka* statues of human beings. When performed on the dead, the Opening of the Mouth rite was supposed not just to enable them to partake in the offerings given to them in the physical world; it also had the effect of awakening them to the reality of the spirit world. Thus in the pyramid of Pepi II, it is stated that through the rite the king "goes and himself speaks with the Great Ennead [of the gods]."[10] It is therefore not hard to see how the rite could, under certain special circumstances, have been used not only on the dead but also on the living. Such special circumstances may well have included "near-death" initiatory rituals like the Sed festival "secret rites," which, significantly, were attended by both a *sem* priest and a priest called "the opener of the mouth."[11]

In the Unas liturgy, the two utterances that conclude the Opening of the Mouth rite (utts. 41–42) indicate that the nourishment to be ingested by the "reborn" king is divine in origin—it is milk from the nipples of Isis or Horus. The suckling of kings by goddesses is a common theme in Old Kingdom as well as much later reliefs depicting kingship ceremonies. Thus, for example, at the temple of Seti I at Abydos there are reliefs depicting various stages of the coronation and investiture of the king in which he is first "baptized" by having a libation poured over him and is then suckled by the goddess Hathor (fig. 7.5).

Figure 7.5. Seti I is suckled by Hathor following his baptism and symbolic rebirth as part of the coronation rites. In the Offering Liturgy of the pyramid of Unas, the offering of milk from the nipples of Isis or Horus to the king may similarly belong to coronation rather than funerary rites. Temple of Abydos.

Something similar is depicted at Luxor temple, where the ceremony of rejuvenating the royal *ka* was held annually.[12] As suckling scenes were depicted alongside Sed festival reliefs in Pepi II's pyramid temple, it is very likely that this also formed part of the Sed festival rites (see fig. 4.22).[13]

In each case the divine suckling of the king symbolizes the mythological reality of his spiritual rebirth. One of the earliest representations of the Egyptian king being suckled is, significantly, a fragment from a relief carving found at the temple adjoining the pyramid of Unas, which portrays him drinking from the nipple of a goddess, possibly Iat (see fig. 7.28). That the theme of rebirth was central to such ceremonies as the coronation of the king, the rejuvenation of the royal *ka*, and the Sed festival suggests that the context in which it appears in the Pyramid Texts is unlikely to be simply funerary.[14] Whether the king was literally suckled is a question that must remain open. In figure 7.6, from the much later tomb of Pet-Amen-Apet, which reproduces the Unas Offering Liturgy, the offering of milk is given in vases.

Part 3: Preliminary Presentation of Offerings (Utts. 32, 43–57)

After the Opening of the Mouth and the "divine suckling," the water purification of utterance 32 is repeated. This marks the beginning of the third phase of the liturgy, which consists of a preliminary presentation of fourteen different "adult" food offerings, which the newborn king can now graduate to.[15] The first seven (utts. 43–49) include wine, beer, bread, and garlic. These having been presented, the *ka* of Unas is now identified with Ra, while the offering table itself is brought in (utt. 50). Then a further seven offerings of cake, meat, beer, and wine are given (utts. 51–57). It is here that we meet the formula that generally

Figure 7.6. The offering of milk in vases. Vignette illustrating utterance 42 from the tomb of Pet-Amen-Apet. Twenty-sixth Dynasty.

precedes the presentation of an offering: "O King, take the Eye of Horus." The symbolism of the presentation of the Eye of Horus derives from the mythological episode in which Seth tears out the eye in their battle for supremacy over Egypt. The loss of the eye constitutes a loss of spiritual vision that it is essential to restore if the king is to be fit to rule the country.

Some light can be shed on the significance of this preliminary presentation of offerings by referring once more to the Ramesseum Dramatic Papyrus. As we have seen in chapter 3, the papyrus dates from the Middle Kingdom, but contains elements that were already old at the time the Pyramid Texts were written. It details a sequence of rituals that were performed either shortly after the accession of each king of Egypt or quite possibly in connection with the Sed festival.[16] The papyrus describes a series of ritual "scenes" leading to the coronation of the Horus-king and his union with his "father" Osiris through the *qeni* garment ritual. Whether the king literally united with his dead predecessor or whether he went through a mystical experience of "dying to be reborn" remains a question of interpretation. But in the overall scheme of the drama, the king's coronation was preceded by seven ritual scenes in which the produce of the land was brought to the king in order to prepare him for his coronation. Each item, whether it was produce from animals (such as meat and milk), produce from plants (such as bread, wine, and the wood used to make furniture), or produce from the mineral kingdom (such as precious stones and metals), was presented to the king as an "Eye of Horus." In other words, the presentation of offerings had the effect of equipping the king with the means of overcoming the spiritual blindness inflicted upon him by Seth. After the presentation of offerings, the king ate a ritual meal, called a *hetep* meal (i.e., an "offering" meal), which, along with the coronation rite, empowered him to proceed with the arduous rites that were to follow—namely, his mystical conjunction with the god Osiris.

An exact parallel to the Ramesseum Dramatic Papyrus sequence of rites can be seen in the Sed festival ceremonies. Just as at the heart of the Ramesseum Dramatic Papyrus rituals there was the mystical union of the king with Osiris through the *qeni* garment episode, so at the heart of the Sed festival there were the "secret rites" that also seem to have involved the *qeni* garment.[17] These secret rites were likewise preceded by the king eating a sacred meal (in the Hall of Eating) and a coronation ceremony that served to empower the king before he underwent the main rite of death and

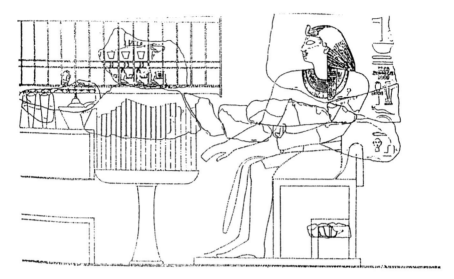

Figure 7.7. Pepi II sits on a throne before a table of offerings. From a relief in the sanctuary of his pyramid temple at Saqqara.

rebirth.[18] Figure 7.7, from the pyramid temple of Pepi II, shows the king sitting before a table of offerings. While scenes such as this are usually interpreted as funerary, there is no compelling reason why it could not be seen as portraying the living king eating a sacred meal prior to undergoing the "secret rites" at the core of the Sed festival.

In the later pyramids of Pepi II, Neith, and Ibi, the preliminary presentation of offerings includes the additional presentation of weapons, garments, and royal insignia, which presumably all had the same purpose: ritually to empower the king (or queen, in the case of Neith).[19] Utterances that require the king to take hold of weapons, to put on garments, and to grasp scepters and sacred staffs seem to indicate a ritual far closer to the Ramesseum Dramatic Papyrus than to any mummification rite. We know from the Ramesseum Dramatic Papyrus as well as from Sed festival texts that equipping the king with "power objects," and the offering and ingesting of symbolically charged food, was a crucial part of the rituals.[20] In both the Ramesseum Dramatic Papyrus ceremonies and those of the Sed festival, there was a concluding "great feast," a fact that is also reflected in part 5 of the Pyramid Texts Offering Liturgy. It is therefore essential that we free ourselves from the notion that the offering texts that we meet in the pyramids are necessarily describing funerary offerings. They actually make as much, or rather more, sense if we read them as part of a ritual, the focus of which was on the living king.

Part 4: Anointing with the Seven Holy Oils (Utts. 72–78, 79, 81)

The fourth ceremony in the Unas liturgy begins at the west end of the second register (see fig. 7.1). It is the anointing with the seven holy oils (utts. 72–78), which have the effect on the mythological plane of "filling the Eye of Horus" (utt. 72). As we have seen, mythologically the Eye of Horus is torn out by Seth in their battle for supremacy over Egypt. This act plunges the night sky into darkness, for the Eye of Horus, cosmically understood, is the moon—the heavenly body that illumines the night. It is Thoth who finds the eye shattered into fragments and, having reassembled them, causes the moon to reappear after its short period of invisibility. In so doing, Thoth restores harmony and wholeness both macrocosmically and microcosmically.[21] On the microcosmic level the restoration of the eye signifies the consolidation of spiritual power in the king.

Through the application of the seven holy oils, then, the Eye of Horus is filled. This is the mythic event that is activated by the application of the holy oils. In utterance 77, we read that through the anointing, the king becomes an *akh* ("shining spirit"), with *sekhem* ("power") in his body. The word for "body" here is *djet*—the living body rather than the corpse. In this

Figure 7.8. The seven holy oils. From right to left, setch-heb *perfume (festival perfume);* hekenu *oil;* sefetch *oil (or sesefetch, in utt. 74);* nekhenem *oil;* tua *oil;* hat-ash *oil (cedar oil); and* hat-tchehennu *oil (Libyan oil). Tomb of Pet-Amen-Apet.*

195

utterance, the king is addressed as Horus, the living king, and the text is concerned with his attainment of both spiritual and physical power. In the other holy oil utterances (utts. 72–76 and utt. 78), the king is addressed as Osiris, but it is important to bear in mind that the king's identification with Osiris may have been only temporary. In the Sed festival "secret rites" of Niuserre, for instance, during which the living king underwent an Osiris identification, we know that *sesefetch* oil (referred to in utt. 74) was used.[22]

The oils that were offered were composed of many different substances mingled together.[23] Their names are descriptive of their healing properties rather than indicative of their composition. Thus the *sesefetch* oil of utterance 74 could be translated as "soothing oil," and was offered with the words:

Osiris Unas, accept the Eye of Horus on account of which he [i.e., Horus] suffered.

The *nekhenem* oil of utterance 75 had protective properties. It could be translated as "keeping safe oil" and was offered with the words:

Osiris Unas, accept the Eye of Horus that he [possibly Thoth] has kept safe.

There is here a paronomasia, or play on words, between the verb used at the end of the sentence (*khenem*) and the name of the oil (*nekhenem* oil). This paronomasia is to be found in several other of the holy oil texts and we shall meet it again in later utterances, where it has the effect of magically enhancing the efficacy of the ritual act.

After the holy oils, linen is offered (fig. 7.9). The offering of the rolls of linen in utterance 81 has the symbolic significance of clothing the king as a resurrected Osiris. The cloth is provided by the cloth goddess Tayet, who has here the role of Isis, mythologically "weaving" the dismembered parts of the body of Osiris together

Figure 7.9. The offering of linen cloth. The "clothing" of the king symbolized his re-memberment after the Osirian dis- memberment. Tomb of Pet-Amen-Apet.

again, thereby making him whole.[24] The clothing of Osiris could be regarded as the feminine counterpart to the filling of the Eye of Horus. It marks the successful accomplishment of the Osirian process of reconstitution after the dismemberment.[25] Thus this stage of the liturgy would seem to correspond to the phase in the Osirian rites when the king is awakened. We know that in the Sed festival "secret rites" of Niuserre, linen cloth was offered to the king, so once again the context of this offering is not necessarily funerary.[26]

Part 5: The Feast (Utts. 25 and 32, 82–96, 108–71)

The transition from the fourth to the final part of the liturgy is marked by the repetition of the two purification rites involving fire and water (utts. 25 and 32). The final part of the liturgy has to do entirely with the great feast. In the Ramesseum Dramatic Papyrus, a great feast was celebrated after the king had successfully undergone a most important "rite of passage" that concluded with his being symbolically reborn.[27] Similarly, at the end of the Sed festival, an immense public feast traditionally was held. The reliefs in the sun temple of Niuserre, who, like Unas, reigned during the Fifth Dynasty, refer to 30,000 meals being provided at the Sed festival of the king.[28] Surviving relief fragments from the pyramid temple of Unas that show offering bearers carrying trays of produce may well be portraying preparations for the public feast at the end of his Sed festival, rather than funerary offerings for the dead king (see figs. 6.8 and 7.10). The pattern of a banquet being held after the successful accomplishment of the most demanding rituals involving the renewal of the kingship can be observed in other kingship festivals, both in Egypt and in neighboring Mesopotamia. At the New Year festival of Niuserre,

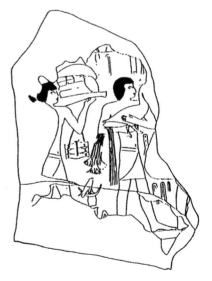

Figure 7.10. Part of a procession of offering bearers: The one on the left carries a tray of food; the one on the right carries a duck and some lotus flowers. From a limestone fragment in the pyramid temple of Unas.

for example, more than 100,000 meals were served.[29] The equivalent festival in Mesopotamia, the Akitil, also concluded with a great feast, following the successful liberation of the god Marduk from the "house of bondage."[30] It is possible therefore that this last part of the offering liturgy took place during the final stages of the Sed festival ceremonies. Certainly the traditions of a great feast serve to remind us once more that the offering and consumption of food did not occur in an exclusively funerary context.

In the Offering Liturgy of the north wall, any public aspect of the banquet is ignored. The focus is entirely on the ritual presentation of food to the king. The banquet commences with Thoth bringing the table of offerings before the king, as an "Eye of Horus" (utt. 82). Then come fourteen utterances, each preceded by the formula "Osiris Unas, take the Eye of Horus," followed by the name of the particular offering presented—cake, bread, beer, and so on (utts. 83–96). After this there is another purification of the king, this time with water and natron (utts. 108–9), then a further fourteen offerings of bread and cakes (utts. 110–23). The number fourteen has both lunar and Osirian significance, since it corresponds both to the cycle of the moon and to the mythological fact that Osiris was cut into fourteen pieces by Seth. It is as if in this first part of the great feast, the full cycle of the death and rebirth of both moon and Osiris is ritually enacted.

After this there are twelve utterances, all of which are meat offerings, save the second, which is of onions (utts. 124–35). As twelve is a number related to the solar cycle (the twelve hours of the day and the twelve hours of the night), it would appear that the great offering feast up to this point occurred against a cosmic backdrop of lunar and solar symbolism. Beyond this point, however, it is less easy to be sure of significant numerological correspondences. The twelve meat offerings are followed by five birds (utts. 136–40) and four more offerings of bread and cakes (utts. 141–44). These are followed by seven drink offerings (mostly different kinds of beer), each of two bowls, making fourteen bowls altogether (utts. 145–51). Then come figs (utt. 152), five different wine offerings (utts. 153–57), two offerings of bread (utts. 158–9), and again seven offerings of two bowls each of fruit and grain (utts. 160–66). The final five offerings are two bowls each of beans, beer, sweets, and so on (utts. 167–71).

If, as seems likely, the Offering Liturgy was not simply a "funerary" ritual but was also performed on and by the living king, then the offering of food in this final part of the liturgy can be understood as a feast celebrating the spiritual awakening of the king. Just as the moon dies for fourteen days and then returns to life again in the next fourteen days, and the sun journeys through the Underworld during the twelve hours of the night and

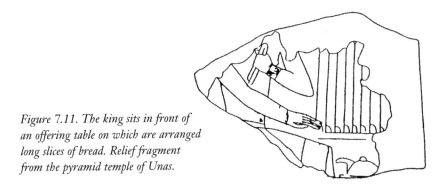

Figure 7.11. The king sits in front of an offering table on which are arranged long slices of bread. Relief fragment from the pyramid temple of Unas.

is then reborn in the morning to travel through the twelve hours of the day, so too does the king die and return to life. The great feast that forms the final part of the Offering Liturgy was a celebration of the king's return to life, and it was precisely this that occasioned the public festivities that in all likelihood accompanied this phase of the liturgy.

There is, in fact, a text on the east wall of the sarcophagus chamber that gives every indication that it is the living king who consumes the offerings, for the text begins with the officiating priest calling to the king:

> **Awake! Turn yourself about! So shout I. O king, stand up and sit down to a thousand of bread, a thousand of beer, roast meat of your rib-joints from the slaughter-house, and *iteh*-bread from the Broad Hall. The god is provided with a god's offering, the king is provided with this bread of his.**[31]

Figure 7.11 shows a relief fragment from the pyramid temple of Unas depicting (in all probability) the king sitting in front of an offering table on which are arranged long slices of bread. In his left hand he holds the *seshed* cloth, which, as we have seen, was a symbol of the triumph of the human spirit over death.[32]

The Twelve South-to-East-Wall Texts (Utts. 213–24)

Opposite the liturgy of offerings of the north wall of the sarcophagus chamber are seven south-wall utterances. The first three (utts. 213–15) and the last three (utts. 217–19) are words spoken by a priest to the king. Sandwiched between these priestly statements, spells, and instructions, the words spoken by the king himself are recorded in the form of a prayer

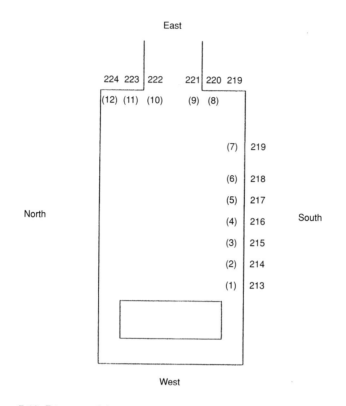

Figure 7.12. Diagram of the sarcophagus chamber showing the twelve south-to-east-wall texts.

(utt. 216).[33] There is thus a symmetry in the distribution of these seven south-wall texts, which is probably not accidental. Nor should we regard as accidental the fact that the last of the south-wall texts (utt. 219) spills over onto the east wall, thus forming a link with the remaining five east-wall texts (utts. 220–24). As this sequence of twelve texts appears in later pyramids with only a slight variation, there is good reason for treating the twelve south-to-east-wall texts as a continuous sequence.[34]

The slight variation just referred to is, however, something that we need to take note of before we proceed any further. In later pyramids the sequence of twelve texts ends not with utterances 223 and 224 as it does on the east wall of Unas's sarcophagus chamber but with utterances 245 and 246, which replace utterances 223 and 224.[35] In Unas's pyramid, utterances 245 and 246 are placed on the south wall of the passage between the sarcophagus chamber and the antechamber and separated from the east-wall texts by an intervening utterance (utt. 244). We shall return to the question of the "right sequence" in the next section, and proceed now on the assumption that the positioning of utterances 223 and 224 at the end of the sequence of twelve in the pyramid of Unas was deliberate and meaningful.

South Wall (Utts. 213–19)

(1) UTTERANCE 213: DEPARTING ALIVE

At the western end of the south wall, nearest to the sarcophagus, the priest addresses Unas with these words:

O Unas, you have not departed dead,
you have departed alive
to sit upon the throne of Osiris,
your 'aba scepter in your hand
that you may give orders to the living,
your lotus-bud scepter in your hand
that you may give orders to those whose seats are hidden[36]

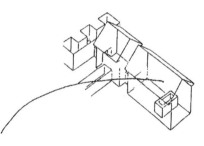

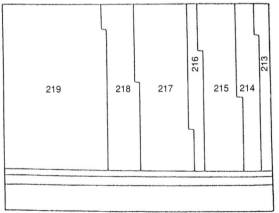

Figure 7.13. The distribution of texts on the south wall of the sarcophagus chamber of the pyramid of Unas. The texts read from west to east (i.e., from right to left).

201

As we have seen in chapter 3, this statement is usually interpreted as a pious denial of the reality of the king's death. However, not only is the king said to be sitting on the throne of Osiris, but he is also said to be grasping a scepter in either hand. The utterance clearly implies a kingship ritual, quite possibly a coronation ceremony, celebrated by the living king.

This ceremony involving the throne of Osiris and the grasping of scepters is said to enable the king to give orders on the one hand to "the living" and on the other hand to "those whose seats are hidden"—that is, the dead. The contrast between the living and the dead is so clearly stated that it would seem perverse to interpret the word *living* as meaning anything other than what the sentence suggests: namely, the living as opposed to the invisible dead, "whose seats are hidden."[37] Since the ability to give orders implies that the king is in some sense "present" in the domain in which his orders are given, we may assume that there is an inner, or mystical, event that lies behind the king's taking up the throne of Osiris and the extension of his authority into the realm of the dead. This mystical event must surely be what is referred to in the sentence that appears at the beginning of the utterance:

O Unas, you have not departed dead,
you have departed alive.

If this were any normal departure, there would be no reason to state so explicitly that the king was departing alive and not dead. It would seem that the destination of the king is the realm of the dead, but he is journeying into it alive.

Journeys into the realm of the dead by the living form part of a long and universal tradition, attested to in a great many cultures all over the world. What is implied in such journeys is that the soul is capable of separating itself from the physical body and "traveling" independently of it. The experience of becoming aware of oneself in a consciousness independent of the physical body—what we would today call an out-of-body experience—is the first step in the process of cosmic ascent referred to in Platonic, Neoplatonic, and Hermetic mystical writings.[38] It is also well attested in shamanism. Eliade has pointed out that one of the characteristics of shamans is that they "are able, *here on earth* and *as often as they wish*, to accomplish 'coming out of the body,' that is, the death that alone has power to transform the rest of mankind into 'birds'; shamans and sorcerers can enjoy the condition of 'souls,' of 'discarnate beings,' which is accessible to the profane only when they die."[39] Eliade's reference to the soul's birdlike condition in the out-of-body state is peculiarly apt, for, as we shall see, in the very next utterance Unas is transformed into a falcon.

Before this occurs, however, the physical body of Unas must be protected. This is achieved through a sevenfold identification of its different parts (arms, shoulders, belly, and so on) with the god Atum, with the exception of Unas's face, which is identified with Anubis.[40] Significantly, the utterance ends with a reference to the king having "encircled" the realms of Horus and Seth.[41] "Encircling" was a very ancient magical ritual, attested to from archaic times to the Ptolemaic and Roman periods. A ritual circumambulation of both fertile land (the realm of Horus) and desert (the realm of Seth) was an integral component of coronation rites, and was repeated during the Sed festival.[42]

This utterance concerning the "departure" of Unas therefore has both ritual and mystical elements. The ritual elements can be seen first in the reference to an enthronement ceremony in which the king's authority over the realm of Osiris is confirmed, second in the protection ritual, and third in the ritual circumambulation that the king enacted in order to secure his power over the realms of Horus and Seth. The main experiential counterpoint to these rituals must have involved the projection of the king's consciousness into the realm of the dead. In shamanic terms, his soul journeys beyond the confines of the physical world.

(2) UTTERANCE 214: BECOMING A FALCON

In utterance 214, Unas's traveling soul is instructed to beware of a lake. It is perhaps a lake of fire in which the king must cleanse himself, for Unas is now instructed to purify himself:

> **Purify yourself!**
> **for your bones are those of the divine falcons**
> **who are in the sky.**[43]

The transformation of the king's bones into those of falcons is a significant stage in the experiences that he is undergoing. The falcon is the form that the sun god Ra takes, and for the king to become transformed into a falcon is a magical act that ensures his inner identity with the solar principle. The falcon in this respect has the same role in ancient Egypt as the eagle in many shamanic traditions, in which the Supreme Being as solar spirit becomes manifest as a sun bird, which usually has the form of an eagle. The eagle is thus the most potent form for the shaman to assume, and it is as a soaring eagle that he rises up to the spirit world.[44] The fact that both Ra

Figure 7.14. The human soul takes the form of a human-headed falcon when journeying into the spirit world either in dream, death, or shamanic flight as described in utterance 214. Tomb of Arinefer, Thebes. New Kingdom.

and Horus, with whom the king is identified, are conceived as falcons is an indication of this shamanic substratum of Egyptian religion. In the passage we are considering, it is not, of course, literally the king's physical bones that are transformed, but rather that the transformation he undergoes is so far-reaching that he acquires the same "celestial" body as the sun god Ra.[45] Thereafter, it is in the form of a falcon that Unas continues his spirit-journey to the stars (fig. 7.14).

The destination of Unas is indicated toward the end of the utterance, where it is stated that the "sun folk" call out to him and the "imperishable stars" raise him up.[46] Here we see that his destination is essentially a realm of light, conceived as linked both to the sun and to the "imperishable" northern stars that are visible all the year round. These two destinations—solar and stellar—are thus not alternatives to each other but rather equally valid celestial images of the king's spiritualization.

(3) UTTERANCE 215: HEALING HORUS AND SETH, EMBRACED BY ATUM

The third stage of this journey is described in utterance 215, in which the king heals the eye of Horus injured by Seth and restores to Seth his testicles, which Horus has torn out. Unas is able to achieve this healing of the two antagonists because he is embraced by the supreme god Atum, whose very being transcends all opposites.[47] By healing the injuries these two antagonists have inflicted on each other, the king is able to unite fully with the royal *ka* energy.[48] It is as if the conflict of Horus and Seth has the effect of locking up and making unavailable this vital energy of the *ka*, holding back all further progress until a reconciliation is accomplished (fig. 7.15). The conflict of these gods can be understood as being waged on the divine, the psychic, and the physical levels: On the divine level it is a clash of the cosmic forces of generation and destruction; on the psychic level it is an objective psychic reality that lives within the human soul; and on the physical level it manifests in the antagonism within the landscape between fertile land and desert.

In the human being, Horus represents the aspiration toward spiritual insight founded on the integration of the energies of the soul, whereas Seth represents the drive of the primitive and elemental forces that—once unleashed—lead to psychic disintegration and spiritual blindness. The resolution of the conflict between these opposing principles in the king has significance both for the divine world and for the whole land of Egypt and its people, because the king's status was such that the effects of his actions ramified through the divine, the human, and the natural realms. Insofar as the *ka* energy of the king is released, the land itself is reinvigorated, and this, of course, was one of the objectives of the Sed festival.[49]

Along with the reconciliation of Horus and Seth, the other salient theme of the utterance is the embrace of the king by Atum and his being protected by Atum in his solar form as Ra-Atum. The latter ensures that Unas will not suffer from the adverse power of any of the gods, most significantly Osiris, who "shall not claim your heart, nor have power over your heart."[50] While it might be odd for a dead king to have to be protected from Osiris, with whom he is supposed to be conjoined at death, this passage reminds us that if the king is

Figure 7.15. The reconciliation of Horus and Seth, as depicted in the New Kingdom mystical text the Book of Gates, tenth division.

living, then it is essential that he not fall wholly under the power of Osiris. The aim is rather to come into direct relationship with the transcendent godhead Atum in his solar aspect, thereby rising beyond the danger of falling into too close an identification with either Horus on the one side, Seth on the other, or Osiris in between.

(4) UTTERANCE 216: IN THE NIGHT BARK OF THE SUN
The next utterance (utt. 216), in the middle of the south wall, marks the end of the first phase of the king's journey. Unas declares:

> **I have come to you O Nephthys;**
> **I have come to you O Night Bark.**[51]

We know from reliefs in the New Kingdom tomb of Kheruef that king Amenhotep III undertook a ritual journey in the night bark of the sun god Ra as part of his Sed festival rites. This probably took place on a lake constructed near his palace at Malqata, and was meant ritually to reinforce the reality of his solar rebirth and his identification with Ra. The text that accompanies the depiction of this event states that these rites were a revival of ceremonies that were very ancient and were enacted "in accordance with writings of old."[52] Since the Pyramid Texts were composed over a thousand years earlier, it is quite possible that these were the "writings of old" that the ceremonies of Amenhotep III's Sed festival were based on. In figure 7.16, we

Figure 7.16. A scene from the Sed festival of Amenhotep III, showing him traveling as Ra on the solar night bark with his queen. Tomb of Kheruef. New Kingdom.

see Amenhotep portrayed as Ra himself, with his queen beside him, traveling on the night bark. While this was enacted as a ritual, the Pyramid Texts seem to be describing something much closer to the actual inner experience that lay behind, and determined, the outer form of the ritual.[53]

In the Unas text, it would seem that the king's identification with Ra at this juncture is to empower him as he descends into the dark netherworld (the Dwat). He prays that he may be remembered by Nephthys, whom he addresses as "She who remembers the *ka*s," for he is himself about to be enveloped by the Underworld. Unas's entry into the Dwat is in the southwestern sky, where he follows the decanal constellations of Orion and Sirius as they are swallowed up or "encircled" by the Dwat. The southern constellations were thought to be governed by Osiris because they disappear for seventy days, going through a symbolic death followed by a rebirth when they reappear again. The leader of the southern constellations was regarded as Orion, with which Osiris was identified (fig. 7.17). Just as the

Figure 7.17. Orion, Sothis, and the southern constellations. Sothis (Sirius), the celestial form of Isis, is on the left; Orion (with whom Osiris was identified) is next to her with the three stars of Orion's belt above him; the stars of the southern constellations are to his right and in the midst of them, apparently, the solar boat, its occupants depicted above it. From the ceiling of the tomb of Senenmut at Deir el-Bahri, circa 1473 B.C.

southern constellations enter the Dwat when they disappear from view, so Unas will be "encircled" by the Dwat. But this experience of being encompassed by the Dwat involves at the same time a process of purification in a mysterious region called the Akhet.

> **Orion is encircled by the Dwat,**
> **When, living, he purifies himself in the Akhet.**
> **Sothis [Sirius] is encircled by the Dwat,**
> **When, living, she purifies herself in the Akhet.**
> **Unas is encircled by the Dwat,**
> **When, living, he purifies himself in the Akhet.**[54]

Now, Akhet is usually translated as "horizon," but it should be understood as the place in which the king undergoes transformation into an *akh*, or "shining spirit."[55] And this is the crucial experience that is undergone here. It is the inward realization that one's essential nature is beyond the opposing principles of Horus and Seth and stems from a higher transcendent source. Thus at the end of utterance 216, the king commits himself "to the arms of my father, to the arms of Atum."[56]

The experience of spiritual transformation in the Akhet is usually interpreted as belonging to ancient Egyptian beliefs about what occurs after death, but we know from New Kingdom sources that the Akhet was also regarded as a place where the living king was initiated. In his coronation inscription at Karnak, Thutmose III describes transforming himself into a falcon and then being taken up into the Akhet, where he communes with the sun god Ra, becoming infused with Ra's "*akh* power."[57] This event was connected with the validation of the king's status as "son of Ra" (a title that he bore from the Fourth Dynasty onward) and the accompanying role of the king as "priest of the sun."[58] It is not hard to see the close parallel between what is described in the Thutmose inscription and the experiences detailed in the pyramid of Unas. In the case of Thutmose, however, there is no question as to the fact that the king is alive, for it is a coronation text. If such experiences as are described in the Pyramid Texts are also found in a coronation text and attributed to a living king, it follows that the Pyramid Texts are not necessarily simply funerary, and that what Unas is said to have undergone he may have undergone while still alive.

(5) UTTERANCE 217: SOLARIZATION

In the utterance that follows (utt. 217) it is affirmed: "You [Atum-Ra and the king] shall traverse the sky being united in the darkness; you shall rise from the Akhet, from the place in which you have become *akh*."[59] This statement is made four times in order to emphasize its importance. How are we to understand this "union in darkness" of the king and Atum-Ra? The union is occurring on the solar night bark in the depths of the Underworld, or Dwat. Here in these netherworld depths, the king comes to the place of renewal, the Akhet, where he is infused with the powers of spiritual regeneration that the sun god taps each night. That which ensures the rebirth of the sun also ensures the rebirth of the king, for the king has become conjoined with the sun god. The king has become consciously connected with the self-regenerating energy of the sun god: He has become "solarized." Now, having incorporated into himself the solar energy of the sun god, he rises up from the Akhet as a "shining spirit"—an *akh*.[60]

The utterance describes how this event of the solarized king traversing the night sky with Atum-Ra is solemnly announced by Seth and Nephthys to the gods of the south, by Osiris and Horus to the gods of the north, by Thoth to the gods of the West, and by Horus to the gods of the east. Unas has achieved the condition of "shining spirit," with power over life and death.

(6) UTTERANCE 218: EMPOWERMENT

Utterance 218 amplifies the same point: The power of the solarized Unas is greater than that of Osiris, to whom the utterance is addressed. It is cosmic, it extends over the four directions, over the heavens, over the Underworld (referred to as the Lower Sky), and over the earth.[61] Once again the repeated references to the king's power extending over those who are on earth militates against a funerary interpretation of this utterance. It is concerned, on the contrary, with an exaltation of his power while still alive, as the next utterance unequivocally affirms.

(7) UTTERANCE 219: A LIVING OSIRIS

The texts of the south wall conclude at the east end with utterance 219. This consists of an affirmation that we have already had cause to discuss in chapter 3, both in relation to problems in the funerary interpretation of the Pyramid Texts and in relation to the episode in the Sed festival "secret rites" in which the king has a visionary encounter with twelve deities. Unas, now identified once more with Osiris, is said to "live." The affirmation is made twelve times to major deities such as Atum, Shu, Tefnut, Geb, Nut, and so on, nearly all of whom appear before Osorkon during his Sed festival in the "secret rites" (fig. 3.4). It is then repeated twelve more times to twelve different manifestations of Osiris, beginning with Nunet, who should possibly be understood as the the tomb personified.[62] The same affirmation is thus repeated twenty-four times altogether. This drives home its message, which mirrors that of utterance 213 at the west end of the wall, where it is said that Unas has departed alive, not dead. Now, addressing each god in turn, it is reiterated that Unas is an Osiris, he is not dead, he lives, and furthermore he is not judged. The utterance begins by addressing Atum:

> **O Atum, this one here is your son Osiris,**
> **whom you have caused to be restored that he may live.**
> **He lives—this Unas lives!**
> **He is not dead—this Unas is not dead!**
> **He is not destroyed—this Unas is not destroyed!**
> **He has not been judged—this Unas has not been judged!**
> **He judges—this Unas judges!**[63]

Each god is then addressed in exactly the same way, and the same formula is repeated word for word twenty-four times.

From a mystical or initiatory point of view, the text may be interpreted as stating that Unas, rather than coming before Osiris in his role of judge of the dead, escapes the fate of being judged altogether. In other words, it is just because his soul is not judged that he can be said still to be alive, with power over his own heart.[64] The utterance thus fulfills the promise of utterance 215, where we read,

> **Ra-Atum will not give you to Osiris,**
> **and he [Osiris] shall not claim your heart**
> **nor have power over your heart.**[65]

It bears comparison with a similar statement in the pyramid of Teti, on the south wall of the passage between the sarcophagus chamber and the antechamber, where the king claims to "give judgment as a god" and says of Ra that

> **he [Ra] will never give me to Osiris,**
> **for I have not died the death.**
> **I have become an *akh* in the Akhet.**[66]

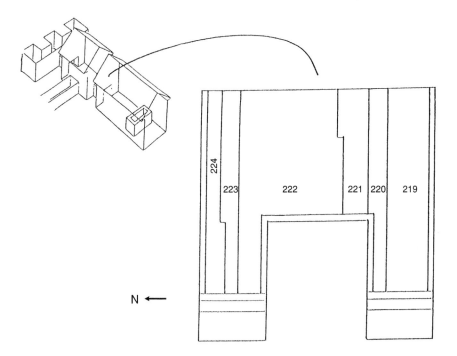

Figure 7.18. The location of texts on the east wall of the sarcophagus chamber of the pyramid of Unas. The texts read from south to north (i.e., from right to left).

East Wall (Utts. 219–24)

(8) UTTERANCE 220: CORONATION AS HORUS—APPROACHING THE CROWN

In the pyramid of Unas, utterance 219 passes from the south wall onto the east wall about four fifths of the way through, so the last fifth (from §188 to §193) is on the east wall (fig. 7.18). Utterance 219 is followed by two closely connected utterances (utts. 220–21) that form part of a coronation ritual. The presence of the coronation texts at this point reinforces our impression that these texts are describing rites and experiences undergone by the living king, and actually make little sense if interpreted as funerary texts. Once again there may well be a relationship with the Sed festival, the climax of which was the dual coronation of the king with the red and the white crowns. In utterances 220–21, the ceremonial for the coronation with the red crown only is given. But, as we shall see, on the other side of the wall (antechamber west wall) the king, referred to as Horus of the

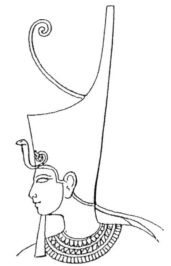

Figure 7.19. The red crown is a manifestation of the fiery cobra goddess Wadjet, who is often depicted raised up and ready to strike at the front of it. Drawing of a relief of Seti I, from his temple at Abydos.

south (utts. 254–55), undergoes coronation on the throne of Horus (utt. 256), presumably with the white crown. The coronation texts on the sarcophagus chamber east wall begin with a hymn to the crown as a goddess, housed in a shrine whose doors are opened at the beginning of utterance 220. The crown is described as a "fiery serpent" full of magic, which the king approaches in dread and awe. The crown is, in fact, the manifestation of the cobra goddess, Wadjet (fig. 7.19).[67]

(9) UTTERANCE 221: CORONATION AS HORUS—THE ROYAL REBIRTH
It is only because he has been through the initiatory ordeal described in the previous utterances of the south wall that Unas can advance toward the crown with impunity, reciting the words:

> **May there be terror of me like the terror of you.**
> **May there be fear of me like the fear of you.**
> **May there be awe of me like the awe of you.**
> **May there be love of me like the love of you.**
> **May my 'aba scepter be at the head of the living,**
> **May my *sekhem* scepter be at the head of the spirits.**[68]

At the end of this recitation, the crown is placed on the king's head while he once again grasps the two scepters. The king is then addressed as follows:

> **The Great One has given birth to you.**
> **The Exalted One has adorned you.**

**For you are Horus
encircled with the protection of his eye.**[69]

In the first of the south-wall texts (utt. 213), we saw how the king was enjoined to "sit upon the throne of Osiris," and throughout utterance 219 immediately prior to the coronation ritual Unas was referred to as Osiris. Now the coronation rite proclaims his rebirth as a Horus. In chapter 3 we discussed the widely held view within Egyptology that the dead king was never referred to as Horus, only Osiris. In terms of the conventional interpretation of the Pyramid Texts as funerary texts, this coronation of the king as Horus in utterance 221 means that either the orthodox view that the dead king is never Horus needs to be revised or else it is not, in fact, the dead king that is being referred to but the living king—in which case the Pyramid Texts are clearly not simply funerary texts. While it could be argued that the coronation texts have been requisitioned here in order to serve essentially funerary purposes, it is more likely that the apparently funerary elements are the elements that have been used within an essentially nonfunerary context.

(10) UTTERANCE 222: JOINING THE COSMIC CIRCUIT OF RA

Utterance 222 is a continuation of the coronation ceremonies, making three coronation texts in total.[70] As a newborn Horus, it is necessary that the king establish his power in relation to the supreme godhead in his manifestation as creator god, Atum-Ra. But in this remarkable utterance, it is not simply the coronation ritual that is described; it is also a mystical experience in which the king unites with Ra by entering into the cosmic orbit of the sun god. Once again, then, mystical experience and outwardly performed ritual are closely intertwined.

The utterance begins with the king being told by the officiating priest to "stand upon it, this earth which issued from Atum."[71] The earth that issued from Atum is the First Land that emerges at the beginning of time from the primordial ocean of Nun. This was replicated in the Sed festival dais upon which the double throne was placed, and which was approached by a staircase at either end. In positioning himself here, the king is positioning himself in the mythical place of origins, the source of creation and the source of power. Going back to this source, he returns to his own spiritual origin, where he is told to

**come into being upon it,
be exalted upon it,**

> **so that your father may see you,**
> **so that Ra may see you.**[72]

While this passage undoubtedly describes an aspect of the coronation ritual, it also includes an experiential dimension that underlies the ritual acts
that are performed. These coronation rites correspond to inner experiences: The coronation of the king has the specific purpose of embodying
inner mythical reality in and through the outwardly performed ritual acts.

The king now advances into that mythical region, addressing Ra eight
times in eight different forms, saying:

> **I have come to you, my father.**
> **I have come to you. . .**

and is finally given a crook to hold in his hand, signifying his dominance of
Lower and Upper Egypt.[73] As in utterance 215, the king once again is said
to integrate within his own being the two warring antagonists, Horus and
Seth. But, as in utterance 215, the integration of the energies of Horus and
Seth is accomplished only insofar as the king is able to transcend the
Osirian state and enter into direct relationship with Atum, who is described
as his father.[74] That the Sed festival coronation ceremony involved the reconciliation of Horus and Seth can be seen in figure 7.20, which depicts the
enthronement of Senwosret III as king of Upper and Lower Egypt. This
image could be taken as an illustration of the text we are here considering.
The coronation dais is raised up like the First Land, and on either side
Horus and Seth are represented, each offering the notched palm branch,
signifying "years" of kingship—i.e., a long reign.

In the south-wall texts, the reconciliation of Horus and Seth and the
embrace of the king by Atum (utt. 215) is followed by the king joining Ra
in his night bark (utt. 216). So here on the east wall, in the middle of utterance 222, the king sheds all his "impurities," the sky opens to him, and he
joins Ra in his sun boat, rising and setting with the sun god as he travels the
cosmic orbit. We saw that the voyage of the king in the night bark of the
sun god (utt. 216) was ritually enacted in the Sed festival of Amenhotep III.
Here, however, it is not just the night bark that the king joins as it travels
through the Dwat, but also the day bark. Whether a similar ritual sailing in
the day bark of Ra took place is not known. The text, which now describes
a second mystical journey of the king traversing the entire cosmic circuit,
hovers on the borders of ritual act and mystical experience. He journeys
from night to day and from day to night, going up and down with the sun

*Figure 7.20. The Twelfth Dynasty king Senwosret III sits upon the Sed festival corona-
tion dais, raised above ground level in imitation of the First Land, which rose up out of
the primordial ocean at the beginning of time. On either side of the dais, the antagonists
Horus and Seth offer the king notched palm branches, signifying a long reign. The integration of their opposing energies was an essential feature of kingship and is an important
theme of both utterances 222 and 215. Relief carving on a lintel at Naq el-Medamud.
Middle Kingdom.*

god, descending below the western horizon and rising above the eastern
horizon as he is swept along in the cosmic orbit of Ra.

> **Ascend and descend;**
> **descend with Ra, darkened with Nedy [an aspect of the**
> **setting sun].**
> **Ascend and descend;**
> **ascend with Ra, rise with the great reed-float user.**
> **Ascend and descend;**
> **descend with Nephthys, sink into the darkness with the**
> **Night-bark.**
> **Ascend and descend;**
> **ascend with Isis, rise with the Day-bark.**[75]

We therefore have two descriptions of mystical flight, both in the form of a "cosmic sailing," one on the south wall describing the king's journey to the southern stars where he travels through the Dwat in the night bark and a second on this east wall, in which the king enters the sun's cosmic orbit and travels around the earth. Whereas the first journey is undertaken as an Osiris, the second is undertaken as a newborn Horus. Two levels or stages of initiation are therefore indicated: The king must first of all go into the Osirian realm, following the decanal constellations in the southwestern sky as they are enveloped by the Dwat, and there meet the forces of death but not succumb to them. He becomes a "living Osiris" (utt. 219) not in virtue of having died, but rather in virtue of having ventured into the spirit world alive and having become solarized there as an *akh*. The fruit of this experience is his spiritual rebirth as a Horus, and precisely as such he is qualified to wear the crown of Egypt. But the coronation of the king as Horus involves a second level of initiation in which the king travels to the source of life and existence itself and experiences the infinite creative power of the godhead Atum-Ra. Again this involves an experience of mystical flight, but no longer in the direction of one portion of the sky, instead encompassing the entire circle of the heavens, through uniting with the light- and life-giving orbit of the sun.

It is significant that cosmic travel is a feature of post-Egyptian mystical traditions, such as the Hellenistic mysteries, Platonism, Neoplatonism, and the Hermetic tradition, in all of which the experience of the divinization of the soul occurs in a cosmic context.[76] Comparable descriptions of cosmic travel abound in the shamanic literature, from the Eskimo shaman's journey to the moon and flight around the earth to the ancient Indian ecstatic's ascent to the eastern and western skies, where he wanders in the track of *apsaras* and *gandharvas*.[77] We are here dealing with a universally attested to mystical pattern, which takes different forms in different cultures, but which nevertheless displays essentially the same fundamental characteristics of the ascent of the soul to the heavens, mystical communion with heavenly beings or gods, and the attainment of a state of inner illumination—and all of this experienced not in a postmortem state but while the initiate, philosopher, mystic, or shaman is still alive.

(11) UTTERANCE 223: AWAKENING

The next utterance (utt. 223) has a completely different tone from the previous utterances. It is concerned with awakening the king from what would appear to be a trancelike state, and ensuring the return of his spirit into his body. Utterance 223 begins with words spoken by a priest or priestess:

Awake! Turn yourself about! So shout I!
O King, stand up. . . .

The scene is no longer the coronation dais but the tomb, where the king's body lies inert:

O King, raise yourself up to me,
betake yourself to me,
do not be far from me
for the tomb (is) is your barrier against me.[78]

One way of understanding the position of this utterance immediately after the mystical experiences described in the previous utterances is that the latter actually took place while the king was lying in trance on the lion bed in "the tomb." These mystical experiences might then have been subsequently enacted in outwardly performed ceremonies. But however we understand the relationship between the rituals performed and the mystical experiences undergone, there is little doubt that both the location and the mood of this utterance have shifted dramatically from what has gone before. The location is no longer cosmic and the mood has an unfamiliar urgency.

Figure 7.21 is one of several reliefs from the Ptolemaic period depicting

Figure 7.21. The awakening of the initiate-king. On the left, the king's soul (in the form of a ba *bird) hovers above the cosmic tree, while to the right of the tree a Horus-priest rouses the king from his lion-headed bed. Temple of Denderah.*

the recall and awakening of the initiate-king. On the left his soul is depicted hovering above the cosmic tree, while to the right of the tree Horus (probably a priest wearing a Horus mask) rouses the king from the initiatory lion-headed bed.

After he has awakened, the king is encouraged to eat and drink. He is invited to

> **sit down to a thousand of bread,**
> **a thousand of beer,**
> **roast meat . . . from the slaughterhouse**
> **and *reteh* bread from the Broad Hall.**[79]

We are now almost adjacent to the north-wall Offering Liturgy already described, the main portion of which is the great feast brought before the king.

(12) UTTERANCE 224: RETURN

The final utterance of the east wall, utterance 224, is closely linked to the previous utterance, and is no less dramatic. The scene would still seem to be the tomb, and a priest calls out to the king:

> **Raise yourself, O King!**
> **Turn yourself about, O King!**[80]

He is reminded that his condition has radically altered, advised to beware of the "border" or "boundary" on earth, and instructed, in the translation of Piankoff, to reenter his body:

> **How changed, how changed [is thy state]!**
> **[Therefore] protect thy children!**
> **Beware of thy border which is in earth!**
> **Put on thy body and come towards them.**[81]

The last line of the same passage, translated by Faulkner and Mercer, is rendered, "Clothe your body." The clothing of the body may equally symbolize the return of the traveling soul to the body.[82] Putting on a garment does seem to have been a ritual act to confirm the successful completion of initiation rites, and there is no doubt as to the symbolic importance of putting on and taking off garments at critical moments of transition during the Sed festival.[83] But whichever way it is translated, either translation is compatible with a nonfunerary interpretation of the text. Instructions to the soul to "put on" its body, or equally to clothe itself, may have had a place in mummification rituals, but in the present context they make considerably more sense if we assume that the king is not in a mummified state. In the variant text (utt. 225), the king proceeds to slaughter an ox, a feat that a dead man could hardly be expected to accomplish.[84]

In this utterance, it is said of the king that he has authority over the regions of both Horus and Seth as well as Osiris—in other words, his authority extends over the realms of the living and the dead. This authority of the king over both worlds is symbolized in his lotus-bud scepter and his staff—the lotus-bud scepter "at the head of the living" and the staff "at the head of the spirits": i.e., the dead.[85] This reflects the statement in the first utterance of the series (utt. 213), in which the king seated himself on the throne of Osiris in order to give orders to the "living" and "those whose seats are hidden" and performed a ritual circumambulation of the realms of Horus and Seth. If the sequence of twelve utterances appears to end where it began, there may be a very good reason for this. And that could be because the "return" at the end of the series of mystical and ritual episodes is to the very same place as that from which the "departure" began.

The Passage between the Chambers

(South Wall: Utts. 244–46; North Wall: Utts. 199, 32, 23, 25, 200)

At the beginning of the last section, we noted that in later pyramids, the sequence of twelve texts on the south and east walls of the sarcophagus chamber of Unas's pyramid end with utterances 245 and 246 rather than utterances 223 and 224. In the pyramid of Unas, utterances 245 and 246 occur on the south wall of the passage between his sarcophagus chamber and his antechamber (see fig. 7.22). On the north wall of this same passage are a familiar series of utterances: utterances 32, 23, and 25, all of which we have met on the north wall, and which functioned as important purification texts, often marking the transition from one phase of the Offering Liturgy to another. There is therefore good reason to view the texts on the south wall of the passage as belonging to the sequence of south-to-east-wall texts and those on the north wall of the passage as belonging to the north-wall Offering Liturgy.

The question, remains, however, as to how exactly we should view the relationship of these texts to the two main sequences of north-wall and

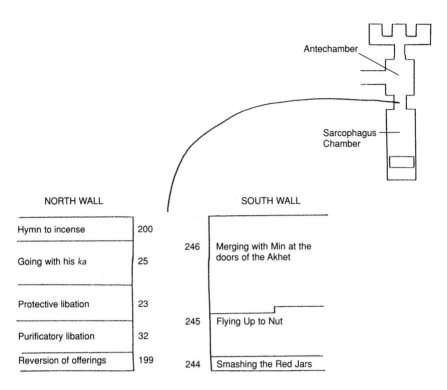

NORTH WALL   SOUTH WALL

Hymn to incense	200		
Going with his *ka*	25	246	Merging with Min at the doors of the Akhet
Protective libation	23		
Purificatory libation	32	245	Flying Up to Nut
Reversion of offerings	199	244	Smashing the Red Jars

Figure 7.22. The placement of texts in the passage between the sarcophagus chamber (bottom) *and the antechamber* (top).

south-to-east-wall texts already discussed. Why, for example, if utterances 245 and 246 replace utterances 223 and 224 in other pyramids, did they not replace them in the pyramid of Unas? It was not a question of lack of space, for utterances 245 and 246 are only a fraction longer than utterances 223 and 224, and could without difficulty have been fitted into the space occupied by utterances 223 and 224. It would seem that the location at the north end of the east wall was felt to be particularly appropriate for these utterances but not appropriate for utterances 245 and 246. The latter are specifically "southern" texts. Thus in other pyramids utterances 245 and 246 are, along with the south-to-east-wall texts of Unas's sarcophagus chamber, incorporated into a single south-wall sequence, leaving the east wall available for other texts.[86] In Unas's pyramid they occur, significantly, on the south wall of the passage. Only one of the utterances from Unas's east wall occurs in a similar position in pyramids subsequent to his, and that is the critical utterance 224 ("Rouse yourself O king, Turn yourself about

O king," ending with the injunction "Put on your body!").[87] It seems, then, that this utterance belongs less to any sequence of texts than to the northeast corner of the sarcophagus chamber: north perhaps through association with the "never wearying" northern stars, east through association with the rising sun and rebirth.

The question thus shifts to why it was felt appropriate for the sequence of texts that in subsequent pyramids was contained on the south wall to be spread across both the south and east walls of Unas's sarcophagus chamber. This question may find its answer when we come in chapter 8 to look at the connection between the texts on the sarcophagus chamber east wall and those of the antechamber west wall. Now we need to return to the passage.

The Passage: South Wall

(1) UTTERANCE 244: SMASHING THE RED JARS

The texts on both sides of the passage read from west to east—that is, from the sarcophagus chamber toward the antechamber, which reinforces the symbolic momentum already established in the sarcophagus chamber from the region of death (the west) toward the region of rebirth (the east). On the south wall of the passage, the texts begin with a short utterance (utt. 244) that describes the ritual smashing of red jars, an act symbolizing the eradication of the enemies of the Horus-king, red being the color associated with Seth.[88] This act of breaking the red jars, insofar as it magically ensures the defeat of the forces of opposition, has the effect of preparing a path for the king to travel on to the next stage of his spirit journey.[89] Directly opposite it, on the north wall, is an equally short text describing the ritual of the "reversion of offerings" (utt. 199), which formally ended the Offering Ceremony. These two texts are like sentinels marking the transition from the sarcophagus chamber to the antechamber. Presumably both the smashing of the red jars and the reversion of offerings rite would have actually taken place here on the threshold of the sarcophagus chamber.

(2) UTTERANCE 245: FLYING UP TO NUT

East of utterance 244, on the south wall, utterance 245 celebrates the king having passed beyond the realm of Osiris, which he leaves far beneath him as he flies up to the sky goddess, Nut. Once again he takes the form of a falcon. The king cries out:

I come to you, O Nut,
I come to you, O Nut.

> I have cast my father [Osiris] to the earth,
> I have left Horus behind me.
> My wings have grown into those of a falcon,
> My two plumes are those of a sacred falcon.
> My *ba* has brought me and its magic (*heka*) has
>   equipped me.

To this, the sky goddess responds:

> May you split open a place for yourself in the sky
> among the stars of the sky.
> For you are the Lone Star,
> the companion of Hu ["authority" or "command"].
> Look down upon Osiris
> when he gives orders to the spirits.
> You stand far above him,
> you are not among them
> and you shall not be among them.[90]

The meaning of the phrase "companion of Hu" is probably that Unas is here identified with Sia (the divine personification of knowledge or insight), since Hu and Sia were the two companions of the sun god.[91] The significance of this identification will become apparent when we look at the texts on the west gable of the antechamber.

(3) UTTERANCE 246: MERGING WITH MIN, AT THE DOORS OF THE AKHET

Having been received by the sky goddess, Nut, in utterance 246, the king assumes the form of a mighty bull, merged with the fertility god, Min. It is significant that during the Sed festival rites, Min had an important role. There was, for example, an elaborate offering ceremony to the god, and he is also depicted as a witness to the dedication of the field rite, during which—as we have seen—the king wore a short kilt with a bull's tail (see fig. 7.23).[92] The annual harvest festival of Min may also have been associated with the Sed festival.[93] The meaning of the king assuming the form of a bull may be that he thereby becomes Kamutef, "bull of his mother," an epithet especially given to Min. The significance of this epithet is that as Kamutef, the king is agent of his own rebirth, brought about through the fertilization of his "mother," the goddess Nut, by whom he has just been welcomed.[94] In this text, however, he is not yet referred to explicitly as

Figure 7.23. The Sed festival dedication of the field rite is witnessed by Min, with whom the king is merged in utterance 246. Relief carving depicting Hatshepsut's Sed festival, Karnak.

Kamutef. He simply appears in bull form as Min, and at his appearance all the gods fall silent, in awe of his spiritual and sexual prowess.

Unas is now positioned "at the doors of the Akhet," and in opening them he opens the way to the firmament, the Cool Region of his apotheosis. Of the king, it is said:

> **You will not go down,**
> **you will not come to an end,**
> **but your name shall endure among men**
> **and your name shall come into being among the gods.**[95]

The Passage: North Wall

(1) UTTERANCES 199, 32, AND 23: REVERSION OF OFFERINGS, PURIFICATORY AND PROTECTIVE LIBATIONS

On the north wall of the passage, following the reversion of offerings (utt. 199, discussed above), utterance 32 describes how a water libation is poured under the soles of the king's feet. To the east of it, utterance 23 is a libation text that invokes the protection of Osiris and Thoth against the king's enemies. Both these libation texts we have met before on the north wall at the beginning of the Offering Liturgy.

(2) UTTERANCES 25 AND 200: THE INCENSE RITE

The libation texts are followed by utterance 25, a fire and incense text, placed directly opposite utterance 246, which describes the king's passage into the realm of the gods as a great bull. Along with the two previous texts, utterance 25 also features in the Offering Liturgy, providing a spell for the king to go forward with his *ka*.

> **O Unas, the arm of your *ka* is before you,**
> **O Unas, the arm of your *ka* is behind you,**
> **O Unas, the leg of your *ka* is before you,**
> **O Unas, the leg of your *ka* is behind you.**[96]

As he goes, he is censed with incense, which suffuses him with a divine fragrance.

Utterance 25 is closely linked to a second censing text adjacent to it—utterance 200. Together they constitute an incense rite through which the king is united with his *ka*. The meaning of this union can be appreciated only when it is realized that the royal *ka* was something more than simply the vital spirit of the king. It was the vital spirit of the kingship—the divine office of kingship as such.[97] Thus the royal *ka* was the human king's link with divinity, and through his union with the *ka* he was effectively divinized. What is being described here is the divinization of the living king in a ritual that is known to have been the precursor to similar New Kingdom royal deification ceremonies.[98]

As in the sarcophagus chamber, the north wall of the passage is liturgical, while the south wall is predominantly experiential. There is thus a thematic continuity between the sarcophagus chamber and the passage, which as we have seen in the case of the south wall probably also represents a textual continuity. Whether the north-wall texts of the passage are to be read as a continuation of the sarcophagus chamber Offering Liturgy is a question that is probably best left open.[99] More important is the fact that it is possible to see a rationale in the placement of the passage texts opposite each other, beginning with the smashing of the red jars on the south wall (utt. 244) and the reversion of offerings on the north wall (utt. 199) at the threshold between the passage and the sarcophagus chamber. As the king flies up to Nut on the south wall (utt. 245), he undergoes purificatory and protective libation on the north wall (utts. 32 and 23). And as he merges with the fertility god, Min, in the form of a bull on the south wall, standing at the doorway to the Akhet (utt. 246), on the north wall he is censed with fire and smoke to enable him to "go with his *ka*" (utts. 25 and 200), signifying the divinization of the king.

The East Gable (Utts. 204, 205, 207, 209, 210–12)

In the sarcophagus chamber of the pyramid of Unas, there are seven east-gable utterances, the main theme of which is the physical and spiritual nourishment of the king. These seven texts are a discrete sequence, as are the seven texts on the other side of the wall on the antechamber west gable.[100] While it may be simply a coincidence that the seven sarcophagus chamber texts are matched by seven antechamber texts, they do seem to complement each other, and elements of both sets of text were incorporated at a later date into a single text, as if they were perceived as belonging together.[101] Although the main theme of the sarcophagus chamber east gable is the nourishment of the king, the main theme of the texts on the antechamber west gable is that of the king's celestial rebirth. There is indeed a possibility that the positioning of these two groups of seven texts either side of the same wall was deliberate, serving magically to reinforce each other. With respect to this possibility, it is helpful to recall an observation made by R. A. Schwaller de Lubicz, who, on the basis of a painstaking analysis of pharaonic architecture in general and Luxor temple in particular, noticed that figures or texts on one side of a partition wall sometimes relate meaningfully to figures or texts on the other side of the same wall. He called this meaningful relationship "transposition." This is how he describes it:

> The complements of an idea set forth in a given room, in which it is developed, are given in another room, dedicated to another development. The accord between the two themes develops through a common element and creates a sequence that explains the true (esoteric) meaning as a logical conclusion. It often happens that the reading of texts and symbols on one wall has meaning only through this indirect superimposition through the wall.[102]

Possible instances of transposition that may be present in the relationship between the sarcophagus chamber east gable and the antechamber west gable will be pointed out as we go along. First of all, we shall look at the

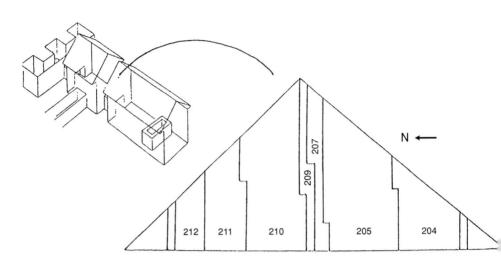

Figure 7.24. The texts of the east gable are concerned mainly with the physical and spiritual nourishment of the king. They read from south to north (right to left).

seven sarcophagus chamber texts, and in chapter 8 we shall examine the seven antechamber texts.

(1) UTTERANCE 204: THE NOURISHMENT PROVIDED BY OSIRIS

The sequence of seven utterances begins at the south end of the sarcophagus chamber with two utterances unique to Unas's pyramid. These are utterances 204 and 205, which together assert that Unas is not hungry because his food is provided by Osiris (utt. 204) and by Ra (utt. 205). In utterance 204 the little finger of the king pulls out what is "in the navel of Osiris," a phrase that may refer to the function of Osiris as god of the fertile earth.[103] Thus the hoers are said to rejoice, presumably because of the fruitfulness of the crop. But while this text may at first seem to be concerned with the provision of nourishment in this world, the reference to the god Ha as well as Osiris suggests that the source of the king's sustenance is in the spirit world. Ha is a god associated with the western necropolis, and like Osiris is a god of the dead.[104] The text states that it is Ha who drives away Unas's hunger. The hunger and thirst of Unas should probably be understood as spiritual rather than physical hunger and thirst, for Unas is in the Otherworld.

(2) Utterance 205: The King Is Transformed into a Bull

That Unas's location is otherworldly is made clear in utterance 205, in which he is given barley, emmer, bread, and beer by Ra. Unas is said to be "unbound." He has been "set free." And we must assume that he has been set free of material conditions, for he appears in the realm of the gods and is "seen" there.[105] What is implied by "being seen" by the gods is that one's spiritual existence is confirmed, perhaps in a manner akin to Berkeley's *Esse est percipi* ("To be is to be perceived"). Being seen has ontological import, conveying to the one who is seen a degree of spiritual substantiality.[106]

The major theme of this text, though, is of the king becoming the son of Ra, and as such taking on the form of a mighty bull. Whereas in utterance 246 in the passage between the sarcophagus chamber and the antechamber, the "Great Bull" epithet linked Unas to Min, here it unites him with the creative, fertilizing, and indomitable energy of the sun god. How are we to understand this transformation of the king into a bull? Was it simply meant as a metaphor for the king's having an almost superhuman power? Was it a title the king was given to link him, perhaps magically, with the sun god? Or was it something more? Did it have an experiential dimension as well? Was the transformation indeed actually accomplished? This latter possibility should not be dismissed out of hand, for we have eyewitness accounts from within the shamanic tradition that describe just such transformations.[107] If we do not believe these accounts, because we do not think it possible for human beings to change themselves into animals, then we deny ourselves access to an important stratum of the religious consciousness of the ancient Egyptians. Mircea Eliade has argued that the magical transformation into an animal form involved a "going out of the self" that was an ecstatic experience:

> There was no question of a regression into pure "animal life"; the animal with which the shaman identified himself was already charged with a mythology, it was in fact, a mythical animal, the Ancestor or Demiurge. By becoming this mythical animal, man became something far greater and stronger than himself. We are justified in supposing that this projection into a mythical being, the center at once of the existence and renewal of the universe, induced the euphoric experience that, before ending in ecstasy, showed the shaman his power and brought him into communion with cosmic life.[108]

This is not to say that the king of Egypt was a shaman, or to argue that shamanism as it is generally understood existed in ancient Egypt, but it is

Figure 7.25. King Narmer as a bull knocks down the walls of an enemy city and tramples his foes. It is in this archetypal role that the bull-king Unas is said to strike Kenzet, a semimythical region at the southern limit of Egypt. Narmer palette. Early Dynastic period.

to suggest that ancient Egyptian religious consciousness had shamanic roots that we need to take into account if we are to understand events such as the transformation of the king into a bull.

This transformation was by no means unique to Unas. There are depictions of the king as a bull from the early dynastic period, knocking down city walls and trampling the enemy (fig. 7.25). These may well be the visual counterparts to the declaration in this utterance that Unas is the great bull who attacked Kenzet. Kenzet was a region located at the southern limit of Egypt, and so identified with Nubia, the traditional enemy of Egypt. Kenzet, however, was also located in the heavens, as a place of purification bordering the heavenly Field of Rushes. So while the text conveys a sense of the king's physical might, there is also a sense of the king's exaltation, and of this transformation occurring on an otherworldly plane, because Kenzet was also—in fact normally in the Pyramid Texts—a region of the Otherworld.[109]

In this utterance we are presented with an image of the king both as a powerful spiritual being, on familiar terms with Ra, and as full of sexual potency. The text states that he eats five meals, three in heaven and two on earth. He then proceeds to copulate with Mowet (possibly a goddess personifying semen), kisses another goddess, Shuset (the dry?), unites with Nekhebut (a goddess personifying fecundity), and makes love to "the

228

Figure 7.26. Unas consorts with two goddesses. Reconstruction drawing from relief fragments from his pyramid temple at Saqqara.

Beautiful One" (fig. 7.26). With such promiscuity, it is not surprising that Unas fears a lack of seed (*tebteb*), but "the Beautiful One gives him bread" and "she does good to him on this day."[110]

What are we to make of this sexual orgy? First of all, we notice that Unas's sexual relations are with goddesses, not with mortal women. Second, they are initially with three goddesses and then a fourth, the Beautiful One, who cares for him and gives bread to him. Here we seem again to touch a shamanic undercurrent to the Pyramid Texts. The idea of a "celestial wife" is a common motif in shamanism, and the shaman's meeting with her is often preceded by his entering into amorous relations with other female spirits.[111] According to Mircea Eliade, "the fact that the shaman has a celestial wife who prepares meals for him in the seventh heaven and sleeps with him is another proof that he shares to some extent in the condition of semidivine beings, that he is a hero who has experienced death and resurrection and who therefore enjoys a second life, in the heavens."[112] This shamanic death/rebirth substratum to the motif of the king's amorous liaisons with goddesses is closely related to the king's assuming a bull form in this utterance. The bull form links him to Kamutef, "the bull of his mother," and it is Kamutef who ensures his own rebirth by becoming the lover of his mother. The Beautiful One is probably an epithet for

Nut, Hathor, or Isis, the celestial goddess through the fecundation of whom the king is enabled to be born again.[113]

(3) AND (4) UTTERANCES 207 AND 209: TWO FOOD TEXTS

There follow two short utterances, the first (utt. 207) describing an "offering of that which is in the eye of Ra"; the second (utt. 209) concerns the relationship of the king to *shu* (emptiness, want) and reads like a Zen koan:

> **If emptiness (*shu*) flourishes,**
> **Unas cannot take his food.**
> **If Unas flourishes,**
> **emptiness cannot take its food.**[114]

To interpret this riddle, we need to understand that the idea of acquiring wisdom or insight was intimately related to the concept of nourishment. The word for "wisdom" (*sai*) is identical with the phrase for "to be sated" or "full up" after a meal. In other words, it is the opposite of emptiness (*shu*).[115] Not only is the desire of Unas for wisdom, but he cannot satisfy this desire while emptiness (lack of spiritual nourishment) flourishes.

In the remaining utterances of this gable (utts. 210–12), we shall see how fervent was the desire of Unas to eat and drink the food of the gods, for only this can provide him with spiritual nourishment. So what was the food of the gods? There is little doubt that the gods were understood to feed principally on Maat, or truth.[116] Since one of the titles of Maat was "eye of Ra," it is possible that it is to Maat that the phrase "that which is in the eye of Ra" in utterance 207 refers.[117] In these two food utterances, while we are superficially meeting offering texts, at a more profound level we are presented with the desire for the spiritual nourishment that leads to the opposite of emptiness or want: namely, satiety or "wisdom." It may be simply coincidental—but, if it is, then it is a remarkable coincidence—that in exactly the same location as utterances 207 and 209 on the other side of the wall in the antechamber there is a text (utt. 250) in which Unas declares himself to be a "master of wisdom" (*her sai*), united with the divine personification of knowledge or insight, Sia—an evident play on words (see fig. 8.2).

(5) UTTERANCE 210: NEGOTIATING THE INVERTED WORLD

The purpose of utterance 210 is to ensure that Unas does not eat feces or drink urine but eats and drinks the divine food of the gods Ra and Thoth. This danger of eating excrement occurs only if one travels into the Otherworld without realizing that it is an inverted world, where everything is the opposite of what it is in the physical world.[118] A New Kingdom depiction of the dangers of traveling upside down in the mirror world of the Dwat is given in figure 7.27. It is a conception that goes back at least as far as the Pyramid Texts. In fact, in the idea of the Otherworld as an inverted world, we touch again upon the shamanic substratum of the Pyramid Texts, for it is found in many shamanic traditions.[119] What this indicates is that it belongs not so much to "belief" as to spiritual experience. We are here meeting a description of a type of danger with which the soul traveling in the spirit world will have to contend.

Unas orients himself by appealing to the two gods who, through the sun and moon, illuminate day and night, and by implication govern the two conditions of consciousness associated with the diurnal rhythm: waking and sleeping. These two gods are Ra and Thoth. While association with Ra links Unas to the creative dynamism of spiritual kingship, Thoth links him to the wisdom required to negotiate the ways of the Otherworld. And so he prays:

O you two companions who cross the sky,
who are Ra and Thoth.

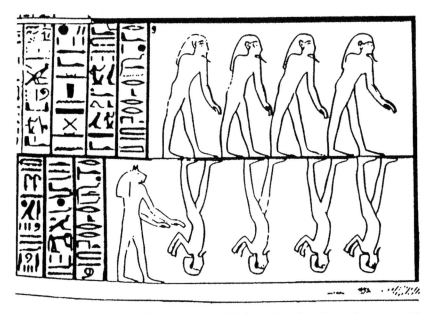

Figure 7.27. The dangers of traveling in the Underworld include the unpleasant possibility not only of traveling upside down but of one's bodily functions being reversed. From the Book of the Earth, Tomb of Ramesses IX.

> Take me with you,
> that I may eat of what you eat,
> that I may drink of what you drink,
> that I may live on what you live on,
> that I may sit on what you sit on,
> that I may be strong through that whereby you are strong,
> that I may sail in that in which you sail.[120]

Thus he finds his sustenance in the divine world, "going round the sky like Ra" and "traversing the sky like Thoth."

(6) UTTERANCE 211: UNAS IS BORN A STAR

Utterance 211 makes it quite clear that the reason why Unas wishes to eat and drink the food of the gods is that he has been spiritually reborn. Something has come to birth in him that is totally indifferent to physical hunger and thirst, yet requires the nourishment of divine food. Thus he is suckled by the milk goddess, Iat, and this may well be the subject of a relief fragment that has survived from Unas's pyramid temple, depicting his being suckled like a newborn baby by a goddess (see fig. 7.28). This is an inner event that had a ritual counterpart in the Sed festival, as we have already seen.[121]

In the text, Unas declares:

> My foster mother is Iat
> and it is she who nourishes me,
> it is indeed she who bore me.
> I was conceived in the night,
> I was born in the night,
> I belong to those who are in the suite of Ra. . . .[122]

Unas has become aware of an element in his own nature that has a purely cosmic origin. This experience must surely be the prototype of similar "cosmic rebirth" motifs in the Hermetic literature.[123] The text explains that Unas was conceived and born in the Nun, the cosmic ocean that is the source of all existence, the progenitor of the gods, which is to say that he becomes conscious that the spiritual source of existence (the Nun) is the source of his own being. Thus he is able to bring nourishment ("bread") to his people. The text describes it as follows:

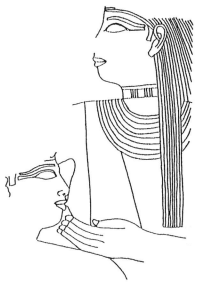

Figure 7.28. Unas is suckled by a goddess, possibly the cosmic milk goddess, Iat, who is referred to in utterance 211. From a relief fragment in the pyramid temple of Unas, Saqqara.

I was conceived in the Nun,
I was born in the Nun,
I have come and I have brought to you
the bread that I found there.[124]

It is worth dwelling on this deed of Unas a little further. The bread that he brings is bread that he found in the Nun. There is only one sort of bread that we know of that exists in the Nun, and that is Maat.[125] In bringing this "spiritual bread" to his people, the king is therefore reestablishing Maat (in the sense of cosmic order and harmony) throughout the land.[126] It is this that constitutes the esoteric meaning of the king's rebirth and coronation as a living Horus. It is not just that he himself has a mystical experience of rebirth, but that he is able to bring the spiritual substance of this experience into connection with the whole land and people of Egypt.

(7) UTTERANCE 212: THE DIVINE NOURISHMENT OF THE KING
The final utterance of the east gable apparently confirms this rebirth of the king as Horus, for Osiris (as Foremost of the Westerners) is said to bring provisions to Horus, and Unas chants:

What he [Horus] lives on, I live on;
What he eats of, I eat of;
What he drinks of, I drink of.[127]

233

Once again the theme of the king being provided with divine nourishment is reiterated. And it is noteworthy that on the other side of the gable wall in the antechamber Unas is hailed as the "wise one" or "sated one" (*sai*) who is reborn, like Ra, from the goddess Nut (utt. 247, first part).

Just as the eye of Horus gives life to Osiris, so Osiris now provides nourishment to Horus, as he did in utterance 204 at the other end of the gable. Osiris is the direct connection of Horus with the divine world. Osiris could here be understood as the king's own experience of himself as having journeyed into the spirit world. Osiris is the king as a "Westerner," one who knows the realm of the dead, who has traveled there and experienced the awesome knowledge of what lies beyond the threshold of death. And who now carries this knowledge back into the realm of the living.

8 THE ANTECHAMBER TEXTS

The West Gable (Utts. 247–53)

On the other side of the wall from the sarcophagus chamber east gable is the antechamber west gable. Like the sarcophagus chamber east gable, the antechamber west gable has seven texts inscribed upon it. These seven texts are concerned primarily with the cosmic rebirth of Unas and his assimilation into the spirit world. As such, they are closely connected thematically with the seven sarcophagus chamber texts on the other side of the wall. As we have already seen, there is a possibility that some of the texts were deliberately positioned so as magically to reinforce the texts on the other side of the wall. We shall continue to notice possible instances of what Schwaller de Lubicz termed "transposition" between the two walls as we proceed.

(1) UTTERANCE 247: THE AWAKENING OF THE INITIATE KING

Utterance 247 begins with Unas addressed as Osiris awakening and coming forth from the Dwat. He is hailed as the "Wise One" (*sai*), or one who is "filled up." He has been reborn, like Ra, from the goddess Nut, referred to here as "She who gives birth to the god." The second part of the utterance consists of words ritually spoken by a priest, taking the role of Horus, to awaken Unas. It is a "resurrection" text, similar to the sarcophagus chamber east-wall utterances 223 and 224. It should be read as part of the ritual reawakening of the initiate king, commanding him to come back into his body and use his senses again. The priest shouts out:

> O Unas, O Unas, SEE!
> O Unas, O Unas, LOOK!
> O Unas, O Unas, HEAR!

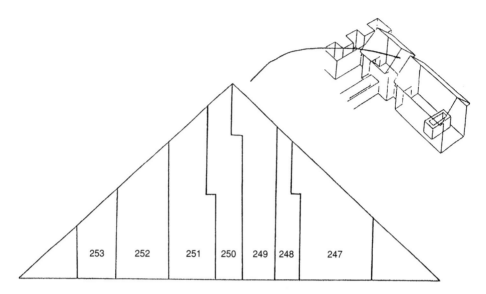

Figure 8.1. The seven texts of the antechamber west gable are mainly concerned with the cosmic rebirth of Unas. They read from north to south (i.e., from right to left).

O Unas, O Unas, BE THERE!
O Unas, O Unas, raise yourself on your side.
Do as I command:
You who hates sleep, but who were made limp, ARISE![1]

It is important to understand that in becoming an "awakened Osiris," the king is at the same time becoming a "reborn Horus": To awaken from the "sleep" of Osiris is to be reborn in a spiritual sense as a Horus-child. Hence the awakening of the initiate king is at the same time his rebirth.

Since this reawakening of the king can also be understood as his rebirth, it is interesting that on the other side of the wall, corresponding spatially to the second part of utterance 247, the theme of utterance 211 is that of the rebirth of the king:

I was conceived in the night,
I was born in the night. . . .[2]

In figure 8.2, the relationship between the texts on either side of the gable wall is shown. It can be seen how utterance 247 straddles both utterances 212 and 211.

Sarcophagus Chamber: East Gable

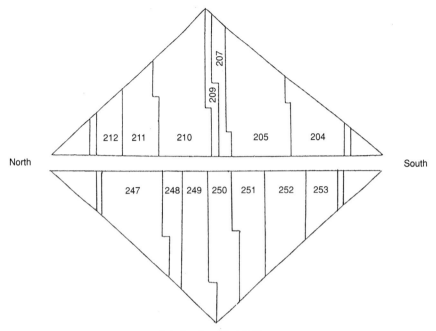

Antechamber: West Gable

Figure 8.2. The seven texts of the sarcophagus chamber east gable correspond thematically with the seven texts of the antechamber west gable on the other side of the wall dividing the two chambers. Note that the orientation is as if looking from the sarcophagus chamber, with the sarcophagus chamber east gable above and north to the left.

(2) UTTERANCE 248: THE FIERY REBIRTH OF UNAS

Utterance 248 gives details of the king's cosmic rebirth. He has been born from the "thighs of the divine world [Ennead]" as a star. Having been conceived by Sekhmet, it was Shesmetet who gave birth to him—these are both fiery leonine goddesses, and Shesmetet could in this context be regarded as an aspect of Sekhmet.[3] We recall here the prominent role of the lion bed in the Sed festival "secret rites," the lion heads of which often appear to be female.[4] The king's rebirth through Sekhmet/Shesmetet enables him to establish a direct relationship to the sun god, Ra. Sekhmet, who was the daughter of Ra and is often depicted with the solar disk on her head, can be seen in figure 8.3. In the utterances that follow, this relationship with Ra is increasingly developed, so that while Unas's rebirth is on one level an

237

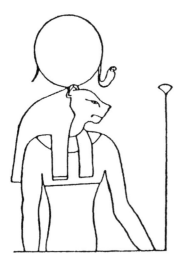

Figure 8.3. Sekhmet, the fiery leonine goddess, who was the daughter of Ra, conceives and then, as Shesmetet, gives birth to Unas.

Osirian event, at a deeper level it involves the solarization of the king.

(3) UTTERANCE 249: THE SUN CHILD

The rebirth theme continues in utterance 249, which describes how Unas rises like the sun god himself from the Island of Fire—that is, from the primeval island that emerges from the dark ocean of Nun every morning at daybreak. There he appears as Nefertem, the son of Sekhmet, the solar child within the lotus of rebirth. The name Nefertem literally means "the new (or young) Atum," the old sun reborn. Like Ra, Unas "will issue from the Akhet every day," and like Ra, the first breath he takes will be filled with the sweet scent of the flower of rebirth (fig. 8.4).[5]

Figure 8.4. The king appears as Nefertem, the solar child within the lotus. Each morning, as Ra rises up from the Akhet, his first breath is the scent of this flower of rebirth. Ptolemaic bronze mirror.

(4) Utterance 250: Uniting with Sia

Physically in the center of the west gable, utterance 250 is also symbolically the central text of the series of seven. Unas declares himself to be a "master of wisdom" (*her sai*, literally, "one who is above wisdom"), united with the divine personification of knowledge or insight, Sia. Sia is one of the "two companions" of Ra, whom we have already met in the passage between the sarcophagus chamber and the antechamber (utt. 245). The other companion is Hu, who personifies "creative utterance" or "command." These two gods are probably best understood in the context of the creation theology of Memphis, according to which the cosmic creator god, Ptah, commands the universe into existence in accordance with the wisdom in his heart. Thus Hu could be seen as the personification of the creator god's creative speech, and Sia the wisdom in his heart. Sia also has affinities with Thoth as "the bearer of the divine book, at the right hand of Ra."[6] Hu and Sia are the constant companions of Ra in New Kingdom mystical texts and are depicted with him in his sun boat (fig. 8.5).

We have already seen that the word *sai*, which is translated as "wisdom," is identical in Egyptian with the word for "to be sated" or "to be full up" after a meal, and that this utterance corresponds spatially to the two food utterances (utts. 207 and 209) on the sarcophagus chamber east gable. While utterance 209 contrasts the state of "emptiness" (*shu*) with Unas being able to take his food, here we see the triumph of "fullness" or wisdom. The wisdom that Unas is master of here is a wisdom gained through ingesting spiritual food that nourishes the heart. In the sarcophagus chamber

Figure 8.5. Hu and Sia accompany Ra on his journey through the sky in the sun boat. In the cabin with Ra are Seti I and Maat. From the New Kingdom Book of Night. The Osireion, Abydos.

239

utterance 209, it is as if the preconditions are set for Unas to become a "master of fullness"—fullness of heart—here in utterance 250.

(5) UTTERANCE 251: BECOMING THE STRONG HORN OF RA

Utterance 251 begins with an address to the stars to prepare a way for Unas so that he may pass through the demonic guardians and attain his throne "behind the great god" Ra. There, in the entourage of Ra, who is described as a bull, Unas becomes the "strong horn" of the god, repelling the enemies of the sun god. Unas is no longer the vulnerable sun child, but is rather the fierce protector of the solar principle that has awakened within him. It is interesting that the only reference to Unas as a bull in the sarcophagus chamber is on the other side of the wall, in exactly the same position, in the second part of utterance 205, in which Ra is said to provide food for Unas because he is "the Great Bull who smote in Kenzet."[7]

(6) UTTERANCE 252: UNION WITH RA

In utterance 252, Unas is entirely assimilated with Ra, wielding power "throughout the domain of Ra." He takes his place on the sun god's boat and

> **commands what is good**
> **and he [Ra] does it,**
> **for the king is the great god.**[8]

Here we see the culmination of the king's solarization, in which he becomes essentially indistinguishable from Ra. On the other side of the wall in the same position, we saw Ra providing Unas with food (utt. 205, first part), and Ra was there described as his father. This antechamber text is like a completion of the sarcophagus chamber utterance, for now Unas is inwardly united with Ra. In this union of the king with Ra, we are once again reminded of the Sed festival rite in which the king sailed in the sun boat as Ra.[9] This rite must surely, as must utterance 252, reflect an inner event in which a living connection is experienced between the self-renewing, self-regenerating solar principle in the sky and an element that resides within the human soul. The sun's light not only shines in the sky, but can be contacted inwardly, and in uniting with it inwardly the soul undergoes apotheosis.[10]

(7) UTTERANCE 253: LIFTED UP BY SHU

At the south end of the west gable, utterance 253 reaffirms the king's union with Ra. His purification in the heavenly Field of Rushes is at the same time Ra's purification. The king's hand is in Ra's hand, and thus is he "lifted up"

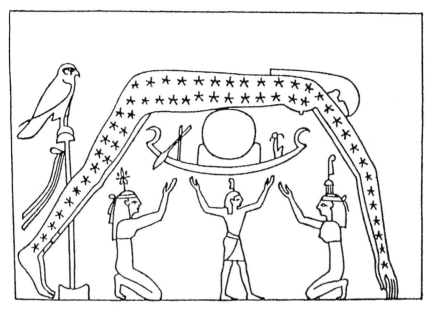

Figure 8.6. Shu lifts up the newborn sun. In utterance 253, the identification of Unas with the sun god, Ra, is so total that he too is lifted up by Shu. New Kingdom papyrus.

by the god Shu. The "lifting up" may be understood as a lifting of the sun disk away from the realm of night into the realm of day. This active engagement of Shu in the elevation of the sun disk into the sky occurs after the successful completion of the journey of the sun through the Underworld, or Dwat.[11] Would it be too far-fetched to see this act of service on the part of Shu as part of the answer to the riddle: "If the king flourishes, *shu* (emptiness) cannot take his meal"? His arms, after all, are full because he is holding the newborn sun at this moment (fig. 8.6). Utterance 204 declares not only that Unas will not thirst or hunger but also that his heart will be "filled" (*mehy*). The text reads: "O fill him, O filler of hearts!"[12]

The Fifteen West-to-South-Wall Texts (Utts. 254–58; 260–63; 267–72)

The fifteen texts of the west and south wall of the antechamber form a continuous sequence, similar to the twelve texts of the sarcophagus chamber south and east walls. Both these sequences have a key utterance that straddles

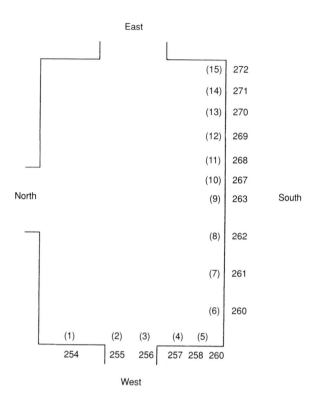

Figure 8.7. The fifteen west-to-south-wall texts in the antechamber form a continuous sequence. They read from the northern end of the west wall to the eastern end of the south wall.

both walls. In the sarcophagus chamber, this was utterance 219. Here in the antechamber it is utterance 260, of which only the first line is on the west wall while the bulk of the text is on the south wall. It would be rash of us to suppose that this was simply fortuitous, for it bears comparison to a practice in Egyptian sacred architecture known as "quoining" (or, to be precise, inverse quoining) of corner blocks. In order to avoid making the joint between two blocks in the corner, a large proportion of the surface area of one block was carved away, with the result that the small proportion that was not carved away "wrapped around" the corner (see fig. 8.8). Thus the right-angle joint with its crack in the corner is replaced by something more organic and flowing. It would seem that a similar principle is being brought into play here with the corner texts, and the reasons for it are more

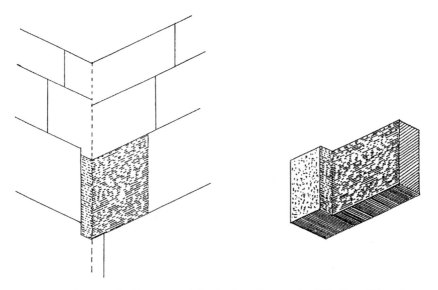

Figure 8.8. An example of inverse quoining in the valley temple of Khafre at Giza. A similar principle seems to be operating in the case of the texts in Unas's pyramid that wrap around the southeast corner of the sarcophagus chamber (utt. 219) and southwest corner of the antechamber (utt. 260). Left: view of an interior corner, made of granite blocks, one of which has most of its surface area carved away. Right: detail of granite block.

likely to be symbolic and magical than due simply to the arbitrariness of the lengths of text in relation to available wall space.[13]

The West Wall (Utts. 254–60)

(1) UTTERANCE 254: THE DEATH AND REBIRTH OF THE HORUS KING

The texts of the west wall start with the long utterance 254 at the northern end. Utterance 254 begins with a reference to Unas as the Bull of Nekhen. Nekhen (Hierakonpolis) was a major center of Horus worship in early dynastic times, and was situated in southern Egypt, just to the south of Abydos. In the text it is clear that Unas, in being identified with the Bull of Nekhen, is the Horus king of the south.[14] It is therefore as Horus that he threatens dire calamities if a place is not made for him by the lord of the Akhet. He will curse the earth god, Geb, and strike him dumb, he will devour whatever stands in his way, he will completely dam up the land so that the two riverbanks unite, and so on. In this early part of the utterance, Unas presents himself as a formidable magician with terrifying power to disrupt the order of nature if a place is not made for him in the heavenly region of transformation and rebirth, the Akhet.[15] His threats, though, are all aimed at Geb, the god of the earth, and by implication that which holds the soul back from becoming spiritualized. Symbolically, the realm of Geb is the realm in which the spiritual is imprisoned. As we shall shortly see, it is here that the solar principle is "held in fetters."

The next part of the utterance (from the middle of §279) begins with a speech by Wer Sekhet (a god who is said to dwell in the Dwat and whose name means "Great Field"), who announces that Unas has "split open the earth" and arisen like Ra as "the Bull of the Sky." Unas in his bull form is now not just Horus; he is also the sun god, Ra. He is greeted by the Beautiful West, a manifestation of the cosmic cow goddess. She welcomes him as her son, for (as in utterance 205) the significance of the king assuming the bull form is that he thereby becomes Kamutef ("the bull of his mother")—both lover and son of the cosmic cow goddess, through whom he is reborn. And so the Beautiful West says to him:

> **Here comes he whom I have borne,**
> **whose horn is upstanding . . . the Bull of the Sky.[16]**

Unas is now urged to travel on to the Field of Offerings (*sekhet hetep*), a heavenly region that could equally be translated "Field of Peace."

The text explains that Unas has been "plowed into the earth," and there in the depths of the earth he saw the sun god Ra "in fetters" and witnessed the liberation of Ra from his fetters.[17] It is this momentous event of the sun god bursting forth from his imprisonment in the earth that Unas reenacts. It was an event later illustrated in the Book of the Dead, in which the earth was depicted in the shape of both a sarcophagus and the primeval mound from which Ra emerged at the beginning of creation (see fig. 8.9).

The plowing into the earth of Unas and the subsequent solar rebirth are best understood in the light of Osirian myth and ritual. The Osirian festival of Khoiak began with a plowing and sowing ceremony, which symbolically corresponded to the death, dismemberment, and interment of Osiris in the earth.[18] Insofar as both Ra and Unas undergo the fate of being plowed into the earth, they do so as Osiris.

This Osirian connection is confirmed in the last part of the utterance (beginning at §286) in which the king boldly tells the female monkeys who cut off heads that he has fixed his head firmly back on his body.[19] The text

Figure 8.9. The liberation of Ra from his imprisonment in the earth is reen-acted by Unas in utterance 254. This became a common motif in the Book of the Dead. Illustration to BD 17, Papyrus of Ani, New Kingdom.

implies that Unas's head had been detached and now it is securely reat-tached, as is that of the Apis bull, with whom Unas is evidently connected here. It was part of the fate of Osiris to be dismembered, and this included his decapitation. Decapitation should be understood as an essential phase in the Osirian process that led to the revirilization and "solar resurrection" of both the god and the king. It will be remembered that one of the episodes in the Sed festival "secret rites" of Niuserre was the restoration of the head of the king immediately prior to his rebirth as a Horus.[20] Figure 8.10 depicts just such a rite of the restoration of the head to the inert and headless Osiris, who rests on the knees of Isis in her two forms of Isis-Hededyt and Sothis

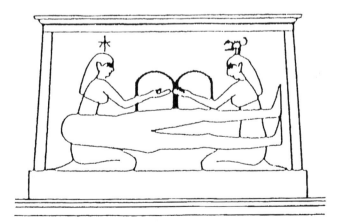

Figure 8.10. Isis-Hededyt and Sothis reconstitute the headless body of Osiris and at the same time conjure up the floodwaters of the Nile. From the Ptolemaic temple of Philae.

245

(Sirius), who conjure forth the waters of the Nile so that the inundation might begin.

The understanding of such events requires that one enter an experiential world that has far more affinities with shamanism than is admitted by most contemporary Egyptologists. The theme of dismemberment is one that we shall return to later, in discussing utterance 267 on the south wall. But here we may in passing note that the decapitation and restoration of the head of the initiate are important submotifs to many shamanic accounts of dismemberment.[21] As we have seen in the case of Niuserre, the condition of headlessness and the restoration of the head were important initiatory experiences within the Egyptian Sed festival "secret rites." This is not to suggest that Niuserre was literally undergoing a shamanic initiation, but rather that the initiatory experiences he was undergoing have clear shamanic parallels. The text describing Niuserre's "secret rites" indicates that the restoration of his head corresponds to his rebirth as a god, that is to his rebirth as one who—like a shaman—is as much at home in the spirit world as in the world of the living. It is presumably this that is the import of the text we are considering here, for once his head is restored, we find Unas being "honored" in the spirit world by those who see him—namely, the gods. At the end of the text, Unas is once more the "bull of the Sky" crushing all those would oppose him. In other words, his identification with the solar principle is complete.

(2) UTTERANCE 255: OVERCOMING THE UGLY ONE

It can be seen in figure 8.11 that utterance 254 is by far the longest utterance on the west wall. It is followed by utterance 255, in which Unas again acts in the role of king of southern Egypt. This is indicated by the fact that he is referred to as Horus of Nekhen three times. It is significant that the main events of the Sed festival, along with other royal ceremonies, were presided over by the ancestral spirits of Nekhen (representing the southern center of Horus worship) along with those of Pe (the equivalent northern center of Horus worship in the Delta).[22] That the spirits of Nekhen are mentioned only here is a clear indication as to the ceremonial role of Unas as king of the south in these utterances. This is in contrast to utterances 220–22 on the other side of the same wall in the sarcophagus chamber, which feature coronation ceremonies in which Unas is crowned with the red crown of the north. The climax of the sarcophagus chamber coronation rites is the mystical union of the king with Ra and Atum in utterance 222. Here on the west wall of the antechamber the emphasis of utterance 254 has been on the union of the king with Ra in an earthly and Osirian setting.

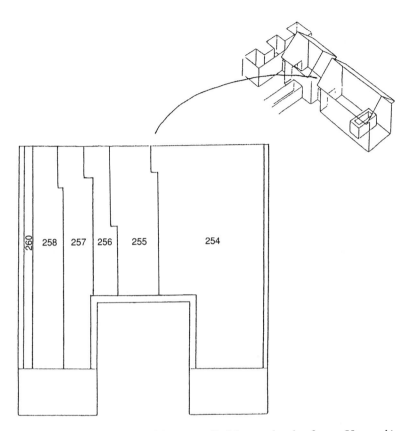

Figure 8.11. The six utterances of the west wall of the antechamber feature Unas as king of the south, and read from north to south (right to left).

Since utterance 222 occupies roughly the same space on the sarcophagus chamber east wall as the second part of utterance 254 and all of utterance 255 on the antechamber west wall, the placement of these texts may not be wholly coincidental (see fig. 8.12). Furthermore, just as there is no reason to regard the sarcophagus chamber east-wall texts as originally funerary, so there is little to support a funerary interpretation of these antechamber west-wall texts.

In utterance 255, Unas as Horus of Nekhen is now located in the Akhet, the place of solar rebirth, where he confronts the Ugly One (*khebedj*) who opposes him. Once again, Unas threatens to bring about a cosmic cataclysm if he is opposed, as he did in the previous utterance. Here Unas identifies with Ra, taking possession of two of his most important attributes—creative utterance (Hu) and knowledge or insight (Sia)—as he did in utterance 249 on the west gable above. Insofar as a king has been through the solar initiation, he acquires these attributes, with Hu coming to reside in his mouth (i.e, in his speech) and Sia in his heart. It is important to note that the acquisition of Hu and Sia was not seen as something that occurred only after the king's death; they were powers that the living king also commanded.[23]

(3) UTTERANCE 256: THE THRONE OF HORUS

In utterance 256, Unas takes his place on the throne of Horus and proclaims himself heir to Geb (the earth) and to Atum (the Cosmic Source):

> **I have succeeded to Geb, I have succeeded to Geb;**
> **I have succeeded to Atum.**
> **I am on the throne of Horus the first-born. . . .**[24]

This again sounds less like a funerary text than a song of the living king's triumphant enthronement. It is a statement of the royal apotheosis, reminiscent of the Sed festival coronation ceremony in which this formula is recited:

> **Horus appears resting on his southern throne**
> **and there occurs a uniting of the sky to the earth.**[25]

In the Pyramid Text version, "sky" or "heaven" is personified as Atum, the spiritual source of the cosmos, while "earth" is personified as Geb. It is interesting to note that on the other side of the wall in the sarcophagus chamber, as if amplifying the statement that Unas is "on the throne of Horus the first-born," we find another coronation text (utt. 221), proclaiming that "the great one has given birth to you" (see fig. 8.12).

In utterance 256, at this moment of the uniting the Above (Atum) and the Below (Geb), all the gods take off their clothes in reverence and, naked, bow down to Unas.[26] This extraordinary image of the gods appearing naked before the king implies that he has complete knowledge of them. But why should they bow down before the king? Perhaps their reverence toward him is owing to the fact that they are unable to accomplish the specifically human feat of uniting heaven and earth, for their sphere is restricted to the heavens alone. The god Horus represents a mode of consciousness both human and divine. In Horus heaven and earth are united in a way that brings into being a new divine–human axis within the person of the king.[27]

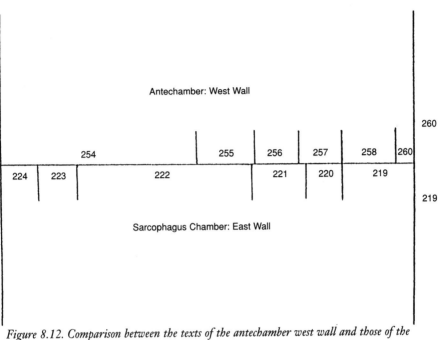

Figure 8.12. Comparison between the texts of the antechamber west wall and those of the sarcophagus chamber east wall.

(4) UTTERANCE 257: BURSTING THROUGH THE SKY

The final stage in the apotheosis of Unas is described in utterance 257, in which the king now "sits on the throne of the Lord of All," causing a sensation in heaven, for this is "something new." This utterance, however, does not describe a coronation ritual. Rather, what it describes is a mystical experience. Unas bursts through the canopy—literally the "basin" (*bia*)—of the sky and penetrates to the supercelestial region beyond space and time.[28] The idea of breaking through the canopy of the sky has shamanic parallels and is explicitly reiterated in the mystical philosophy of Plato.[29] It is not unique to Unas's pyramid, but can be found elsewhere in the Pyramid Texts—for example, in the pyramid of Pepi I, where it is similarly placed on the antechamber west wall. There we read:

> **The doors of the basin (*bia*) of the starry sky**
> **are thrown open to me,**
> **and I go through them.**
> **My leopard skin is on me**
> **and my scepter is in my hand.**[30]

Immediately before this statement, Pepi says that he takes his seat in the solar bark and rows Ra across the sky to the west. In the pyramid of Unas, there is a similar association of breaking out of the basin of the sky and joining Ra. But, unlike Pepi, Unas is here identified with Ra. As Ra, he rises as Kheprer, descends in the west, and travels through the Dwat in order to shine anew in the east. That the idea of the king joining the cosmic circuit of Ra should be linked with his transcendence of the celestial sphere is owing to the fact that the one makes the other possible. It is just because he has transcended the celestial world—the realm of the gods—that the human king is able to travel with the Being from whom all the gods originate. His identification with the sun god is an identification with One whose essential nature lies beyond the world of form. Although Ra may manifest in the sun, he is far greater than the shining disk by which he illumines the world below, and which the Egyptians regarded merely as his "eye" (fig. 8.13).

As the essential nature of Ra is beyond manifestation, the course of the sun imitates the divine nature in the world of form by moving in circles, this according to a principle later articulated by Plato that the circular movement of celestial bodies is a "moving image of eternity."[31] In Egyptian thought, eternity (*neheh*) is an attribute preeminently belonging to Ra, who transcends the temporal order. Thus the utterance concludes with Unas once again taking possession of the solar attributes not only of Hu and Sia, but also of Neheh (the personification of eternity).

(5) UTTERANCE 258: A LIVING OSIRIS

Utterance 258, which follows, features Unas no longer as Horus but as an Osiris rising up to the heavens in a dust storm. He has not entered into the earth (Geb), he has been healed by the Eye of Horus, and all his injuries have been effaced.

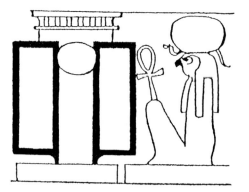

Figure 8.13. Ra watches the sun disk emerge from the eastern gate of the Akhet. This image makes a clear distinction between the god Ra, who is beyond all form, and the disk of the sun.

> **Unas is on the way to heaven,**
> **Unas is on the way to heaven,**
> **with the wind, with the wind.**
> **He will not be hindered,**
> **there is no one who might hinder him.**[32]

Significantly, there will be no session on him in the tribunal: He will not be judged, but rather he "bestows powers (*ka*s) and takes away powers (*ka*s)," and he "punishes and effaces injuries."[33] The only other reference to Unas not being judged, but—on the contrary—actively judging, is on the other side of the wall in the sarcophagus chamber. There we find utterance 219 occupying exactly the same wall space (seven lines of text) as utterance 258 and the beginning of utterance 260 here in the antechamber. Utterance 219 is a very long utterance that has the same formula repeated twenty-four times:

> **He has not been judged—this Unas has not been judged!**
> **He judges—this Unas judges!**

(6) Utterance 260: The One Who Went and Came Back

At the southern end of the west wall is the beginning of the sixth utterance (utt. 260), which then continues onto the south wall of the antechamber. In the first line of this utterance, Unas claims to be a Horus once more:

> **I am Horus, my father's heir.**
> **I am one who went and came back.**

As this statement is placed right after utterance 258, in which Unas is an Osiris, the implication is that he has been through an "Osiris experience" from which he has successfully returned, for now he has come back as Horus: that is, as the living king.[34] Utterance 260 occupies only one vertical line of text on the west wall before it is continued on the south wall (just after the word "purification" in §316). As there is only one other instance of an utterance spilling over from one wall to another in the whole pyramid, and that is on the other side of the same wall—the east wall of the sarcophagus chamber—so there is a kind of mirroring taking place here between the southern ends of the west wall of the antechamber and the east wall of the sarcophagus chamber. The mirroring extends beyond the simple placement of the texts to their underlying message. Reflecting the statement

"I am one who went and came back" in the antechamber, on the other side of the wall in the sarcophagus chamber in exactly the same position we read, as if in chorus,

He lives—this Unas lives!
He is not dead—this Unas is not dead![35]

The South Wall (Utts. 260–63; 267–72)

The south wall of the antechamber is noteworthy for three themes that are especially emphasized. First, there is the theme of the king's ascent to the sky, second his crossing the heavenly Field of Rushes, and third his overcoming various difficulties and dangers. While the theme of the king's

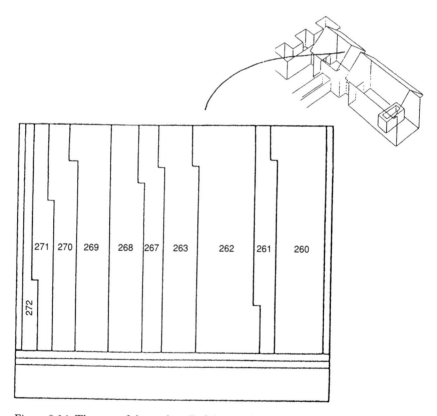

Figure 8.14. The texts of the south wall of the antechamber are concerned mainly with the king's ascent to the sky, his crossing the Field of Rushes, and his overcoming various difficulties and dangers. They read from west to east (i.e., from right to left).

ascent to the sky is prominent in the sarcophagus chamber, the Field of Rushes is not mentioned there at all, and the concept of difficulties and dangers is only briefly alluded to on the east gable in utterance 210. In both the pyramid of Unas and, it seems, in other pyramids as well, the three themes of ascent to the sky, transit across the Field of Rushes, and the overcoming of difficulties and dangers were felt to be especially appropriate for the antechamber south wall.[36]

(6) Utterance 260: The One Who Went and Came Back

We have seen that utterance 260 begins on the west wall of the antechamber, with the declaration that Unas is Horus, "the one who went and came back." This declaration sets the scene for the whole utterance. Almost immediately we encounter a reference to the "Two Truths" (Double Maat):

> **The Two Truths have judged,**
> **though a witness [lit., "a tongue"] was lacking.**
> **The Two Truths have commanded**
> **that the thrones of Geb shall revert to me,**
> **so that I may raise myself to what I have desired.**[37]

This is the only reference to the Two Truths, or Double Maat, in the Pyramid Texts —Maat is elsewhere referred to in the singular. Double Maat is shown in figure 8.15. Because of this reference to Maat in her dual form, it might seem that what is being described is the judgment of the soul that later became prominent in the Book of the Dead, and in which Double Maat plays a major part. In this passage, however, it is not the soul of the king that Double Maat has judged, but rather his claim as Horus to the throne of Geb (i.e., the double throne of Egypt). This particular passage is concerned with the mythical vindication of Horus in the legal contest between him and Seth for the right to rule over Egypt after Osiris. In other

Figure 8.15. The Two Truths, or "Double Maat," typically portrayed as two goddesses wearing an ostrich feather and holding the ankh cross.

words, it is concerned with the right of the living king to the throne.[38]

What this passage refers to, therefore, is a mythical event that may well stand behind the Sed festival ritual of the dedication of the field, in which the king holds in his hand a document known as the "Secret of the Two Partners" (i.e., Horus and Seth) that gives the king legal entitlement to rule over the land (fig. 8.16).[39] It will be recalled that this ritual was performed immediately after "the secret rites" during which the king underwent the Osirian death, dismemberment, and rebirth. Not only does this utterance begin by referring to the king as a (reborn) Horus who "went and came back," it also states that the king's limbs, which were hidden or concealed, are now reunited, and that he goes forth as a "living spirit" (*akh*). We have already seen in chapter 7 that the transformation into an *akh* was undergone by the living king Thutmose III, who had the "*akh*-power" of Ra bestowed upon him in an initiatory experience.[40] The connotation of the word *akh* is that of inner illumination as well as primordial creative power. Used in its initiatory sense, an *akh* might best be translated as "an enlightened being"—one whose consciousness has become open to the reality of the spirit world.[41] In the present utterance it is as an *akh* that Unas is said to oppose disorder (*khennu*) and act as the guardian or protector of *maat*, both typical functions of the living king.[42] All of these references point to the possibility of a Sed festival context, rather than a funerary context, for this passage.

Figure 8.16. King Niuserre "dedicates the field" during his Sed festival. In his left hand he holds the document known as the The Secret of the Two Partners (i.e., Horus and Seth) that gives him legal entitlement to rule over the land. Abu Gurob, Fifth Dynasty.

While the trial of the king as Horus is one difficulty triumphantly overcome in the first part of the utterance, in the second part we encounter the fear of being encompassed by darkness, and its attendant danger of traveling upside down. This danger we have already met in utterance 210 on the sarcophagus chamber east gable, with reference to the reversal of bodily functions. Here it is more explicitly stated:

> **I detest traveling in darkness,**
> **for then I cannot see**
> **but go upside down.**
> **I go forth today**
> **and I bring Truth (*maat*) with me.**
> **I will not be given over to your fire, O gods.**[43]

Not to travel upside down was later to become an obsessive theme of the Coffin Texts. Here, on the south wall of the antechamber, it is referred to as one of the adverse circumstances of traveling in darkness, and as leading to the possibility of being given over to the fire of the gods. Darkness and fire are both conditions experienced in the Underworld and were later elaborated on in the Coffin Texts.[44]

(7) UTTERANCE 261: THE LIGHTNING ASCENT

The next utterance describes Unas as a flash of lightning, "a blinding light . . . a flame moving before the wind to the end of the sky and the end of the earth." Thus he comes to stand on the eastern side of the sky, where he is greeted by those who dwell in the spirit world. This is the first of the "ascension texts" of the south wall.

(8) UTTERANCE 262: THE REGENERATIVE JOURNEY

Utterance 262 begins with one of the most beautiful and profound prayers of the Pyramid Texts. This prayer reveals the process of transformation that is undergone by the king as the inner counterpart of his journey to the stars. The stages of transformation are stages in the Osirian process of suffering destruction in order to undergo regeneration. The prayer is addressed to a series of gods, and begins with the following words:

> **Do not be unaware of me O god;**
> **Know me, for I know you.**
> **Do not be unaware of me, O god.**
> **Of me it is said: "the transitory one."**
> **Do not be unaware of me, O Ra.**
> **Know me, for I know you.**
> **Do not be unaware of me, O Ra.**
> **Of me it is said: "Great One who is destroyed."**[45]

One god after another is addressed in the same way, while each time Unas receives a different title of Osiris. He is "the solitary one at rest" and "the unfortunate one." But as the prayer proceeds, the names of Osiris Unas become more positive, ending with "He who awakes in good health" and finally "This *nekhekh* star." The word *nekhekh* has connotations of growing old and being rejuvenated (for example, Ra as the setting sun that will rise again is called *nekhekh*). In order to become a brilliant *nekhekh* star, Unas's knowledge of the gods must be reciprocated by them in a supportive act of recognition of the deep transformative stages that he passes through. As we saw in utterance 205 (sarcophagus chamber, east gable), "being seen" by the gods has ontological import. At each stage of his crisis, disintegration, rehabilitation, and inner illumination, Unas prays that the gods, as it were, hold him in their consciousness. Thus his divinization as a star occurs against the background of a mutual gnosis between the human and divine worlds.

After the opening prayer, the second part of the utterance returns to the theme of the king's ascent to the sky. But in this utterance there are various dangers to be overcome. A "dangerous place," a "great lake," a "ferryboat," and then a "shrine" or "palace" (*het*) of the Great Ones mark the hazardous route that the king must take:

> **Unas has passed by his dangerous place,**
> **the fury of the great lake has missed him.**
> **His fare for the ferryboat has not been taken from him,**
> **the shrine (*het*) of the Great Ones cannot oppose him**
> **on the path of the *sehedu* stars.**[46]

Whereas in the last utterance, his ascent to the sky appeared dramatically swift in the lightning flash, in this utterance the ascent seems slower and the way is fraught with obstacles. There are dangerous regions to be traveled through and perils to be avoided in order finally to approach the sun god Ra and gain a place in the solar night bark and day bark.

(9) UTTERANCE 263: CROSSING ON REED FLOATS, MEETING THE DEAD

In utterance 263, Unas crosses over to the Akhet on two reed floats:

> **The reed floats of the sky are set in place for me,**
> **that I may cross on them to the Akhet, to Ra. . . .**[47]

What is being crossed is evidently envisaged as a watery expanse. Up until

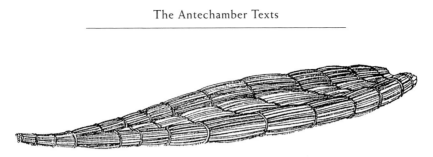

Figure 8.17. A reed float raft, in common use on the Nile up until the beginning of the twentieth century. It consists of two bundles of reeds lashed together. On a simple raft such as this, Unas traveled to the eastern part of the sky.

the beginning of the twentieth century, such reed floats were commonly used by peasants to cross the Nile. They consisted of two fat bundles of dried reeds, tied together side by side (see fig. 8.17).[48] Unas is here at the border between worlds, on his way to the eastern part of the sky, the place of dawning light, which is also the place of transformation into a shining spirit, an *akh*. This borderland is the Field of Rushes, which Unas enters with his *ka*. He wears a leopard-skin loincloth and carries two power objects: the Horus weapon (*ames* scepter) on his arm and the lotus-bud scepter (*'aba* scepter) in his hand. He goes forward armed like King Pepi when he broke through the basin of the sky.[49]

Having crossed over the watery expanse, what Unas encounters are the spirits of the dead, who bring to him four ancient spirits who act as border guards to the Otherworld. These ancient spirits who lean on their staffs are also paradoxically youthful, for they are said to wear the sidelock of youth. They are perhaps examples of what it means to have become *nekhekh*. It is only with their approval that Unas can proceed to cross the Field of Rushes. This encounter with the spirits of the dead does not mean that Unas is himself dead. In the shamanic tradition, the spirits of the dead play a crucial role in instructing the shaman in how to participate in the mode of being of the dead, thereby enabling him to enter into contact with the gods. It is quite possible that something similar is being described here.[50]

(10) UTTERANCE 267: RE-MEMBERMENT AND ASCENT TO THE SKY
Unas's position between two states of being is the main theme of utterance 267, which is roughly in the middle of the wall. On the one hand, Unas is an Osiris who has been through the experience of dismemberment and now knows that he once more has his heart, his legs, his arms—a fact already alluded to in utterance 260. On the other hand, as we have seen in utterance 262, his task as a re-membered Osiris is to rise up to heaven to

join Ra. It is often supposed that Osirian and solar texts represent two quite distinct cults that are artificially brought together in the Pyramid Texts. The present utterance is held to be a good example of the artificial juxtaposition of texts belonging to the two different cults of Osiris and Ra.[51] But is this juxtaposition artificial? The deeper relationship between the cults of Osiris and Ra will be missed if they are seen as simply expressing the beliefs of two rival priesthoods or as representing different historical strata in the development of Egyptian religion.

The experience of physical dismemberment, followed by the renewal of internal organs and reconstitution of the body, conforms to a universal pattern of initiation, well attested within the shamanic literature. The later stages involve an ascent to the sky and dialogue with gods and ancestral spirits, which can culminate in a meeting with the Supreme Being, who bestows upon the shaman his power to shamanize.[52] The Osirian and solar elements in utterance 267 follow this archetypal pattern of shamanic initiation experiences, even to the extent that the ways the king reaches the sky are typically shamanic. In the shamanic tradition, the ascent to the sky takes place through a variety of means, but the most frequently attested to are climbing a ladder or stairway and flying up as a bird.[53] So while it is possible to distinguish Osirian and solar themes in utterance 267, this does not mean that we have to explain them in terms of rival priesthoods or of different historical strata in the text. What we are dealing with first and foremost are levels of mystical experience that correspond remarkably closely to those documented in the literature of shamanism.

Utterance 267 begins with Unas identified with Osiris and assured that, like Osiris, he has been reconstituted. His prior dismemberment is assumed to have taken place, and now his body is whole:

> **You have your heart, O Osiris,**
> **you have your legs, O Osiris,**
> **you have your arms, O Osiris,**
> **[so too] my heart is my own,**
> **my legs are my own,**
> **my arms are my own.**[54]

The physical "wholeness" of Unas having been established, the text immediately goes on to describe his ascent to the sky, where he joins Ra in the solar boat. This is accomplished by his climbing a stairway, ascending on smoke, and flying up as a bird:

A stairway to the sky is set up for me
that I may ascend on it to the sky,
and I ascend on the smoke of the great censing.
I fly up as a bird and alight as a beetle (*kheprer*),
I fly up as a bird and alight as a beetle (*kheprer*)
on the empty throne which is in your bark, O Ra.[55]

In these two passages, then, we are meeting two different levels of mystical experience that, far from being arbitrarily juxtaposed, are inwardly linked. Just as in shamanic initiation rites the torture, dismemberment, death, and rebirth of the shaman is followed by what Eliade calls "the initiation proper," which consists in the candidate's triumphant journey to the sky, so in the Pyramid Texts we meet a similar experiential sequence.[56] Figure 8.18 is one

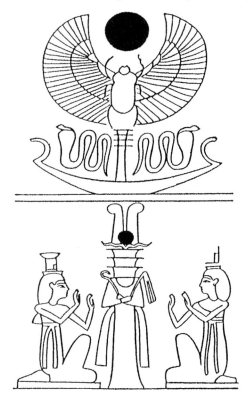

Figure 8.18. The reconstituted Osiris is represented by the upright djed *pillar, on either side of which Isis and Nephthys kneel. Above, the scarab beetle alights on the bark of Ra. This image very clearly depicts the two mystical levels of initiation described in utterance 267: the Osirian and the solar. From the New Kingdom papyrus of Khonsu-Renep.*

image selected from a large number that make up a whole genre of images that appear in New Kingdom mystical papyri, all of which express in different ways the theme of the two levels of initiation: the Osirian below and the solar above.[57] This particular illustration, from the papyrus of Khonsu-Renep, could almost be a meditation on utterance 267, for it shows the reconstituted and upright Osiris in the form of a *djed*, on either side of which are Isis and Nephthys. Above it, on a second level, the scarab beetle alights on the solar bark. Here the *djed* itself is like the "stairway to the sky," fully occupying the space between earth and heaven. Certain representations of the *djed* do in fact depict it with rungs, just like a ladder, as we shall shortly see.

What we are dealing with here is not just inner experience, for it was probably also enacted as ritual. It is possible that utterance 267 may in fact have originally accompanied a ritual enactment of a search for the "dismembered king" and his subsequent celestial ascent, for this is precisely what is described as taking place in the Ramesseum Dramatic Papyrus. As we have already seen, the Ramesseum Dramatic Papyrus describes kingship rituals performed in the reign of Senwosret I in the Middle Kingdom, but it is also regarded as an important source for more ancient kingship rites that Senwosret was deliberately reviving in his reign. In the sequence of rituals described in the papyrus, Osiris is sought for by the "Embracers of the Akh," who were also identified as the "Children of Horus," wearing jackal and baboon masks. It has been suggested that these Children of Horus (who in the New Kingdom became the guardians of the canopic jars in which the viscera were preserved after mummification) could have been searching for the viscera of the king who had gone through the dismemberment experience,[58] in which case a shamanic substratum to their later role as guardians of the extracted viscera, and indeed the whole practice of removing the viscera, is implied. The very next phase of the ritual described in the papyrus has the same Children of Horus ("the Embracers of the Akh") forming a great celestial ladder for the revived Osiris to ascend.[59]

(11) UTTERANCE 268: UNITING WITH THE *KA*

What is described in utterance 268 is the purification of the king, his being suckled by Isis and Nephthys and his drawing close to Horus, literally "at his two fingers" (§372). These are all elements in the coronation rites, and it is therefore not surprising to find that, interweaving these events are coronation motifs such as the king's taking hold of the white crown (§371) and the presentation of the antenna-like wire (*hematj*) at the front of the red crown (§373). Also not surprising is the festival atmosphere of the first part of the utterance, in which we read of the standard of Seth ("He of Ombos") raised high in front of the *iteret* palace (of Upper Egypt).[60] The context seems less to be funerary than that of a festival involving coronation ceremonies in which both Horus and Seth, along with the red and white crowns, are implicated.

Corresponding to these ceremonials is an inner event of utmost importance: the uniting of the king with his *ka*. This event has already been referred to on the south wall of the sarcophagus chamber (utt. 215) and in the censing rite in the passage between the chambers (utts. 25 and 200). Here in the antechamber we return to it once more. In the text, both the king and his *ka* are purified by Horus in the Jackal Lake, which is in the Osirian Dwat, as the necessary preliminary to their union. That Horus should preside over this is appropriate because it is precisely insofar as the king integrates his *ka* energy that he achieves Horus-consciousness.[61] For the ancient Egyptians, the vital energy that is associated with the *ka* was felt to emanate from the ancestors. Thus an opening of contact with the ancestors, and hence with the spirit world in general, was necessary for the *ka* energy to become individualized or "owned" by the living king. The event of Unas meeting his *ka* and it becoming integral to his self-consciousness follows naturally from his encounter with the spirits of the dead and his celestial ascent described in the previous two utterances. As a result of the king's union with his *ka*, he becomes suffused with a new daimonic power, a superhuman potency:

> **Omnipotent is Unas,**
> **his arms do not fail him.**
> **Preeminent is Unas,**
> **his *ka* comes to him.**[62]

(12) Utterance 269: Ascent to the Sky, Suckled by Ipy

Utterance 269 begins with a beautiful censing prayer. The prayer echoes the prayer of utterance 262, in which, by a reciprocal gnosis, the king both became conscious of the gods and was held in the consciousness of the gods. Now, through the kindling of the incense, its fragrance mingles with that of the king and brings the king into contact with the gods just as it attracts the gods to the king. The incense prayer is the liturgical counterpart to the king's ascent on "the smoke of the great censing" in utterance 267:

> **The fire is laid, the fire sparkles;**
> **the incense is laid on the fire, the incense sparkles.**

> Your fragrance comes to me, O incense,
> my fragrance comes to you O incense.
> Your fragrance comes to me, O gods,
> my fragrance comes to you, O gods.
> May I be with you, O gods,
> may you be with me, O gods.
> May I live with you, O gods,
> may you live with me, O gods.
> May I love you, O gods,
> may you love me, O gods.[63]

In the second part of the utterance, the theme of celestial ascent is elaborated with the king climbing up to the sky on the thighs of Isis and Nephthys, while his "father" Atum takes hold of his arm. The king is now suckled by the hippopotamus goddess, Ipy, a goddess associated with the northern stars as well as being a protectress of childbirth. In figure 8.19, Ipy is portrayed with her left hand resting on the *sa* symbol of protection. She is depicted here, as usual, with the legs and arms of a lion and a crocodile's tail.[64] Unas prays to her:

> O my mother Ipy, give me this breast of yours,
> that I may apply it to my mouth
> and suck this your white, gleaming sweet milk.
> As for yonder land in which I walk,
> I will neither thirst nor hunger in it for ever.[65]

While Ipy's suckling Unas symbolizes his spiritual rebirth and his nourishment with divine food (reminding us of the sarcophagus chamber east-gable texts), it is also something more than that, for Ipy was not just associated in a vague way with the northern stars. The ancient Egyptian constellation of the hippopotamus goddess corresponds approximately to our Draco, and it is likely that a

Figure 8.19. The hippopotamus goddess, Ipy, was a protectress of childbirth; she is shown here with her left hand resting on the sign of protection.

point on her breast represented the North Celestial Pole.⁶⁶ This makes the suckling of Unas all the more significant, for it takes place at the center point around which the universe turns. It is because of the cosmic centrality of the celestial hippopotamus that she is usually portrayed with her left hand resting not on the *sa* sign of protection, but on a mooring post that symbolically stabilizes the whole universe (fig. 8.20).

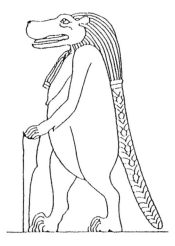

Figure 8.20. The constellation of the celestial hippopotamus, whose left hand rests on the mooring post of the universe. She corresponds approximately to the modern constellation Draco. A point on her breast probably corresponded to the North Celestial Pole, near Thuban, around which the northern stars revolved in ancient Egyptian times. Tomb of Seti I. Nineteenth Dynasty.

Should we begin to think that this celestial symbolism is peculiarly Egyptian, we would be seriously mistaken. While the form it takes is obviously specific to Egypt, the rationale behind it arises out of a far more universal perception, for the northern stars, and particularly the Pole Star, have had an important place in shamanic traditions worldwide.⁶⁷ In shamanic cosmology, the North Celestial Pole is both the axis around which the cosmos turns and the opening through which the gods descend to earth. The three great cosmic regions of Sky, Earth, and Underworld, recognized in practically all shamanic cosmologies, are connected along this central axis. It is specifically through the celestial opening in the northern sky that shamans are said to make their ascent to the realm of the gods. Only shamans have the power to reach the sky through this central opening, in a profound mystical experience. Mircea Eliade has rightly emphasized that the shamans did not create the cosmology, the mythology, and the theology of their respective tribes: They experienced it, and used it as the itinerary for their ecstatic journeys.⁶⁸ If there existed only one point of connection between shamanism and ancient Egyptian religion, it would be that the Egyptians likewise did not so much create as experience their cosmology, mythology, and theology. The suckling of the king by Ipy will be understood far better if it is seen not so much as a funerary belief than as a concrete mystical experience.

(13) UTTERANCE 270: AWAKENING THE FERRYMAN

In utterance 270, we return again to the theme of crossing over waters. Whether these waters are the Field of Rushes is not stated in the text, but the ferryboat that Unas calls for is the ferryboat used by the gods. The location of the waters is therefore celestial. The king needs to wake up the ferryman by calling out to him,

> **Awake in peace!**
> **O you whose face is behind him, in peace!**
> **O you who sees behind him, in peace!**
> **O ferryman of the sky, in peace!**
> **O ferryman of Nut, in peace!**
> **O ferryman of the gods, in peace!**[69]

Figure 8.21. Osiris in his celestial manifestation as the constellation Orion is always depicted with his face behind him, looking backward. It would seem that the celestial ferryman of utterance 270 is none other than Osiris. Tomb of Senenmut. Eighteenth Dynasty.

In the Coffin Texts and the Book of the Dead, the summoning of the ferryman "whose face is behind him" is an essential phase in the Otherworld journey, and fraught with difficulties.[70] Here in the Pyramid Texts, the difficulties are only hinted at—the ferryman needs to be awakened and the king must show that he is free of any accusation against him—but these are not serious problems and the king is able to invoke Thoth's aid should the ferryman fail to comply with his wishes.

In this utterance we are presented with the enigma of the curious name of the ferryman "whose face is behind him"—it is a name that recurs in the Middle Kingdom Coffin Texts and the New Kingdom Book of the Dead. Since the god Osiris is represented with his face behind him in his celestial manifestation as the constellation Orion (fig. 8.21), it seems plausible to interpret the "waking the ferryman" episode as connected to the awakening of Osiris. The ferryman, then, would seem to be none other than Osiris reconstituted and hence ready for the celestial ascent that follows his regeneration. That this is probably the case can also be gleaned from the fact that in the later ferryman texts of the Middle and New Kingdom, we learn not only that the ferryman is "asleep" but also that his boat has been taken to pieces and needs to be reassembled. The boat thus symbolizes the dismembered body of Osiris. To drive home the point, in these later texts the traveler who is seeking to be ferried across to the eastern sky has to assure both the ferryman's agent and the ferryman (once he is woken) that he or she is "whole" with arms and legs restored.[71]

(14) UTTERANCE 271: PULLING PAPYRUS, RAISING THE DJED

The scene shifts in utterance 271 with a reference to a ritual in honor of the wild cow goddess, Hathor, performed by the living king: pulling up papyrus and offering it to the goddess. Papyrus was sacred to Hathor, who is sometimes depicted as a wild cow pushing her head through a papyrus thicket (fig. 8.22). The papyrus symbolized the powers of fertility, and the pulling of the papyrus served both to affirm the king's vitality and to ensure the inundation of the land.[72] In this utterance, the cow goddess is one form that Unas's heavenly mother takes. The other form is the *sehseh* bird—probably a vulture, a manifestation of the goddess Nekhbet.[73] The wild cow and the *sehseh* bird thus represent here the goddesses of the north and south of Egypt, the "two mothers" of the king.

The inner scenario is that "Osiris Unas" has been reborn a Horus, and it is as such that he performs the papyrus-pulling ritual. The reference to the two *djed*

Figure 8.22. The cow goddess, Hathor, is shown in a papyrus thicket, growing at the bottom of the Mountain of the West, from behind which her head emerges. Papyrus of Ani. Nineteenth Dynasty.

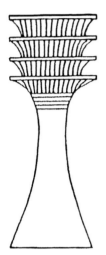

Figure 8.23. The djed *pillar was originally made of papyrus bundled together, and symbolized the mother goddess, as Hathor, "pregnant" with the king.*

pillars "standing" is an oblique reference to this fact: The *djed* pillar was originally made of papyrus bundled together, and was a representation of the mother goddess, as Hathor, "pregnant" with the king (fig. 8.23). As the rebirth of the king from Hathor was celebrated toward the end of the Sed festival, there is the possibility of a Sed festival connection with this utterance.[74]

The "pregnancy," of course, could also be seen as the king's sojourn within the body of the cosmic goddess, which was understood to be the Dwat. Hence the pregnant *djed* also symbolized the king's death prior to his rebirth. As much as the symbolism of the *djed* is Hathorian, it is also Osirian, and its status as either lying horizontally on the ground or standing upright is an allusion to Osiris's condition as on the one hand "asleep" (i.e., dead) or on the other hand "awake" (i.e., reborn as Horus). The fact that the raising of the *djed* was a ritual probably enacted at the end of the Sed festival to symbolize the regeneration of Osiris and his rebirth as Horus reinforces the likelihood of a Sed festival background to this utterance (see fig. 8.24).[75] The raising of the *djed* may also have been the preliminary to the king's ascent to the sky, for it also symbolized the world pillar or pillars that, once raised, support the sky. In this utterance, it seems that because the two *djed*s are standing, Unas is able to make his ascent, assisted by Horus and Seth.[76] What we meet in this utterance, then, is a complex and multilayered symbolism with both ritual and experiential components that may well also relate to the Sed festival.

(15) UTTERANCE 272: THE GATE OF NUN

The south wall ends with the short utterance 272, in which the king reaches the gate of Nun and demands that it be opened for him, for though he is small, he is at the head of the followers of Ra. The location of this gate of Nun is not specified, but it seems most likely that it was located at that "opening" in the sky marked by the North Celestial Pole, where in utterance 269 Unas was nurtured by the hippopotamus goddess, Ipy.[77] While it is ostensibly but a tiny opening, it is also vast, for the gods pass through it

Figure 8.24. The raising of the djed *pillar during the Sed festival of Amenhotep III. From the New Kingdom tomb of Kheruef.*

into the world of manifestation. Perhaps it is best understood as a transition point to another plane of being, quite other than what is experienced between heaven and earth. It is at this point, then, that the south-wall texts end, with Unas brought to the threshold of the very source of existence, the fount and origin of the gods themselves.[78]

The Eleven North-Wall Texts (Utts. 302–12)

Whereas the ten south-wall texts clearly belong together with the west-wall texts in a sequence, the eleven north-wall texts seem to stand as an independent grouping. Many of them reappear on the north wall of Pepi II's antechamber, a fact that suggests that they were probably regarded as specifically "north-wall" texts.[79] Whether they should be read after the west-to-south-wall sequence, or whether it would be more appropriate to turn to the east-wall or east-gable texts at this point is a question that is perhaps best not to press too hard.[80] We need to be aware that the quest for a linear "right sequence" is an anxiety of the modern mentality unwilling to accept that the Pyramid Texts are wedded to the walls on which they are inscribed. Walls do not come "one after another" like the pages of a book: They occupy space, they have a certain orientation, they mutually support each other as part of a three-dimensional architectural organism. This is not to deny that sequences of text such as the west-to-south-wall sequence are genuine, but the texts may also be meaningfully related to each other in a nonsequential manner. And anyway, the actual placement of a text on a certain wall is quite possibly just as significant as the relationship of texts one to another. There are nevertheless good reasons why we should approach the north-wall texts next. First of all, several of the themes of the north-wall texts are similar to, and seem to be echoing, those of the west-to-south-wall sequence: The king is hailed as a mighty bull; he flies up to the sky as a bird; he ascends by a ladder; he encounters a ferryman, crosses the waters on reed floats, and joins Ra. Second, the north-wall texts have an unusual and extremely interesting feature, which is that whereas normally hieroglyphs face the direction in which they are to be read, here on this north wall they are reversed. So, although the hieroglyphs are facing east rather than west, they are actually to be read from west to east, as on the south wall. This may be to emphasize their commitment to the direction symbolic of rebirth (the east), but it also

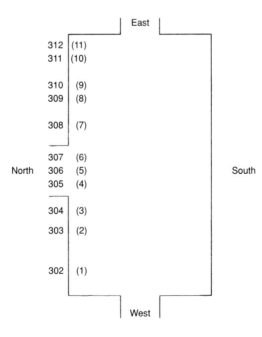

Figure 8.25. The eleven texts of the north wall (utts. 302–12).

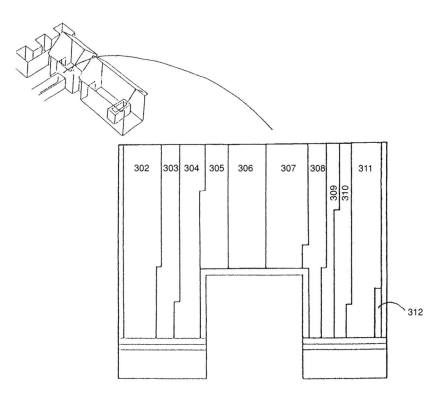

Figure 8.26. The eleven texts of the north wall are preoccupied with the ascent of the king to the sky, as are those of the south wall. They also include the theme of the king as a bull. They read from west to east (i.e., left to right).

means that, like their south-wall counterparts, they take their starting point from the west end. Furthermore, in certain of the later pyramids, important texts that one would expect to find on the north wall appear on their west walls, implying a degree of interchangeability between the north and west walls of the antechamber.[81] It would seem, then, that although the north-wall texts may not be a continuation of the west-to-south-wall sequence, both thematically and in terms of spatial symbolism, they are nevertheless closely related to it.

(1) Utterance 302: Becoming a Falcon, Flying Up to Ra

The north wall begins with utterance 302, in which the king declares himself to be "a living one, the son of Sothis [Sopedet]." Now, Sothis is the star Sirius, the celestial manifestation of Isis (see fig. 8.27), and her son was the

Figure 8.27. Sothis (the star Sirius), the celestial manifestation of Isis, who is declared the mother of Unas in utterance 302. From the tomb of Seti I. Nineteenth Dynasty.

falcon god, Horus-Soped. The "son of Sothis" is therefore a stellar manifestation of Horus. If his mother is the celestial manifestation of Isis, his father is the celestial manifestation of Osiris, who is none other than the king himself in his astral form. We learn of this in an utterance that occurs in the later pyramids—utterance 366—which describes how the king as Osiris impregnates Sothis in order to be born again as Horus-Soped.[82] The "living one, the son of Sothis," is therefore to be understood here as the reborn Osiris.[83] Unas is thus declaring that he has regenerated himself and is born again now as a living Horus. He is, however, a Horus who has both a "house in the sky" and a "throne on earth." The fact that he has a throne on the earth as well as a house in the sky must surely mean that in this utterance the king is not considered dead.

The text explains that Sothis has enabled Unas to fly up to the sky into the realm of the gods. Whereas ordinary mortals have their habitation on earth, those who are divinized fly up to the sky into the company of the gods.[84] As in utterance 267, on the south wall, the initial allusion to the death and rebirth motif is followed by the motif of ascent to the sky. The ability of Unas to fly up to the sky is due to the fact that as Horus-Soped he has assumed the form of a falcon. We have already seen that ascent to the sky in the form of a bird is typically shamanic. Figure 8.28 shows a remarkable image of a human being putting on the form of Horus-Soped in a manner reminiscent of the preparation for a shamanic ritual performance, in which the shaman dons the costume of a particular spirit. As there is evidence that the masks and costumes of gods were used in ancient Egyptian ritual, it seems possible that this is what is being depicted here.[85] The image may, on the other hand, be depicting a purely inner experience of metamorphosis into the falcon god.

In the second part of the utterance, the ascent is specifically directed

Figure 8.28. Horus-Soped, the falcon son of the star goddess Sothis.

toward union with Ra. Unas flies up to Ra as a bird: His face and claws are those of another falcon god, Anti, while his wings are those of a goose.[86] In this utterance, the jackal god, Wepwawet, whose name means "the opener of ways," is said to be instrumental in causing this ascent. The text actually states that it is Wepwawet who "has caused Unas to fly up to the sky among his brothers, the gods."[87] The jackal god, in his form as either Wepwawet or Anubis, has been described as "the Egyptian shamanic deity par excellence," for it is he who not only presides over the initiatory rituals of death, dismemberment, and renewal but also provides the "celestial sledge" (*shed-shed*) on which the king travels to the sky.[88] He thus links the Osirian and the solar phases of the king's initiation. It is significant that Wepwawet played a prominent role in the Sed festival, especially just prior to the "secret rites." This fact may point us toward the ritual context for our understanding of this utterance.[89] Of the relatively few surviving relief fragments from the pyramid temple of Unas, there are three that depict the jackal god. One of these is shown in figure 8.29.

Figure 8.29. A depiction of the jackal god on one of the surviving relief fragments from the pyramid temple of Unas.

271

(2) UTTERANCE 303: THE DAWNING OF THE SECOND HORUS
In utterance 303, Unas appeals to the gods of the four directions that reed floats be set down for him so that he may cross over toward the Cool Region. The utterance is reminiscent of utterance 263, on the south wall, where the reed floats of the sky are set in place for the king, just as they are for Ra and Harakhti, so that he may cross over to the eastern part of heaven. But here the prototype is neither Ra nor Harakhti but Osiris, and the gods of the four directions are not quite so amenable. They subject Unas to an interrogation:

> **Are you Horus, son of Osiris?**
> **Are you the god, the eldest one, the son of Hathor?**
> **Are you the seed of Geb?**[90]

Unas replies that he has appeared (*khai*, literally, "dawned") as a second Horus, and this has been recorded in the spirit world. Once again, then, we find the king referring to himself as a Horus, the implication being that his inner identity has metamorphosed to a stage beyond that of Osiris, for he has been reborn through the celestial cow goddess, Hathor.[91] As we have seen in utterance 271, on the south wall, the rebirth of the king through the cow goddess is not only an important theme of the Pyramid Texts, but it was also an event celebrated during the Sed festival.

(3) UTTERANCE 304: THE OPENINGS OF THE SKY
Utterance 304 begins with Unas asking the daughter of the jackal god, Anubis, who stands by the "openings" or "windows" of the sky, to let him through. The daughter of Anubis was a serpent goddess called Kebehut, and her gatekeeper role is presumably similar to that of Anubis, who, as well as causing the king to ascend to the sky, also often has the role of gatekeeper.[92] In the text, the word for "opening" or "window" is *peter*, which as a verb means "to see," implying some kind of aperture in the sky that opens onto the spirit realm. Shamanic accounts of passing through such apertures relate that they open for just an instant, and only the initiate is able to go through them into the Otherworld.[93] The meeting with the daughter of Anubis is followed by a meeting with an ostrich (possibly symbolizing Maat) on the banks of the Winding Waterway and the Bull of Ra. In this latter meeting, the gods of the four directions become compacted into one image of the Bull of Ra, who has four horns, one for each of the four directions. Interestingly, it is the western horn that Unas requests the bull to lower so that he may pass. The bull asks: "Are you a pure Westerner?" "I have come

from Falcon City," replies the king, thereby declaring his royal credentials. Falcon City should probably be understood as the royal residence on earth, once again implying that the king is traveling alive rather than dead.[94] In this utterance, we note also that the king is traveling to the west, rather than to the east. The utterance ends with Unas addressing the Field of Offerings and greeting the "honorable ones" (the dead) who are in it.[95]

(4) UTTERANCE 305: THE SKY LADDER

In utterance 305, Unas, now at the top of the celestial ladder, is subjected to a third interrogation. This ladder was mentioned in passing in the previous utterance. Now it figures more prominently as Unas's mode of ascent. The image of the sky ladder or stairway is, along with transformation into a bird, one of the most pervasive symbols of the means of ascent from the world we normally inhabit with our ordinary consciousness to the spirit world, accessible only to visionary consciousness. The symbolism is primal, and it emerges in such varied accounts as the dream-vision of Jacob in the Book of Genesis, the mystical ladders of both the Orphic and Mithraic mysteries, and later Christian depictions of the "ladder of virtues" that must be scaled by the soul in its ascent to heaven.[96] The root of this ladder symbolism is shamanic: In shamanic traditions worldwide, ascent to the spirit world by means of a ladder is commonly reported and indeed ritually enacted.[97] In utterance 305, the sky ladder is thought of as being made of rope, knotted together by Ra and Horus for Osiris. Apart from the possible allusion here to the theme of reassembling the vehicle of Osiris (as in the later versions of the ferryboat utterance 270) by having to knot it together, the Osirian symbolism can also be seen in the fact that the *djed* pillar is sometimes represented with crossbars to give it the appearance of a ladder (fig. 8.30).

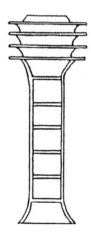

The mystical ascent of Osiris-Unas to his illuminated state as an *akh*, which he reaches at the top of the ladder, is witnessed by Horus and Seth, whose integration, as we have already noted in utterances 215 and 221, is necessary if the inner transfiguration from *ba* to *akh* is to take place. In the second part of the present utterance, we find a metaphysical

Figure 8.30. The ladder as a djed *pillar with crossbars. Vignette to BD 155, Papyrus of Ani. Nineteenth Dynasty.*

statement that foreshadows both the mystical philosophy of Plato and that of the Hermetic tradition:

> **The spirit (akh) belongs to the sky,**
> **the body (khat) to the earth.**[98]

This statement sums up the cosmic perspective of the Pyramid Texts, which is that the human spirit is celestial in origin and in essence, and thus human beings realize their true nature in a cosmic rather than an earthly ambience.

(5) UTTERANCE 306: THE LINKING OF HEAVEN AND EARTH

In utterance 306, however, we find an apparently contradictory teaching in which both heaven and earth are "given" to Unas. As in utterance 256, on the west wall of the antechamber, it is Atum who gives Unas heaven and Geb who gives him the earth.[99] This event occurs in the semimystical, semiritual context of Unas meeting the divinized ancestral spirits of Pe (ancient capital of the north) and Nekhen (ancient capital of the south). These royal ancestors had an important role in the Sed festival, and respectively represented not only Lower and Upper Egypt but also heaven and earth.

> **They come to you, the divine souls of Pe,**
> **they come to you, the divine souls of Nekhen,**
> **the gods who are in heaven,**
> **the gods who are on earth.**
> **They make supports for you with their arms,**
> **and you ascend to the sky,**
> **climbing up on it in its name of "Ladder."**
> **"The sky is given to you,**
> **the earth is given to you," says Atum.**
> **He who spoke about it is Geb.**[100]

What is being described is a linking of heaven and earth. The function of the ladder here is not simply to provide a means of ascent away from the earth; it is also to bring about a connection between earth and heaven. It is possible that, just as with utterances 255 and 256, on the west wall, which in many respects resemble the present utterance, what we are dealing with here is an aspect of the coronation ritual. Geb declares that not only do the realms of Horus and Seth that lie within his (i.e., Geb's) kingdom worship

Unas, but so also does the heavenly Field of Rushes, thereby once more emphasizing the union of the earthly and the heavenly within Unas.

A powerful symbol of this union of the earthly (or physical) and heavenly (or spiritual) realms is the bull, which was written with the same hieroglyph as the *ka*. For the Egyptians, the vital and generative energy of the *ka* was felt to derive from the spirit world. The *ka* energy was held by the ancestors. In this utterance, it seems that the metamorphosis of Unas into a bull is a direct result of his meeting the royal ancestors of Pe and Nekhen. The climax of the utterance comes with a description of Unas in his new state:

> **Behold, you have become the enduring bull**
> **of the wild bulls. . . .**
> **Endure, endure, O enduring bull,**
> **that you may be enduring at their head,**
> **at the head of the spirits (*akhu*) forever.**[101]

It was as much to symbolize the king's integration of the ancestral *ka* energies as to indicate his generative power and renewed vitality that a bull's tail hung from the kilt that the king wore for the dedication of the field during the Sed festival. Whether or not this utterance is connected with the Sed festival, it seems far more likely that it is part of a kingship ritual than a funerary rite.[102]

(6) UTTERANCE 307: THE BULL OF HELIOPOLIS

In utterance 307, the theme of the king's identity as a bull continues, but now it is made explicit that the energy of the bull is solar (see fig. 8.31). The bull-king Unas knows himself to be one with Ra, the god whose cult center is Heliopolis. At Heliopolis, the solar bull was known as the Mnevis (*menwer*) bull, and his cult was long established there.[103] In the Sed festival of Osorkon II, the Mnevis bull appears along with the sacred pillar of Heliopolis (see fig. 8.32). In fact, the head of the Mnevis bull alone is shown, attached to the Heliopolitan pillar (Heliopolis is Greek for the Egyptian Iunu, literally the "pillar" city). It is probably with this Mnevis bull that Unas is identified when we read that he is "the great-faced bull which came out of Heliopolis."[104] At the very beginning of the utterance, Unas says:

> **A Heliopolitan is in me, O god,**
> **a Heliopolitan such as you are is in me, O god.**

A Heliopolitan is in me, O Ra,
a Heliopolitan such as you are is in me, O Ra.[105]

Insofar as Unas experiences this inner identification with Ra, he experiences the bull energy within himself so strongly that he can say to Ra:

I come to you.
I am the wild bull of the grassland,
the bull with the great head
who comes from Heliopolis.
I come to you,
the wild bull of the grassland.
For it is I who generates you,
and continuously generates you.[106]

Figure 8.31. The solar Mnevis (menwer) bull, whose cult center was at Heliopolis (Iunu), is here depicted on an Eighteenth Dynasty stela.

The divine-human king experiences his divinity through unlocking the solar bull energy within himself, so that it is experienced as freely accessible to him. In this mystical experience, the king locates himself at the generative source of the divine creative power. Thus he can say to Ra: "It is I who generates you."

On the west wall, in utterance 254, we saw Unas described as "a bull of heaven" and subsequently in utterance 256 inheriting both earth and heaven. On this north wall, we have the uniting of earth and heaven in the king's person (utt. 306) immediately followed by his being hailed as a bull (utt. 307). The deeper meaning of this image of the king becoming a bull would seem to be that the bull-king unites within himself both the physical and the spiritual aspects of human nature. The Heliopolitan bull symbolizes the inexhaustible fecundity and creativity of the spiritual source, Ra, that the king experiences within his own being. At the same time, the bull is such a creature of nature, exuding sexual and physical prowess, that to interpret the bull-king of utterance 307 as a dead king who has thrown off his physical body and is physically disempowered seems a contradiction in terms. Should we not, rather, say that the utterance is describing the living king who has united within himself the instinctive and the spiritual? Something similar perhaps to what Jung referred to when he wrote: "In the mental make-up of the most spiritual you discern the traits of the living primitive."[107]

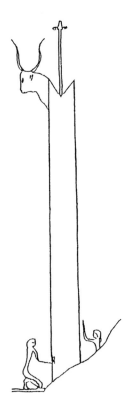

Figure 8.32. The head of the Mnevis (men-wer) *bull is attached to a pillar representing Heliopolis. From the Sed festival of Osorkon II.*

(7) Utterance 308: The Naked Daughters of the Gods

The central event of utterance 308 is that Unas sees certain goddesses naked—an event that perhaps parallels the west wall utterance 256 in which the gods come bowing naked before the king. If here it is goddesses rather than gods that Unas meets, this may be due to the fact that having transformed himself into a bull, the king has accessed the solar regenerative energy through which the sun god (as Kamutef—"the bull of his mother") both fertilizes and is then born from the cosmic cow goddess, who harbors within herself the Dwat, or spirit realm. A rebirth is thus implied by the metamorphosis into a bull, for the bull metamorphosis is the precondition of the king's rebirth. The newborn infant-king then requires suckling. We have already met a similar pattern of the king transforming into a bull and then receiving divine nourishment and suckling from goddesses in the sarcophagus chamber east-gable texts. The imagery of the naked goddesses is therefore as much maternal as sexual. They come bearing their breasts so that they can suckle the king, and he looks at them "as Horus looked at Isis."[108]

(8) UTTERANCE 309: THE SERVANT OF RA

In utterance 309, Unas is described as having been born of the "wish" (*nehet*) of the gods. This wish of the gods is probably a synonym of Maat, for Nehet is said to be in the prow of the sun boat, where normally we would expect to find Maat. It is Maat therefore who in this utterance is the spiritual mother of Unas.[109] As she is the daughter of Ra, a place in the sun boat of Ra is ensured for the king, who makes himself into Ra's servant, "doing what he [Ra] tells me." Thus the king "opens his [Ra's] boxes, breaks open his edicts, seals his papyrus rolls, sends forth his messengers," and so on.[110] While this image of the king as servant of the sun god is usually thought of in terms of a somewhat modest, even comic, role for the deceased pharaoh to aspire to, the relationship implies that the king has put his own will to the service of the deeper "solar will" of the sun god. There is, furthermore, no indication in the text that this is a postmortem scenario. It actually makes considerably more sense if we consider the boxes, edicts, papyrus rolls, and messengers as those of the living king, whose "solarized" consciousness regards them as issuing from Ra.

(9) UTTERANCE 310: HORUS WHO CAME AFTER OSIRIS

Utterance 310 begins with a protective spell in which the king redirects toward Atum any evil words or deeds directed against himself, to the detriment of his antagonist. Unas declares himself to be Horus, who has "come after his father" Osiris. This is another of the many Pyramid Texts in which the king is said to be Horus rather than Osiris. We have already met a good few. The fact that so many of the utterances make this assertion must mean that either the dead king was not necessarily regarded as an Osiris or else these "Horus texts" are not funerary texts. In the case of the present utterance, there is surely an experiential basis to the statement,

I am Horus,
I have come after my father,
I have come after Osiris.[111]

It is a statement that reminds us of the beginning of utterance 260, on the west wall:

I am Horus, my father's heir.
I am the one who went and came back.

In the present utterance, though, Unas as Horus is said to "come after" Osiris. This is a coming after in time: Osiris must come first, and only after the Osiris stage has been passed through is it possible for the king to be reborn as Horus. Utterance 260, on the west wall, implied that he "goes" as Osiris but he "comes back" as Horus. It would seem that something similar is being suggested here. The mythological relationship of father to son is lived out experientially as a death or disintegration in the Osiris phase, followed by a rebirth as Horus.

The utterance ends with a fragment of a ferryman text in which the ferryman is described not just as having "his face behind him" as in utterance 270 (directly opposite on the south wall) but as being able to see both ways—both forward and backward. We are reminded of the ancient Latin god Janus, the god of the doorway (*janua*), who guarded and watched all that went out and came in. Janus stood at the "gateway" of birth, at the opening of the year, and at the beginnings of all enterprises. Could it be that his image originated in ancient Egypt? The Egyptians portrayed the planet Venus, who as evening and morning star heralds both night and day, as two-headed. And in the New Kingdom Book of What Is in the Underworld, two-headed gods appear in the eleventh division, just before the rebirth of the sun god in the twelfth division (see fig. 8.33).[112] It would seem that the ferryman is similarly positioned in the present utterance between two mythological and existential conditions. Unas declares himself to be Horus who has been Osiris: He is no longer what he was. What he was (Osiris) is father to—that is, the generator of—what he has now become (Horus).

(10) UTTERANCE 311: BEING KNOWN BY AND KNOWING RA

The north-wall texts conclude at the east end with utterance 311 and the very short utterance 312 (a food spell). Utterance 311 begins with a brief prayer addressed to Ra, similar to the prayer in the south-wall utterance

Figure 8.33. Left: *one of the two-headed gods who appear in the New Kingdom Book of What Is in the Underworld just before the rebirth of the sun. He is named Two-Headed, and may be related to the two-faced ferryman of utterance 310.* Right: *the ancient Latin "gateway" god, Janus.*

262 ("Do not be unaware of me O god; know me for I know you . . ."). In utterance 311, the king prays:

> **See me, O Ra,**
> **recognize me, O Ra.**
> **I belong to those that know you,**
> **so know me.**[113]

We have already observed in utterance 205 (sarcophagus chamber, east gable) that to be seen by the gods has ontological weight, insofar as it confirms one's existence as a spiritual being. This appeal to be recognized and known by Ra surely has the same import.

Unas prays that the goddess who guards the doors of the Akhet will open them for Ra's morning boat, and he also claims to have knowledge of the place from which Ra enters the night boat. This place is the booth of the royal throne, set on a platform with steps, identical to the one shown in depictions of the Sed festival.[114] Figure 8.34 is an early depiction of the booth set on its platform, as it appears in the early dynastic tablet portraying the Sed festival of King Den. That this is where Ra enters his night boat signifies that this is where the journey through the Dwat begins. As

Figure 8.34. King Den's Sed festival. The king is seated on the left on a throne within a booth set on a stepped platform, as described in utterance 311. First Dynasty tablet.

we have seen, the purpose of the coronation before the Sed festival "secret rites" was to empower the king before his own departure into this region.[115] For this reason, the king is entitled to claim that he has knowledge of the place from which Ra embarks on his night boat, for he himself has been there.

Unas prays that "the four raging ones" who are around Ra will not oppose him when he comes to Ra. We encounter here the terrible aspect of the sun god, who, through the raging ones, could utterly destroy those who are not fit to come into his presence.[116] The utterance ends with some of the most fervently devotional lines in the whole of the Pyramid Texts. Wishing with his whole being to join the sun boat on its cosmic circuit so that he might travel in the luminous presence of the great god of light, wishing, that is, that he himself may be, like Ra, inwardly radiant because united with the cosmic source of radiance, Unas prays:

> **I will not be blind,**
> **though you leave me in darkness,**
> **I will not be deaf,**
> **though I do not hear your voice.**
> **Take me with you, with you.**
> **I will drive away the storm for you,**
> **I will dispel the clouds for you,**

Figure 8.35. Adoration before Ra. Eighteenth Dynasty papyrus.

I will break up the hail for you.
I will make for you adoration upon adoration,
I will make for you praise upon praise.[117]

(11) UTTERANCE 312: THE BREAD THAT FLIES UP

The last vertical line of hieroglyphs on the antechamber north wall is taken up mostly by the end of this beautiful prayer to Ra. At the end of the prayer there is a brief reference to the vulture goddess of Upper Egypt and, with this, utterance 311 rather abruptly stops—about two thirds of the way down the wall. There, as if tacked on as an afterthought, is an enigmatic "food spell"—utterance 312. It is a spell for the offering bread to "fly up" to the "houses of the crown of Lower Egypt." The flight of the bread perhaps follows the flight of the spirit (*akh*) described in utterance 305. The houses of the Lower Egyptian crown are probably Pe and Dep, both ancient cities under the patronage of the cobra goddess, Wadjet. As goddess of the north she complements Nekhbet, the vulture goddess of the south, referred to at the end of the previous utterance.[118] The "houses of the crown of Lower Egypt" are also mentioned in utterance 81, on the north wall of the sarcophagus chamber, where they appear in connection with the cloth goddess, Tayet, who has the mythological role of Isis in weaving the dismembered parts of Osiris together and making him whole.[119] In this brief food spell there would seem, then, to be a veiled reference to the supportive role of the divine feminine in the process by which the king undergoes solarization.

9 FROM THE ANTECHAMBER TO THE ENTRANCE CORRIDOR

The East Gable (Utts. 273–76)

The principal text of the east gable is the so-called Cannibal Hymn (utts. 273–74), probably the most famous and frequently quoted of all the Pyramid Texts. It reads as the climax of the texts of the antechamber, whose easterly course brings them up to this architectural point in the pyramid. Its physical location on the east gable is, however, from the point of view of its relationship to the other antechamber texts, relatively self-contained, and it probably should not be considered as part of any sequence.[1] In the hymn, the king is portrayed as a figure with supernatural power, whose appearance in the spirit world is so terrible that the whole celestial realm quakes in terror:

> The sky is overcast,
> the stars are darkened,
> the celestial expanses quiver,
> the bones of the earth gods tremble,
> the planets stand still
> when they see Unas rising in power.[2]

The word translated as "power" here is in fact *ba*, which in this context means far more than just "soul." It refers to the awesome appearance of divinity.[3]

Just as in the antechamber west-gable utterance 250, Unas was described

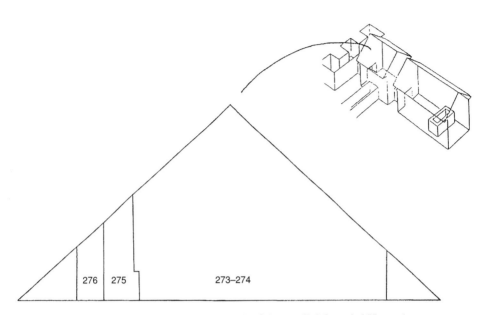

Figure 9.1. The east-gable texts consist mainly of the so-called Cannibal Hymn (utts. 273–74) in which the king "eats the magic" and "gulps down the spirits" of the gods.

as a "master of wisdom" (literally "one who is above wisdom"—*her sai*), so he is here said to be a "lord of wisdom" (*neb saibut*). The word *saibut* is written with the jackal ideogram. As we have already seen, the jackal has the function of opening the ways into the Otherworld, so the connotations of *saibut* are more shamanic than intellectual.[4]

The text proclaims that Unas has been reborn, and his progenitor is none other than Atum, the creative source of all that exists. And for this reason the root of Unas's power is that place of spiritual regeneration and renewal that only gods know of—the Akhet:

> **His power (*user*) is in the Akhet**
> **like his father Atum, who has begotten him.**
> **Unas is even more powerful than he [Atum] is.**[5]

This extraordinary final statement, that Unas is even more powerful than Atum, bears comparison with a similar statement in utterance 307 on the north wall, where the bull-king Unas, in uniting with Ra, says:

> **It is I who generates you**
> **and continuously generates you.**[6]

What these statements imply is that the king's consciousness has deepened to a level at which he experiences himself merged with the pure creativity that is the divine source of all that comes into manifestation.

The present text can also be compared to utterance 254, on the west wall, where we saw Unas hailed as a Bull of the Sky who had been reborn from the Underworld womb of the cosmic cow goddess. It will be recalled that in the last part of utterance 254, the king stated that his head was firmly back on his body. He had, in other words, been through the Osirian ritual of the restoration of the head. In the present utterance, we meet the same two motifs of the king appearing as a Bull of the Sky with his head firmly fixed on his body.[7] It would seem that these two motifs belong together, as if the Osirian loss of and subsequent restoration of the head is the prerequisite for the king's transformation into the heavenly bull.

As the Bull of the Sky, Unas emerges from the Akhet with complete command of his life energies, referred to as including both the male *ka*s and the female *hemsut*. The *ka*s and *hemsut* would seem to be male and female helping spirits, closely linked to the king's own vital energies. Like a shaman, suffused with a wild potency, he now "assembles his spirits" and "summons his helpers" so that he can capture, kill, cook, and eat the magic of the gods.[8] Although the text has been dubbed the Cannibal Hymn because in one phrase Unas is said to "live on his fathers and feed on his mothers" and in another to "eat men and feed on the gods," the cosmic setting of the hymn leaves little doubt that the mothers and fathers and "men" in question are spirits (perhaps ancestral spirits) rather than living people. The acquisition of their magic power through ingesting it is Unas's paramount concern. It is also interesting to notice that nowhere does the king actually eat the gods themselves. Rather, he ravenously consumes various attributes or qualities of the gods—their "magic" (*heka*) or their spirits (*akhu*):

> **Unas eats their magic**
> **and gulps down their spirits.**
> **Their big ones are for his morning meal,**
> **their middle-sized ones are for his evening meal,**
> **their little ones are for his night meal. . . .[9]**

It is not, then, the gods that Unas eats. It is rather that he feeds on, and absorbs into himself, their spiritual power. Elsewhere he seizes their hearts, feeds on their lungs, swallows their knowledge, and digests their souls in his belly.[10] He engages in this orgy of consumption in order to achieve a specific end: that "those who are in heaven serve Unas," for he has become "a great power who has power over the powers."[11]

The practice of eating or consuming spiritual qualities in order to obtain magic power (and also for healing purposes) is well attested to in ancient Egyptian texts and is by no means unique to the Cannibal Hymn.[12] By ingesting something, its traits become integrated within the being of the person who ingests them. To ingest a spiritual quality is to know it so thoroughly that it has become part of oneself. Even today the vocabulary of understanding includes such "metabolic" phrases as "absorbing the meaning of" something or simply "taking something in." Here we encounter once again a thoroughly shamanic motif, for in shamanism we also find prominence given to the idea of ingesting spiritual power. In some shamanic traditions, the shaman is said to store his magic power as a thick white phlegm in the upper part of his stomach. This phlegm contains spirit helpers that the shaman can call upon in need.[13] The great Russian ethnographer Shirokogoroff has defined shamans as people who have "mastered spirits," and this mastery is demonstrated in their ability to "introduce these spirits into themselves and use their power over the spirits. . . ."[14] The underlying motive of Unas's eating the attributes and qualities of the gods needs to be understood as a magical means of his acquiring control and mastery over them. They become his servants through his having ingested them and absorbed them into his own being.

But we should not see this mastery of spirits simply as concerned with boosting the king's magical prowess, for we have already noted that the text begins by describing Unas's power (*user*) as being in the Akhet "like his father Atum." Unas can achieve mastery over the gods because he is himself centered in the place of spiritual creativity, the place that is the generative source of everything that comes into manifestation, including the gods. Thus his absorption of the magic and spirits of the gods is an expression of the fact that his consciousness is functioning at a deeper, more interior, and more potent spiritual level than theirs. It is because he has grounded his own consciousness in the Akhet that he can master them.

All these considerations make a funerary interpretation of the utterance seem almost poignantly irrelevant. While the text is certainly describing the king in relationship to the spirit world, every line of it palpably conveys that Unas is a man possessed with a furious, unstoppable daimonic energy—not dead but terrifyingly full of life. This is not to say that there is no ritual context to the Cannibal Hymn. It has been argued that it is the text of a bull sacrifice and butchery ritual.[15] If this were the case, and it is by no means certain that it was, then it seems more likely that the context would have been the cult of the living, rather than the dead, king.[16] The whole hymn can be read as a hymn of spiritual empowerment. The king draws into himself, and is transmuted by, the divine energies that he encounters, gathering up the substance of the celestial and supercelestial spheres into his own being, as he identifies increasingly closely with the source of all existence, the source of all manifestation, until he can at last claim that

my lifetime is eternity,
my limit is everlastingness

and that he dwells "in the Akhet for all eternity." Dwelling here, in the place of eternal spiritual renewal, Unas is

he whose appearance is Appearance itself,
whose endurance is Endurance itself.[17]

If much of the imagery and tone of the Cannibal Hymn seems violent and primitive, its ultimate end is nevertheless exalted and sublime. The apparent savagery of the king's dealings with the spirit world serves to promote his progress toward, and mystical union with, the Absolute, on the lines of the Hermetic maxim, "Unless you make yourself equal to God, you cannot understand Him."[18] In the Cannibal Hymn we have a *unio mystica* in reverse: Rather than the king becoming absorbed into the godhead, all the divine powers are one by one absorbed into the king.

Apart from the Cannibal Hymn, there are just two further texts on the east gable: Utterance 276 is a very short snake spell, no doubt part of the group below it on the east wall that we shall shortly come to, but utterance 275 is a somewhat longer, more significant text. It relates how the king opens the double doors that are at the limits of the Akhet. This action is accompanied by two "costume rituals" in which the king is said to have put on a *maarek* garment—a kilt or girdle made from the hide of a baboon and worn around the waist—having taken off the *mesedet* garment, which, according to Piankoff, is a "robe with a tail."[19] Whether or not the *mesedet* should be understood as the Sed festival kilt with the bull's tail, such ritual changes of clothing are in themselves reminiscent of kingship ceremonies, during which the king could change garments several times. The reason why the king puts on a garment made from the hide of a baboon will become clear when we look at the entrance-corridor texts. This aside, it is evident that if the king is putting on and taking off garments, it seems more likely that this text is linked to a kingship ritual rather than to funerary rites. The utterance ends with Unas being identified with "the Great One in Shedet." Shedet was a town near the Faiyum, known to the Greeks as Crocodilopolis, for it was a cult center of the crocodile god, Sobek. The significance of this identification will be discussed when we come to the entrance-corridor texts, where Unas is once again identified with Sobek (utt. 317).

The Snake Spells (Utts. 277–99 and Utts. 226–43)

The final wall to consider in the antechamber is the east wall, underneath the gable containing the Cannibal Hymn. We noted in the last section that on the east gable there is one very short spell against snakes (utt. 276). On the wall below, there are a great many more snake spells. A full two thirds of the wall is taken up with spells against obnoxious creatures—most of which are snakes (utts. 277–99). Since there are twenty-three of these spells on the wall and one on the gable, we have twenty-four spells in total at this east end of the pyramid. The remaining one third of wall space (at the northern end of the east wall) is occupied by just two texts (utts. 300–301), which we shall consider in the next section. Figure 9.2 shows the distribution of texts on the antechamber east wall.

There is only one other place in the pyramid where we find an equivalent gathering of spells, and that is on the west gable of the sarcophagus chamber. In chapter 7, these were deliberately passed over because—for reasons that will soon become apparent—it seems best to treat them together with the antechamber east-wall spells. The eighteen texts of the sarcophagus chamber west gable (utts 226–43) are—like the twenty-four spells at the east end of the antechamber—nearly all directed against snakes, making a total of forty-two spells against malevolent creatures. As the number forty-two has a certain magical significance in ancient Egyptian religion, it is possible that the number of these protective spells was not arbitrary.[20] The distribution of the spells on the sarcophagus chamber west-gable wall is shown in figure 9.3.

As the likelihood of snakes entering the pyramid through its well-constructed walls or down its sealed corridor was minimal, these spells against snakes should not be taken literally. The snakes against which the spells are directed are not actual physical snakes, but rather evil influences that are visualized as having serpentine form. Ancient Egyptian snake symbolism is highly complex and by no means always negative. But in these spells in the pyramid of Unas, the negative connotation of the snake is clearly paramount. The mythological root of the negative snake image is

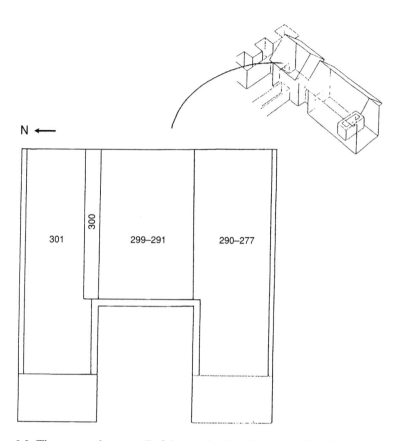

Figure 9.2. The texts on the east wall of the antechamber. Utterances 277–99 are nearly all spells against snakes. They read from south to north (i.e., from right to left).

that at the beginning of time, it is a snake (in the form of a python) that traps Atum in the world of nonmanifestation by coiling itself around him in the watery Nun (see fig. 9.4).[21]

In order to break out of the coils of the serpent, Atum changes himself into a mongoose or into a cat or lynx, and bites or cuts off the head of his antagonist (see fig. 9.6).[22] In the New Kingdom Underworld books, it is again a giant python that tries to prevent Ra from completing his journey through the night, its aim being to hold the world in perpetual darkness. The python, a manifestation of Apophis (or Apep), must be overcome in order for the sun god to be reborn each morning. The new birth of the light-bearing god depends upon this opposing serpent being overcome. In

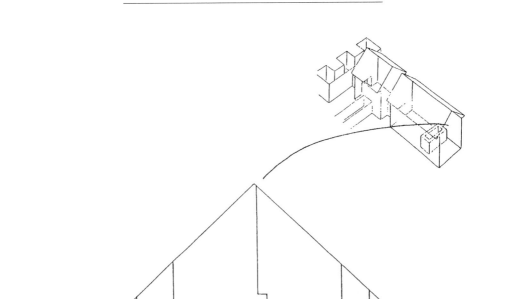

N ⟵

| 243 | 242–241 | 240 | 239–231 | 230 | 229–228 | 227 | 226 |

Figure 9.3. The eighteen texts of the west gable of the sarcophagus chamber are nearly all magical spells against snakes. They read from north to south (i.e., from right to left).

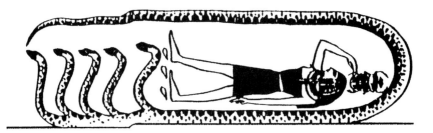

Figure 9.4. Atum in the coils of the primeval snake that traps him in the realm of non-manifestation. From The Book of What Is in the Underworld, sixth division. Tomb of Amenhotep II. Valley of the Kings.

Figure 9.5. The serpent Apophis, who opposes the rebirth of the sun god, is transfixed with knives and fettered with rope in the seventh hour of the night. The Book of What Is in the Underworld, seventh division. Tomb of Amenhotep II. Valley of the Kings.

figure 9.5, the opposing serpent of the Book of What Is in the Underworld *(Amduat)* is shown transfixed with knives and fettered with rope in the seventh hour of the night.

For the Egyptians, then, the python was a lover of nonmanifestation, of entropy and darkness. Since the destiny of the king is to become a "shining spirit" like Ra, this snake presents itself as the main opponent of his spiritualization. The snake spells were therefore designed to ward off the malevolent forces that would prevent the inner transformation of the king into a being of light. Their aim was magically to ensure a safe environment for the king's spiritual rebirth.

Many of the spells on the west gable of the sarcophagus chamber and the east wall of the antechamber are enigmatic and their meaning at times virtually impenetrable to the modern reader. But their very impenetrability is indicative of their magical power: Here are words that take on a life of their own, independent of the meaning that we can glean from them. Often this is achieved through punning, which, for the Egyptians, was a way of ensuring that linguistic statements became organic entities with their own internal rhythm and harmony. Utterance 281, on the east wall of the antechamber, is a good example. It completely defeated Faulkner, who pronounced it untranslatable. Piankoff was braver:

> **Chastise *Heku*, *Kebeb-he-heruby*,**
> **O lion of *Pehty*, O lion of *Pethety*, the *Pehty* [and]**
> ***Pethety*.**
> **Give me now, *Heru-thubes*, meat, now! One pot!**
> **Go, go serpent, serpent!**[23]

This utterance is a spell against two serpents that are addressed as "lions," but the effectiveness of the spell lies less in any objective meaning that it may convey than in the magical sounds upon which it plays. In this spell we meet language as an autonomous force.[24]

A more accessible spell is utterance 226, from the first of the west-gable spells. It begins:

A snake is enveloped by another
when is enveloped the toothless calf
which came forth from the pasture. . . .[25]

The text appears to be designed to protect a young calf, but it reads like a riddle whose meaning is deliberately obscure. The spell continues with the command:

O earth, swallow what went forth from you!

and then, addressing the snake:

O monster, lie down, crawl away!

This last command is often used at the end of snake charms. But the utterance continues with another riddle:

The Majesty of the Pelican has fallen into the water.
O snake, turn round, for Ra sees you!

The "Majesty of the Pelican" is an epithet of Osiris, and this part of the utterance could be a spell designed to protect the king from the fate of Osiris, which was to drown.[26] But however this and other of the utterances are interpreted, we should remember that the snake spells—like many of the Pyramid Texts—were not intended to be, as a modern book is, simply a medium of communication. The intention was to cast a web of enchantment. The snake spells were first and foremost potent magic formulas from which the magic emanated like a powerful scent, impregnating the space that the spells were meant to protect.

This space was the whole of the interior of the pyramid. Between the sarcophagus chamber spells and the antechamber spells, there is not only a shared protective purpose but in many cases a striking similarity of content as well. It is as if the spells of the west gable of the sarcophagus chamber and the east wall of the antechamber echo each other. For example, we have just seen that the west-gable utterance 226 refers to "the Majesty of the Pelican" (Osiris) that has "fallen into water." Over on the east wall of the antechamber, utterance 293 refers to the same "Majesty of the Pelican" that "falls into the Nile."[27] A kind of mirroring of the texts seems to have been deliberately set up here.

Likewise, the west-gable utterance 228 speaks enigmatically of how "one face falls on another" and of how "a mottled black and green knife" is used against the enemy (presumably a snake). The utterance is reflected on the east wall of the antechamber in utterance 290, where again "one face falls on another" and a "black knife" is used against the enemy (snake).[28] In utterance 238, on the west gable, reference is made to a "gold collar and *hekenu* oil" and to the god Khaitau. The utterance is repeated almost word for word in utterance 282 on the east wall of the antechamber.[29]

More revealing still is utterance 229 on the west gable, which states that "the fingernail of Atum" is pressed "on the spine of the Neheb-kau" serpent.[30] On the east wall of the antechamber, Unas (now evidently in the role of Atum) himself speaks: "Indeed I dart this left thumbnail of mine against you." He goes on to explain that he "strikes a blow" (or according to Piankoff makes a magic sign) on behalf of Min and the "defenders" (*ikiu*), and that this is to deter robbers.[31] The east-wall text is clearly amplifying what is stated more cryptically on the west gable.

We see the same pattern of amplification in the next west-gable spell, utterance 230, where mention is made of the lynx goddess, Mafdet, who is said to "close the mouth" of "the instrument of punishment." Mafdet was a form that Atum could take in order to liberate himself from the bonds of the primeval serpent.[32] No more is said in the west-gable spell of Mafdet's deed, but over on the east wall of the antechamber, utterance 297 gives a fuller account of Mafdet's dealings with the serpent:

> **she [Mafdet] strikes you on your face,**
> **she scratches you on your eyes,**
> **so that you fall into your faeces**
> **and crawl into your urine.**[33]

Figure 9.6 shows Mafdet's battle with the serpent from a vignette to chapter 17 of the New Kingdom Book of the Dead.

In these spells, then, there is something more than just an echo; there is an amplification. We have the impression of one spell being completed by the other, almost as if we are dealing with a single spell divided spa-

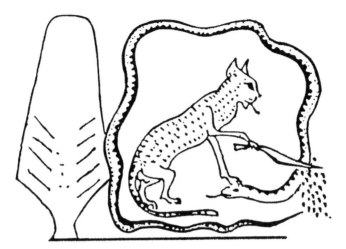

Figure 9.6. The lynx goddess, Mafdet, as portrayed in a vignette to chapter 17 of the Book of the Dead, attacks the opposing serpent. In this illustration, she is the form taken by Atum in order to break out of the serpent's bonds. Papyrus of Hunefer. Nineteenth Dynasty.

tially into two parts. It appears to be another instance of what Schwaller de Lubicz called "transposition" that we have already noticed might be operating between the east gable of the sarcophagus chamber and the west gable of the antechamber.[34] Here, however, it is taking place between one end of the pyramid and the other. If this is the case, then we may surmise that it was done as a deliberate ploy to reinforce the "energy field" that was set up between the two walls by the interacting spells.[35] Altogether, there would appear to be seven spells that are linked textually to each other. Other spells may also be contextually linked, but an attempt to establish their relationship is beyond the scope of this study. The seven textually linked spells are here listed as they are linked in figure 9.7:

SARCOPHAGUS CHAMBER		ANTECHAMBER
West gable		East wall
226	a	293
228	b	290
229	c	283
230	d	297
235	e	280
238	f	282
240	g	299

In figure 9.7, the relative positions of these spells in the pyramid are marked and connected by straight lines, in order to show the "field of protective energy" that is created by their interrelationship.

The Two Remaining East-Wall Utterances (Utts. 300–301)

UTTERANCE 300: ACQUIRING A FERRYBOAT, BECOMING SOKAR

The snake spells occupy the southern two thirds of the east wall of the antechamber. The remaining one third is taken up by two texts. The first (utt. 300) is very short and is concerned with the king's acquisition of a ferryboat—a scenario that we are already familiar with from utterance 270 on

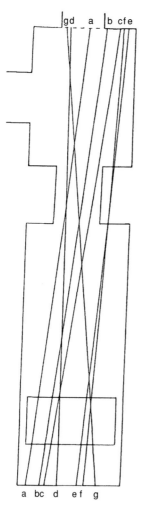

Figure 9.7. The snake spells on the west gable of the sarcophagus chamber of the pyramid of Unas relate to similar spells on the east wall of the antechamber, so that a "protective field" is formed between the two chambers.

the antechamber south wall and utterance 310 directly opposite it on the north wall. In both of these utterances, we have seen that the symbolism of the ferryboat is related to the reconstitution of Osiris and his rebirth as Horus. The ferryboat symbolizes the transition from the old Osirian state to becoming a reborn Horus. It is the symbolic vehicle of celestial rebirth. Here at the east end of the antechamber, Unas now identifies himself with the god Sokar of Ro-Setawe.[36] Sokar was an ancient deity, portrayed as a mummiform god like Osiris, but with a falcon head like Ra or Horus (fig. 9.8). He can be understood as representing an amalgam of Osirian and solar energies. Closely associated with Anubis, Sokar presided with him over the "gateway" or passage between worlds known as Ro-Setawe.[37] Ro-Setawe was also conceived in terms of the labyrinthine paths that had to be traversed in order to come to the place of inner regeneration. These paths were located in the Dwat, or Underworld, and this was essentially Sokar's realm. But Sokar had a specific function in the Underworld, for it was through him that the germination of new solar life occurred.[38] In this utterance Unas both identifies with Sokar and says that he is bound for the place where Sokar dwells.

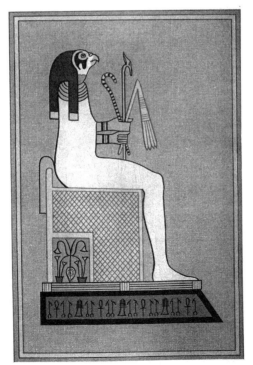

Figure 9.8. The god Sokar, with whom Unas identifies in utterance 300.

UTTERANCE 301: CROSSING TO THE FATHER GOD

The much longer utterance 301 begins with Unas presenting a series of food offerings to the creator gods of Hermopolis and Heliopolis. These are the deepest gods—Nun and Naunet (the primeval waters), Amun and Amaunet (the hidden ones), Atum (the complete) and the double-lion god Ruti, identified as Shu and Tefnut. They are (excepting Shu and Tefnut) the gods behind the gods, the nonmanifest primeval sources of the gods, the self-generating sources of divinity itself.[39] Unas addresses each pair and propitiates them with offerings so that they will not obstruct him in his "crossing" to their "father." These deepest gods are not yet the very deepest, for they have a father. And Unas intends to cross over to the father, as it were, from one spiritual plane to another, at the Akhet. Finally he declares that he knows the name of their "father"—and declares it to be "the eternal" (*nehi*). He also identifies the father god as "Horus who is over the stars of the sky, who brings Ra to life every day." This Horus, then, is a supercelestial power greater even than Ra. Just as He re-creates Ra each day, so He re-creates the king and "brings the king to life every day."[40] The first part of this utterance, therefore, takes us beyond even the sources of the gods to the source of the sources—the eternal father god, to whom the king acknowledges the daily renewal of his own life.

The second part of the utterance is another offering ritual in which the king presents the healed left eye of Horus (in the form of unguent) to three forms of the sun god, each of which is addressed as a Horus, and each of which is probably related to the rising sun.[41] We could understand the rising sun to be rising out of the matrix of the deep, nonmanifest gods of the first part of the utterance.

Then in the third and final part of the utterance, there is a prayer (probably recited by Unas) to the rising sun.

> **Arise, O great reed float,**
> **like Wepwawet [Opener of the Ways],**
> **filled with your spiritual power (akh),**
> **come forth from the Akhet.**[42]

Coming forth from the Akhet as an *akh* is something that Unas aspires to, and that the sun god accomplishes each day. Ra thereby "opens the way" for Unas—as Horus—to make the same journey. The idea of Unas being embarked upon a journey of spiritual transformation is indicated both in the reference to the jackal god, Wepwawet, in the quotation above and at the end of the utterance where we read of the king being purified in the Jackal Lake where the gods are purified. It is there, in the Jackal Lake, that Unas is made "bright," and at the end of the text Unas is hailed as "powerful" (*ba*) and "sharp" (*seped*). The meaning of *seped*, which is written with the determinative of a knife, could perhaps be to do with the king's inner refinement.[43]

There is little in utterance 301 to suggest that it is a funerary text. The episodes that it describes seem to require the king to be alive, for otherwise it is difficult to see how he could present bread offerings to the primeval gods at the beginning of the utterance and unguent to the three Horus-forms of the sun god later. These are clearly rituals performed by the living king. But the text is also describing levels of mystical knowledge that Unas is demonstrating. The king knows the secret name of the father god who is deeper even than the source gods, and he knows that this god is the life energy within both Ra and himself. Thus the way is opened for the king to undergo spiritual transformation in the Jackal Lake, where he is made bright, powerful, and sharp. While there is little to suggest that utterance 301 is a funerary text, its mystical content would appear to be undeniable.

The Entrance Corridor (Utts. 313–21)

From a textual standpoint, the entrance corridor to the pyramid would be better termed the exit, as the texts that line the walls of the corridor read from south to north: that is, away from the chambers of the pyramid toward the exit (see fig. 9.9). It has been argued, on the basis of comparison with the later Middle Kingdom tomb of Imhotep at Lisht, that the west- and east-wall texts of the corridor form a single sequence, beginning at the southern end of the west wall at utterance 313 and ending at the northern end of the east wall at utterance 321.[44] While this may be the case, it is nevertheless important to bear in mind that in the pyramid of Unas, from an architectural point of view, we are presented with two sequences that run on opposite walls. They are arranged in such a way that the west-wall sequence, which spreads over twenty lines of text, is exactly matched by the east-wall sequence, which also has twenty lines of text. There are, furthermore, certain resonances between the content of the utterances of the two walls. For example, at the south end of the west wall (utt. 313), the baboon god, Babi, figures prominently, but he also appears again at the northern end of the east wall (utt. 320). Babi is a guardian of the threshold between the human and divine worlds, and mastery of the power wielded by Babi is necessary for the king to ascend to the sky. Thus in utterance 313, the doors of the sky are only opened when Babi draws back the bolt that locks them, while in utterance 320 the king actually becomes Babi in order—in the final utterance of the east wall (utt. 321)—to ascend to the sky. It can hardly be coincidence that these two episodes, which clearly relate to each other, are strategically placed at opposite ends of the two wall sequences. Similarly, the motif of the king's fecundity in the long utterance 317, which dominates the west wall, is taken up in the east-wall utterance 319, which, from a spatial perspective, partially overlaps it. Let us look, then, more closely at the actual content of these texts.

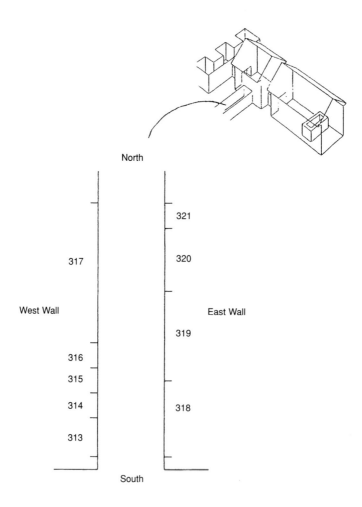

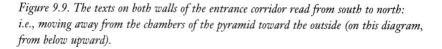

Figure 9.9. The texts on both walls of the entrance corridor read from south to north: i.e., moving away from the chambers of the pyramid toward the outside (on this diagram, from below upward).

300

The West Wall

UTTERANCE 313: THE ENCOUNTER WITH BABI

The west wall begins with utterance 313, in which the baboon god, Babi, is commanded to "draw back the bolt" so that the double doors of the sky open for Unas.[45] Babi is a fierce guardian spirit who has a great phallus (in some texts identified with the door bolt), red ears, and purple buttocks, and lives on the entrails of "the old ones."[46] The energy of Babi is Sethian, to be treated with caution and respect, for it is primal energy, both sexual and potentially violent. When Babi draws back the bolt, the way forward is through fire. Only Horus, the divinized human being, can find a path through the flames of which Babi is the guardian spirit, and in this utterance Unas is decisively identified with Horus.[47] The situation is illustrated in figure 9.10, in which Babi and Horus confront each other on either side of a doorway.

UTTERANCE 315: THE VOLUNTARY DEATH

The opening of the doors of the sky in utterance 313 is followed by a short spell, possibly to calm an ox that is being dragged to the slaughter (utt. 314).[48] Utterance 315 begins with Unas greeting three different kinds of baboon and ends with his saying that he will sit among them. These three baboons are probably three of the four who sit on the eastern side of the sky to do homage to the rising sun, and by joining them Unas becomes the fourth (fig. 9.11).[49] This may be the significance of Unas having put on

Figure 9.10 The baboon god, Babi, wielding a bow, guards the doorway to the sky. Only one whose consciousness has become that of Horus can pass through this door. From the sarcophagus of Psusennes, Twenty-first Dynasty.

the *maarek* garment (made from the hide of a baboon) in utterance 275 on the antechamber east gable, as part of the ceremony for opening the double doors at the limit of the Akhet. Integral to Unas becoming a baboon worshipper of the rising sun as it appears from the Akhet—an event that symbolizes spiritual rebirth—is the statement in the middle of the utterance made by the king:

> **My death (*aret*) is at my own wish,**
> **My spiritualization (*imakhu*) is at my own will.**[50]

This statement, so reminiscent of the idea of the "voluntary death" of later Greek and Hellenistic mysticism, clearly points away from a funerary interpretation of this utterance.

UTTERANCE 316: CALLING THE CELESTIAL FERRYMAN

Utterance 316 is probably another ferryman text, for the person to whom Unas calls is named Hemi, a name similar to that of other known ferrymen. He is linked in this utterance to a star (*sehed*), firmly placing the event of being ferried in a celestial location.[51] This utterance once again shows a thematic link between these corridor texts and the utterances of the east wall and gable of the antechamber, where there is also a ferryman text.[52]

Figure 9.11. Four baboons do homage to the sun as it rises at dawn. Eighteenth Dynasty papyrus of Userhat.

Utterance 317: Becoming Sobek

The final text of the west wall of the corridor is utterance 317. In this utterance, the king is identified with the crocodile god, Sobek, rising up out of the waters of the inundation, energetic, alert, and very fierce. Sobek is the son of Neith, a warrior goddess as well as goddess of the primordial flood, from which he emerges with a green feather on his head (fig. 9.12). The color green symbolizes the fecundity of the god, who in this image of his emergence from the primordial flood should be understood as a form of the sun god Ra.[53] Identified with Sobek, the crocodile-king is thus situated in the watery landscape of emergent life:

> **Unas comes to his flowing water**
> **in the land of the great flood,**
> **to the places of peace (*hetepu*) with green fields**
> **which are in the Akhet.[54]**

Unas is no longer at the doors to the Akhet, or the doors to the sky: He has gone through to "the land of the great flood" that lies beyond these doors. And there, in the Akhet, the place of transformation and rebirth, he makes the grass green and brings fertility to the fields. He also brings fecundity (greenness) to "the eye of the Great One," who is here feminine and should be understood as the cosmic goddess from whom he was born, the "Great Flood" herself.[55] He thus both emerges from and fecundates her, as

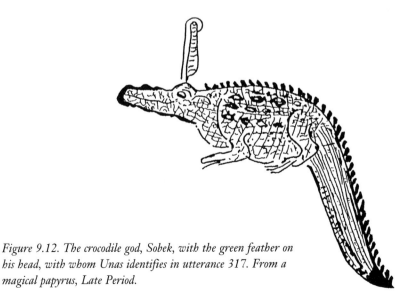

Figure 9.12. The crocodile god, Sobek, with the green feather on his head, with whom Unas identifies in utterance 317. From a magical papyrus, Late Period.

does the sun god, and this cosmic fertilization spills over into the natural world. And so Unas, enthroned in the Akhet, the mythical place of regeneration, "causes the grass to become green." We have already seen in chapter 4 that the spiritual regeneration of the king during the Sed festival involved at the same time the renewal of the powers of fertility throughout the land. A Sed festival backdrop to this utterance therefore seems quite plausible.[56]

The utterance ends with Unas's identification with Sobek reaffirmed as he sits enthroned in the Akhet. There he celebrates the abundance of his own overflowing libido:

> **Unas eats with his mouth,**
> **Unas urinates,**
> **Unas copulates with his phallus.**
> **Unas is lord of seed,**
> **who takes women from their husbands**
> **whenever he wants,**
> **as his heart urges.**[57]

If this passage seems, in the words of Mercer, to be "a barbarity second only to the famous Cannibal Text," it needs to be understood in the total context of Unas's embodying the primal, cosmic, and solar forces of creativity represented in the figure of Sobek. The sacred import of the passage may be glimpsed through the following remark of Mircea Eliade: "In premodern societies, sexuality, like all other functions of life, is fraught with sacredness. It is a way of participating in the fundamental mystery of life and fertility."[58]

The libido of the king participates in the cosmic libido of the sun god, and what Unas enacts is on a cosmic scale. In this specific sense, the ancient Egyptian king ruled from a sexual as well as a spiritual base.[59] The integration of the spiritual and the instinctual level—the heavenly and the earthly—of spiritual power and overwhelming sexual fecundity is central to the religious consciousness that comes to expression in the Pyramid Texts.

The East Wall

UTTERANCE 318: BECOMING THE *NAU* SNAKE

In utterance 318, at the south end of the east wall, Unas is described as "the *nau* snake, the leading bull," who absorbs into himself primordial ser-

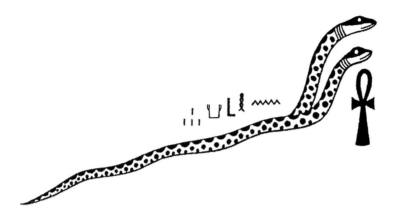

Figure 9.13. The Nehebkau snake, "bestower of kas," is probably the prototype of the nau *snake that Unas is identified with in utterance 318. From The Book of What Is in the Underworld, fourth division. Tomb of Amenhotep II. Valley of the Kings.*

pentine power so that he can command the gods. The image of Unas as a snake returns us to the watery setting of utterance 317 and the king's wielding primal creative power. In the present utterance he is said to both take away and bestow life-giving *ka* energy. In this respect, the *nau* snake is like the original snake of the precreation world named Nehebkau. Nehebkau (literally, "bestower of *ka*s") may well be the prototype of the *nau* snake, or the *nau* snake a form of Nehebkau (fig. 9.13).[60] Usually, but not always, Nehebkau is portrayed in the Pyramid Texts as a benevolent companion of the sun god, Ra, so there is a solar undercurrent to his bestowal of *ka* energy. In one text Nehebkau also aids the king's ascent to the sky.[61]

UTTERANCE 319: THE BULL-KING

In utterance 319, the king is described as a bull, an epithet that—as we know—unites him to the creative power of the sun god. Breathing fire, the bull-king rules over the gods in heaven and makes the lapis lazuli and *tun* plant grow on earth. In a possible reference to a baptismal ceremony associated with his accession, the king is described as "the third at his accession." As a third, he would be between Horus and Seth (or Horus and Thoth), who would be standing on either side of him and would pour baptismal water over him.[62] The position of the king between the dual gods, receiving blessings from both, symbolizes his union of their opposing natures within himself (fig. 9.14).

The reference at the end of the utterance to the accession is supported by the whole of the second part of the utterance that precedes it, the tone of which seems far removed from anything funereal and much more like a description of the living king:

> **Unas has tied the cords of the *shem-shem* plant,**
> **Unas has united the heavens,**
> **Unas rules over the lands, the South and the North,**
> **as the gods of long ago.**
> **Unas has built a divine city as it should be,**
> **Unas is the third at his accession.**[63]

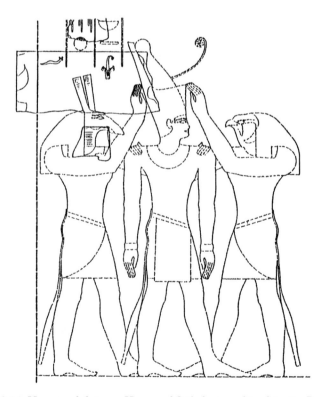

Figure 9.14. Unas stands between Horus and Seth during a kingship rite. Reconstruction from relief fragments found at his pyramid temple at Saqqara.

UTTERANCE 320: BABI, LORD OF THE NIGHT

In utterance 313, we have already met the fierce baboon god, Babi, as the guardian of the double doors of the sky. Now he appears again, not in his role of guardian but as "Lord of the Night Sky," and as such Unas is identified with him (fig. 9.15). Whereas hitherto Unas's transformations into various animals—crocodile, snake, and bull—have all had a solar symbolism, Babi as the Lord of the Night represents the opposite: darkness and violent destruction. The text reads:

> **Humble yourselves, you Lords,**
> **hide yourselves, you subjects,**
> **in the presence of Unas.**
> **For Unas is Babi, lord of the night sky,**
> **the bull of the baboons**
> **who lives on those who do not know him.**[64]

Just as in utterance 313, Babi must draw back the phallic door bolt for the king to go out into the sky, so here in utterance 320 the king's ascent to the sky (in the following utterance, 321) is dependent on his having encountered and integrated within himself the energies represented by Babi.

Babi "lives on those who do not know him." His are essentially Sethian energies of elemental sexuality and aggression that belong to the night. In utterance 316, on the west wall of the corridor, we saw Unas call for a

Figure 9.15. The fierce baboon god, Babi, Lord of the Night, with whom Unas identifies in utterance 320. From a Twenty-first Dynasty papyrus.

Figure 9.16. In the Middle Kingdom Coffin Texts, the mast of the ferryboat that trans-ports the celestial traveler across the sky is said to be the phallus of Babi. This illustration of the ferryboat is from the Eighteenth Dynasty papyrus of Nu.

ferryman to take him across the sky. From later ferryman texts that appear on Middle Kingdom coffins, a vivid image of what constitutes the right relationship to Babi is given. In these Coffin Texts, the mast of the ferry-boat is said to be Babi's phallus.[65] The phallus that kept the doors to the sky locked and bolted is the same phallus that becomes the mast of the ferry-boat that transports the king across the heavens to Ra (fig. 9.16).

UTTERANCE 321: THE FAITHFUL COMPANION OF RA

The final east-wall utterance is a short text to enable the king to ascend to the sky so that he may join Ra. In it, Unas calls for a *seferet-hetepet* that will act as the means of his ascent. It has been suggested that the *seferet hetepet* is a ferryboat or a ladder. The two words do not occur anywhere else, so we cannot be sure of their meaning. *Seferet* may be derived from the root *sef*, a word meaning "to be mild," "merciful," "kindly"; *hetepet* derives from *hetep*, meaning "peace" or "satisfaction." It seems likely, then, that it is these two qualities conjoined—of outward kindliness and inner peace—that here act

Figure 9.17. The mystical goal of having become the faithful companion of Ra, as portrayed in the Nineteenth Dynasty papyrus of Neferrenpet.

as the vehicle of the king's ascent. Perhaps there is a degree of poetic aptness in our not being able to name with complete certainty what the qualities are that are conveyed by the word *seferet-hetepet* that will enable Unas to ascend to the sky. All we do know for sure from this utterance (and others like it) is that through this ascent, Unas achieves the mystical goal of becoming the "faithful companion" of Ra (fig. 9.17).[66]

10 THE RECOVERY OF ANCIENT EGYPTIAN MYSTICISM

The Features of Ancient Egyptian Mysticism

In part 2, layers of meaning have been uncovered in the Pyramid Texts that consistently support a mystical interpretation of their content. The type of mysticism that they reveal is a "visionary mysticism" that entails a range of experiences, often expressed in striking imagery, that the king undergoes in relation to the spirit world. Not to regard these experiences as authentically mystical would only result in a distorted assessment of the real significance of what is related in the Pyramid Texts. What is related in these texts goes beyond mere intellectual speculation or beliefs concerning the afterlife, beyond also the liturgical accompaniment of funerary rituals: What the texts describe are direct encounters with a spiritual dimension of existence.

Alongside these visionary experiences, there is also an undercurrent of longing for union with such cosmic gods as Ra and Atum and the goddess Nut, the realization of which is also vividly and repeatedly expressed, so even were we to adopt the narrow definition of mysticism as "identity or union with the ultimate source of reality," the Pyramid Texts should still be regarded as mystical texts. On both the broad and the narrow definition of mysticism, the Pyramid Texts belong among the classics of world mystical literature. What has prevented their being appreciated as such is the erroneous assumption that they are simply and solely funerary texts. The deeply entrenched view that the content of the Pyramid Texts relates either to funerary rituals or to beliefs of the Egyptians concerning the afterlife and does not relate to the experiences of the living king is incompatible with the texts themselves and stands in the way of a true perception of their meaning.

In our exploration of their meaning, strong affinities have been revealed between the Pyramid Texts and the literature of shamanism. Rather than simply being viewed as a sociological phenomenon, shamanism is itself best understood as a type of mysticism, as Mircea Eliade has shown.[1] What is distinctive about shamanism when viewed as a type of mysticism is that it involves the living encounter with the spirit world that occurs in a state of consciousness in which the shaman temporarily crosses the threshold of death. It is experiences at this threshold of death that constitute both the mystical core of shamanism and the mystical content of the Pyramid Texts. This is why we may refer to the content of the Pyramid Texts as articulating a shamanic wisdom, for they are expressing direct spiritual experiences arising when the boundary between worlds is consciously crossed.

It is in this respect, then, that these texts are first and foremost to be understood as mystical texts. It is quite conceivable that the same texts could have been used in a variety of ritual and ceremonial contexts. Indeed, there is no problem in accepting that one of these contexts was funerary, for the simple reason that the type of mysticism that existed in ancient Egypt involved crossing the threshold of death while still alive. It would be entirely appropriate that mystical texts concerned with traveling into the realm of the dead while still alive should be employed for funerary purposes. But the texts themselves are clearly describing experiences of the living, not of the dead. That is why they are mystical.

Unlike historically more recent, and therefore more familiar, accounts of visionary mystics, the Pyramid Texts do not have a narrative form, with a clear beginning and end and various episodes in between. As we have seen, their distribution on the walls of the pyramids is determined less by the demands of any narrative sequence than by the architectural symbolism of the inner chambers of the pyramid.[2] Nevertheless, there are salient themes in the texts that are indicative of stages of a mystical journey. Although the attempt to arrange them in a sequential order is fraught with hazard, two factors come to our aid. The first is that a comparison between the pyramid of Unas with later pyramids, and also with the later copy of the Unas texts in the tomb of Senwosret-Ankh, shows certain sequences of text to have been relatively constant. Individual utterances do seem to "belong together" within these short sequences.[3] A second helpful factor is the manifest parallels that we have repeatedly found between certain themes in the Pyramid Texts and other mystical traditions, such as Platonism, the Hermetic tradition, and the literature of shamanism. These parallels provide us with a ready key with which to unlock meaningful patterns of mystical experience within the Pyramid Texts, five of which can be singled out.

(1) Death and Rebirth

The fundamental underlying pattern in the Pyramid Texts is one that can be found in all initiatory traditions: It is that of death and rebirth. Osiris must die in order for Horus to be born. Horus is the reborn Osiris. At the same time, Horus is intimately related to the solar principle. As well as being son of Osiris, Horus is also "son of Ra," and the intimacy of the relationship between Horus and Ra is shown in the fact that they both manifest in the same animal form: They are both falcons. Thus the Osirian death leads to a solar rebirth, and just as falcons are creatures that seem to belong less to the earth than to the sky, so the solar rebirth occurs in a cosmic setting, far away from terrestrial existence. Within Egyptology, the standard funerary interpretation of the relationship between Osiris and Horus is that the two gods correspond to two different kings: the deceased king and his successor, the living king who occupies the throne. Only when it is seen that the two gods can also correspond to two different existential phases, or states of consciousness, of one and the same king is it possible to grasp the potential initiatory significance of their relationship: for then it would be one and the same king who goes through the death experience of being identified with Osiris in order for him to experience rebirth as Horus.

This death-rebirth pattern is readily discernible in the sarcophagus chamber south-to-east-wall sequence of texts in the pyramid of Unas (utts. 213–24). At the beginning of the sequence, the king "departs alive" to sit upon the throne of Osiris, the Lord of the Dwat. The prospect that the king should sit upon the throne of Osiris clearly implies an identification between the king and the god of the dead. The king is going to enter the realm of death, he is himself going to experience death. But although he is to journey into the realm of the dead, it is explicitly stated that he journeys into it alive. The death, then, is a "voluntary death"—a death experience undergone while still alive rather than a literal physical death. We have seen in chapter 7 that such journeys by the living into the realm of the dead are widely attested to both in the literature of shamanism and in Orphic, Platonic, Neoplatonic, and Hermetic mystical writings.[4] Indeed, it is such a pervasive theme in initiatory literature that we would be blind not to see that an initiatory interpretation of Unas's "departing alive" is just as viable as that of the standard funerary interpretation.

In the very next utterance in the south-to-east-wall sequence (utt. 214), the king is transformed into a falcon, inwardly identifying with the solar principle as he soars into the heavens. The "sun folk" call out to him as he flies toward realms of spiritual light. But before he can join Ra in his sun boat, he is required to heal and reconcile the opposing forces of Horus and Seth. That is, he is required to bring into harmony the opposites of creativity and destruction, of order (Horus) and the wild, primal, but ultimately unproductive energies of Seth. This reconciliation of the opposites is en route to the union with Ra in his sun boat, a union that occurs initially in the depths of the night. It occurs, in fact, in the depths of the Dwat, the realm of Osiris, the realm of death (utts. 216–17). But what this night union with the solar principle entails is the inner rebirth of the king so that he realizes within himself what the Egyptians termed *akh*. The king becomes *akh*—a shining spirit, with power over both life and death (utt. 217). Thus, by journeying into the realm of death, into the Osirian realm, Unas is able to find new life. Normally, we think of life as something that will inevitably succumb to and be extinguished by the forces of death. But what Unas finds is a new kind of life that is kindled within the very heart of death (utt. 219). It is therefore a different order of life that he finds: Spiritual life that can be sustained even in the midst of the sphere of death.

It is on the basis of having had this inner experience of spiritual rebirth that the king is proclaimed a Horus (utts. 220–21) and undergoes coronation as Horus. Horus is the god, or state of being, that is born from the condition of death and dismemberment represented by Osiris. The inner experience of the birth of Horus comes about when one is able to tap the source of life in the midst of the realm of death.

Although this underlying initiatory pattern of death (as Osiris) and rebirth (as Horus) is most clearly seen in the sarcophagus chamber south-to-east-wall sequence, it is reiterated or alluded to in a great many other texts and sequences of text in the pyramid of Unas. It is a fundamental motif of the Pyramid Texts, and the latter cannot be understood without a recognition of the root significance of this initiatory motif.[5]

(2) Cosmic Self-Realization

Another important theme of the Pyramid Texts is that human self-realization occurs in a cosmic rather than a simply terrestrial context. By "self-realization" is meant the experiential knowledge of one's deepest nature, the divine within oneself. In the Pyramid Texts, many utterances (often referred to as "ascension texts") describe the experience of rising up and away from the earth and into the heavens. In the shamanic tradition, the ascent to heaven typically follows the ordeal of dismemberment, and this is a pattern that we also find in the texts of the pyramid of Unas. The dismemberment of Osiris is never referred to directly, but his re-memberment is, and in certain sequences of text this is the prelude to the ascent to the sky.[6] Often, however, the prior phase of re-memberment is not even alluded to, and all the emphasis goes on the ascent alone. In the pyramid of Unas, we have already seen that in utterance 214 the king assumes the form of a falcon and soars into the sky. Elsewhere he streaks like lightning, ascends in a dust storm, a cloud of smoke, or more prosaically climbs a stairway or ladder in order to reach the heavens.[7] In each case the mode of ascent expresses Unas's transcendence of the earth plane as the precondition of the experience of that higher or deeper level of reality upon which all things earthly depend.

Similar descriptions of rising up to the heavens abound in the mystical literature of the world. Comparable to the many accounts within the shamanic tradition is the flight of the Mesopotamian king Etana on the back of an eagle that takes him up through the heavenly spheres. We also have Plato's description of the soul's levitation in *Phaedrus*, Paul's experience of being raised to the "third heaven" in 2 Corinthians, the ecstatic Hermetic "Discourse on the Eighth and the Ninth," and Muhammad's *mi'râj*, or night journey, through the heavenly spheres.[8] In each case, we see a similar pattern of movement away from the sphere of the earth as the precondition of direct vision of spiritual realities, otherwise concealed from view. This, of course, is not to deny obvious differences in content among these descriptions of mystical ascent, but it is to recognize a similar pattern of experience that categorically belongs within the sphere of mysticism.[9]

The accounts in the Pyramid Texts rank as the first in world literature to articulate this pattern of mystical ascent and spiritual vision. Once in the cosmic spheres, it is as if the spiritual eye is opened and conscious encounters with ancestral spirits and gods then become possible, culminating in the union of the king with the cosmic deities, Nut, Atum, and Ra. Encounters with gods and mystic union are not the only experiences, however. There is also—as we have seen—the experience of being spiritually reborn that occurs specifically in the cosmic spheres. On the east gable of the sarcophagus chamber (utts. 211–12), Unas acquires a new celestial body that needs a quite different kind of nourishment from that which the physical body demands on earth. The motif of celestial rebirth and nourishment (mostly in the form of being suckled by goddesses) recurs several times in the Pyramid Texts. It is both a dramatic and a deeply mysterious event in which the divine feminine has a central cosmic role.[10]

According to the Pyramid Texts, wisdom *(sai)* and knowledge or insight *(sia)* are attainable only in realms beyond the earth. Just as for Plato true wisdom can only be found in the realm of the dead (i.e., the spirit world) and hence philosophers should devote themselves to dying and death, so in the Pyramid Texts wisdom and knowledge or insight are dependent upon the celestial rebirth of the soul.[11] Symbolically, these qualities are the spiritual nourishment given by heavenly goddesses like the milk goddess, Iat, or the hippopotamus goddess, Ipy. The reborn spirit is suckled on wisdom and insight—a wisdom of the heart that is based on insight into the reality of unseen worlds. The Pyramid Texts make it transparently clear that the human being is not just a terrestrial being. This presumption is a modern one, and the Pyramid Texts call it into question. We belong to a superterrestrial world as well, and this should be understood in the sense of the greater cosmos that exists above the small sphere of the earth and also at a more interior and mostly invisible level of being. It is both a celestial and an interior mode of being that we take on when we die or equally when the human spirit rises into the heavens in the kind of ecstatic ascent described in the literature of shamanism, the Hermetic and Platonic traditions, and paramountly in the Pyramid Texts.

(3) Negotiating the Spirit World

Along with many other ancient cultures, as indeed for mainstream Western culture up until as recently as the seventeenth century, the superterrestrial world was regarded by the ancient Egyptians as the abode of spirits. The stars that shine in the night sky shine with an otherworldly light, for they are at the boundary between outwardly visible existence and the inward reality of the spirit world, or Dwat. One way in which the Dwat was pictured by the ancient Egyptians, and this was especially elaborated in the New Kingdom, was that it was located in the interior of the body of the cosmic star goddess, Nut. Looking up to the heavens, they saw the night sky as her dark flesh spangled with stars, and they conceived that this was but the outermost manifestation of a rich inner world, hidden from view because it was literally interior to the body of the goddess. Thus there existed a reverent, awe-filled feeling for the cosmos as sheltering a different kind of reality from that which is ordinarily perceived on the terrestrial plane with the physical senses.[12]

Here, then, is a "cosmology" that is at once both outer and inner. Specific regions of the sky—the south, the east, the north, and the west, the Milky Way, certain key constellations (such as Orion, the southern constellations, and the Great Bear), and stars (such as Sirius), as well as the sun and moon—all open onto inner realities. They point inward toward the unseen, toward inner zones of experience, toward the location of inner events that the human being must undergo on the journey of spiritual self-realization. Then there are other celestial/spiritual regions such as the Field of Rushes, the Akhet or place of rebirth and transfiguration (often translated as "horizon"), and the mysterious watery expanse of the Nun that also belong to this cosmology but at a more unmanifest level that is hard (and also fairly pointless) to equate with anything externally perceptible. Orientation in the spirit world cannot ultimately be achieved by reference to anything familiar to us from the standpoint of the terrestrial world. Despite being for the most part invisible, the transcendent reality that we refer to in shorthand as the spirit world was, for the Egyptians, a very full world. It was a multilayered and infinitely complex world that the human spirit must negotiate, gain knowledge of and power over, in order to attain full human-divine stature. In this respect the cosmology of the Pyramid Texts bears comparison to other mystical cosmologies in which manifold regions, corresponding to states or levels of being, are incorporated within a picture of the stages of human spiritual development.[13]

Inhabiting these inner worlds are a number of different spiritual beings. There are the dead, the royal ancestors in particular, who come to meet the king as he stands on the threshold of the spirit world (utt. 306).[14] There are also helping spirits, in the form of spirit wives who consort with the king (utt. 205), spirit mothers who suckle him (utts. 41–42, 211, 269, and 308) and spirit guides who guide him through the Otherworld regions (both Sothis and Wepwawet in utt. 302). Various gods observe the arrival of the king, welcome him, and may also assist him in his ascent to heaven by providing or holding a celestial ladder (utts. 271, 305, 306, and 269). There are also formidable opponents, whose wish seems only to obstruct the king: the Ugly One (utt. 255), for example, who confronts him at the Akhet, the very place of transfiguration; the "four raging ones" (utt. 311), who encircle the sun god Ra, opposing all who are unfit to come into his presence; the fierce baboon god, Babi (utt. 313), who guards the doors of the sky; and so on. These beings must be confronted and overcome or transformed into spirits that no longer oppose but aid the king on his journey, their energies integrated. There are also more ambivalent beings who are partly benevolent, partly obstructive, such as the celestial ferryman (utts. 270 and 310), who is an Osirian figure; and at times even Osiris himself is portrayed as an opposing force (utts. 215, 219, and 245).

For the Egyptians, then, the spiritual dimension is full of beings. The breakthrough in plane is a breakthrough not into simplicity but into a complex and multifaceted world that presents many challenges to the human being who accomplishes it. The spirit world is a dangerous world that requires both knowledge and skill to negotiate, and not a little magic power. In the famous Cannibal Hymn (utts. 273–74), the king breaks into the spirit world as a mighty magician, storming heaven and absorbing the energies of the gods into himself in order to master them. We would have to be peculiarly thick-skinned to regard the cosmology of the Pyramid Texts as merely the product of "priestly speculations" and to see it only as so many intellectual constructs. What we are presented with are extreme existential situations and lived encounters with extraordinary realities.

(4) Union with the Gods

We have seen that those who deny the existence of a mystical tradition in ancient Egypt do so on the grounds that Egyptian religious texts do not refer to the experience of mystic union.[15] Yet the Pyramid Texts describe countless meetings and interactions with the gods, and frequent identifications or mergings of the individual with divine beings. Most obviously, the king is identified with either Osiris or Horus in a great many utterances.[16] Whether we are entitled to describe these identifications as "mystic" unions depends, of course, on how we choose to define mysticism. If we accept the broad definition, there would be no problem in describing them as mystic unions. But from the perspective of the narrow definition of mysticism as union or identity with the ultimate source of reality, these identifications with Osiris and Horus would not pass the test. Neither god could really be said to be the ultimate source of reality. They are each specific manifestations of the divine, exemplars of archetypal processes that the human soul suffers (in the case of Osiris) and wins through to (in the case of Horus).

The same may also be said of other divine identifications that are featured in the Pyramid Texts, with such gods as Nefertem, Sia, Sobek, and Babi. They each belong to a specific spiritual context, express a degree of attainment, a certain quality or power that is gained. These identifications indicate that the king has gone beyond himself, and is participating in or acting out of an energy that is transpersonal and archetypal. But he is not yet identified or united with the ultimate source of existence. The Pyramid Texts, however, do not stop at this level. There is a greater longing that forms the spiritual undercurrent of the texts, a longing to reach out beyond identification with any particular god and to stand in the presence of the deities that are closest to the source of existence: Nut, the cosmic mother; Nun, the primordial source and father of the gods; Atum, the most all-encompassing of the gods; and Ra, the source of light and creativity who corresponds cosmically to the human-divine archetype on earth, Horus.

In the pyramid of Unas, utterance 245 expresses the longing of the king to come to Nut, who may be said to represent the whole superterrestrial cosmos. This longing for union with Nut arises out of a profound awareness that our nature as human beings is cosmic as well as earthly. The greater cosmic reality of Nut metaphysically as well as literally encompasses and encloses all that is earthly within its embrace, and provides the setting in which the human spirit realizes its intrinsic divinity.[17] Nut is the cosmic matrix within which spiritual rebirth takes place. Thus, for example, Unas is born from the womb of Nut as the Bull of the Sky (utt. 254)—having realized within himself both solar and cosmic power. At a deeper level even than Nut lies the Nun, the cosmic ocean that is the source of all existence, and we read in utterance 211 that the spiritual rebirth of Unas occurs in the Nun. The text clearly implies that Unas has been immersed in these primordial waters that symbolize the formless reality of the infinite. Such an experience, then, must surely approximate "classic" mystic union with the source of reality. It is expressed again in utterance 301, where Unas is said to cross over to the "father" of the gods, who should probably be identified with Nun.

Again, the embrace of the king by the supreme god Atum in utterance 215 is expressive of a nondual state that transcends the opposites symbolized by Horus and Seth. This embrace is the prelude to the king's inner identification with Ra in the solar night bark and his solar rebirth and transfiguration in the Akhet. From the Akhet, the king rises as an *akh*, an inwardly illumined, "solarized" being (utts. 216–17). Atum is again the progenitor of Unas in the Cannibal Hymn (utts. 273–74), where the root of the king's power is said to be in the Akhet "like his father Atum who has begotten him." The relationship to Nut, Nun, and Atum would seem in each case to be that union with them leads to spiritual rebirth. The model or prototype of this spiritual rebirth—the god upon whom it is based—is Ra.

In the Pyramid Texts, union with Ra has a different ontological status from union with the great cosmic divinities, Nut, Nun, and Atum. It is more intimate, more final. Unlike these other deities, Ra is the cosmic divine archetype that the human being is able to realize on earth as Horus. To become one with Ra signifies that the king has access to the self-generating and self-regenerating energy of the sun god, an energy that transcends the duality of life and death. As a solarized being, the king is able to live in the invisible as well as the visible worlds, the cosmic as well as the earthly, the spiritual as well as the physical. Union with Ra, therefore, should probably be regarded as closer to—or at least a more realized phase of—the classic form of mystic union with the godhead, than union with Nut, Nun, or Atum, albeit expressed in the language and imagery of Egyptian religion. Ra is "the great god," and both identity and conscious union with Ra (in the sense of being in the god's presence) are repeatedly portrayed as the ultimate goal and the deepest fulfillment of our human divine nature.[18]

Even on the narrow definition of mysticism as "union or identity with the source of reality," the case for the existence of mysticism in Old Kingdom Egypt is overwhelming and its denial requires ignoring all the evidence cited above and referred to in chapters 7, 8, and 9 for the attainment of unitive states of consciousness in the Pyramid Texts. Those arguing against mysticism can do so only by doggedly maintaining that the Pyramid Texts were exclusively funerary texts. Their argument then rests on the presumption that only dead Egyptians were mystical: Living Egyptians were practical and down-to-earth.[19] Were we to accept such a view, the ancient Egyptians and their religion would remain an oddity of world history: the only culture that we know of in which mysticism did not exist, or if it did exist, then it existed in a curious postmortem form. Throughout the present study, the aim has been to show that this unfortunate characterization of the Egyptians is palpably and demonstrably false.

(5) Return

Nevertheless, one qualification does need to be made concerning the character of ancient Egyptian mysticism as this is portrayed in the Pyramid Texts. This is that although such potent inner experiences as the ascent to the sky, direct knowledge of and access to the spirit world, encounters with spirits and gods, the experience of mystic union, and spiritual rebirth are all major themes in the Pyramid Texts, there is also one further theme that we need to take into account. This is the theme of "return"—the return of the king to earth, his taking up his throne and his acting as a mediator between the worlds. The goal of the mystical journey is not simply to enter into relationship with the divine, but also to bring the divine into relationship with the earthly.

We have seen that in the south-to-east-wall sequence of the sarcophagus chamber in the pyramid of Unas, the ascent of the king to the sky and his solarization is followed by his coronation as a living Horus (utts.

319

220–21). In other words, the king is crowned as ruler of the two lands of Egypt. At the end of this same sequence describing the king's journey to the sky we find two texts that explicitly recall the king back to terrestrial existence (utts. 223–24). In the first text, he is told to move around, to stand up and sit down, and then to eat and drink. In the second he takes hold of two symbols of kingship: One is a scepter that symbolizes his rulership over the world of the living, the other a staff that symbolizes his rulership over the realm of the dead. The point of his journey into the spirit world was to become a master of both spheres of reality.

On the antechamber west wall, the theme of the coronation of the king recurs again (utts. 255–56). And this time Unas declares himself the heir of both the cosmic god Atum and the earth god, Geb. As Horus—the god who has been through the Osirian death and dismemberment, flown up to the heavens, and experienced spiritual rebirth—the king unites in himself the Above and the Below, and brings into manifestation a new divine-human axis, a channel for the energies of the spirit world to flow into the terrestrial world. He is "the one who went and came back," who makes the link between worlds (utt. 260). And the consequence of his having made this link is that he becomes the mediator of the fertilizing powers that flow into the terrestrial sphere, into the land of Egypt, from the spirit world. He channels the vitalizing energies of the spirit world into the realm of the living. In so doing he establishes Maat, or cosmic harmony, on earth, one of the most important functions of kingship (utts. 317 and 319). The goal of the spiritual journey described in the Pyramid Texts is therefore not simply the king's enlightenment or absorption in the godhead; it is for him to seal the connection between worlds, to unite the realms of heaven and earth for the benefit of all Egypt, and thereby to establish Maat—universal harmony and order—throughout the kingdom.

The Phenomenological Approach to Ancient Egyptian Religion

If in the preceding pages we have seen the Pyramid Texts reveal themselves as mystical rather than as simply funerary texts, this has been due largely to a methodological decision to allow the texts themselves to guide us toward their inner meaning, rather than by seeking to fit the texts into a preconceived theory concerning their funerary purpose or ritual function. Following the methodology of the phenomenology of religion, we have approached the texts as specifically religious phenomena to be understood primarily on the religious plane of reference. A prerequisite of pursuing such an approach is that the very idea of a "religious plane of reference" means something to the researcher. If it were not meaningful and deemed to have intrinsic value, then the phenomena would lose their significance as *religious*, for the idea of a religious plane of reference provides the ground of our understanding the content of the texts precisely as religious phenomena. If, for example, we are to understand such episodes as the Osirian dismemberment and the mystical flight to the stars religiously, it is incumbent on us, the researchers, to deepen our own relationship to the religious import that these experiences might have. And this requires our active and empathetic engagement with both the religious content of the texts and the religious dimension to which they refer. The two go together.

The question of method, then, is at root a question of fundamental attitude and comes down to whether the researcher's orientation to the sphere of religion is one of personal interest and engagement or of relative indifference. Henri Corbin more than once referred to the "agnostic reflex" within academia as one of the greatest stumbling blocks to a true perception of the meaning of religious texts.[20] While the "agnostic reflex" may be the necessary basis of explanatory reductionism, its opposite is the necessary ground from which a phenomenological study would work. Without a personal interest in the religious dimension, there can be no real empathetic engagement with the religious texts that one is trying to understand, and empathetic engagement is at the heart of the phenomenological method. According to van der Leeuw, "to him who does not love, nothing whatever is manifested."[21] While the disengaged stance of explanatory reductionism will seek to explain religious phenomena in terms of the nonreligious contexts with which the secular mind feels comfortable, the phenomenological approach depends upon engagement, passionate engagement, with the religious sphere in order to penetrate the existential significance of the religious texts it endeavors to understand.

This does not mean that the texts are thereby interpreted in a context vacuum. The argument that religious experience needs to be understood in relation to the historical and cultural context in which it occurs is not a point of contention, and throughout the present study the scholarship of Egyptologists has been essential in unraveling the meaning of the Pyramid Texts. What is a point of contention, however, is the argument that religious experience is necessarily determined by its historical and cultural contexts, and this argument has been categorically rejected in chapter 5. Were this argument to be accepted, then the only discipline capable of studying ancient Egyptian religion would be Egyptology itself, for it alone specializes in the study of these contexts. The purpose of the present study, however, has been to focus on the experiential basis of the Pyramid Texts, a focus that previous Egyptological studies of the texts have not been able to sustain, because of the general assumption within Egyptology that the texts relate to funerary beliefs and the rituals associated with them, and not to religious or mystical experiences.

One of the main reasons why previous studies of the Pyramid Texts (discussed in chapter 6) have failed to lay hold of their mystical content is not, therefore, because it is absent but because the fundamental presuppositions and methodological parameters of these previous studies have actually hindered rather than helped its discovery. Three general criticisms may be made, from a strictly methodological standpoint, concerning these previous studies. First, their approach to the Pyramid Texts has been distorted by the unquestioned presupposition that the texts are purely funerary. This presupposition has never been proved, but its adoption has ensured that the mystical content of the Pyramid Texts has been ignored. For this reason the present study has deliberately approached the texts free of this presupposition. In so doing, a deeper initiatory level of meaning has been uncovered that can only cause us to question the extent to which reference to a funerary interpretation of the texts can be helpful in further studies of them. This is not to deny that the texts may have been used in a funerary context, but only to point out that if their primary meaning is initiatory, then the primary context in which they were used would clearly have been initiatory rather than funerary. Further studies are therefore more likely to bear fruit if they approach the Pyramid Texts within an initiatory rather than a funerary matrix of understanding.

In chapter 4, detailed evidence was presented for a connection between the pyramids of the Old Kingdom and the Sed festival of the kings to whom the pyramids belonged. This evidence, consistently appearing in pyramid complexes from the Third to the Sixth Dynasties, poses one of the most cogent challenges to the funerary interpretation of the Old Kingdom pyramids by suggesting that they had an initiatory rather than a simply funerary purpose. As we have seen in chapter 3, at the center of the Sed festival were initiatory rites in which the king went through an Osiris identification, "died," and was reborn. Because of the location of the Pyramid Texts in the heart of the pyramid complexes of the Fifth and Sixth Dynasties, it would be odd if a relationship did not exist between the content of these texts and the purpose of the pyramid complexes. Furthermore, the frequent reference in the texts to kingship rites and the many allusions in them to ceremonies that resemble those of the Sed festival specifically point to the likelihood of a Sed festival connection.[22]

But although there are strong reasons for regarding the Sed festival as providing the ritual context for many of the Pyramid Texts, this does not necessarily mean that the Pyramid Texts were "Sed festival texts," and the central argument of this book does not stand or fall with the successful demonstration of this relationship. Rather, the invocation of the Sed festival as an alternative context for the interpretation of the Pyramid Texts has served to enable us to loosen the stranglehold of the funerary interpretation on these texts in order to release their existential and experiential content to view. It is precisely this that previous studies, beholden to the funerary interpretation, have not been able to do.

This brings us to the second point. Previous studies of the Pyramid Texts have tended to focus on the contexts of ritual practice, belief systems, and other cultural factors on the assumption that only by placing the texts within such contexts is it then possible to arrive at a satisfactory explanation of them. While this kind of focus is obviously important, it nevertheless remains of limited value if the experiential dimension is overlooked, for that is where the deeper meaning of the texts resides. From a phenomenological perspective, it would therefore make little sense to press the case for a Sed festival context for the Pyramid Texts, as if this were all we needed to do to explain them. This would come too close to the kind of reductive "explanation in terms of" that phenomenology seeks to avoid. In order to understand the Pyramid Texts, the primary task, from a phenomenological standpoint, is to recognize their experiential content; it then becomes possible to understand the nature of the rituals that would have supported or induced these experiences. The point here is about focus. While it has been argued in chapters 3 and 4 that the Sed festival provides a viable alternative to the funerary context for understanding the Pyramid Texts, the main purpose of this study has been to lay bare the meaning that these texts hold *as expressions of religious experience.* It is precisely because the focus of previous Egyptological studies has been on the contexts of funerary ritual or afterlife beliefs rather than on actual experiences that the inherent mystical content of the texts has been missed. When the question of whether mysticism existed in ancient Egypt is asked, therefore, the answer given depends to a very large extent on the assumptions and the methodology of the researcher. Both the assumptions and the methodology of previous Egyptological studies have had the consequence that the mystical significance of the Pyramid Texts has either been entirely overlooked or else projected into a safely neutralized postmortem scenario to fall under the category of "afterlife beliefs."

We now come to the third criticism of the kind of methods employed in earlier studies. It is that previous attempts to understand the Pyramid Texts have often been highly conjectural, with the result that the meaning of the texts has repeatedly been squeezed into the confines of a narrow hypothesis, rather than being allowed to flow from the texts themselves. As a result, the flaws within these previous theories have been easily exposed, and subsequent commentators, such as, for example, Henri Frankfort and Winfried Barta, have been able to subject them to withering criticism, as we have seen in chapter 6.[23] What Frankfort and Barta failed to do, however, was to challenge them sufficiently strongly on grounds of methodology. There is a fundamental difference between the methodology of "conjecture and refutation" (to which both Frankfort and Barta implicitly subscribe) and the methodology of gaining insight through an empathetic engagement with the experiential content of a text. Because the phenomenological approach avoids conjecture, and seeks rather to lay hold of the meaning inherent within the phenomena by uncovering their experiential basis, it is the most appropriate method for understanding their religious significance. It is precisely in virtue of its methodology that the phenomenological approach is able to reveal the mystical content of the Pyramid Texts that to previous studies has remained concealed.

A central aim of the phenomenological approach is—in the words of Mircea Eliade—"to lay bare the existential situation" that underlies what is expressed in religious texts.[24] It is just because the phenomenology of religion has the existential and experiential significance of religious phenomena as its principal focus that it is able to provide a much needed complement to the researches of Egyptologists that generally do not have this focus. It requires above all openness, empathy, and a meditative relationship to the texts, which enables the researcher to become receptive to their religious content and understand them in specifically religious terms. If the present study has been able to demonstrate that there was a mystical tradition in ancient Egypt, and that the Pyramid Texts should be regarded as mystical texts, then hopefully it has also been able to show how a phenomenological approach can make a positive contribution, alongside Egyptology, to the understanding of ancient Egyptian religion.

There is, then, an important role for phenomenology in the study of ancient Egyptian religion, as there is by implication in the study of other religions of antiquity. The focus of the phenomenology of religion is on the experience of the sacred, in whatever different cultural and historical circumstances it presents itself. While the religions of antiquity may from a purely historical standpoint be regarded as belonging to the past, from the standpoint of the phenomenology of religion it would be inappropriate to regard them only in this way. They belong to the general existential situation of humanity, revealing to us often raw, frequently profound, and sometimes disturbing relationships to a transhistorical religious dimension. At the most fundamental level of ontology, meaning, and truth, they are not containable within history. For this reason they have direct relevance to us today. And this relevance is all the greater for our contemporary culture, which sadly expends so much effort in defending itself from exposure to the sacred.

Ancient Egypt and Western Esotericism

The Pyramid Texts are the oldest version of a literary genre of religious texts produced during the course of Egyptian history. This includes the Middle Kingdom Coffin Texts and the New Kingdom Book of the Dead papyri, both of which derive from, and are developments of, the earlier Pyramid Texts. If the Pyramid Texts are mystical rather than just funerary, then clearly a reassessment of the funerary nature of the later Coffin Texts and Book of the Dead needs to be undertaken. We have seen at the end of chapter 2 that several studies have already been made that support a mystical interpretation of many of the Coffin Texts and a significant number of chapters of the Book of the Dead. Similarly, the New Kingdom royal Underworld books that appear in the tombs of the Valley of the Kings and elsewhere are highly susceptible to a mystical interpretation.[25] The task is not so much one of more textual analysis, however, as the adoption of a methodological approach sensitive to the mystical content of these texts.

The Pyramid Texts, Coffin Texts, and Book of the Dead, along with the royal Underworld books, together constitute the backbone of ancient Egyptian religious literature. We have seen in chapters 2 and 3 that in the eyes of the Greeks, Egyptian religion was essentially mystical.[26] The reinterpretation that has been proposed in this study would clearly validate this Greek perception of Egyptian religion. It was a perception that was shared by European scholars, philosophers, and esotericists up until the nineteenth century. Indeed, several important Western esoteric traditions claim not only Egyptian origins, but also to represent authentic Egyptian mystical teachings and ritual practices derived from Egypt.[27] If ancient Egyptian texts hitherto regarded as funerary are seen to be primarily mystical and based upon an initiatory "core experience," then an actual connection between these later traditions and ancient Egyptian spiritual wisdom should no longer be dismissed out of hand.

As we have seen in chapter 1, Egyptology has, since its inception as a bona fide academic discipline in the late nineteenth century, strongly resisted any such connection.[28] One of the main arguments it has used to support this resistance is that ancient Egyptian religion in fact has very little in common with later esoteric movements that claim to have ancient Egyptian roots. In particular, initiation rites purported to be derived from Egypt in reality played no part in ancient Egyptian religion. Thus Erik Hornung, in his recent survey of Western esoteric traditions claiming Egyptian origins, *The Secret Lore of Egypt*, feels it necessary to distinguish "Egyptosophy" from Egyptology proper. The former is based upon an "imaginary Egypt viewed as the profound source of all esoteric lore. This Egypt is a timeless idea bearing only a loose relationship to the historical reality."[29] For Hornung, it is of course Egyptology that studies the historical reality, and Egyptology knows of no initiation rites in ancient Egypt.[30] In contrast to Hornung, those Egyptologists who are more open to the idea that modern esoteric traditions do have their roots in a real rather than an imaginary ancient Egypt are at the same time more open to a mystical as opposed to a funerary interpretation of ancient Egyptian religious texts, imagery, and rituals. It is precisely through accepting the fact that there were initiatory rituals involving death and rebirth in ancient Egypt that Alison Roberts sees the need to reevaluate ancient Egypt's contribution to later religious developments such as Hermeticism and Gnosticism.[31]

With the growing interest in the academic study of Western esotericism, as exemplified in the work of Antoine Faivre, Wouter Hanegraaff, Arthur Versluis, and others,[32] it is all the more important that the question of the actual nature of ancient Egyptian religion become a focus of concern not only for Egyptologists but also for historians of religion—how this question is answered has a direct bearing on our understanding of the relationship between Western esoteric streams and ancient Egypt. With the standard view still being that the sources of Western esotericism go no farther back than the Hellenistic period, the relatively young academic study of Western esotericism is needlessly stunting itself.[33] Even mainstream Egyptologists are now prepared to accept that the Hermetic tradition really does have ancient Egyptian roots, and it seems just a question of time before it is generally acknowledged that alchemy too has pharaonic origins. The same could well be said of major streams of Gnostic thought, which, like alchemy, sprang from Egyptian soil.[34]

By wresting the Pyramid Texts free of an exclusively funerary interpretation, and by showing that their primary meaning and purpose was mystical, the present study has hopefully made a contribution toward the vital task of reconnecting Western esoteric traditions to their mystical and initiatic roots in ancient Egypt. The implications of the reinterpretation of the

Pyramid Texts as mystical texts thus extend far beyond a simply historical understanding of ancient Egyptian religion. Within the academic discipline of religious studies, there has been a tendency to steer clear of historical religions, perhaps in the belief that so-called dead religions of the past have little to offer us today. Roots can seem to be the most "dead" part of a tree, and they are certainly the most hidden. But they both anchor and nourish all that we see growing above ground. The relationship of ancient Egypt to Western esoteric traditions such as Hermeticism, Gnosticism, and alchemy (and perhaps also to later movements like Rosicrucianism and esoteric Freemasonry that claim to draw inspiration from Egypt) could be seen as that of roots to the rest of the tree. We have something of an obligation today to bend ourselves to the task of reaching back to the mystical and initiatory core of ancient Egyptian religion, for if this core runs through Western esotericism, then its rehabilitation has profound implications for the spiritual life of the contemporary Western world.

But it is not simply our understanding of Western esoteric traditions that would be enlivened by showing the extent to which they are irradiated by the spiritual legacy of ancient Egypt. Our understanding of ancient Egyptian religion too can be illumined by the light that may be thrown upon it from later esoteric sources. In the foregoing chapters, we have repeatedly seen how Hermetic and Platonic perspectives have been helpful in orientating one toward the deeper meaning of certain passages in the Pyramid Texts. There is no reason why the same illuminative relationship may not also exist between, for example, later alchemical texts and the understanding of certain stages of the Osirian initiation.[35] The possibility of a reciprocally illuminative relationship between ancient Egyptian religion and Western esoteric traditions depends less on our being able to trace an exoteric historical transmission (as can be done with alchemy) than the extent to which the teachings, imagery, ritual practices, and so on of these traditions reach into the same archetypal territory as that occupied by ancient Egyptian religion. To what extent a specific esoteric tradition could be said to represent genuine Egyptian teachings or practices, and equally to what extent it could be employed as an aid to our understanding of religious experience in ancient Egypt, should be judged less by the outer forms it assumes than by the degree to which it connects with and transmits the pattern typical of Egyptian initiatory experience.

As mystical texts, the Pyramid Texts describe the human encounter with spiritual realities. The spiritual world that the Pyramid Texts disclose is one that is revealed only once a certain existential threshold has been reached and consciously crossed. Rather than speculations or beliefs, the content of the Pyramid Texts should be regarded as knowledge, or gnosis, of an order of reality quite "other" than that of which we today are normally aware. In this respect, the study of ancient Egyptian religion goes beyond archaeology and cultural history. It is primarily a study of the religious dimension as such. Although expressed in Egyptian terms, the realms of experience that we encounter in the Pyramid Texts are not exclusive to ancient Egypt. Of course the Pyramid Texts belong to, and need to be understood within, the cultural context of Old Kingdom Egypt. But to understand them simply within this cultural context is to miss something in them that has a more universal relevance, as the texts speak of the religious experience of human beings, no doubt very different from us, but human nevertheless.

By attempting to "get inside" the consciousness—and the worlds accessed by this consciousness—that the Pyramid Texts describe, we discover a very different "reality principle" from that by which modernity lives, upon the basis of which a whole civilization was organized. A new and quite different perspective on life is presented to us that we can usefully hold up as a mirror to ourselves. These ancient texts put us in touch with dimensions of human experience that are at once unfamiliar, even shocking, but also strangely familiar. The central motifs of the mysticism that we find in the Pyramid Texts have a certain resonance with contemporary spiritual longings. And it is a remarkable fact that they have become available to the modern world at precisely this point in history when it seems that we have most need of what they have to offer. One of the principal reasons for studying them is that they reconnect us with something vital that our culture has forgotten.

It is because Egypt reminds us of transpersonal realities that are mostly vague and obscure to contemporary consciousness that it constitutes a valid and relevant subject of study for human beings living today. In order to understand the Pyramid Texts, the modern reader is required to become awake to a different dimension of human experience. The fruit of genuine insight can be attained only to the extent that an empathetic "living into" the material leads to a certain inner "waking up" to the religious dimension. The study of ancient Egyptian religion, then, demands that we do more than simply familiarize ourselves with the world of the ancient Egyptians. It demands that we also become more sensitive to what impinges on our own. Wrestling with the content of the Pyramid Texts then becomes a wrestling with both the conceptual and the experiential limitations that we today are subject to in our monolithically secular culture. It also becomes an exploration of pathways by which we might effect an escape from these limitations.

And so the study of ancient Egyptian religion may lead us to conceive of a task that we have to fulfill in the present day. This task is to open ourselves once more to those realms of spirit that we are presented with in the mystical literature of Egypt. This could lead to the possibility of a new Egyptian-inspired Renaissance, in which Western spiritual culture is given fresh vigor by its reconnecting to its Egyptian roots. While it would make little sense to try to resurrect the religion of ancient Egypt today, the spiritual impulse that issues from ancient Egypt into contemporary culture may nevertheless encourage us to pursue paths of inner development appropriate to our own period in history, paths that once again put us in touch with realms of experience that have for too long been neglected. The study of ancient Egyptian religion paradoxically points us toward our own future, which is surely to develop new capacities of consciousness that would awaken us once more to the spiritual realities of which the mystical literature of ancient Egypt speaks.

APPENDIX 1

Summary of Utterances in the Pyramid of Unas

Sarcophagus Chamber

West Gable

Utts. 226–43: Eighteen Snake Spells

North Wall

1 Purification: Utts. 23, 25, 32, 34, 35, and 36
2 Opening the Mouth: Utts. 37–42
3 Preliminary Presentation of Offerings: Utts. 32 and 43–57
4 Anointing with the Seven Holy Oils: Utts. 72–78, 79, and 81
5 The Feast: Utts. 25 and 32, 82–96, 108–71

South and East Walls

1 Utt. 213: Departing Alive
2 Utt. 214: Becoming a Falcon
3 Utt. 215: Healing Horus and Seth, Embraced by Atum
4 Utt. 216: In the Night Bark of the Sun
5 Utt. 217: Solarization
6 Utt. 218: Empowerment
7 Utt. 219: A Living Osiris
8 Utt. 220: Coronation as Horus—Approaching the Crown
9 Utt. 221: Coronation of Horus—The Royal Rebirth
10 Utt. 222: Joining the Cosmic Circuit of Ra
11 Utt. 223: Awakening
12 Utt. 224: Return

Passage between Chambers

SOUTH

1. Utt. 244: Smashing the Red Jars
2. Utt. 245: Flying Up to Nut
3. Utt. 246: Merging with Min at the Doors of the Akhet

NORTH

1. Utt. 199: Reversion of Offerings
1. Utt. 32: Purificatory Libation
1. Utt. 23: Protective Libation
2. Utt. 25: Going with His *Ka*
2. Utt. 200: Hymn to Incense

East Gable

1. Utt. 204: The Nourishment Provided by Osiris
2. Utt. 205: The King Is Transformed into a Bull
3–4. Utts. 207 and 209: Two Food Texts
5. Utt. 210: Negotiating the Inverted World
6. Utt. 211: Unas Is Born a Star
7. Utt. 212: The Divine Nourishment of the King

Antechamber

West Gable

1. Utt. 247: The Awakening of the Initiate King
2. Utt. 248: The Fiery Rebirth of Unas
3. Utt. 249: The Sun Child
4. Utt. 250: Uniting with Sia
5. Utt. 251: Becoming the Strong Horn of Ra
6. Utt. 252: Union with Ra
7. Utt. 253: Lifted Up by Shu

West and South Walls

1. Utt. 254: The Death and Rebirth of the Horus King
2. Utt. 255: Overcoming the Ugly One
3. Utt. 256: The Throne of Horus
4. Utt. 257: Bursting through the Sky

5 Utt. 258: A Living Osiris
6 Utt. 260: The One Who Went and Came Back
7 Utt. 261: The Lightning Ascent
8 Utt. 262: The Regenerative Journey
9 Utt. 263: Crossing on Reed Floats, Meeting the Dead
10 Utt. 267: Re-memberment and Ascent to the Sky
11 Utt. 268: Uniting with the *Ka*
12 Utt. 269: Ascent to the Sky, Suckled by Ipy
13 Utt. 270: Awakening the Ferryman
14 Utt. 271: Pulling Papyrus, Raising the Djed
15 Utt. 272: The Gate of Nun

North Wall

1 Utt. 302: Becoming a Falcon, Flying Up to Ra
2 Utt. 303: The Dawning of the Second Horus
3 Utt. 304: The Openings of the Sky
4 Utt. 305: The Sky Ladder
5 Utt. 306: The Linking of Heaven and Earth
6 Utt. 307: The Bull of Heliopolis
7 Utt. 308: The Naked Daughters of the Gods
8 Utt. 309: The Servant of Ra
9 Utt. 310: Horus Who Came After Osiris
10 Utt. 311: Being Known By and Knowing Ra
11 Utt. 312: The Bread That Flies Up

East Gable

1 Utt. 273–74: The Cannibal Hymn
2 Utt. 275: The Baboon-hide Garment
3 Utt. 276: Snake Spell

East Wall

Utts. 277–99: Twenty-three Snake Spells
Utt. 300: Acquiring a Ferryboat, Becoming Sokar
Utt. 301: Crossing to the Father God

The Entrance Corridor

WEST WALL

Utt. 313: The Encounter with Babi

Utt. 314: Ox-Calming Spell

Utt. 315: The Voluntary Death

Utt. 316: Calling the Celestial Ferryman

Utt. 317: Becoming Sobek

EAST WALL

Utt. 318: Becoming the *Nau* Snake

Utt. 319: The Bull-King

Utt. 320: Babi, Lord of the Night

Utt. 321: The Faithful Companion of Ra

APPENDIX 2

List of Utterances in the Five Double-Chamber Pyramids at Saqqara

The table of utterances given below lists the utterances in the five main pyramids wall by wall. To make quick reference easier, these utterances are listed in numerical sequence, according to the numbers given them by Sethe. The tables therefore neither give information as to the actual position of an utterance on the walls of the pyramid nor indicate the sequence of the utterances as they occur on the walls. The tables simply give information regarding which utterances occur on which walls in the five main pyramids. A more exact treatment of this material would take up too many pages and would also make it a much more complicated process for the reader to locate various utterances.

For more detailed information as to the exact placement of texts, in both the five main pyramids and the four single-chamber pyramids, the reader is referred to Kurt Sethe, *Die Altägyptischen Pyramidentexte*, and T. G. Allen, *Occurrences of Pyramid Texts*. For some supplementary information, see also J. P. Allen, "Reading a Pyramid" in *Hommages à Jean Leclant* 1:5–28.

The following abbreviations are used:

fr., frs.: fragment, fragments
beg.: beginning of utterance only
end: end of utterance only
?: possibly present

334

SARCOPHAGUS CHAMBER

North Wall

Unas	Teti	Pepi I	Merenre	Pepi II
23, 25	lost	frs of	lost	some lost
32		33–34		9, 11–199
34–57		108–71		223–25
72–79		660		268, 272
81–96				326–27
108–71				330–31
				412 beg
				598
				624–53
				(654–58)?

South Wall

Unas	Teti	Pepi I	Merenre	Pepi II
213–19	mostly	mostly	lost	damaged:
	lost	lost		213–22
	frs of	frs of		245–46
	213–22	213–22		262, 267
	and	and		302, 309
	245–46	245–46		358, 458
				509, 537
				591–92, 603
				658 fr
				663–64 fr
				665–72

East Wall

Unas	Teti	Pepi I	Merenre	Pepi II
219–24	142–73	wall lost	some lost	201–3
	224	except	199	352–53
	355–58	407, 456	206, 208	355, 357
			210–12	401–3
			224, 244	405 end
			338–46	407
			348–51	414, 418
			353	439, 456
			400–404	459
			436, 460	591
			598–604	593–97
				599
				600–602
				604–5
				637
				659–62

SARCOPHAGUS CHAMBER (*continued*)

East Gable

Unas	Teti	Pepi I	Merenre	Pepi II
204–5	208	355–57	355–57	206, 208
207	210–12	457–61	407	210–12
209	338–51		459	338–49
210–12	353–54		593–97	400
				404–5 beg
				406

West Wall

Unas	Teti	Pepi I	Merenre	Pepi II
none	none	335–36	10, 332	9
		356	373, 414	332, 336
		367–68	424–34	356
		425–55	437	365–71
			439–44	373
			446–55	412 end
			588–92	422
				425–34
				443–44
				446–55
				589–90
				621–23

West Gable

Unas	Teti	Pepi I	Merenre	Pepi II
226–43	322–37	365–66	335–36	335
		370–72	365–68	423–24
		422–25	370–72	436–38
			422	440–42
				620

PASSAGE BETWEEN ANTECHAMBER AND SARCOPHAGUS CHAMBER

North Wall

Unas	Teti	Pepi I	Merenre	Pepi II
23	359–63	some	lost	462
25		lost		674–77
32		462–64		
199				
200				

PASSAGE (*continued*)

South Wall

Unas	Teti	Pepi I	Merenre	Pepi II
244–46	262	lost	lost	360–61
	264			463–64
	272			587
				673

ANTECHAMBER

West Wall and Gable

Unas	Teti	Pepi I	Merenre	Pepi II
wall:	wall and	wall and	wall:	wall:
254–58	gable	gable	270	270, 271
260	together:	together	467–68	457, 461
	253–59	(some	472	470–81
gable:	364–74	damaged):	477–79	
247–53		265, 270	481–83	gable:
		310, 337		467–68
		363, 407	gable:	482–83
		465–87	310	487
			473–76	678–80
			487	

East Wall and Gable

Unas	Teti	Pepi I	Merenre	Pepi II
wall:	wall and	wall and	wall	wall:
277–301	gable	gable	damaged	227, 233
	together:	together	(most	240
gable:	206, 240	(some	lost):	280–82
273–76	273–74	lost):	470, 484	284 beg
	277	233, 280		285 end–87
	280–83	284–86	gable:	289–92
	285–93	289	364	295–99
	295–96	292–93	418–21	301, 363–64
	299, 318	384, 408	456, 461	406, 418
	375–410	489–502	466	421, 466
			605	469, 493
				499, 500
				502, 524
				gable:
				420, 456
				460
				693–96

ANTECHAMBER (*continued*)

North Wall

Unas	Teti	Pepi I	Merenre	Pepi II
302–12	lost	mostly lost 302? fr 594 or 626? 627B? 704?	lost	303–5 308, 310 fr 606 679 681–90 691A–G

South Wall

Unas	Teti	Pepi I	Merenre	Pepi II
260–63 267–272	411	488	lost	damaged fr 160? 265? fr 269? fr 325 333, 419 end 508, 509 fr 524? fr 555? 565 fr 682? fr 703?

Passage to Serdab (Triple Chamber)

Unas	Teti	Pepi I	Merenre	Pepi II
none	north wall: 412–13 \ south wall: 414–21	none	none	none

ENTRANCE CORRIDOR

East Wall

Unas	Teti	Pepi I	Merenre	Pepi II
318–21	lost	south end: 323 503–9	south end: 510 515–20 573	south end: 322, 503 558–60 609
		north end: 357 534–38	north end: lost	middle: 486 515–19 565
				north end: 337, 359 532, 535 573

West Wall

Unas	Teti	Pepi I	Merenre	Pepi II
313–17	fr 480 fr 705	south end: 322–23 510–14	south end: 323 504–7 521–23 525–31 563 606–8	south end: 504 511
		north end: 266 515–33		middle: 507, 512 521–23 525, 531 555, 563 607–8 697
			north end: 269 558–60 565 609	north end: 506, 513 606

DESCENDING PASSAGE

East Wall

Unas	Teti	Pepi I	Merenre	Pepi II
none	none	south end: 206 348–51 353 401–5 fr 439? fr 684? north end: 587	none	none

West Wall

Unas	Teti	Pepi I	Merenre	Pepi II
none	none	south end: 325, 474 569–70 584–86 north end: lost	none	none

VESTIBULE

Unas	Teti	Pepi I	Merenre	Pepi II
none	none	south wall: 539–52	south wall: 610–12	south wall: 556 mostly lost
		east wall: fr 262? 271 fr 328? 553–61 fr 706–8?	east wall: 555 569–70 572 613–16	east wall: 306, 331 553, 566–68 574–75 610–12 617, 619 698–701
		west wall: 269, 307 359 562–83	west wall: lost	west wall: 478 beg 569–70 beg 571, 579 581, 613
		north wall: lost	north wall: 306, 583 617–19	north wall: 562, 564 582 702–3

NOTES

Chapter 1: Introduction: The Encounter with the Sacred

1. Robert S. Ellwood Jr., *Mysticism and Religion*, 1st ed. (Eaglewood Cliffs, N.J.: Prentice Hall, 1980), xi, defines mysticism as an "encounter with ultimate divine reality in a direct nonrational way which engenders a deep sense of unity." See also R. C. Zaehner, *Mysticism Sacred and Profane* (London: Oxford University Press, 1961), 35.

2. For Zaehner, *Mysticism Sacred and Profane*, 31 f., mystical experience "has nothing to do with visions, auditions, telepathy, telekinesis, or any other praeternatural phenomenon which may be experienced by saint and sinner alike and which are usually connected with an hysterical temperament."

3. W. T. Stace, *Mysticism and Philosophy* (London: Macmillan and Co., 1961), 47–55. See also Rudolf Otto, *Mysticism East and West* (London: Macmillan and Co., 1932), 70.

4. For example, Evelyn Underhill, *Mysticism* (New York: New American Library, 1974); Otto, *Mysticism East and West*; Stace, *Mysticism and Philosophy*; Zaehner, *Mysticism Sacred and Profane*; Robert K. C. Forman, ed., *The Problem of Pure Consciousness* (New York: Oxford University Press, 1990); Nelson Pike, *Mystic Union: An Essay in the Phenomenology of Mysticism* (Ithaca: Cornell University Press, 1992); and William J. Wainwright, *Mysticism: A Study of Its Nature, Cognitive Value and Moral Implications* (Brighton, U.K.: Harvester Press, 1981).

5. William James, *The Varieties of Religious Experience* (London: Longmans, Green and Co., 1928), 55. For the spectrum of mystical experiences, see 382 ff. On the importance of images, see W. James, *Varieties of Religious Experience*, 406 f. See also W. Barnard, *Exploring Unseen Worlds: William James and the Philosophy of Mysticism* (Albany: State University of New York Press, 1997), 41.

6. M. Eliade, *Myths, Dreams and Mysteries* (London: Collins, 1960); Henry Corbin, *Spiritual Body and Celestial Earth*, trans. Nancy Pearson (London: I. B. Tauris and Co., 1990) and *Creative Imagination in the Sufism of Ibn 'Arabi*, trans. Ralph Manheim (Princeton: Princeton University Press, 1969); Gerda

Walther, *Phänomenologie der Mystik* (Olten und Freiburg im Breisgau: Walter Verlag, 1955); J. C. Hollenback, *Mysticism: Experience, Response and Empowerment* (University Park: Pennsylvania State University Press, 1996); Andrew Rawlinson, *The Book of Enlightened Masters* (Chicago: Open Court, 1997).

7. The term *imaginal realm* is used here in Corbin's sense of a perfectly real but supersensible reality that is accessed by imaginative perception. See Henry Corbin, "*Mundus Imaginalis*, or the Imaginary and the Imaginal," in *Swedenborg and Esoteric Islam*, trans. Leonard Fox (West Chester, Penn.: Swedenborg Foundation, 1995), 18 f. For Corbin, the visionary imagination is directed toward "a world as ontologically real as the world of the senses" (9). It therefore "does not construct something unreal but *unveils* the hidden reality." See also his *Spiritual Body and Celestial Earth*, 12.

8. Stace, *Mysticism and Philosophy*, 50. See also Zaehner, *Mysticism Sacred and Profane*, 130 and 136–39.

9. Hollenback, *Mysticism: Experience, Response and Empowerment*, ix. See also Eliade, *Myths, Dreams and Mysteries*, chap. 4. In twentieth-century mysticism studies, a certain alliance has been forged between Western scholars and the nondualistic traditions of the East, largely, it seems, in an attempt to carve out an area of spiritual experience secure from reductionist assault. This motivation can be seen to underlie, for example, Stace, *Mysticism and Philosophy*, Zaehner, *Mysticism Sacred and Profane*, and more recently Forman, *The Problem of Pure Consciousness*. It has, however, had the effect of promulgating a reduced view of mysticism itself.

10. See, for example, the discussions in Henri Frankfort, *Kingship and the Gods* (Chicago: University of Chicago Press, 1978), 16, 62, 163–67, and 201 f.

11. For an insightful "taxonomy" of mystical traditions in which a number of different types of mystical path are carefully distinguished, see Rawlinson, *The Book of Enlightened Masters*, chap. 3. The type that most closely approximates that of ancient Egypt is what Rawlinson terms the "hot-structured." This, broadly speaking, is characterized by an ontology that recognizes a multiplicity of spiritual powers, a labyrinthine cosmology, a view of the human being as having a microcosmic relationship to the macrocosm, and a concept of the spiritual goal as attainable only through a great initiatic journey. See Rawlinson, 102. See also Leon Schlamm, "Ken Wilber's Spectrum Model," in *Religion* 31, no. 1 (2001): 22–27, for a helpful summary of Rawlinson's taxonomy and 31–33 for the "hot-structured" tradition in particular.

12. For Black Elk, see Hollenback, *Mysticism: Experience, Response and Empowerment*, 325–55. The coronation text is discussed in J. Assmann, "Death and Initiation," in *Religion and Philosophy in Ancient Egypt*, ed. W. K. Simpson (New Haven: Yale University Press, 1989), 142, n. 41.

13. Otto, *Mysticism East and West*, 70.

14. Erik Hornung, *Conceptions of God in Ancient Egypt: The One and the Many*, trans. John Baines (New York: Cornell University Press, 1982), 182.

15. Rawlinson, *The Book of Enlightened Masters*, 103 ff.

16. G. Englund, *Akh. Une notion religieuse dans l'Égypte pharaonique* (Boreas: Uppsala, 1978), 17. J. Assmann, *The Search for God in Ancient Egypt*, trans. David Lorton (Ithaca and London: Cornell University Press, 2001), 87; C. Jacq, *La tradition primordiale de l'Egypte ancienne selon les Textes des Pyramides* (Paris: Bernard Grasset, 1998), 59–61.

17. Jacq, *La tradition primordiale*, 31–34; Frankfort, *Kingship and the Gods*, 51–52; A. Versluis, *The Egyptian Mysteries* (London: Arkana, 1988), chap. 2. It should be pointed out that Hornung is himself well aware of the importance given by the Egyptians to attuning the world to Maat. See Hornung, *Conceptions of God*, 213–16, and the essay "The Concept of Maat" in E. Hornung, *Idea into Image: Essays on Ancient Egyptian Thought*, trans. Elizabeth Bredeck (New York: Timken, 1992).

18. The union of the king with Ra and his being embraced by Atum or Nut are experiences that approximate to a cosmic *unio mystica*. See Pyramid Texts, utt. 252, for union with Ra; utt. 215 for the king embraced by Atum; utts. 429–35 for union with Nut.

19. For the term *visionary mysticism*, see Corbin, *Spiritual Body and Celestial Earth*, 111. The two key elements of the definition for the purposes of this study are direct experience on the one hand and the access that this experience gives to the spiritual dimension of existence on the other. In this respect, "visionary mysticism" entails gnosis—knowledge or direct perception of spiritual realities. It is this kind of knowledge that lies at the root of esotericism, for which see A. Versluis, "What Is Esoteric?" *Esoterica* 4 (2002): 2. Versluis uses the term *cosmological gnosis* in more or less the same way as the term *visionary mysticism* is used here.

20. Eliade, *Myths, Dreams and Mysteries*, 59: "The shamanistic complex represents, in 'primitive' societies, that which is usually known in the more highly developed religions as *mysticism* and *mystical experience*." See also Eliade, *Shamanism*, 8.

21. According to M. Eliade, *The Quest: History and Meaning in Religion* (Chicago: University of Chicago Press, 1984), 6, "A religious datum reveals its deeper meaning when it is considered on its own plane of reference, and not when it is reduced to one of its secondary aspects or contexts." For Eliade, *Myths, Dreams and Mysteries*, i, religion, and hence the religious plane of reference, denotes all that is experienced by the human being as sacred. For the importance of approaching historic religion as an autonomous expression of religious thought and experience that must be viewed in and through itself and

its own principles and standards, see J. M. Kitagawa, "The History of Religions in America," in *The History of Religions: Essays in Methodology*, ed. M. Eliade and J. M. Kitagawa (Chicago: University of Chicago Press, 1959), 26.

22. See, for example, Wayne Proudfoot, *Religious Experience* (Berkeley: University of California Press, 1985), 223, for whom historical or cultural explanation for religious experience is preferable to a religious explanation; see also Gavin Flood, *Beyond Phenomenology* (London, New York: Casell, 1999), 7, who seeks to "deprivilege" consciousness, experience, and inner states so as to "place religion squarely within culture and history." Among Egyptologists, Assmann is a good example of this approach. In his *The Search for God*, 7, he champions "a historico-analytical perspective that occupies an external standpoint vis-à-vis the religion to be described. From this standpoint, the deities and their actions, to whose reality human activity responds, are a cultural creation." For the experiential focus of the phenomenology of religion, see G. van der Leeuw, *Religion in Essence and Manifestation*, trans. J. E. Turner (London: George Allen and Unwin, 1938), 674–75; C. J. Bleeker, *The Sacred Bridge* (Leiden: E. J. Brill, 1963), 11; W. Brede Kristensen, *The Meaning of Religion* (The Hague: Martinus Nijhoff, 1960), 13; Eliade, *The Quest*, 3.

23. For this argument, see J. Baines, "Restricted Knowledge, Hierarchy and Decorum," in *JARCE* 27 (1990): 5.

24. With respect to the question as to the degree to which social, political, historical, and cultural factors exercise a determining influence on religious experience, the approach taken in this study is the opposite of that of "contextualists" like Ivan Strenski, Steven Katz, Wayne Proudfoot, J. B. Hollenback, and others who believe that essentially nonreligious contexts determine the content of religious or mystical experience. For a concise summary of the contextualist position, see Hollenback, *Mysticism: Experience, Response and Empowerment*, 4–12. What contextualists like to think of as nonreligious determining factors were, in the case of ancient Egypt, less determining of than determined by the religious consciousness that infused the whole culture. The advantage of the phenomenological approach is that it enables us to see the fundamental primacy of the religious consciousness over the social, political, and cultural contexts upon which it exercised such a profound influence. For further discussion, see chap. 5, pp. 136–40.

25. This is acknowledged, for instance, in J. Baines and J. Málek, *Atlas of Ancient Egypt* (Oxford: Andromeda, 1980), 29.

26. Whereas Egyptology may remain agnostic or indifferent toward the ontological status of the religious dimension, such an attitude would make little sense within religious studies. For the phenomenologist, the religious dimension includes not just religious experience but also *what* is experienced (the spirit world, the gods, etc.). To ignore or deny this aspect of the religious

dimension would be to surrender to what Henri Corbin called "the agnostic reflex," so pervasive in academia, by which religious consciousness is artificially isolated from its object so as surreptitiously to place the latter in doubt. See Corbin, *"Mundus Imaginalis,"* 7 and 32. See also chap. 1, notes 44 and 47, and chap. 5, p. 138f.

27. Eliade, *The Quest*, 61–62.

28. Kristensen, *The Meaning of Religion*, 10.

29. G. van der Leeuw, "Some Recent Achievements of Psychological Research and Their Application to History, in Particular the History of Religion," in *Classical Approaches to the Study of Religion*, ed. J. Waardenburg (The Hague: Mouton, 1973), 400. On the importance of "subjective engagement," see chap. 5, p. 136ff.

30. J. Assmann, *Egyptian Solar Religion in the New Kingdom*, trans. Anthony Alcock (New York: Kegan Paul International, 1995), 3–4.

31. Baines, "Restricted Knowledge, Hierarchy and Decorum," 2ff.

32. Assmann, *Egyptian Solar Religion*, 9.

33. Van der Leeuw, *Religion in Essence and Manifestation*, 677; Bleeker, *The Sacred Bridge*, 12.

34. See Kristensen, *The Meaning of Religion*, 7, for whom the historian "by means of empathy . . . tries to relive in his own experience that which is alien." See also van der Leeuw, "Some Recent Achievements of Psychological Research," 403, where he writes that the basis of the phenomenological approach to the study of the history of religion "remains forever the living and loving devotion to experience *(Erlebnis)*, and this basis is empathy *(Einfühlung)* itself."

35. The phenomenological method is described in detail in chapter 5.

36. M. Eliade, *The Two and the One* (London: Harvill Press, 1965), 200. See also M. Eliade, "Methodological Remarks on the Study of Religious Symbolism," in *The History of Religions*, ed. M. Eliade and J. Kitagawa (Chicago: University of Chicago Press, 1959), 92–93. It would, of course, be unfair to claim that no Egyptologists have worked in this way. Examples of Egyptological studies of ancient Egyptian religion that pursue the kind of approach advocated by Eliade include R. T. Rundle Clark, *Myth and Symbol in Ancient Egypt* (London: Thames and Hudson, 1978); H. te Velde, *Seth: God of Confusion* (Leiden: E. J. Brill, 1967); W. Brede Kristensen, *Life Out of Death: Studies in the Religions of Egypt and of Ancient Greece*, trans. H. J. Franken and G. R. H. Wright (Louvain: Peeters Press, 1992); A. Roberts, *Hathor Rising* (Totnes: Northgate Publishers, 1995), and idem, *My Heart, My Mother: Death and Rebirth in Ancient Egypt* (Rottingdean: Northgate Publishers, 2000).

37. Terence DuQuesne, "Anubis e il Ponte dell'Arcobaleno. Aspetti dello sciamanismo nell'antico Egitto," in *La religione della terra*, ed. G. Marchianò (Como: Red Edizioni, 1991), 115.

38. I. M. Lewis, *Ecstatic Religion* (Harmondsworth: Penguin Books, 1971), 51.

39. W. Helck, "Schamane und Zauberer," in *Mélanges Adolphe Gutbub* (Montpellier: Université de Montpellier, 1984), 103–8, has pointed to the shamanic role of the *sem* priest. DuQuesne, in a number of essays, notably "Anubis e il Ponte," and in *Jackal at the Shaman's Gate* (Thame, England: Darengo, 1991), has argued for a shamanic interpretation of the god Anubis and sees his priests functioning shamanistically. H. W. Fischer-Elfert, *Die Vision von der Statue im Stein* (Heidelberg: Universitätsverlag, 1998), 65, has referred to the tradition of a shamanic healer practicing at Deir el-Medina. C. Jacq, *Egyptian Magic*, trans. Janet M. Davis (Warminster: Aris and Phillips, 1985), gives an evocatively shamanistic picture of the Egyptian magician. For which, see also R. K. Ritner, *The Mechanics of Ancient Egyptian Magical Practice* (Chicago: Oriental Institute of the University of Chicago, 1993), 220–33. W. R. Fix, *Star Maps* (London: Octopus, 1979), has argued for a shamanic interpretation of the king's journey to the sky in the Pyramid Texts.

Fischer-Elfert, *Die Vision von der Statue im Stein*, 67–68, arguing against the existence of shamanism in ancient Egypt, has attempted to list specifically religious—as distinct from merely sociological—elements of classical shamanism absent from ancient Egyptian religion. But his argument is severely weakened by the narrowness of his focus, which is entirely on the role of the *sem* priest, and is particularly aimed at countering Helck. Many of the typically shamanic practices he lists were undertaken by other kinds of priests, by magicians and healers, or indeed in rituals undergone by the king himself.

40. M. Eliade, *Shamanism: Archaic Techniques of Ecstasy* (1964; reprint, London: Arkana, 1989), 8. For shamanism as a type of mysticism, see Shirley Nicholson, ed., *Shamanism* (London: Theosophical Publishing House, 1987), part 4. Since the concept of shamanism is the creation of historians of religion and anthropologists extrapolating from the original Tungus word *shaman*, there is an interminable debate as to how shamanism as a general category should be defined. It is such a rich and multifaceted phenomenon that no single definition seems adequate, and perhaps it is best left unencumbered by an overarching definition. For a general discussion on definitions of shamanism, see I. M. Lewis, "What Is a Shaman?" in *Folk* 23 (1981), an extended version of which appears in I. M. Lewis, *Religion in Context* (Cambridge: Cambridge University Press, 1996), chap. 6. See also M. D. Jakobsen, *Shamanism* (New York: Berghahn Books, 1999), chap. 1. For a thorough deconstruction of the Western "creation" of shamanism, see Ronald Hutton, *Shamans: Siberian Spirituality and the Western Imagination* (London: Hambledon and London, 2001).

41. For the Greek and Hellenistic mysteries following primordial and archaic patterns reminiscent of shamanism, see M. Eliade, *Rites and Symbols of Initiation* (New York: Harper and Row, 1958), 111–14. For the shamanic underpinnings of Platonism, see E. R. Dodds, *The Greeks and the Irrational* (Berkeley: University of California Press, 1973), 209–10.

42. This is essentially the argument of Helck, "Schamane und Zauberer," in relation to ancient Egypt.

43. See, for example, Assmann, *The Search for God*, 153, where he comments: "Reading the works of Mircea Eliade, one could arrive at the impression that shamanism is a universal phenomenon. In Egypt, however, one searches in vain for the relevant phenomena." Assmann's denial of shamanism includes any form of intoxication, trance, or ecstasy, mysticism, meditation, or contemplation. For Assmann, it is an essential feature of Egyptian religion that all of the above are absent (or only rudimentarily present) in the religious life. These views are reiterated in Fischer-Elfert, *Die Vision von der Statue im Stein*, 69.

44. Eliade, *The Quest*, 6, writes that in relation to "the universe of religion," we have to do with "individual experiences" on the one hand and "transpersonal realities" on the other. These correspond respectively to Husserl's *noesis* (the meaning-giving act of consciousness) and *noema* (the meaningfully structured object of consciousness), for which see chap. 5, n. 22.

45. For "cosmologies," see, for example, James P. Allen, "The Cosmology of the Pyramid Texts," in *Religion and Philosophy*, ed. W. K. Simpson (New Haven: Yale University Press, 1989); for "cosmographies," see Assmann, *Egyptian Solar Religion*, 26; for "ideologies," see B. J. Kemp, *Ancient Egypt: Anatomy of a Civilization* (London: Routledge, 1989), 19 ff.

46. Corbin, *Spiritual Body and Celestial Earth*, viii. See also chap. 1, n. 26.

47. See John Hick, *An Interpretation of Religion: Human Responses to the Transcendent* (New Haven: Yale University Press, 1989), 3, whose "religious definition of religion" runs parallel to the use of the term *mysticism* that is adopted here. Hick writes: "Religion (or a particular religious tradition) centers upon an awareness of and response to a reality that transcends ourselves and our world, whether the 'direction' of transcendence be beyond or within or both. Such definitions presuppose the reality of the intentional object of religious thought and experience."

48. M. Eliade, *Images and Symbols: Studies in Religious Symbolism* (Princeton: Princeton Univesity Press, 1991), 35.

Chapter 2: Egyptology: The Death and Rebirth of Mysticism in Ancient Egypt

1. For the ancient Egyptian conception of the Dwat, see J. P. Allen, "The Cosmology of the Pyramid Texts," 21–25. See also Clark, *Myth and Symbol in Ancient Egypt*, 165 f., and Jacq, *La tradition primordiale*, chap. 14.

2. J. P. Allen, "The Cosmology of the Pyramid Texts," 19–21. Jacq, *La tradition primordiale*, 85.

3. Translation from A. Piankoff, *The Tomb of Ramesses VI* (New York: Pantheon Books, 1954), 1:230. See also Erik Hornung, *Das Amduat: Die Schrift des Verborgenen Raumes* (Wiesbaden: Otto Harrassowitz, 1963–67), 2:2. That the contents of the text were "useful for those on earth" and not simply for the dead is explicitly stated at the end of the first division of the Book of What Is in the Underworld (Piankoff, *The Tomb of Ramesses VI*, 1:239; Hornung, *Das Amduat*, 33).

4. M. Eliade, *A History of Religious Ideas* (Chicago: University of Chicago Press, 1978–85), 3:20.

5. The text is translated in Assmann, "Death and Initiation," 142, n. 41.

6. "Master of secrets" is the translation of *hery sesheta*. For a survey of the use of the title, see K. T. Rydström, *"Hery Sesheta* 'In Charge of Secrets': The 3000-Year Evolution of a Title," *DE* 28 (1994): 54–93. Although Rydström argues that the title was mostly administrative or honorific, he accepts that after the Old Kingdom its usage was increasingly restricted to the religious sphere—particularly in connection with the funerary cult. Difficulties with a purely administrative or honorific interpretation of the title occur in phrases such as "master of secrets concerning the unique seeing/vision *(maa)*" and, indeed "master of secrets of heaven, earth and the Dwat," which latter Rydström does not discuss. The title *hery sesheta* was, according to Ritner, *The Mechanics of Ancient Egyptian Magical Practice*, 232 (with n. 1074 and n. 1076 and also pages 61–64), indicative of both ritual and magical mastery and was by no means simply administrative or honorific. For the initiatory significance of the phrase "master of secrets in heaven, earth and Dwat," see T. DuQuesne, "Anubis, Master of Secrets *(Hery Sesheta)* and the Egyptian Conception of Mysteries," *DE* 36 (1996): 26 ff., and idem, "Effective in Heaven and on Earth," in *Ägyptische Mysterien?*, ed. J. Assmann and M. Bommas (München: Fink, 2002), 39–40. For a general discussion of the title, including the statement about Rekhmire, see J. Naydler, *Temple of the Cosmos* (Rochester, Vt.: Inner Traditions International, 1996), 132.

7. Chaeremon, fr. 10 (= Porphyry, *De abstinentia* 4.6), trans. in G. Fowden, *The Egyptian Hermes* (Princeton: Princeton University Press, 1986), 55.

8. On the admiration and veneration felt toward Egypt by Greek philosophers, see Erik Iversen, *The Myth of Egypt and Its Hieroglyphs* (Princeton: Princeton University Press, 1961), 38–39. For the Roman perception of Egypt, see J. Godwin, *Mystery Religions in the Ancient World* (London: Thames and Hudson, 1981), 120; for the Roman view of Egypt harboring "deep mysteries," see Hornung, *Conceptions of God*, 15. For a general overview of Greek and Roman reverence for Egypt and its wisdom, see Erik Hornung, *The*

Secret Lore of Egypt: Its Impact on the West, trans. David Lorton (Ithaca: Cornell University Press, 2001), chaps. 2 and 8.

9. Thus Herodotus refers to Egyptian mystery rites in *Histories* 2:65 and 2:170, trans. A. de Sélincourt (Harmondsworth: Penguin, 1972), (see also 12:132), and describes a festival of great antiquity that was still celebrated in his own day that involved "descending alive into what the Greeks call Hades," for which see *Histories* 1:122. Plutarch, who, like Herodotus also had firsthand knowledge of Egypt, refers in *De Iside et Osiride*, ed., trans., and comm. J. G. Griffiths (Swansea: University of Wales Press, 1970), para. 2, to the Osiris myth as "sacred teaching" and from the account that he gives of its meaning in *De Iside et Osiride*, para. 49 and 53, he evidently regarded it as an initiatory myth. See also *De Iside et Osiride*, para. 68 and 77, and n. 10 below. Nowhere in Plutarch's treatise on Isis and Osiris do we find the funerary interpretation of the myth as espoused in modern Egyptology. Iamblichus, in his treatise *On the Mysteries of the Egyptians*, trans. T. Taylor (1821; 3rd edition reprint, London: Stuart and Watkins, 1968), is equally silent on the funerary religion of Egypt. He focuses instead on "theurgy," or practical mysticism, which he believed the Egyptians excelled at. In *On the Mysteries*, 8:4, he describes how "through the sacerdotal theurgy, they announce that they are able to ascend to more elevated and universal essences, and to those that are established above Fate, namely to God and the Demiurgus. . . ." For the Egyptian cultivation of ecstatic out-of-the-body experiences, see n. 10 below.

10. This is frequently indicated by Plutarch in *De Iside et Osiride*. See, for example, *De Iside et Osiride*, para. 68, where he refers to the robe worn by the Osiris initiate, and tells us that it is worn only once because "the understanding of what is spiritually intelligible and pure and holy" shines through the soul "like lightning," affording "only one chance to touch and behold it." See also *De Iside et Osiride*, para. 49, 53, and 77. Another important source is Iamblichus, *On the Mysteries*, who describes the Egyptians as "theurgists" able to have out-of-body experiences of the spirit world, "for there is a time when we become wholly soul, are out of the body, and sublimely revolve on high, in conjunction with all the immaterial gods" (*On the Mysteries*, 5:3). Such experiences were open only to those few who "while they are yet in body" (i.e., alive) were nevertheless capable of becoming "separated from bodies," and thus to be "led round to their eternal and intelligible principle" (*On the Mysteries*, 1:12).

11. For Greek religion in general being derived from Egyptian religion, see Herodotus, *Histories*, 2:49–60. For a discussion of commentators such as Herodotus, Diodorus Siculus, and others who believed that Egyptian religion was the source of Greek religion, see M. Bernal, *Black Athena*, vol. 1 (London: Free Association Books, 1987), chap. 1. For Greek philosophy being derived from Egyptian sources, Plutarch, *De Iside et Osiride*, para. 34, maintained that the pre-Socratic philosopher Thales "relied on Egyptian

knowledge" when he formulated his cosmological philosophy. Ancient com-
mentators understood that Pythagoras, too, derived his teaching from the
Egyptians. For Pythagoras, see Herodotus, *Histories*, 2:123; Porphyry, *Vita
Pythagorae*, 19, in *The Presocratic Philosophers*, ed. G. Kirk and J. Raven
(Cambridge: Cambridge University Press, 1957), 223; Isocrates, *Busiris*, 28,
in *Early Greek Philosophy*, ed. Jonathan Barnes (London: Penguin, 1987), 84.
Plato himself acknowledged his own debt to the ancient Egyptians in *The
Laws*, 656, trans. T. J. Sanders (Harmondsworth: Penguin, 1976). See also
Plato, *Phaedrus*, 274, trans. W. Hamilton (Harmondsworth: Penguin, 1973),
where he attributes to the Egyptian god Thoth not only the invention of
writing but also number, calculation, geometry, and astronomy. According to
the early Greek commentator Krantor, all Plato's contemporaries assumed
the *Republic* was based on Egyptian institutions, for which see Bernal, *Black
Athena* 1:106. Plutarch noted the indebtedness of the *Timaeus* to ancient
Egyptian teachings in *De Iside et Osiride*, para. 53. Both Iamblichus's *On the
Mysteries of the Egyptians* and the *Corpus Hermeticum* are based on the presupposition that Egypt is the source of true philosophy, and both present a view
of Egyptian wisdom as rooted in mystical experience. For Iamblichus, see
chap. 2, n. 10. For the ancient view of the Hermetica as Greek translations
of Egyptian sacred texts, see Fowden, *The Egyptian Hermes*, 29–31 and
136–41. For mystical experience in the Hermetica, see especially *Corpus
Hermeticum*, books 10 and 13, in Brian P. Copenhaver, *Hermetica: The Greek
Corpus Hermeticum and the Latin Asclepius in a New English Translation with
Notes and Introduction* (Cambridge: Cambridge University Press, 1992), and
"Discourse on the Eighth and the Ninth," in *The Nag Hammadi Library in
English*, ed. J. Robinson (Leiden: E. J. Brill, 1970), 292–97.

12. Herodotus's sensitivity to the Osirian mysteries is evidenced in the fact that
he declined to give any details of the sacred rites of Osiris performed at night
on the sacred lake of the temple of Sais. He would not even mention Osiris's
name in the context of his mystery rites, and simply refers to him as "that
being whose name I will not speak." See Herodotus, *Histories*, 2:170; also
2:65 and 12:132. We know of Plutarch's initiation into the mysteries of
Dionysus from a letter to his wife, for which see W. Burkert, *Ancient Mystery
Cults* (Cambridge: Harvard University Press, 1987), 105. It was clearly from
an awareness of the mystery traditions that both the Hermetica and
Iamblichus's treatise *On the Mysteries* were written.

13. Versluis, *The Egyptian Mysteries*, 46, writes: "What matters, ultimately, is
not the particular names and manifestations of the Gods, but the Mysteries
by which they are revealed, to which the ancient Greek and Roman writers
still had access, and to which we, whatever our 'discoveries,' do not. . . . And
this direct contact with the Mysteries, which travel like a stream through
ancient history, is far more crucial to true understanding than any wealth of
mere 'information.' It is this contact, either direct—through initiation—or

indirectly through cultural irradiation, which still affected and inspired the writers of that time, including Plutarch, Xenophon and Apuleius directly, and Herodotus indirectly." For Pythagoras's ability to read hieroglyphs, see Diogenes Laertius, *Lives of Eminent Philosophers*, trans. R. D. Hinks (Cambridge: Harvard University Press, 1972), 8.3.

14. Medieval and Renaissance scholarship relied heavily on the available classical sources. In the Renaissance these were considerably augmented by the works of Ammianus Marcellinus, Horapollo, and most notably the *Corpus Hermeticum*, which stimulated a new fervor for "Egyptian" philosophy. See F. A. Yates, *Giordano Bruno and the Hermetic Tradition* (London: Routledge and Kegan Paul, 1964); Iversen, *The Myth of Egypt and Its Hieroglyphs*; J. S. Curl, *The Egyptian Revival* (London: George Allen and Unwin, 1982); and Hornung, *The Secret Lore of Egypt*, chap. 10.

15. For the eighteenth century and a discussion of such scholarly works as Abbé Banier, *The Mythology of the Ancients Explained* (1739), Jacob Bryant, *A New System: Or an Analysis of Ancient Mythology* (1774), and William Mitford, *History of Greece* (1784), see Bernal, *Black Athena* 1, chap. 3.

16. Charles-François Dupuis, *The Origin of All Cults* (1795) discussed in Bernal, *Black Athena* 1:182 ff.

17. According to Bernal, *Black Athena* 1:184,

> Plans for the colonization of Egypt had in fact been made long before the Revolution, in the 1770s at the height of French Masonic enthusiasm for Egypt. While there were important political and economic reasons for the Expedition, there is no doubt that the ideas of France reviving the "cradle of civilization" that Rome had destroyed, and the desire to understand the Egyptian mysteries, also provided important motivation.

18. Ibid., 258.

19. G. Maspero, *Études de mythologie et d'archéologie égyptiennes* (Paris: E. Leroux, 1893), 2:277. For Maspero, the fact that Egyptian religion was polytheistic was in itself a mark of its barbarity:

> I take [the Egyptian religion] to be what it says it is, a polytheism with all its contradictions, repetitions, doctrines that are to modern eyes sometimes indecent, sometimes cruel, sometimes ridiculous. . . . (2:278)

20. A. Erman, *Handbook of Egyptian Religion* (London: Archibald Constable, 1907), 98–99 and 113. Commenting on the New Kingdom mystical text, the Book of What Is in the Underworld, Erman wrote in exasperation:

> What is the meaning of all this? In vain we search in the text for an explanation. . . . We need not, however, greatly lament our ignorance, for what is incomprehensible to us here does not represent

> popular ideas, nor does it contain deep speculation. It is the phantasy of a strange people . . . who were nothing more than compilers of magic spells. (113)

21. A. Erman, *Life in Ancient Egypt*, trans. H. M. Tirard (1894; reprint, New York: Dover, 1971), 2. A similar view is expressed in Cyril Aldred's highly acclaimed and much reprinted *The Egyptians* (London: Thames and Hudson, 1984), 14:

> Classical authors . . . never really understood Egyptian religion and were inclined to see in inexplicable acts and beliefs a more profound significance than actually existed.

22. T. E. Peet, *The Present Position of Egyptological Studies* (Oxford: Oxford University Press, 1934), 18.

23. Ibid. This view of the limitations of the "concrete" ancient Egyptian mind goes back at least as far as Budge, and is reiterated in J. H. Breasted's *The Development of Religion and Thought in Ancient Egypt* (1912; reprint, Philadelphia: University of Pennsylvania Press, 1972), 7–8.

24. B. L. Goff, *Symbols of Ancient Egypt in the Late Period* (New York: Mouton, 1979), 19–20.

25. O. Neugebauer, *The Exact Sciences in Antiquity* (Copenhagen: E. Munksgaard, 1951; reprint, New York: Harper Torchbooks, 1962), 91.

26. B. Russell, *The Wisdom of the West* (London: MacDonald, 1969), 10.

27. Hornung, *Idea into Image*, 14.

28. Ibid., 13. Studies such as Frankfort et al., *Before Philosophy: The Intellectual Adventure of Ancient Man* (Harmondsworth: Penguin Books, 1949), Kristensen, *Life Out of Death* (first published in 1949), and Clark, *Myth and Symbol in Ancient Egypt* (1959) all contributed to a much greater respect for Egyptian ways of thinking within Egyptology after World War II.

29. J. P. Allen, *Genesis in Egypt* (New Haven: Yale University Press, 1989), 1–2. The same point was repeatedly made by Schwaller de Lubicz, who referred to the "theological philosophy" of ancient Egypt expressing itself through myths and symbols rather than through abstract principles arrived at through cerebral analysis. See, for example, R. A. Schwaller de Lubicz, *The Temple of Man*, trans. Deborah Lawlor and Robert Lawlor (Rochester, Vt.: Inner Traditions International, 1998), 1:2, 1:89, and 1:456. See also Jacq, *La tradition primordiale*, 8.

30. Assmann, *Egyptian Solar Religion*, 7.

31. Ibid., 7–8 and 26. The same view is expressed in Baines, "Restricted Knowledge, Hierarchy and Decorum," 22, where he writes:

> Restricted knowledge is socially competitive or divisive, enhancing competition within a social group and accentuating divisions between groups to which knowledge is available and others to which

> it is not. The character of the knowledge is not as significant as is
> the question of who knows it. . . . It does not matter what the
> "Eastern Souls" sing at sunrise; what is important is that the king
> knows it (and others do not).

Such a view clearly signals where Egyptology and phenomenology of religion must part company.

32. For Hornung's denial of mysticism, see *Conceptions of God*, 182; *Idea into Image*, 112, and *The Secret Lore of Egypt*, 15 f.

33. A. Piankoff, *The Pyramid of Unas* (Princeton: Princeton University Press, 1968), 3, and J. P. Allen, "The Cosmology of the Pyramid Texts," 1. This view also underpins such influential studies as J. Spiegel, *Das Auferstehungsritual der Unas-Pyramide* (Wiesbaden, Germany: Otto Harrassowitz, 1971), and H. Altenmüller, *Die Texte zum Begräbnisritual in den Pyramiden des Alten Reiches, ÄgAb* (Wiesbaden, Germany: Otto Harrassowitz, 1972).

34. For example, R. David, *Cult of the Sun: Myth and Magic in Ancient Egypt* (London: J. M. Dent, 1980), 94–95, laments the lack of "logical order" in the Pyramid Texts and the "confused" and "even contradictory" content of the utterances. M. Lichtheim, *Ancient Egyptian Literature*, 3 vols. (Berkeley: University of California Press, 1975–80), 1:131, characterizes the Coffin Texts as "oscillating between grandiose claims and petty fears" and claims that they "show the human imagination at its most abstruse." Indeed they "accord so little with the observed facts of life as to appear paranoid." I. E. S. Edwards, *The Pyramids of Egypt* (Harmondsworth: Penguin, 1993), 12, referring to the religious literature as a whole, complains that "elements which had once been admitted into the canon continued side by side with later innovations, even though they were logically superfluous and sometimes irreconcilable." For Edwards, "the impression made on the mind is that of a people searching in the dark for a key to truth." Further examples of negative late-twentieth-century assessments of ancient Egyptian religious literature will be given in the course of this chapter.

35. For an excellent account of the ongoing significance of Francis Bacon, see T. Roszak, *Where the Wasteland Ends* (London: Faber and Faber, 1972), chap. 5.

36. Warburton, *The Divine Legation of Moses* (1739) 4:229–41, discussed in Bernal, *Black Athena* 1:197.

37. This was the view of influential ancient sources such as Chaeremon, Plutarch, Iamblichus, and the *Corpus Hermeticum*. See chap. 2, nn. 7–12 and nn. 14–16.

38. Goff, *Symbols of Ancient Egypt in the Late Period*, 19. A view similar to Goff's is expressed in Esmond Wright, ed., *The Ancient World* (Secaucus, N.J.: Chartwell Books, 1979), 75:

> Imprisoned within this mental framework of a non-mechanical uni-
> verse, accepting without question the validity of ancient documents,

the Egyptians were doomed to pursue a course of thought which, while it grew broader and more elaborately patterned at every step, ultimately led nowhere.

39. Kemp, *Ancient Egypt: Anatomy of a Civilization*, 6.

40. The groundwork for this view was laid by Bacon and developed in the nineteenth century by Comte, Tylor, and Frazer, all of whom will be discussed in the next section. Among twentieth-century historians of science, Benjamin Farington and James Jeans are typical in their assumption that the priesthood held back the development of a real understanding of the world. For Farington, *Science in Antiquity* (London: Thornton Butterworth, 1936), 36, scientific knowledge was "the creation and property, not of priests who claimed to represent the gods, but of men whose only claim to be listened to lay in their appeal to the common reason of mankind." For Jeans, *The Growth of Physical Science* (Cambridge: Cambridge University Press, 1950), 14, the "true scientific spirit" first began to flourish only with "the liberation of knowledge from the priesthood and its transfer to the laiety. . . ."

41. Bernal, *Black Athena* 1:276–79. In his study *Le problème des pyramides d'Égypte* (Paris: Payot, 1948), 190, Jean-Philippe Lauer wrote, concerning the pyramids at Giza:

> From the mathematical point of view, the study of the pyramids, and especially the Great Pyramid, reveals very remarkable geometrical properties as well as numerical rapports that deserve attention. But the whole problem that this poses is to establish the extent to which the builders were aware of these properties.

Compare with Toomer's comments in *The Legacy of Egypt*, ed. J. R. Harris (Oxford: Oxford University Press, 1971), 45, who writes:

> The truth is that Egyptian mathematics remained at much too low a level to be able to contribute anything of value. . . . its interest for us lies in its primitive character.

Such attitudes contrast markedly with the detailed examination of Egyptian mathematical thought in Schwaller de Lubicz, *The Temple of Man*, vol. 1, parts 2 and 3.

42. Aristotle *Metaphysics*, 1.1.981b; *De Caelo* 2.14.298a.

43. Strabo, *Geography*, trans. H. L. Jones (Cambridge, Mass.: Loeb Classical Library, 1930), 17.1.29; Diogenes Laertius, *Lives of Eminent Philosophers*, 8.86–89. Thales' visit to Egypt is testified to in several ancient sources, for which see Kirk and Raven, *The Presocratic Philosophers*, 76. An early source for Pythagoras's visit to Egypt is Isocrates, *Busiris*, 28–29, in Barnes, *Early Greek Philosophy*, 84; see also Diogenes Laertius, *Lives of Eminent Philosophers*, 8.3, on Pythagoras's mastery of the Egyptian language. For Plato's visit to Egypt, see Strabo, *Geography*, 17.1.29, where Strabo indicates the exact place where Plato spent thirteen years studying with Egyptian priests at Heliopolis. For

Plato, see also Diogenes Laertius, *Lives of Eminent Philosophers*, 1.3.6; Plutarch, *De Iside et Osiride*, para. 10; and Iamblichus, *On the Mysteries*, 1.1.3.

44. For a full discussion of these authors, see P. Tompkins, *Secrets of the Great Pyramid* (New York: Harper and Row, 1971), 44–51 and 77–146. See also Bernal, *Black Athena* 1:272–80.

45. Schwaller de Lubicz, *The Temple of Man*, vol. 1, parts 2 and 3. See also his more accessible *Sacred Science*, trans. André VandenBroeck (Rochester, Vt.: Inner Traditions International, 1985), for Egyptian esotericism and symbolism. For an introduction to the thought of Schwaller de Lubicz, see J. A. West, *Serpent in the Sky* (London: Wildwood House, 1979).

46. Schwaller de Lubicz, *The Temple of Man*, 1:456. See also S. H. Nasr, *Religion and the Order of Nature* (Oxford: Oxford University Press, 1996), 241.

47. Schwaller de Lubicz, *The Temple of Man*, 1:54.

48. Quoted in Fowden, *The Egyptian Hermes*, 55. Chaeremon's account is preserved in Porphyry, *De abstinentia*, 4.6.

49. Fowden, *The Egyptian Hermes*, 55.

50. This ancient perspective is to be found in Mesopotamia, India, Persia, and Greece as well as in Egypt. In India, Persia, and Greece it is expressed in the doctrine of the four (or sometimes five) ages or *yugas*, beginning with the golden age and then proceeding through a silver, bronze, and iron age, with each age being characterized by ever greater divorce from, and forgetfulness of, our divine origins. See Eliade, *The Myth of the Eternal Return* (Princeton: Princeton University Press, 1965), 112–30. In Mesopotamia and Egypt, the main sources for the view of history as decline are the king lists that in both cultures begin with the earlier kings reigning for staggering lengths of time, which gradually reduce as they near the present. In Egypt the earliest kings are the gods, and their reigns correspond to cosmic cycles, implying that conditions on earth were at that time assimilated to heavenly conditions. See Naydler, *Temple of the Cosmos*, chap. 5.

51. J. B. Bury, in *The Idea of Progress* (1932; reprint, New York: Dover, 1955), 54, has succinctly summarized Bacon's stance:

> What we call antiquity and are accustomed to revere as such was the youth of the world. But it is the old age and increasing years of the world—the time in which we are now living—that deserves in truth to be called antiquity. We are really the ancients, the Greeks and Romans were younger than we, in respect to the age of the world. And as we look to an old man for greater knowledge of the world than from a young man, so we have good reason to expect far greater things from our own age than from antiquity, because in the meantime the stock of knowledge has been increased by an endless number of observations and experiments. Time is the great discoverer, and truth is the daughter of time, not of authority.

52. Bury, *The Idea of Progress*, 291 f.

53. Ibid., 295–99.

54. Twelve years after the *Origin of Species*, Darwin drove home the point in his *Descent of Man* (1871). There we read in the penultimate paragraph of the concluding chapter: "The main conclusion arrived at in this work, namely, that man is descended from some lowly organised form will, I regret to think, be highly distasteful to many. But there can hardly be a doubt that we are descended from barbarians."

55. E. B. Tylor, *Primitive Culture* (London: John Murray, 1971), 425.

56. Ibid., 133. See E. E. Evans-Pritchard, *Theories of Primitive Religion* (Oxford: Oxford University Press, 1965), 25–29, for a succinct summary of Tylor's views.

57. In *The Golden Bough* (London: MacMillan, 1929), 57, James Frazer wrote,

> I would suggest that a tardy recognition of the inherent falsehood and barrenness of magic set the more thoughtful part of mankind to cast about for a truer theory of nature and a more fruitful method of turning her resources to account. The shrewder intelligences must in time have come to perceive that magical ceremonies and incantations did not really effect the results which they were designed to produce.... It was a confession of human ignorance and weakness. Man saw that he had taken for causes what were no causes, and that all his efforts to work by means of these imaginary causes had been in vain.

For the confusion of magic and religion in Egypt, see *The Golden Bough*, 52 f.

58. Frazer, *The Golden Bough*, 711 f.

59. For a review of various nineteenth- and early-twentieth-century theories of religion influenced by evolutionary perspectives, see Eric J. Sharpe, *Comparative Religion: A History* (London: Duckworth, 1986), chap. 3.

60. Sir John Lubbock, *The Origin of Civilization and the Primitive Condition of Man* (1870), summarized in Sharpe, *Comparative Religion: A History*, 52.

61. A. C. Bouquet's popular survey (it ran to several editions during the 1940s and 1950s) of the history of religion, *Comparative Religion* (Harmondsworth: Penguin, 1954), provides a good example of such attitudes. Bouquet subscribed to the view that "magic is religious practice that has lost its theology" (53) and regarded the shaman as "an epileptic or neurotic—or even drunkard, who in his potations has his tongue loosed" (56). For Bouquet, there was little doubt that ethical monotheism is the highest form of religion and that it corresponds more or less exactly to Christianity (212 and 221). Interestingly, he regarded the pharaoh Akhenaten as an early ethical monotheist (73–74).

62. Breasted, *The Development of Religion and Thought*, 8.

63. Ibid., 334. Breasted was obviously deeply moved by Akhenaten, and regarded his "gospel of the beauty and beneficence of the natural order" as a precursor of eighteenth- and nineteenth-century Romanticism (335). Akhenaten was, for Breasted, a peculiarly modern soul born several thousand years before his time, the "earliest idealist," almost a Baconian—who "appeals to no myths, to no ancient and widely accepted versions of the dominion of the gods, to no customs sanctified by the centuries" (339).

64. Ibid., 363.

65. A. Gardiner, *Egyptian Grammar*, 3rd ed. (London: Oxford University Press, 1973), 4.

66. Ibid., 24c.

67. B. Watterson, *The Gods of Ancient Egypt* (London: B. T. Batsford, 1984), 32. Ritner, *The Mechanics of Ancient Egyptian Magical Practice*, 9 f., has complained that Frazer's *The Golden Bough* still underlies all discussions of magic in Egyptology, and states that "Egyptology has yet to question its Frazerian attitude to the subject" (10).

68. For a discussion of Freud's views, see Evans-Pritchard, *Theories of Primitive Religion*, 41 f. See also Radin's study, *Primitive Religion*, in which he argues that in "primitive" religions the "neurotic-epileptoid mentality" dominates. This observation (or diagnosis) applies both to shamans and priests in more complex civilizations such as ancient Egypt. See P. Radin, *Primitive Religion* (New York: Dover, 1957), 110.

69. Julian Jaynes, *The Origins of Consciousness in the Breakdown of the Bicameral Mind* (Harmondsworth: Penguin, 1976), 186. See also Vincent Tobin, "The Bicameral Mind as a Rationale of Egyptian Religion," in *Studies in Egyptology: Presented to Miriam Lichtheim*, vol. 2, ed. Sara Israelit-Groll, 994–1018 (Jerusalem: Magnes Press, Hebrew Univeristy, 1990). While Tobin is sympathetic to Jaynes, he points to a range of instances in ancient Egypt that do not support the bicameral theory.

70. Ken Wilber, *Up From Eden: A Transpersonal View of Human Evolution* (1981; reprint, Wheaton, Ill.: Theosophical Publishing House, 1996), 123 ff. Wilber's account of Egyptian religion is remarkably ill informed.

71. C. G. Jung writes in *Psychology and Religion*, vol. 11 of *The Collected Works of C. G. Jung* (Princeton: Princeton University Press, 1969), para. 141:

> Since the development of consciousness requires the withdrawal of all the projections we can lay our hands on, it is not possible to maintain any non-psychological doctrine about the gods. If the historical process continues as hitherto, then everything of a divine or daemonic character outside us must return to the psyche, to the inside of the unknown man, whence it apparently originated.

72. Neumann, *The Origins and History of Consciousness*, 304f. and 325.

73. Ibid., xvi: "In the course of its ontogenetic development, the individual ego consciousness has to pass through the same archetypal stages which determined the evolution of consciousness of the life of humanity. The individual has in his own life to follow the road that humanity has trod before him."

74. F. G. Fleay, *Egyptian Chronology* (London: David Nutt, 1899), 98. For the cosmic cycles that underlie the long reigns of the gods, see Naydler, *Temple of the Cosmos*, 98f.

75. This principle is adhered to in the New Kingdom Turin Canon, the Saite scheme recorded by Herodotus, the Manethonic chronology, and the scheme of Eratosthenes preserved by Eusebius. See Fleay, *Egyptian Chronology*, 19f.

76. Naydler, *Temple of the Cosmos*, 91–93. See also Jacq, *La tradition primordiale*, 31–34, and Versluis, *The Egyptian Mysteries*, 16f. and 21f.

77. See chapter 2, n. 27.

78. *Corpus Hermeticum*, 16.1, in *Hermetica*, 58.

79. Ibid.

80. Plato, *Timaeus*, 22b.

81. John A. Wilson, *The Culture of Ancient Egypt* (Chicago: University of Chicago Press, 1956), 145 and 146.

82. William J. Murnane, *The Penguin Guide to Ancient Egypt* (Harmondsworth: Penguin Books, 1983), 25.

83. P. Derchain, "Symbols and Metaphors in Literature and Representations of Private Life," in *RAIN* 15 (1976): 7–10; W. Westendorf, "Symbol, Symbolik," in *Lexikon der Ägyptologie*, 6:122–28; Ritner, *The Mechanics of Ancient Egyptian Magical Practice*; and R. Wilkinson, *Symbol and Magic in Ancient Egyptian Art* (London: Thames and Hudson, 1994).

84. On the religious historians' understanding of the relationship of daily-life activities to religion, see M. Eliade, *Patterns in Comparative Religion* (London: Sheed and Ward, 1958), 125. See also R. Pettazoni, "The Supreme Being: Phenomenological Structure and Historical Development," in *The History of Religions*, ed. M. Eliade and J. Kitagawa, 65. See also J. A. West, *Serpent in the Sky*, 94. For a symbolist interpretation of the Old Kingdom tombs of Ti, Ptah-hotep, Mereruka, and Kagemni at Saqqara, see J. A. West, *The Traveller's Key to Ancient Egypt* (London: Harrap Columbus, 1987), 170–89.

85. Edwards, *The Pyramids of Egypt*, 25.

86. A. Gardiner, *Egypt of the Pharaohs* (Oxford: Oxford University Press, 1966), 427.

87. C. Aldred, *Art in Ancient Egypt*, vol. 3 (London: Alec Tiranti, 1972), 3.

88. Erman, *Life in Ancient Egypt*, 261, 263, 34.

89. Hornung, *Conceptions of God*, 182.

90. One of the few contemporary Egyptologists to recognize the far-reaching implications of accepting the existence of mysticism in ancient Egypt is Roberts, who, in *My Heart, My Mother*, 175, writes:

    Accepting that ancient Egyptian religion involved a journey of return to primal origins—and that the ancient Egyptians practised rituals in their temples aimed at such a rebirth—necessitates a complete re-evaluation, not only of the Underworld Books, but also of ancient Egypt's possible contribution to much later religious developments including the Hermetic tradition. In particular, it must raise serious questions about the methodological adequacy of studying Hermetic and Gnostic texts . . . with little or no consideration of how they might have been influenced by earlier Egyptian religion.

91. According to Bernal, *Black Athena* 1:259, during the 1880s and '90s:

    [T]he last traces of the Platonic, Hermetic and Masonic respect for Egypt were being expelled from academia, and a full-scale attack on the older Egyptology was launched.

92. Baines, "Restricted Knowledge, Hierarchy and Decorum," 2. It is for this reason, as G. Pinch, *Magic in Ancient Egypt* (London: British Museum Press, 1994), 9, has recently confirmed, that

    Professional Egyptologists prefer to distance themselves from the popular image of Egypt as the source of occult knowledge. They tend to stress the numerous practical achievements of Egyptian civilization and those Egyptian writings that expound a pragmatic and cheerful philosophy of life.

    For Hornung, *The Secret Lore of Egypt*, 3, the notion that Egypt is a source of esoteric wisdom is the defining mark of "Egyptosophy," to be distinguished from the academic discipline of Egyptology by the fact that Egyptosophy is the study of an "imaginary Egypt" that bears "only a loose relationship to the historical reality."

93. A. Moret, *Mystères égyptiens* (Paris: Armand Colin, 1922), 42–71.

94. S. Mayassis, *Mystères et initiation de l'Égypte ancienne* (Athens: Bibliothèque d'Archéologie Orientale d'Athènes, 1957), 160.

95. Ibid., 218 and 226. See also F. Daumas, "Y eut-il des mystères en Égypte?" *Le Bulletin Annuel de "L'Atelier d'Alexandrie"* 1 (1972): 44f. See also Kristensen, *Life Out of Death*, for whom "Egyptian religion was a mystery religion 'par excellence'" (102) because it was based on an understanding that the mystical experience of dying prior to one's actual physical death put one in touch with the normally hidden spiritual source of life (78).

96. Their work has for the most part been ignored, save for the occasional acid review. See, for example, T. G. Allen's review of S. Mayassis, *Le Livre des Morts de l'Égypte ancienne est un Livre d'Initiation* (Athens: Bibliothèque d'Archéologie

Orientale d'Athènes, 1955), in *JNES* 17 (1958): 147f. See also Baines's remarks in "Restricted Knowledge, Hierarchy and Decorum," 4f.

97. E. F. Wente, "Mysticism in Pharaonic Egypt?" in *JNES* 41 (1982): 175f. The texts in question are the Book of What Is in the Underworld (*Amduat*) and the Book of Gates. See also Daumas, "Y eut-il des mystères en Égypte?" 45–48.

98. Wente, "Mysticism in Pharaonic Egypt?" 178. See also Kristensen, *Life Out of Death*, 113:

> The funerary text also operates for life here on earth; the eternal blessing is connected with earthly happiness, which was also the idea in the Greek mystery religion.

99. Assmann, *Egyptian Solar Religion*, 26. A similar perspective is offered in S. Quirke, *The Cult of Ra* (London: Thames and Hudson, 2001), 58.

100. Assmann, *Egyptian Solar Religion*, 17:

> The Egyptian expression for the "inner aspect" of the cult is *seshetau* (lit. that which has been made inaccessible). If we translate this by the word "mysteries," we have to dispense with some of the meanings of the Greek, e.g. initiation and anticipation of death and apotheosis of the initiate.

Note, however, that Assmann's stance in his essay "Death and Initiation" is more ambivalent (see, for example, 152–55).

101. Roberts, *My Heart, My Mother*, 178.

102. Ibid., 174–78. For the Book of the Dead being intended for use by the living, it is interesting to find that R. Lepsius, as far back as 1867, in his *Aelteste Texte des Todtenbuchs nach Sarkophagen des Altägyptischen Reichs im BerlinerMuseum* (Berlin: Wilhelm Hertz, 1867), 8, saw it as "a book of practical instruction . . . to inform the individual, intent on his spiritual welfare, about what already on earth should be known and prepared by him for his death," quoted in W. Federn, "The 'Transformations' in the Coffin Texts: A New Approach," in *JNES* 19 (1960): 245. See also T. DuQuesne, *A Coptic Initiatory Invocation* (Thame, England: Darengo, 1991), 52, n. 112, who compares the Book of the Dead to the Tibetan *Bardo Thödol* and claims that "both works are clearly intended to be for spiritual (or magical) practice." See also G. Thausing, *Der Auferstehungsgedanke in ägyptischen religiösen Texten* (Leipzig: O. Harrassowitz, 1943), 15.

103. Federn, "The 'Transformations' in the Coffin Texts," 246–49.

104. Ibid., 251f. Not surprisingly, Federn's views have been criticized from the orthodox standpoint of the funerary interpretation. See Willems, *The Coffin of Heqata* (Leuven: Uitgeverij Peeters en Departement Oriëntalistiek, 1996), 278–86. Willems's criticism includes the work of Wente.

Chapter 3: The Mystical versus the Funerary Interpretation of Ancient Egyptian Religion

1. The term *mysteries* has often been used rather loosely by Egyptologists during the twentieth century, mostly in relation to Osirian rites. For example, H. Schäfer, *Die Mysterien des Osiris in Abydos* (Leipzig: J. C. Hinrichs, 1903), applied it to the ritual (much of it could be described as pageant) of Osiris at Abydos; H. Junker, "Die Mysterien des Osiris," in *Internationale Woche für Religions-Ethnologie* 3, 414–26 (Paris: P. Guenthner, 1922), and E. Chassinat, *Le Mystère d'Osiris au mois de Khoiak* (Cairo: Institut français d'archéologie orientale, 1966–68), also refer to Osirian ceremonies during Khoiak as "mysteries." For Moret, *Mystères égyptiens*, and Mayassis, *Mystères et initiations de l'Egypte ancienne*, a number of non-Osirian rituals are also covered by the term.

   DuQuesne, "Effective in Heaven and on Earth," 37, has sought to link the term *mysteries* to rites used for specifically mystical ends. This linkage is essential, but in the ancient Egyptian religious context it requires that what is understood to constitute a "mystical end" is broader than that of mystic union alone. DuQuesne is not completely clear where he stands on this issue, but he does appear to regard traveling to other worlds and altered states of consciousness as mystical ends (43–46), despite his original definition of mysticism in the narrower terms of mystic union (37).

   For the use of the term *mysteries* as involving secret initiatory rites, see J. G. Griffiths, "Mysterien," in *Lexikon der Ägyptologie* 4:276–77. For Griffiths, the dramatic presentation of the myth of the relevant god or gods was also a necessary part of any mystery rite. This view is also taken by Daumas, "Y eut-il des mystères en Egypte?" 38f. and 49. From a phenomenological standpoint, however, the external performance of any drama is less necessary than the inner experiences that occurred. This is clearly understood by Kristensen, *Life Out of Death*, 111–13. See also chap. 2, n. 95, in this book.

2. S. Morenz, *Egyptian Religion*, trans. Ann E. Keep (London: Methuen, 1973), 250.

3. Hornung, *Idea into Image*, 112.

4. Hornung, *Conceptions of God*, 182.

5. Assmann, "Death and Initiation," 143f. For speculative "cosmography," see Assmann, *Egyptian Solar Religion*, 26.

6. For the denial of trance, ecstasy, mystical contemplation, etc., see Assmann, *The Search for God*, 153ff. For Assmann, mysticism and ecstasy were "deeply contrary to Egyptian thought" and for this reason "the mystical path was as little realized in Egypt as the ecstatic." Assmann, *The Search for God*, 155.

7. See chap. 2, n. 9 and n. 10.

8. For example, *Corpus Hermeticum* 10.16 (in Copenhaver, *Hermetica*), where it is made clear that while the soul's release from the body and its realization of its inner divinity parallels what occurs after death, it is nevertheless an expe-

rience attainable while one is still alive, and in its attainment the human being realizes his or her divine potential. See also *Corpus Hermeticum* 13.3, where the mystical experience of spiritual rebirth occurs in an implicitly celestial environment, which elsewhere in the Hermetic literature is the environment that the dead find themselves in (e.g., *Corpus Hermeticum* 1.24–26). The celestial context of the mystical experience of spiritual rebirth is entirely explicit in the Hermetic "Discourse on the Eighth and Ninth" in J. Robinson, ed., *The Nag Hammadi Library in English*, 292–97.

9. *Corpus Hermeticum*, 10.25. The concept of the human being having the ability to acquire knowledge of things heavenly or spiritual while still on earth goes back to the Pyramid Texts, utt. 256, §301, and utt. 302, §458, where we read how the Horus-king is established both in heaven and on earth. Later sources include the New Kingdom *Amduat* (The Book of What Is in the Underworld), for which see chap. 2, n. 3, and the Book of the Dead, for example, BD 64 Rubric.

For the relationship between the Hermetic treatises and ancient Egyptian doctrine, see B. H. Stricker, *De Brief van Aristeas* (Amsterdam: Noord-Hollandsche Uitg. Mij.,1956); P. Derchain, "L'authenticité de l'inspiration égyptienne dans le Corpus Hermeticum," in *Revue de l'histoire des religions* 61 (1962): 175–98; J.-P. Mahé, *Hermès en haute-Egypte* (Québec: Presses de l'Université Laval, 1978–82); F. Daumas, "Le fonds égyptien de l'hermétisme," in *Gnosticisme et monde hellénistique*, ed. J. Ries (Louvain-la-Neuve, France: 1982), 1–23; and E. Iversen, *Egyptian and Hermetic Doctrine* (Copenhagen: Museum Tusculanum Press, 1984). See also Fowden, *The Egyptian Hermes*, and P. Kingsley, "Poimandres: The Etymology of the Name and the Origins of the Hermetica," in *JWCI* 56 (1993): 3–25. For a brief summary of the debate on the Egyptian/non-Egyptian origins of the *Corpus Hermeticum*, see Copenhaver, *Hermetica*, xlv–lix.

10. Eliade, *Rites and Symbols of Initiation*, 91.

11. Ibid., chap. 6; Burkert, *Ancient Mystery Cults*, 97–101; Godwin, *Mystery Religions in the Ancient World*, 34–37. See also P. Kingsley, *Ancient Philosophy, Mystery and Magic: Empedocles and Pythagorean Tradition* (Oxford: Oxford University Press, 1995), 259f and 264; R. Steiner, *Egyptian Myths and Mysteries* (New York: Anthroposophic Press, 1971), 121–24.

12. See chap. 2, n. 43.

13. Burkert, *Ancient Mystery Cults*, 92.

14. Plato, *Phaedrus*, 246–47.

15. Ibid., 248.

16. Ibid., 249.

17. Plato, *Phaedo*, 68b, trans. H. Tredennick (Harmondsworth: Penguin, 1969).

18. Ibid., 64a.

19. *Phaedrus*, 250bc, trans. in Burkert, *Ancient Mystery Cults*, 92.

20. For a thoroughly researched case for the Egyptian origin of the Eleusinian mysteries, see P. Foucart, *Les Mystères d'Éleusis* (Paris: A. Picard, 1914), part 1 and especially chap. 1. See also Bernal, *Black Athena* 1:69, who comments:

     > The late 15th century was a period of great Egyptian power after the conquests of Tuthmosis III, and one in which the mystery cults of Isis and Osiris seem to have been well established in Egypt and the Levant. Since Egyptian faience plaques of the type placed under the corners of temples have been found at Mycenae dated to the reign of Amenophis III (1405–1367), I have no difficulty in accepting the possibility that the Eleusinian cult of Archaic Greece was the descendant of an Egyptian foundation made there 700 years earlier.

     Against the derivation of the Eleusinian cult from Egypt is the lack of any object or artifact of Egyptian origin in either the sanctuary or a nearby cemetery dating from the second millennium. See C. Picard, "Sur la patrie et les pérégrinations de Déméter," in *Revues des Études Grecques* 40 (1927): 320–69, and G. Mylonas, *Eleusis and the Eleusinian Mysteries* (Princeton: Princeton University Press, 1961). However, see also Burkert, *Ancient Mystery Cults*, 20f., for Egyptian influence on the Eleusinian cult.

21. C. Kerényi, *Eleusis*, trans. R. Manheim (Princeton: Princeton University Press, 1967), 93; Eliade, *Rites and Symbols of Initiation*, 111. For the divine child, see W. Burkert, *Greek Religion* (Oxford: Basil Blackwell, 1985), 288.

22. For a detailed account of the Eleusinian rites, see Mylonas, *Eleusis and the Eleusinian Mysteries*, chap. 9. See also Burkert, *Greek Religion*, 285 ff.; Eliade, *History of Religious Ideas*, 1:294 ff.; and Kerényi, *Eleusis*, chaps. 3 and 4.

23. Aristotle fr. 15 (Rose), trans. in Burkert, *Ancient Mystery Cults*, 89.

24. For the statements of Pindar, Sophocles, and Isocrates and the Homeric Hymn to Demeter, see Burkert, *Greek Religion*, 289. For further ancient testimonies on the effects of the Eleusinian mysteries on those participating, see Kerényi, *Eleusis*, 13–16.

25. Plutarch fr. 168 (Sanbach). The same statement is wrongly attributed by Stobaeus to Themistios. See Burkert, *Ancient Mystery Cults*, 162, n. 11.

26. Kerényi, *Eleusis*, 95–102.

27. Burkert, *Ancient Mystery Cults*, 21.

28. Cicero, *De Legibus*, 2.36, quoted in Burkert, *Ancient Mystery Cults*, 21.

29. Apuleius, *The Golden Ass*, trans. Robert Graves (Harmondsworth: Penguin, 1950), 285–86.

30. Eliade, *Shamanism*, chap. 2. For the shamanic underpinnings of Plato's philosophy, see Dodds, *The Greeks and the Irrational*, 210. For shamanic themes in the Eleusinian and Hellenistic mysteries, see Eliade, *Rites and Symbols of Initiation*, 109–15.

31. Eliade, *Rites and Symbols of Initiation*, 112–13. A particularly telling example is the inscribed gold plate found at Hipponium in 1969, similar to many gold plates placed in graves in Crete, Thessaly, and southern Italy dating from around 400 B.C. These gold plates give detailed descriptions of what the dead person should expect to experience in the journey into the Underworld. The 1969 discovery, however, presents exactly the same information in an explicit context of initiation into the Bacchic mysteries. See P. Kingsley, *Ancient Philosophy, Myth and Magic* (Oxford: Oxford University Press, 1995), 259. According to Kingsley, it is possible that the gold-plate tradition has Egyptian origins (264). For further sources, see also chapter 3, n. 11.

32. S. A. Pallis, *The Babylonian Akitu Festival* (København: Hovedkommissionaer: A. F. Høst, 1926), 249. Frankfort, *Kingship and the Gods*, 315 and 321 ff., contrary to Pallis, does not accept that the death of the god was enacted by the king, because no proof of the enactment exists. Yet the evidence of the major role of the king in the rites immediately before and immediately after the god's "confinement in the mountain" is incontrovertible. As Eliade points out, insofar as the Mesopotamian kings incarnated the god in the Sacred Marriage Rite that took place after the god's "confinement in the mountain," it is only reasonable to suppose that they also went through the "confinement." See Eliade, *History of Religious Ideas*, 1:64–66.

33. Eliade, *History of Religious Ideas*, 1:74.

34. Pyramid Texts, utt. 317. In certain utterances, the king lives in the trees and fruits and scents of the earth. See Utts. 403 and 409. See also Jacq, *La tradition primordiale*, 24.

35. The Babylonian New Year festival was modeled on much earlier Sumerian rites. There is good reason to believe that an early version of the *Akitu* was already well established by the twenty-first century B.C. (Third Dynasty of Ur). See T. Jacobsen, *The Treasures of Darkness* (New Haven: Yale University Press, 1976), 124; also N. K. Sandars, *Poems of Heaven and Hell from Ancient Mesopotamia* (Harmondsworth: Penguin, 1971), 44 ff.

36. For ancient Minoan mystery rites (second millennium B.C.) and their relationship to the Eleusinian mysteries, see J. Harrison, *Prolegomena to the Study of Greek Religion* (London: Merlin Press, 1962), 564–67. Diodorus Siculus, *Library of History*, trans. C. H. Oldfather et al., Loeb Classical Library (London: Heinemann, 1933–67), 5.64 and 5.77, states that whereas the Greeks performed their rites of initiation secretly, the Cretans did so openly. For the Ugaritic myth of Baal and Mot, closely paralleling the initiatory Mesopotamian descent myths, see S. H. Hooke, *Middle Eastern Mythology* (Harmondsworth: Penguin Books, 1963), 84 ff. For the Hittite version, see 100 ff. in the same book.

37. H. W. Fairman, "Kingship Rituals of Egypt," in *Myth, Ritual and Kingship*, ed. S. H. Hooke (Oxford: Oxford University Press), 75.

38. According to Baines, "Restricted Knowledge, Hierarchy and Decorum," 3, "Schwaller de Lubicz comes at the cautious end of such approaches, which range as far afield as Joan Grant, who was the reincarnation of an ancient Egyptian—royal, of course—and Bulbul Abdel Meguid or Umm Sety. The claims of these people to inspired knowledge of their subject bypass academic endeavour and cannot be integrated with it."

39. It is embryonically present in Erman, *A Handbook of Egyptian Religion*, 95–98, but is more crystallized in Erman, *Life in Ancient Egypt*, 308. Interestingly, Budge holds back from the full formulation of the theory that the dead king is always Osiris and the living king Horus, being aware of the lack of textual support. See, for example, Budge, *The Egyptian Book of the Dead (The Papyrus of Ani)* (1895; reprint, New York: Dover, 1967), lxxiii. For Breasted's funerary interpretation of the Osiris myth, see *The Development of Religion and Thought*, 145 ff.

40. In the Unas texts, the king is explicitly identified with Horus in utts. 212, 220, 221, 222, 254, 255, 256, 302, 303, 308, 310, and 313. The identification is implicit in a great many other utterances. For example, the south-to-east-wall sequence of the sarcophagus chamber as well as both the west-wall and north-wall sequences of the antechamber are best understood as Horus sequences. Apart from the sarcophagus chamber north-wall offering texts and the related texts on the passage between the chambers, explicit references to the king as Osiris are relatively rare, and are far outnumbered by references to the king as Horus.

41. Utt. 260, trans. Faulkner, *The Ancient Egyptian Pyramid Texts* (Oxford: Oxford University Press, 1969).

42. Utt. 257, trans. Faulkner.

43. For example, in 1915, Gardiner could write in his "Review of J. Frazer's *The Golden Bough*," in *JEA* 2 (1915): 124:

> I know of no evidence anywhere among Egyptian texts in which the living pharaoh is assimilated with Osiris, or the dead pharaoh to Horus; in other words, it is in death alone that the monarch's transformation from Horus to Osiris was effected.

This view has since been reiterated countless times. A few examples may help to convey the extent to which it has become an unquestioned dogma of the funerary interpretation of the Osiris myth. For example, Griffiths, *The Origins of the Osiris Cult* (Leiden: E. J. Brill, 1980), 3:

> The Egyptian treatment of the myth of Osiris is constantly presented . . . in the setting of death; and it is also constantly related in its early phases to the fact of kingship. Horus as the living pharaoh and his father Osiris as the dead pharaoh: these are the basic elements of the royal funerary cult. Osiris per se is king of the domain of the dead, so that the dead pharaoh is naturally regarded as aspir-

ing to sovereignty in the afterworld in the form of Osiris. At the same time the royal burial rites adumbrate the birth of a new Horus in the son who succeeds the deceased.

For Wilson, *The Culture of Ancient Egypt*, 66:

Thus the deceased pharaoh came to be Osiris, and his son who followed him on the throne came to be the dutiful son Horus.

In Aldred, *The Egyptians*, 179:

and when he [the king] died and was asimilated to Osiris, the king of the dead, his son the new Horus would reign in his stead.

And S. Mercer, *The Religion of Ancient Egypt* (London: Luzac, 1949), 118:

Horus, in the form of "Horus"-kings, reigned over Egypt in this world; Osiris, in the form of the resurrected "Osiris"-king, that is, the god Osiris himself . . . reigned over Egypt of the Underworld, the realm of the dead. Moreover, each reigning king during his lifetime was a "Horus"; but as soon as he died he became an "Osiris."

44. Utt. 373, trans. Faulkner, referred to in Breasted, *The Development of Religion and Thought*, 145, n. 4.

45. Eliade, *Shamanism*, chap. 2. See also L. Lamy, *Egyptian Mysteries* (London: Thames and Hudson, 1981), 24, who refers to the "striking parallelism between these [Pyramid] texts and those of various ecstatic or initiatic visions." The parallelism has been noted in J. A. West, *Serpent in the Sky*, 146, and *The Traveller's Key to Ancient Egypt*, 97. For parallels in the Coffin Texts, see Federn, "The 'Transformations' in the Coffin Texts," 251. For a fuller exploration of the shamanic initiatory pattern underlying the Pyramid Texts, see Fix, *Star Maps*, chaps. 5–7.

46. Utt. 373, §657.

47. Utt. 219, §167, trans. in Piankoff, *The Pyramid of Unas*.

48. Breasted, *The Development of Religion and Thought*, 146.

49. Ibid., 33. Examples of resurrection utterances include utts. 219, 223, 224, 225, 355, 364, 498, and 690.

50. Griffiths, *The Origins of the Osiris Cult*, 64.

51. Utt. 219, §193. See also utt. 225, §224, and utt. 690, §2092–94.

52. Griffiths, *The Origins of the Osiris Cult*, 66. Griffiths compares this view with later Christian teaching concerning the resurrection of the body (67). By implying that an ancient Egyptian precursor of the Christian doctrine of the resurrection of the body can be found in the Pyramid Texts, an essentially alien religious belief is projected onto the ancient Egyptians. While the projection may serve to give the funerary interpretation of these very explicit passages of the king taking possession of his body an air of familiarity to a Christian readership, its effect is to saddle the Egyptians with a credo that not only offends common sense, but also belies the subtlety of their own understanding of

postmortem states, as conveyed by concepts such as the *ka, ba, sahu,* and *akh.* S. Mercer, *The Pyramid Texts,* 3:648, makes the same comparison.

53. Griffiths, *The Origins of the Osiris Cult,* 6. See also chapter 3, n. 43.

54. Utts. 26 and 449. See also utt. 600, where the king is addressed as follows: Hail Horus! This king is Osiris.

55. This is the view of both Moret and Mayassis; see n. 61 below. Mayassis, *Mystères et initiation de l'Égypte ancienne,* 92, comments:

    Osiris resuscitates himself in Horus. Horus is the "becoming" of Osiris.

56. Griffiths, *The Origins of the Osiris Cult,* 46. For Griffiths, inconsistencies within the funerary interpretation are to be explained in terms of inconsistencies within the texts themselves, due to the mixing up of the two myths. Thus on page 16 f. he writes:

    The Osiris-myth in the Pyramid Texts shows a complexity that involves inconsistencies, and it seems that the only rational explanation of these is the theory of the conflation of a Horus-legend and an Osiris-myth.

57. H. te Velde, *Seth: God of Confusion,* 74–80, has criticized Griffiths for attempting to explain essentially religious phenomena as a reflection of social conditions and historical events. See also E. F. Wente, "Review of J. Gwyn Griffiths, *The Conflict of Horus and Seth from Egyptian and Classical Sourcs,*" in *JNES* 22 (1963): 273–76, for doubts on the viability of the "two myths" approach.

58. Utt. 677, §2022–23, trans. Faulkner.

59. Breasted, *The Development of Religion and Thought,* 146.

60. Ibid., 146, n. 5:

    There is little distinction between the passages where the dead king receives the throne of Osiris, because identified with him, and others in which he receives it as the heir of Osiris [i.e., Horus].

61. According to Moret, *Mystères égyptiens,* 73, the divinization of the living king (as Horus) was achieved precisely by means of his passing through an identification with Osiris:

    The king became god through the Osirian rites; but also, from as early as his accession, he was supposed to have passed through the Osirian death and to have been redeemed as Osiris had been.

    A similar view is stated in Mayassis, *Mystères et initiation de l'Égypte ancienne,* 92. See also Clark, *Myth and Symbol in Ancient Egypt,* 161, where we read that "the heart of the [Osirian] mystery lies in the change of the speaker's soul identity."

62. For example, utts. 57–71 and utts. 220–22.

63. Assmann, "Death and Initiation," 141 f.

64. Utt. 213, §134, trans. Faulkner, discussed in Griffiths, *The Origins of the Osiris Cult*, 175.

65. Griffiths, *The Origins of the Osiris Cult*, 40.

66. For example, in a New Kingdom description of kingship, attested to on a dozen monuments, we read:

> Ra has placed the king on the earth of the living for ever and eternity, in order to judge humankind, to satisfy the gods, to make Right happen and to annihilate Wrong, so that he gives divine offerings to the gods, funerary offerings to the blessed dead.

Quoted in Quirke, *The Cult of Ra*, 20. There is no doubt that "the living" here are the literally living as contrasted with the "blessed dead."

67. For example, G. Hart, *Dictionary of Egyptian Gods and Goddesses* (London: Routledge and Kegan Paul, 1986), 154, writes:

> The belief that the king has undergone a transformation of state and has not on death reached a termination of existence is further emphasized by graphic phraseology, such as asserting that he has departed "alive" to sit on the throne of Osiris to give orders to the "living."

For similar statements, see Griffiths, *The Origins of the Osiris Cult*, 176; Wilson, *The Culture of Ancient Egypt*, 66; Aldred, *The Egyptians*, 179; Murnane, *The Penguin Guide to Ancient Egypt*, 67; and S. Quirke, *Ancient Egyptian Religion* (London: British Museum Press, 1992), 154.

68. Frankfort, *Kingship and the Gods*, 123. In this section, I shall be following the order of rites as proposed originally by K. Sethe, *Dramatische Texte zu altägyptische Mysterienspielen* (Leipzig: J. C. Hinrichs, 1928), 81–258, and followed by Frankfort, *Kingship and the Gods*, chap. 11, and A. Roberts, "The Mystery Drama of Renewal: An Archaic Ritual" (unpublished paper, 1989).

69. Frankfort, *Kingship and the Gods*, 123.

70. W. Helck, "Bemerkungen zum Ritual des Dramatischen Ramesseum-papyrus," in *Orientalia* 23 (1954): 383–441. See also *Lexikon der Ägyptologie*, ed. W. Helck and E. Otto (Wiesbaden: O. Harrassowitz, 1975–89), 5: c. 896.

71. Scene 33, trans. Roberts, "The Mystery Drama of Renewal."

72. Frankfort, *Kingship and the Gods*, 134.

73. Ibid., 133.

74. The dating of the Memphite Theology is particularly difficult, partly because it is written in archaic language resembling that of the Pyramid Texts, and itself purports to be a copy of a very ancient work, and partly because it has features that compare with the Middle Kingdom Coffin Texts. Sethe believed it to have originated in the First Dynasty, but this view is no longer held by most Egyptologists. For a translation of the text, see Lichtheim, *Ancient*

Egyptian Literature, 1:51–57. For the New Kingdom "Ancestor Ritual," see Roberts, *My Heart, My Mother*, chap. 7, especially 76 f., and chap. 8, especially 102 f.

75. Memphite Theology 62–64, trans. in Lichtheim, *Ancient Egyptian Literature*, 1:55–6.

76. Frankfort, *Kingship and the Gods*, 32 f.

77. Utt. 368, §636. The latter part is repeated word for word in utt. 357, §585a–b. I have used J. P. Allen's literal translation, from "The Cosmology of the Pyramid Texts," 19. This text appears on the symbolically significant east wall of the sarcophagus chambers of Teti and Pepi II. In the pyramid of Unas, this location is reserved for the coronation texts.

78. According to J. P. Allen, "The Cosmology of the Pyramid Texts," 19–20,

> The *akhet* is the place in which the king, like the sun and other celestial beings, undergoes the final transformation from the inertness of death and night to the form that allows him to live effectively—that is, as an *akh*—in his new world.

79. For the term "Embracers of the *Akh*," Frankfort, following Sethe, gives "Spirit *[akh]* Seekers." See Frankfort, *Kingship and the Gods*, 127, with n. 8.

80. Eliade, *Shamanism*, 127 ff. and 403 ff., gives many examples of such ascents in purely shamanic contexts. In relation to Egypt, see 487 ff.

81. For example, utt. 267 from the Pyramid of Unas:

> A stairway to the sky is set up for me, that I may ascend on it to the sky.

And again, utt. 478, from the pyramids of Pepi I, Pepi II, and Merenre:

> When I ascend to the sky on the ladder of the god, my bones are reassembled for me, my limbs are gathered for me, and I leap up to the sky in the presence of the Lord of the Ladder.

82. The two main sources that will be drawn on in this section are the reliefs of the Old Kingdom sun temple of Niuserre at Abu Gurob and the festival-hall gateway of Osorkon II at Bubastis. For the Niuserre reliefs, see W. F. von Bissing and H. Kees, *Das Re-Heiligtum des Königs Ne-woser-re (Rathures)*, 3 vols. (Leipzig: 1923). For the Osorkon reliefs, see E. Naville, *The Festival-Hall of Osorkon II in the Great Temple of Bubastis (1887–1889)* (London: Egypt Exploration Fund, 1892). Two further important sources for the Sed festival are the reliefs in the Eighteenth Dynasty temple of Amenhotep III at Soleb, summarized in J. Gohary, *Akhenaten's Sed-Festival at Karnak* (London and New York: Kegan Paul International, 1992), 11–18, and the tomb of Kheruef, described in Epigraphic Survey, *The Tomb of Kheruef: Theban Tomb 192* (Chicago: Oriental Institute Publications, 1980). For a brief survey of evidence of other Sed festivals, see Gohary, *Akhenaten's Sed-Festival at Karnak*, 6–9. For a fuller survey, see E. Hornung and E. Staehelin, *Studien zum Sedfest*, in *Aegyptiaca Helvetica* 1 (Geneva: Éditions de Belles-Lettres, 1974).

83. Although the thirtieth year of the king's reign may have been the original timing of the festival, even by the First Dynasty some kings were celebrating it before the thirtieth regnal year had elapsed. For example, Anedjib, Semerkhet, and Ka-a. In the Old Kingdom we know that Zoser, Khufu, Sahure, and Menkauhor all celebrated a Sed festival but their reigns were shorter than thirty years. The period of thirty years, therefore, may not have been calculated from the actual accession. D. Redford, *Pharaonic King-Lists, Annals and Day Books* (Mississauga, Ontario: Benben Publications, 1986), 180, comments:

> The festival was, from the 12th Dynasty at least, associated with the 30th year of the ruler qua king, but for the ancient Egyptian this need not mean the beginning of the king's sole reign. The heir apparent could become king when his father or predecessor, still living, had him undergo a coronation, as happened to Hatshepsut, Amenophis II and Ramesses II, to name a few; or since mythologically pharaoh had been designated king while still "in the egg" the 30 years could conceivably be counted from the king's birth. Only thus, it seems to me, can we explain the certain, though not numerous, cases in which a sed-festival is alluded to as having been celebrated before the 30th regnal year.

Redford argues that the celebration of the festival fell into abeyance after the end of the Twelfth Dynasty until it was revived in the Eighteenth Dynasty by Amenhotep III (185–86). The most regularly recorded series of celebrations of the festival is that of Ramesses II (Nineteenth Dynasty), who held a Sed in years 30, 34, 37, 40, 43, and 46 of his reign. See P. O'Mara, *The Chronology of the Palermo and Turin Canons* (La Canada, Calif.: Paulette Publishing Co., 1980), 29. See also W. J. Murnane, "The Sed Festival: A Problem in Historical Method," in *MDAIK* 37 (1981): 369–76. For a general discussion, see Gohary, *Akhenaten's Sed-Festival at Karnak*, 2–4.

84. For a brief survey of different theories about the meaning of the word, see Gohary, *Akhenaten's Sed-Festival at Karnak*, 2. There is a noun *sed*, meaning "tail." There is also a verb *sed*, meaning "to clothe." According to Frankfort, *Kingship and the Gods*, 366, n. 1, *sed* is also an ancient name of the god Wepwawet.

85. The next paragraphs mainly follow Frankfort, *Kingship and the Gods*, chap. 6, and E. Uphill, "The Egyptian Sed-Festival Rites," in *JNES* 24 (1965): 365–83.

86. For Niuserre's bed, see figs. 3.5 and 3.8. The possible use of a sarcophagus in Sed festival rites is attested to in four inscriptions cut by working parties in the quarries of Hammamat (trans. in J. H. Breasted, *Ancient Records of Egypt*, 5 vols. [Chicago: University of Chicago Press, 1906–7], 1:211–16). These reveal that in the second year of the reign of the Middle Kingdom king, Mentuhotep IV, a royal sarcophagus was prepared under the direction of the vizier Amenemhat during the year of the king's Sed festival. Amenemhat led

a huge expedition of quarrymen, artisans, and sculptors plus a force of 10,000 soldiers in order to excavate, construct, decorate, and then bring back the sarcophagus, which was intended as "an eternal memorial" so that the king "might celebrate very many [Sed Jubilees], living like Re, forever." (Breasted, *Ancient Records of Egypt*, 1:213 f.). See also Lichtheim, *Ancient Egyptian Literature*, 1:114 f.

87. Frankfort places the coronation at the end of the festival, but Uphill, basing his account on Osorkon's reliefs, also places it at the beginning. For both Uphill and Moret, the enactment of the coronation at the beginning as well as at the end was an essential part of the scheme. See Uphill, "The Egyptian Sed-Festival Rites," 380, n. 69, and Moret, *Mystères égyptiens*, 187 ff.

88. Uphill, "The Egyptian Sed-Festival Rites," 377.

89. According to Uphill, this was the "climax of the festival" (ibid., 377). Surprisingly, Frankfort does not refer to the "secret rites." Perhaps his overlooking this crucial event is linked to his insistence in *Kingship and the Gods*, 79, that "the Sed festival, in contrast to the coronation, does not refer to Osiris at all" and that there was "no relation between the Sed festival and Osiris, since the festival renews the existing kingship and is not concerned with the succession" (367, n. 2). The fact is, however, that the renewal of the kingship depended precisely on the king entering into a relationship with Osiris. See n. 91 below.

90. According to Helck, "Schamane und Zauberer," 104, the *sem* priest entered the realm of the dead in a state of trance, similar to that of north European–Asiatic shamans in their journeys into the spirit world.

91. According Moret, *Mystères égyptiens*, 73, the Sed festival "consists essentially of an Osirification of the king." See also p. 189. For Breasted, as well, *The Development of Religion and Thought*, 39, during the Sed festival, "the king assumed the costume and insignia of Osiris, and undoubtedly impersonated him." Breasted's interpretation is supported by Mercer, *The Religion of Ancient Egypt*, 122, and many others, including Frazer, Petrie, and Margaret Murray. The depiction of the king during the "secret rites" in Amenhotep III's temple at Soleb seems decisive, for although the relief is damaged, the king is clearly mummiform. This relief is reproduced in n. 93 on the next page. Egyptological opinion has, however, always remained sharply divided on this crucial point of interpretation. Thus Gardiner, "Review of J. G. Frazer's *The Golden Bough*," 124, argued against those who believed that the king was identified with Osiris in the Sed festival on the grounds that the resemblance of costume was due to Osiris being a king, hence wearing royal regalia, rather than the king being Osiris! J. G. Griffiths, "The Costume and Insignia of the King in the Sed-Festival," in *JEA* 41 (1955): 127 f., also denies any Osiris identification. The argument for a fusion of the king with Osiris probably should not be settled merely on the interpretation of his costume and

insignia. We have also to look at the rites that he was engaged in, the inscriptional evidence, and what the reliefs actually show.

92. The word *is* (and *iset*) is somewhat ambiguous and could refer to a shrine, chapel, or palace rather than the actual tomb. Uphill, "The Egyptian Sed-Festival Rites," 378, with n. 56, argues against the view of Naville that the word *is* here refers to a shrine rather than the actual tomb of the king on the grounds that (1) in Old Kingdom inscriptions *is* commonly means "tomb" and (2) the reliefs adjacent to "the secret rites" have a decidedly funereal character. The discovery of Osorkon's burial place at Tanis on the site where his Sed festival was likely to have taken place, i.e., near to the great temple with its large courts, certainly adds weight to his argument that the secret rites took place in his tomb and not in a shrine. Even if the translation "tomb" is debatable, the main point at issue is not so much the type of building in which the secret rites took place as what they consisted of: in particular, the fact that they had a distinctly funereal character, and that there is good reason to believe that during them the king seems to have undergone certain transcendent experiences.

93. Naville, *The Festival-Hall of Osorkon II*, pl. X, fig. 5. See also Uphill, "The Egyptian Sed-Festival Rites," 378. The scene closely resembles a similar scene in Amenhotep III's temple at Soleb, in which the king in his shrine is represented mummiform, for which see M. S. Giorgini, *Soleb* (Firenze: Sonsoni, 1965–71), 1:100, fig. 81, which is reproduced here.

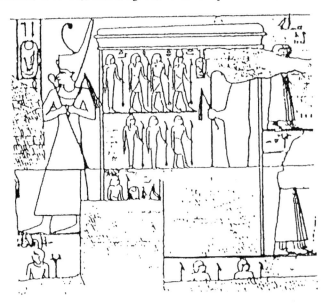

Amenhotep III is represented mummiform during his Sed festival.

94. The verb *iry* is used in a wide variety of contexts and can be translated in many different ways. See R. O. Faulkner, *A Concise Dictionary of Middle Egyptian* (Oxford: Griffith Institute, Ashmolean Museum, 1962), 25–27, for the range of options, all of which are concerned with some sort of activity. In the present context, the activity of "attending to" is possibly what is meant, but this must remain a matter of speculation.

95. D. Meeks, "Dieu masqué, dieu sans tête," in *Archéo-Nil* 1 (1991): 9–11. See also Berlandini, "L' 'acéphale' et le rituel de revirilisation," in *OMRO* 73 (1993): 33.

96. In utt. 13, these words are spoken to the king: "I give you your head, I fasten your head to the bones for you." In utt. 373, the restoration of the head is related to the revivification of the king:

> Oho! Oho! Raise yourself, O king;
> Receive your head, collect your bones,
> Gather your limbs together,
> Throw off the earth from your flesh. . . .

See also utt. 254, which appears on the west wall of the antechamber of the pyramid of Unas, where the restoration of the head motif also occurs, for which see pp. 245–46, with chap. 8, n. 21. See also Coffin Texts 229 and 532 for this important theme.

The birth of the Horus principle is referred to in utt. 221, where it is announced:

> The Great One has given birth to you,
> The exalted One has adorned you.
> For you are Horus. . . .

See also utts. 211, 248, and 302, also from the pyramid of Unas, which all emphasize the celestial context of the birth of the Horus principle. In utt 302, for example, he is referred to as the "son of Sothis" (i.e., Isis in her celestial aspect).

97. Utt. 74. For the seven holy oils, see utts. 72–78. For a commentary on the seven holy oils, see E. A. Wallis Budge, *Herb Doctors and Physicians in the Ancient World* (Chicago: Ares Publishers, 1978), 30. Budge transliterates *sesefetch* as Sefth. See also A. M. Roth, "The *psš-kf* and the 'Opening of the Mouth' Ceremony: A Ritual of Birth and Rebirth," in *JEA* 78 (1992): 121 f.

98. Uphill, "The Egyptian Sed-Festival Rites," 379. Another scene similar to fig. 3.9 can be found in the tomb of Ramesses IX, reproduced in E. Lefébure, *Les hypogées royaux de Thèbes. Première division: Le tombeau de Séti I*, Mémoires publiés par les membres de la Mission archéologique française au Caire, 3 (Paris: E. Leroux, 1886), pl. XXI.

99. Uphill, "The Egyptian Sed-Festival Rites," 380. Scenes in the tomb of Kheruef showing the raising of the *djed* during the Sed festival of Amenhotep III suggest that in his festival the *djed* was raised as a preliminary

rite at the beginning of the festival. See Gohary, *Akhenaten's Sed-Festival at Karnak*, 16.

100. Uphill, "The Egyptian Sed-Festival Rites," 379 f.

Chapter 4: The Pyramids as the Locus of Secret Rites

1. For the ancient Egyptian conception of the Dwat, see chap. 2, n. 1.

2. For the cycles of manifestation in relation to the goddess Nut, see Roberts, *My Heart, My Mother*, 182–88.

3. This is made clear in the New Kingdom mystical text, the Book of What Is in the Underworld *(Amduat)* div. 3, in Hornung, *Das Amduat*, 2:64; Piankoff, *The Tomb of Ramesses VI*, vol. 1, 248. The tradition that the Nile flood issues from the Dwat goes back at least to the Sixth Dynasty. See G. Maspero, *The Dawn of Civilization* (London: Society for Promoting Christian Knowledge, 1894), 19 f. and 38 f.

4. Kristensen, *Life Out of Death*, 28, comments on the ancient Egyptian conception of the realm of death as follows: "The world of death secreted greater powers and contained richer possibilities than the world of finite experience. It was the basis for the whole existence which we are apt to call worldly life."

5. See Frankfort, *Kingship and the Gods*, 62–69. It is, however, Clark who understands this best: "The ancestors, the custodians of the source of life, were the reservoir of power and vitality, the source whence flowed all the forces of vigour, sustenance and growth. Hence they were not only departed souls but still active, the keepers of life and fortune." Clark, *Myth and Symbol in Ancient Egypt*, 119 ff.

6. For the king's role as mediator between worlds, see Clark, *Myth and Symbol in Ancient Egypt*, 107 and 121. See also DuQuesne, "Anubis e il Ponte," 115. See also n. 11 and n. 12 below.

7. Frankfort, *Kingship and the Gods*, 57–60; also chaps. 14–15. See also G. A. Wainwright, *The Sky-Religion in Egypt* (Cambridge: Cambridge University Press, 1938), 16–20.

8. See chap. 3, n. 83. See also Frankfort, *Kingship and the Gods*, 366 f.

9. Frankfort, *Kingship and the Gods*, 84.

10. Spencer, "Two Enigmatic Hieroglyphs and Their Relation to the Sed-Festival," in *JEA* 64 (1978): 54 f.

11. According to R. Wilkinson, *Symbol and Magic in Egyptian Art*, 171, "[T]he area crossed or encircled in the *heb-sed* 'race' represented not only the extent of the king's earthly domain, but also his celestial realm, for the rule of the king was identified with the rule of the god Horus over heaven and earth." See also Reeder, "Running the Heb Sed," in *KMT* 4, no. 4 (1993–94), 68, who comments: "The celebrant not only traversed the field (i.e., Egypt) in a

public ceremony, but also traversed the heavens in, understandably, a much less public form."

12. Quoted in Frankfort, *Kingship and the Gods*, 86. The text suggests that the king is in an altered state of consciousness. In certain shamanic initiations, dance is used to induce precisely such a state. Thus H. Kalweit, *Dreamtime and Inner Space: The World of the Shaman*, trans. Werner Wünsche (Boston and London: Shambhala, 1988), 228, writes: "The initiate therefore dances not only on earth—in our reality . . . his dance is also performed in an altered state of consciousness or in another world."

13. For the Otherworldly field, see J. P. Allen, "The Cosmology of the Pyramid Texts," 6.

14. For the Mesopotamian *Akitu*, see chap. 3, 56f. According to Wainwright, *The Sky-Religion in Egypt*, 20–24, the Sed festival was primarily a fertility festival, and the purpose of the king's Sed dance was to ensure the fertility of the fields magically.

15. R. Wilkinson, *Reading Egyptian Art* (London: Thames and Hudson, 1994), 151.

16. Quirke, *Ancient Egyptian Religion*, 90.

17. Frankfort, *Kingship and the Gods*, 83–88.

18. This is given special emphasis from the Fifth Dynasty onward. According to Wente and van Siclen, "A Chronology of the New Kingdom," in *Studies in Honour of George R. Hughes*, eds. Janet H. Johnson and Edward F. Wente, 221, "[A] culminating point in the traditional Sed-festival was the apotheosis of the king identifying him with the sungod." For a discussion of the solarization of Amenhotep III at his Sed festival, see W. Raymond Johnson, "Amenhotep III and Amarna: Some New Considerations," in *JEA* 82 (1996): 67 ff.

19. Uphill, "The Egyptian Sed-Festival Rites," 371.

20. Quirke, *Ancient Egyptian Religion*, 91.

21. The position of Niuserre's coronation in the sequence of Sed festival ceremonies is, according to Kaiser, "Die Kleine Hebseddarstellung im Sonnenheiligtum des Neuserre," in *BÄBA* 12 (1971): 87–105, after the "secret rites" (which he refers to as the "lion furniture" sequence). This would explain the difference in costume.

22. Uphill, "The Egyptian Sed-Festival Rites," 374. Uphill places this coronation at the beginning of the Sed festival rites but Frankfort believes it belongs at the end, which does seem to make more sense. See "The Egyptian Sed-Festival Rites," 370; also Frankfort, *Kingship and the Gods*, 88.

23. Gohary, *Akhenaten's Sed-Festival at Karnak*, 14.

24. Uphill, "The Egyptian Sed-Festival Rites," 381; Naville, *The Festival-Hall of Osorkon II*, pl. XV.

25. Uphill, "The Egyptian Sed-Festival Rites," 369, n. 9. Also W. C. Hayes, "Inscriptions from the Palace of Amenhotep III," in *JNES* 10 (1951): 35 ff.

26. Von Bissing and Kees, *Das Re-Heiligtum des Königs Ne-woser-re*, vol. 3, plates 20 and 21. The king's presence is evident in vol. 3, pl. 20. Other reliefs show oxen and other animals intended for slaughter (vol. 1, pls. 6 and 7; vol. 3, pl. 16) and the actual slaughter of an ox (vol. 3, pl. 23). It is recorded at the sun temple that 30,000 meals were provided at the king's Sed festival. According to Z. Hawass, "Funerary Establishments of Khufu, Khafra, and Menkaura during the Old Kindom" (Ph.D. diss., University of Pennsylvania, 1987; Ann Arbor: University Microfilms International, 1987), 497, such offering scenes should be understood as depicting "the powers that are renewed through the festival," i.e., the powers of life and fertility in the land.

27. Quirke, *Ancient Egyptian Religion*, 90. See also Quirke, *The Cult of Ra*, 122, where he argues that the pyramid was primarily an object of the cult of the living king, and only secondarily his tomb. Kemp, "Old Kingdom, Middle Kingdom, and Second Intermediate Period," in *Ancient Egypt: A Social History*, ed. B. G. Trigger et al. (Cambridge: Cambridge University Press, 1983), 85, has commented: "While it is common to emphasize the mortuary character of the pyramids and to see them as tombs with temples attached to them, the way in which they were in fact organized and referred to suggests that the emphasis should be reversed, and they be regarded first and foremost as temples for the royal statues with a royal tomb attached to each." See also D. Arnold, "Royal Cult Complexes of the Old and Middle Kingdoms," in *Temples of Ancient Egypt*, ed. Byron E. Shafer (Ithaca: Cornell University Press, 1997), 31 and 85.

28. Kristensen, *Life Out of Death*, 76 f.

29. E. O. James, *Myth and Ritual*, 88. See also Frankfort, *Kingship and the Gods*, 148–49.

30. Kristensen, *Life Out of Death*, 111. While the symbolism of the step pyramid as a staircase is often noted, few scholars have made the further connection with the Sed festival coronation dais, because the pyramid is supposed to have served only funerary purposes.

31. Firth and Quibell, *The Step Pyramid*, 2 vols. (Cairo: Institut français d'Archéologie Orientale, 1935–36), vol. 1, introduction; Gardiner, "Horus the Behdetite," in *JEA* 30 (1944): 27 f.; Frankfort, *Kingship and the Gods*, 80; Kemp, *Ancient Egypt: Anatomy of a Civilization*, 62.

32. These include the North and South Houses, the structure known as Temple T, identified by Firth as the robing chamber used by the king during the Sed festival, and the Southern Tomb. See Reeder, "Running the Heb Sed," 63 f. Reeder challenges the view that the whole site served a purely commemorative purpose and was designed only for Zoser's use in the afterlife. See also Hawass, "A Fragmentary Monument of Djoser from Saqqara," in *JEA* 80

(1994): 56, n. 22, where he states that the complex of Zoser was not only funerary but also included the palace of the living king.

33. Strouhal et al., "Re-investigation of the remains thought to be of King Djoser," in *Anthropologie* 32, no. 3 (1994): 225–42.

34. See Edwards, *The Pyramids of Egypt*, 50; Reeder, "Running the Heb Sed," 68.

35. Lehner, *The Complete Pyramids* (London: Thames and Hudson, 1997), 92, argues that the southern tomb was intended for the king's *ka* statue, and was the precursor of the Fourth, Fifth, and Sixth Dynasty "satellite" pyramids, which probably served the same function. If he is right, the likelihood that the "secret rites" of the Sed festival took place in one of the chambers underneath the step pyramid is considerably strengthened.

36. Goneim, *Excavations at Saqqara: Horus Sekhem-khet: The Unfinished Pyramid*, 1:13 ff. and 21.

37. Ibid., 34.

38. Ibid., 19. A readily accessible account of the excavation of the pyramid of Sekhemkhet can be found in Edwards, *The Pyramids of Egypt*, 58–64; see also Fakhry, *The Pyramids* (Chicago: Chicago University Press, 1969), 42–48. Curiously, neither mentions the alabaster dish with the Sed festival inscription.

39. See chap. 3, p. 71, with n. 86. For evidence of "funerary ceremonies" performed by the living, see Kristensen, *Life Out of Death*, 112 f., where he describes an official under Senwosret I who underwent a symbolic burial in his tomb at Abydos. According to Kristensen, the many empty tombs or cenotaphs at Abydos served precisely this purpose. See also Assmann, "Death and Initiation," 149, and *The Search for God*, 156, for the incorporation of funerary elements in initiation ceremonies of priests.

40. Edwards, *The Pyramids of Egypt*, 69.

41. Lehner, *The Complete Pyramids*, 100. See also Stadelmann, "Scheintür oder Stelen im Totentempel des AR," in *MDAIK* 39 (1983): 237–41.

42. Lehner, *The Complete Pyramids*, 92.

43. Ibid., 103. See also Stadelmann, "Snofru und die Pyramiden von Meidum und Dahschur," in *MDAIK* 36 (1980): 437 ff.

44. A. Fakhry, *The Monuments of Sneferu at Dahshur*, vol. 1, *The Bent Pyramid* (Cairo: General Organisation for Government Printing Offices, 1959), 89.

45. Ibid., vol. 2, *The Valley Temple*, part 1, 60–117. Other reliefs in the valley temple, while not directly depicting Sed festival rites, are in all likelihood closely associated with the Sed festival. These include offerings from the estates of both Upper and Lower Egypt and the king consorting with various deities. See Hawass, "The Funerary Establishments," 497 f. and 500 f. with plan 32.

46. Fakhry, *The Monuments of Sneferu at Dahshur*, 2:98. There are also fragments of the fertility god, Min; see Fakhry, 107.

47. Lehner, *The Complete Pyramids*, 104 f. See Edwards, *The Pyramids of Egypt*, 93 f. for a discussion on the question of the length of Sneferu's reign and the biennual census records. See also Stadelmann, "Snofru und die Pyramiden von Meidum und Dahschur," 437–49.

48. Edwards, *The Pyramids of Egypt*, 91 f. See also Stadelmann, "Die Pyramiden des Snofru in Dahschur," in *MDAIK* 38 (1982): 379–93.

49. Edwards, *The Pyramids of Egypt*, 93; Stadelmann, "Snofru und die Pyramiden von Meidum und Dahschur," 437–49.

50. S. Hassan, *Excavations at Giza*, vol. 10 (Cairo: General Organisation for Government Printing Offices, 1960), 22 f. and plates VIA and VIB.

51. Ibid., 23. Note that Hassan translates the first sentence "The great wild ox."

52. See, for example, utts. 205, 254, 273–74 and 306 in the pyramid of Unas.

53. Hassan, *Excavations at Giza*, 23.

54. Hawass, "The Funerary Establishments," 352–54 with plan 24; 364–89.

55. These blocks were reused in the core of the pyramid of the Middle Kingdom king, Amenemhet I at Lisht. See Goedicke, *Re-used Blocks from the Pyramid of Amenemhet I at Lisht* (New York: Metropolitan Museum of Art, 1971), for the upper temple 29 ff., for the valley temple 13, 16 ff., and 100 ff. For their original positions in the temples, see Hawass, "The Funerary Establishments," 803, plan 35.

56. Arnold, "Royal Cult Complexes of the Old and Middle Kingdoms," 51. The interpretation of the court of the upper temple of Khufu as a Sed festival court is made in J. Brinks, *Die Entwicklung der königlichen Grabanlagen des Alten Reiches* (Hildesheim: Gerstenberg, 1979), 121 with pl. 5. See also Hawass, "The Funerary Establishments," 467 and 518 f. with plan 35.

57. Arnold, "Royal Cult Complexes of the Old and Middle Kingdoms," 57.

58. Hawass, "The Funerary Establishments," 352 f. and 364–89. Another piece of evidence for a Sed festival connection with Khafre's pyramid is a damaged fragment of a statue of Khafre apparently wearing the Sed festival garment found at Giza, for which see Uvo Holscher, *Das Grabdenkmal des Königs Chephren* (Leipzig: Hinrichs, 1912), 94. The lack of evidence for a Sed festival intention in Menkaure's pyramid complex has led Brinks, *Die Entwicklung der königlichen Grabanlagen des Alten Reiches*, 129 f., to doubt that it served any Sed festival purpose. See, however, Hawass, "The Funerary Establishments," 283–85.

59. Mummy remains discovered in the sarcophagus chamber of Menkaure's pyramid have been dated to early Christian times. See Edwards, *The Pyramids of Egypt*, 143. For the bones in the sarcophagus of Khafre, see Lehner, *The Complete Pyramids*, 124.

60. Edwards, *The Pyramids of Egypt*, 146 f.

61. Firth, "Excavations of the Department of Antiquities at Saqqara," in *ASAE* 29 (1929): 65–67.

62. See chap. 4, n. 26.

63. Gardiner, *Egyptian Grammar*, 495. That fertility and renewal symbolism are intrinsic to the meaning of fishing, fowling, and hunting scenes has been demonstrated by Derchain, Westendorf, and others. For which, see R. Wilkinson, *Symbol and Magic in Egyptian Art*, 182 and 189, which gives further references.

64. Firth, "Excavations," 67. But see also Lauer, "Le temple haut de la pyramide du roi Ouserkaf Saqqarah," in *ASAE* 53 (1955): 119–33, who argues that the satellite pyramid was used for funerary rites rather than the Sed festival. The implication is that if the "secret rites" did take place on this site, then the main pyramid would have been used.

65. For other early depictions of this motif, see Aldred, *Egypt to the End of the Old Kingdom* (London: Thames and Hudson, 1965), 64, ill. 55 (King Den) and ill. 54 (King Sekhemkhet). For a discussion of the magical, symbolic, and mythological aspects of this motif, see Ritner, *The Mechanics of Ancient Egyptian Magical Practice*, 113 ff. and 131; R. Wilkinson, *Symbol and Magic in Ancient Egyptian Art*, 176 f. and 188; and Naydler, *Temple of the Cosmos*, 109 f.

66. Uphill, "The Egyptian Sed-Festival Rites," 380. Interestingly, in the sarcophagus chamber of Pepi II's pyramid, we read (utt. 650) of how the king not only sets Upper and Lower Egypt in order for Ra, but also "hacks up the fortresses of Asia" and "quells all the hostile peoples," activities that are scarcely comprehensible in a funerary context, and make considerably more sense if read in the light of standard Sed festival iconography and inscriptional statements. See also Hawass, "The Funerary Establishments," 496–98, who argues that "the smiting of the Libyan" theme relates to the Sed festival.

67. For other relief fragments depicting the Sed festival in Sahure's temples, see Gardiner, "Horus the Behdetite," 28–30. Gardiner refers to important reliefs that were copied in the antechamber to Pepi II's pyramid temple.

68. Uphill, "The Egyptian Sed-Festival Rites," 378, n. 56.

69. For the alabaster vessel, see L. Borchardt, *Das Grabdenkmal des Königs Neuser-Re* (Leipzig: J. C. Hinrichs, 1907), pl. 119. For the king suckled by Sekhmet, see plates 21 and 23.

70. Strouhal and Gaballah, "King Djedkare-Isesi and His Daughters," in *Biological Anthropology and the Study of Ancient Egypt*, eds. W. V. Davies and R. Walker (London: British Museum Press, 1993), 104–18.

71. Quibell, *Excavations at Saqqara 1907–1908* (Cairo: Institut français d'archéologie orientale, 1909), 20 and pl. LIV.3.

72. J.-Ph. Lauer and J. Leclant, *Le temple haut du complexe funéraire du roi Téti* (Cairo: Institut français d'archéologie orientale, 1972), 91, fr. 12.

73. For the jar and ointment vessel, see Hayes, *Scepter of Egypt*, vol. 1 (New York: Harper Brothers with Metropolitan Museum of Art, 1953), 126–27 and fig. 77. Hayes also refers to a large cylinder in glass steatite bearing an inscription mentioning Pepi's Sed festival. Unfortunately the provenance of these artifacts is unknown. See also Minault-Gout, "Sur les vases jubilaires et leur diffusion," in *Études sur l'ancien empire et la nécropole de Saqqara dédiées à Jean-Philippe Lauer*, Orientalia Monspelansia, vol. 9, eds. C. Berger and B. Mathieu (Montpellier: Université Paul Valéry, 1997), 305–14. For further artifacts and inscriptions commemorating Pepi I's Sed festival, see Hornung and Staehelin, *Studien zum Sedfest*, 23–24.

74. Von Bissing and Kees, *Das Re-Heiligtum des Königs Ne-woser-re*, vol. 3, pl. 23.

75. For the symbolism of the *seshed* cloth, see Kristensen, *Life Out of Death*, 47–49, with figs. 21–23. Herodotus apparently refers to this cloth in an initiatory context in *Histories*, 2.122. See also Moret, *Mystères égyptiens*, 74f. That it had Sed festival associations can be gleaned from the reliefs in the antechamber of the pyramid temple of Pepi II, who is shown holding it while he communes with the gods of Egypt, a scene that was probably part of the Sed festival rites. See Gardiner, "Horus the Behdetite," in *JEA* 30 (1944): 30. Unas is also shown holding it in a relief in his pyramid temple, as he partakes in a sacred meal, for which see Labrousse et al., *Le temple haut du complex funéraire de roi Ounas* (Cairo: Institut français d'archéologie orientale, 1977), 89, doc. 38, fig. 64, and pl. XXXII. The question may remain as to whether these scenes were depicting the Sed festival or funerary rites, but there can be little doubt that the weight of the contextual evidence is on the side of a Sed festival interpretation.

76. Leclant, *Recherches dans la pyramide et au temple haut du pharaon Pépi 1er Saqqarah* (Leiden: Nederlands Institut voor Het Nabije Oosten, 1979), pl.XVII, fig. 25. For the "smiting of the Libyan" and other scenes, see Leclant, "Fouilles et travaux en Égypte," in *Orientalia* 45 (1976), 285.

77. Lauer, *Saqqara: The Royal Cemetery of Memphis* (London: Thames and Hudson, 1976), 184.

78. Hornung and Staehelin, *Studien zum Sedfest*, 24f. and 67.

79. Lehner, *The Complete Pyramids*, 161. Evidence for this comes from the fact that the girdle was composed of blocks from a preexisting sanctuary within the pyramid complex that was adorned with reliefs relating to the royal cult. The symbolism of dismantling the sanctuary and then reincorporating certain blocks from it within a new structure would match well the regeneration theme of the Sed festival. See Schwaller de Lubicz, *The Temple of Man*, 2:984f., for the concept of "seed-stones" from one sacred structure being placed in the foundations of a new structure.

80. Ritner, *The Mechanics of Ancient Egyptian Magical Practice*, 113ff.; R. Wilkinson, *Symbol and Magic in Egyptian Art*, 177 and fig. 139.

81. Edwards, *The Pyramids of Egypt*, 184, comments: "The scene is not merely

reminiscent of that in the temple of Sahure, but is actually a replica of it, even the names of the wife and two sons [of a Libyan chieftain] being repeated. This almost exact duplication of a scene in the temples of two kings whose reigns were separated by about two centuries furnishes conclusive proof that temple reliefs did not necessarily record historical episodes from the life of the king." See also Naydler, *Temple of the Cosmos*, 108f., for a discussion of this and other examples of the "mythologization of history" in ancient Egypt.

82. Edwards, *The Pyramids of Egypt*, 185. For images of, and commentary on, the ceremony, see Roberts, *Hathor Rising*, 96, pl. 104, and Schwaller de Lubicz, *The Egyptian Miracle*, 221, fig. 39.

83. Jéquier, *Le monument funéraire de Pepi II*, vol. 2, *Le temple* (Cairo: Institut français d'archéologie orientale, 1936–41), plates 46–60. According to Edwards, *The Pyramids of Egypt*, 186, the deities of Egypt and high sacerdotal and secular officials have "assembled to greet him as he entered the temple by way of the sanctuary from his tomb." For Edwards this scene is "reminiscent" of the Sed festival, not least because the antechamber is the functional equivalent of an apartment in the royal palace at Memphis used during Sed festival ceremonies, and closely related to a similar structure at Zoser's pyramid complex.

84. For the prominent role of the *sem* priest in the "secret rites," see Uphill, "The Egyptian Sed-Festival Rites," 377f. See also Gardiner, "Horus the Behdetite," 28–30, who argues that the reliefs belong to the Sed festival. For the view that the reliefs portray the king in the hereafter, see Frankfort, *Kingship and the Gods*, 367, n. 5.

85. According to Arnold, "Royal Cult Complexes of the Old and Middle Kingdoms," 68f., there is no doubt at all that the reliefs in the square antechamber are Sed festival reliefs. For the fragment mentioning the date of the Sed festival and its implications, see Gardiner, "Horus the Behdetite," 30.

86. Gardiner, "Horus the Behdetite," 28, n. 1, suggests Memphis was the main Sed festival site during the Old Kingdom. Heliopolis is clearly another possibility.

87. For the dedication of the upper temple to Sed festival rites, see Brinks, *Die Entwicklung der königlichen Grabanlagen des Alten Reiches*, 121 and pl. 5; Hawass, "The Funerary Establishments," 467 and 518f. with plan 35. For the possible Sed festival function of the satellite pyramid, see Brinks, *Die Entwicklung der königlichen Grabanlagen des Alten Reiches*, 76–94; Lehner, *The Pyramid Tomb of Queen Hetep-heres and the Satellite Pyramid* (Mainz: P. von Zabern, 1985), 35 ff.; Hawass, "The Funerary Establishments," 118. For evidence of robing chambers, see Hawass, "The Funerary Establishments," 352–54 and 364–89. See also Reeder, "Running the Heb Sed," 63 f.; and Arnold, "Royal Cult Complexes of the Old and Middle Kingdoms," 51. See also chap. 4, n. 32.

88. Edwards, *The Pyramids of Egypt*, 188f.

89. Lauer, *Saqqara: The Royal Cemetery of Memphis*, 184. Only the decoration remained incomplete.

90. Quirke, *Ancient Egyptian Religion*, 81. Quirke's bold statement needs to be treated with some caution. We know, for instance, that the Fifth Dynasty king Neferirkare's pyramid and pyramid temple were completed by his sons owing to his early death. See M. Verner, "The Fifth Dynasty's Mysterious Sun Temples," in *KMT* 14, no. 1 (2003), 52.

91. Quirke, *The Cult of Ra*, 122, asserts that the pyramids are "only secondarily tombs: their first purpose is the cult of the king as a divine being, from the Fourth Dynasty as son of the sun god. There is no reason why this cult should await the death of the king. . . . ." See also Hawass, "The Funerary Establishments," ix, who states that "the pyramid complex was not established for the royal funerary procession nor the king's mummification. It was built to celebrate the myth of kingship and the worship of the triad [Ra, Horus, Hathor]." See also Kemp, "Old Kingdom, Middle Kingdom, and Second Intermediate Period," 85.

92. §406, trans. Faulkner. The words translated as "travelling around" and "circumambulating" are, respectively, *deben* and *pekher*, both of which have ritual and magical connotations, for which see Ritner, *The Mechanics of Ancient Egyptian Magical Practice*, 57–67.

93. Spencer, "Two Enigmatic Hieroglyphs and Their Relation to the Sed-Festival," 54, where he comments that this passage in utts. 273–74 "seems to reflect exactly what the king achieved by running between these emblems." See also Reeder, "Running the Heb Sed," 68. See also Ritner, *The Mechanics of Ancient Egyptian Magical Practice*, 58 f. and n. 271.

94. It goes back at least to the time of Sneferu. See Fakhry, *The Monuments of Sneferu at Dahshur*, 2:98. Portrayals of the king running with a bull can be seen in Seti's temple at Abydos and Hatshepsut's Sed festival pavilion reliefs, located at Karnak.

95. See, for example, utt. 254 and utts. 304–7 in the pyramid of Unas. See also utts. 365, 474, 480, etc.

96. Utt. 58, §41, trans. Faulkner.

97. Utt. 221, §196–97, trans. Faulkner. See also Faulkner's introduction to this utterance in *The Ancient Egyptian Pyramid Texts*, 48.

98. Uphill, "The Egyptian Sed-Festival Rites," 379 f.

99. Plato, *Phaedrus* 246–47; *Corpus Hermeticum*, books 1, 10, and 13; also the Hermetic "Discourse on the Eighth and the Ninth," 292–97. For celestial ascent in shamanism, see Eliade, *Shamanism*, chap. 6.

100. Plato, *Phaedrus* 246; Apuleius, *The Golden Ass*, trans. Robert Graves (Harmondsworth: Penguin, 1950), 285–86; *Corpus Hermeticum* 1.26; and

"The Discourse on the Eighth and the Ninth," 59. For visions of gods in shamanism, see Eliade, *Shamanism*, 186 ff.

101. For the direct experience of one's immortal core, see Plato, *Phaedrus*, 245–48. The language of rebirth is particularly characteristic of the Hermetic dialogues. See, for example, *Corpus Hermeticum* 13.10 and 13.13, and "The Discourse on the Eighth and the Ninth," 57–58. For the rebirth motif in shamanism, see Eliade, *Shamanism*, 37 f., and Eliade, *Rites and Symbols of Initiation*, 87 ff.

102. There are several other means of ascent besides these. See Breasted, *The Development of Religion and Thought*, 109–15; also Davis, "The Ascension-Myth in the Pyramid Texts," in *JNES* 36, no. 3 (1977): 161–79. For the cosmic ascent in the pyramid of Unas, see, for example, utts. 214, 216, 222, 257, 267, and 269, among others.

103. Some examples from the pyramid of Unas are utts. 222, 257, 262, 302, 306, 308, and 311, among others.

104. For the rebirth theme, see utts. 1–11, 211, 248, 269, 279, and 302, among others.

Chapter 5: A Question of Method

1. Assmann, *Egyptian Solar Religion*, 9.

2. For the quality of devotion, see van der Leeuw, "Some Recent Achievements of Psychological Research and Their Application to History, in Particular the History of Religion," in *Classical Approaches to the Study of Religion*, ed. J. Waardenburg (The Hague: Mouton, 1973), 403. For the importance of considering phenomena on their own plane of reference, see Eliade, *The Quest*, 6.

3. Eliade, *The Quest*, 6. Some phenomenologists, however, choose to remain neutral as regards the existential status of religious phenomena and the truth of religious statements. See, for example, Smart, *The Science of Religion and the Sociology of Knowledge* (Princeton: Princeton University Press, 1973), 54, and Bleeker, *The Sacred Bridge*, 3.

4. See Heinemann, "Goethe's Phenomenological Method," *Philosophy* 9 (1934): 67–81. Goethe's writings on scientific method are collected in *Goethe on Science: An Anthology of Goethe's Scientific Writings*, ed. Jeremy Naydler (Edinburgh: Floris Books, 1996).

5. Quoted in Naydler, *Goethe on Science*, 32.

6. Husserl, *Ideas: General Introduction to Pure Phenomenology*, trans. W. R. Boyce Gibson (London: George Allen and Unwin, 1931), §27.

7. Husserl, "Phenomenology," in *Encyclopaedia Brittanica*, 14th ed., 1927, reproduced in Kockelmans and Husserl, *Phenomenology* (West Lafayette, Ind.: Purdue University Press, 1994), 28–30.

8. Husserl, *Ideas*, §31.

9. Ibid., §33 f.

10. Van der Leeuw's studies of ancient Egyptian religion include *Godvoor-stellingen in de oudaigyptische pyramidetexten* (1916), *Achnaton* (1927), and *Egyptische Eschatologie* (1949).

11. Van der Leeuw, "On Phenomenology and Its Relation to Theology," in *Classical Approaches to the Study of Religion*, ed. J. Waardenburg (The Hague: Mouton, 1973), 406–7.

12. Van der Leeuw, *Religion in Essence and Manifestation*, 677 f.

13. Ibid., 675.

14. Ibid., 672–73.

15. Van der Leeuw, "On Phenomenology and Its Relation to Theology," 407.

16. Kristensen, *The Meaning of Religion*, 13.

17. Ibid.

18. Bleeker, "The Phenomenological Method," in *The Sacred Bridge*, 3.

19. Ibid., 11.

20. "The essentially human always remains essentially human, and is, as such, comprehensible." Van der Leeuw, *Religion in Essence and Manifestation*, 675.

21. Husserl, *Ideas*, §129. For the mediating role of empathy, see *Ideas*, §151.

22. Husserl discusses at great length how it is possible for the act of consciousness by which meaning is conferred onto the world to be at one and the same time the means by which the meaningfulness inherent in the world can be revealed. See *Ideas*, §87–135. In particular, his celebrated discussion of the relationship between *noesis* (the meaning-giving act of consciousness) and *noema* (the meaningfully structured object of consciousness) underpins his concept of objectivity as a "seeing into" the essential noematic structures of a phenomenon, or the essential relationships between phenomena. For which, see especially *Ideas*, §93 and §137.

23. Husserl, *Cartesian Meditations: An Introduction to Phenomenology*, trans. Dorion Cairns (Dordrecht, Boston, and London: Kluwer Academic Publishers, 1993), 135.

24. Van der Leeuw's *Religion in Essence and Manifestation* was published in 1933, just two years after Husserl's *Cartesian Meditations*. In it, van der Leeuw writes:
    Understanding, in fact, itself presupposes intellectual restraint. But it is never the attitude of the cold-blooded spectator: it is, on the contrary, the loving gaze of the lover on the beloved object. (684)

25. Ibid., 684.

26. It should be pointed out that van der Leeuw does not attempt to substitute a mere feeling of "sympathetic identification" with a religious phenomenon for the act of comprehension in which its meaning is grasped. For him it is "the

sphere of meaning" that is the third realm, subsisting above mere subjectivity and mere objectivity: "my meaning and its meaning, which have become irrevocably one in the act of comprehension." *Religion in Essence and Manifestation*, 673.

27. Ibid., 674.

28. Van der Leeuw, "Confession Scientifique," 10, quoted in Eric J. Sharpe, *Comparative Religion: A History* (London: Duckworth, 1986), 231. In this respect, van der Leeuw departed from the earlier "descriptive phenomenology" of Chantepie de la Saussaye. For the history of the phenomenology of religion, see Sharpe, *Comparative Religion*, chap. 10.

29. Eliade, *The Two and the One*, 12.

30. Kristensen, *The Meaning of Religion*, 6. See also 10, where Kristensen is clear that this kind of insight does not and should not require a literal reexperiencing of the religious experiences of, say, an ancient Egyptian, still less a reenactment or revival of ancient Egyptian religious forms. The aim of the historian of religion is to understand, not to revive, the religions of the past.

31. Thus for Bleeker, *The Sacred Bridge*, 12, in the phenomenology of religion, direct access to sources provides the necessary "control" on wild speculation. See also Smart, *The Science of Religion and the Sociology of Knowledge*, 3, where he seeks to "deal with religion scientifically and, at the same time, warmly." In *Concept and Empathy* (London: Macmillan, 1986), 218f., Smart uses phrases such as "structured empathy" and "evocative dispassion" to try to express the two sides of the phenomenological approach. More recently, Versluis, "What is Esoteric?" 4, has used the phrase "sympathetic empiricism" to express the same idea. He writes:

> Sympathetic empiricism means that one seeks, as much as possible, to enter into and understand the phenomenon one is studying from the inside out. The further removed historically that one is from such a religious phenomenon, the more valuable historiography is in recreating context, but without a sympathetic approach . . . misunderstanding and reductionism become inevitable. (30)

32. See Hall, "Methodological Reflections" in T. William Hall, ed., *Introduction to the Study of Religion* (New York: Harper and Row, 1978), 255.

33. Van der Leeuw, *Religion in Essence and Manifestation*, 677.

34. Ibid. See also Pettazoni, "The Supreme Being: Phenomenological Structure and Historical Development," in *The History of Religions: Essays in Methodology*, eds. Eliade and Kitagawa (Chicago: University of Chicago Press, 1959), 66.

35. Gadamer, *Truth and Method*, 2nd ed. (London: Sheed and Ward, 1989), 305.

36. The conditioning factors or "forms of mediation" that are said to stand in the way of direct, unmediated knowledge have been listed in Rothberg,

"Contemporary Epistemology and the Study of Mysticism," in *The Problem of Pure Consciousness*, ed. Robert K. C. Forman (Oxford: Oxford University Press, 1990), 171–73. They include sociohistorical conditions, economic and political relations, gender politics, linguistic traditions, emotions, passions, unconscious motivations, libidinal drives, traumas, and complexes.

37. This view goes back to Kant's *Critique of Pure Reason*, where in A.104, for example, we read: "Appearances are themselves nothing but sensible representations, which, as such and in themselves must not be taken as objects capable of existing outside our power of representation" (trans. Norman Kemp Smith [London: Macmillan, 1933]). In the twentieth century, it was reformulated by Karl Popper. See, for example, K. Popper, *Objective Knowledge* (Oxford: Oxford University Press, 1972), 342.

38. Gadamer, *Philosophical Hermeneutics* (Berkeley and Los Angeles: University of California Press, 1977), 6.

39. Proudfoot, *Religious Experience*, 64.

40. Strenski, *Religion in Relation* (Basingstoke: Macmillan, 1993), 40.

41. For the contextualist argument, see Steven Katz, "Language, Epistemology and Mysticism," in *Mysticism and Philosophical Analysis*, ed. Steven Katz (New York: Oxford University Press, 1978). It is also put forward in Proudfoot, *Religious Experience*. It is criticized in *The Problem of Pure Consciousness*, ed. R. Forman. For a concise summary of the constructivist argument and its rebuttal, see Forman, ed., *The Innate Capacity* (Oxford: Oxford University Press, 1998), intro.

42. Proudfoot, *Religious Experience*, 35. See also Katz, "Language, Epistemology and Mysticism," 46.

43. Proudfoot, *Religious Experience*, 196–97 and 201. See also 223, where Proudfoot clearly states that a historical or cultural explanation for religious experience is preferable to a religious explanation.

44. This is the approach taken, for instance, in Griffiths, *The Conflict of Horus and Seth from Egyptian and Classical Sources* (Liverpool: Liverpool University Press, 1960), 16f. and 39f., and in W. B. Emery, *Archaic Egypt* (Harmondsworth: Penguin, 1961), 119. Griffiths and Emery are criticized in te Velde, *Seth: God of Confusion*, 74–80, for failing to explain why a supposed historical record came to function as a religious myth. Te Velde's is one of the best critiques of this kind of "explanatory reductionism" so often met with in Egyptology.

45. Flood, *Beyond Phenomenology*, 7. For Flood, "The shift to the sign deprivileges consciousness, experience and inner states, and places religion squarely within culture and history, that is, within narrative" (118).

46. Ibid., 148 and 111.

47. Ibid., 72.

48. Ibid., 152.

49. See Henri Bortoft, *The Wholeness of Nature: Goethe's Way of Science* (Edinburgh: Floris Books, 1996), part 3, chap. 6.

50. Ibid., 307. The idea of "intensification" *(Steigerung)* was crucially important for Goethe. Only through the willingness to intensify one's observation of, or "living with," the phenomena is it possible to pass through the hypotheses, theories, and judgments and to gain a direct awareness of what is there at a deeper level. See especially Heinemann, "Goethe's Phenomenological Method," 73. What is there at a deeper level is the *Urphänomen*, which, in the case of religious phenomena, would be the originating religious experience that the phenomenologist endeavors to recapture or "reexperience."

51. Proudfoot, *Religious Experience*, 222 f.

52. Ibid., 222.

53. Eliade, *The Quest*, 2, writes: "The scholar has not finished his work when he has reconstructed the history of a religious form or brought out its sociological, economic, or political contexts. In addition, he must understand its meaning—that is, identify and elucidate the situations and positions that have induced or made possible its appearance."

54. Goethe recognized this as crucial to the development of a nonreductionist "delicate empiricism": "There is a delicate empiricism which makes itself utterly identical with the object, thereby becoming true theory. But this enhancement of our mental powers belongs to a highly evolved age." Quoted in Naydler, *Goethe on Science*, 72.

55. See Frederick Amrine, "Goethe's Science in the Twentieth Century," in *Goethe in the Twentieth Century*, ed. Alexej Ugrinsky (New York: Greenwood Press, 1987), 91, who refers to the need of the Goethean scientist to "restructure his intentional faculty" in order to fully participate in the *Urphänomen*. See n. 50 above.

56. Van der Leeuw, *Religion in Essence and Manifestation*, 672–73. See also Brady, "Goethe's Natural Science: Some Non-Cartesian Meditations," in *Toward a Man-Centred Medical Science*, ed. K. E. Schaeffer et al. (New York: Futura Publishing Co., 1977), 160, for whom it is possible "to come to a point in experience where we are most intimately ourselves—the activity of our own will—and yet are most definitely the other at the same time, since the activity in which we participate is the constitutional structure of the object contemplated."

57. Eliade, *The Quest*, 125. It is revealing that the initiatory comparison has also been made by John Baines, professor of Egyptology at Oxford Universtiy, who compares Egyptologists to initiates in a secret society that has elaborate initiation rituals designed to exclude outsiders. Whereas for Baines, the model of initiation is that of the secret society in which a small elite jealously guard their privileged position, the model of initiation that Eliade uses is a

model in which the consciousness of the novice is altered so that a more meaningful level of reality becomes available. This contrasting use of the analogy of initiation could be seen to illustrate the gulf between the two mind-sets of Egyptology and the phenomenology of religion. See Baines, "Restricted Knowledge, Hierarchy and Decorum," 4 f.

58. Strenski, "Eliade's Theory of Myth and the 'History of Religions,'" in *Four Theories of Myth in Twentieth Century History* (Basingstoke: Macmillan, 1987), 119. A comparable criticism of van der Leeuw is made by Waardenburg in *Reflections on the Study of Religion* (The Hague: Mouton, 1973), 234 f., where van der Leeuw is castigated for seeing the act of understanding as religious or mystical, and "absolutizing" the notion of meaning.

59. Rothberg, "Contemporary Epistemology and the Study of Mysticism," especially 179–86. For Rothberg, the epistemology adopted by contextualists is essentially secular because it rejects the possibility of unmediated experience or knowledge. It thereby implicitly devalues the mystical traditions it studies, regarding them as deluded. See 181 f.

60. Eliade, *Shamanism*, 69–71 and 157 f.; Joan Halifax, *Shaman: The Wounded Healer* (London: Thames and Hudson, 1982), 23 f.

61. For magicians holding high offices of state, see Jacq, *Egyptian Magic*, 12 f. According to Jacq, "Magic was considered to be a primordial activity by the state of Egypt. The books of magic were not written by authors acting on whim, but were rather the work of official institutions" (8). See also Naydler, *Temple of the Cosmos*, 128–32.

62. Frankfort, *Kingship and the Gods*, chap. 4. Also Jacq, *Egyptian Magic*, 8–9.

63. Eliade, *The Two and the One*, 12–13. In *Myths, Dreams and Mysteries*, 14, Eliade writes: "If the discovery of the unconscious has compelled Western man to confront his own individual, secret and larval 'history,' the encounter with non-Western cultures will oblige him to delve very profoundly into the history of the human spirit, and will perhaps persuade him to admit that history as an integral part of his own being."

64. Strenski, "Eliade's Theory of Myth and the 'History of Religions,'" 120.

65. Eliade, *The Quest*, 62.

66. Thus Eliade, *The Quest*, 62, comments: "In the end, the creative hermeneutics changes man; it is more than instruction, it is also a spiritual technique susceptible of modifying the quality of existence itself. This is true above all for the historico-religious hermeneutics."

Chapter 6: The Pyramid of Unas

1. G. Maspero, *Les Inscriptions des pyramides de Saqqarah* (Paris: E. Bouillon, 1884), 3.

2. Herodotus, *Histories*, 2.125. The gullible Herodotus was told by his guide

that the inscriptions merely recorded the amount spent on radishes, onions, and leeks for the laborers. Later Arab travelers such as Ibn Haukal (tenth century A.D.) and Abdel Latif (thirteenth century A.D.) also recorded the existence of inscriptions on the casing stones in their own time. Abdel Latif claimed that the inscriptions, if copied, would fill 10,000 pages. See Fahkry, *The Pyramids*, 101.

3. For the accessibility of the pyramid of Unas, at least into the early Middle Kingdom, and then again possibly during the Saite period (Twenty-sixth Dynasty), see Eyre, *The Cannibal Hymn: A Cultural and Literary Study* (Liverpool: Liverpool University Press, 2002), 12, with n. 6.

4. For the later occurrences of Pyramid Texts, see T. G. Allen, *Occurrences of Pyramid Texts with Cross Indexes of These and Other Mortuary Texts* (Chicago: University of Chicago Press, 1950), 103 ff. For the final appearance of Pyramid Texts at Philae, see Zabkar, "Adaptation of Ancient Egyptian Texts to the Temple Ritual at Philae," in *JEA* 66 (1980): 127–36.

5. Mercer, *The Pyramid Texts*, 1:1.

6. Faulkner, *The Ancient Egyptian Pyramid Texts*, vii.

7. Sethe, *Die Altägyptische Pyramidentexte.*

8. Gardiner, "Horus the Behdetite," in *JEA* 30 (1944): 28, n. 1.

9. On Sokar's gazelle-headed boat, Osiris is "lifted up" and spiritualized by the Horus principle. See utt. 364.

10. "Complete" in the sense that none is missing. However, certain utterances that appear in later pyramids may have been left out of the pyramid of Unas owing to lack of space. See J. P. Allen, "Reading a Pyramid," in *Hommages à Jean Leclant*, 2 vols., ed. Catherine Berger et al. (Cairo: Bibliothéque d'Étude, 1994), 1:7 and 9.

11. It is for this reason that major attempts to interpret the Pyramid Texts, such as those of Spiegel, Altenmüller, Osing, and J. P. Allen, have all focused on the Unas texts.

12. Edwards, *The Pyramids of Egypt*, 175.

13. Petrie, *A History of Egypt*, 5th ed., vol. 1 (London: Methuen, 1903), 82.

14. Ibid., 84.

15. The second boat pit, parallel to the first, was discovered in 1949. See U. Schweitzer, "Archäologischer Bericht aus Ägypten," in *Orientalia* 19 (1950), 120, pl. 1, fig. 2.

16. For the solar interpretation of the two boats, see Cerny, "A Note on the Boat of Cheops," in *JEA* 41 (1955): 79. For the ritual sailing of Amenhotep III, see chap. 7, fig. 7.16.

17. See chap. 4, p. 112 f.

18. Labrousse et al., *Le temple haut du complex funéraire du roi Ounas*. The Sed festival scenes include figs. 5–61, 105, and probably a number of others.

19. Ibid., figs. 67–79.

20. See chap. 4, p. 89 f.

21. Faulkner, "The King and the Star-Religion in the Pyramid Texts," in *JNES* 25 (1966): 155 ff.

22. Spiegel, *Das Auferstehungsritual der Unas-Pyramide*, 95–105 and 251–307. This view has been challenged by Mathieu, "La signification du serdab dans la pyramide d'Ounas," in *Études sur l'Ancien Empire*, 289–302, according to whom the *serdab* represents the House of Osiris, into which the deceased must descend in order to undergo resurrection. See n. 23 below.

23. The *serdab* utterances in the pyramid of Teti are utts. 412–13 on the north wall and utts. 414–21 on the south wall. Mathieu, "La signification du serdab dans la pyramide d'Ounas," 291 ff., has brought together a good deal of textual evidence from a wide range of sources in support of the view that the *serdab* symbolized the House of Osiris, from which we may draw the implication that rites of death and resurrection could have been performed in it. As Mathieu points out (298), the very fact that the *serdab* was not inscribed gives to it an additional "charge," and his suggestion that it played an essential role as a place of regeneration and inner illumination seems intuitively more plausible than Spiegel's idea that it was a statue chamber.

24. Utts. 447–53 on the west walls of Pepi I, Merenre, and Pepi II; also utts. 365–72 on the west gables of Pepi I and Merenre and the west wall of Pepi II.

25. Utts. 447–53.

26. Utts. 624–33, which should be read in reverse order.

27. Utt. 591 and the fragmentary utt. 509. Comparison with the pyramids of Neith, Oudjebten, Apouit, and Ibi is not made here because they have only one chamber.

28. The only reference to the re-membering of Osiris in the pyramid of Unas is on the antechamber south wall (utts. 262 and 267), where it occurs as part of a larger sequence in which the king is united with his *ka*, ascends to the sky, and is suckled by various goddesses.

29. Strictly speaking, the alabaster should be called travertine. Alabaster today is understood to be calcium sulfate, whereas the material employed by the Egyptians and generally referred to as alabaster by Egyptologists is a crystalline and compact form of calcium carbonate. True alabaster and travertine do, however, look very similar to each other. See Lucas, *Ancient Egyptian Materials and Industries*, 4th ed., revised and enlarged by J. R. Harris (London: Edward Arnold, 1962), 59; and Barbara G. Aston et al., "Stone," in *Ancient Egyptian Materials and Technology*, eds. Paul T. Nicholson and Ian Shaw (Cambridge: Cambridge University Press, 2000), 21 f. and 59 f.

30. Schwaller de Lubicz, *Sacred Science*, 102, observes: "[It] is as if this matter were in a state of becoming from a more terrestrial state toward a more subtle, flowing state that could be compared to cream rising to the top of milk. It is curious, in this connection, to note that *ankh uas* (the sap of life) is one of the designations of milk, and that *ankh* (life) sometimes also serves to designate alabaster or some object executed in this material."

31. For the Hatnub quarry, see Schwaller de Lubicz, *Sacred Science*, 102 f.; Aston et al., "Stone," 59. See also Baines and Málek, *Atlas of Ancient Egypt*, 19 and 126. For the use of the phrase to designate the sarcophagus chamber, see Schwaller de Lubicz, *Sacred Science*, 103. The phrase *per neb* was also used. See also R. Wilkinson, *Symbol and Magic in Egyptian Art*, 83 f.

32. Schwaller de Lubicz, *Sacred Science*, 99. The difficulties of this interpretation are illustrated in the fact that where the word *mat* occurs, for example, in BD 27.4, T. G. Allen, *The Book of the Dead* (Chicago: University of Chicago Press, 1974), 38, gives it a quite different shade of meaning by translating it as "to devise." Faulkner, however, in *The Ancient Egyptian Book of the Dead* (London: British Museum Publications, 1985), 53, departs completely from any hint of a connotation of some form of mental activity by translating the same *mat* as "to announce." See also Faulkner, *A Concise Dictionary of Middle Egyptian* (Oxford: Griffith Institute, Ashmolean Museum, 1962), 103 and 104, where *match* is translated "(to) proclaim."

33. R. Wilkinson, *Symbol and Magic in Egyptian Art*, 109.

34. Ibid, 109; Budge, *An Egyptian Hieroglyphic Dictionary*, 2 vols. (1920; reprint, New York: Dover, 1978) 1:522 f.; Faulkner, *A Concise Dictionary of Middle Egyptian*, 181.

35. For larger units and text sequences, see Osing, "Zur Disposition der Pyramidentexte des Unas," in *MDAIK* 42 (1986): 131–44; Englund, "La Lumière et la répartition des textes," in *Hommages à Jean Leclant*, ed. Berger et al. (Cairo: Bibliotheque d'Étude, 1994) 1:170–73; and J. P. Allen, "Reading a Pyramid," 5–24.

36. The Dwat is described as "at the place where Orion is" in utt. 437, §802 and utt. 610, §1717. Since Orion is the principal southern constellation, the Dwat was evidently regarded as having a southern location. Orion was also the stellar manifestation of the god Osiris, the Lord of the Dwat. See Sellers, *The Death of Gods*, 39 f. See also James P. Allen, "The Cosmology of the Pyramid Texts," 21 ff. According to Allen, although the celestial location of the Dwat is at the southeastern rim of the sky, the entrance to the Dwat is at the opposite end of the sky, in the northwest. See also chap. 7, n. 54, in this book.

37. J. P. Allen, "The Cosmology of the Pyramid Texts," 23.

38. Schwaller de Lubicz, *The Temple in Man*, trans. Deborah Lawlor and Robert Lawlor. (Rochester, Vt.: Inner Traditions International, 1977), 44.

39. Sethe, "Die Totenliteratur der alten Ägypter," in *SPAW* 18 (1931): 524.

40. Ibid., 540.

41. W. Barta, *Die Bedeutung der Pyramidentexte* (Berlin: Deutscher Kunstverlag, 1981), 57. See also S. Mercer, *Literary Criticism of the Pyramid Texts* (London: Luzac and Co., 1956), 16.

42. S. Schott, *Bemerkungen zur Ägyptischen Pyramidenkult* (Cairo: Schweizerisches Institut für Ägyptische Bauforschung und Alterumskunde in Kairo, 1950), 149 ff. For Ricke's interpretation of Old Kingdom royal monuments based on Schott's analysis of the relationship between pyramid complexes and Pyramid Texts, see Ricke, *Bemerkungen zur Ägyptishen Baukunst*, 2, and "Der Harmarchistempel des Chefren in Giseh," in *BÄBA* 10 (1970): 1–43.

43. Schott, *Bemerkungen zur Ägyptischen Pyramidenkult*, 149 f. and 223 f. Although Piankoff concurs with Schott regarding the order in which the Pyramid Texts should be read, he does so on quite different grounds. See Piankoff, *The Pyramid of Unas*, 9 ff. with n. 27.

44. Frankfort, "Pyramid Temples and the Religion of the Old Kingdom," in *BO* 10 (1953): 158–60. See also Bonnet, "Ägyptische Baukunst und Pyramiden-kult," in *JNES* 12 (1953): 257–73.

45. Arnold, "Rituale und pyramidentempel," in *MDAIK* 33 (1977): 1–4. For Arnold, 13 f., the pyramid complex served a symbolic rather than a ritual purpose. For a discussion of Arnold's criticism of Ricke and Schott, see Hawass, "The Funerary Establishments," 435–64.

46. Arnold, "Rituale und pyramidentempel," 1–14.

47. Spiegel, "Die religionsgeschichtliche Stellung der Pyramidentexte," in *Orientalia* 22 (1953), 129–57; "Das Auferstehungsritual der Unaspyramide," in *ASAE* 53 (1955): 339–439; *Das Auferstehungsritual der Unas-Pyramide*.

48. Spiegel, *Das Auferstehungsritual*, 21–26 and fig. 2.

49. Ibid., 78–83 and 160–205; 84 f. and 206–17; 95 ff. and 251–84.

50. Thus the last two utterances of the east wall of the entrance corridor (utts. 320 and 321), respectively, identify Unas with Babi in his form of moon god and portray Unas as servant of Ra. Spiegel, *Das Auferstehungsritual*, 107 f. and 329–42.

51. Spiegel, "Die religionsgeschichtliche Stellung," 140 f.

52. Spiegel, *Das Auferstehungsritual*, 34.

53. Barta, *Die Bedeutung der Pyramidentexte*, 21–28. For example, utt. 199 on the north wall of the passage between the chambers is, in the sequence proposed by Spiegel, positioned between the processional entry into the pyramid and the Offering Liturgy on the north wall of the sarcophagus chamber. But in the pyramid of Merenre, this text is located within the sarcophagus chamber on the east wall, and in the pyramid of Pepi II it is on the north wall of the sarcophagus chamber.

54. Barta, *Die Bedeutung der Pyramidentexte*, 21–28, points to the incompatability of Spiegel's interpretative scheme for Unas with other pyramids in the case of utts. 199, 220–22, 245, 263–64, 267, 270, 272, 302 306–7, 309–10, and 318–20.

55. Spiegel, "Die religionsgeschichtliche Stellung der Pyramidentexte," 138.

56. Griffiths, *The Origins of the Osiris Cult*, 223–28, has criticized Spiegel on these grounds. For the importance of the bull sacrifice in the funerary ritual, see Eyre, *The Cannibal Hymn*, chap. 9. Eyre, like Schott before him (Schott, *Bemerkungen zur Ägyptischen Pyramidenkult*, 197–200) regards the Cannibal Hymn (utts. 273–74) as a butchery ritual text. Schott believed this ritual was performed in the pyramid temple. Spiegel interprets the Cannibal Hymn quite differently, as designed magically to empower the *ba* statue (*Das Auferstehungsritual*, 96–99 and 260–71). Nevertheless, explicit references to the slaughter of a bull in the Pyramid Texts include utt. 225 on the north wall of the sarcophagus chamber of the pyramid of Pepi II and utt. 580 on the west wall of the vestibule in the pyramid of Pepi I.

57. As Eyre, *The Cannibal Hymn*, 43, has observed, the attempt to reconstruct the texts as a single ritual sequence making up the burial ritual has the effect of "[forcing] the interpretation of individual units of text into the procrustean bed of a continuous narrative, when the organisation of spells on the wall is a mixture of thematic, ritual and architectural sequences. Moreover, the logic of such treatment is that a separate ritual should be constructed for each pyramid, as the order and content of spells in the royal burial ritual changed from reign to reign."

58. As J. P. Allen has argued, "Reading a Pyramid," 12–28.

59. Altenmüller, *Die Texte zum Begräbnisritual*, 112 ff. The funerary procession sequence comprises utts. 213–22 on the south and east walls of the sarcophagus chamber, utts. 245–46 on the south wall of the passage between the chambers, and utts. 302–12 on the north wall of the antechamber.

60. Ibid., 75 ff. In the offering ritual sequence are included utts. 204–12 on the sarcophagus chamber east gable, utts. 223 and 224 on the east wall of the sarcophagus chamber, and utts. 199 and 32 on the north wall of the passage between the chambers.

61. Utts. 247–58. See Altenmüller, *Die Texte zum Begräbnisritual*, 174 ff.

62. Altenmüller, *Die Texte zum Begräbnisritual*, 193 ff. The ritual for the royal statue is in utts. 260–63 and 267–72 (both on the antechamber south wall) along with utts. 273–76 (on the east gable of the antechamber).

63. Ibid., 212 ff. The protection rites are in utts. 313–21 (entrance corridor) and snake spells 226–43 and 277–301.

64. Barta, *Die Bedeutung der Pyramidentexte*, 32–35. For the discrepancies between the Unas text and the version in the tomb of Senwosret-Ankh, see J. P. Allen, "Reading a Pyramid," 5–12.

65. Fairman, "The Kingship Rituals of Egypt," 94. The later illustrations have been studied in Settgast, *Untersuchungen zu Altägyptischen Bestattungsdarstellungen* (Glückstadt, Hamburg, and New York: J. J. Augustin, 1963), upon which Altenmüller draws.

66. Altenmüller, *Die Texte zum Begräbnisritual*, 159 ff. Altenmüller attempts to support this interpretation by referring to utterance 306 nearby, which describes Unas ascending to the sky and being greeted by the gods and ancestors. In this utterance, the phrase "you shall die because of him" *(mutek en ef)* occurs. According to Altenmüller, 146 f., this is a play on words and in fact relates to the *tekenu*, and so a link is made between these utterances and the phase in the funerary rites when the *tekenu* appears.

67. Ibid., 56 f.

68. Ibid., 140.

69. Utterance 252 appears beside a picture of a priest in the tomb of Rekhmire, but in the tomb of Puimre is not connected with any funerary illustration and is placed on the false door of the north chapel. See Altenmüller, *Die Texte zum Begräbnisritual*, 180.

70. Barta, *Die Bedeutung der Pyramidentexte*, 51.

71. Ibid., 50 ff.

72. Ibid., 52 f.

73. Ibid., 148 ff.

74. Faulkner, *The Ancient Egyptian Pyramid Texts*, v.

75. Faulkner, "The King and the Star-Religion in the Pyramid Texts," in *JNES* 25 (1966): 153–61.

76. Mercer, *The Pyramid Texts*, 1:3.

77. Piankoff, *The Pyramid of Unas*, 11.

78. Ibid., 10, with n. 28.

79. Ibid., 11–12.

80. Ibid., 10, with n. 28.

81. Eyre, *The Cannibal Hymn*, 4–6.

82. Osing, "Zur Disposition der Pyramidentexte des Unas," 143, with n. 40; J. P. Allen, "Reading a Pyramid," 23 f. and 24–28.

83. J. P. Allen, "Reading a Pyramid," 24–28. See also chap. 6, n. 48 of this book. This interpretation is also developed in Englund, "La Lumière et la Répartition des Textes," 171–73.

84. The fact that later pyramids fail consistently to support the symbolic designation of the chambers as conceived by J. P. Allen for the pyramid of Unas is a stumbling block, as is the fact that Piankoff is able to find the Unas texts telling more or less the same story but in the reverse order. See Englund, "La

Lumière et la Répartition des Textes," 179, for a note of caution on the Spiegel-Allen interpretation of the architectural metaphor.

85. The one outstanding contribution to the uncovering of a level of meaning in the Unas texts that is nonfunerary, by attempting to show that the texts belong rather to the shamanic tradition, is the pioneering analysis of a non-Egyptologist, William Fix. See his *Star Maps*, 89–105.

86. Here the approach of the present study differs from that recently pursued by Eyre, *The Cannibal Hymn*, for whom the explication of the ritual or performative frame of reference of a given text is seen as tantamount to explaining its meaning. Its existential significance is thereby overlooked. See *The Cannibal Hymn*, 47–50, 54 ff., and 148.

Chapter 7: The Sarcophagus Chamber Texts

1. The use of offering lists goes as far back as the Archaic Period. See Barta, *Die altägyptische Opferliste*, MÄS 3 (Berlin: Verlag Bruno Hessling, 1963), 5 ff.; Budge, *The Liturgy of Funerary Offerings* (1909; reprint, New York: Dover, 1994), 7.

2. Barta, *Die altägyptische Opferliste*, 78; Budge, *The Liturgy of Funerary Offerings*, 40–41. Of the Sixth Dynasty pyramids, the north-wall texts of Teti and Merenre are almost completely lost. The north wall of Pepi I is damaged but the catalog of offerings making up the great feast is present (utts. 108–71). Pepi II's north wall contains the complete liturgy of Unas's north wall plus the additional offering texts of utts. 172–92. This is also the case with that of his queen Neith, and probably his other two queens, Apouit and Oudjebten, whose north walls are badly damaged. Iby's north wall also contains the complete set of Unas texts with the additional utts. 108–98. J. P. Allen, "Reading a Pyramid," 9, has suggested that the additional utterances (utts. 172–98) were left out of the Unas sequence because of lack of space. They would all fall under part 5 of the liturgy. The liturgy was subsequently used through every period to the end of ancient Egyptian history. See Barta, *Die altägyptische Opferliste*, 82–154; Budge, *The Liturgy of Funerary Offerings*, 15 and 37–41.

3. Budge, *The Liturgy of Funerary Offerings*, 43 f. A purification ritual of this type is known to have been performed on the king just before "the secret rites" during the Sed festival. See above, chap. 3, p. 72, with fig. 3.2.

4. This is reflected in the Egyptian word for incense, *senetcher*, which is related to the verb *senetcheri*, meaning "to make divine." See R. Wilkinson, *Symbol and Magic in Egyptian Art*, 93.

5. Frankfort, *Kingship and the Gods*, 130–32.

6. Mercer, *The Pyramid Texts*, 2:19. See also Roth, "The *pss-kf* and the 'Opening of the Mouth' Ceremony: A Ritual of Birth and Rebirth," 118–20, for this sequence of purificatory offerings as symbolizing the process of birth.

7. J. P. Allen, "Reading a Pyramid," 12, believes that utts. 32 and 43 conclude the Opening of the Mouth sequence, but if utt. 32 is seen as a transitional ritual, it makes more sense to see it and utt. 43 as opening the next phase of the ceremonies.

8. Van Walsem, "The *pss-kf*: An Investigation of an Ancient Egyptian Funerary Instrument," in *OMRO* 59 (1978–79): 203f; Roth, "The *pss-kf* and the 'Opening of the Mouth' Ceremony: A Ritual of Birth and Rebirth," 116.

9. For Seth as demonic initiator, see te Velde, *Seth: God of Confusion*, 98. See also Roth, "The *pss-kf* and the 'Opening of the Mouth' Ceremony: A Ritual of Birth and Rebirth," 138–40. For the use of the *peseshkef* in midwifery, and for its rebirth symbolism, see 23 and 127.

10. Utt. 21, §14 (trans. Faulkner).

11. An "opener of the mouth" along with a *sem* priest were present immediately before the "secret rites." See Uphill, "The Egyptian Sed-Festival Rites," 377f.

12. Bell, "Luxor Temple and the Cult of the Royal Ka," in *JNES* 44 (1985): 251–94.

13. Uphill, "The Egyptian Sed-Festival Rites," 379–80. See also chap. 4, p. 114f.

14. Eliade has noted that in the later Hellenistic age, the mystery cult of the Phrygian Great Mother involved the burial of the *mystes* in a tomb, which was followed by a spiritual rebirth. Sallustius records that the new initiates "received nourishment of milk as if they were being reborn." Since the Phrygian ceremonies involved ritual lament, nocturnal rites, and so on, and were based on a dismemberment myth, they must surely owe much to an original Egyptian prototype. See Eliade, *Rites and Symbols of Initiation*, 112; Burkert, *Ancient Mystery Cults*, 75; Marvin Meyer, ed., *The Ancient Mysteries* (San Francisco: Harper and Row, 1987), 131f.

15. According to Roth, "The *pss-kf* and the 'Opening of the Mouth' Ceremony: A Ritual of Birth and Rebirth," 121, the sequence of the ritual represents the weaning and teething of a child.

16. Helck, "Bemerkungen zum Ritual des Dramatischen Ramesseumpapyrus," 383–441.

17. Uphill, "The Egyptian Sed-Festival Rites," 377.

18. Ibid., 373 and 377.

19. Utts. 57–71.

20. Uphill, "The Egyptian Sed-Festival Rites," 379–80, where utts. 57–71 are directly related to the Sed festival.

21. Clark, *Myth and Symbol in Ancient Egypt*, 224–25. The myth is explained in CT 335 and BD 17. See also te Velde, *Seth: God of Confusion*, 48, who points out that Thoth does not simply return the universe to an original state of

perfection, but designs "a new image of reality, which takes account of the existence of Seth."

22. See chap. 3, p. 78, with fig. 3.8.

23. We know their ingredients during the Ptolemaic period from an inscription in the temple of Horus at Edfu, translated in Lise Manniche, *Sacred Luxuries: Aromatherapy and Cosmetics in Ancient Egypt* (Ithaca: Cornell University Press, 1999), 108.

24. Mercer, *The Pyramid Texts* 1:35ff; R. Wilkinson, *Reading Egyptian Art*, 175. See also n. 25 below.

25. This can be seen particularly clearly in the sequence of utterances in the pyramid of Teti. On the south wall of the passage to the *serdab* in Teti's pyramid, the "clothing" of the king with the Eye of Horus through the presentation of garments (utts. 414 and 416) immediately follows a "resurrection" spell (utt. 413) and is accompanied by invocations to Tayet, goddess of woven cloth, to guard the king, who is still vulnerable to the danger of falling apart again (utts. 415 and 417). A similar sequence occurs on the sarcophagus chamber south and east wall of the pyramid of Pepi II (utts. 447–53).

These sequences parallel the resurrection rites described in the Ramesseum Dramatic Papyrus, and were clearly the prototype of what is described in the Book of What Is in the Underworld, divs. 8 and 9. Here the theme of "putting on cloth" is directly associated with resurrection from the sarcophagus. Twelve recently resurrected gods are addressed by Ra as follows (in the translation of Piankoff, *The Tomb of Ramesses VI*, 295): "You are provided with your cloth, your glory is in your garments. Horus has clothed you there as he did his father in the Dwat."

26. Uphill, "The Egyptian Sed-Festival Rites," 379. For the clothing ritual in the Ramesseum Dramatic Papyrus, see chap. 3, p. 70. See also Frankfort, *Kingship and the Gods*, 137.

27. Frankfort, *Kingship and the Gods*, 133.

28. Uphill, "The Egyptian Sed-Festival Rites," 369, n. 9.

29. Ibid.

30. This took place on the tenth day of the festival. See Frankfort, *Kingship and the Gods*, 319–29.

31. Utt. 223 (trans. Faulkner). J. P. Allen, "Reading a Pyramid," 12, has argued that this utterance and utt. 224, both of which are adjacent to the north wall, belong to the north-wall Liturgy of Offerings, whereas the rest of the east-wall utterances belong to the south-to-east-wall sequence. Certainly utts. 223 and 224 do relate closely to the north-wall liturgy, but they can also be understood as concluding the south-to-east-wall sequence (see p. 217f.). They could be regarded therefore as linking the latter sequence with the north-wall liturgy.

32. See chap. 4, p. 110, with n. 75.

33. While J. P. Allen, "Reading a Pyramid," 16, may be right to include utts. 217 and 218 as spoken by the king, the fact remains that we only can be certain that utt. 216 was spoken by the king because it alone uses the first person.

34. Ibid., "Reading a Pyramid," 11.

35. This is the case with the pyramids of Teti, Pepi I, Pepi II, Queen Neith, and Iby. See ibid., 11, n. 10.

36. Utt. 213, §134.

37. See chap. 3, p. 64.

38. See, for example, Plato, *Phaedrus*, 245-47; Plotinus, *Enneads*, 6.9.11, trans. S. MacKenna (London: Faber and Faber, 1956); *Corpus Hermeticum*, 10.19 and 13.3. See also the Hermetic "Discourse on the Eighth and the Ninth," 292–97.

39. Eliade, *Shamanism*, 479 (italics in original).

40. Utt. 213, §135.

41. Literally, the sentence reads: "You have encircled [*pekher*] the mounds of Horus, you have gone round [*deben*] the mounds of Seth." For the realms of Horus and Seth, see te Velde, *Seth: God of Confusion*, 60 f.

42. For the magical significance of "encircling," see Ritner, *The Mechanics of Ancient Egyptian Magical Practice*, 5–67. For the ritual of "encircling" during the Sed festival, see also 58 f. with n. 271.

43. Utt. 214, §137.

44. Halifax, *Shaman: The Wounded Healer*, 23–24, has noted that

> For the Buryats of Siberia, the eagle is the prototype of the shaman. The Gilyaks of Siberia have the same word for eagle and shaman. The Yenissei Ostyaks believe that the first shaman was a two-headed eagle. The Teleuts say that the eagle is a shaman-bird, because it assists the shaman in his or her celestial ascent. Some Siberian peoples directly associate the eagle with the Supreme Being and the Creator of Light. . . . In some Siberian tales, the first shaman is the eagle or Sun Bird. The shaman's transformation via fire allows for a parallel transformation of neophyte shaman into soaring bird—Sun Bird—and return to source—the sun or Sun Father."

See also Eliade, *Shamanism*, 69–71 and 157 f.

45. Interestingly, the bones of the king are transformed into those of falcon goddesses. This is perhaps because the feminine principle is the necessary medium of the king's celestial rebirth.

46. Utt. 214, §139.

47. Utt. 215, §140. For the reconciliation of Horus and Seth as a *coincidentia oppositorum*, see te Velde, *Seth: God of Confusion*, 69. For a discussion of the motif of the reconciliation of opposing principles in Egyptian religion from

a Jungian perspective, see Michael Rice, *Egypt's Legacy* (London: Routledge, 1997), 35 f.

48. This is made explicit at the end of the utterance (§149), where it is said of Unas: "You do not perish, your *ka* does not perish, you are *ka*."

49. G. A. Wainwright, *The Sky-Religion in Egypt*, 20–24. According to te Velde, *Seth: God of Confusion*, 72, "It is the co-operation of both gods in the king which guarantees the welfare of the world."

50. Utt. 215, §145.

51. Utt. 216, §150.

52. The Epigraphic Survey, *The Tomb of Kheruef*, 43, pl. 24. See also Johnson, "Amenhotep III and Armana," 67.

53. For shamanic parallels of travel into the spirit world by means of a boat, see Eliade, *Shamanism*, 355–58, and P. Vitebsky, *The Shaman* (London: Macmillan, 1995), 44 and 71 f.

54. Utt. 216, §151. For the identification of the constellation Orion with the Dwat, see utt. 437 (§802) and its variant, utt. 610 (§1717); §151 is usually interpreted as referring to the fading of the southern stars at dawn. However, the context is clearly stated at the beginning of the utterance as being that of the sun's descent in the night boat—i.e., at dusk, not dawn. What Unas is experiencing is an envelopment by the Dwat, separate from, yet paralleling, the descent of the sun god into the Dwat. Compare utt. 466, in which the king sails with Orion in the Dwat through the night. See also chap. 6, n. 36 above.

55. J. P. Allen, "The Cosmology of the Pyramid Texts," 19–20, writes: "The *Akhet* is the place in which the king, like the sun and other celestial beings, undergoes the final transformation from the inertness of death and night to the form that allows him to live effectively—that is, as an *akh*—in his new world. It is for this reason that the king and his celestial companions are said to 'rise from the *Akhet*,' and not because the *Akhet* is a place on the horizon or—as some have suggested—because it is a place of light." See also Jacq, *La tradition primordiale*, chap. 9.

56. Utt. 216, §151.

57. Assmann, "Death and Initiation," 142, n. 41. Assmann's translation of the text reads:

> He opened the door-leaves of heaven / and unfolded the gates of his horizon (*akhet*). / I rose to heaven as a divine falcon / and saw his secret image in heaven. . . . / Re himself established me / by distinguishing me with the crowns on his head, / his Uraeus remaining at my forehead./ I was furnished with his *akh*-power / and acquainted with the wisdom of the gods.

See also Roberts, *My Heart, My Mother*, 242, n. 5.

58. For the role of the king as solar priest, see Assmann, *Egyptian Solar Religion*,

17 ff.; also Quirke, *The Cult of Ra*, 20. A treatise concerning the king's role as solar priest is preserved in certain Theban temples, and documents the king's knowledge of the secrets concerning Ra's birth in the eastern Akhet. There can be no shadow of a doubt that this knowledge was possessed by the living king. See Quirke, *The Cult of Ra*, 53, who comments: "These lines ascribe the secrets quite explicitly to the king: the secrets themselves define kingship, and make the king something more divine, more solar, than human."

59. Utt. 217, §152.

60. For the shamanic sources of solarization as an initiatory experience, see Eliade, *Patterns in Comparative Religion*, 135–38 and 147–51. See also Halifax, *Shaman: The Wounded Healer*, 90 f.

61. Utt. 218, §164–66. The fact that the transformation of the king into an *akh* in the Akhet features so prominently here on the south wall of the sarcophagus chamber must make us cautious with respect to blanket interpretations of the sarcophagus chamber as representing the Dwat and the antechamber the Akhet (with the passage between the chambers symbolizing the doorway between these two regions). This interpretation, first put forward by Spiegel in the 1950s, has more recently been championed by J. P. Allen, "Reading a Pyramid," 24. For a summary of Spiegel's argument, see Fairman, "The Kingship Rituals of Egypt," 95 ff. See also n. 99 below.

62. Faulkner, *The Ancient Egyptian Pyramid Texts*, 48, n. 2. Faulkner translates *nunet* as "the City," in the absence of the determinative for "lower Sky," on the assumption that it is the city where Osiris is buried. The play on words is no doubt deliberate. According to Mercer, *The Pyramid Texts*, 2:89, Nunet is possibly interchangeable with Nut. For the identification of Nut with the sarcophagus as opposed to the tomb, see James P. Allen, "Reading a Pyramid," 25, with fig. 5, 24.

63. Utt. 219, §167 (trans. Faulkner, adapted. See n. 64 below).

64. For this interpretation, see Fix, *Star Maps*, 93 ff. The word *nehep* is translated by Sethe, Mercer, and Piankoff as "to judge." Faulkner is alone in translating it as "to mourn," which, although it alters the meaning, does not substantially undermine the interpretation suggested here—namely, that the king is not dead.

65. Utt. 215, §145.

66. Utt. 264, §350.

67. Mercer, *The Pyramid Texts*, 2:92–93, believes the text to be very ancient, probably predynastic, and to refer to the crowning of the king in Buto in Lower Egypt. Hence, the crown is identified with the cobra goddess of Buto—Wadjet. For the coronation ceremony, see Frankfort, *Kingship and the Gods*, 107 ff.

68. Utt. 221, §197. Note that the sphere of the king's rule is over both the living (*ankhu*) and the "spirits" (*akhu*), i.e., the dead. See p. 219 and n. 85 below.

69. Utt. 221, §198.

70. Frankfort, *Kingship and the Gods*, 108. Mercer, *The Pyramid Texts*, 2:95, regards utt. 222 as an old Heliopolitan text concerned with the coronation of the king in Heliopolis, which has been "worked over to serve as a mortuary, and especially ascension text. . . . In other words, from the beginning of the text to §206c we have to do with the living king, and in the second part with the deceased king accompanying the sun-god in heaven and the underworld." This is a view Mercer shares with Sethe. The initiatory implications of the utterance are thus overlooked, but are virtually unmissable to anyone who is open to the possibility of an initiatory understanding of what is described.

71. Utt. 222, §199.

72. Ibid. (trans. Faulkner).

73. Utt. 222, §200–202.

74. Utt. 222, §207.

75. §209–10 (trans. Faulkner, slightly adapted). The mystical union with Ra is strongly confirmed in utt. 407 (on the east walls of the sarcophagus chambers of Pepi I, Merenre, and Pepi II), where the king asumes his "pure throne in the sky" in the boat of the sun god and is conveyed with Ra "round about the Akhet."

76. See chap. 4, p. 120f. and chap. 4, nn. 99–101.

77. Eliade, *Shamanism*, 289ff. and 407ff. See also Eliade, *Patterns in Comparative Religion*, 104–8.

78. Utt. 223, §214–16 (trans. Faulkner). The word *tomb* in §216 translates *is*.

79. Utt. 223, §214.

80. Utt. 224, §218 (trans. Faulkner).

81. Utt. 224, §221 (trans. Piankoff). The reference to the "border" (Piankoff) or "boundary" (Faulkner) is possibly to the soul's experience of severe restriction when it reenters the physical body.

82. The word is *wenekh*, which can mean "to clothe," "to put on," or "to assume." In this passage it is written without the cloth determinative, so strictly speaking, "to put on" is more accurate. The choice of the verb "to clothe" is, however, supported by the variant of the utterance in the pyramid of Pepi II (utt. 225), in which the king puts on two garments plus sandals. For the Hermetic doctrine of the physical body as a "garment" or "cloak" that the soul wraps itself in, see *Corpus Hermeticum* 7.2 and 10.16.

83. According to Bleeker, *Egyptian Festivals*, 120, the Sed festival was "a festival of clothing," or reinvestiture, and the root meaning of *sed* is "cloth." For the meaning of the word *sed*, see chap. 3, n. 84, above. For the initiatory significance of ritual clothing, see Mayassis, *Mystères et initiations*, 400ff. For the purple cloth worn by the king following his identification with the awakened

Osiris during the ritual described in the Ramesseum Dramatic Papyrus, see chap. 3, p. 70.

84. Utt. 225, §223. This occurs on Pepi II's sarcophagus chamber north wall.

85. Utt. 224, §220. The reading of "spirits" as "the dead" is confirmed in the next phrase, "like Anubis, at the head of the Westerners."

86. These generally continue the broad themes of the king's coronation as a Horus, his mystical union with Ra, his recall to the body, and his partaking of a banquet. In some of the pyramids, special emphasis is placed on the triumph of Horus over Seth and the resurrection of Osiris, themes that figure prominently in the Ramesseum Dramatic Papyrus, and hence were probably ritually enacted. See, for example, utt. 357, which occurs on the east walls of Teti and Pepi II and the east gable of Merenre. See also utts. 404 and 602, both on the east wall of the sarcophagus chambers of Merenre, Pepi II, and Iby. See also n. 75 above and appendix 2.

87. This is located at the north ends of the east walls of both Merenre and Teti's sarcophagus chamber, in a position similar to that in which it is placed in the pyramid of Unas. While it is not on the east wall of Pepi II and Neith's sarcophagus chamber, it is at least at the east end of the north wall. Since the theme of the utterance is the resurrection and rebirth of the king, it is only right that it be associated with the east. Note that J. P. Allen, "Reading a Pyramid," 14, regards utts. 223 and 224 as belonging to the Offering Liturgy. He sees utt. 223 as a "general food offering" and utt. 224 as a "general offering of clothing and insignia." He thereby overlooks their mystical significance.

88. Piankoff, *The Pyramid of Unas*, 55. See also Ritner, *The Mechanics of Ancient Egyptian Magical Practice*, 144 f. and 147 f.

89. Ritner, *The Mechanics of Ancient Egyptian Magical Practice*, 149, quotes CT 425 in which the smashing of water pots is connected with a path being opened "to the place where the great god is."

90. Utt. 245 (trans. Faulkner, slightly adapted).

91. Mercer, *The Pyramid Texts*, 2:115. The explicit identification of the king with Sia occurs in the antechamber, on the west gable immediately above the entrance passage.

92. For the offering ceremony to Min in the Sed festival reliefs of Niuserre's sun temple, see Kaiser, "Die Kleine Hebseddarstellung im Sonnenheiligtum des Neuserre," Falttafel 4, fourth row. For a similar ceremony in Amenhotep III's Sed festival, see Gohary, *Akhenaten's Sed-festival at Karnak*, 15. Min's role as witness to the dedication of the field rite can be seen in the reliefs of Hatshepsut's Sed festival at Karnak, of which fig. 7.23 is one example.

93. For the association of the Sed festival and the harvest festival of Min, see Jéquier, *Le monument funéraire de Pepi II*, vol. 2, pl. 12, where the festival of Min and the Sed festival dedication of the field rite are shown next to each other.

94. Roberts, *Hathor Rising*, 82. See also Frankfort, *Kingship and the Gods*, 188.

95. Utt. 246, §256.

96. Utt. 25, §18.

97. Fairman, "The Kingship Rituals of Egypt," 99 with n. 3. Bell, "The New Kingdom Divine Temple," in *Temples of Ancient Egypt*, ed. Byron E. Shafer (Ithaca: Cornell University Press, 1997), 140, puts it as follows: "The royal *ka* was the immortal creative spirit of divine kingship, a form of the Creator's collective *ka*. The *ka* of a particular king was but a specific instance, or fragment, of the royal *ka*."

98. For the "incense rite," see Bell, "Luxor Temple and the Cult of the Royal Ka," 283–85.

99. J. P. Allen, "Reading a Pyramid," 11. According to Allen (who follows the earlier interpretation of Spiegel), the passage between the two chambers represents the threshold between the two cosmological regions of the Dwat (symbolized by the sarcophagus chamber) and the Akhet (symbolized by the antechamber). Allen's thesis, while appealing, does not seem to be borne out by the texts on the walls of the chambers. The Akhet is referred to many times in the sarcophagus chamber, just as the Dwat is referred to in the antechamber, and the theme of the king's resurrection and celestial ascent belongs as much to the sarcophagus chamber as it does to the antechamber. See Allen, "Reading a Pyramid," 24–28. See also chap. 7, n. 61.

100. Ibid., 9. Allen bases this assessment on comparison with the Middle Kingdom tomb of Senwosret-Ankh. Comparison with later pyramids shows that utts. 210–12 appear on the east gable of the pyramids of Teti and Pepi II and the east wall of Merenre. The orientation to the east was evidently felt by Merenre to be a more important factor than their height in the pyramid.

101. The full east-gable sequence reappears in the Eighteenth Dynasty Book of the Dead papyrus of Nebseni (BM 9900) as BD 178b–h in T. G. Allen, *The Book of the Dead*, 186–87. Some of the west gable of the antechamber is also incorporated in BD 178: namely, utt. 249, §266 (BD 178t); utt. 251, §269 (BD 178s); and utt. 252, §272 (BD 178u), suggesting that certain elements of the two sequences were regarded as belonging together in the New Kingdom. See T. G. Allen, *Occurrences of Pyramid Texts*, 103.

102. Schwaller de Lubicz, *The Temple in Man*, 44. "Transposition" is to be distinguished from a similar concept that de Lubicz termed "transparency," in which an image on one side of the wall is deliberately left incomplete and "completed" by an image on the other side of the wall occupying exactly the same position, so that one needs to "look through the wall" in order to see the whole picture.

103. Piankoff, *The Pyramid of Unas*, 72.

104. Mercer, *The Pyramid Texts*, 2:63.

105. Utt. 205, §122 (trans. Piankoff).

106. Thus, for example, in utt. 306, §476, it is significant that as the king ascends to the sky, the gods exclaim, "How lovely to see! how pleasing to behold!" And in utt. 311, §495, Unas prays to Ra, "See me O Ra; recognize me, O Ra. I belong to those that know you, so know me." See also utt. 262 for the importance of being known by the gods.

107. Joseph Campbell, *The Masks of God: Primitive Mythology* (Harmondsworth: Penguin Books, 1976), 265, quotes an eyewitness account of Yakut shamans turning into bulls. The witness recalls that "the shamans bellowed during the seance like bulls. And there would grow on their heads pure, opaque horns. I once saw such a thing myself. There used to live in our village a shaman whose name was Konnor. When his older sister died, he shamanized. When he did so, horns grew on his head. He stirred up the dry clay floor with them and ran about on all fours . . . and bellowed like a bull."

108. Eliade, *Shamanism*, 460.

109. For Kenzet as having an otherworldly location, see utt. 210, §126; utt. 471, §920; utt. 510, §1141; utt. 525, §1245; and utt. 578, §1541. Kenzet probably referred originally to the cataract region near Aswan, where the Nile was thought to emerge from the Dwat. At this entrance to the Dwat, the dead would undergo purification. According to Mercer, Kenzet represents the eastern part of heaven. See Frankfort, *Kingship and the Gods*, 374, n. 13, and Mercer, *The Pyramid Texts*, 2:64.

110. Utt. 205, §123.

111. Eliade, *Shamanism*, 75.

112. Ibid., 77. For a discussion of shamanic spirit marriages, see Lewis, *Ecstatic Religion*, 57–64; also Kalweit, *Dreamtime and Inner Space*, chap. 11.

113. Piankoff, *The Pyramid of Unas*, 73, sees her as the "personified West," i.e., a form of Nut or Hathor. In utt. 366, §632, the celestial wife of the king is Isis (as Sothis or Sirius), and his sexual relations with her cause a celestial Horus (Horus-Soped) to be born.

114. Utt. 209, §125.

115. Gardiner, *Egyptian Grammar*, 588; Faulkner, *A Concise Dictionary of Middle Egyptian*, 208.

116. Hornung, *Conceptions of God*, 213 f.; Meeks and Favard-Meeks, *Daily Life of the Egyptian Gods* (London: Pimlico, 1999), 66; Naydler, *Temple of the Cosmos*, 93 f.

117. Utt. 207, §124. See Budge, *The Gods of the Egyptians*, 2 vols. (1904; reprint, New York: Dover, 1969), 1:418.

118. Jacq, *Egyptian Magic*, 41 and 118; Hornung, "The Discovery of the Unconscious in Ancient Egypt," in *Spring* (1986), 22 f.; Naydler, *Temple of the Cosmos*, 221 ff.

119. See, for example, Eliade, *Shamanism*, 205, who writes: "The peoples of North Asia conceive the otherworld as an inverted image of this world. Everything takes place as it does here, but in reverse. . . . In the Underworld rivers flow backward to their sources. And everything that is inverted on earth is in its normal position among the dead. . . ." See also Kalweit, *Dreamtime and Inner Space*, 59.

120. Utt. 210, §128–29 (trans. Faulkner).

121. See chap. 7, p. 191 f., with n. 13.

122. Utt. 211, §131–32 (trans. Faulkner).

123. *Corpus Hermeticum*, 10.7, 13.10, and 13; "The Discourse on the Eighth and the Ninth," 57 f. It also has parallels in the shamanic tradition, for which see Vitebsky, *The Shaman*, 66.

124. Utt. 211, §132.

125. According to the Coffin Texts, when Atum emerged from the waters of the Nun, Nun admonished him to "eat of your daughter Maat." CT 80, §35. See also Breasted, *Ancient Records*, 2.299, where Maat is described as the "bread" on which Ra lives. See also n. 116 above.

126. This was one of the king's primary functions. See Jacq, *La tradition primordiale*, chap. 2; Frankfort, *Kingship and the Gods*, 54 ff.; and Quirke, *The Cult of Ra*, 20.

127. Utt. 212, §133 (trans. Faulkner). The utterance is a little ambiguous, for it is not explicitly stated who "he" is, though the sense of it does seem to be that "he" is Horus, nourished by Osiris as he was in utt. 204. That this is the case may be gleaned by comparison with utt. 400, which begins in the same way, but in which the "Foremost of the Westerners" is replaced by the "two Horuses." In this utterance it is the two Horuses who are providing the king with food, and hence the king can be assumed to be Osiris. It follows, therefore, that in utt. 212, where Osiris (as Foremost of the Westerners) is in exactly the same position as the two Horuses, the reverse will hold, i.e., the king is Horus.

Chapter 8: The Antechamber Texts

1. Utt. 247, §259–60.

2. Utt. 211, §132.

3. Hart, *Dictionary of Egyptian Gods and Goddesses*, 198.

4. As in the Niuserre reliefs. For the lion-bed motif, see chap. 3, pp. 75–78 and figs. 3.5 to 3.10. Sekhmet was immensely significant in the Sed festival rites of Amenhotep III, for which literally hundreds of statues of the goddess were made. See B. M. Bryan, "The Statue for the Mortuary Temple of Amenhotep III," in *The Temple in Ancient Egypt*, ed. Stephen Quirke (London: British

Museum Press, 1997), 60. It is also interesting to note the presence of the leonine goddess Bastet just before "the secret rites" during the Sed festival of Osorkon. She is depicted twice facing the king, once while he sits enthroned and once while he walks toward the tomb wearing the long Osirian cloak. The latter figure is reproduced below.

5. Utt. 249, §266. For Nefertem, see Mercer, *The Pyramid Texts*, 2:124. Also Hart, *Dictionary of Egyptian Gods and Goddesses*, 130.

6. Hart, *A Dictionary of Egyptian Gods and Goddesses*, 201. Also Quirke, *Ancient Egyptian Religion*, 46. For the Memphite theology, see Lichtheim, *Ancient Egyptian Literature*, 1:51–57. For an excellent account of the Memphite theology, see Roberts, *My Heart, My Mother*, 14–20. For the affinities between Sia and Thoth, see Mercer, *The Pyramid Texts*, 2:124.

7. Utt. 205, §121.

8. Utt. 252, §274 (trans. Faulkner).

9. See chap. 7, p. 206, and fig. 7.16.

10. As Wente and van Siclen have noted in their study "A Chronology of the New Kingdom," 221, "A culminating point in the traditional Sed-festival was the apotheosis of the king identifying him with the sun-god." See also Johnson, "Amenhotep III and Amarna: Some New Considerations," 66 f., who refers to the deification of Amenhotep III during his Sed festival as a "theological event" and adds, "[T]his king experienced living deification." The New Kingdom Underworld books are another important source for this inner event. As Hornung, "The Discovery of the Unconscious in Ancient Egypt,"

25, has written, "Whoever goes down into the Underworld meets the gods face to face, looks into the 'Face of the Sun' which . . . is drawn through the underworld to shine in its depth." Such was the experience of the Greek and Hellenistic mysteries, as witness Apuleius, *The Golden Ass*, 285, "At midnight I saw the sun shining as if it were noon," an inner experience that quite possibly has its precursor in the solarization of the king during the Sed festival.

11. E. Hornung, *The Ancient Egyptian Books of the Afterlife*, trans. D. Lorton (Ithaca: Cornell University Press, 1999), 41.

12. Utt. 204, §119 (trans. Mercer).

13. For the symbolism of the practice of inverse quoining in Egyptian temple architecture, see West, *The Traveller's Key to Ancient Egypt*, 146 f.

14. Mercer, *The Pyramid Texts*, 2:129.

15. For the use of threats in the practice of magic in ancient Egypt, see Jacq, *Egyptian Magic*, 102 f.; Naydler, *Temple of the Cosmos*, 162–64.

16. Utt. 254, §282–83 (trans. Faulkner).

17. §285. Piankoff translates "plowed into" as "fall to pieces in," Mercer as "decay in," and Faulkner as "sink into." The word *hb* is, however, written with the determinative of a plow, and it does seem appropriate to translate it literally here.

18. The classic study is Chassinat, *Le Mystère d'Osiris au mois de Khoiak*. The main events of the festival of Khoiak are described in Frazer, *The Golden Bough*, 375 f. See also Frankfort, *Kingship and the Gods*, 193.

19. In so doing he affirms his identity with Ra. In *The Litany of Ra*, col. 26, Ra is hailed as "supreme power with attached head" and later, in col. 64, as "chief of the she-monkeys." See Piankoff, *The Litany of Ra* (Princeton: Princeton University Press, 1961), 24 and 27. While Faulkner translates them as apes, both Mercer and Piankoff call them monkeys. Judging by their hieroglyphic depiction in the pyramid of Unas, they are monkeys and not apes. Houlihan, *The Animal World of the Pharaohs* (London: Thames and Hudson, 1996), 95, notes that there is no evidence to suggest that the Egyptians were acquainted with great apes. It is, however, frustratingly difficult to know exactly what to make of these female monkeys, whose appearance in religious texts is very rare and whose religious symbolism is obscure.

20. See chap. 3, p. 78 and fig. 3.8, with nn. 95–96. See also Meeks, "Dieu masqué, dieu sans tête," 5–15. See also Berlandini, "L' 'acéphale' et le rituel de revirilisation," 29–41.

21. In certain shamanic sources, the forging of a new head in a blacksmith's furnace was considered necessary if the shaman was to acquire the ability to shamanize. See Eliade, *Shamanism*, 41 f. and 471. For the Osirian rite of restoring and consecrating the head in Middle Kingdom, New Kingdom, and later sources, see Meeks, "Dieu masqué, dieu sans tête," 5–15. See also

Moret, *Mystères égyptiens*, 57 f. and 69 f., and DuQuesne, *At the Court of Osiris* (London: Darengo, 1994), 56. For the theme of the "headless Osiris," documented in a variety of Ptolemaic and later sources, and its relationship to the alchemical tradition, see Roberts, *My Heart, My Mother*, 211 f. and 247, n. 28 f.

22. Frankfort, *Kingship and the Gods*, 83 ff. and 93 ff.

23. Wilson, "Egypt," in Frankfort et al., *Before Philosophy*, 93 f.; and Frankfort, *Kingship and the Gods*, 51 f.

24. Utt. 256, §301 (trans. Faulkner).

25. Uphill, "The Egyptian Sed-Festival Rites," 371. That it is not a funerary text is also affirmed in Mercer, *The Pyramid Texts*, 2:140.

26. Utt. 256, §303. See also utt. 518, §1197, in the entrance corridor of the pyramids of Merenre, Pepi I, and Pepi II, which is another instance of the gods disrobing. It reads as follows: "I found the gods standing wrapped in their garments, with their white sandals on their feet; they threw off their sandals on the ground and discarded their garments; 'We were not happy until you came down,' they said. . . ."

27. The following statement in *Corpus Hermeticum*, 10.24–25, reiterates this profound truth: "The true human being is above even the gods. . . . For none of the heavenly gods will leave the heavenly frontiers and descend to earth, yet the human being rises up to the heavens . . . and knows their heights and depths. . . . And what is even more remarkable than all of this, is that the human can become established on high WITHOUT EVEN LEAVING THE EARTH." What is spoken of as a universal human possibility in the *Corpus Hermeticum* was in Old Kingdom Egypt restricted to the king and a small spiritual elite.

28. For the understanding of *bia* as "basin," see J. P. Allen, "The Cosmology of the Pyramid Texts," 9. According to Faulkner, *The Ancient Egyptian Pyramid Texts*, 67, *bia* should be understood as "the visible canopy of the sky."

29. See Plato, *Phaedrus*, 247, where he describes the immortal souls as "going outside" the vault of heaven and "standing upon the back of the universe," where they are able to "contemplate what lies outside the heavens." Compare with utt. 503, §1080, in the pyramid of Pepi I, where the king states: "I am back to back with those northern gods of the sky, the circumpolar stars, therefore I shall not perish."

   For the shamanic counterpart to this cosmic breakthrough in plane, see Kalweit, *Dreamtime and Inner Space*, 213, where he gives several examples of shamans entering the supercelestial spirit realm through "holes" or "windows" in the sky. The concept is that the stars are like little openings in the heavenly canopy, through which the supercelestial world of pure light sends its beams. In many shamanic traditions, the most important of these openings is the Pole Star, for it is on the cosmic axis of the world (*axis mundi*) that connects the different planes of reality and through which a breakthrough in plane can most easily be accomplished. For this cosmological concept, see Eliade, *Shamanism*, chap. 8. Whether the ancient Egyptians subscribed to a similar concept is hard to tell. Militating against it is the evidence from the New Kingdom Book of Nut in the cenotaph of Seti I, which describes the realm beyond the sky as one of infinite darkness rather than of light. This view, however, does belong to a period over a thousand years later than the Unas texts, and we must allow for both changes in theology and the changes in consciousness that the theology of Seti's time would reflect. In the Pyramid Texts, the infinite darkness of the Nun was the progenitor of the light-bearing creator god, Atum-Ra. It is possible that—in line with many mystical accounts of God's "darkness"—it is the only way we can experience the dazzling brilliance of the divine light-source. For the Heliopolitan creation account in the Pyramid Texts, see J. P. Allen, *Genesis in Egypt* (New Haven: Yale University Press, 1988), 13 f.; also 30 ff. For a translation and commentary on the Book of Nut, see *Genesis in Egypt*, 1–7. A brief discussion of what lies beyond the canopy of the sky is also to be found in J. P. Allen, "The Cosmology of the Pyramid Texts," 11 f.

30. PT 469, §907. Note that, wearing the leopard skin, Unas is clothed like a *sem* priest.

31. Plato, *Timaeus*, 37.

32. Utt. 258, §308 (trans. Piankoff).

33. Utt. 258, §311 (trans. Piankoff).

34. According to Mercer, *The Pyramid Texts*, 2:148 f., the "dead" king is here unequivocally identified with Horus, and the phrase "I am one who went and came back" can only mean that "the deceased king defines himself as he who died and now lives again." But the text actually states that he "came back" or "returned"—not "returned to life" but simply "returned" (in ancient Egyptian, *ii*). The sense of the phrase as a whole is mystical or initiatory rather than mortuary.

35. The first line of text in the sarcophagus chamber (corresponding to the last line in the antechamber) is §188cde–189a ("He lives—this Unas lives! He is not dead—this Unas is not dead. He is not destroyed—this Unas is not destroyed! He has not been judged—this Unas has not been judged! He judges—this Unas judges!") The last line in the antechamber is §316abc ("O Geb, bull of the sky, I am Horus, my father's heir. I have gone and returned, the fourth of these four gods who have brought water, who have made a purification").

36. Only one fragmentary utterance (utt. 411) survives from the south wall of the pyramid of Teti, apparently a ferryman text. In the pyramid of Pepi I, on the antechamber south wall there is just one short ascension text (utt. 488),

in which the king "grows wings as a falcon" in order to ascend to the sky. Merenre's south-wall texts are lost altogether, but on the antechamber south wall of Pepi II's pyramid there are four complete texts in which the ascension motif is strong (utts. 333, 508, 509, and 565) and various fragments in which crossing the Field of Rushes is featured (utts. 419 end, 265?, and 325) and also overcoming obstacles or dangers (utts. fr. 524? and fr. 703). See appendix 2.

37. Utt. 260, §317 (trans. Faulkner). The word "lacking" is *shu*, and the passage could equally well be translated "while Shu was a witness," which is how Piankoff chooses to translate it. Note that toward the end of the Old Kingdom, Shu's partner Tefnut was increasingly identified with Maat, for which see Clark, *Myth and Symbol in Ancient Egypt*, 45 f.

38. Breasted, *The Development of Religion and Thought*, 34. See also Griffiths, *The Conflict of Horus and Seth*, 54 ff. Whether this judgment by Double Maat, set in the context of the Horus-Seth conflict, became the prototype for the judgment of the soul in the later Book of the Dead should probably remain an open question, but there can be no doubt as to its nonfunerary context here. Griffiths, *The Conflict of Horus and Seth*, chap. 3, argues that gradually Horus—the original plaintiff in the trial—was replaced by Osiris, and cites CT 29 as an important transitional text (64).

39. Frankfort, *Kingship and the Gods*, 86. See also chap. 4, pp. 85–87, and chap. 7, p. 214f.

40. See chap. 7, p. 208 with n. 57 and n. 58.

41. Englund, *Akh. Une notion religieuse*, 172 and 205 ff. See also Englund, "La lumière et la répartition des textes," 173–80.

42. Utt. 260, §318–19. For the primary function of the kingship as being to establish and maintain *maat* throughout the land, see Frankfort, *Kingship and the Gods*, 51 f.; Morenz, *Egyptian Religion*, 113 ff.; and Quirke, *The Cult of Ra*, 17–20. See also chap. 7, p. 233 and chap. 7, n. 126.

43. Utt. 260, §323.

44. One of the most famous sequences of Coffin Texts is the Book of the Two Ways, in which the Underworld traveler has to negotiate a Gate of Fire and a Gate of Darkness. See CT 1037.

45. Utt. 262, §327–28. The phrase "Do not be unaware of" (or "ignorant of") translates the Egyptian *khem*; in the next line, "know" translates the Egyptian *rekh*.

46. Utt. 262, §334. Faulkner, *The Ancient Egyptian Pyramid Texts*, 72, n. 11, interprets "the path of the *sehedu* stars" as the Milky Way, while Mercer, *The Pyramid Texts*, 2:157, argues that they occupy the zodiacal belt and may be the planets. See also J. P. Allen, "The Cosmology of the Pyramid Texts," 4 and 7.

47. Utt. 263, §337.

48. Breasted, *The Development of Religion and Thought*, 108.

49. Utt. 469. See p. 249f. above.

50. Eliade, *Shamanism*, 85; Vitebsky, *The Shaman*, 66f.

51. Mercer, *The Pyramid Texts*, 2:170. This view was originally propounded by Breasted in *The Development of Religion and Thought*, 139f. and 142ff. and has continued to be the "standard" view. The two cults were supposedly syncretized for entirely nonreligious, political reasons. See, for example, Aldred, *The Egyptians*, 100f.

52. Eliade, *Shamanism*, 34. For the role of the Supreme Being, see Eliade, *Shamanism*, chap. 4. For general discussions of dismemberment as an initiatory pattern, see R. N. Walsh, *The Spirit of Shamanism* (London: HarperCollins, 1990), 59f.; Vitebsky, *The Shaman*, 60f.; and Eliade, *Shamanism*, 39–45.

53. According to Eliade, *Shamanism*, 391, "[S]ymbolic ascent to heaven by stairs is typically shamanic." Examples of ascent to the sky by ladder or stairway abound in his book. See, for example, 121–29 and 487–94. See also p. 273 with n. 95 of this book. With respect to ascent in the form of a bird Eliade, *Shamanism*, 403, comments: "[T]he ability to turn into a bird is the common property of all kinds of shamanism, not only the Turko-Mongol but also the Arctic, American, and Oceanian."

54. Utt. 267, §364 (trans. Faulkner). While the Pyramid Texts are generally reticent about the dismemberment, Unas's pyramid texts are also more reticent than most about the reconstitution of the body. For example, in the pyramid of Teti, the antechamber west wall includes an important "reconstitution ritual" sequence (utts. 364–74), most of which is repeated on Pepi I's, Merenre's, and Pepi II's sarcophagus chamber west wall. A second reconstitution sequence, utts. 447–53, also appears on the same sarcophagus chamber west wall (in full in Pepi I, and with minor variation in the others). It will be recalled that Unas's sarcophagus chamber west wall was not inscribed with texts, as if the subject of dismemberment and reconstitution were too delicate a matter to express in writing.

55. Utt. 267, §365–66 (trans. Faulkner).

56. Eliade, *Shamanism*, 76, distinguishes between the "consecration" and the "initiation proper," the former involving the dismemberment experience, the latter the ascent to the sky. See also Eliade, *Rites and Symbols of Initiation*, 90–99.

57. N. Rambova, "The Symbolism of the Papyri," in *Mythological Papyri*, vol. 1, ed. A. Piankoff (New York: Pantheon Books Inc., 1957), 56–65.

58. Roberts, "The Mystery Drama of Renewal: An Archaic Ritual" (unpublished paper on the Ramesseum Dramatic Papyrus, 1989).

59. Ramesseum Dramatic Papyrus, scene 38. See also chap. 3, p. 70.

60. Utt. 268, §370. Mercer, *The Pyramid Texts*, 2:172, comments that the word *kai* ("to be high") is used here "in reference to the brilliant symbols of the gods on standards raised aloft and carried in processions on feast days."

61. Naydler, *Temple of the Cosmos*, 193–97.

62. Utt. 268, §375. The word "omnipotent" translates *menekh* written twice. Literally, *"menekh* is this Unas, being *menekh."*

63. Utt. 269, §376–78.

64. She is more usually depicted, however, with the face of a hippopotamus.

65. Utt. 269, §38–82 (trans. Faulkner).

66. Sellers, *The Death of Gods in Ancient Egypt*, 320.

67. Eliade, *Shamanism*, 259–66.

68. Ibid., 266.

69. Utt. 270, §383–84.

70. In the Coffin Texts, the traveler is subjected to a lengthy cross-examination. See CT 395 ff., but especially CT 397. In the Book of the Dead, the main ferryman text is BD 99, which parallels CT 397.

71. CT 397, BD 99.

72. Mercer, *The Pyramid Texts*, 2:178.

73. Ibid., 180. See also utt. 508, §1118, where two vulture goddesses appear on the mountain of Sehseh.

74. For the *djed* as Hathor, see Frankfort, *Kingship and the Gods*, 178. For the Sed festival connection with utt. 271, see E. F. Wente, "Hathor at the Jubilee," in E. B. Hauser, ed., *Studies in Honor of John A. Wilson, September 12, 1969* (Chicago: Oriental Institute of the University of Chicago, 1969), 90, who argues that during the Sed festival of Amenhotep III, there was a sacred marriage of Hathor and the king (identified with the sun god): "This ritual enactment of the cosmological union of the sungod with his mother insured the king's symbolic rebirth at the end of the jubilee." For the rebirth motif in the Sed festival of Amenhotep III, see Roberts, *Hathor Rising*, 29–32

75. The *djed* was raised at the end of the third festival of Amenhotep III, for which see Fakhry, "A Note on the Tomb of Kheruef at Thebes," in *ASAE* 42 (1943): 477 f. and pl. XXXIX; also Moret, *Mystères égyptiens*, 15. While there is some evidence for its being raised at the end of other Sed festivals (e.g., the *djed* motif in the chambers under Zoser's pyramid), we cannot be absolutely certain that this was the case.

76. Utt. 271, §390. For the *djed* as world pillar, see Mercer, *The Pyramid Texts*, 2:180; Clark, *Myth and Symbol in Ancient Egypt*, 237; Fix, *Star Maps*, 29–37.

77. The shamanic literature would certainly support this. See Eliade, *Shamanism*, 259 and 262 f.

78. For Nun as the fount and origin of the gods, see J. P. Allen, *Genesis in Egypt*, 1.

79. The texts that appear on the north wall of Pepi II's antechamber are utts. 303, 304, 305, 308, and 310. The north-wall texts from the pyramids of both Teti and Merenre are lost, and only a few fragments survive from the pyramid of Pepi I. These fragments are mostly of ascension texts in which the king flies up as a bird to the sky (see utts. 302, 626, 627, and 704). The pyramid of Pepi II is alone in preserving intact a sequence of texts, although its north wall has also suffered damage. See n. 81 below.

80. The argument of Allen, "Reading a Pyramid," 11, that the antechamber east-gable texts should be read after the south-wall texts is seriously weakened by the fact that only two Middle Kingdom tombs (of Senwosret-Ankh and of Siese) adopt this order, whereas several later copies of the Unas texts treat utt. 272 (at the end of Unas's south wall) as terminating the sequence (254–72). Since one of these later copies follows utt. 272 with utt. 302 (the beginning of the ten north-wall texts), and another with utt. 213 (the beginning of the sarcophagus chamber south wall), the question of a "right sequence" seems to have run out of steam here. See J. P. Allen, "Reading a Pyramid," n. 13. See also the discussion in Eyre, *The Cannibal Hymn*, 61.

81. Although neither of the bull texts (utts. 306 and 307) is exactly replicated in Pepi II's pyramid, the closely parallel utts. 474 and 480 feature prominently on Pepi II's west wall, as they do on Pepi I's west wall. Utt. 474 also appears on Merenre's west wall.

82. Utt. 366, §632, reads as follows: "Your sister Isis comes to you, rejoicing for love of you. You have placed her on your phallus and your seed issues into her, she being ready as Sothis, and Horus-Soped has come forth from you as Horus who is in Sothis." This utterance occurs in the pyramids of Merenre, Pepi I, Teti, and Pepi II. See also the variant utt. 593, §1633 ff., which occurs in the pyramids of Pepi I, Merenre, and Pepi II.

83. This is made clear in §460. For the relationships between Sothis/Orion/Soped and Isis/Osiris/Horus see Hart, *A Dictionary of Egyptian Gods and Goddesses*, 205–7.

84. In the phrase translated by Faulkner as "Men hide (*dekh*), the gods fly away" (§459), the word *dekh* has the determinative of a hut with a low entrance near to the ground. Mercer, *The Pyramid Texts*, 1:102, suggests, "Men bury themselves," thereby bringing out the Osirian implications of the contrast. The word translated as "men" is *remetj*, which could be rendered as "ordinary people" in contrast to the divinized king.

85. For evidence of the use of masks in Egyptian ritual, see Ritner, *The Mechanics of Ancient Egyptian Magical Practice*, 249, n. 1142; and Naydler, *Temple of the Cosmos*, 153 f. For costumes in shamanic ritual, see Vitebsky, *The Shaman*, 82 ff. and 120 f.

86. The claws of Unas are said to be "the fangs of Him of the Cerastes (horned viper) Mountain nome" (§461). The Cerastes Mountain nome (*djuf*-nome) worshipped Anti, a falcon god named The Clawed One (Dunanwy), a form of Horus associated especially with the eastern sky.

87. Utt. 302, §463.

88. DuQuesne, "Anubis e il Ponte," 116. For traveling to the sky on the celestial sledge, see DuQuesne, *Jackal at the Shaman's Gate*, 11 f. and 18. References in the Pyramid Texts to this event include utt. 330, §539; utt. 437, §800; and utt. 485C, §1036.

89. For the role of Wepwawet in the Sed festival, see Frankfort, *Kingship and the Gods*, 83 and 85 f. Also Uphill, "The Egyptian Sed-Festival Rites," 374 f. and 376 f. The appearance of both the Wepwawet standard and the tambourine or drum, which is his special instrument, carried in procession as the king stands in front of the tomb, can be seen in the Sed festival reliefs of both Niuserre and Osorkon. See von Bissing and Kees, *Das Re-Heiligtum des Königs Ne-woser-re*, vol. 2, pl. 18; and Naville, *The Festival Hall of Osorkon II*, pl. XI. For the tambourine as the instrument of Anubis/Wepwawet, see DuQuesne, *Jackal at the Shaman's Gate*, 20. For the relationship of the *shedshed* to the Sed festival, see Moret, *Mystères égyptiens*, 74–79, who believes it possible that the name of the Sed festival may be derived from the *shedshed*.

90. Utt. 303, §466 (trans. Faulkner).

91. §466. The text is quite clear as to the identity of Unas as Horus. See Mercer, *The Pyramid Texts*, 2:218 f.

92. DuQuesne, *Jackal at the Shaman's Gate*, 12 ff.

93. Eliade, *Shamanism*, 482–86. For the meaning of *peter*, see Faulkner, *A Concise Dictionary of Middle Egyptian*, 96; and Mercer, *The Pyramid Texts*, 2:219.

94. For Falcon City being the royal residence on earth, see Faulkner, *The Ancient Egyptian Pyramid Texts*, 93, n. 3.

95. "Honourable ones" is Mercer's translation. Piankoff gives "honoured dead." Faulkner, however, gives "herbs," which seems unlikely. See Mercer, *The Pyramid Texts*, 2:221 f., for the reasons why the reference is almost certainly to the dead.

96. For Jacob's ladder, see Genesis 28:12. For the Orphic ladder, see A. B. Cook, *Zeus: A Study in Ancient Religion*, 3 vols. (Cambridge: Cambridge University Press, 1914–40), 2:124 f. For the Mithraic ladder, see F. Cumont, *Astrology and Religion among the Greeks and Romans* (1912; reprint, New York: Dover,

1960), 101. An illustration of the Christian ladder of virtues, from a fifteenth-century Italian engraving, is reproduced below.

97. For the ladder in shamanic tradition, see Eliade, *Shamanism*, 121–27, 275 ff., and 487–94. For photographs of shamanic rituals involving ladders, see Halifax, *Shaman: The Wounded Healer*, 84 f. See also chap. 8, pp. 258–60, with n. 52.

98. Utt. 305, §474. The transliteration *khat* should strictly speaking be *shat*, but after the Old Kingdom, *sh* is often replaced by *kh*, and *shat* came to be spelled *khat*.

99. Utt. 306, §479–80. The text is not completely clear, but this seems the most likely interpretation. See Piankoff, *The Pyramid of Unas*, 23.

100. Utt. 306, §478–79. For the role of the spirits of Pe and Nekhen in the Sed festival, see Frankfort, *Kingship and the Gods*, 87 f. The spirits of Pe appear falcon-headed on monuments, while the spirits of Nekhen are jackal-headed. For this and their representing, respectively, heaven and earth, see Mercer, *The Pyramid Texts*, 2:225, and Frankfort, *Kingship and the Gods*, 94 f. Note that the spirits of Nekhen witnessed the rites performed by the king in utt. 255, immediately preceding his coronation in utt. 256 on the antechamber west wall.

101. Utt. 306, §481.

102. Utt. 306 appears in variant form in the pyramids of Pepi I, Merenre, and Pepi II as utt. 474, which belongs to a sequence of eight utterances (utts. 470–77) in the middle of Pepi I's west wall. The sequence begins (utt. 470) with an address to the red and white crowns as the "mothers" of the reborn king, who is also referred to as a "great wild bull" (§913). He ascends to the sky, where he meets the ancestors (the Followers of Horus) and gods (utt. 471); encounters the "bull of the gods" (utt. 472); crosses the celestial river; and is reborn as Horus in the Akhet (utt. 473). Finally, in utt. 474, the king is met by Isis and Nephthys as he ascends the ladder to the stars. As in utt. 306, the king meets the divinized ancestral spirits of Pe and Nekhen, while the realms of the earth god Geb are given to the king, who is then hailed as "the firmest of the Wild Bulls." Clearly describing a ritual, the utterance (§945) ends with the directions: "Recite four times: O King, long endure! You are long enduring!" The parallel with the Unas north wall is clear, but so also is the fact that we are dealing here with a kingship ritual that does not necessarily have any funerary implications.

103. For the cult of the Mnevis bull at Heliopolis, see Frankfort, *Kingship and the Gods*, 63, 67, and 381, with n. 27. See also Quirke, *The Cult of Ra*, 109 f.

104. Utt. 307, §486.

105. Ibid., §482.

106. Ibid., §486. The word "generates" translates *mesi* (literally, "gives birth"). The word "continuously" translates *djeretch*, implying continuity in the past as well as the future. See Faulkner, *The Ancient Egyptian Pyramid Texts*, 95, n. 9. For *djer*, see Faulkner, *A Concise Dictionary of Middle Egyptian*, 323. Both Faulkner and Piankoff emphasize the continuity of the generative process in their translations of the last sentence of this passage, while Mercer, *The Pyramid Texts*, 2:230 states: "[t]he sentence is an echo of what is true of Re that he daily comes forth from the earth and the sky."

107. "What India Can Teach Us" (1939), in *Civilization in Transition*, vol. 10 of *The Collected Works of C. G. Jung* (London: Routledge and Kegan Paul, 1970), para. 1011.

108. Utt. 308, §489. The other similes in the text are also of maternal relationships: Nehebkau to Selkit, Sobek to Neith, and Seth (more problematically) to the "two harmonious ones," whose identity is not stated.

109. Mercer, *The Pyramid Texts*, 2:232.

110. Utt. 309, §491.

111. Utt. 310, §493.

112. The two-headed planet Venus reproduced below is from Budge, *The Gods of the Egyptians*, 2:303, and belongs to a later period. For the two-headed gods of the Book of What Is in the Underworld, see Piankoff, *The Tomb of Ramesses VI*, 30.

113. Utt. 311, §495 (trans. Faulkner, slightly modified).

114. For the hieroglyph of the platform wih steps, see Piankoff, *The Pyramid of Unas*, pl. 10. Depictions of the throne within the booth set on a stepped platform abound in Sed festival representations, from that of King Narmer to those of Amenhotep III and Osorkon II.

115. See chap. 3, p. 72.

116. Utt. 311, §498.

117. Utt. 311, §499f.

118. For Wadjet, see Mercer, *The Pyramid Texts*, 2:36. For Wadjet in relation to Nekhbet, see Frankfort, *Kingship and the Gods*, 96.

119. See chap. 7, p. 196f.

Chapter 9: From the Antechamber to the Entrance Corridor

1. See Eyre, *The Cannibal Hymn*, 61, who also notes the similarly self-contained positioning of this text in the pyramid of Teti—the only other pyramid in which it is found—where it straddles the east wall and gable between utts. 399 and 400. For a discussion of the difficulty of assigning the antechamber east-gable texts to a specific sequence, see chap. 8, n. 79 of the present study.

2. Utts. 273–74, §393.

3. Hornung, *Conceptions of God*, 61 f.

4. Utts. 273–74, §394. DuQuesne, *Jackal at the Shaman's Gate*, 11 f. See also chap. 8, p. 217, of the present study.

5. Utts. 273–74, §395.

6. Utt. 307, §486. See chap. 8, p. 276, with n. 104.

7. Utts. 273–74, §396–97. See chap. 8, pp. 244–46 for comparison with utt. 254.

8. Utts. 273–74, §398. These spirits and helpers are revealed in §400–403 to include spirit messengers, a "horn grasper" who lassoes other spirits, a serpent guardian, a spirit who binds other spirits, one who kills them, another who cuts them up, and another who cooks them. For helping spirits in shamanism, see Eliade, *Shamanism*, 88–95. See also n. 15 below for a rather different interpretation of the meaning of this passage.

9. Utts. 273–74, §403–4 (trans. Faulkner).

10. §409, §410, §411, §413.

11. §406 and §407. The word "power" translates *sekhem*.

12. Ritner, *The Mechanics of Ancient Egyptian Magical Practice*, 103.

13. Vitebsky, *The Shaman*, 24. According to Vitebsky, in Peru the shaman's phlegm is called *yachay*, which is derived from a verb meaning "to know." It therefore represents power as knowledge. The shaman is also able to regurgitate some of this phlegm and give it to a pupil to drink, in order to pass on his knowledge and power.

14. Shirokogoroff, *The Psychomental Complex of the Tungus* (London, 1935), 269, quoted in Jakobsen, *Shamanism*, 5.

15. An interpretation first proposed by Schott, *Bemerkungen zur Ägyptischen Pyramidenkult*, 194–200, and more recently by Eyre, *The Cannibal Hymn*, chap. 9. According to Eyre, reference to "the magic of the gods" in §400–403 should be interpreted as the parts of the sacrificial bull, but it is hard to see why. The only explicit bull imagery in the Cannibal Hymn relates to the king as the victorious bull of the sky, rather than to any sacrificial bull. Eyre argues that the sacrificial bull is at the beginning of the text initially identified with the king (76–80), but subsequently with "the magic of the gods" (85 ff.), which the king himself (no longer a bull) then consumes. For the bull's identity to change in this way during such a highly charged ritual does intuitively seem implausible, and casts serious doubt on the interpretation of this text as a slaughter ritual text. While the bull itself may be, as Eyre argues (145), a contradictory symbol, representing the forces both of destructive chaos and of power, dominance, and virility, it is questionable whether this symbolic ambivalence of the bull would have been ritually enacted with one and the same bull taking on the role of both "victorious king" and "victim to be slaughtered."

16. Eyre, *The Cannibal Hymn*, 57, has stated: "There is nothing in the text that necessarily relates it to a purely funerary context, but everything to assert the king's role as heritor of divine power." There are possible indications of a Sed festival context to the Cannibal Hymn. Two thirds of the way through, at §406, we meet two phrases discussed in chap. 4, p. 119, with n. 92 and n. 93. The king is said to have "traveled around the whole of the two skies" and "circumambulated the Two Banks." These phrases in all probability refer to the Sed festival dedication of the field rite. The fact that the king is earlier referred to as "the Bull of Heaven" could also be taken as an indicator of a possible Sed festival background to this text.

17. §412–13, "Appearance" here is literally "dawning." This is a particularly hard stanza to translate. Mercer gives us: "He is as that which dawns, which dawns, which endures, which endures." The doubling of the participles, however, carries the metaphysical connotation of the "dawningness of dawning," the "enduringness of enduring."

18. *Corpus Hermeticum*, 11.20. The text continues: "Like is understood by like. Grow to immeasurable size, be free from every body, transcend all time, become eternity and thus you will understand God." See C. Salaman et al. trans., *The Way of Hermes* (London: Duckworth, 1999), 57.

19. Piankoff, *The Pyramid of Unas*, 47. Mercer, *The Pyramid Texts*, 2:193, concurs. But Faulkner, *The Ancient Egyptian Pyramid Texts*, 84, n. 5, sees it as "something in the nature of a cloak." The problem is in whether we interpret the *sed* in *mesedet* as being derived from the noun "tail" or from the verb "to clothe." If we choose the former, we could, with Fix, *Star Maps*, 99 ff., see this episode as yet another link to the Sed festival, since the *mesedet* garment would then become the Sed festival kilt with the bull's tail hanging from it. For the translation of the first garment as "hide of a baboon," see Piankoff, *The Pyramid of Unas*, 46, and Mercer, *The Pyramid Texts*, 2:193.

20. For the magical signicance of the number forty-two (as a multiple of seven), see R. Wilkinson, *Symbol and Magic*, 136. It is unlikely that this number related to the nomes or administrative regions of Egypt, as in the Old Kingdom there were only thirty-eight or thirty-nine nomes.

21. Clark, *Myth and Symbol in Ancient Egypt*, 50–54. See also CT 321.

22. Clark, *Myth and Symbol in Ancient Egypt*. See also utts. 22 and 297. See also BD 17, 18–22.

23. Utt. 281 (trans. Piankoff).

24. Piankoff, *The Pyramid of Unas*, 48. This spell is perhaps an example of what the *Corpus Hermeticum* refers to as "the pure spirit of the words" of the Egyptian language. "For the very quality of the sound and the pronunciation of the Egyptian language carries in itself the power of what is being spoken." *Corpus Hermeticum* 16.2, trans. Salaman et al., *The Way of Hermes*, 74.

25. Utt. 226, §225 (trans. Faulkner).

26. Utt. 226, §226 (trans. Faulkner). Piankoff, *The Pyramid of Unas*, 95; Mercer, *The Pyramid Texts*, 2:104f. To appreciate what death by "drowning" might have meant, it is necessary to remember that travel in the celestial regions was normally by boat.

27. Utt. 293, §435 (trans. Faulkner).

28. Utt. 228, §228; utt. 290, §431.

29. Utt. 238, §242; utt. 282, §423. The god Khaitau is, according to Mercer, *The Pyramid Texts*, 2:112, the ox god of a district near Byblos.

30. Utt. 229, §229 (trans. Faulkner). For the role of the Nehebkau snake as the primeval opponent of Atum, see Clark, *Myth and Symbol in Ancient Egypt*, 52f.

31. Utt. 283, §424 (trans. Faulkner). See Piankoff, *The Pyramid of Unas*, 48.

32. Clark, *Myth and Symbol in Ancient Egypt*, 52f.; BD 17, 18–22.

33. Utt. 297, §440 (trans. Faulkner).

34. See chap. 7, p. 225.

35. I am grateful to Maria Narancic for this suggestion in her unpublished paper "Snake Spells in the Pyramid Texts," written in 1996.

36. Utt. 300, §445.

37. For the relationship between Anubis and Sokar in connection with Ro-Setawe, see Terence DuQuesne, *Jackal at the Shaman's Gate*, 14–24.

38. This is most clearly expressed in the New Kingdom Book of What Is in the Underworld *(Amduat)*, div 5. See also CT 1150, where Ro-Setawe is described as a place of birth and associated with the Akhet.

39. Utt. 301, §447.

40. Utt. 301, §449–50 (trans. Faulkner).

41. Mercer, *The Pyramid Texts*, 2:211.

42. Utt. 301, §455.

43. Utt. 301, §457. For meanings of *seped*, see Faulkner, *A Concise Dictionary of Middle Egyptian*, 223. It is also not wholly certain that it is Unas who is being referred to as *ba* and *seped*. The text attributes these qualities to Horus, Lord of the Greenstone, with whom—according to Piankoff—Unas is here identified. See Piankoff, *The Pyramid of Unas*, 53. Mercer thinks otherwise, but the sense of the text supports Piankoff.

44. J. P. Allen, "Reading a Pyramid," 19.

45. Utt. 313 is notoriously difficult to translate. For an illuminating discussion, see West, *Serpent in the Sky*, 149–56. Note that West misleadingly refers to it as utt. 316.

46. In the Unas text, there is no mention of "phallus," which appears in so many translations. The substitution of "phallus" for "bolt" is justified on the grounds that it occurs in a later version of the utterance in the Middle Kingdom mastaba tomb of Senwosret-Ankh at Lisht. See Piankoff, *The Pyramid of Unas*, 17. The phallus of Babi forms the subject of spells in the Coffin Texts (e.g., CT 576 and CT 822). For his red ears and purple buttocks, see PT utt. 549. For his living on the entrails of "the old ones," see BD 125. For a discussion of Babi (Baba), see te Velde, *Seth: God of Confusion*, 54 and 106.

47. Utt. 313, §503b.

48. The resistance of the ox is envisaged as having a malevolent serpentine form, hence the final words of the spell are directed against a snake. See Mercer, *The Pyramid Texts*, 2:236f.

49. Ibid., 237. Roberts, *Hathor Rising*, 197–98, describes "becoming like one of Thoth's baboons" as the climax of a sequence of initiatory experiences on the mystical "way of Thoth," which continued into the Roman period.

50. Utt. 315, §505b. "Wish" translates *saar*. "At my own will" translates *her tep Wenis* (literally, "upon the head of Unas"). See the discussion of the meaning of these two phrases in Mercer, *The Pyramid Texts*, 2:237.

51. It is possible that *sehed* is another name of Hemi, or else a second ferryman, for which see Mercer, *The Pyramid Texts*, 2:238. For ferrymen with names similar to Hemi, see Hem in utt. 556, §1382. See also Imheti in utt. 507, §1102; and utt. 678, §202.

52. The ferryman text on the east wall of the antechamber is utt. 300. Note that Babi also appears among the east-wall snake spells in utt. 278, where he is said to "stand up."

53. Utt. 317, §507. Quirke, *Ancient Egyptian Religion*, 51.

54. Ibid., §508.

55. Ibid., §509. "Great Flood" translates *mehet weret*, often conceived in the form of a cow.

56. For the Sed festival as a fertility festival, see G. A. Wainwright, *The Sky-Religion in Egypt*, 20–24. For the Hathorian aspects of the Sed festival that may well underly this utterance, see Roberts, *Hathor Rising*, chap. 3.

57. Utt. 317, §510.

58. Eliade, *Rites and Symbols of Initiation*, 25. Mercer's comment is in *The Pyramid Texts*, 2:240. For many examples of the interrelationship of the divine, cosmic, natural, and human levels in ancient fertility rites that shed light on this part of utt. 317, see Frazer, *The Golden Bough*, chap. 11.

59. For the sexual basis of the king's rule, see Roberts, *Hathor Rising*, 49.

60. Piankoff, *The Pyramid of Unas*, 19, and Mercer, *The Pyramid Texts*, 2:242. See also chap. 9, p. 294, with n. 30 above.

61. For Nehebkau as malevolent, see utt. 229, discussed on p. 294. For Nehebkau as the benevolent companion to the sun god, see utt 263, §340; utt. 264, §346; utt. 265, §356; and utt. 266, §361. For Nehebkau in relation to the primordial waters, see utt 510, §1146. For Nehebkau aiding the king's cosmic ascent, see utt. 667, §1934.

62. Faulkner, *The Ancient Egyptian Pyramid Texts*, 101, utt. 319, n. 4.

63. Utt. 319, §514.

64. Utt. 320, §516.

65. CT 38 (5.132); CT 473 (6.11).

66. "Faithful companion" translates *setep za*. For this phrase in other utterances, see utt. 475, §948; utt. 478, §971 and §975; utt. 569, §1442; and utt. 576, §1517. Of these, it is utt. 569 (which is positioned in the vestibule to the entrance corridor in the pyramids of Pepi I, Merenre, and Pepi II) that most strikingly and beautifully affirms the mystical meaning of the phrase: "I have come to you, O Ra, I have come to you, O Limitless One, and I will row you, I will be your faithful companion, I will love you with my body, I will love you with my heart."

Chapter 10: The Recovery of Ancient Egyptian Mysticism

1. Eliade, *Myths, Dreams and Mysteries*, 59–65, 80-84; *Shamanism*, 8. See also Campbell, *The Masks of God: Primitive Mythology*, 263-4.

2. See the discussion in chap. 6, p. 183 f. See also Osing, "Zur Disposition der Pyramidentexte des Unas," 131–44; J. P. Allen, "Reading a Pyramid," 5–28.

3. An important example is the sequence of twelve utterances on the south and east walls of the sarcophagus chamber of the pyramid of Unas (Osing's sequence C, Allen's sequence E). Most of this sequence is replicated in the later pyramids of Pepi II and his queen Neith, and in fragmentary form in the pyramids of Teti and Pepi I. In each case it appears on their south walls. It is also replicated in the Middle Kingdom tomb of Senwosret-Ankh. See Osing, "Zur Disposition der Pyramidentexte des Unas," 138 f.; J. P. Allen, "Reading a Pyramid," 15 ff.

4. See chap. 7, p. 202, with nn. 38–39.

5. The death and rebirth motif is strong in the antechamber west-to-south-wall sequence (utts. 254–72), which architecturally is a mirror image of the sarcophagus chamber south-to-east-wall sequence. The theme of cosmic rebirth is key to the antechamber west-gable texts. Solarization and union with Ra is a recurrent theme in the antechamber west-gable and west-wall, south-, and north-wall texts (e.g., utts. 249, 251, 252, 268, 302, 309, and 311). The idea of Horus as a reborn Osiris, or as a condition that supersedes the Osirian condition, can be found in utts. 254, 256, 258, 260, 267–69, 303, and 310.

6. In the antechamber south-wall sequence, this is particularly clear. See utts. 260–62 and utt. 267.

7. Utts. 261 and 267. See also utts. 269, 302, 305, 273–74, and 318. For modes of ascent in the Pyramid Texts, see Davis, "The Ascension-Myth in the Pyramid Texts," 161–79.

8. For shamanic ascent, see Eliade, *Shamanism*, chap. 6. The mystical flight of Etana is translated in Stephanie Dalley, *Myths from Mesopotamia* (Oxford: Oxford University Press, 1991), 196–200; see also J. Black and G. Green, *Gods, Demons and Symbols of Ancient Mesopotamia* (London: British Museum Press, 1992), 78. For Plato's description of the ascent of the soul, see *Phaedrus*, 246–47. For Paul's, see 2 Corinthians 12:1–7. The Hermetic "Discourse on the Eighth and the Ninth" is published in Robinson (ed.), *The Nag Hammadi Library in English*, 292–97. Muhammad's *mi'râj* is discussed in Eliade, *A History of Religious Ideas*, 3:70f.

9. Eliade, *Myths, Dreams and Mysteries*, 110, comments: "It would be absurd to minimize the differences of content that diversify examples of 'flight,' 'ecstasy' and 'ascension.' But it would be just as absurd not to recognize the correspondence of structure which emerges from such comparisons. And in the history of religions, as in other mental disciplines, it is knowledge of structure which makes it possible to understand meanings." The classic Egyptological study of the motif of ascension in the Pyramid Texts, Davis, "The Ascension-Myth in the Pyramid Texts," 161–79, is typically oblivious of the vast literature concerning mystical ascent, and fails to mention that the "ascension myth" in the Pyramid Texts conforms to a basic mystical pattern. Davis, predictably, sees it rather as belonging to the ancient Egyptian "system of [funerary] belief" (163).

10. In utt. 211, the king is said to be conceived and born in the night, and also in the Nun—the watery source of all existence. In utt. 248, it is Sekhmet who is said to have conceived him and Shesmetet who gives birth to him—both fiery leonine goddesses. In utt. 249, he appears as Nefertem, the solar child and son of Sekhmet. He is suckled by the milk goddess, Iat, in utt. 211 and by the hippopotamus goddess, Ipy, in utt. 269.

11. This doctrine is expounded in Plato, *Phaedrus*, 246ff., and *Phaedo*, 64ff. In the pyramid of Unas, the Egyptian precursor of this doctrine is expressed in the delicate relationship between the sarcophagus chamber east-gable and the antechamber west-gable texts, especially utts. 207, 209, and 212 (on the sarcophagus chamber west gable), and utts. 247–50 on the antechamber west gable. See the discussion in chap. 7, pp. 231–34, and chap. 8, pp. 235–40.

12. In the Pyramid Texts, the exact location of the Dwat is not made explicit, but since it is written with the star determinative, it was clearly conceived as having a starry location. It has been suggested that it was visualized by the authors of the Pyramid Texts as lying beneath the earth, for which see J. P. Allen, "The

Cosmology of the Pyramid Texts," 23. While this is possible, Allen accepts that it was also conceived as a cosmic region (22). Even taking account of the changes in religious consciousness during the Middle Kingdom and the New Kingdom, it seems improbable that the conception of the location of the Dwat within the body of Nut would have been a completely new conception introduced in the New Kingdom. It is more likely that this idea was an elaboration of an already existing conception.

13. See Versluis, *Song of the Cosmos: An Introduction to Traditional Cosmology* (Bridport, Prism Press, 1991), chap. 2. Such cosmologies are described by Rawlinson, *The Book of Enlightened Masters*, chap. 3, as "hot-structured," for which see chap. 1, n. 11 in this book.

14. See also utts. 263 and 304.

15. Hornung, *Conceptions of God*, 167 f., 182, 191; Assmann, *The Search for God*, 155–57. See also chap. 1, p. 7.

16. In the sarcophagus chamber of the pyramid of Unas, Unas is explicitly identified with Osiris eighty-eight times and implicitly thirteen times (all in the north-wall Offering Liturgy), explicitly with Horus four times and implicitly eight times. In the antechamber, he is explicitly identified with Osiris only once (utt. 258) and explicitly with Horus eight times, implicitly ten times. In the passage between the chambers and the entrance corridor are a further five identifications with Osiris and five (mostly implicit) identifications with Horus. See also chap. 3, n. 40.

17. This understanding of Nut is encapsulated in utt. 432, where it is stated of Nut: "[Y]ou have enclosed the earth and all things within your embrace, and you have set this king as an imperishable star who is within you."

18. The king is identified with Ra in utts. 252, 253, and 257, and with the solar Mnevis bull in utt. 307. His longing to be in the presence of Ra is expressed in utts. 262, 302, and 311. He is said to be in the presence of Ra in utt. 309 (as Ra's servant) and in utt. 321 (as Ra's faithful companion). He joins the cosmic circuit of Ra in utt. 222 in a state of identification or very close companionship with the god. See also utts. 216–17 for union with Ra.

19. As Hornung argued in *Conceptions of God*, 101. See also chap. 2, p. 43, in this book. A view similar to Hornung's can be inferred for those Egyptologists who regard the Pyramid Texts as reflecting beliefs about the afterlife. See the discussion in chap. 6, pp. 181–84.

20. Corbin, *"Mundus Imaginalis"* in *Swedenborg and Esoteric Islam*, 7 and 32; *Spiritual Body and Celestial Earth*, viii.

21. Van der Leeuw, *Religion in Essence and Manifestation*, 684.

22. These references and allusions refer to practically every phase of the Sed festival, from the initial purification rites and offering rituals to the circumambulation of the "mounds" of Horus and Seth, the dedication of the field, the

communion with the Spirits of Pe and Nekhen, the double coronation, solarization, the ritual sailing, vision of the gods, the union of heaven and earth, and the channeling of the forces of fertility into the land of Egypt, all discussed in chaps. 7–9.

23. For Frankfort's criticism of Schott, see "Pyramid Temples and the Religion of the Old Kingdom," 157–62. Barta's assault on previous Pyramid Texts theories is to be found in *Die Bedeutung der Pyramidentexte*, references to which are given in chap. 6.

24. Eliade, *The Two and the One*, 46.

25. Chap. 2, pp. 45–47.

26. Ibid., p. 22 f.; chap. 3, p. 51.

27. General studies of Western esoteric traditions and their relationship to ancient Egyptian include Curl, *The Egyptian Revival;* Iversen, *The Myth of Egypt;* and Hornung, *The Secret Lore of Egypt*. See also chap. 2, p. 24, with n. 18.

28. See chap. 1, p. 12, with n. 31.

29. Hornung, *The Secret Lore of Egypt*, 3.

30. Ibid., 16.

31. Roberts, *My Heart, My Mother*, 175 f., quoted in chap. 2, n. 90.

32. See Faivre, *Access to Western Esotericism* (Albany: State University of New York Press, 1994); W. J. Hanegraaff, *New Age Religion and Western Culture: Esotericism in the Mirror of Secular Thought* (Albany: State University of New York Press, 1998); the collections of essays in A. Faivre and J. Needleman (eds.), *Modern Esoteric Spirituality* (New York: SCM Press, 1992) and in W. J. Hanegraaff and R. van den Broek, eds., *Gnosis and Hermeticism from Antiquity to Modern Times* (Albany: State University of New York Press, 1998); and the numerous publications of Versluis, most recently *Restoring Paradise: Esoteric Transmission through Literature and Art* (Albany: State University of New York Press, 2004). See also the electronic journal *Esoterica* at www.esoteric.msu.edu.

33. The standard view is represented by Faivre, "Ancient and Medieval Sources of Modern Esoteric Movements," in Faivre and Needleman (eds.), *Modern Esoteric Spirituality*, 1–70. See also Faivre, *Access to Western Esotericism*, 51–53. Compare, however, with the dissenting view of Versluis, *The Egyptian Mysteries*, 1, who asserts that for the understanding of the Western tradition—especially Neoplatonism and Hermeticism—"an understanding of the Egyptian Mysteries and tradition is virtually indispensable."

34. The Valentinian School in particular, for which see Jonas, *The Gnostic Religion* (Boston: Beacon Press, 1963), chap. 8. See also Doresse, *The Secret Books of the Egyptian Gnostics* (Rochester, Vt.: Inner Traditions International, 1986),

272–74. For the indebtedness of the Hermetic tradition to ancient Egyptian sources, see chap. 3, n. 9, of the present study. Even Hornung seems to accept that the sources of the Hermetic tradition lie in "real" rather than simply imaginary Egypt. See Hornung, *The Secret Lore of Egypt*, 51. For the pharaonic roots of alchemy, see the discussion in Hornung, *The Secret Lore of Egypt*, chap. 4. More usefully, Roberts, *My Heart, My Mother*, 202–5, discusses the ancient Egyptian-alchemical transmission. See also 205–16 for a pioneering discussion of the sixteenth-century alchemical text *Splendor Solis* in relation to the New Kingdom Book of Night.

35. In the writings of the early alchemist Zosimus, the Osirian nature of the alchemical process of transmutation is made quite explicit. An English translation of the *Visions of Zosimus* is given in Jung, *Alchemical Studies*, vol. 13 of *The Collected Works of C. G. Jung* (Princeton: Princeton University Press, 1967), 59–65, with an extensive commentary by Jung, 66–108. See also the discussion in Roberts, *My Heart, My Mother*, 202 f. Apart from the *Visions of Zosimus*, ancient Egyptian mythical and initiatory motifs are present in such major alchemical works as the *Turba Philosophorum* (of which there was an early-tenth-century Arabic protoype); the fourteenth-century illustrated texts of Petrus Bonus, *Pretiosa Margarita Novella*, and Pseudo-Thomas Aquinas, *Aurora Consurgens*; as well as the sixteenth-century *Splendor Solis*. While reference may not be explicitly made to ancient Egyptian sources in these texts, it is nevertheless perfectly evident to anyone familiar with ancient Egyptian religion that Egyptian motifs are present in them. Sometimes, however, alchemical texts do refer explicitly to ancient Egypt, as, for example, when in Michael Maier's *Arcana arcanissima* (1614), refererence is made to the myth of Osiris as representing the alchemical process, for which see Hornung, *The Secret Law of Egypt*, 39.

BIBLIOGRAPHY

Aldred, Cyril. *Art in Ancient Egypt*. 3 vols. London: Alec Tiranti, 1968–72.

———. *Egypt to the End of the Old Kingdom*. London: Thames and Hudson, 1965.

———. *The Egyptians*. London: Thames and Hudson, 1984.

Allen, James P. "The Cosmology of the Pyramid Texts." In *Religion and Philosophy in Ancient Egypt*, edited by William K. Simpson, 1–28. New Haven: Yale University Press, 1989.

———. *Genesis in Egypt*. New Haven: Yale University Press, 1988.

———. "Reading a Pyramid." In *Hommages à Jean Leclant*, 2 vols., edited by Catherine Berger et al., 5–28. Cairo: Bibliothéque d'Étude, 1994.

Allen, T. G. *The Book of the Dead*. Chicago: University of Chicago Press, 1974.

———. *Occurrences of Pyramid Texts with Cross Indexes of These and Other Mortuary Texts*. Chicago: University of Chicago Press, 1950.

Altenmüller, H. *Die Texte zum Begräbnisritual in den Pyramiden des Alten Reiches*, ÄgAb 24. Wiesbaden, Germany: O. Harrassowitz, 1972.

Amrine, Frederick. "Goethe's Science in the Twentieth Century." In *Goethe in the Twentieth Century*, edited by Alexej Ugrinsky, 87–93. New York: Greenwood Press, 1987.

Apuleius. *The Golden Ass*. Translated by Robert Graves. Harmondsworth: Penguin, 1950.

Aristotle. *Physics*. Translated by P. H. Wicksteed and F. M. Cornford. Loeb Classical Library. London: Heinemann, 1970.

———. *Metaphysics*. Translated by Hugh Tredennick. Loeb Classical Library. London: Heinemann, 1977.

———. *De Caelo*. Translated by W. K. C. Guthrie. Loeb Classical Library. London: Heinemann, 1939.

Armstrong, A. H. *An Introduction to Ancient Philosophy*. Boston: Beacon Press, 1963.

Arnold, Dieter. "Rituale und pyramidentempel." In *MDAIK* 33 (1977): 1–14.

———. "Royal Cult Complexes of the Old and Middle Kingdoms." In *Temples of Ancient Egypt*, edited by Byron E. Shafer, 31–85. Ithaca: Cornell University Press, 1997.

Assmann, J. "Death and Initiation in the Funerary Religion of Ancient Egypt." In *Religion and Philosophy in Ancient Egypt*, edited by William Kelly Simpson. New Haven: Yale University Press, 1989.

———. *Egyptian Solar Religion in the New Kingdom*. Translated by Anthony Alcock. New York: Kegan Paul International, 1995.

———. *The Search for God in Ancient Egypt*. Translated by David Lorton. Ithaca and London: Cornell University Press, 2001.

Assmann, J., and Martin Bommas, eds. *Ägyptische Mysterien?* München: Fink, 2002.

Aston, Barbara G., et al. "Stone." In *Ancient Egyptian Materials and Technology*, edited by Paul T. Nicholson and Ian Shaw. Cambridge: Cambridge University Press, 2000.

Baines, J. "Restricted Knowledge, Hierarchy and Decorum." In *JARCE* 27 (1990): 1–22.

Baines, J., and J. Málek. *Atlas of Ancient Egypt*. Oxford: Andromeda, 1980.

Barnard, W. *Exploring Unseen Worlds: William James and the Philosophy of Mysticism*. Albany: State University of New York Press, 1997.

Barnes, Jonathan. *Early Greek Philosophy*. London: Penguin, 1987.

Barta, Winfried. *Die altägyptische Opferliste*, *MÄS* 3. Berlin: Verlag Bruno Hessling, 1963.

———. *Die Bedeutung der Pyramidentexte für den verstorben König*, *MÄS* 39. Berlin: Deutscher Kunstverlag, 1981.

Bell, L. "Luxor Temple and the Cult of the Royal Ka." In *JNES* 44, no. 4 (1985): 251–94.

———. "The New Kingdom Divine Temple." In *Temples of Ancient Egypt*, edited by Byron E. Shafer, 127–84. Ithaca: Cornell University Press, 1997.

Berlandini, J. "L''acéphale' et le rituel de revirilisation." In *OMRO* 73 (1993): 29–41.

Bernal, Martin. *Black Athena*. 2 vols. London: Free Association Books, 1987.

Bissing, W. F. von, and H. Kees. *Das Re-Heiligtum des Königs Ne-woser-re (Rathures)*. 3 vols. Leipzig: J. C. Hinrichs, 1923.

Black, J., and G. Green. *Gods, Demons and Symbols of Ancient Mesopotamia*. London: British Museum Press, 1992.

Bleeker, C. J. *Egyptian Festivals*. Leiden: E. J. Brill, 1967.

———. "Initiation in Ancient Egypt." In *Initiation*, edited by C. J. Bleeker, 49–58. Leiden: E. J. Brill, 1965.

———. *The Sacred Bridge*. Leiden: E. J. Brill, 1963.

Bonnet, H. "Ägyptische Baukunst und Pyramidenkult." In *JNES* 12 (1953): 257–73.

Borchardt, L. *Das Grabdenkmal des Königs Sa3-hu-re*. 2 vols. Leipzig: J. C. Hinrichs, 1910–13.

Bortoft, Henri. *The Wholeness of Nature: Goethe's Way of Science*. Edinburgh: Floris Books, 1996.

Bouquet, A. C. *Comparative Religion*. Harmondsworth: Penguin, 1954.

Brady, R. "Goethe's Natural Science: Some Non-Cartesian Meditations." In *Toward a Man-Centred Medical Science*, edited by K. E. Schaefer et al., 135–65. New York: Futura Publishing Co., 1977.

Breasted, J. H. *Ancient Records of Egypt*. 5 vols. Chicago: University of Chicago Press, 1906–7.

——. *The Development of Religion and Thought in Ancient Egypt.* 1912. Reprint, Philadelphia: University of Pennsylvania Press, 1972.

Brinks, J. *Die Entwicklung der königlichen Grabanlagen des Alten Reiches.* Hildesheim: Gerstenberg, 1979.

Brodrick, M., and A. A. Morton. *A Concise Dictionary of Egyptian Archaeology.* Chicago: Ares Publishers Inc., 1924.

Bryan, B. M. "The Statue for the Mortuary Temple of Amenhotep III." In *The Temple in Ancient Egypt,* edited by Stephen Quirke, 57–81. London: British Museum Press, 1997.

Budge, E. A. Wallis. *The Book of the Dead.* 1923. Reprint, Routledge and Kegan Paul, 1985.

——. *The Book of Opening the Mouth.* 2 vols. London: Kegan Paul, Trench, Trubner and Co., 1909.

——. *The Egyptian Book of the Dead (The Papyrus of Ani).* 1895. Reprint, New York: Dover, 1967.

——. *The Egyptian Heaven and Hell.* LaSalle, Ill.: Open Court, 1925.

——. *An Egyptian Hieroglyphic Dictionary.* 2 vols. 1920. Reprint, New York: Dover, 1978.

——. *From Fetish to God in Ancient Egypt.* London: Oxford University Press, 1934.

——. *The Gods of the Egyptians,* 2 vols. 1904. Reprint, New York: Dover, 1969.

——. *Herb Doctors and Physicians in the Ancient World.* 1928. Reprint, Chicago: Ares Publishers, 1978.

——. *The Liturgy of Funerary Offerings.* 1909. Reprint, New York: Dover, 1994.

——. *Osiris and the Egyptian Resurrection.* 2 vols. 1891. Reprint, New York: Dover, 1973.

Burkert, W. *Ancient Mystery Cults.* Cambridge: Harvard University Press, 1987.

——. *Greek Religion.* Oxford: Basil Blackwell, 1985.

Bury, J. B. *The Idea of Progress.* 1932. Reprint, New York: Dover, 1955.

Campbell, Joseph. *The Masks of God: Primitive Mythology.* Harmondsworth: Penguin Books, 1976.

Černý, J. "A Note on the Recently Discovered Boat of Cheops." In *JEA* 41 (1955): 75–79.

Chassinat, E. *Le Mystère d'Osiris au mois de Khoiak.* 2 vols. Cairo: Institut français d'archéologie orientale, 1966–68.

Clark, R. T. Rundle. *Myth and Symbol in Ancient Egypt.* London: Thames and Hudson, 1978.

Collingwood, R. G. *The Idea of History.* New York: Oxford University Press, 1956.

Cook, A. B. *Zeus: A Study in Ancient Religion.* 3 vols. Cambridge: Cambridge University Press, 1914–40.

Copenhaver, Brian P. *Hermetica: The Greek* Corpus Hermeticum *and the Latin* Asclepius *in a New English Translation with Notes and Introduction.* Cambridge: Cambridge University Press, 1992.

Corbin, Henri. *Creative Imagination in the Sufism of Ibn Arabi*. Translated by Ralph Manheim. Princeton: Princeton University Press, 1969.

———. *"Mundus Imaginalis*, or the Imaginary and the Imaginal."* In *Swedenborg and Esoteric Islam*, translated by Leonard Fox, 1–33. West Chester, Penn.: Swedenborg Foundation, 1995.

———. *Spiritual Body and Celestial Earth*. Translated by Nancy Pearson. London: I. B. Tauris and Co., 1990.

Cumont, F. *Astrology and Religion among the Greeks and Romans*. 1912. Reprint, New York: Dover, 1960.

Curl, James Stevens. *The Egyptian Revival*. London: George Allen and Unwin, 1982.

Dalley, Stephanie. *Myths from Mesopotamia*. Oxford: Oxford University Press, 1991.

Darwin, Charles. *The Descent of Man*. 2nd ed. London: John Murray, 1874.

Daumas, François. "Le fonds égyptien de l'hermétisme." In *Gnosticism et monde hellenistique: Actes du Colloque de Louvain-la-Neuve (11–14 mars 1980)*, edited by J. Ries, 3–25. Louvain-la-Neuve, France, 1982.

———. "Y eut-il des mystères en Égypte?" In *Le Bulletin Annuel de "L'Atelier d'Alexandrie"* 1 (1972): 37–52.

David, R. *Cult of the Sun: Myth and Magic in Ancient Egypt*. London: J. M. Dent, 1980.

———. *A Guide to Religious Ritual at Abydos*. Warminster: Aris and Phillips, 1981.

Davies, W. V., and R. Walker, eds. *Biological Anthropology and the Study of Ancient Egypt*. London: British Museum Press, 1993.

Davis, Whitney M. "The Ascension-Myth in the Pyramid Texts." In *JNES* 36 (1977): 161–79.

Derchain, P. "L'authenticité de l'inspiration égyptienne dans le Corpus Hermeticum." In *RHR* 161 (1962): 175–98.

———. "Symbols and Metaphors in Literature and Representations of Private Life." In *RAIN* 15 (1976): 7–10.

Dilthey, W. *Hermeneutics and the Study of History*. Edited by Rudolf A. Makkreel and Frthjof Rodi. Princeton: Princeton University Press, 1996.

Diodorus Siculus. *Library of History*. Translated by C. H. Oldfather et al. Loeb Classical Library. London: Heinemann, 1933–67.

Diogenes Laertius. *Lives of Eminent Philosophers*. Translated by R. D. Hinks. Cambridge: Harvard University Press, 1972.

Dodds, E. R. *The Greeks and the Irrational*. Berkeley: University of California Press, 1973.

Doresse, Jean. *The Secret Books of the Egyptian Gnostics*. Rochester, Vt.: Inner Traditions International, 1986.

Dümichen, J. *Der Grabpalast der Patuamenap*. Leipzig: J. C. Hinrichs, 1884–85.

Dunham, A. G. *The History of Miletus*. London: University of London Press, 1915.

DuQuesne, Terence. "Anubis, Master of Secrets *(Hery Sesheta)* and the Egyptian Conception of Mysteries." In *DE* 36 (1996): 25–38.

———. "Anubis e il Ponte dell'Arcobaleno. Aspetti dello sciamanismo nell'antico Egitto." In *La religione della terra*, edited by Grazia Marchianò, 115–35. Como: Red Edizioni, 1991.

———. *Anubis and the Spirits of the West*. Thame, England: Darengo, 1990.

———. *At the Court of Osiris*. London: Darengo, 1994.

———. *A Coptic Initiatory Invocation*. Thame, England: Darengo, 1991.

———. *Demeter, Anubis and the Eleusinian Mysteries*. Thame, England: Mandrake Press, 1990.

———. "Effective in Heaven and on Earth." In *Ägyptische Mysterien?*, edited by Jan Assmann and Martin Bommas, 37–46. München: Fink, 2002.

———. *Jackal at the Shaman's Gate*. Thame, England: Darengo, 1991.

Edwards, I. E. S. *The Pyramids of Egypt*. Harmondsworth: Penguin, 1993.

Eliade, Mircea. *History of Religious Ideas*, 3 vols. Chicago: University of Chicago Press, 1978–85.

———. *Images and Symbols: Studies in Religious Symbolism*. Princeton: Princeton University Press, 1991.

———. "Methodological Remarks on the Study of Religious Symbolism." In *The History of Religions: Essays in Methodology*, edited by Mircea Eliade and Joseph M. Kitagawa, 86–95. Chicago: University of Chicago Press, 1959.

———. *The Myth of the Eternal Return*. Prineton: Princeton University Press, 1965.

———. *Myths, Dreams and Mysteries*. London: Collins, 1960.

———. *Patterns in Comparative Religion*. London: Sheed and Ward, 1958.

———. *The Quest: History and Meaning in Religion*. Chicago: University of Chicago Press, 1984.

———. *Rites and Symbols of Initiation*. New York: Harper and Row, 1958.

———. *Shamanism: Archaic Techniques of Ecstasy*. 1964. Reprint, London: Arkana, 1989.

———. *The Two and the One*. London: Harvill Press, 1965.

Eliade, Mircea, and J. Kitagawa, eds. *The History of Religions: Essays in Methodology*. Chicago: University of Chicago Press, 1959.

Ellwood, Robert S., Jr. *Mysticism and Religion*. 1st ed. Englewood Cliffs, N.J.: Prentice Hall, 1980.

Emery, W. B. *Archaic Egypt*. Harmondsworth: Penguin, 1961.

Englund, G. *Akh. Une notion religieuse dans l'Égypte pharaonique*. Acta Universitatis Upsaliensis, Uppsala Studies in Ancient Mediterranean and Near Eastern Civilizations 11. Boreas: Uppsala, 1978.

———. "La Lumière et la Répartition des Textes dans la Pyramide." In *Hommages à Jean Leclant*, vol. 1, edited by Catherine Berger et al., 169–80. Cairo: Bibliotheque d'Étude, 1994.

Epigraphic Survey. *The Tomb of Kheruef: Theban Tomb 192*. Chicago: Oriental Institute Publications, 1980.

Erman, Adolf. *A Handbook of Egyptian Religion*. London: Archibald Constable, 1907.

———. *Life in Ancient Egypt*. Translated by H. M. Tirard. 1894. Reprint, New York: Dover, 1971.

Evans-Pritchard, E. E. *Theories of Primitive Religion*. Oxford: Oxford University Press, 1965.

Eyre, C. *The Cannibal Hymn: A Cultural and Literary Study*. Liverpool: Liverpool University Press, 2002.

Fairman, H. W. "The Kingship Rituals of Egypt." In *Myth, Ritual and Kingship*, edited by S. H. Hooke, 74–104. Oxford: Oxford University Press, 1958.

Faivre, A. *Access to Western Esotericism*. Albany: State University of New York Press, 1994.

———. "Ancient and Medieval Sources of Modern Esoteric Movements." In *Modern Esoteric Spirituality*, edited by A. Faivre and J. Needleman, 1–70. New York: SCM Press, 1992.

Faivre, A., and J. Needleman, eds. *Modern Esoteric Spirituality*. New York: SCM Press, 1992.

Fakhry, Ahmed. *The Monuments of Sneferu at Dashur*. 2 vols. Cairo: General Organisation for Government Printing Offices, 1959.

———. "A Note on the Tomb of Kheruef at Thebes." In *ASAE* 42 (1943): 447–532.

———. *The Pyramids*. Chicago: Chicago University Press, 1969.

Farington, Benjamin. *Science in Antiquity*. London: Thornton Butterworth, 1936.

Faulkner, R. O. *The Ancient Egyptian Book of the Dead*. London: British Museum Publications, 1985.

———. *The Ancient Egyptian Coffin Texts*. 3 vols. Warminster: Aris and Phillips, 1973–78.

———. *The Ancient Egyptian Pyramid Texts*. Oxford: Oxford University Press, 1969.

———. *A Concise Dictionary of Middle Egyptian*. Oxford: Griffith Institute, Ashmolean Museum, 1962.

———. "The King and the Star Religion in the Pyramid Texts." In *JNES* 25 (1966): 153–61.

Federn, W. "The 'Transformations' in the Coffin Texts: A New Approach." In *JNES* 19 (1960): 241–57.

Ferguson, John. *An Illustrated Encyclopaedia of Mysticism*. London: Thames and Hudson, 1976.

———. *The Religions of the Roman Empire*. London: Thames and Hudson, 1970.

Firth, C. M. "Excavations of the Department of Antiquities at Saqqara (October 1928 to March 1929)." In *ASAE* 29 (1929): 64–70.

Firth, C. M., and J. E. Quibell. *The Step Pyramid*. 2 vols. Cairo: Institut français d'Archéologie Orientale, 1935–36.

Fischer-Elfert, H. W. *Die Vision von der Statue im Stein*. Heidelberg: Universitäts-verlag, 1998.

Fix, W. R. *Star Maps*. London: Octopus, 1979.

Fleay, F. G. *Egyptian Chronology*. London: David Nutt, 1899.

Flood, Gavin. *Beyond Phenomenology*. London, New York: Cassell, 1999.

Forman, Robert K. C., *The Innate Capacity*. Oxford: Oxford University Press, 1998.

————, ed. *The Problem of Pure Consciousness*. Oxford: Oxford University Press, 1990.

Foucart, Paul. *Les Mystères d'Éleusis*. Paris: A. Picard, 1914.

Fowden, Garth. *The Egyptian Hermes*. Princeton: Princeton University Press, 1986.

Frankfort, Henri. *Ancient Egyptian Religion*. 1948. Reprint, London: Harper and Row, 1961.

————. *Kingship and the Gods*. Chicago: University of Chicago Press, 1978.

————. "Pyramid Temples and the Religion of the Old Kingdom." In *BO* 10 (1953): 157–62.

Frankfort, Henri, et al. *Before Philosophy: The Intellectual Adventure of Ancient Man, an Essay on Speculative Thought in the Ancient Near East*. Harmondsworth: Penguin Books, 1949.

Frankfort, Henri, A. de Buck, and B. Gunn. *The Cenotaph of Seti I at Abydos*. 2 vols. London: Egypt Exploration Fund, 1933.

Frazer, James. *The Golden Bough*. Abridged ed. London: MacMillan, 1929.

Gadamer, Hans-Georg. *Philosophical Hermeneutics*. Berkeley and Los Angeles: University of California Press, 1977.

————. *Truth and Method*. 2nd ed. London: Sheed and Ward, 1989.

Gardiner, A. *Egypt of the Pharaohs*. Oxford: Oxford University Press, 1966.

————. *Egyptian Grammar*. 3rd ed. London: Oxford University Press, 1973.

————. "Horus the Behdetite." In *JEA* 30 (1944): 23–60.

————. "Review of J. Frazer's *The Golden Bough*." In *JEA* 2 (1915): 121–26.

Godwin, Joscelyn. *Mystery Religions in the Ancient World*. London: Thames and Hudson, 1981.

Goedicke, H. *Re-used Blocks from the Pyramid of Amenemhet I at Lisht*. New York: Metropolitan Museum of Art, 1971.

Goethe, J. W. von. *Goethe's Werke*. Hamburger Ausgabe, 14 vols. Edited by Erich Trunz et al. Hamburg: Wegner, 1948–60.

Goff, B. L. *Symbols of Ancient Egypt in the Late Period*. New York: Mouton, 1979.

Gohary, J. *Akhenaten's Sed-Festival at Karnak*. London and New York: Kegan Paul International, 1992.

Goneim, Z. M. *Excavations at Saqqara: Horus Sekhem-khet: The Unfinished Step Pyramid at Saqqara*. Vol. 1. Cairo: Institut français d'archéologie orientale, 1957.

Griffiths, J. Gwyn. *The Conflict of Horus and Seth from Egyptian and Classical Sources*. Liverpool: Liverpool University Press, 1960.

————. "The Costume and Insignia of the King in the Sed-Festival." In *JEA* 41 (1955): 127–128.

————. *De Iside et Osiride*. Swansea: University of Wales Press, 1970.

————. "Mysterien." In *LÄ* 4: 276–77.

————. *The Origins of the Osiris Cult*. Leiden: E. J. Brill, 1980.

Guilmant, F. *Le Tombeau de Ramsès IX*. Le Caire: Institut français d'archéologie orientale, 1907.

Halifax, Joan. *Shaman: The Wounded Healer*. London: Thames and Hudson, 1982.

Hall, W. T., ed. *Introduction to the Study of Religion*. New York: Harper and Row, 1978.

Hanegraaff, W. J. *New Age Religion and Western Culture: Esotericism in the Mirror of Secular Thought*. Albany: State University of New York Press, 1998.

Hanegraaff, W. J., and R. van den Broek, eds. *Gnosis and Hermeticism from Antiquity to Modern Times*. Albany: State University of New York Press, 1998.

Harris, J. R., ed. *The Legacy of Egypt*. Oxford: Oxford University Press, 1971.

Harrison, Jane. *Prolegomena to the Study of Greek Religion*. London: Merlin Press, 1962.

Hart, George. *A Dictionary of Egyptian Gods and Goddesses*. London: Routledge and Kegan Paul, 1986.

Hassan, Selim. *Excavations at Giza*. Vol. 10. Cairo: General Organisation for Government Printing Offices, 1960.

Hawass, Z. "A Fragmentary Monument of Djoser from Saqqara." In *JEA* 80 (1994): 45–56.

———. "The Funerary Establishments of Khufu, Khafra and Menkaura during the Old Kingdom." Ph.D. diss., University of Pennsylvania, 1987; Ann Arbor: University Microfilms International, 1987.

Hayes, W. C. "Inscriptions from the Palace of Amenhotep III." In *JNES* 10 (1951), 35 ff.

———. *Scepter of Egypt*. Vol. 1. New York: Harper Brothers with Metropolitan Museum of Art, 1953.

———. *The Texts in the Mastabeh of Se'n-Wosret-'nkh at Lisht*. New York: Publications of the Metropolitan Museum of Art Egyptian Expedition 12, 1935.

Heinemann, Fritz. "Goethe's Phenomenological Method." In *Philosophy* 9 (1934): 67–81.

Helck, W. "Bemerkungen zum Ritual des Dramatischen Ramesseumpapyrus." In *Orientalia* 23 (1954): 383–411.

———. "Schamane und Zauberer." In *Mélanges Adolphe Gutbub*, 103–8. Montpellier: Université de Montpellier, 1984.

Herodotus, *Histories*. Translated by Aubrey de Sélincourt. Harmondsworth: Penguin, 1972.

Hick, John. *An Interpretation of Religion: Human Responses to the Transcendent*. New Haven: Yale University Press, 1989.

Hodel-Hoenes, S. *Life and Death in Ancient Egypt*. Ithaca: Cornell University Press, 1991.

Hollenback, J. C. *Mysticism: Experience, Response and Empowerment*. University Park: Pennsylvania State University Press, 1996.

Holscher, U. *Das Grabdenkmal des Königs Chephren*. Leipzig: J. C. Hinrichs, 1912.

Hooke, S. H. *Middle Eastern Mythology*. Harmondsworth: Penguin Books, 1963.

Hornung, Erik. *Das Amduat: Die Schrift des Verborgenen Raumes*. 3 vols. Wiesbaden: Otto Harrassowitz, 1963–67.

———. *The Ancient Egyptian Books of the Afterlife.* Translated by David Lorton. Ithaca: Cornell University Press, 1999.

———. *Conceptions of God in Ancient Egypt: The One and the Many.* Translated by John Baines. Ithaca: Cornell University Press, 1982.

———. "The Discovery of the Unconscious in Ancient Egypt." In *Spring* (1986): 16–28. Dallas: Spring Publications, 1986.

———. *Idea into Image: Essays on Ancient Egyptian Thought.* Translated by Elizabeth Bredeck. New York: Timken, 1992.

———. *The Secret Lore of Egypt: Its Impact on the West.* Translated by David Lorton. Ithaca: Cornell University Press, 2001.

———. *The Valley of the Kings.* Translated by David Warburton. New York: Timken, 1990.

Hornung, Erik, and E. Staehelin. *Studien zum Sedfest*, Aegyptiaca Helvetica 1. Geneva: Éditions de Belles-Lettres, 1974.

Houlihan, Patrick F. *The Animal World of the Pharaohs.* London: Thames and Hudson, 1996.

Husserl, Edmund. *Cartesian Meditations: An Introduction to Phenomenology.* Translated by Dorion Cairns. Dordrecht, Boston, and London: Kluwer Academic Publishers, 1993.

———. *Ideas: General Introduction to Pure Phenomenology.* Translated by W. R. Boyce Gibson. London: George Allen and Unwin, 1931.

———. "Phenomenology." In *Encyclopaedia Brittanica*, 14th ed., 1927. Reprinted in *Phenomenology*, by Joseph J. Kockelmans and Edmund Husserl, 28–30. West Lafayette, Ind.: Purdue University Press, 1994.

Hutton, Ronald. *Shamans: Siberian Spirituality and the Western Imagination.* London: Hambledon and London, 2001.

Iamblichus. *On the Mysteries of the Egyptians, Chaldeans, and Assyrians.* Translated by Thomas Taylor. 1821. 3rd-edition reprint, London: Stuart and Watkins, 1968.

Israelit-Groll, Sara. *Studies in Egyptology: Presented to Miriam Lichtheim.* 2 vols. Jerusalem: Magnes Press, Hebrew University, 1990.

Iversen, Erik. *Egyptian and Hermetic Doctrine.* Copenhagen: Museum Tusculanum Press, 1984.

———. *The Myth of Egypt and Its Hieroglyphs.* Princeton: Princeton University Press, 1961.

Jacq, C. *Egyptian Magic.* Translated by Janet M. Davis. Warminster: Aris and Phillips, 1985.

———. *La tradition primordiale de l'Egypte ancienne selon les Textes des Pyramides.* Paris: Bernard Grasset, 1998.

Jacobsen, Thorkild. *The Treasures of Darkness.* New Haven: Yale University Press, 1976.

Jakobsen, M. D. *Shamanism.* New York: Berghahn Books, 1999.

James, E. O. *Myth and Ritual in the Ancient Near East.* London: Thames and Hudson, 1958.

James, William. *The Varieties of Religious Experience*. London: Longmans, Green and Co., 1928.

Jaynes, Julian. *The Origins of Consciousness in the Breakdown of the Bicameral Mind*. Harmondsworth: Penguin, 1976.

Jeans, James. *The Growth of Physical Science*. Cambridge: Cambridge University Press, 1950.

Jéquier, G. *Le monument funéraire de Pepi II*. 3 vols. Cairo: Institut français d'archéologie orientale, 1936–41.

Johnson, W. Raymond. "Amenhotep III and Amarna: Some New Considerations." In *JEA* 82 (1996): 65–82.

Johnson, W. Raymond, and Edward F. Wente, eds. *Studies in Honor of George R. Hughes (Jan 12th, 1977)*. In *Studies in Ancient Oriental Civilization* 39. Chicago: Oriental Institute of the University of Chicago, 1976.

Jonas, Hans. *The Gnostic Religion*. Boston: Beacon Press, 1963.

Jung, C. G. *Alchemical Studies*. Vol. 13 of *The Collected Works of C. G. Jung*. Princeton: Princeton University Press, 1967.

———. *Mysterium Coniunctionis*. Vol. 14 of *The Collected Works of C. G. Jung*. 2nd ed. Princeton: Princeton University Press, 1974.

———. *Psychology and Religion: West and East*. Vol. 11 of *The Collected Works of C. G. Jung*. 2nd ed. Princeton: Princeton University Press, 1969.

———. "What India Can Teach Us." In *Civilization in Transition*, vol. 10 of *The Collected Works of C. G. Jung*. London: Routledge and Kegan Paul, 1970.

Junker, H. "Die Mysterien des Osiris." In *Internationale Woche für Religions-Ethnologie* 3, 414–26. Paris: P. Geuthner, 1922.

Kaiser, W. "Die Kleine Hebseddarstellung im Sonnenheiligtum des Neuserre." In *BÄBA* 12 (1971): 87–105.

Kákosy, László. "Hermes and Egypt." In *Studies in Pharaonic Religion and Society in Honour of J. Gwyn Griffiths*, edited by A. B. Lloyd, 258–61. London: Egypt Exploration Society, 1972.

Kalweit, Holger. *Dreamtime and Inner Space: The World of the Shaman*. Translated by Werner Wünsche. Boston and London: Shambhala, 1988.

Kant, Immanuel. *Critique of Pure Reason*. Translated by Norman Kemp Smith. London: Macmillan, 1933.

Katz, Steven, ed. *Mysticism and Philosophical Analysis*. New York: Oxford University Press, 1978.

Kemp, Barry J. *Ancient Egypt: Anatomy of a Civilization*. London: Routledge, 1989.

———. "Old Kingdom, Middle Kingdom, and Second Intermediate Period c. 2686–1552 B.C." In *Ancient Egypt: A Social History*, edited by B. G. Trigger et al., 71–182. Cambridge: Cambridge University Press, 1983.

Kerényi, Carl. *Eleusis*. Translated by Ralph Manheim. Princeton: Princeton University Press, 1967.

Kingsley, Peter. *Ancient Philosophy, Mystery and Magic: Empedocles and Pythagorean Tradition*. Oxford: Oxford University Press, 1995.

———. "From Pythagoras to the *Turba Philosophorum*: Egypt and Pythagorean Tradition." In *JWCI* 57 (1994): 1–13.

———. "Poimandres: The Etymology of the Name and the Origins of the Hermetica." In *JWCI* 56 (1993): 1–24.

Kirk, G. S., and J. E. Raven. *The Presocratic Philosophers*. Cambridge: Cambridge University Press, 1957.

Kitagawa, Joseph M. "The History of Religions in America." In *The History of Religions: Essays in Methodology*, edited by Mircea Eliade and Joseph M. Kitagawa, 1–30. Chicago: University of Chicago Press, 1959.

Kockelmans, J. *Edmund Husserl's Phenomenology*. West Lafayette, Ind.: Purdue University Press, 1994.

Kristensen, W. Brede. *Life Out of Death: Studies in the Religions of Egypt and of Ancient Greece*. Translated by H. J. Franken and G. R. H. Wright. Louvain: Peeters Press, 1992.

———. *The Meaning of Religion*. The Hague: Martinus Nijhoff, 1960.

Labrousse, Audran, and Ahmed M. Moussa. *Le temple d'accueil du complexe funéraire du roi Ounas*. Cairo: Institut français d'archéologie orientale, 1996.

Labrousse, Audran, J.-Ph. Lauer, and J. Leclant. *Le temple haut du complexe funéraire du roi Ounas*. Cairo: Institut français d'archéologie orientale, 1977.

Lamy, Lucy. *Egyptian Mysteries*. London: Thames and Hudson, 1981.

Lauer, J.-Ph. *Le problème des pyramides d'Égypte*. Paris: Payot, 1948.

———. *La pyramide à degrees*. 3 vols. Cairo: Institut français d'archéologie orientale, 1936–39.

———. *Saqqara: The Royal Cemetery of Memphis*. London: Thames and Hudson, 1976.

———. "Le temple haut de la pyramide du roi Ouserkaf à Saqqarah." In *ASAE* 53 (1955): 119–33.

Lauer, J.-Ph., and J. Leclant. *Le temple haut du complexe funéraire du roi Téti*. Cairo: Institut français d'archéologie orientale, 1972.

Leclant, J. "Fouilles et travaux en Égypte et au Soudan, 1974–75." In *Orientalia* 45 (1976): 275–318.

———. *Recherches dans la pyramide et au temple haut du pharaon Pépi 1er à Saqqarah*. Leiden: Nederlands Instituut voor Het Nabije Oosten, 1979.

Lefébure, E. *Les hypogées royaux de Thèbes. Première division: Le tombeau de Séti I*. Mémoires publiés par les membres de la Mission archéologique française au Caire, 3. Paris: E. Leroux, 1886.

Lehner, Mark. *The Complete Pyramids*. London: Thames and Hudson, 1997.

———. *The Pyramid Tomb of Queen Hetep-heres and the Satellite Pyramid*. Mainz: P. von Zabern, 1985.

Lepsius, R. *Aelteste Texte des Todtenbuchs nach Sarkophagen des Altaegyptischen Reichs im BerlinerMuseum*. Berlin: Wilhelm Hertz, 1867.

Lewis, I. M. *Ecstatic Religion*. Harmondsworth: Penguin Books, 1971.

———. *Religion in Context*. Cambridge: Cambridge University Press, 1996.

———. "What Is a Shaman?" In *Folk* 23 (1981).

Lichtheim, Miriam. *Ancient Egyptian Literature*. 3 vols. Berkeley: University of California Press, 1975–80.

Lucas, A. *Ancient Egyptian Materials and Industries*. 4th ed. Revised and enlarged by J. R. Harris. London: Edward Arnold, 1962.

Mahé, Jean-Pierre. *Hermès en haute-Egypte*. 2 vols. Québec: Presses de l'Université Laval, 1978–82.

Manniche, Lise. *Sacred Luxuries: Aromatherapy and Cosmetics in Ancient Egypt*. Ithaca: Cornell University Press, 1999.

Maspero, Gaston. *The Dawn of Civilization*. Translated by A. H. Sayce. London: Society for Promoting Christian Knowledge, 1894.

———. *Études de mythologie et d'archéologie égyptiennes*. Paris: E. Leroux, 1893.

———. *Les Inscriptions des pyramides de Saqqarah*. Paris: E. Bouillon, 1884.

Mathieu, B. "La signification du serdab dans la pyramide d'Ounas." In *Études sur l'Ancien Empire et la nécropole de Saqqâra dédiées à Jean-Philippe Lauer*, Orientalia Monspelansia, vol. 9, edited by C. Berger and B. Mathieu, 289–304. Montpellier: Université Paul Valéry, 1997.

Mayassis, S. *Le Livre des Morts de l'Égypte ancienne est un Livre d'Initiation*. Athens: Bibliothèque d'Archéologie Orientale d'Athènes, 1955.

———. *Mystères et initiations de l'Égypte ancienne*. Athens: Bibliothèque d'Archéologie Orientale d'Athènes, 1957.

Meeks, Dimitri. "Dieu masqué, dieu sans tête." In *Archéo-Nil* 1 (1991): 5–15.

Meeks, Dimitri, and Christine Favard-Meeks. *Daily Life of the Egyptian Gods*. London: Pimlico, 1999.

Mercer, Samuel A. B. *Literary Criticism of the Pyramid Texts*. London: Luzac and Co, 1956.

———. *The Pyramid Texts*. 3 vols. Toronto: Longmans, Green and Co., 1952.

———. *The Religion of Ancient Egypt*. London: Luzac, 1949.

Meyer, Marvin W., ed. *The Ancient Mysteries*. San Francisco: Harper and Row, 1987.

Minault-Gout, A. "Sur les vases jubilaires et leur diffusion." In *Études sur l'Ancien Empire et la nécropole de Saqqâra dédiées à Jean-Philippe Lauer*. Orientalia Monspelansia, vol. 9, edited by C. Berger and B. Mathieu, 305–14. Montpellier: Université Paul Valéry, 1997.

Montet, Pierre. *Les constructions et le tombeau de Psousennès à Tanis*. Paris, 1951.

———. *Everyday Life in Egypt in the Days of Ramesses the Great*. Translated by A. R. Maxwell-Hyslop and Margaret S. Drower. London: E. Arnold, 1958.

Morenz, S. *Egyptian Religion*. Translated by Ann E. Keep. London: Methuen, 1973.

Moret, A. *Mystères égyptiens*. Paris: Armand Colin, 1922.

Müller, W. M. *Egyptian Mythology*. London: G. G. Harrap, n.d.

Murnane, William J. *The Penguin Guide to Ancient Egypt*. Harmondsworth: Penguin Books, 1983.

———. "The Sed Festival: A Problem in Historical Method." In *MDAIK* 37 (1981): 369–76.

Mylonas, G. *Eleusis and the Eleusinian Mysteries*. Princeton: Princeton University Press, 1961.

Narancic, Maria. "Snake Spells in the Pyramid of Unas." Unpublished paper. 1996.

Nasr, S. H. *Religion and the Order of Nature*. Oxford: Oxford University Press, 1996.

Naville, E. *The Festival-Hall of Osorkon II in the Great Temple of Bubastis (1887–1889)*. London: Egypt Exploration Fund, 1892.

Naydler, J. *Temple of the Cosmos*. Rochester, Vt.: Inner Traditions International, 1996.

———, ed. *Goethe on Science: An Anthology of Goethe's Scientific Writings*. Edinburgh: Floris Books, 1996.

Neugebauer, O. *The Exact Sciences in Antiquity*. Copenhagen: E. Munksgaard, 1951. Reprint, New York: Harper Torchbooks, 1962.

Neumann, Erich. *The Origins and History of Consciousness*. Princeton: Princeton University Press, 1970.

Neusner, J., ed. *Religions in Antiquity*. Leiden: E. J. Brill, 1968.

Nicholson, Paul T., and L. Shaw, eds. *Ancient Egyptian Materials and Technology*. Cambridge: Cambridge University Press, 2000.

Nicholson, Shirley, ed. *Shamanism*. London: Theosophical Publishing House, 1987.

O'Mara, Patrick. *The Chronology of the Palermo and Turin Canons*. La Canada, Calif.: Paulette Publishing Co., 1980.

Osing, J. "Zur Disposition der Pyramidtexte des Unas." In *MDAIK* 42 (1986): 131–44.

Otto, Rudolf. *Mysticism East and West*. London: Macmillan and Co., 1932.

Pallis, S. A. *The Babylonian Akitu Festival*. København, Hovedkommissionaer: A. F. Høst, 1926.

Peet, T. Eric. *The Present Position of Egyptological Studies*. Oxford: Oxford University Press, 1934.

Petrie, W. M. Flinders. *A History of Egypt*. 5th ed., vol. 1. London: Methuen, 1903.

Pettazoni, Rafaele. "The Supreme Being: Phenomenological Structure and Historical Development." In *The History of Religions: Essays in Methodology*, edited by Mircea Eliade and Joseph Kitagawa, 59–66. Chicago: University of Chicago Press, 1959.

Piankoff, A. *Mythological Papyri*. 2 vols. New York: Pantheon Books, 1957.

———. *The Litany of Ra*. Princeton: Princeton University Press, 1961.

———. *The Pyramid of Unas*. Princeton: Princeton University Press, 1968.

———. *The Tomb of Ramesses VI*. 2 vols. New York: Pantheon Books, 1954.

Picard, Charles. "Sur la patrie et les pérégrinations de Déméter." In *Revue des Études Grecques* 40, (1927): 320–69.

Pike, Nelson. *Mystic Union: An Essay in the Phenomenology of Mysticism*. Ithaca: Cornell University Press, 1992.

Pinch, Geraldine. *Magic in Ancient Egypt*. London: British Museum Press, 1994.

Plato. *The Laws*. Translated by T. J. Sanders. Harmondsworth: Penguin, 1976.

———. *Phaedo*. Translated by H. Tredennick. Harmondsworth: Penguin, 1969.

———. *Phaedrus*. Translated by W. Hamilton. Harmondsworth: Penguin, 1973.

———. *Timaeus*. Translated by B. Jowett. London: Sphere Books, 1970.

Plotinus. *The Enneads*. Translated by Stephen MacKenna. London: Faber and Faber, 1956.

Plutarch. *De profectu in virtute in Moralia*. Translated by Frank Cole Babbitt et al. London: Loeb Classical Library, 1927.

———. *De Iside et Osiride*. Edited, translated, and commentary by J. Gwyn Griffiths. Swansea: University of Wales Press, 1970.

Popper, Karl. *Objective Knowledge*. Oxford: Oxford University Press, 1972.

Porphyry. *De Abstinentia: On abstinence from killing animals*. Translated by Gillian Clark. London: Duckworth, 2000.

Proudfoot, Wayne. *Religious Experience*. Berkeley: University of California Press, 1985.

Quibell, J. E. *Excavations at Saqqara, 1907–1908*. Cairo: Institut français d'archéologie orientale, 1909.

Quirke, Stephen. *Ancient Egyptian Religion*. London: British Museum Press, 1992.

———. *The Cult of Ra*. London: Thames and Hudson, 2001.

———. *Hieroglyphs and the Afterlife*. Norman, Okla.: University of Oklahoma Press, 1996.

———, ed. *The Temple in Ancient Egypt*. London: British Museum Press, 1997.

Radin, Paul. *Primitive Religion*. New York: Dover, 1957.

Rambova, N. "The Symbolism of the Papyri." In *Mythological Papyri*, vol. 1, edited by A. Piankoff, 29–65. New York: Pantheon Books, 1957.

Rawlinson, Andrew. *The Book of Enlightened Masters*. Chicago: Open Court, 1997.

Redford, Donald B. *Pharaonic King-Lists, Annals and Day Books*. Mississauga, Ontario: Benben Publications, 1986.

Reeder, Greg. "Running the Heb Sed." In *KMT* 4, no. 4 (1993–94): 60–71.

Rice, Michael. *Egypt's Legacy*. London: Routledge, 1997.

Ricke, H. *Bemerkungen zur ägyptischen Baukunst des Alten Reiches* 2. BÄBA 5. Cairo: Schweizerisches Institut für Ägyptische Bauforschung und Alterumskunde in Kairo, 1950.

Ritner, R. K. *The Mechanics of Ancient Egyptian Magical Practice*. Chicago: Oriental Institute of the University of Chicago, 1993.

Roberts, A. *Hathor Rising*. Totnes: Northgate Publishers, 1995.

———. *My Heart, My Mother: Death and Rebirth in Ancient Egypt*. Rottingdean: Northgate Publishers, 2000.

———. "The Mystery Drama of Renewal: An Archaic Ritual." Unpublished paper, 1989.

Robinson, James, ed. *The Nag Hammadi Library in English*. Leiden: E. J. Brill, 1970.

Roszak, Theodore. *Where the Wasteland Ends*. London: Faber and Faber, 1972.

Roth, Ann Macy. "The *pss-kf* and the 'Opening of the Mouth' Ceremony: A Ritual of Birth and Rebirth." In *JEA* 78 (1992): 113–47.

Rothberg, Donald. "Contemporary Epistemology and the Study of Mysticism." In *The Problem of Pure Consciousness*, edited by Robert K. C. Forman, 163–91. New York: Oxford University Press, 1990.

Roulin, G. *Le Livre de la Nuit: Une composition égyptienne de l'au-delá.* 2 vols. Freiburg and Göttingen: Editions Universitaires, Vendenhoeck and Ruprecht, 1996.

Russell, B. *The Wisdom of the West.* London: MacDonald, 1969.

Rydström, Kjell T. "*Hery Sesheta* 'In Charge of Secrets': The 3000-Year Evolution of a Title." In *DE* 28 (1994): 53–94.

Salaman, C., et al. *The Way of Hermes.* London: Duckworth, 1999.

Sandars, N. K. *Poems of Heaven and Hell from Ancient Mesopotamia.* Harmondsworth: Penguin, 1971.

Schäfer, H. *Die Mysterien des Osiris in Abydos.* Leipzig: J. C. Hinrichs, 1903.

Schiff Giorgini, M. *Soleb.* 2 vols. In collaboration with C. Robichon and J. Lechart. Firenze: Sonsoni, 1965–71.

Schlamm, Leon. "Ken Wilber's Spectrum Model: Identifying Alternative Soteriological Perspectives." In *Religion* 31, no. 1 (2001): 19–39.

Schott, S. *Bemerkungen zur Ägyptischen Pyramidenkult.* BÄBA 5, 135–252. Cairo: Schweizerisches Institut für Ägyptische Bauforschung und Alterumskunde in Kairo, 1950.

———. *Mythe und Mythenbildung im Alten Ägypten.* UGAÄ 15. Leipzig: J. C. Hinrichs, 1945.

Schwaller de Lubicz, R. A. *The Egyptian Miracle.* Translated by André VandenBroeck. Rochester Vt.: Inner Traditions International, 1985.

———. *Sacred Science.* Translated by André VandenBroeck. Rochester Vt.: Inner Traditions International, 1982.

———. *The Temple in Man.* Translated by Deborah Lawlor and Robert Lawlor. Rochester, Vt.: Inner Traditions International, 1977.

———. *The Temple of Man.* 2 vols. Translated by Deborah Lawlor and Robert Lawlor. Rochester, Vt.: Inner Traditions International, 1998.

Schweitzer, U. "Archäologischer Bericht aus Ägypten." In *Orientalia* 19 (1950): 118–122.

Scott, Walter, ed. and trans. *Hermetica.* vol 1. 1924. Reprint, Trowbridge: Solos Press, 1992.

Sellers, Jane B. *The Death of Gods in Ancient Egypt.* London: Penguin, 1992.

Sethe, K. *Die Altägyptischen Pyramidentexte.* 4 vols. Leipzig: J. C. Hinrichs, 1908–22.

———. *Dramatische Texte zu altägyptische Mysterienspielen.* Leipzig: J. C. Hinrichs, 1928.

———. "Die Totenliteratur der alten Ägypter." In *SPAW* 18 (1931): 520–43.

Settgast, J. *Untersuchungen zu Altägyptischen Bestattungsdarstellungen.* Glückstadt, Hamburg, and New York: J. J. Augustin, 1963.

Shafer, Byron E., ed. *Temples of Ancient Egypt.* Ithaca: Cornell University Press, 1997.

Sharpe, Eric J. *Comparative Religion: A History.* London: Duckworth, 1986.

Smart, Ninian. "Beyond Eliade: The Future of Theory in Religion." In *Numen* 25 (1978): 171–83.

———. *Concept and Empathy.* London: Macmillan, 1986.

———. *The Science of Religion and the Sociology of Knowledge.* Princeton: Princeton University Press, 1973.

Bibliography

Sørensen, J. P. "Ancient Egyptian Religious Thought and the XVIth Hermetic Tractate." In *The Religion of the Ancient Egyptians*, edited by G. Englund, 41–57. Uppsala, 1987.

Spencer, A. J. "Two Enigmatic Hieroglyphs and Their Relation to the Sed-Festival." In *JEA* 64 (1978): 52–56.

Spiegel, J. "Das Auferstehungsritual der Unaspyramide." In *ASAE* 53 (1955): 339–439.

———. *Das Auferstehungsritual der Unas-Pyramide*. Wiesbaden, Germany: O. Harrassowitz, 1971.

———. "Die religiongeschichtliche Stellung der Pyramidentexte." In *Or* 22 (1953): 129–57.

Stace, W. T. *Mysticism and Philosophy*. London: Macmillan and Co., 1961.

Stadelmann, R. "Die Pyramiden des Snofru in Daschur." In *MDAIK* 38 (1982): 379–93.

———. "Scheintür oder Stelen im Totentempel des AR." In *MDAIK* 39 (1983): 237–41.

———. "Snofru und die Pyramiden von Meidum und Dahschur." In *MDAIK* 36 (1980): 437–49.

Steiner, Rudolf. *Egyptian Myths and Mysteries*. New York: Anthroposophic Press, 1971.

Strabo. *Geography*. Translated by H. L. Jones. Cambridge, Mass.: Loeb Classical Library, 1930.

Strenski, Ivan. *Four Theories of Myth in Twentieth Century History*. London: Macmillan Press, 1987.

———. *Religion in Relation*. London: Macmillan Press, 1993.

Stricker, B. H. *De Brief van Aristeas*. Amsterdam: Noord-Hollandsche Uitg. Mij, 1956.

Strouhal, E. *Life in Ancient Egypt*. Cambridge: Cambridge University Press, 1992.

Strouhal, E., and M. F. Gaballah. "King Djedkare-Isesi and His Daughters." In *Biological Anthropology and the Study of Ancient Egypt*, edited by W. V. Davies and R. Walker, 104–18. London: British Museum Press, 1993.

Strouhal, E., and M. F. Gaballah. "Re-investigation of the remains thought to be of King Djoser and those of an unidentified female from the Step Pyramid at Saqqarah." In *Anthropologie* 32, no. 3 (1994): 225–42.

Thausing, G. *Der Auferstehungsgedanke in ägyptischen religiösen Texten*. Leipzig: O. Harrassowitz, 1943.

Tobin, Vincent. "The Bicameral Mind as a Rationale of Egyptian Religion." In *Studies in Egyptology: Presented to Miriam Lichtheim*, 2 vols., edited by Sara Israelit-Groll, 994–1018. Jerusalem: Magnes Press, Hebrew University, 1990.

Tompkins, P. *Secrets of the Great Pyramid*. New York: Harper and Row, 1971.

Toynbee, Arnold. *A Study of History*. Oxford: Oxford University Press, 1972.

Tylor, Edward Burnett. *Primitive Culture*. London: John Murray, 1971.

Underhill, Evelyn. *Mysticism*. New York: New American Library, 1974.

Uphill, Eric. "The Egyptian Sed-Festival Rites." In *JNES* 24 (1965): 365–83.

van der Leeuw, G. "On Phenomenology and Its Relation to Theology." In *Classical Approaches to the Study of Religion*, edited by J. Waardenburg, 406–7. The Hague: Mouton, 1973.

———. *Religion in Essence and Manifestation*. Translated by J. E. Turner. London: George Allen and Unwin, 1938.

———. "Some Recent Achievements of Psychological Research and Their Application to History, in Particular the History of Religion." In *Classical Approaches to the Study of Religion*, edited by J. Waardenburg, 399–405. The Hague: Mouton, 1973.

———. "Confession scientifique." In *Numen* 1 (1954), 8 ff.

Velde, H. te. *Seth: God of Confusion*. Leiden: E. J. Brill, 1967.

Verner, Miroslav. "The Fifth Dynasty's Mysterious Sun Temples." In *KMT* 14, no. 1 (2003): 44–57.

Versluis, Arthur. *The Egyptian Mysteries*. London: Arkana, 1988.

———. *Restoring Paradise: Esoteric Transmission through Literature and Art*. Albany: State University of New York Press, 2004.

———. *Song of the Cosmos: An Introduction to Traditional Cosmology*. Bridport, Prism Press, 1991.

———. *TheoSophia: Hidden Dimensions of Christianity*. New York: Lindisfarne Press, 1994.

———. "What Is Esoteric? Methods in the Study of Western Esotericism." In *Esoterica* 4 (2002): 1–15. http:www.esoteric.msu.edu.

Vitebsky, P. *The Shaman*. London: Macmillan, 1995.

Waardenburg, J., ed. *Classical Approaches to the Study of Religion*. The Hague: Mouton, 1973.

———. *Reflections on the Study of Religion*. The Hague: Mouton, 1978.

Wainwright, G. A. *The Sky-Religion in Ancient Egypt*. Cambridge: Cambridge University Press, 1938.

Wainwright, William J. *Mysticism: A Study of Its Nature, Cognitive Value and Moral Implications*. Brighton, U.K.: Harvester Press, 1981.

Walsem, R. van. "The *psš-kf*: An Investigation of an Ancient Egyptian Funerary Instrument." In *OMRO* 59 (1978–79): 193–249.

Walsh, Roger N., *The Spirit of Shamanism*. London: HarperCollins, 1990.

Walther, Gerda. *Phänomenologie der Mystik*. Olten und Freiburg im Breisgau: Walter Verlag, 1955.

Watterson, B. *The Gods of Ancient Egypt*. London: B. T. Batsford, 1984.

Wente, Edward F. "Hathor at the Jubilee." In E.B. Hauser ed., *Studies in Honor of John A. Wilson, September 12, 1969. Studies in Ancient Oriental Civilization* 35, 83–91. Chicago: The Oriental Institute of the University of Chicago, 1969.

———. "Mysticism in Pharaonic Egypt?" In *JNES* 41 (1982): 161–79.

———. "Review of J. Gwyn Griffiths, *The Conflict of Horus and Seth from Egyptian and Classical Sources*." In *JNES* 22 (1963): 273–76.

Wente, Edward F., and Charles van Siclen III. "A Chronology of the New Kingdom." In *Studies in Honour of George R. Hughes (Jan. 12th 1977)*, edited by Janet H. Johnson and Edward F. Wente. In *Studies in Ancient Oriental Civilization* 39. Chicago: Chicago University Press, 1976.

West, J. A. *Serpent in the Sky*. London: Wildwood House, 1979.

———. *The Traveller's Key to Ancient Egypt*. London: Harrap Columbus, 1987.

Westendorf, Wolfhart. "Bemerkungen zur "Kammer der Wiedergeburt" im Tutanchamungrab." In *ZÄS* 94 (1967): 139–50.

———. "Symbol, Symbolik." In *LÄ* 6:122–28.

Whaling, Frank, ed. *Contemporary Approaches to the Study of Religion*. 2 vols. Berlin: Mouton, 1983.

White, Jon Manchip. *Everyday Life in Ancient Egypt*. London: B. T. Batsford, 1963.

Wilber, Ken. *Up From Eden: A Transpersonal View of Human Evolution*. 1981. Reprint, Wheaton, Ill.: Theosophical Publishing House, 1996.

Wilkinson, J. G. *The Ancient Egyptians*. 2 vols. London: John Murray, 1853.

Wilkinson, Richard. *Reading Egyptian Art*. London: Thames and Hudson, 1992.

———. *Symbol and Magic in Ancient Egyptian Art*. London: Thames and Hudson, 1994.

Willems, H. *The Coffin of Heqata*. Leuven: Uitgeverij Peeters en Departement Oriëntalistiek, 1996.

Wilson, John A. *The Culture of Ancient Egypt*. Chicago: University of Chicago Press, 1956.

———. "Egypt." In *Before Philosophy*, Henri Frankfort et al., 39–133. Harmondsworth: Penguin, 1961.

Wright, Esmond, ed. *The Ancient World*. Secaucus, N.J.: Chartwell Books, 1979.

Yates, Frances A. *Giordano Bruno and the Hermetic Tradition*. London: Routledge and Kegan Paul, 1964.

Zaehner, R. C. *Mysticism Sacred and Profane*. London: Oxford University Press, 1961.

Zabkar, L. V. "Adaptation of Ancient Egyptian Texts to the Temple Ritual at Philae." In *JEA* 66 (1980): 127–36.

ILLUSTRATION CREDITS

N.b.: Full citations for the sources listed here can be found in the bibliography.

Chapter 3: The Mystical versus the Funerary Interpretation of Ancient Egyptian Religion

3.1. The *qeni* worn by a *sem* priest. Tomb of Tausert, New Kingdom. (Author's drawing).

3.2. The "secret rites" of the Sed festival: King Osorkon II is purified. Relief from his ceremonial gateway at Bubastis. (Naville, *The Festival Hall of Osorkon II*, pl. 11).

3.3. Osiris with Isis. Osiris wears the white crown. Papyrus of Ani, New Kingdom. (Budge, *The Book of the Dead*, 71).

3.4. The "secret rites" of the Sed festival. King Osorkon II enters a shrine or tomb. From his ceremonial gateway, Bubastis. (Naville, *The Festival Hall of Osorkon II*, pl. 10).

3.5. The "secret rites" of the Sed festival. King Niuserre stands beside a double bed. Relief from his sun temple at Abu Gurob. (Von Bissing and Kees, *Das Re-Heiligtum des Königs Ne-woser-re*, vol. 3, pl. 56B).

3.6. A mummy lies on a lion-headed bier. Papyrus of Ani, vignette to BD 89. New Kingdom. (Budge, *The Book of the Dead*, 279p).

3.7. The conception of Horus. Temple of Hathor, Denderah. (Budge, *The Gods of the Egyptians*, 2:137, fig. 20).

3.8. King Niuserre is reborn as a god. Relief from his sun temple at Abu Gurob. (Von Bissing and Kees, *Das Re-Heiligtum des Königs Ne-woser-re*, vol. 3, pl. 56B).

3.9. King Seti I lies prone on a lion bed. From his cenotaph at Abydos. (Frankfort et al., *The Cenotaph of Seti I at Abydos*, 1:68).

3.10. The king turns over on his stomach to face Horus. Relief from the temple of Hathor, Denderah. (Budge, *Osiris and the Egyptian Resurrection*, 2:54).

Chapter 4: The Pyramids As the Locus of Secret Rites

4.1. King Zoser performs the Sed festival rite of "dedicating the field." From a relief within his pyramid at Saqqara. (Firth and Quibell, *The Step Pyramid*, vol. 2, pl. 3.4.)

4.2. King Osorkon II is crowned with the red crown and wears the long Osirian cloak. Relief from his ceremonial gateway at Bubastis. (Naville, *The Festival Hall of Osorkon II*, pl. 23.)

4.3. Sed festival offerings placed before Niuserre. A relief fragment from his sun temple at Abu Gurob. (Von Bissing and Kees, *Das Re Heiligtum des Königs Ne-woser-re*, vol. 3, pl. 20.318.)

4.4. The coronation of King Niuserre at his Sed festival. (Von Bissing and Kees, *Das Re Heiligtum des Königs Ne-woser-re*, vol. 2, pl. 11a.)

4.5. The primordial mound and the Sed festival dais both have the same form. (Kristensen, *Life Out of Death*, 68, fig. 30.) Reproduced by kind permission of Peeters Press.

4.6. The pyramid complex of Zoser at Saqqara. (Lauer, La pyramide *à degrés*, vol. 2, pl. 4.)

4.7. King Zoser visits the shrine of the god Horus. From a relief within his pyramid at Saqqara. (Firth and Quibell, *The Step Pyramid*, vol. 2, pl. 16.)

4.8. Location of the seven provincial pyramids. (Lehner, *The Complete Pyramids*, 96.) Reproduced by kind permission of Mark Lehner.

4.9. Map showing the positions of the pyramids at Seila, Meidum, and Dahshur, all attributed to Sneferu. (Adapted from illustration by Mark Lehner.)

4.10. Sneferu's Bent Pyramid at Dahshur. (Fakhry, *The Pyramids*, 78, fig. 43.) Reproduced by kind permission of University of Chicago Press.

4.11. Stela of King Sneferu from the Bent Pyramid complex.(Fakhry, *The Monuments of Sneferu at Dahshur*, vol. 1, fig. 53.) Reproduced by kind permission of the General Organization for Government Printing Offices, Cairo.

4.12. King Sneferu "dedicates the field." Valley temple to the Bent Pyramid at Dahshur. (Fakhry, *The Monuments of Sneferu at Dahshur*, 2:66, fig. 43.) Reproduced by kind permission of the General Organization for Government Printing Offices, Cairo.

4.13. The king engages in a rite known as the "going round of the Apis bull." Valley temple to Sneferu's Bent Pyramid at Dahshur. (Fakhry, *The Monuments of Sneferu at Dahshur*, 2:99, fig. 96.) Reproduced by kind permission of the General Organization for Government Printing Offices, Cairo.

4.14. King Sneferu is embraced by the goddess Seshat. Valley temple to Sneferu's Bent Pyramid at Dahshur. (Fakhry, *The Monuments of Sneferu at Dahshur*, 2:95, fig. 81.) Reproduced by kind permission of the General Organization for Government Printing Offices, Cairo.

4.15. Khufu, wearing the short Sed festival tunic, sits enthroned. Relief fragment from the northern wall of the causeway to his pyramid at Giza. (After Hassan, *Excavations at Giza*, vol. 10, pl. 6B.)

4.16. One of the earliest depictions of the Egyptian king wearing the Sed festival kilt with the bull's tail and "smiting the enemy." From the Narmer palette, First Dynasty. (Schwaller de Lubicz, *Sacred Science*, 116, fig. 17.)

4.17. King Sahure sits in an open booth, enthroned and wearing the short Sed festival tunic. Relief from his pyramid temple at Abusir. (Borchardt, *Das Grabdenkmal des Königs Sa-hu-Re*, vol. 2, pl. 45.)

4.18. Map showing the Fifth and Sixth Dynasty pyramid fields at Saqqara. (Adapted from Fakhry, *The Pyramids*, 190, fig. 105.)

4.19. Plan of the pyramid and pyramid temple of Pepi II at Saqqara. (Jéquier, *Le monument funéraire de Pepi II*, vol. 3, pl. 1.)

4.20. Relief showing the king performing the "dedication of the field" rite. Reconstruction drawing from the central transverse corridor of his pyramid temple. (From Jéquier, *Le monument funéraire de Pepi II*, vol. 3, pl. 8.)

4.21. The king smites the Libyan. Reconstruction drawing of relief in the central transverse corridor of the pyramid temple of Pepi II. (Jéquier, *Le monument funéraire de Pepi II*, vol. 2, pl. 8.)

4.22. Pepi II is suckled by a goddess. From the niche on stairway, north wall of the central transverse corridor, pyramid temple of Pepi II. (Jéquier, *Le monument funéraire de Pepi II*, vol. 2, pl. 30.)

4.23. Part of a scene from the antechamber (east wall) of Pepi II's pyramid temple showing the king holding the *seshed* cloth. (Jéquier, *Le monument funéraire de Pepi II*, vol. 2, pl. 50.)

Chapter 6: The Pyramid of Unas

6.1. The locations of the main pyramids at Saqqara. (Adapted from Fakhry, *The Pyramids*, 190.)

6.2. Reconstruction drawing of the valley temple of Unas. (Labrousse and Moussa, *Le temple d'accueil du complexe funéraire du roi Ounas*, fig.38.) Reproduced by kind permission of Institut français d'archéologie orientale.

6.3. Map showing the valley temple, causeway, pyramid temple, and pyramid of Unas. (Adapted from Murnane, *The Penguin Guide to Ancient Egypt*, 164.)

6.4. The pyramid temple and pyramid of Unas. Reconstruction drawing. (Labrousse and Moussa, *Le temple d'accueil du complexe funéraire du roi Ounas*, fig. 39.) Reproduced by kind permission of Institut français d'archéologie orientale.

6.5. Plan of the pyramid temple of Unas. (Fakhry, *The Pyramids*, 183.) Reproduced by kind permission of Chicago University Press.

6.6. Fragment of the king performing "the dedication of the field" dance of the Sed festival. Drawing of a relief fragment from pyramid temple of Unas. (Labrousse et al., *Le temple haut du complexe funéraire du roi Ounas*, 85, fig. 56.) Reproduced by kind permission of Institut français d'archéologie orientale.

6.7. The king, wearing a false beard and short Sed festival tunic, sits enthroned. Drawing of relief fragment from pyramid temple of Unas. (Labrousse et al., *Le temple haut du complexe funéraire du roi Ounas*, 86, fig. 57.) Reproduced by kind permission of Institut français d'archéologie orientale.

6.8. Offering bearers carrying trays of fruit. Drawing of limestone fragment from pyramid temple of Unas. (Labrousse et al., *Le temple haut du complexe funéraire du roi Ounas*, 110, fig. 102.) Reproduced by kind permission of Institut français d'archéologie orientale.

6.9. Cross-section of pyramid of Unas. (Author's drawing.)

6.10. Drawing of the pyramid of Unas. (Author's drawing, adapted from Lehner, *The Complete Pyramids*, 33.)

6.11. Plan of entrance passage, corridor, and chambers of pyramid of Unas. (Author's drawing.)

6.12. View into the sarcophagus chamber of the pyramid of Unas. (Photo by Louanne Richards.)

6.13. An example of the so-called palace façade design from sarcophagus chamber of pyramid of Unas. (Photo by Louanne Richards.)

6.14. Diagram showing location of texts in the sarcophagus chamber. (Author's drawing.)

6.15. Diagram showing location of texts in the antechamber. (Author's drawing.)

6.16. Diagram of order of utterances for recitation according to Spiegel. (Barta, *Die Bedeutung der Pyramidentexte*, 180, abb. 5.)

6.17. Diagram of order of utterances according to Altenmüller. (Barta, *Die Bedeutung der Pyramidentexte*, 180, abb. 8.)

6.18. Diagram of cosmological symbolism of the chambers of the pyramid, according to Allen. (Allen, "Reading a Pyramid," 24, fig. 24.) Reproduced by kind permission of Institut français d'archéologie orientale.

Chapter 7: The Sarcophagus Chamber Texts

7.1. The Offering Liturgy on the north wall of the sarcophagus chamber. (Author's drawing.)

7.2. A *sem* priest performs the incense rite. Drawing of relief in temple of Seti. New Kingdom. (Wilkinson, *Symbol and Magic in Egyptian Art*, 103, fig. 70.) Illustration by Troy Sagrillo.

7.3. A libation is poured "under the sandals" of King Niuserre. Relief from his sun temple at Abu Gurob. (Von Bissing and Kees, *Das Re-Heiligtum des Königs Ne-woser-re*, vol. 2, pl. 9.)

7.4. Opening of the Mouth with the *peseshkef*. Tomb of Pet-Amen-Apet, Twenty-sixth Dynasty. (Budge, *The Book of Opening the Mouth*, 2:162.)

7.5. Seti I is suckled by Hathor. Temple of Abydos. (David, *A Guide to Religious Ritual at Abydos*, 22.) Reproduced by kind permission of Aris and Phillips.

7.6. The offering of milk in vases. Tomb of Pet-Amen-Apet, Twenty-sixth Dynasty. (Budge, *The Liturgy of Funerary Offerings*, 69.)

7.7. Pepi II sits on a throne before a table of offerings. Reconstruction from relief fragments in the sanctuary of his pyramid temple at Saqqara. (Jéquier, *Le Monument Funéraire de Pepi II*, vol. 2, pl. 61.)

7.8. The seven holy oils. From the tomb of Pet-Amen-Apet, Twenty-Sixth Dynasty. (Budge, *The Liturgy of Funerary Offerings*, 89.)

7.9. The offering of linen cloth. From the tomb of Pet-Amen-Apet, Twenty-Sixth Dynasty. (Budge, *The Book of Opening the Mouth*, 2:182.)

7.10. Part of a procession of offering bearers. Limestone fragment from the pyramid temple of Unas. (Labrousse et al., *Le temple haut du complexe funéraire du roi Ounas*, 108, fig. 99.) Reproduced by kind permission of Institut français d'archéologie orientale.

7.11. The king sits in front of an offering table. Relief fragment from the pyramid temple of Unas. (Labrousse et al., *Le temple haut du complexe funéraire du roi Ounas*, 89, fig. 64.) Reproduced by kind permission of Institut français d'archéologie orientale.

7.12. Diagram of the sarcophagus chamber, pyramid of Unas. (Author's drawing.)

7.13. The distribution of texts on the south wall of the sarcophagus chamber of the pyramid of Unas. (Author's drawing.)

7.14. The human soul takes the form of a human-headed falcon. From the New Kingdom tomb of Arinefer, Thebes. (Naydler, *Temple of the Cosmos*, 206.)

7.15. The reconciliation of Horus and Seth. Book of Gates, tenth division. (Budge, *The Gods of the Egyptians*, 2:242.)

7.16. Scene from the Sed festival of Amenhotep III, showing him traveling as Ra on the solar night bark. From the New Kingdom tomb of Kheruef. (Adapted from the Epigraphic Survey, *Tomb of Kheruef*, pl. 24.)

7.17. Orion, Sothis, and the southern constellations. From the New Kingdom tomb of Senenmut, Deir el-Bahri. (Schwaller de Lubicz, *Sacred Science*, 176, fig. 35.)

7.18. Location of texts on the east wall of the sarcophagus chamber of the pyramid of Unas. (Author's drawing.)

7.19. The red crown is a manifestation of the fiery cobra goddess Wadjet. Drawing of a relief of Seti I, from his temple at Abydos. (Erman, *Life in Egypt*, 226.)

7.20. Senwosret III sits upon the Sed festival coronation dais. From a lintel in Naq el-Medamud. (Wilkinson, *Reading Egyptian Art*, 119, fig. 1.) Illustration by Troy Sagrillo.

7.21. The awakening of the initiate-king. Temple of Denderah. (Budge, *Osiris and the Egyptian Resurrection*, 40.)

7.22. The placement of texts in the passage between the sarcophagus chamber and the antechamber. (Author's drawing.)

7.23. Sed festival "dedication of the field" rite is witnessed by Min. Relief carving at Karnak, depicting Hatshepsut's Sed festival. (Author's drawing.)

7.24. The texts of the east gable concerned with the nourishment of the king. (Author's drawing.)

7.25. King Narmer as a bull. Detail from the Narmer palette. Early Dynastic period, circa 3100 B.C. (Schwaller de Lubicz, *Sacred Science*, 118.)

7.26. Unas consorts with two goddesses. Relief fragment from his pyramid temple at Saqqara. (Labrousse et al., *Le temple haut du complexe funéraire du roi Ounas*, 82, fig. 52.) Reproduced by kind permission of Institut français d'archéologie orientale.

7.27. The dangers of traveling in the Underworld. From the New Kingdom Book of the Earth. Tomb of Ramesses IX, Valley of the Kings. (Guilmant, *Le tombeau de Ramsès IX*, pl. 56.)

7.28. Unas is suckled by a goddess. Drawing from a relief fragment found at his pyramid temple. (Author's drawing.)

Chapter 8: The Antechamber Texts

8.1. The seven texts of the antechamber west gable. (Author's drawing).

8.2. The seven texts of the sarcophagus chamber east gable compared with the seven texts of the antechamber west gable. (Author's drawing.)

8.3. Sekhmet, the fiery leonine goddess. (Brodrick and Morton, *A Concise Dictionary of Egyptian Archaeology*, 156.)

8.4. The king appears as Nefertem, the solar child within the lotus. Ptolemaic bronze mirror, from a tomb at Faras. (Drawing by Barry Cottrell.)

8.5. Hu and Sia accompany Ra on his journey through the sky in the sun boat. The New Kingdom Book of Night, Osireion, Abydos. (Roulin, *Le Livre de la Nuit: Une composition égyptienne de l'au-delà*, vol. 2, pl. 1, adapted.) Reproduced by kind permission of Éditions Saint-Paul, Fribourg.

8.6. Shu lifts up the newborn sun. (Brodrick and Morton, *A Concise Dictionary of Egyptian Archaeology*, 118.)

8.7. The fifteen west-to-south-wall antechamber texts. (Author's drawing.)

8.8. An example of inverse quoining in the valley temple of Khafre at Giza. (Drawing by Iain Geddes.)

8.9. The liberation of Ra from his imprisonment in the earth. BD 17, Papyrus of Ani. New Kingdom. (Budge, *The Book of the Dead*, 99.)

8.10. Isis-Hededyt and Sothis reconstitute the headless body of Osiris. Ptolemaic temple of Philae. (Adapted from Lamy, *Egyptian Mysteries*, 86.)

8.11. The six utterances of the west wall of the antechamber, pyramid of Unas. (Author's drawing.)

8.12. Comparison between the texts of the antechamber west wall and those of the sarcophagus chamber east wall. (Author's drawing.)

8.13. Ra watches the sun disk emerge from the eastern gate of the Akhet. (Müller, *Egyptian Mythology*, 24.)

8.14. The texts of the south wall of the antechamber. (Author's drawing.)

8.15. The Two Truths or "Double Maat." (Wilkinson, *The Ancient Egyptians*, 2:205.)

8.16. King Niuserre "dedicates the field." From his sun temple at Abu Gurob. (Von Bissing and Kees, *Das Re-Heiligtum des Königs Ne-woser-re*, vol. 2, pl. 13, fig. 33B.)

8.17. A reed float raft. (Baines and Málek, *An Atlas of Ancient Egypt*, 68.) Reproduced courtesy of Andromeda Oxford Limited.

8.18. The reconstituted Osiris is represented by the upright *djed*. New Kingdom papyrus of Khonsu Renep. (Piankoff and Rambova, *Mythological Papyri*, 61, fig. 48.) Reproduced by kind permission of Princeton University Press.

8.19. The hippopotamus goddess Ipy. (Budge, *The Gods of the Egyptians*, 2:29.)

8.20. The constellation of the celestial hippopotamus. Tomb of Seti I. (Budge, *The Gods of the Egyptians*, 2:313.)

8.21. Osiris in his celestial manifestation as the constellation Orion. Ceiling of the tomb of Senenmut. Eighteenth Dynasty. (Schwaller de Lubicz, *Sacred Science*, 176.)

8.22. The cow goddess Hathor in a papyrus thicket. Papyrus of Ani. (Budge, *From Fetish to God in Ancient Egypt*, 59.)

8.23. Djed pillar made of papyrus stems. (Clark, *Myth and Symbol in Ancient Egypt*, 235, fig. 35.) Reproduced by kind permission of Thames and Hudson.

8.24. The raising of the Djed pillar. Tomb of Kheruef. (Adapted from the Epigraphic Survey, *The Tomb of Kheruef*, pl. 47.)

8.25. The eleven texts of the north wall. (Author's drawing.)

8.26. The eleven texts of the north wall. (Author's drawing.)

8.27. Sothis (Sirius), the celestial manifestation of Isis. From the tomb of Seti I. Nineteenth Dynasty. (Schwaller de Lubicz, *Sacred Science*, 27.)

8.28. Horus-Soped, the falcon son of the star goddess Sothis. (Budge, *From Fetish to God in Ancient Egypt*, 62. No provenance is given.)

8.29. A depiction of the jackal god on one of the surviving relief fragments from the pyramid temple of Unas. (Labrousse et al., *Le temple haut du complexe funeraire du roi Ounas*, 98, fig. 76B.) Reproduced by kind permission of Institut français d'archéologie orientale.

8.30. The ladder as a *djed* pillar with crossbars. Papyrus of Ani, New Kingdom. Vignette to BD 155. (Budge, *The Book of the Dead*, 521.)

8.31. The solar Mnevis bull. From an Eighteenth Dynasty stele. (Quirke, *The Cult of Ra*, 109, fig. 52.) Reproduced by kind permission of Thames and Hudson.

8.32. The head of the Mnevis bull is attached to a pillar representing Heliopolis. From the Sed festival reliefs of Osorkon II. (Naville, *The Festival Hall of Osorkon II*, pl. 9.)

8.33. *Left*, two-headed Egyptian deity, from the Book of What Is in the Underworld, eleventh division. (Budge, *The Egyptian Heaven and Hell*, 1:243.) *Right*, two-headed Janus figure. First-century B.C. coin. (Marindin, *A Smaller Classical Dictionary*, 316.)

8.34. King Den's Sed festival. First Dynasty tablet. (Emery, *Archaic Egypt*, 76, fig. 37.) Reproduced by kind permission of Penguin Books, Ltd.

8.35. Adoration before Ra. Papyrus of Ani. Eighteenth Dynasty. Vignette to BD 15. (Budge, *The Book of the Dead*, 63.)

Chapter 9: From the Antechamber to the Entrance Corridor

9.1. The antechamber east-gable texts. (Author's drawing.)

9.2. The texts on the east wall of the antechamber. (Author's drawing.)

9.3. The eighteen texts of the sarcophagus chamber west gable. (Author's drawing.)

9.4. Atum in the coils of the primeval snake. From the Book of What Is in the Underworld, div. 6. New Kingdom. (Budge, *The Egyptian Heaven and Hell*, 1:120.)

9.5. The serpent Apophis, who opposes the rebirth of the sun god. From the Book of What Is in the Underworld, div. 7. New Kingdom. (Budge, *The Egyptian Heaven and Hell*, 1:142.)

9.6. The lynx goddess Mafdet. Vignette to BD 17. Papyrus of Hunefer. New Kingdom. (Budge, *The Egyptian Book of the Dead*, 280.)

9.7. The snake spells on the west gable of the sarcophagus chamber. (Author's drawing.)

9.8. The god Sokar. (Budge, *The Gods of the Egyptians*, 1:507.)

9.9. The texts on both walls of the entrance corridor. (Author's drawing.)

9.10. The baboon god Babi guards the doorway to the sky. Sarcophagus of Psusennes, royal necropolis at Tanis, Twenty-first Dynasty. (Montet, *Les Constructions et le tombeau de Psousennès à Tanis*, vol. 2, pl. 88.)

9.11. Four baboons do homage to the sun. From papyrus of Userhat. Eighteenth Dynasty. (Author's drawing.)

9.12. The crocodile god Sobek. Detail from a magical papyrus. (Author's drawing.)

9.13. The Nehebkau snake. From The Book of What Is in the Underworld, div. 4. New Kingdom. (Budge, *The Egyptian Heaven and Hell*, 1:79.)

9.14. Unas stands between Horus and Seth. Reconstruction drawing from relief fragments. Pyramid temple of Unas, Saqqara. (Labrousse et al., *Le temple haut du complexe funéraire du roi Ounas*, 96, fig. 73.) Reproduced by kind permission of Institut français d'archéologie orientale.

9.15. The fierce baboon god Babi, Lord of the Night. From the Papyrus of Muthetepti. Twenty-first Dynasty. (Author's drawing.)

9.16. Ferry boat with mast and sail. Papyrus of Nu. New Kingdom. (Budge, *The Book of the Dead*, 297.)

9.17. The mystical goal of having become the faithful companion of Ra. Papyrus of Neferenpet. Nineteenth Dynasty. (Author's drawing.)

Notes

Chapter 3, note 93. Amenhotep III is represented mummiform during his Sed festival. Amenhotep III's temple at Soleb. (Giorgini, *Soleb*, 1:100, fig. 81.)

Chapter 8, note 4. Osorkon stands before the leonine goddess Bastet at his Sed festival as he walks toward the tomb. (Naville, *The Festival Hall of Osorkon II*, pl. 23.)

Chapter 8, note 96. Christian ladder of virtues, from a fifteenth-century Italian engraving from Antonio Bettini, *Il Monte Sancto di Dio*, 1477. (Toynbee, *A Study of History*, 87, fig. 57.) Reproduced by kind permission of the British Museum, London.

Chapter 8, note 112. The two-headed planet Venus. (Budge, *The Gods of the Egyptians*, 2:303.)

INDEX